Prove All Things

a response to
Women in Ministry

Mercedes H. Dyer, Ph.D., Editor

ADVENTISTS AFFIRM

This book is lovingly dedicated to the memory of

C. Mervyn Maxwell, Ph.D.,
January 13, 1925–June 21, 1999,

minister, teacher, church historian, theologian, writer, editor, storyteller, poet, and musician. He gave himself and his talents to encouraging Seventh-day Adventists diligently to study God's Word, the Bible, and His counsels in the writings of Ellen G. White. He inspired countless church members with a new appreciation for God's leading in the history of the Seventh-day Adventist movement. His contributions to the preparation of this book, even on the morning of the day he died, constitute his last gift of service to the church he loved. It was his hope that *Prove All Things* would bless the church by providing clarity on an issue which has confused and divided God's people, and that believers everywhere would respond in faith and love to trust God fully and obey Him reverently.

Table of Contents

Prologue

Mercedes H. Dyer, Editor

~

Prove All Things: A Response to Women In Ministry, as the title of our book suggests, examines the recently published book *Women in Ministry* and points out its merits as well as its shortcomings. The authors of *Women in Ministry* claim to have shown that the Bible supports women's serving in the headship roles of elder and pastor and that, therefore, the Seventh-day Adventist church should encourage women to seek these roles and should proceed with the process of ordaining them in these capacities.

ADVENTISTS AFFIRM, the sponsor and publisher of *Prove All Things,* does not agree with this claim. In this book, we explain why biblical and historical evidence does not support the ordination of women as elders and pastors, nor does it support their serving in these headship roles.

Where We Agree

The book *Women in Ministry* (1998), prepared by an Ad Hoc Committee from the Seventh-day Adventist Theological Seminary in Berrien Springs, Michigan, invites dialogue with readers who take issue with its point of view on women's ordination. Its editor recognizes that there are two sides to the question of women's ordination to the gospel ministry and that her authors have presented only one side of the issue, favoring the ordination of women pastors.

We respect the authors of *Women in Ministry.* They are our friends and co-workers. And we commend them for their invitation to dialogue. They have been

Mercedes H. Dyer, Ph.D., *is Professor of Educational Psychology and Counseling, Emerita, Andrews University.*

gracious to acknowledge that not everyone agrees with them. But there is much that we can indeed agree on.

We agree with the authors of *Women in Ministry* on most of the hermeneutical stance (though not all of it) that they have cited on their pages three and four. We want to commend them for asserting that they believe in interpreting the Bible by the Bible itself, taking the entire Bible as a unit which does not contradict itself when interpreted rightly.

We share their view that men and women are equal, equally created by God in His image and equally saved by Christ's precious blood (Gen 1:26, 27; Gal 3:28; 1 Pet 1:19).

We commend their desire to see more women in the service of the Lord. All true followers of Christ are to be fruit bearers. One cannot live for self, enjoying the vain pleasures of the world, and at the same time have fellowship with Him who gave His life on the cross to save us from self and sin. The spirit of heaven is the spirit of service.

We share the same belief that both men and women have been called to soul-winning ministry, to utilize their skills and spiritual gifts (Joel 2:28, 29; 1 Cor 12). Indeed, God has appointed a specific place on earth for each one. If we choose to follow Him and to give Him our lives, He will equip us to do His bidding, whether we are men or women. All are to put on the cloak of righteousness and live godly lives of service, be that service great or small. God sees the intents of the heart and knows our motives and desires.

We applaud their concern for women to be paid a fair wage and that women as well as men should have opportunities for service in the church. The Bible is very clear that all of Christ's followers are to minister in one way or another and that "the worker deserves his wages" (1 Tim 5:17, 18; cf. 1 Cor 9:7-12). Ellen G. White used several strong terms to describe the denial of just wages for the labor of women in the cause of God. She called this "making a difference" (discrimination), "selfishly withholding . . . their due," "exaction," "partiality," "selfishness," and "injustice." She said, "the tithe should go to those who labor in word and doctrine, *be they men or women*" (*Evangelism*, pp. 491-493, emphasis added).

We agree with our friends, the authors of *Women in Ministry*, that God has called women to public service in Seventh-day Adventist history as in Bible times (though we challenge their claim that some Adventist women in the days of our pioneers served as regular pastors).

We join our *Women in Ministry* colleagues in asserting that ordination or the laying on of hands does not confer any special grace or holiness upon the one ordained. The long-standing Adventist position maintains that ordination does not bestow some special magical power of the Holy Spirit; neither does it confer upon the elder or pastor some special character which sets the person apart as a "priest." Correctly understood, ordination is the act of the church in choosing, appointing, and setting apart certain individuals for assigned services through the laying on of hands.

But while agreeing on so much, we differ on some crucial issues.

Points of Contention

The key theological issue that divides us and our friends who wrote for *Women in Ministry* is this: Since, through an act of dedication ("the laying on of hands"), both men and women can be commissioned *to perform certain specific functions* on behalf of the church, the disagreement is whether, among the varied ministries of the church, women may legitimately be commissioned through ordination to perform *the headship roles of elders or pastors.* The issue then is not ordination *per se,* but ordination to *what function.* In other words, our disagreement with the authors of *Women in Ministry* is over whether or not the Bible *permits* women to be appointed and commissioned *as elders or pastors.*

In addressing the above issue, those of us opposing the ordination of women as elders and pastors have called attention to the fact that (1) there is no biblical *precedent* in either the Old or New Testament for women being ordained to serve in the headship roles of priest, apostle, and elder or pastor; (2) some explicit biblical *prohibitions* seem to militate against the practice (1 Tim 3:2; Titus 1:6; 1 Tim 2:11-15; 1 Cor 14:34, 35); and (3) there is no evidence of the ordination of women in early Adventist history. We have argued that this stems not from mere sociological or cultural factors but rather from God's divine arrangement established at creation—when God created male and female equal but different.

Our *Women in Ministry* colleagues, however, disagree with this, claiming that there is, after all, *precedent* in the Bible and early Adventist history for women serving in the headship roles of priest, apostle, and elder or pastor, and that the specific biblical *prohibitions* noted above, correctly understood, are culturally conditioned to the Bible writers' times. In the *Women in Ministry* authors' opinion, when God created male and female He made them "fully equal" with "total role-interchangeability." Male headship and female submission, they argue, were introduced not at Creation but *after* the Fall. While the headship principle may still be valid in the home, it is not valid in the church.

Clearly, on the matter of ordaining women as elders and pastors, we disagree with our friends and colleagues, the authors of *Women in Ministry*, on how to interpret the biblical and historical data.

To help the reader appreciate the nature and extent of our disagreement, a brief historical review will explain how *Women in Ministry* came to be written and why we have felt the need to respond.

Historical Review

When requests for permission to ordain women were presented at the General Conference sessions of 1990 (Indianapolis) and 1995 (Utrecht), opponents cited many biblical reasons why our church ought not to ordain women as pastors and elders. On the other hand, those proposing such ordination also argued that the Bible supported their position and that anyone could prove it if they took the time to study. This difference was observed by our church leaders, who do not want our church to take positions that cannot be supported by Scripture.

After the ordination proposal was defeated at Utrecht, the presidents of several North American Unions went to the Seventh-day Adventist Theological Seminary and asked the theologians and scholars there to find that long-promised biblical support. In response, the Seminary set up a committee with no other task than to find the Bible passages which proponents need. Fifteen men and women were selected from among the best scholars and theologians our denomination has to offer. The committee was called the Ad Hoc Committee on Hermeneutics and Ordination.

Before going further, let us pause to look at that name. The name itself goes a long way to explain *Women in Ministry. Ad Hoc* means "for this one purpose." *Hermeneutics* comes from a Greek word meaning "interpretation," and in our context it refers to principles for how to interpret the Bible. When we put "Ad Hoc Committee on Hermeneutics and Ordination" into ordinary language we get "Committee Appointed With the One Purpose of Correctly Interpreting the Bible to Discover Whether the Scriptures Will Support Ordaining Women as Elders and Pastors."

But as will become evident in the following pages, the North American Division Union presidents who made the request wanted the Seminary to come out with a book *supporting* women's ordination. Readers can, therefore, understand why the Ad Hoc Committee that published the book chose not to include views opposed to women's ordination. No wonder the committee's report, published as *Women in Ministry,* attempts to interpret the Bible to support ordaining women!

Is It Right to Reinterpret the Bible?

It is not wrong to search for ways to interpret a problem text so it will agree with the rest of the Bible. We do this with Jesus' statement to the thief on the cross, "Verily I say unto thee, Today shalt thou be with me in paradise" (Luke 23:43). We find that a translator put the comma in the wrong place. Moving it from before "today" to after "today" dates Christ's *conversation* to that Friday afternoon rather than saying that the *meeting in Paradise* occurred then—and the passage agrees with the consistent thrust of Scripture.

No, it is not wrong to find ways to interpret a text so that it agrees with the rest of the Bible. It is quite another matter, however, to try to interpret the Bible so it will agree with what we want the Bible to say. An example of this kind of interpreting Scripture is the habit of Christians for many centuries of interpreting the seventh day of the week as the first, thereby justifying treating Sunday as the Lord's day.

Interpreting Sunday as the Sabbath was wrong. When God decided that the time had come to correct that long-standing mistake, He led our pioneers to find an abundance of clear evidence in Scripture that the seventh day is the Sabbath. The same may be said regarding the condition of man in death, the imminence of the Second Coming, the correct form of baptism, and so many other Adventist doctrines which may be seen as corrections of previously held false interpretation of Scripture. Always there has been clear biblical evidence as well as confirming messages through the ministry of Ellen G. White for the correction.

But now we come to this change in ordination practices, which proponents claim is a belated correction in Scriptural interpretation. *Women in Ministry* makes such claims as these:

• the equality of men and women in Christ means they have identical roles;

• role distinctions between men and women did not originate at Creation, but after the Fall;

• the spiritual leadership of men is applicable only in the home, and not necessarily in the church;

• there was at least one woman priest in the Old Testament;

• women served as apostles and ministers in the New Testament;

• 1 Corinthians 11 and 14 and 1 Timothy 2, when correctly understood as culturally conditioned to the New Testament times, do not prohibit women from exercising headship roles as elders or pastors;

• Ellen G. White called for women's ordination in 1895;

• women served as pastors in early Seventh-day Adventist history;

• the 1881 General Conference session voted to ordain women.

But are the above claims true? Despite their noble intention and motives, it is our contention in *Prove All Things* that *none* of these claims are true. In fact, we find there is no solid evidence, either in the Bible or in the writings of Ellen G. White, for what our friends are claiming in *Women in Ministry.*

The Scholars and Theologians

Though we are challenging the claims and conclusions in *Women in Ministry,* we want to make it clear that:

We are acquainted with the scholars and theologians who sat on the Ad Hoc Committee and wrote for *Women in Ministry.* We worship together in the same Adventist churches. They are our friends. Good Seventh-day Adventists, all of them. And we appreciate the devoted effort they have put into producing their report. The entire Seventh-day Adventist church should be grateful to them. Not grateful, to be sure, that their work endeavors to support ordaining women as pastors and elders. But the church can be doubly grateful because they have made the best case possible for their positions, even though a careful study of the claims in *Women in Ministry* shows conclusively that the Bible does not support such ordination.

Our book points out that no scholar known to have published articles opposing women's ordination was invited to sit with the Ad Hoc Committee. Only those known to be enthusiastic about women's ordination—or at least open to it—were chosen. Some observers have criticized the committee for this, calling it prejudiced or worse. But others see it as a good thing. The Ad Hoc Committee met frequently over a period of two years with much earnestness and prayer and with their efforts exclusively directed at finding ways to interpret the Bible to support women's ordination. Now the church may examine the best that they came up with, weigh it, and decide whether or not it is wanting.

The Lack of Clear Evidence

From the start, the editor of *Women in Ministry* admits honestly that where "clear evidence" is "lacking" from the Bible the authors used "sanctified judgment and imagination." A few examples will show to what lengths this led.

The Results of "Sanctified Judgment and Imagination"

The General Conference session of 1881 considered women's ordination and declined to approve it. *Women in Ministry,* however, says that the session voted to ordain women as pastors.

Women in Ministry says that the doctrine of the priesthood of all believers justifies ordaining women as pastors. Are not Korah, Dathan, and Abiram an example of the consequences of seeking the priesthood for those whom God has not appointed?

One *Women in Ministry* author says that in the Garden of Eden, following Eve's partaking of the forbidden fruit, God appointed her a priest. The basis for this assertion is that God clothed Eve in an animal's skin, which, we agree, He did, but not to appoint her a priest. The true interpretation for this act is that evening was coming on; for the first time in her life, Eve was feeling cold. "The Lord mercifully provided" both Adam and Eve "with garments of animal skins *as a protection from the extremes of heat and cold"* (*Patriarchs and Prophets,* p. 61, emphasis added).

If these are the kinds of proofs *Women in Ministry* offers, if there is no hard biblical evidence supporting appointing and ordaining women as elders or pastors, and if the editor of *Women in Ministry* freely admits that the authors sometimes used "sanctified judgment and imagination" to make up for this lack, why have we devoted many months and much prayer to refuting *Women in Ministry?*

Why This Book?

We have prepared this book because we are aware that not everyone who reads *Women in Ministry* will discern where the evidence—such as it is—leaves off and the "sanctified judgment and imagination" begins. Bible texts on male-female role relationships have been reinterpreted to accommodate women's ordination. Passages have been selected from Ellen G. White's writings to make it appear that Mrs. White supported ordaining women as elders and pastors when a study of all of her writings shows that this is not the case.

In *Prove All Things* we have tried to make these distinctions clear.

The reader will find several scholarly chapters filled with theology. There are also shorter chapters relating personal experiences, demonstrating how effectively unordained women have worked for God. Read of the two young women, ordained as elders, who later rejected that ordination. They are too busy winning souls full time in the mission field to spend time being elders—a practice foreign to the religion of the Bible and the Seventh-day Adventist pioneers. Read, too, of the Adventist woman who has done much more than most ordained men to share God's truth in forbidden countries—without the ordination of laying on of hands; without even a husband.

A Road Map for Reading

Part I of *Prove All Things,* "Background and Methods in *Women in Ministry,*" provides the reader with background and overview for understanding the basic issue and the reasons for the concerns to be elaborated in *Prove All Things.* First, Samuel Koranteng-Pipim looks at the Seminary book's origin and purposes. Then, P. Gerard Damsteegt examines specifically the methods of interpretation found in *Women in Ministry.* These chapters will help the reader see something of the "big picture" before moving into a more detailed look at certain key aspects.

Part II, "Biblical Issues," grapples with *Women in Ministry's* handling of the relevant Bible material. Samuele Bacchiocchi responds in detail to one of the major chapters of the book, examining the issues of headship, submission, and equality in Scripture, especially in Genesis 1-3 and in the writings of Paul. Next, P. Gerard Damsteegt analyzes the four chapters of *Women in Ministry* which treat "Ministry in the Bible," using both Scripture and the writings of Mrs. White to evaluate the authors' claims. C. Raymond Holmes offers an exegetical study of 1 Timothy 2:11-15, showing that the passage in its context is quite plain and straightforward. S. Lawrence Maxwell's chapter, "One Chilling Word," compares popular arguments heard today with those which brought disaster in Israel's day. Filling out this section and summarizing concerns from many chapters of *Women in Ministry* is Samuel Koranteng-Pipim's provocative challenge, "Are Those Things So?—Part I." These chapters have much valuable information and insight regarding the Bible's position on qualifications for pastoral ministry.

Part III, "Historical and Theological Issues," delves into matters of Seventh-day Adventist history, recent as well as early. For a survey of some events in the last 30 years which have contributed to our current situation, be sure to read C. Mervyn Maxwell's chapter that begins this section. The following three chapters in the section relate to Ellen G. White and Seventh-day Adventist history. Larry Kirkpatrick reviews the use of Mrs. White's writings by several authors in *Women in Ministry.* Laurel Damsteegt examines the feminist connection to spiritualism, which Mrs. White noted and commented on, and which one author in *Women in Ministry* downplays for the contemporary scene. Two articles by William Fagal from *Ministry* magazine in the late 1980s, combined into one chapter in this book, look at often-heard arguments regarding Mrs. White and the role of women in the church. The section climaxes with Samuel Koranteng-Pipim's perspectives on historical and theological concerns regarding *Women in Ministry* and his proposals on how the church may resolve its conflicts on this matter in a way that is both true to Scripture and true to God's call for women to take a significant, active part in His work.

In Part IV, "Ordination and Women in Ministry," several authors present their personal experiences with various aspects of the question of women in ministry. Wellesley Muir and Carolyn Stuyvesant both speak from a missionary's perspective. Jay Gallimore, a conference president, reflects on the controversy in recent years over women's ordination in the Seventh-day Adventist church.

Readers will find a few issues on which more than one author comments. Despite some duplication, each author brings to the discussion his own perspective, making their comments supplement one another rather than simply repeat the same observations.

Four appendices present material which ADVENTISTS AFFIRM has published previously, outlining the issues which confront the church and suggesting ways to address them. Even our first publication in 1987 (see Appendix A) seems remarkably up-to-date in today's discussions.

Along the way in your journey through the book, we hope the personal testimonies will be an encouragement and a blessing to you.

Our Prayer

This book is the result of much prayer and reflection. Its title, *Prove All Things,* comes from 1 Thessalonians 5:21: "Prove all things; hold fast that which is good." This is what we must always do when confronted by new interpretations of Scripture. We believe the Bible is our standard, and we take the Bible at its word. We have tried not to rationalize or to imagine conclusions based (for example) on our limited awareness of ancient conditions and cultures. We take all of the Bible to interpret any part of the Bible. When we take it as a whole, we see a beautiful harmony and design, which we believe is strong evidence that all parts of Scripture are given by inspiration of God for our good. We believe God means what He has inspired. We hope our church will consider carefully the biblical indications of God's will concerning the relationship between male and female in the home as well as in the church.

Just as we have invested much prayer and reflection in the preparation of this book, we trust that the reader will study its positions prayerfully and with reverential fear, knowing that God knows the end from the beginning. He has created and ordered the world in the only way that can be good for all His people, both men and women. In the sight of God, men and women are His children, created by Him with intrinsic value. Sin cost heaven a tremendous sacrifice. But all heaven was willing to cooperate to buy back what humanity had lost through the sin of Adam and Eve.

That *Prove All Things* will help guide our beloved church to make the right decision about women as elders and pastors is the sincere prayer of all who work with ADVENTISTS AFFIRM.

Part 1

Backgrounds and Methods in Women in Ministry

Chapter 1

Theology or Ideology?
Background, Methodology, and Content of
Women in Ministry

Samuel Koranteng-Pipim

~

Introduction

"What is your view on women's ordination?" one of my Seminary professors asked me several years ago.

"I have no position on the issue. It does not matter to me one way or the other," I responded, trying to hide the fact that up until that time I had not carefully studied the question.

In those days, my apathy was stronger than my conviction on this controversial theological issue. I prized the feeling of being "neutral" more than paying the price for taking a stand either for or against women's ordination. This explains why I chose the "neither for nor against" position.

But my professor would not let me remain neutral: "Would it matter to you if you discovered from the Bible and the writings of Ellen G. White that the ordination of women is right, fair, just, and essential to rightly representing God to the world, and that excluding women from ordination is a denial of their spiritual gifts and their call to ministry?"

A simple rhetorical question from a teacher. But, needless to say, it led me to become a believer in women's ordination. At that time, I saw the issue as a question of equality, justice, and fundamental fairness. Refusing to ordain women was,

Samuel Koranteng-Pipim, Ph.D., *is Director of Public Campus Ministries for the Michigan Conference of Seventh-day Adventists.*

in my view, a form of discrimination. And didn't both the Bible and the writings of Ellen G. White teach that injustice was un-Christian?

For about five years I enjoyed the fellowship, respect, and admiration of those with whom I was championing the cause of women's ordination. I was not a radical feminist nor an unbelieving liberal. I was a committed Seventh-day Adventist, upholding the tradition of the Protestant Reformers and Adventist pioneers in standing for what I thought was biblical truth. Our cause was right and our motives were noble.

But was the ordination of women as elders or pastors biblical? Do the Bible and Mrs. White's counsels really support it? Though my motives were noble, were they biblical? These questions ultimately led me, almost ten years ago, to change my mind on women's ordination.

I still believe that women have a legitimate place in the soul-winning ministry of the church and that the Seventh-day Adventist church should make provision to encourage a greater participation of women in ministry. I still believe that the church should show stronger support for the training of women at the Seminary and should offer adequate and fair remuneration to women for their labor and, in some cases (such as in team ministries), should authoritatively commission women for roles and duties that do not violate biblical teaching.

I still believe that, among many lines of ministry, women could be encouraged to participate in the study, teaching and preaching of the gospel in personal and public evangelism; to be involved in ministries of prayer, visitation, counseling, writing and singing; to labor as literature evangelists or health evangelists, to raise new churches, and to minister to the needy; to serve in positions of responsibility that do not require ordination as elders or pastors, serving as colleagues in partnership with ordained men at the various levels of the church organization; to teach in our institutions and seminaries; and above all, to minister to their children at home. But while I affirm the legitimacy of women in ministry, I do not believe that the Bible permits women to be ordained *as elders or pastors,* or that the writings of Mrs. White provide support for it.[1]

Even though today I no longer believe in the biblical correctness of women's ordination, I am grateful to my pro-ordination teacher for helping me realize that a true Adventist cannot (and must not) remain neutral on disputed *theological* issues. The world today may honor indifference to truth as a sign of "open-mindedness," "tolerance," or even "maturity"; but the Bible condemns the attitude as betrayal or cowardice.

In a real sense, the book I am about to review in this chapter and in two later chapters represents the position I once held. The twenty authors who have contributed to the volume deserve our praise for offering the best biblical and historical arguments that Adventist proponents of women's ordination are capable of presenting to a Bible-believing Seventh-day Adventist church. It takes real courage to put one's views in print, allow them to be examined by others, and risk being criticized and even proven wrong. But it is a small price to pay for a genuine search for truth. The Lord always rewards those who make an effort to know Him and His revealed will, regardless of the cost.

In another sense, my biblical and historical evaluation in two subsequent chapters may be read as reasons why I can no longer believe in women's ordination. If my critique at times appears vigorous, it is because I'm disputing with my own earlier views. I invite you, therefore, to put emotions and personalities aside and join me as we reason together on the most divisive and politicized issue to have plagued our church in recent times.

Why Review *Women in Ministry?*

Why should one evaluate *Women in Ministry: Biblical and Historical Perspectives* (1998)? After all, its authors describe the book as the product of two years of regular meetings which always began with "prayer, often several prayers—pleading with God for wisdom and understanding, love and firmness, but most of all for God's leading that His will might be done in the meeting and in the book." Why assess a work its writers already believe to be "a contribution to an ongoing dialog"?[2]

Again, why should one take another look at a 438-page volume the editor claims has the "support" of the ministerial department of the General Conference?[3] And why re-examine a book that a respected scholar and General Conference vice-president has already acclaimed as a "deeply spiritual, highly reasoned, consistently logical approach to the issue of women's ordination"?[4]

First, even a Spirit-guided scholarly contribution deserves careful evaluation. God's inspired Word obliges every Christian to do so: "Quench not the Spirit. Despise not prophesyings. *Prove all things; hold fast that which is good*" (1 Thess 5:19-21).

Second, the twenty authors of the book have invited those who disagree with the volume's findings to engage them in a dialogue: "This volume represents the understanding of the Seminary Ad Hoc Committee on Hermeneutics and Ordination. We do not claim to speak for others, either at the Seminary or in church administration. Some may disagree with our findings. That is their privilege. We welcome their responses and invite them to dialogue."[5]

Third, *Women in Ministry* is the latest attempt by a group of Seventh-day Adventist scholars to find biblical and historical justification for ordaining women *as elders or pastors.* Coming from the Seventh-day Adventist Theological Seminary at Andrews University, the book will undoubtedly influence those members of the worldwide Seventh-day Adventist church who look to the Seminary for sound biblical teaching, training, and guidance.[6] It is this need for safe and discerning theological direction that may have prompted "several" North American Division leaders, shortly after the 1995 Utrecht General Conference session, to approach the Seminary faculty for answers to questions raised by their petition to the world body of Seventh-day Adventists for divisional ordinations.[7]

Fourth, the book provides a critical component in a carefully thought-out, step-by-step strategy to legislate, if not legitimize, the practice of women's ordination in the Seventh-day Adventist church.[8] One such effort is contained in a very significant document that was formally accepted at the October 9, 1997, North American Division year-end meeting. The document is the Division's "President's Commission on Women in Ministry—Report."[9]

Fifth, *Women in Ministry* contains some of the most creative arguments ever marshaled by church scholars to change the minds of a Bible-believing church that has twice overwhelmingly rejected the call to ordain women as pastors.[10] We need to ascertain whether or not the arguments found in the volume will stand the test of biblical and historical scrutiny.

Sixth, the book is being promoted in certain quarters of the Adventist church as the official position of the Seminary and as the product of "sound Biblical and historical scholarship."[11] Even if such statements are dismissed as unfounded, the fact still remains that some Adventists and non-Adventists will consider this work a model of thorough, profound Adventist scholarship on a divisive and controversial issue.[12]

These six reasons offer the justification for this present review of *Women in Ministry*. If the book's conclusions are proven to be valid, they should be incorporated into the Seventh-day Adventist church's Bible-based beliefs and lifestyle. And the church should be encouraged immediately to rectify its 150-year-old practice of ministry and ordination.[13] On the other hand, if the evidence and reasoning in the volume are found wanting biblically and historically, then the campaign during the past two or three decades by a few influential scholars and leaders to impose women's ordination on the church should be rejected as a tragic mistake and a misguided endeavor.

In this chapter I will review *Women in Ministry*, paying close attention to the implications of (1) how the book came into being, (2) the hermeneutical stance of the volume, (3) the major conclusions of the work, and (4) how the book fits into a well-orchestrated strategy to legislate and legitimize women's ordination in the Seventh-day Adventist church. In two other chapters, later in the book, I will offer an evaluation of the book's biblical and historical arguments. Taking issue with the authors, some of whom I esteem as close friends, does not involve questioning their sincerity as well-meaning Adventist scholars. Neither does it mean that whatever they have written in other areas is necessarily suspect or invalid.

A. How *Women in Ministry* Came into Being

Women in Ministry was published against a backdrop of an ongoing controversy in the church between "liberals" (Adventist scholars who believe in the use of modified versions of contemporary higher criticism) and "conservatives" (those who reject the liberal method).[14] The Seminary Ad Hoc Committee on Hermeneutics and Ordination, the group responsible for producing the book, was a gathering of pro-ordination scholars who, though disagreeing on the appropriateness of the higher-critical method, are nonetheless united in their view that women should be ordained as elders or pastors.

The first challenge that faced the committee was how to construct a theological justification for women's ordination without tripping the explosive hermeneutical land mine (the use of contemporary higher criticism) that for years a number of scholars at the Seminary have avoided handling and defusing. Another challenge was how to craft a justification for women's ordination that would appeal to a conservative Adventist church which shows no interest in liberal and feminist reinterpretations of Scripture.

After two years of regular meetings and "animated" discussions, "a spirit of camaraderie developed" among these scholars. With this spirit of friendship, "eventually all the chapters [of the book] were written, rewritten, and approved by the committee."[15] Introducing the book at a special Seminary assembly on October 7, 1998, the chair of the Ad Hoc Committee stated that "no chapter was accepted until all members felt they could live with the document." Even though "each chapter was written by a different author and retains the writer's individual style," explains the book's editor, "careful readers will notice slight differences of opinions between chapters. Our agreement was on the big picture."[16]

The "big picture" that kept the pro-ordination committee together was its members' shared belief that the Bible is not against ordaining women *as elders or pastors*. Without doubt, theirs was a daunting task in pursuit of today's "unity in diversity"—*theological* unity (women's ordination) amidst *hermeneutical* diversity (conflicting approaches to the Bible). But the authors believe that they accomplished their mission: "We believe that the biblical, theological, and historical perspectives elaborated in this book affirm women in pastoral leadership."[17]

In two later chapters I will evaluate the validity of their conclusion. Presently, however, we shall make some important observations on how *Women in Ministry* came into being.

1. The Reason Behind the Book

The initial request for the book came from "several union presidents of the North American Division" who, before and during the 1995 Utrecht General Conference session, had urged the North American Division President that there be "no turning back" in their campaign for women's ordination.[18] When their petition was rejected by the world body at Utrecht, certain leaders in the North American Division began calling for "a clarification of the Adventist theology of ordination, *culminating in the ordination of women,*" and for steps that would lead to "clear understanding and member education regarding valid Adventist hermeneutical principles [of biblical interpretation]."[19]

Notice that the call for "a clarification of Adventist theology of ordination" was really a quest for a scholarly work that would "culminate in the ordination of women." The meaning of "valid Adventist hermeneutical principles" was later made explicit at the October 1995 Year-end meeting of the North American Division leaders to be an approach to Scripture that would ultimately justify their belief in the biblical correctness of women's ordination.

At that October 1995 Year-end Meeting in Battle Creek, just three months after the Utrecht vote, the North American leadership announced that a commission was being appointed to recommend ways to "expand the role of women in ministry," recognize and deploy the gifts God has given to women, and "affirm women in pastoral and other spiritual ministries."[20] In their *Statement of Commitment to Women in Gospel Ministry,* adopted on October 13, 1995, the Union presidents of North America also reaffirmed their belief *"in the biblical rightness of women's ordination"* and pledged their support for a clarification of the church's theology of ordination.[21]

This brief background leads one to conclude that the initial request to the Seminary faculty by "several" of these union presidents for a clarification of the Adventist theology of ordination and for a clear understanding regarding valid Adventist hermeneutical principles was a search for a scholarly work that would justify the ordination of women. Some three months *before* the Seminary appointed its Ad Hoc Committee in January 1996 to study issues related to hermeneutics and ordination, some of the North American Division leaders were already convinced of the "biblical rightness of women's ordination."

Why was there a need for the Seminary to clarify the church's principles for interpreting the Bible when the church already had done so—in the "Methods of Bible Study" document, approved by the church's worldwide leaders in 1986 in Rio de Janeiro, Brazil?[22] And why was there a need to clarify the church's theology of ordination, when the church already had articulated its position in the 1988 volume *Seventh-day Adventists Believe . . . : A Biblical Exposition of 27 Fundamental Doctrines* (pp. 142-150)[23] and our *Minister's Manual* (pp. 75-79 [1992 edition]; pp. 83-86 [1997 edition])?[24]

The answer seems obvious. It wasn't because the church had no valid hermeneutical principles for interpreting the Bible, nor a sound theology of ordination. It already had these. Instead, some of the pro-ordination leaders wanted a theological validation of their stance on ordination. This was the only way they could justify earlier church policy revisions and *Church Manual* alterations in response to problems resulting from the North American Division's desire to enjoy United States income tax benefits.[25]

Thus, in the production of the Seminary book *Women in Ministry,* the interests of pro-ordination leaders and that of pro-ordination scholars kissed each other. Or as the book's editor later explained, the North American Division leadership, feeling "let down" at Utrecht, wanted the Seminary to *"do something about it [the Utrecht vote]."*[26]

The conclusion is inescapable. After several years of unsuccessful attempts at *legislating the ideology* of women's ordination, the proponents decided that the time had come to try another strategy: the *proclamation of the theology* of women's ordination. Using one of the leading and most influential church institutions, the Seventh-day Adventist Theological Seminary at Andrews University, some of the North American Division leaders sought to shift their strategy of women's ordination *from ideology to theology.* The Seminary book *Women in Ministry* is the result of this strategy.

2. The Partners in the Seminary "Dialogue"

There is another indication that the Seminary volume was an attempt to justify theologically the ideology of women's ordination, not a quest for an openminded investigation into what the Bible has to say on a divisive and controversial issue in the church. The Seminary committee's "dialogue" did not include Andrews University scholars opposed to women's ordination, some of whom, through their earlier published works, had demonstrated a grasp of the crucial issues in the debate.[27] Though twenty authors collaborated to produce the book, the Seminary Ad Hoc Committee allowed no other viewpoints in the book except those favoring women's ordination.[28]

Although dissenting scholarly views were not represented in the committee, readers are informed that during its two years of regular meetings, "sensitivity to the positions of others, both for and against women's ordination was evident."[29] Lamentably, this is typical of the manner in which the issue has been discussed even in official church publications.[30]

Is it not ironic—and unfortunate—that the views of scholars upholding the long-established Seventh-day Adventist convictions on this question are not always welcome today in church publications and even in the book originating from the Seminary? Whose interest is served when, on *unresolved* theological issues, opposing views are excluded even when those views are still embraced by the overwhelming majority of the church through official action?

The authors of *Women in Ministry* sincerely believe that the church made a great mistake at Utrecht, a mistake that they believe constitutes a hindrance to God's purpose and therefore needs to be ameliorated and/or corrected in order for the church to fulfill God's purpose. Does belief in the rightness of a cause justify the excluding of opposing views from a volume promoted and financed by the church's leading theological Seminary?

The Seminary book under review would have gained much credibility and, as we shall later show, would have avoided some of its theological and historical shortcomings if it had allowed for challenges by opposing views during its two years of "animated" discussions.[31]

Women in Ministry would also have escaped justifiable criticisms that the Seminary's name and resources are being (mis)used to promote the ideological agenda of women's ordination. Since the authors "do not claim to speak for others, either at the seminary or in church administration,"[32] would it not have been better for the pro-ordination scholars of the Seminary to have published and financed their private views independently (as other scholars both for and against ordination had previously done), instead of using the Seminary's prestige and resources to gain credibility for their one-sided view?

3. Expected Use of the Book

The authors claim that their book is not to be seen as "the final answer to whether or not the Seventh-day Adventist Church should ordain its women in ministry, but rather as a resource tool for decision making." They "hope and pray that this volume may assist individuals, leaders, and the community of faith at large in deciding how to deal with the issue of ordination and, more specifically, the relationship of ordination to women."[33]

Since the worldwide Seventh-day Adventist church has already decided on the issue of women's ordination at the 1990 and 1995 General Conference sessions, one wonders why the book is being offered "as a resource tool for decision making." Could it be that the authors anticipate the use of the book in providing a theological basis to overturn the worldwide decision?[34]

This seems to be the case. For, in the opinion of some post-Utrecht advocates of women's ordination, (1) the 1990 vote was not a categorical No to women's ordination; instead of a theological reason against the practice, proponents claim that the General Conference session simply cited pragmatic reasons—"the widespread lack of support" for it and "the possible risk of disunity, dissension, and diversion from the mission of the Church" that could result had the church gone ahead *at that time* in ordaining women as pastors;[35] (2) the 1995 General Conference session addressed "only the procedural recommendation" of the North American Division, not "the theological appropriateness of women's ordination"; thus a pro-ordination book from the Seminary could be used to justify theologically a future push to overturn the Utrecht vote;[36] (3) unlike opponents of women's ordination who allegedly defied a 1988 "moratorium" or "ban" by the General Conference president on publishing and distributing materials on the issue, proponents loyal to the church chose not to present and publicize their theological defense of women's ordination, in compliance with the supposed "moratorium"; the alleged ban was apparently lifted in 1995 when "several" North American Division leaders met with the Seminary professors and urged them to "do something about Utrecht."[37]

The above justification for *Women in Ministry* is based on a creative reinterpretation of church actions on women's ordination (see endnotes 35-37). Yet, building upon these arguments, advocates and promoters believe that a pro-ordination book from the Seminary would not only create the much-needed consensus for women's ordination but could also be used to theologically bolster a future push to overturn the Utrecht vote.

We have already noted that *Women in Ministry* was produced at the urging of some North American leaders to *"do something about it"* [Utrecht]. In fact, a year and a half before the book was released, the "prospectus" of the Seminary book (detailing how it came into being, its objective, a partial listing of the authors and their topics, the target audience, its wide distribution in Latin America, and the marketing strategies) was published in a non-official pro-ordination Adventist publication.[38]

Barely six months into the two years of regular meetings "which always began with prayer, often several prayers—pleading with God for wisdom and understanding,"[39] at least some of the Seminary Ad Hoc Committee members were already convinced that the 150-year-old practice of the Seventh-day Adventist church was wrong and needed to be changed. Before all the chapters of the pro-ordination book were written, the tentative thrust of the Seminary volume was to suggest that the "Adventist church structure, however legitimate, has not been, historically, an exact replica of biblical patterns of ministry. While accepting the decision of the Adventist church not to ordain women *at this time* as voted at the 1995 General Conference Session in Utrecht, *the book will attempt to provide data on which to base future decisions.*"[40]

Also, following the book's publication, a press release from the public relations office of Andrews University announcing the book-signing concluded: "Whether the book will signal a shift in the worldwide Adventist Church remains to be seen. In Utrecht, conservative factions from Latin America and Africa voted down the women's ordination question. The next General Conference session, to be held in Toronto, Canada, in the year 2000, *could be the site of another theological firestorm if the North American Church pushes the issue.*"[41]

Could the plan to *"do something about Utrecht"* and the possibility of the North American Division "pushing the issue" again at the year 2000 General Conference session in Toronto be behind the Seminary's wide distribution of the book to church leaders around the world, ostensibly to "foster dialogue"?[42] There is nothing wrong in attempting to overturn a General Conference session decision that is believed to be biblically flawed. But if we choose to do so, as sometimes we ought, at least we must be candid about our intentions.

Perhaps the pro-ordination General Conference vice-president who chaired the women's ordination business session at Utrecht and who enthusiastically endorsed the book in *Adventist Review* may have spoken for many of the book's authors when he wrote: "Though unfortunately too late to inform prior [Utrecht] debate, my opinion is that *Women in Ministry* has the *potential to be determinative in future* [General Conference?] *discussion.*"[43]

If indeed the intent of the Seminary book is to overturn the worldwide decision at Utrecht, some major questions arise: Is it ever right for the Seventh-day Adventist Theological Seminary to allow its prestige and resources to be hijacked for some ideological agenda rejected by the church? If, for instance, a General Conference session votes against homosexuality, can a group of pro-gay theologians in a church institution use the name and resources of the institution to advance their homosexual agenda?

This question is not about the biblical rightness of women's ordination, homosexuality, or any other issue. My point here is simply about the responsibility of the church's leading theological institution to the community of faith at large. What kind of precedent do we set when the Seminary begins to cave in to ideological pressure or "appeals" from some quarters of church leadership?

Also, the concern here is not about whether theologians may legitimately mass-distribute their published works; they have a right to do so. The issue being raised is simply this: Since the book's editor states in the prologue that the authors of *Women in Ministry* "do not claim to speak for others, either at the Seminary or in church administration," is it appropriate for the Seminary (or Andrews University, or any other church institution) to use its resources, name, and influence to promote some privately held opinions that are contrary to official church actions? Would the Seminary (or Andrews University, or some other church institution) do the same for other scholars holding opposing views on this question, and perhaps on another controversial issue like homosexuality?

I raise these questions in an effort to highlight the real reason behind the Seminary book ("doing something about Utrecht"), the unfortunate silencing of views opposing women's ordination, and the potential use of such an ideological document to overturn a worldwide General Conference session decision. But perhaps this background glimpse into how the book came into being is not the most important thing at this point. The book is already out, is being widely distributed around the world in the name of the Seminary, and is being used by advocates of women's ordination to push their agenda.[44]

Perhaps we should now turn our attention to another aspect of my review: the hermeneutical approach adopted by the authors of the volume. Focusing on questions about the authors' methodology will shed some light on conclusions in *Women in Ministry*, enabling us later to evaluate the validity of the book's message.

B. The Hermeneutical Approach of *Women in Ministry*

Women in Ministry should be read against the backdrop of an earlier work by another team of pro-ordination scholars. The 1995 volume, *The Welcome Table: Setting a Table for Ordained Women,* was authored by 14 thought leaders.[45] Although not published by any Seventh-day Adventist institution, like the present work under review it also was widely promoted in the church as "a definitive collection of essays for our time from respected church leaders—both women and men. Informed, balanced, mission-oriented, and thoroughly Adventist, this book—like Esther of old—has 'come to the kindom [sic] for such a time as this.'"[46] The book's release was timed to influence the 1995 Utrecht General Conference session's debate on the North American Division's request for divisional ordinations. Upon closer inspection, however, thoughtful Adventists rejected its conclusions because of its revisionist interpretation of the Bible and Adventist history.[47]

Observe that in *The Welcome Table* some of the authors argued that Bible passages (like Eph 5:22-33; Col 3:18-19; 1 Pet 3:1-7; 1 Cor 11:3, 11-12; 14:34-35; 1 Tim 2:11-14; 3:2; and Titus 1:6) which Adventists historically understood as having a bearing on male-female role relations in both the home and the church are the product of the Bible writers' faulty logic or mistaken rabbinic interpretations in vogue in their day. Reasoning along feminist and higher-critical lines, some of the writers maintained that the apostle Paul erred in his interpretation of Genesis 1-3 when he grounded his teaching of role distinctions between male and female in Creation and the Fall. They claimed that the apostle Paul's statements were merely expressions of uninspired personal opinions—opinions that reflect his culture and hence do not apply to us. To these authors, Paul was "a man of his own time." He occasionally glimpsed the ideal that Jesus established during His time on earth; yet he never fully arrived at "the gospel ideal" of "full equality" or complete role interchangeability in both the home and the church.[48]

In contrast to the authors of *The Welcome Table,* the authors of *Women in Ministry* consciously underscore the claim that their approach to the Bible is not the same as that of their distant ideological cousins. Significantly, the editor of *Women in Ministry* states that "all the chapters" in the book are based on the "time-honored approaches" reflected in such "recognized Adventist publications" as the 1986 "Methods of Bible Study" document, an officially approved church document that rejects even a "modified use of the historical-critical method."[49]

Given that some authors of *Women in Ministry* also still subscribe to a modified use of contemporary higher criticism,[50] some readers may wonder if the carefully-worded statement on the use of the church's time-honored approaches to the Bible is not calculated to appeal to conservative church members who are now waking up to the baneful effects of the historical-critical method in the church.[51]

Still, to the extent that the authors have put themselves on record as not using aspects of the historical-critical method, readers should see the hermeneutical stance professed in *Women in Ministry* as a step in the right direction. Whether the actual practice in the book is consistent with the claim remains to be seen. Insofar as the authors claim to uphold the church's generally accepted approach to Scripture on this particular issue, I personally sense a far closer affinity with the authors of the Seminary book than with those of *The Welcome Table,* many of whom seem to put their liberal and feminist commitments above Scripture.

My point is this: There are two major defects plaguing the arguments of liberal and conservative *proponents* of women's ordination—defects arising from the use of a wrong methodology, and those arising from an inconsistent use of a right methodology. Whereas *The Welcome Table* should justifiably be criticized for using a *wrong* methodology (liberal and feminist hermeneutics), *Women in Ministry,* if truly adopting the traditional Adventist approach, should be evaluated on the basis of whether the book consistently uses the *right* methodology (the "time-honored" approach). It is this latter issue that divides the views of conservative *opponents* of women's ordination from those of conservative *proponents* (the conservative image the Seminary writers seek to project when they all claim to subscribe to Adventism's time-honored principles of interpretation).

C. The Content of *Women in Ministry*

Women in Ministry should also be read against the backdrop of the long-standing Seventh-day Adventist belief and practice of ministry. Regardless of one's position on women's ordination, this one fact is incontrovertible: Ordaining women as elders or pastors is "new light" which the worldwide Seventh-day Adventist church is being urged to embrace.[52] Until recently, Adventists have been unanimous in their view that no precedent for the practice of ordaining women can be found in Scripture, nor in the writings of Ellen G. White and the early Seventh-day Adventist church.[53]

Thus, in order for the authors of the book to overthrow what has been understood as the universal consensus of the Old Testament, New Testament, and early Seventh-day Adventist belief, and thus succeed in "doing something about Utrecht," they must come up with compelling reasons for women's ordination. The writers believe they have done exactly that: "Our conclusion is that ordination and women can go together, that 'women in pastoral leadership' is not an oxymoron, but a manifestation of God's grace in the church." Or as the prologue states: "We believe that the biblical, theological, and historical perspectives elaborated in this book affirm women in pastoral leadership."[54]

Perceptive readers of *Women in Ministry* will notice slight variations in the views of the authors regarding the above conclusions. A majority of the writers are fully convinced that the New Testament "affirms new roles for women in the church that do not preclude women's ordination to ministry" or that it "never" prohibits women from taking "positions of leadership, including headship positions over men."[55]

But a minority is more modest: "It is time for the Adventist Church to calmly admit that the Scriptures are silent on the matter and that we have no direct word from the Lord either in Scripture or in the writings of Ellen White. This is an opportunity therefore for the exercise of prayerful study and sound judgment. It is our responsibility to seek divine guidance and make a decision as best we can in the light of the Adventist understanding of the church and its mission."[56]

Despite the slight differences among the convinced voices ("there are compelling reasons to ordain women") and the cautious voices ("there are no compelling reasons not to ordain"), the two years of animated discussions, writing, re-writing, careful editing, cross-referencing, and approval by all members of the committee has produced a work in which there seem to be ten basic lines of argument for the ordination of women as elders or pastors. I suggest the following as the essential contours of the biblical and historical arguments advanced by *Women in Ministry*.[57]

(1) Genesis 1-3 teaches that God did not institute headship and submission or male-female role distinctions *at creation*. Adam and Eve enjoyed "full equality" of "shared leadership" or "shared headship." Male headship and female submission were introduced by God *after the Fall;* even then, this was a non-ideal arrangement designed only for the governance of the home, not the church or covenant community.

(2) New Testament teaching on headship and submission (Eph 5:21-33; Col 3:18-19; 1 Pet 3:1-7) suggests that today Christians should aim at reaching the creation ideal of "total equality," understood to mean the obliteration of any gender-based role differentiation.

(3) A careful study of the Bible reveals that there was actually at least one "woman priest" in the Old Testament. God Himself ordained Eve as a priest alongside Adam when, after the Fall, He dressed both as priests in the garden of Eden using animal skins. Prophetesses Miriam, Deborah, and Huldah exercised headship or leadership roles over men.

(4) The Bible also reveals that there were actually "women apostles and leaders" in the New Testament. Junia (Rom 16:7), for example, was an outstanding "female apostle," and Phoebe (Rom 16:1-2) was a "female minister."

(5) The New Testament teaching of "the priesthood of all believers" suggests that women may be ordained as elders or pastors.

(6) When correctly understood, biblical texts (like 1 Tim 2:11ff., 1 Cor 14:34ff., etc.) which seem to preclude women from headship responsibilities in the home as husbands and fathers and in the church as elders or pastors are temporary restrictions that applied only to specific situations during New Testament times.

(7) Careful study of early Seventh-day Adventist history reveals that women actually served as pastors in those days and were issued ministerial certificates. Ellen G. White apparently endorsed the call of such women to the gospel ministry.

(8) The 1881 General Conference session voted to ordain women. This vote, however, was apparently ignored or killed by the all-male General Conference Committee (comprised of George I. Butler, Stephen Haskell, and Uriah Smith).

(9) A landmark statement in 1895 by Ellen G. White called for ordaining women to the gospel ministry. This statement could have spurred on the male brethren who were reluctant to implement the alleged 1881 General Conference decision.

(10) Ellen G. White was herself ordained and was issued ministerial credentials.

In two later chapters I will argue that the above assertions are based on speculative and questionable reinterpretations of Scripture as well as misleading and erroneous claims regarding Adventist history. Yet on the basis of such "biblical, theological, and historical" evidence, *Women in Ministry* seeks to convince readers of the "new light" of ordaining women *as elders or pastors.*

But there is also a moral-ethical argument. Emphasizing the ethical necessity of ordaining women as elders or pastors, some of the *Women in Ministry* authors argue that "it is morally reprehensible to hold back from women the one thing that formally recognizes their work within the church." "It is imperative" that the church act "with justice, with mercy, and with courage on behalf of its women." The failure of the church to act ethically, or a delay on its part to do so, will compel "the forces of history" (such as the churches in North America which unilaterally engaged in "congregational ordinations") to drag the church along.[58]

Moreover, we are told, unless the new light of women's ordination is implemented, the witness of the church will not only be discredited in countries where it is wrong to "discriminate" against women, but it will make God "look bad." Thus, the church's rejection of women's ordination will be an affront to the character of God, even as slavery was in the nineteenth century.[59]

If the reader is not yet convinced by *Women in Ministry*'s biblical, theological, historical, and moral or ethical arguments, there is one final argument: We must listen to the voice of the Holy Spirit as He calls upon us today to change our patterns of ministry in response to the pragmatic needs of a growing church. Writes the editor in her summation chapter:

"If circumcision, based on divine [Old Testament] mandate, could be changed [by the apostles, elders, and believers, together with the Holy Spirit, at the Jerusalem Council of Acts 15], how much more could patterns of ministry [ordaining women as elders and pastors], which lack a clear 'Thus says the Lord,' be modified to suit the needs of a growing church?"[60]

Because my later chapters will evaluate the contents of the book, for now I will simply make the following comments in response to the "moral imperative" argument and the appeal to the Holy Spirit's leading to meet the pragmatic needs of a growing church: (1) For believing Christians, there is a "moral imperative" always to trust and obey biblical truth. Whenever they are compelled to believe and practice error, that imperative is not moral—it is coercion. (2) The Holy Spirit cannot lead believers today into "new truths" or "new light" that contradict those already established in His inspired Word.

Therefore, *Women in Ministry*'s arguments concerning ethics and the Holy Spirit can only be sustained if the book's biblical, theological, and historical arguments are compelling enough to overthrow the historic understanding of Seventh-day Adventists that ordaining women is an unbiblical practice.

Before embarking upon a biblical and historical evaluation of *Women in Ministry*, it may be helpful to show how this pro-ordination book from the Seminary fits into a carefully orchestrated strategy to impose women's ordination upon the Seventh-day Adventist church.

D. *Women in Ministry:* Theology or Ideology?

As we have noted earlier, the initiative for *Women in Ministry* came from some leaders in the North American Division in response to pressure from a relatively small but influential group which has been pushing for women's ordination during the past thirty or more years. Initially, advocates convinced *church leaders* at the 1975 Spring Council meeting to approve the biblically-compromising practice of ordaining women as *local elders* in the North American Division if "the greatest discretion and caution" were exercised. Later, they succeeded in persuading *church leaders* at the Fall 1984 Annual Council meeting to re-affirm and expand the 1975 decision, voting to "advise each division that it is free to make provisions as it may deem necessary for the election and ordination of women as local elders."[61]

Thus, even though the 1975 provision departed from the New Testament model of church leadership which assigns to men, not women, the headship roles of elder or pastor, and even though the world church had not formally approved of the provision at a General Conference session, in 1984 ordination of women as *elders* was extended from North America to the world field.

Emboldened by their success in influencing church leaders to allow "women elders," pro-ordination advocates proceeded then to urge the *world church* in General Conference session to ordain women as *pastors,* at least in divisions favorable to it. However, at the General Conference sessions both in 1990 (Indianapolis) and 1995 (Utrecht), the representatives of the world church overwhelmingly *rejected* the pleas to ordain women into the gospel ministry. The votes were 1173 to 377 (in 1990) and 1481 to 673 (in 1995). In spite of these decisions, proponents of women's ordination determined upon an all-out campaign, including unilateral ordinations in some influential North American churches and institutions. At the same time that these rebellious ordinations were taking place, advocates were also employing a tactic that had served their cause well in the past—namely, working through church leaders to legislate the unbiblical practice.

Without doubt, the most subtle, and yet most ambitious, effort by pro-ordinationists to overturn the worldwide decision is the proposal contained in the North American Division's document "President's Commission on Women in Ministry—Report." The document was voted during the October 7-10, 1997 year-end meeting of the North American church leaders (see Appendix D of this present volume). If fully implemented, it will allow women to occupy the highest headship positions of church leadership, including local church pastor, conference president, union president, division president, and even General Conference president.

I summarize below the major strategies which the document outlines, offering possible reasons behind some of its provisions. Readers familiar with what is going on will recognize that advocates are already energetically implementing these strategies in church publications, print and video media, schools, local churches, conferences and unions.

1. To make "women pastors" a common fixture in the church, conferences are encouraged "to hire more women in pastoral positions"; they are also requested "to set realistic goals to increase the number of women in pastoral ministry in their field [*sic*] during the next three years [culminating in the year 2000—the year of the Toronto General Conference session]";

2. To enlist young people and their parents and teachers in the pro-ordination campaign, Adventist colleges and universities in North America are encouraged "to recruit young women who sense a call to pastoral ministry to pursue ministerial studies";

3. To get people used to the *concept* of women serving in same roles as men, "the NAD edition of the *Adventist Review* and other general church papers [are to] be asked to publish profiles of women serving in pastoral ministry several times a year";

4. To ensure that church members become accustomed to *seeing* "women pastors," the latter must be given "multiple exposures . . . in congregations throughout the NAD," including the "use of print and video media" and "indirect portrayals of women with men in creative approaches to pastoral ministry";

5. To legislate or make official the ordination of women in the Seventh-day Adventist church without risking another General Conference session defeat, the document encourages the world church "to modify the language" in relevant sections of the current *Church Manual* and North American Division working policy so that wherever the words "ordain" or "ordination" occur they will be replaced by

"ordain/commission" or "ordination/commissioning"; this modification makes "commissioning" the functional equivalent of "ordination."

6. To implement modifications suggested in the *Church Manual* and North American Division Working Policy, unions and local conferences are encouraged "to promptly conduct commissioning services for those women who are eligible";

7. To skillfully quiet opposition to women's ordination/"commissioning" at both the local and higher levels of the church, "the Ministerial Association and/or any appropriate structure" should appoint "an 'ombudsman'—a person with insight in the system and denominational policies who can provide feedback and guidance when women in ministry encounter conflict with employing organizations, as well as provide mediation if necessary";

8. To ensure that pro-ordination views are constantly carried in materials produced by the church, "more of the advocacy for women in ministry [should] be channeled through the union papers and other media of mass distribution"; "preparation and dissemination of educational materials in multiple media designed to raise awareness about women in pastoral ministry and the role of women in the church" should be carried out;

9. To silence or censor views opposing women's ordination, "the Church Resources Consortium [should] monitor and audit all NAD-produced and endorsed materials for compliance with a gender-inclusive model for ministry";

10. To make dissenting church members feel as though *they* are out of harmony with the Bible or the official Seventh-day Adventist position, "the division president [should] issue a clear call to the church for gender-inclusiveness at all levels of the church—boards, committees, pastoral assignments, etc."

11. To ensure the eventual possibility for all conference, union or division pastors to be guided by a "woman pastor," the North American Division is urged to "move with a sense of urgency to include a woman with ministerial background as ministerial secretary or an associate ministerial secretary";

12. To give biblical and historical justification for the women's ordination agenda, there should be "(i) multiple articles in denominational periodicals" and "(ii) a hermeneutics conference by the NAD and/or the GC" to "clarify" the church's understanding of biblical interpretation towards the "goals for gender inclusiveness in church organization."

Actually, most of these strategies had been in operation for many years prior to the voting of the document. Advocates had employed them as they had worked through church leaders in their campaign for ordaining women as *elders*. But now, for the first time, the document puts these strategies clearly into print.

Of the twelve strategies listed above, the last one seems to be the most daunting. This is because an overwhelming majority of Seventh-day Adventists in North America and other parts of the world are theological conservatives—Bible-believers. As such they will strongly oppose the pro-ordination campaign, unless advocates are able to come up with ways to interpret the Bible (hermeneutics) to justify the ordaining of women as elders or pastors. This is one reason why some

North American leaders approached the Seminary, urging it to "do something about Utrecht."

The rest is now history. As requested, the Seminary's "Ad Hoc Committee on Hermeneutics and Ordination" has carried out its assignment, producing the book *Women in Ministry*. And consistent with the strategies already outlined in the North American Division's "President's Commission on Women in Ministry—Report," the book has been one-sidedly promoted in church publications and widely distributed around the world. Its producers and promoters believe that they have offered the long-awaited reasons for the "new light" urging women's ordination as a "moral imperative." The question I will address in later chapters is this: Are the book's methods and conclusions biblically and historically valid? A response to this question will reveal to what extent *Women in Ministry* is part of a well-orchestrated campaign to legitimize an unbiblical ideology.

Conclusion

"Doing something about Utrecht" is what *Women in Ministry* is all about. It is an attempt by well-meaning scholars to provide a much-desired biblical and historical justification for the ordination of women as elders and pastors. Their motives are noble. But are their conclusions biblical?

While a majority of the worldwide Seventh-day Adventist church has twice voted against women's ordination, a majority of scholars at the Seminary is believed to favor the practice. How should a theological institution of the church conduct itself when the "scholarly" opinion conflicts with the "churchly" decision? Should an ideological majority at the Seminary exclude opposing views on theological questions they contend are *unresolved?*

The authors of *Women in Ministry* "do not claim to speak for the others, either at the Seminary or in church administration." Yet the resources, name, and influence of the Seminary at Andrews University have been employed to publish and promote their privately-held opinions. Is this appropriate? Should a church institution allow its prestige or resources to be used by *some* church leaders (or even some influential individuals or ideological organizations) to promote controversial views that run contrary to positions taken by the worldwide church?

These questions bring into focus the role we must accord to the opinions of scholars, the voice of the majority, political pressure from some church leaders, and the decisions of church councils, whenever we are called upon to decide on unresolved theological issues.

Ellen G. White reminded us that "God will have a people upon the earth to maintain the Bible, and the Bible only, as the standard of all doctrines and the basis of all reforms. The *opinions of learned men, the deductions of science, the creeds or decisions of ecclesiastical councils,* as numerous and discordant as are the churches which they represent, *the voice of the majority—not one nor all of these* should be regarded as evidence for or against any point of religious faith. Before accepting any doctrine or precept, we should demand a plain 'Thus said the Lord' in its support" (*The Great Controversy*, p. 595, emphasis mine).

Heeding the above counsel, in two later chapters I will attempt to evaluate the biblical and historical evidence marshaled by *Women in Ministry* in support of ordaining women as elders or pastors. As I mentioned earlier, if the book's conclusions are proven to be valid, they should be incorporated into the Seventh-day Adventist church's Bible-based beliefs and lifestyle. And the church should be encouraged immediately to rectify its 150-year-old practice of ministry and ordination. On the other hand, if the evidence and reasoning in the volume are found wanting biblically and historically, then the campaign during the past two or three decades by a few influential scholars and leaders to impose women's ordination on the worldwide church should be rejected as a tragic mistake and a misguided endeavor. Only as we "prove all things," examining "whether those things are so," can we fully decide whether the determined effort to "do something about Utrecht" is inspired by biblical theology or political ideology.

Endnotes

1. For the biblical basis for my present position, see my *Searching the Scriptures: Women's Ordination and the Call to Biblical Fidelity* (Berrien Springs, Mich.: Adventists Affirm, 1995).

2. Quoted portions are from the prologue and epilogue of the book *Women in Ministry: Biblical and Historical Perspectives,* ed. Nancy Vyhmeister (Berrien Springs, Mich.: Andrews University Press, 1998), pp. 2, 436.

3. Nancy Vyhmeister, the editor of *Women in Ministry,* is quoted as making this comment during her October 1998 presentation at the meeting of the pro-ordination group Association of Adventist Women held in Loma Linda, California. For an account of her presentation, see Colleen Moore Tinker, "Seminary States Position in *Women in Ministry*," *Adventist Today,* November-December 1998, pp. 24, 10.

4. Calvin B. Rock, "Review of *Women in Ministry*," *Adventist Review,* April 15, 1999, p. 29. Coming from "a general vice president of the General Conference . . . [and a holder of] doctoral degrees in ministry and Christian ethics," the above statement is designed to be taken seriously by readers of *Adventist Review.* Dr. Rock chaired the business session at the 1995 Utrecht General Conference session. In his opinion, the pro-ordination book of the Seminary "offers a sterling challenge to those who see Scripture as forbidding women's ordination. And it provides welcome data for those who support women's ordination but who lack professional materials to bolster their belief and convincing insights for those who have not known quite how or what to decide" (ibid.). Our re-examination of the pro-ordination volume will put the above book review into a better perspective (see my later chapters in the present book).

5. Vyhmeister, "Prologue," in *Women in Ministry,* p. 5. Of the 20 scholars whose works are published in *Women in Ministry,* 15 were appointed by the Seminary Dean's Council—a chair of the Ad Hoc Committee and editor of the book (Nancy Vyhmeister) and representatives from each of the six departments of the Seminary (Jo Ann Davidson, Richard Davidson, Walter Douglas, Jacques Doukhan, Roger Dudley, Jon Dybdahl, Denis Fortin, Robert Johnston, George Knight, Jerry Moon, Larry Richards, Russell Staples, Peter van Bemmelen, Randal Wisbey). Of the five remaining writers whose works appear in the book, two were Master of Divinity students (Michael Bernoi, Alicia Worley), and three others are Andrews University scholars, apparently invited because of their pro-ordination stance

(Daniel Augsburger, Raoul Dederen, Keith Mattingly). Of the three scholars invited by the committee, the first two are retired (emeritus) Seminary professors and the last is a faculty member in the undergraduate religion department at Andrews University.

6. One favorable reviewer of the book writes: "It is both appropriate and timely for Seminary professors to lead the church in a study of the theology of women's ordination as it relates to the mission of the Adventist Church. What does the Bible say about this? What is theologically sound? What does our Adventist heritage lead us to do now?" See Beverly Beem, "What If . . . Women in Ministry," *Focus* [Andrews University alumni magazine], Winter 1999, p. 30. Beem is chair of the Department of English at Walla Walla College. In her opinion, the Seminary book presents such a "powerful argument" for women's ordination that "to say that the ordination of women is contrary to Scripture or to the tradition of the Adventist Church means going against an impressive array of evidence otherwise" (ibid., p. 31). In later chapters, I will challenge what our pro-ordination reviewer describes as the Seminary authors' "impressive array of evidence" for women's ordination.

7. According to the editor of the book, "less than one month after the Utrecht vote [rejecting autonomy for Divisions regarding women's ordination], several union presidents of the North American Division met with the faculty of the Seventh-day Adventist Theological Seminary, still asking the same question: May a woman legitimately be ordained to pastoral ministry? If so, on what basis? If not, why not? What are the issues involved—hermeneutics? Bible and theology? custom and culture? history and tradition? pragmatism and missiological needs? And furthermore, how could all these facets of the issue be presented in a logical, coherent manner? Would the Seminary faculty please address these questions and provide answers?" (Vyhmeister, "Prologue," in *Women in Ministry,* p. 1).

8. Though historically Seventh-day Adventists did not have women elders and pastors, many women have served the church well in positions of responsibility and outreach, from the local church to the General Conference level. They did so without ordination. However, for about thirty years a small but influential group of people has been working to move the Seventh-day Adventist church a little at a time to legislate the ordination of women as elders and pastors. In the course of their campaign, those pushing for women's ordination have received endorsements from some church leaders who have effected a series of Annual Council policy revisions and *Church Manual* alterations, allowing for a change in the church's long-standing policy regarding the ministry of ordained elders and pastors. For a brief history of how tax-benefit considerations led the church into redefinitions of Adventist practice of ministry, see [C. Mervyn Maxwell,] "A Very Surprising (and Interesting) History," *Adventists Affirm* 12/3 (Fall 1998): 18-22 (included in this volume on pp. 225-230); cf. Laurel Damsteegt, "Pushing the Brethren," ibid., pp. 24-27.

9. Among the 13 recommendations aimed at "affirming and encouraging women in ministry," the document expresses an "urgent need to study and clarify the church's understanding and application of biblical hermeneutics" and that "this should take the form of: (i) multiple articles in denominational periodicals" and (ii) "a hermeneutics conference by the NAD and/ or the GC." See Article XII of the North American Division "President's Commission on Women in Ministry—Report." The entire document, with an analysis, is found in *Adventists Affirm* 12/3 (Fall 1998): 5-17, and is included in this volume Appendix D, pp. 391-404. As I will attempt to show in the next section, the initial request to the Seminary faculty by "several" North American Division union presidents for a clarification of Adventist theology of ordination and for a clear understanding regarding valid Adventist hermeneutical principles was really a search for a scholarly work that would justify the ordination of women. Observe that the generic phrase "women in ministry," employed by the Seminary's Ad Hoc Committee on Hermeneutics and Ordination as a title for their book, is misleading. Like the North American Division President's commission on "Women in Ministry," the Seminary authors' goal was not simply the ministry of women in the church (which has never been opposed by the Adventist church), but rather ordaining women as elders and pastors.

10. At the 1990 Indianapolis session of the General Conference, by a vote of 1173 to 377, the world field rejected the call to ordain women as pastors. Also, at the 1995 Utrecht session of the General Conference, by a vote of 1481 to 673, the worldwide church refused to grant the North American Division's request to ordain women in its own territory. Despite the "spin" by pro-ordination advocates to the effect that the delegates at the two General Conference sessions didn't quite understand what they were voting for, the fact remains that at these two world assemblies, the Bible-believing Seventh-day Adventist family, 90% of which lives outside the industrialized countries of North America, Europe, and Australia, made it clear that the arguments for women's ordination are not biblically convincing.

11. For example, Roger L. Dudley, the author of one of the chapters of the volume, recently stated: "It is important to note that *Women in Ministry* represents the official view of the Seminary and the position of virtually all of its faculty. Whatever the book may accomplish in the church at large, it is the hope of the [Seminary Ad Hoc] committee that it will demonstrate that the Seminary faculty stands for sound Biblical and historical scholarship on this contemporary and controversial issue" (see Roger L. Dudley, "[Letter to the Editor Regarding] *Women in Ministry,*" *Adventist Today,* January-February 1999, p. 6). Similarly, an article titled "Seminary States Position in *Women in Ministry*" quotes Nancy Vyhmeister, the editor of the Seminary book, as saying: "With the total support of the university and the seminary administration and with the support of about 90% of the seminary faculty [who are believed to favor women's ordination], the book came out." Nancy Vyhmeister made this comment at the annual convention of the Association of Adventist Women held in Loma Linda, California, in October 1998 (see Colleen Moore Tinker, "Seminary States Position in Women in Ministry," *Adventist Today,* November-December, 1998). Apparently, it is the comment by the book's editor that *Women in Ministry* enjoys the "total support of the university and the seminary administration" that has been misunderstood as an official Seminary endorsement of the book. But the chair of the Seminary Ad Hoc Committee and editor of the book has categorically repudiated such a claim (see Vyhmeister, "Prologue," in *Women in Ministry,* p. 5).

12. Calvin Rock writes that "the Seventh-day Adventist Church, and the broader Christian community, are indebted to the 20 authors of *Women in Ministry*" for "producing such a thoughtful, thorough treatment of the major aspects of the question 'Should women be ordained as pastors in the Seventh-day Adventist Church?'" In his estimation, the book employs "skillful exegesis of Scripture and careful examination of relevant E. G. White materials," showing why "liberating knowledge of contextual and linguistic backgrounds is absolutely vital in ecclesiastical debate" (Rock, "Review of *Women in Ministry,*" *Adventist Review,* April 15, 1999, p. 29). Given the one-sided book reviews that have been presented in several Adventist publications, Doug Jones's editorial comment in *Focus* magazine is worth remembering: "The faculty in the Seminary are to be commended for their earnest and critical exploration of women and Christian ministry. . . . I encourage *Focus* readers to read *Women in Ministry* with care as an important step in achieving balance" (see Jones's editorial note to Malcolm Dwyer's letter to the editor, "Seeking Solid Backing," in *Focus,* Spring 1999, p. 5).

13. Until very recently, the Seventh-day Adventist practice has limited ordination of *elders* and *pastors* to males alone. (Biblically speaking there is no distinction between elder and pastor.) However, through a series of Annual Council church policy revisions, a theologically and ethically-inconsistent practice has been instituted in recent times that allows women to be ordained as elders, but not as pastors. We must not miss the implication of this biblically-untenable practice. If women can be ordained as local elders, it is equally valid for them to be ordained as pastors. But by the same token, if the practice of ordaining women as local elders is unbiblical, it is also unbiblical to ordain them as pastors. So the question really facing the church is this: Is ordaining women as *elders* biblical? If it is, we must continue the practice and extend it to include ordaining women as pastors. On the other hand, if ordain-

ing women as local elders is not scriptural, we must *reconsider* previous church council actions in order to come into harmony with the Bible. In an earlier work, *Searching the Scriptures: Women's Ordination and the Call to Biblical Fidelity* (Berrien Springs, Mich.: Adventists Affirm, 1995), I have argued for the latter option—namely for the church to reconsider previous church council actions in order to come into harmony with the Bible. This approach alone preserves the 150-year-old biblical practice of the Adventist church.

14. See my *Receiving the Word: How New Approaches to the Bible Impact Our Biblical Faith and Lifestyle* (Berrien Springs, Mich.: Berean Books, 1996).

15. Nancy Vyhmeister, "Prologue," in *Women in Ministry,* p. 2.

16. Ibid., p. 4.

17. Ibid., p. 5.

18. See, for example, Alfred C. McClure, "NAD's President Speaks on Women's Ordination: Why Should Ordination be Gender Inclusive?" *Adventist Review* [North American Division edition], February 1995, pp. 14-15; cf. Gary Patterson, "Let Divisions Decide When to Ordain Women," *Spectrum* 24/2 (April 1995), pp. 36-42. For responses to the above view, see the articles by Ethel R. Nelson, "'No Turning Back' on Ordination?" and C. Mervyn Maxwell, "Response to NAD President's Request to Annual Council" in *Adventists Affirm* 9/1 (Spring 1995): 42-46, 30-37, 67; cf. Samuel Koranteng-Pipim, *Searching the Scriptures: Women's Ordination and the Call to Biblical Fidelity* (Berrien Springs, Mich.: Adventists Affirm, 1995), pp. 9-14, 88-90.

19. After the rejection of the North American Division's petition at Utrecht, the Pacific Union Conference, one of the largest North American union conferences, took an action they considered to be a road map to eventually ordaining women. Among other things, the union executive committee passed a resolution calling upon the General Conference, through the North American Division, to initiate a process that leads to: (A) "a clarification of the Adventist theology of ordination, *culminating in the ordination of women";* and (B) "action steps that leads to a clear understanding and member education regarding valid Adventist hermeneutical principles." The executive committee of the Pacific Union also released a document affirming the group's commitment to the goal of women's ordination and to working towards the day when it will be realized. See "Pacific Union Executive Committee Maps Course for Women," *Pacific Union Recorder,* October 2, 1995, pp. 3, 11, emphasis mine.

20. See the introduction to "President's Commission on Women in Ministry—Report" reproduced in *Adventists Affirm* 12/3 (Fall 1998): 13 and in this volume on p. 399.

21. "A Statement of Commitment to Women in Gospel Ministry from the North American Division Union Presidents," October 13, 1995, emphasis mine. Two years after the North American Division President's commission was appointed, its report was formally accepted on October 9, 1997. Among the specific recommendations for "gender inclusiveness in church organization" is an "urgent need to study and clarify the church's understanding and application of biblical hermeneutics. This should take the form of: (i) multiple articles in denominational periodicals; (ii) a hermeneutics conference sponsored by the NAD and/or the GC." See Article XII of the Report of the "President's Commission on Women in Ministry." The entire document is worth reading, if one is to capture the scope of the strategies to achieve a gender-inclusive ministry (see pp. 399-404 in this volume).

22. At the 1986 Annual Council meeting in Rio de Janeiro, Brazil, church leaders representing all the world fields of the Seventh-day Adventist church approved the report of the General Conference's "Methods of Bible Study Committee" as representative of the church's hermeneutical position. This document was published in the *Adventist Review,* January 22, 1987, pages 18-20, and reproduced as Appendix C in my *Receiving the Word,* pp. 355-362. Generally, loyal Adventists embrace the 1986 "Methods of Bible Study" document as reflecting Adventism's historic principles of interpretation. For a discussion of how Adventist scholars have reacted to the "Methods of Bible Study" document, see my *Receiving the Word,* pp. 75-99. For more on the history of Adventist Bible interpretation, see C. Mervyn Maxwell,

"A Brief History of Adventist Hermeneutics," *Journal of the Adventist Theological Society* 4/ 2 (1993): 209-226; Don F. Neufeld, "Biblical Interpretation in the Advent Movement," in *Symposium on Biblical Hermeneutics,* ed. Gordon Hyde (Washington, D.C.: Biblical Research Institute, 1974), pp. 109-125; George Reid, "Another Look At Adventist Hermeneutics," *Journal of the Adventist Theological Society* 2/1 (1991): 69-76.

23. *Seventh-day Adventists Believe . . . : A Biblical Exposition of 27 Fundamental Doctrines* (Washington, D.C.: Ministerial Association of the General Conference of Seventh-day Adventists, 1988), esp. pp. 142-150. Produced by some 194 Seventh-day Adventist thought leaders around the world, this "carefully researched" volume is to be received "as representative of . . . [what] Seventh-day Adventists around the globe cherish and proclaim," and as furnishing "reliable information on the beliefs of our [Seventh-day Adventist] church" (ibid., pp. vii, iv, v).

24. *Seventh-day Adventist Minister's Handbook* (Silver Spring, Md.: Ministerial Association of the General Conference of Seventh-day Adventists, 1997), pp. 83-86. The "Ordination Statement" in the *Minister's Handbook* sets forth Adventists' understanding of the nature, significance, qualifications, and the responsibility of ordination. A note attached to "Statement of Ordination" reads: "This section reproduces the statement on ministerial ordination prepared by the General Conference Ministerial Association and the GC Biblical Research Institute. The statement received broad input from the world field and went through numerous revisions. It purposely omits the gender issue in ministerial ordination, seeking rather to lay down basic principles by which all ministerial ordination issues can be measured" (ibid., p. 83 [1997 edition]).

25. For more on the relationship between the issues of income-tax benefits and ordination, see [C. Mervyn Maxwell, editor] "A Very Surprising (and Interesting) History," *Adventists Affirm* 12/3 (Fall 1998): 18-23, appearing on pp. 225-230 of the present volume; cf. *Receiving the Word,* pp. 125-126; p. 140, notes 43 and 44.

26. The editor of the unofficial magazine *Adventist Today* summarizes the circumstances leading to the production of the Seminary book, as narrated by Nancy Vyhmeister, chair of the Seminary Ad Hoc Committee and editor of the book, at the October 1998 meeting of the pro-ordination group Association of Adventist Women held in Loma Linda, California. On the circumstances leading to the feeling of "let down," Vyhmeister mentioned that in the wake of the Utrecht defeat of the North American Division petition for women's ordination, people from opposite ends of the ordination spectrum blamed or praised the Seminary for sending two representatives with opposing viewpoints. She, however, explained that the two professors who spoke at Utrecht (Raoul Dederen and P. Gerard Damsteegt) did not speak for the Seminary: "Those people were invited by 'someone else,' and they agreed to speak long before the seminary knew anything about it." When, therefore, less than a month after Utrecht "several" North American leaders met with the Seminary faculty and told them, "you let us down [at Utrecht]; you're against women's ordination," reports *Adventist Today*'s editor, "every representative of the seminary who was attending the meeting insisted that they were not against women's ordination. In fact, Nancy said, about 90% of the seminary faculty favor women's ordination." What follows is significant: *"'Then do something about it,'* one union president said. Dr. [Werner] Vyhmeister, dean of the seminary and Nancy's husband, agreed and said that the Dean's Council would decide what to do. The outcome of that decision was a fifteen-person committee which [was] formed to study the subject of hermeneutics and ordination" (see Colleen Moore Tinker, "Seminary States Position in *Women in Ministry,"Adventist Today,* November-December, 1998, pp. 24, 10; emphasis mine). "Doing something about Utrecht" is what the Seminary book is all about, rather than being a quest for an open-minded investigation of what the Bible actually teaches on the subject of women in ministry. Some North American leaders wanted the scholars at the Seminary to speak with one voice in favor of women's ordination.

27. See, for example, Samuele Bacchiocchi, *Women in the Church: A Biblical Study on the Role of Women in the Church* (Berrien Springs, Mich.: Biblical Perspectives, 1987); C. Raymond

Holmes, *The Tip of An Iceberg: Biblical Authority, Biblical Interpretation, and the Ordination of Women in Ministry* (Berrien Springs, Mich.: Adventists Affirm and Wakefield, Mich.: Pointer Publications, 1994); Samuel Koranteng-Pipim, *Searching the Scriptures: Women's Ordination and the Call to Biblical Fidelity* (Berrien Springs, Mich.: Adventists Affirm, 1995). At the time they published their works, Samuele Bacchiocchi was a professor of church history and theology in the religion department of Andrews University; C. Raymond Holmes was the director of the Doctor of Ministry Program and professor of Worship and Preaching at the Theological Seminary; and Samuel Koranteng-Pipim was a Ph.D. candidate in systematic theology at the Theological Seminary, having served there as a contract teacher in theology and ethics (see also next note).

28. Of the 20 authors who collaborated to produce the book, one was the Seminary professor who presented the pro-ordination view at Utrecht (Raoul Dederen); but the other Seminary faculty member who presented the opposing view at Utrecht was excluded (P. Gerard Damsteegt, the principal author of the church's *Seventh-day Adventists Believe*). *Women in Ministry* contains an article by an associate professor in the religion department at Andrews University (Keith Mattingly); but a well-known professor in the same department who had published an opposing view (*Women in the Church*) was left out (Samuele Bacchiocchi). Though not part of the initial committee of 15, other Seminary scholars, including a retired faculty member, were allowed to publish their views in the book (George Knight, Denis Fortin, and Daniel Augsburger); but another equally competent retired faculty member who had earlier challenged women's ordination (in his *The Tip of An Iceberg*) was not invited to contribute a chapter (C. Raymond Holmes). Two Seminary students' works appear in the book (Michael Bernoi and Alicia Worley); but not a single Seminary student opposing women's ordination was included (at that time Samuel Koranteng-Pipim was a doctoral candidate and had authored the book *Searching the Scriptures*). It is clear that the Seminary Ad Hoc Committee decided that no other viewpoints should be known in the book except those favoring women's ordination. The pro-ordination bias of the committee is also evidenced by the manner in which some cite the works and authors of non-ordination publications (see especially Randal Wisbey, "SDA Women in Ministry, 1970-1998," *Women in Ministry*, pp. 241, 245, 254 note 31).

29. Vyhmeister, "Prologue," p. 2.

30. Space limitations will not permit me to document how, prior to Utrecht, official church publications presented mainly pro-ordination views in their pages. But one of the authors of *Women in Ministry*, despite his pro-ordination bias in chronicling the history of Seventh-day Adventist discussions of the issue, has correctly noted that prior to the 1995 Utrecht General Conference Session, "the *Adventist Review* and *Ministry* published articles dealing with ordination in which the editors took pro-ordination stands" (Randal R. Wisbey, "SDA Women in Ministry: 1970-1998," in *Women in Ministry*, p. 246). For a recent attempt by editors of a church publication to discredit the works of those attempting to uphold the church's official position, see the editorial comment preceding the article by P. Gerard Damsteegt, "Scripture Faces Current Issues," *Ministry*, April 1999, p. 23. For a possible explanation of the pro-ordination bias in church publications, see Articles X and XII in the "[North American Division] President's Commission on Women in Ministry—Report," reproduced on pp. 403-404 of the present volume.

31. How can the committee legitimately invite a "dialogue" when its very actions show that it is more committed to a "monologue" among the different stripes of pro-ordination scholars who had accepted some North American leaders' assignment to *"do something about it [Utrecht]"* than to grappling with the concerns raised by those opposing women's ordination?

32. Vyhmeister, "Prologue" in *Women in Ministry*, p. 5.

33. Ibid.

34. We are not suggesting that there is anything wrong with attempts by scholars to overturn a General Conference session decision if that decision is biblically indefensible. Our point is

simply that the Seminary authors should be candid about their intention, instead of mask-
ing it under euphemistic phrases.

35. Observe, however, that the above pragmatic reasons—namely, "the widespread lack of support" for it and "the possible risk of disunity, dissension, and diversion from the mission of
the Church"—were the secondary reasons stated at the 1990 General Conference session
against ordaining women as pastors. Despite the contrary claims of proponents, the primary reason given by those opposing the practice of ordaining women as pastors was that it
was unbiblical and out of harmony with the writings of Ellen G. White. Thus, in the opinion of those opposed to women's ordination, to go ahead with a practice that lacked widespread *theological* support could result in "disunity, dissension, and diversion from the mission of the Church." The following are the two recommendations from the "Role of Women
Commission" that the 1989 Annual Council brought to the 1990 General Conference
session: "1. While the Commission does not have a consensus as to whether or not the
Scriptures and the writings of Ellen G. White explicitly advocate or deny the ordination of
women to pastoral ministry, it concludes unanimously that these sources affirm a significant, wide ranging, and continuing ministry for women which is being expressed and will
be evidenced in the varied and expanding gifts according to the infilling of the Holy Spirit.
2. Further, in view of the widespread lack of support for the ordination of women to the
gospel ministry in the world Church and in view of the possible risk of disunity, dissension,
and diversion from the mission of the Church, we do not approve ordination of women to
the gospel ministry." Notice that whereas the first reason is theological (lack of theological
consensus) the second is pragmatic (lack of support and possible risks). By a vote of 1173 to
377, the world church voted against women's ordination. (See *Adventist Review,* July 13,
1990, p. 15.

36. One pro-ordination reviewer of the Seminary book sums up the reason for *Women in Ministry* and how the book could be used to justify theologically a possible North American
Division "push" of the issue at a future General Conference session: "So why this book?
Why now? *Utrecht.* That is the answer given in the prologue to the book. One might think
that after the 1995 General Conference session in Utrecht, the discussion would be over
and that everyone would go home and quit talking about it. But that has not happened.
How could it? The motion voted at Utrecht did not address the theological appropriateness
of women's ordination. It addressed only the procedural recommendation of the North
American Division that the decision be made by each division. The increasing dissonance
between theological understandings and church practice remained unresolved. . . . Now, it
is both appropriate and timely for Seminary professors to lead the church in a study of the
theology of women's ordination as it relates with the mission of the Adventist church"
(Beverly Beem, "What If . . . Women in Ministry," *Focus,* Winter 1999, p. 30, emphasis
hers). In response to the so-called procedural argument, a respected North American church
leader has correctly noted: "Though the issue had been presented as a policy matter, whether
to allow divisions to decide for themselves about ordination, most delegates knew that they
were really voting on the biblical legitimacy of women's ordination. How could the world
church make so fundamental a change unless it could find biblical support? How could it
allow itself to be divided on something so essential to its unity and function? So as it had
done five years earlier, the world church gave an emphatic No" (Jay Gallimore, "The Larger
Issues," on p. 343 in this volume).

37. In view of these oft-repeated claims by proponents of women's ordination, the following
questions deserve a brief response: (1) Was there a ban on publishing and distributing
materials on women's ordination between 1988 and 1995? (2) Were advocates of women's
ordination relatively silent during the period of the "moratorium" or "ban," while opponents published two books (*The Tip of An Iceberg* [1994] and *Searching the Scriptures* [1995])?
These are the facts: In May 1988, while awaiting the July 1989 meeting and recommendation of the "Role of Women Commission," General Conference president Elder Neal C.

Wilson appealed to all church members "to abstain from circulating books, pamphlets, letters, and tapes that stir up debate and often generate more confusion [on women's ordination]." Proponents of women's ordination often misinterpret this specific appeal by the General Conference president to mean a permanent moratorium or ban on publishing works on women's ordination. They claim that out of loyalty to the General Conference president they honored his moratorium while those opposed undermined it by publishing and distributing their works. In making these claims, advocates are either unaware of or overlook the facts concerning the General Conference president's appeal and the aggressive campaign mounted by pro-ordination entities. First of all, the president's appeal was not a permanent "ban" or moratorium. Elder Wilson's statement reads: "The 1985 General Conference session action called upon the church to prepare a recommendation by the time of the 1989 Annual Council, so a further meeting of the commission [the Commission on the Role of Women] will be held in July of 1989. Indeed, in such important matters we must at all costs avoid hasty action, and so we will set aside one week to pray together, listen to each other, discuss further papers that will be prepared, and—I hope—come together in a decision dictated by the Holy Spirit. *In the meantime,* I appeal to all members of the church, whatever their particular convictions on this matter, to avoid further controversy and argument. I request you to abstain from circulating books, pamphlets, letters, and tapes that stir up debate and often generate more confusion. I think it would be much better if we prayed and fasted, and studied the Bible and the writings of Ellen White for ourselves" (Neal C. Wilson, "Role of Women Commission Meets: The General Conference President Reports to the Church," *Adventist Review,* May 12, 1988, p. 7, emphasis mine). Notice that the president's appeal was not a permanent moratorium or "ban"; it was limited to the period between May 12, 1988 and July 1989 when the Commission was expected to present its theological findings. Even then, the appeal was directed against works that "stir up debate and often generate more confusion." Second, if the moratorium did indeed exist as proponents of women's ordination often claim, (1) then editors of church publications like *Adventist Review* and *Ministry* contravened it when they published several pro-ordination articles during the period between 1988 and 1995; (2) then the pro-ordination authors and some church institutions like Pacific Press, Review and Herald, Andrews University Press, and Loma Linda University Press broke the ban when they published and distributed pro-ordination books like Caleb Rosado's *Broken Walls* (Pacific Press, 1989), and *Women, Church, God: A Socio-Biblical Study* (Loma Linda University Press, 1990), Josephine Benton's *Called by God* (Blackberry Hill Publishers, 1990), V. Norskov Olsen's *Myth and Truth: Church, Priesthood and Ordination* (Loma Linda University Press, 1990), Jennifer Knight's, et al., *The Adventist Woman in the Secular World: Her Ministry and Her Church* (North Ryde, N.S.W., Australia, 1991), Rosa Taylor Banks's, ed., *A Woman's Place* (Review and Herald, 1992), Sakae Kubo's *The God of Relationships* (Review and Herald, 1993), Patricia A. Habada and Rebecca Frost Brillhart's, eds., *The Welcome Table* (TEAMPress, 1995), Lourdes Morales-Gudmundsson's, ed., *Women and the Church: The Feminine Perspective* (Andrews University Press, 1995); (3) then certain authors of the Seminary book violated the alleged "moratorium" by publishing articles in favor of women's ordination; see, for example, Richard M. Davidson's "The Theology of Sexuality in the Beginning: Genesis 1-2" and "The Theology of Sexuality in the Beginning: Genesis 3," *Andrews University Seminary Studies* 26 (1988); Nancy Vyhmeister, "Review of *The Tip of An Iceberg*," *Ministry,* February 1995, pp. 26-28; etc. Space limitations will not allow me to document the fact that during and after the alleged seven-year "moratorium," advocates of women's ordination, including a number of the Seminary authors of *Women in Ministry,* used a number of means to publicize their pro-ordination views. But in spite of their aggressive campaign, proponents failed to convince the world church of the soundness of their theological arguments for women's ordination. A pro-ordination scholar of ethics puts to rest the oft-repeated claim that until the publication of *Women in Ministry* proponents of women's ordination had been relatively silent. He correctly noted that, prior to the more than 2-to-1 defeat of the women's ordination request at Utrecht, "denominational leaders, with others, had backed ordination with speeches at Annual Council, the speech in Utrecht, and a special strategy committee. The Southeastern California Conference Gender Inclusiveness Commission and others had sent materials to all General Conference delegates. The *Adventist Review* had run special covers, issues, and features promoting women. . . . Some ordination proponents thought that they might win if they got enough materials to the delegates, but found themselves wrong" (Jim Walters, "General Conference Delegates Say NO on Women's Ordination," *Adventist Today,* July-August, 1995, pp. 12-13).

38. See Susan Walters, "Prospectus Revealed for Book on Ordination of Women," *Adventist Today,* March-April, 1997, p. 24.

39. Vyhmeister, "Prologue," p. 2.

40. Susan Walters, "Prospectus Revealed for Book on Ordination of Women," *Adventist Today,* March-April, 1997, p. 24, emphasis mine.

41. Jack Stenger (Public Information Officer, Andrews University), "Andrews Professors Address Women's Ordination" Press Release, dated October 22, 1998, emphasis mine.

42. The book has been widely distributed to church leaders around the world. In an accompanying letter on the stationery of the Seventh-day Adventist Theological Seminary, the rationale for the free distribution of the book is explained: "Because of your position as a thought leader in the Seventh-day Adventist Church, you have been selected to receive a gift copy of this important study of the place of women in the church's ministry. The book is not intended to incite polemics on ordination, but to provide carefully researched information and foster dialogue. If you have questions or comments, feel free to direct them to the individual authors or to the editor of the book, all of them at Andrews University. May God bless your service in His cause." Could the "carefully researched information" to "foster dialogue" be a veiled reference to the year 2000 General Conference session in Toronto?

43. Calvin Rock, "Review of *Women in Ministry,*" *Adventist Review,* April 15, 1999, p. 29, emphasis mine.

44. Besides the official introduction of the book at a special Seminary chapel assembly on October 7, 1998, the press release by the public relations office of Andrews University, and the book's use as textbook and required reading material in some Seventh-day Adventist institutions, there have also been one-sided book reviews in church publications like *Adventist Review* (see Calvin Rock's review in the April 15, 1999 issue, p. 29) and *Ministry* (see Fritz Guy's book review in the January 1999 issue, pp. 28-29). It has also been favorably reviewed in the Andrews University publication *Focus* (see Beverly Beem's review in the Winter 1999 issue, pp. 30-34), a magazine sent worldwide to alumni of the university. As we have mentioned earlier, the book has also been mass-distributed to church leaders around the world "to provide carefully researched information and foster dialogue." Finally, one of the church's leading publishing houses, Pacific Press Publishing Association, is distributing the book in Adventist Book Centers around the world. The book's editor is also quoted as saying that their book has "the total support" of Andrews University, the Seminary, and the ministerial department of the General Conference. For the strategy behind much of this publicity of works promoting women's ordination in the church, see the North American Division's "President's Commission on Women in Ministry—Report," especially Articles X and XII, reproduced in this volume, pp. 403-404.

45. *The Welcome Table: Setting A Place for Ordained Women,* edited by Patricia A. Habada and Rebecca Frost Brillhart (Langley Park, Md.: TEAMPress, 1995). The "fourteen prominent SDA historians, theologians, and professionals" who contributed essays to the book are: Bert Haloviak, Kit Watts, Raymond F. Cottrell, Donna Jeane Haerich, David R. Larson, Fritz Guy, Edwin Zackrison, Halcyon Westphal Wilson, Sheryll Prinz-McMillan, Joyce Hanscom Lorntz, V. Norskov Olsen, Ralph Neall, Ginger Hanks Harwood, and Iris M. Yob.

46. This comment from Lawrence T. Geraty appears on the back of *The Welcome Table*.

47. Although the book's introduction and back-cover recommendations state that *The Welcome Table* comprises "carefully thought-through expositions by some of our most competent writers" and "is a definitive collection of essays for our time from respected church leaders," others have observed that, regarding the key hermeneutical issues of women's ordination, this volume is more noteworthy for its breadth than for its depth. For example, Keith A. Burton, an Adventist New Testament scholar, has exposed the historical-critical assumptions underlying some of the essays in *The Welcome Table*. He concludes his insightful critique of this pro-ordination book: "The table around which we are warmly invited to sit is one that already accommodates those who have attacked the relevance of biblical authority; those who wish to pretend that the gnostic image of the primeval and eschatological androgyne is the one toward which Adventists should be moving; those whose interest is in the acquisition of corporate power rather than the evangelization of a dying world; and finally, those who confuse the undiscriminating limitation of the familial and ecclesiastical roles that have been defined by the same Spirit." See Burton, "The Welcome Table: A Critical Evaluation" (unpublished manuscript, 1995), available at the Adventist Heritage Center, James White Library, Andrews University. In my earlier work *Receiving the Word* (pp. 119-129), I spotlighted a few of the troubling aspects of *The Welcome Table's* arguments for women's ordination.

48. For a brief evaluation of the pro-ordination arguments by some of the authors in *The Welcome Table*, see my *Receiving the Word*, chapter 5, part 2, pp. 126-129.

49. See Vyhmeister, "Prologue," in *Women in Ministry*, pp. 3, 5, note 1. Observe the careful wording of the statement: "Rather than having a section on hermeneutics in each chapter containing biblical material, the group decided that one presentation, in the introduction, should be sufficient. Thus, the principles of interpretation described here apply to all chapters on biblical materials. The principles applied are time-honored approaches; similar rules appear in recognized Adventist publications" (ibid., p. 3).

50. Contrary to the church's official position in "The Methods of Bible Study" document, Robert M. Johnston (a *Women in Ministry* author), for example, has recently argued for the use of the historical-critical method. See his "The Case for a Balanced Hermeneutic," *Ministry*, March 1999, pp. 10-12.

51. See my unpublished article, "A Bug in Adventist Hermeneutic," 1999, a summary version of which is to be published in a future issue of *Ministry* under the title, "Questions in the Quest for a Unifying Hermeneutic."

52. Christians must always welcome "new light" from God's Word, as long as the proposed "new light" does not contradict an established biblical truth. For a careful summary of what Ellen G. White taught about "new light," see P. Gerard Damsteegt, "New Light in the Last Days," *Adventists Affirm* 10/1 (Spring 1996): 5-13.

53. In my *Receiving the Word* (pp. 123-126), I have challenged revisionist re-interpretations of Adventist beliefs and practice of ministry (see also pp. 138-140, notes 34-44 of my book).

54. Vyhmeister, *Women in Ministry*, pp. 436, 5.

55. See the following authors in *Women in Ministry*: Richard M. Davidson, pp. 283, 284; Jo Ann Davidson, p. 179; cf. Nancy Vyhmeister, p. 350; Robert M. Johnston, pp. 52-53; Peter van Bemmelen, p. 306-307; Jacques Doukhan, p. 39; Daniel Augsburger, p. 96; Keith Mattingly, pp. 71-72; Randal Wisbey, p. 251; Denis Fortin, pp. 127-129; Michael Bernoi, p. 229; Alicia Worley, pp. 370-372; Walter B. T. Douglas, p. 394; Roger L. Dudley, pp. 414-415.

56. Russell Staples, in *Women in Ministry*, p. 251. Jon L. Dybdahl also writes: "Let us be honest. There is no clear specific biblical statement on the issue. No verse gives permission to ordain women, and no passage specifically forbids it" (p. 430); cf. Raoul Dederen, pp. 22-23; Jerry Moon, p. 204; George Knight, pp. 111-112; W. Larry Richards, p. 327-328.

57. Source references from *Women in Ministry* for each of the following points will be provided in my evaluation of the book (see my two other chapters in this volume).

58. Randal R. Wisbey, "SDA Women in Ministry: 1970-1998," *Women in Ministry*, p. 251. For my response to the unilateral post-Utrecht ordinations, see my "How the Holy Spirit Leads the Church," *Adventists Affirm* 12/3 (Fall 1998): 28-35.

59. Roger L. Dudley, "The Ordination of Women in Light of the Character of God," in *Women in Ministry*, pp. 400, 413-414; Walter B. T. Douglas, "The Distance and the Difference: Reflections on Issues of Slavery and Women's Ordination in Adventism," ibid., pp. 379-398; Nancy Vyhmeister, "Epilogue," ibid., pp. 434-435.

60. Vyhmeister, "Epilogue," p. 436.

61. Refer to the minutes of the General Conference Spring Meeting (April 1975) and the General Conference Annual Council (October 1984).

Chapter 2

A Look at the Methods of Interpretation in *Women in Ministry*

P. Gerard Damsteegt

～

During the 1995 General Conference session, the Seventh-day Adventist world church delegates voted overwhelmingly (1481 to 673) against a request of the North American Division that would have allowed each division to ordain women as ministers within its territory. An earlier request for women to be ordained as ministers had been soundly defeated at the 1990 General Conference session.

Soon after the 1995 decision several of the disappointed North American Division union presidents met with some of the faculty of the Seventh-day Adventist Theological Seminary and requested help. A major issue had surfaced during the 1995 General Conference. It had become obvious that the significant barrier to women's ordination was hermeneutics, the way people interpret Scripture. The presidents asked the Seminary to investigate the question of women's ordination.

In response, a Seminary "Ad Hoc" Committee was set up. (*Ad hoc* means "for this one purpose.") Members of the committee were selected so as to avoid the inclusion of well-known opponents of women's ordination. For more than two and a half years the committee met, first assigning topics to various authors, then going over their papers again and again. The result was published by Andrews University Press in October of 1998 as the book, *Women in Ministry: Biblical & Historical Perspectives.*

As one might have anticipated, given the committee's assignment and its exclusive membership, the committee's conclusion was that the Bible, rightly interpreted, is not

P. Gerard Damsteegt, Dr. Theol., *is Associate Professor of Church History, Seventh-day Adventist Theological Seminary, Andrews University.*

opposed to the ordination of women as ministers and that for women to function in positions of pastoral leadership is "a manifestation of God's grace in the church."[1]

The press release issued by Andrews University announced the book as a "watershed" that makes a convincing "biblical case for women's ordination."[2] Both *Ministry* magazine (January 1999, pp. 28, 29) and *Adventist Review* (April 15, 1999, p. 29) published positive reviews of the book.

Such powerful claims deserve our attention. In this chapter we will focus on the principles of interpreting the Bible set forth by the book. Since hermeneutical issues were the very reason the book was requested, the underlying interpretive methodology deserves careful review and evaluation.

1. The Principles of Bible Interpretation

In the prologue of the book, Professor of World Mission Dr. Nancy Vyhmeister, the committee's chair and the book's editor, lists the scriptural principles of interpretation that she says lie at the foundation of the book.

The Bible is divinely inspired, she says, and is the authoritative rule of faith, presenting God's word for all people in all times. The different authors, she observes, stress that the Bible must be allowed to interpret itself, one part explaining another. And because the Bible forms an intrinsic unity, the whole Bible must be taken into account before firm conclusions can be made, meaning that Scripture must be compared with Scripture to find the true meaning of any passage.

The prologue further states that although readers do profit from a simple reading of the Bible, the understanding of a passage is enhanced by a study of the literary and historical context of any passage. It cautions against imposing external interpretations on the Bible.

Wisely, the prologue points out that one needs to approach Scripture in faith, with a willingness to obey. For a correct interpretation, one must have the aid of the Holy Spirit, making prayer a necessity.

Finally it mentions that "absolute uniformity of understanding was not possible or desirable."[3] On this point the prologue quotes Ellen G. White, who wrote, "We cannot then take a position that the unity of the church consists in viewing every text of Scripture in the very same light. The church may pass resolution upon resolution to put down all disagreement of opinions, but we cannot force the mind and will, and thus root out disagreement. These resolutions may conceal the discord, but they cannot quench it and establish perfect agreement. Nothing can perfect unity in the church but the spirit of Christlike forbearance."[4]

So far, so good. These principles we can fully endorse.

There is, however, a very significant additional "rule" of Bible interpretation that the prologue mentions which raises major questions as to how it should be applied. This additional rule is intended to deal with the question, "What do we do with matters of faith on which Scripture is silent?" In view of the significance of this rule in the reasoning of *Women in Ministry*, the whole paragraph in which it appears deserves our attention here:

"On matters on which Scripture is silent, one must search for biblical principles that relate to the situation and apply them with sanctified reasoning. For example, the Bible does not prohibit smoking, but it does admonish us to care for the body temple. Church organization is not spelled out in the Bible. In the 1850s and 1860s Adventist pioneers agonized over whether or not to organize the little flock. James White put forth his position: 'All means which, according to sound judgment, will advance the cause of truth, and are not forbidden by plain scripture declarations, should be employed.' While some Christians have taken the position that whatever Scripture does not specially command is prohibited, Seventh-day Adventists have followed James White's thinking. Our committee did likewise."[5]

As the committee was not clear that women were excluded from pastoral leadership, they found this rule helpful in their investigation of the question of women's ordination.

We readily acknowledge that when confronted with such modern problems as incorporating under state law in order to hold property, selection of a name for the church organization, and applying for insurance, James White could not find explicit instructions "spelled out in the Bible." In such cases he did indeed seek out "biblical principles" and apply them with "sanctified reasoning." At the same time, we must ask whether James White found that the Bible did not spell out church organization. More specifically, we must ask whether James White would have used his rule and sanctified reasoning to allow for the ordination (or commissioning) of women pastors.

It is their use of James White's rule that seems to have enabled the authors of *Women in Ministry* to present their case for women's ordination as elders and ministers. The Seminary committee claims to have done what James White did. Candid attention to the evidence suggests the opposite. This current chapter in *Prove All Things* examines Elder White's perception of church organization as presented in the Bible and his manner of applying what he found. *Women in Ministry* attaches great importance to his example. This chapter does also—though from a different perspective.

2. The Misuse of James White's Rule

In the earliest printed Adventist literature, James White, along with his wife, deplored the confusion and disorganization current among Sabbath-keeping Adventists. They appealed for order and unity. As early as 1853, in a series of articles called "Gospel Order" (James White's name for church organization), Elder White showed his strong support for following the *biblical model* of church organization and leadership.

Elder White wrote that the fundamentals of church organization, or gospel order, were spelled out in the Bible. He urged that "vigorous efforts should be put forth to restore as fast as possible the order of the gospel."[6] He declared that "the divine order of the New Testament is sufficient to organize the church of Christ" and added significantly, "If more were needed, it would have been given by inspiration."[7]

The New Testament was James White's model for church leadership. First, a minister should be called by the Lord to the responsibility of such a position. Second, he said, the prospective minister must meet the "necessary qualifications" that "are plainly stated in the Word."[8] These qualifications, Elder White wrote, were listed by Paul in his counsel to Timothy: "This is a true saying," White quoted, "'If a man desire the office of a bishop, he desireth a good work. A bishop then must be blameless, the husband of one wife, vigilant, sober, of good behaviour, given to hospitality, apt to teach; not given to wine, no striker, not greedy of filthy lucre; but patient, not a brawler, not covetous; one that ruleth well his own house, having his children in subjection with all gravity; (for if a man know not how to rule his own house, how shall he take care of the church of God?) Not a novice, lest being lifted up with pride he fall into the condemnation of the devil. Moreover, he must have a good report of them which are without; lest he fall into reproach and the snare of the devil.' (1 Tim. 3:1-7)."[9]

Commenting on the requirements for the office of elder or minister, James White remarked: "Many seem to desire the office of a bishop, or elder, who fail in many points named here by the Apostle. He must be 'blameless,' 'vigilant,' 'sober,' 'patient,' 'not a brawler.' He must rule well his own house. How is it possible that the Holy Ghost should make a man an overseer of the precious flock, to rule over them [Heb. 13: 17], who knows not how, or neglects to govern his children at home?—Here the Apostle appeals to our reason. And it seems the greatest absurdity that such a man should be called to rule the church. God does not call them. He will not trust souls to their care."[10]

From these comments it is obvious that Elder White did *not* believe that church organization is not spelled out in Scripture. He said the Bible was the guidebook for the selection of church leaders. Judging by the specific requirements he quoted from the Bible, he believed that elders or ministers must be persons with one wife who are successful leaders in their home. This obviously disqualified women from serving as elders or pastors. And not just any man could qualify, but only men who had proven themselves to be successful leaders in their own families.

To use James White's rule—that "all means which, according to sound judgment, will advance the cause of truth, and are not forbidden by plain scripture declarations, should be employed"—to allow the ordination of women as elders and ministers violates his plain intent.

By using Elder White's rule out of context, *Women in Ministry* moves startlingly away from the solid Adventist practice of following the Bible and the Bible only. This departure is seen in the many unwarranted conclusions of the book.

3. What Does James White's Rule Mean?

Women in Ministry emphasizes a point that James White made in 1860 and uses it as an additional rule for interpreting the Bible. We have just seen that Elder White was *not* arguing in defense of women pastors or for church organization as a whole. So what specific problems did he have in mind? What was the historical setting in which he used this rule? For this we need to go back to the years prior to the official organization of the believers into the Seventh-day Adventist movement.

In 1860 Sabbath-keeping Adventists were wrestling with the issue whether they as a church could *legally hold church property*. Donations had been made to James White for the operation of a publishing office for which capital of $5000 was felt to be necessary.[11] Some held Elder White responsible for handling the money, but he declined, arguing that the publishing office was not his personal property but belonged to the church at large. He said, "We do object to being in any way responsible for money lent to this Office, used in printing books while the Office property is not insured."[12]

To prevent total loss in the case of a fire, the office would have to be insured, and he pointed out that to insure the publishing office the believers would have to be incorporated officially as a religious body under the laws of the state of Michigan. This meant that Sabbath-keepers would have to adopt a name for their organization.

But to some strong-minded individuals among the small number of Sabbath-keepers (we numbered about 3000 at that time), organizing as a church was un-thinkable. It would make us just like the other churches that constituted Babylon. And to be legally incorporated as a religious body was out of the question because it would unite God's people with the state—with the United States, the two-horned beast of Revelation 13.[13]

To counteract these objections Elder White asked opponents for clear *scriptural proof* that it was objectionable *to hold church property legally*. He could not see that there was anything in Scripture that prohibited it. He pointed out that there were no biblical counsels for having a weekly church paper or a publishing press, yet it was perfectly proper to have these things. This is the setting in which he suggested that when the Bible does not specifically address an issue, we should follow the rule that "all means which, according to sound judgment, will advance the cause of truth, and are not forbidden by plain scripture declarations, should be employed."

To avoid confusion among believers, Elder White invited everyone to exam-ine his rule, saying, "If this rule be defective, let its defects be shown; if right, then let it be adopted, that confusion *on this question* be prevented."[14]

There certainly can be no objection to James White's rule when it concerns matters that the Bible does not address, such as publishing a weekly church paper or owning a printing press. It is obvious that the Bible is silent on these matters. Here we can fully endorse the use of this rule. However, when it comes to applying his rule to the basic structure of church organization that deals with the qualifica-tions for ministers and elders, we find that his rule does not fit at all. Contrary to the suggestion of *Women in Ministry's* prologue, we have seen that Elder White taught that the Bible does indeed address the basic structure of church organiza-tion. The prologue's claim that "church organization is not spelled out" comes as a surprise in view of the many references to church organization in the Bible to be found in the early Adventist literature.

4. The Bible Teachings on Church Organization

In light of the prologue's assertion that the Bible does not spell out church organization, we need to look extensively at what God has said on this subject. To do this, it is appropriate to investigate the testimonies of Ellen G. White, given to protect the remnant church against almost overwhelming last-day deceptions.

In words that have become famous, Mrs. White observed in 1892 that "the church of Christ, enfeebled and defective as it may be, is the only object on earth on which He bestows His supreme regard."[15] Christ is constantly watching His church with "solicitude, and is strengthening it by His Holy Spirit."[16] If God loves His church this much, we ask, would He have left it to develop without operating instructions? Hardly! And throughout the history of the remnant church, the Lord has given abundant counsels on how it should operate.

During the early days, when some were suspicious of organizing, the believers sought God's counsel earnestly, and He answered. Ellen White wrote: "We sought the Lord with earnest prayer that we might understand His will, and light was given by His Spirit, that there must be *order and thorough discipline* in the church, that *organization was essential.* System and order are manifest in all the works of God throughout the universe. Order is the law of heaven, and it should be the law of God's people on the earth."[17]

Through His Spirit Jesus gave early Adventists testimony after testimony. When the believers accepted this light, they prospered. "Marked prosperity," Mrs. White wrote, attended the progress of the movement. "What is the secret of our prosperity?" she asked. "We have moved under the order of the Captain of our salvation. God has blessed our united efforts. The truth has spread and flourished. Institutions have multiplied. The mustard seed has grown to a great tree. The system of organization has proved a grand success."[18]

Among the counsels given by God's inspiration was instruction to study the excellent organization developed by Moses in the Old Testament. As we shall see, we have considerable information to guide us in our quest for organization that follows the Bible pattern.

5. Church Organization in the Old Testament

The ancient Israelites constituted God's church. Today we should take notice of how God organized this church. "Has God changed from a God of order? No; He is the same in the present dispensation as in the former. Paul says, 'God is not the author of confusion, but of peace' [1 Cor 14:33]. He is as particular now as then. *And He designs that we should learn lessons of order and organization from the perfect order instituted in the days of Moses,* for the benefit of the children of Israel."[19]

The Old Testament's Model of Perfect Organization. The organization of Israel under Moses was characterized by completeness and simplicity. God, the One in control, delegated His authority through leaders. Moses, the highest human leader, was assisted by a council of elders. Spiritual responsibilities were assigned to priests. Each tribe had rulers who delegated responsibilities to subordinates.

"The government of Israel was characterized by the most thorough organization, wonderful alike for its completeness and its simplicity. The order so strikingly displayed in the perfection and arrangement of all God's created works was manifest in the Hebrew economy. God was the center of authority and government, the sovereign of Israel. Moses stood as their visible leader, by God's appointment, to administer the laws in His name. From the elders of the tribes a council of seventy was afterward chosen to assist Moses in the general affairs of the nation. Next came the priests, who consulted the Lord in the sanctuary. Chiefs, or princes, ruled over the tribes. Under these were 'captains over thousands, and captains over hundreds, and captains over fifties, and captains over tens,' and, lastly, officers who might be employed for special duties. Deut. 1:15."[20]

An Organization With No Equality in Ministry. It is noteworthy that even though leadership responsibilities were widely distributed, there was no sense of "equal opportunity" for everyone to select his or her own choice of a life calling. God gave minute and specific instructions, and no one was allowed to depart from them. Anyone who did paid a terrible price. For example:

"The Lord did not leave His holy tabernacle to be borne [carried] indiscriminately by any tribe that might choose. He was so particular as to specify the order He would have observed in bearing the sacred ark and to designate a special family of the tribe of the Levites to bear it."[21] When Uzzah disregarded this order, he died instantly.

When the tribes moved forward, "The head officer of each company gave definite directions in regard to the movements they were required to make, and none who gave attention were left in ignorance of what they were to do. If any failed to comply with the requirements given by the Lord to Moses, and by Moses to the people, they were punished with death. It would be no excuse to plead that they knew not the nature of these requirements, for they would only prove themselves willingly ignorant, and would receive the just punishment for their transgression. If they did not know the will of God concerning them, it was their own fault. They had the same opportunities to obtain the knowledge imparted as others of the people had, therefore their sin of not knowing, not understanding, was as great in the sight of God as if they had heard and then transgressed.

"The Lord designated a special family of the tribe of Levi to bear the ark; and others of the Levites were specially appointed of God to bear the tabernacle and all its furniture, and to perform the work of setting up and taking down the tabernacle. And if any man from curiosity or from lack of order got out of his place and touched any part of the sanctuary or furniture, or even came near any of the workmen, he was to be put to death. God did not leave His holy tabernacle to be borne, erected, and taken down, indiscriminately, by any tribe who might choose the office; but persons were chosen who could appreciate the sacredness of the work in which they were engaged."[22]

Israel's "perfect organization," their subsequent rebellion, and their punishments have all been recorded for us as a warning. The reason for their severe punishment was simply "because of their unwillingness to submit to God's wise arrangements—this faithful picture is hung up before us as a warning lest we follow their example of disobedience and fall like them."[23]

Growth in population led to a refinement of national organization that greatly increased the number of participants and is upheld as a model for today.

Organizational Refinements Lead to Greater Involvement. Under King Solomon the organizational structure was further expanded. "The thoroughness and completeness of the organization perfected at the beginning of Solomon's reign; the comprehensiveness of the plans for bringing the largest number possible of all the people into active service; the wide distribution of responsibility, so that the service of God and of the king should not be unduly burdensome to any individual or class—these are lessons which all may study with profit, and which the leaders of the Christian church should understand and follow."[24]

But there still was no "equality in ministry"; all were still assigned specific tasks. "So far as possible, they followed the system of organization given Israel soon after the deliverance from Egypt. The Levites were assigned the work connected with the temple service, including the ministry of song and instrumental music, and the keeping of the treasures."[25]

6. Church Organization in the New Testament

As with the Old Testament, so the New Testament provides us considerable specific information about church organization for our guidance. Organization of the New Testament church began when Jesus ordained His twelve disciples. "It was at the ordination of the twelve that the first step was taken in the organization of the church that after Christ's departure was to carry on His work on the earth. Of this ordination the record says, 'He goeth up into a mountain, and calleth unto Him whom He would: and they came unto Him. And He ordained twelve, that they should be with Him, and that He might send them forth to preach.' Mark 3:13, 14."[26] We notice that Jesus called "whom He would."

The Jerusalem Church a Model of Church Organization. When difficulty developed in the young Jerusalem church after Christ's ascension, the apostles were led by the Holy Spirit to appoint seven assistants (Acts 6:1-7), who came to be known as the seven deacons. There were now two classes of church leaders or officers: the apostles or elders, with the general oversight of the church, and the deacons, with supportive roles. This simple but effective organization the Lord recommended as a model for future churches: "The organization of the church at Jerusalem was to serve as *a model* for the organization of churches in every other place where messengers of truth should win converts to the gospel."[27]

Spiritual Gifts. "Later in the history of the early church, when in various parts of the world many groups of believers had been formed into churches, the organization of the church was further perfected, so that order and harmonious action might be maintained. Every member was exhorted to act well his part. Each was to make a wise use of the talents entrusted to him. Some were endowed by the Holy Spirit with special gifts—'first apostles, secondarily prophets, thirdly teachers, after that miracles, then gifts of healings, helps, governments, diversities of tongues.' 1 Corinthians 12:28. But all these classes of workers were to labor in harmony."[28]

Again, although we observe harmonious action, not everyone is qualified for whatever position he or she would like to occupy. There were restrictions on the roles church members were called to fill, just as in the Old Testament church.

To help assure optimum cooperation within the church, God specified qualifications so that the right leaders might be selected.

Requirements for Elected Officers. Near the end of his long ministry Paul, under divine inspiration, listed the leadership qualifications for the two leading officers of the church: the elders, the highest elected officers, whose function is oversight of the church, and the deacons, who have supportive duties.

A study of these requirements makes it plain that the Lord, as head of the church (Eph 5:30), is interested in having His church under leaders who have a proven record of success. They must have been successful as leaders in their own families. The elder or minister must be "one who rules his own house well . . . for if a man does not know how to rule his own house, how will he take care of the church of God?" (1 Tim 3: 4, 5).

7. Church Organization in the Seventh-day Adventist Church

Is the model of church organization that God gave to the first Christians still the model that He wants Seventh-day Adventists to follow until the second advent? Through the prophetic ministry of Ellen G. White, the Lord fully endorses the relevance of Paul's list of qualifications for the office of elder and minister.

In 1852, during the formative stages of church organization of the Seventh-day Adventist church, the Lord gave Ellen White a vision calling attention to the need for our churches to follow the "gospel order" of the Bible.[29] At this time the believers were plagued by various persons who felt that God had called them to the ministry. In reality they had not been called by God at all. Mrs. White was shown that they were false teachers planted by Satan to bring confusion into the church. When she asked the angel in the vision what could be done to stop this, he answered that they were to follow the Bible on church organization. He said, "The church must flee to God's Word and become established upon gospel order, which has been overlooked and neglected."[30]

Ellen White saw that the church in the days of the apostles was in danger of false teachers. To counteract this problem the New Testament church, by divine guidance, was given a list of qualifications so church leaders could safely select and appoint those truly called by God, distinguishing them from false teachers. Thus "the brethren chose men who had given good evidence that they were capable of ruling well their own house and preserving order in their own families, and who could enlighten those who were in darkness."[31] These persons who gave evidence of successful leadership in the home were chosen to be ordained "by the laying on of hands."[32]

Ellen G. White was shown that Adventists should follow the apostles' example. Said she, "I saw that we are no more secure from false teachers now than they were in the apostles' days; and, if we do no more, we should take as special measures as they did to secure the peace, harmony, and union of the flock. We have their example, and should follow it."[33]

Ellen White added that we have to follow the Bible in determining whether persons are called by God. When these persons have met the Bible criteria, then they may be ordained. She wrote, "Brethren of experience and of sound minds should assemble, and following the Word of God and the sanction of the Holy Spirit, should, with fervent prayer, lay hands upon those who have given full proof that they have received their commission of God, and set them apart to devote themselves entirely to His work. This act would show the sanction of the church to their going forth as messengers to carry the most solemn message ever given to men."[34]

Persons' claims that they had a call from God were not sufficient. Unless they met the biblical qualifications for elder or minister, they were not to be ordained. Ellen White strongly warned against so-called "self-sent" persons. "Men are hurried into the field who lack wisdom and judgment, perhaps not ruling well their own house, and not having order or government over the few that God has given them charge of at home; yet they feel capable of having charge of the flock."[35] Here she clearly endorsed the validity of the qualifications for leadership of elders and ministers that are listed in 1 Timothy 3 and Titus 1 given nearly 2000 years ago. Men are to be successful leaders in the "church" in their homes before they should be appointed to take care of a church congregation. Throughout her ministry she recommended that Seventh-day Adventists follow these Bible qualifications.[36]

8. What Would Be Ellen White's Solution to the Issue?

The Prologue of *Women in Ministry* mentioned that "absolute uniformity of understanding was not possible or desirable," supporting this view with an Ellen White statement. In a conversation the editor mentioned to me that we could maintain church unity without having uniformity on women's ordination. Evidently, in this unity some may look at a series of texts and conclude that the Bible allows the ordination of women, while others looking at the very same texts may conclude that women's ordination is unbiblical. Is this really the unity Ellen White wrote of?

Let us look more carefully at the Ellen White statement quoted in *Women in Ministry*. The quotation begins with the sentence that "we cannot *then* take the position that the unity of the church consists in viewing every text in Scripture in the very same light."[37] The word "then" indicates that the statement offers a conclusion to something that was said before. To help the reader see what Ellen White was talking about, we will quote more of the paragraph than was quoted in the book.

"One man may be conversant with the Scriptures, and *some particular portion of the Scripture* may be especially appreciated by him; another sees *another portion* as very important, and thus one may present *one point*, and another, *another point*, and *both may be of highest value. This is all in the order of God.* But if a man makes a mistake in his interpretation of some portion of the Scripture, shall this cause diversity and disunion? God forbid. We cannot *then* take a position that the unity of the church consists in viewing every text of Scripture in the very same light."[38]

In this paragraph Ellen White mentions that some believers see one section of the Bible as important, others another portion. Some present one point, others stress another point, but that "both may be of highest value. This is all in the order of God." It is important to notice that she is dealing here with views that are not mutually exclusive. They are, she says, "all in the order of God." And even if a person makes a mistake in the interpretation of a text, it should not disturb the unity of the church.

The question we have to ask ourselves is whether the contradicting positions taken on numerous Bible passages related to women's ordination are "of the highest value" and "all in the order of God."

The conflict over the ordination of women to the role of elder or minister amounts to more than just differences of opinion. It involves the biblical doctrines of Christian leadership in the home and in the church, together with the unique divinely-ordained roles of men and women which God instituted at creation and after the Fall. One's understanding of these doctrines has a far-reaching impact on the organizational structure and operation of the home and the church and how men, women, and children relate to each other. It affects not only the operation of the local church, but also that of the conferences, unions, and world divisions.

The dispute over women's ordination involves not only the meaning of many biblical passages but also two different approaches to the Bible, one of which is foreign to the way that Adventists have used the Bible in their studies of Scripture and the conclusions they draw. Even though the Seminary committee seems to be sincerely convinced that the unity of the church can be preserved while both positions are allowed to operate side by side, it is difficult to support this with the Ellen White quotation in the Prologue.

In reading the complete Ellen White manuscript, one cannot but be impressed with the thought that studying the Bible together is the real answer to our conflicts: "If brethren would meet together once or twice a week, and with humble minds, feeling their weakness and realizing their defects, would then ask the Lord to enlighten their understanding and fill their hearts with His love, examining not one another, but the Scriptures, Satan would be defeated."[39]

Conclusion

We have seen that *Women in Ministry* puts forth some excellent principles of Bible interpretation, one of them being that "doctrine cannot be construed on the basis of one text alone" but "the whole Bible message must be taken into account." It is one thing to state these principles and another to implement them. Unfortunately, *Women in Ministry* has not followed its own principle of taking the whole Bible's message into account, as I will demonstrate in subsequent chapters of this book.

The question of ordination involves many dimensions, such as the priesthood of all believers, the relationship between male and female at creation, the impact of the fall, the male and female roles throughout the Bible, the impact of Christ's incarnation on gender relations, the model of church organization throughout the Scriptures, the laying on of hands, the distinction between spiritual gifts and appointed church offices, the qualifications for church leadership, and Ellen G. White's interpretation of the Bible passages. Without looking at each of these factors one cannot make a sound judgment on the ordination of women as ministers.

In *Women in Ministry* one author focused on the biblical topic of the priesthood of all believers. His presentation was helpful in many respects. Yet, on this limited set of biblical data, without grappling with the Bible's own stated qualifications for church leadership, he concluded that the distinctions between men and women are no longer valid considerations for the ministry. Another author capably addressed the biblical teaching of the laying on of hands. But he too concluded, without dealing with the biblical leadership qualifications affecting ordination, that women can be ordained as ministers. Other chapters of the book are open to similar observations. The data these authors considered were too limited to support their conclusions regarding ordaining women.

Women in Ministry, then, has followed a fragmented approach to women's ordination, each author dealing with one aspect of the subject, yet not considering the whole message of the Bible before endorsing women's ordination. The same can be said of the historical and cultural studies in the book. These can be helpful when based on solid evidence. But the authors are not qualified to make sound recommendations in favor of ordination unless they take into consideration what the whole Bible teaches on this subject. It is the responsibility of an editor to make sure that the authors do not jump to conclusions too quickly but faithfully adhere to the principles of Bible interpretation set forth in the prologue. Unfortunately this has not been done, and as a result the book has set forth conclusions that are invalid.

As the book claims to be a scholarly production one may wonder why this important practice of evaluating every chapter in the light of the whole Bible has not been rigidly followed. One plausible reason is that the committee assumed that the Bible did not spell out a church organization concept in which women were not supposed to function as elders and ministers. This incorrect assumption seems to dominate the whole book and explains the adoption and misuse of James White's rule of interpretation.

At the beginning of this chapter we noted how the editor's prologue to *Women in Ministry* said that "church organization is not spelled out in the Bible," allowing its authors to use James White's rule in a search for principles and to use sanctified reasoning. Readers may very well get the impression that the editor thinks James White would doubtless approve of women pastors, even though this provision is not spelled out in Scripture.

Perhaps, as often happens, the editor did not express her full mind regarding which aspects of church organization are spelled out in the Bible, but we have seen from the Bible itself and from Ellen G. White's use of it that in fact, the Bible says a great deal about the basic structure of church organization. Specifically, in a passage that Elder White cited, the Bible does indeed spell out the qualifications for the elder or pastor. The passage says that an elder is to be "the husband of one wife," one who "rules his own house well."

The editor says that *Women in Ministry* has followed James White's example. His example was one of deep, careful Bible study, letting the Bible speak for itself. Very likely, *Women in Ministry* intended to do the same; but with all due respect to the serious writers who contributed to its pages, evidence seems to indicate that his example was not followed.

By assuming that church organization is not spelled out in the Bible, the writers of *Women in Ministry* generally pass over the list of biblical qualifications for elders given in Paul's letters to Timothy and Titus. It seems that they have taken for granted that these lists are not an important consideration for the election of women as elders and ministers.

From their early beginnings Adventists, however, have taken the Bible as their standard to test all their practices. Therefore, they take seriously the lists of qualifications the Lord inspired Paul to write. Today, on the brink of a new millennium, Seventh-day Adventists will still take these lists of qualifications in 1 Timothy 3 and Titus 1 seriously in determining whether women may be ordained to the function of elder or minister.

One would have hoped, however, to see the prologue include a reference to a fundamental principle in the Adventist approach to Scripture, stating that the conclusions and recommendations on the ordination of women in each chapter have been tested by the Bible. In conversations with the editor it became clear to me that this was not the purpose of the book. Its authors had adopted a broader approach, studying the subject of ordination from a much wider perspective that included not only the biblical but also the theological and historical dimensions of women's ordination. Nevertheless, the committee would have done well to follow Mrs. White's counsel on matters that are controversial.

"The word of God is the great detector of error; to it we believe everything must be brought. The Bible must be our standard for every doctrine and practice. We must study it reverentially. We are to receive no one's opinion without comparing it with the Scriptures. Here is divine authority which is supreme in matters of faith.

"It is the word of the living God that is to decide all controversies."[40]

Failing to make the Scriptures the final test in evaluating all the research presented in the twenty chapters of the book, *Women in Ministry* will be an *unreliable* "resource tool for decision making" and will fall short in affirming women in pastoral leadership as the committee hoped to do.[41]

Finally, one can agree with the Andrews University press release that the book signifies a watershed, but not the kind the press secretary had hoped for. Instead of being a convincing "biblical case for women's ordination,"[42] the book reveals a major departure from the standard Adventist practice of evaluating all research by the Bible before making final conclusions and recommendations.

We must be willing to set aside personal agendas and go to Scripture with hearts that are willing to hear and obey. "If any man will do His will," Jesus promised, "he shall know of the doctrine, whether it be of God, or whether I speak of myself" (John 7:17). The church need not be in conflict over matters such as these. Ellen White pointed the way for us as a people as well as individuals: "It is obedience and faith that unite us with Jesus Christ. You must learn the simple art of taking God at His word. Then you have solid ground beneath your feet."[43]

Endnotes

1. Ad Hoc Committee on Hermeneutics and Ordination, Epilogue, *Women in Ministry*, p. 436.
2. Andrews University press release, Oct. 22, 1998.
3. Nancy Vyhmeister, Prologue, *Women in Ministry*, p. 4.
4. Ellen G. White, *The Ellen G. White 1888 Materials*, p. 1092; *Manuscript Releases*, 11:266.
5. Nancy Vyhmeister, *Women in Ministry*, p. 3. The reference to James White was from J. White, "Making Us a Name," *Review and Herald*, April 26, 1860, p. 180.
6. [J. White], "Gospel Order," *Review and Herald*, Dec. 6, 1853, p. 173.
7. Ibid.
8. [J. White], "Gospel Order," *Review and Herald*, Dec. 20, 1853, p. 189.
9. Ibid.
10. Ibid.
11. J. White, "Making Us a Name," *Review and Herald*, April 26, 1860, p. 181.
12. Ibid., p. 182.
13. Some assumed that the number 666 (Rev. 13:18) was the number of the apostate churches in the United States of America. They felt that to become legally organized as a church meant becoming a part of the apostasy (ibid., pp. 181, 182).
14. Ibid., p. 180, emphasis mine.
15. Ellen G. White, *Testimonies to Ministers*, p. 15.
16. Ellen G. White, Ms. 155, 1902, pp. 5, 6 (sermon preached Sabbath, Nov. 22, 1902, "On the Study of the Book of Revelation"), *Manuscript Releases*, 1:154.
17. Ellen G. White, *General Conference Daily Bulletin*, Jan. 29, 1893, p. 22, emphasis mine.
18. "Lessons from the Life of Solomon—N. 5: Order and Organization," *Review and Herald*, October 12, 1905, p. 9.
19. *General Conference Daily Bulletin*, Jan. 29, 1893, p. 23; Ellen G. White, *Testimonies for the Church*, 1:653, emphasis mine.
20. Ellen G. White, *Patriarchs and Prophets*, p. 374. See also Ellen G. White, "Order and Organization," *Review and Herald*, October 12, 1905, p. 8.
21. *Testimonies for the Church*, 1:650.

22. Ibid., pp. 651, 652.
23. Ibid., p. 652.
24. "Order and Organization," *Review and Herald*, October 12, 1905, p. 8.
25. Ibid.
26. Ellen G. White, *The Acts of the Apostles*, p. 18.
27. Ibid., p. 91, emphasis mine.
28. Ibid., pp. 91, 92.
29. Arthur L. White, *Ellen G. White: The Early Years, 1827-1862*, 1:286.
30. Ellen G. White, *Early Writings*, p. 100.
31. Ibid., pp. 100, 101.
32. Ibid., p. 101.
33. Ibid.
34. Ibid.
35. Ibid., p. 97.
36. See, for example, *Testimonies for the Church*, 5:617; ibid., 2:620, 621; Ms. 104, 1901 and Ms. 67, 1900 in *Manuscript Releases,* 5:449, 450; Letter 164, 1902 in ibid., 21:98. See also Ellen G. White's comments in *SDA Bible Commentary*, 2:1009.
37. *Ellen G. White 1888 Materials*, p. 1092, emphasis mine.
38. Ibid., emphasis mine.
39. Ibid., *Ellen G. White 1888 Materials*, p. 1087.
40. Letter, Ellen G. White to Dear Brethren Who Shall Assemble in General Conference, Aug. 5, 1888 in *Ellen G. White 1888 Materials*, pp. 44, 45, emphasis mine.
41. Nancy Vyhmeister, *Women in Ministry*, p. 5.
42. Andrews University press release, Oct. 22, 1998.
43. Ellen G. White, "The Mirror," *The Youth's Instructor*, Aug. 18, 1886.

Chapter 3

Testimony:
What Is a Woman Worth?

Rosalie Haffner Zinke

~

"It's a man's world." This slogan, which has covered a multitude of feminine frustrations for generations, is probably still true today, the women's movement notwithstanding. As a young professional in my early ministry, I faced this situation head on. How would I relate to the predominance of males in my chosen profession?

I had three options. In our male-dominated society, I could rebel against my peers; I could become competitive with males and seek to beat them by their own rules and standards; or I could accept the differences between my role and theirs and find fulfillment by excelling within the framework of my personal God-given abilities and talents.

A period of struggle and uncertainty in my professional life led me to the "blueprint" for the role of women in ministry. After carefully and prayerfully studying the inspired writings I came to the settled conclusion that God had a work for me to do, a work which, according to Ellen G. White, could best be done by women. "They [women] can do in families a work that men cannot do, a work that reaches the inner life" (*Evangelism,* p. 464).

This process demanded that I deal with the issue of worth. How was my worth as a professional woman to be determined? Would I be trapped into the "man's world" philosophy that determines worth by male roles? Or would I have

Rosalie Haffner Zinke *is a retired Bible Instructor and trainer of Bible Instructors. Among the works she has authored are two quarters of the Adult Sabbath School Lessons.*

the courage to resist the pressure of societal norms and measure my worth in ministry by God's value system?

My determination to choose the latter has not been without pain and even rejection at times. It has not been a popular road. I have often walked alone. It has been a costly choice in many ways. For example, the issue of fair pay for a woman's role has dogged my steps throughout my professional life. How often someone has quipped, "You wouldn't be facing this issue if you were a man," implying that if I were doing a man's work, there would be no question about what I was worth.

But in spite of the frustrations I refused to accept the concept that a woman must either compete or involve herself in male roles in order to be fulfilled. I refused to believe that only a man's role is worthwhile and valuable, making feminine roles second rate and undesirable.

I concluded that the women's movement, instead of freeing women to be themselves and do their best, has virtually enslaved them into accepting the male role as an imposed norm. Tragically, viewing things that way makes the old saying, "It's a man's world," more true today than it ever was! I choose to believe the biblical concept that God created men and women as equals yet gave them each distinct roles in personal relationships and in professional outlets. As the privilege of child bearing is the most important responsibility a person can have, I discovered that in ministry, the role of spiritual birthing and nurturing, for which women have special gifts, brings deep and lasting fulfillment.

My life has been richly blessed by my spiritual children. Whatever accomplishments I have achieved in my career, whatever successes might have been mine had I taken a different course, none compare with the joy of knowing that I have had a part in the lives of my spiritual children and in their growth toward the kingdom.

Part II
Biblical Issues

Chapter 4

Headship, Submission, and Equality in Scripture

Samuele Bacchiocchi

~

Recently the question of whether women should be ordained to serve in the church in the headship role of elders and pastors has been hotly debated in many Christian churches. Some churches, like the Lutheran church, have actually been split over this issue. At the root of the controversy is one's understanding of the biblical teaching regarding headship, submission, and equality in male-female relationships. This fact is clearly recognized by the special pro-ordination committee set up by the Seventh-day Adventist Theological Seminary to supervise the production of the symposium, a collection of chapters by different authors, called *Women in Ministry: Biblical and Historical Perspectives*. In the introduction to the part of the book dealing with "Perceived Impediments to Women in Ministry," the committee lists as the first of four "serious obstacles" to the ordination of women "the concept of the headship of all males over all females."[1]

The symposium, made up mostly of teachers at the Seminary, attempts to overcome this "serious obstacle" by arguing that the role distinctions of male headship and female submission derive from the Fall (Gen 3:16) and that they apply exclusively to the home. In the church, women can serve in the headship positions of elders and pastors. The methodology used to construct this position consists primarily of two strategies. First, the Genesis passages (Gen 1:26-31; 2:18-25; 3:1-24) are interpreted in isolation from the rest of Scripture as teaching "perfect egalitarianism," that is, full equality with no role distinctions between Adam and Eve. Second, the crucial Pauline passages, which interpret the Genesis passages as prohibiting women

Samuele Bacchiocchi, Ph.D., *is Professor of Religion, Andrews University.*

from serving in a headship role in the church (1 Tim 2:11-15; 1 Cor 11:3-12; 14:34-36), are interpreted as temporary restrictions which apply exclusively to the home, or perhaps to problematic women who caused disorder in the church.

An Overview of the Assumptions of the Symposium

The fundamental assumption of the symposium is that the role distinctions of male headship and female submission were not divinely ordained at creation but were introduced after the Fall and are limited to the governance of the home, not to the community of faith. Thus, Christians are called to return to the creation ideal of "perfect equality," understood as obliteration of gender-based role distinctions.

Before we examine the specific arguments used to construct this position, some general observations are in order regarding *Women in Ministry*'s perception of the problem and the moral implications of the position adopted by the contributors to the symposium.

First, we have already noted that the symposium sets out to examine "perceived impediments to women in ministry," among which it lists "the concept of the headship of all males over all females." Yet I have never seen this concept expressed in the Seventh-day Adventist church. It is certainly not the view of opponents of women's ordination known to me. *Women in Ministry* offered no references to books by Adventist authors which set forth such a view. By framing the issue in this extreme way and arguing against it, the book imputes to its opponents a view which they do not hold while failing to deal adequately with the views they do hold.

Further, by listing this view of headship as a "perceived impediment to women in ministry," the book implies that those who do not share its views are opposed to women in ministry. In fact, the opposite is true, as I shall observe in more detail below. The authors of the book you are now reading believe that there is a significant place for women in ministry and a genuine need for their services. They believe that respect for the biblical view of roles and headship in the home and church does not prevent women from ministering, but channels their ministry into the areas where it may be most effective.

To turn next to the moral implications, *Women in Ministry*'s assumption that male headship and female submission reflect "God's plan for fallen human beings rather than an original mandate for the sinless world"[2] implies that functional role distinctions are intrinsically evil. But we must ask, Is this true? The answer is, Absolutely not! The most compelling proof is the fact that functional role distinctions exist within the Trinity itself! The Bible tells us that "the head of Christ is God" (1 Cor 11:3) and that the Son Himself "will be subjected to him [the Father]" for all eternity (1 Cor 14:28). If there is nothing morally wrong with functional distinctions within the Trinity, why is it morally wrong for functional distinctions to exist within male-female relationships?

This leads us to another observation, examining the assumption that male headship entails superiority and female submission inferiority—a subtle and deceptive assumption that underlies the whole symposium. We ask, do functional male-female role distinctions imply superiority and inferiority? Absolutely not! This is true in the Trinity and is also true in male-female relationships. In the Trinity the headship of the Father does not make the Son inferior. Christ Himself affirmed, "I and the Father are one" (John 10:30). In human relationships, male headship does not make women inferior because of their submissive roles. We "are all one in Christ," and consequently there is no male superiority or female inferiority (Gal 3:28-29).

The fact that I am a man called by God to serve as the head of my family does not make me superior to my wife. In a certain sense she is "the boss," because she has constantly reminded me through the years of my God-given responsibility to serve as the spiritual head of our home. Functional role distinctions have nothing to do with superiority or inferiority but only with the different—and complementary—roles God has called men and women to fulfill in the home and in the church.

The Real Issue

The real issue in the debate over women's ordination is not whether men were created superior and women inferior. No Adventist scholar opposed to women's ordination holds such a view. Rather, the real issue is whether God created men and women equal in nature and worth yet different in function, with the man called to serve in the servant headship role and the woman in the submissive helper role.

It is most unfortunate that the symposium fails to address this fundamental crucial issue, choosing instead arguments about superiority and inferiority—arguments that are foreign to the Bible and to the whole question of women's ordination.

Those of us who for biblical reasons oppose the ordination of women to the headship roles of elders and pastors are often thought to be trying to deprive women of the opportunity to minister in the church. Nothing could be further from the truth. We strongly believe that if ever there were a time when the ministry of women in the church was needed, it is today. The many broken homes, single parents, and abused children inside and outside the church call today more than ever for the ministry of women who have been trained theologically and psychologically to meet such situations.

Simply stated, the issue is not whether women should minister in the church. On this point we are all in full agreement. Rather the issue is, should women serve in the headship roles of elders and pastors? The answer of Scripture is abundantly clear. In both the Old and New Testaments women were precluded from serving as priests, elders, and pastors, not because they were inferior or less capable than men, but because these offices entail the headship role of a spiritual father and not the supportive role of a spiritual mother. This does not mean that the church has no need of spiritual mothers. The contrary is true. As a home without a mother lacks the tender, loving care that only mothers can give, so a church without spiritual mothers lacks the warmth, care, and compassion that spiritual mothers can best give. Summing up, the biblical teaching is that men and women are equally called by God to minister in the home and in the church, but in different, complementary roles.

A Review of the Pivotal Chapter

This review focuses on the fundamental issue of "Headship, Submission, and Equality in Scripture," which is examined in chapter 13 of *Women in Ministry.* The chapter's author chairs the Old Testament department at the Seventh-day Adventist Theological Seminary. Over the years I have learned to respect him, not only for his outstanding scholarship but also for his commitment to the Lord. Though I must differ with what he has written in this chapter, I intend no negative reflection on his scholarship as a whole or on his personal character. In several of my books I have quoted extensively from his writings. My review here is limited to the chapter under consideration. It examines exclusively the chapter's methodology and arguments, with no intent to question its author's sincerity or integrity.

The *Women in Ministry* chapter offers a reinterpretation of the biblical data relating to the headship-submission pattern in attempting to provide a biblical justification for the ordination of women. This chapter is fundamental to the whole symposium. The author himself acknowledges that a definition of the biblical teaching on headship-submission is "foundational to determining whether or not women should be ordained as elders and pastors in the church."[3]

In many ways the whole symposium *Women in Ministry* stands or falls on this chapter's interpretation of the biblical teaching on headship and submission in male-female relationships, because the other nineteen chapters are built upon the premises laid down in chapter 13. If the conclusions of this chapter are found to be based on a misinterpretation of the biblical data, then much of the work set forth by the other contributors collapses for the lack of an adequate biblical foundation. In view of the foundational importance of this chapter, we must closely examine the methodology the author used to reach his conclusions.

The Chapter's Conclusions

It may be helpful at the outset to state the *Women in Ministry* chapter's conclusions. Fortunately, they are expressed with enviable clarity at the end. "Before the Fall there was full equality with no headship-submission in the relationship between Adam and Eve (Gen 2:24). But after the Fall, according to Genesis 3:16, the husband was given a servant headship role to preserve the harmony of the home, while at the same time the model of equal partnership was still set forth as the ideal. This post-Fall prescription of husband headship and wife submission was limited to the husband-wife relationship. In the divine revelation throughout the rest of the Old Testament and the New Testament witness, servant headship and voluntary submission on the part of husband and wife, respectively, are affirmed, but these are *never* broadened to the covenant community in such a way as to prohibit women from taking positions of leadership, including headship positions over men."[4]

Simply stated, our author believes the Bible to teach that before the Fall there was perfect equality with no functional distinctions between the man and the woman. The role distinctions of husband-headship and wife-submission originated as a result of the Fall (Gen 3:16), and they apply exclusively to the home. Consequently, in the church women can serve even in "headship positions over men" without violating a biblical principle.

Can these conclusions be drawn legitimately from the Bible? Are functional role distinctions between men and women a post-Fall phenomenon, applying exclusively to the home and not to the church? My study shows otherwise. Both male-female equality *and* role distinctions, properly defined, are part of God's creational design for the harmonious functioning of humanity. God created the man and the woman perfectly equal in their moral worth and spiritual status but clearly distinct in their biological and functional roles. In the partnership of these two spiritually equal human beings, man and woman, God created man to function in the servant-headship role of husband and father, and woman to function in the submissive role of wife and mother. These distinctive roles apply equally to both the home and the church, because from a biblical perspective the church is an extended spiritual family, often referred to as "the household of God" (Eph 2:19; 1 Tim 3:15; 1 Pet 4:17; Gal 6:10).

To determine which of the two paradigms rightly interprets the biblical data, we must begin our investigation with Genesis 1 to 3. The author acknowledges that these Bible chapters are foundational for defining the role relationships of men and women.[5] The three passages of Genesis which are central for our understanding of the relationships between man and woman are (1) Genesis 1:26-31, the creation of the human race; (2) Genesis 2:18-25, the creation of woman; and (3) Genesis 3:1-24, the story of the Fall and its consequences. Let us examine what each passage says.

PART I – GENESIS 1: MALE AND FEMALE

1. Equal, Yet Different Before the Fall

Genesis 1:26-31 contains three key statements: (1) God created mankind in His own image and likeness; (2) God created mankind as male and female; (3) God gave mankind dominion over all the living things with power to increase and multiply, that is, to become a race. These three statements embody two vital concepts, equality in being and differentiation in gender.

Equal Yet Different. Equality is suggested by the fact that both man and woman were created in the image of God. Genesis 1:26-27 says, "Then God said: 'Let us make man in our image, after our likeness, and let them have dominion over the fish of the sea . . . .' So God created man in his own image, in the image of God he created him; male and female he created them." "Man" is mentioned twice here and refers inclusively to man and woman. This is indicated first by the Hebrew word for "man" (*'adam*) which can be translated as "mankind, humanity": "Let us make mankind in our own image." The second indication is the plural "them," which points to "man" as being a plurality consisting of both man and woman. The fact that Genesis 1:26-27 moves back and forth three times between the singular "man" and the plural "them" clearly indicates that the term "man" is used collectively to refer to both man and woman.

Genesis 1:27 corroborates this conclusion. The statement, "So God created man in his own image, in the image of God he created him," is clarified by the following statement, "male and female he created them." From these data, our *Women in Ministry* chapter argues that "the equal pairing of male *and* female in parallel with *ha'adam* [man] in this verse [shows that] there is no hint of ontological or functional superiority-inferiority or headship-submission between male and female. . . . Both participate equally in the image of God."[6]

The conclusion that the "pairing of male *and* female in parallel with *ha'adam* [man]" excludes any hint of a headship-submission distinction between male and female ignores two important considerations. First, equality must not obscure the sexual differentiation which is made unavoidably clear in this passage: "male and female he created them" (Gen 1:27). The two sexes are part of God's original purpose for the human race and both are good. Both men and women are essential to the proper functioning of the human race. Denying or perverting sexual differentiation is a rejection of the order established at creation and is condemned in the Bible as "abomination" (Deut 22:5; Rom 1:26-27).

Genesis 1 does not say much about the roles of men and women. It simply affirms that man and woman are equally created in the image of God but are sexually different. The implications of the gender distinctions are explained subsequently in the Bible, beginning with Genesis 2.

The second important consideration is the fact God designated both the male and the female as "man—*ha'adam.*" We see this again in Genesis 5:2, where the word *man* denotes both male and female: "He created them male and female; at the time they were created, *he blessed them and called them 'man.'*"

Paul's Use of Genesis 1:26-27. Supporting the above conclusion is Paul's use of the terms "image" and "glory" in 1 Corinthians 11:7 in his discussion of the manner in which men and women ought to participate in public worship.

Paul alludes to Genesis 1:26-27 when he writes, "For a man ought not to cover his head, since he is the image and glory of God; but woman is the glory of man" (1 Cor 11:7). Paul is not implying that a woman reflects the image of God to a lesser degree than does man. The focus of his discussion is not the personal dignity or worth of men and women implied in Genesis 1:26-28, but rather the headship of man in marriage and worship implied in Genesis 2:18-23. Paul refers specifically to the man's headship in 1 Corinthians 11:8-9. It is in this context that man images God and that woman does not. It is obvious that women bear God's image in *other senses,* as Paul himself recognizes in Ephesians 4:24, where he speaks of all believers as being renewed according to God's image in terms of "righteousness and holiness" (cf. Col 3:10).

Paul is careful in 1 Corinthians 11:7 not to say that the woman is man's image. Rather he says that "woman is the glory of man." The language of Genesis 1:26-27 in the Septuagint is "image" (*eikon*) and "likeness" (*homoioma*) and not image and glory (*doxa*). Thus Paul's use of the term "glory" is significant. To understand its meaning we must note that Paul uses "glory" in the context of the relation of man to God and of woman to man. Man images God and gives Him glory by being submissive to Him and by being a loving, self-sacrificing head (Eph 5:25-29). The wife is the glory of her husband in the way she honors his headship by her life and attitude. This meaning is well expressed in the Septuagint version of Proverbs 11:16, which says, "A gracious wife brings glory to her husband" (cf. Prov 12:4).

What is significant about Paul's use of "image" and "glory" is the fact that he interprets Genesis 1:26-27 in the light of Genesis 2 to explain why the woman is the glory of man, namely, because she was created from and for man and not vice versa (1 Cor 11:8-9). All of this shows that Paul understood the image of God in man and woman mentioned in Genesis 1:26-27, not in the light of the egalitarian model but in terms of the functional distinctions mentioned in Genesis 2:20-22.

In light of these considerations we conclude that Genesis 1:26-27 does affirm male-female equality, but that it also alludes to male headship by twice calling the human race, "man—*ha'adam*" rather than "woman." Furthermore, by differentiating between man as "the image and glory of God" and woman as the "glory of man," Paul shows that the equality between men and women implied by Genesis 1:26-27 does not negate their functional distinction implied in Genesis 2:18-23.

PART II – GENESIS 2: EQUALITY AND SUBMISSION

Genesis 2 expands on the creation of mankind covered in Genesis 1:26-31. While Genesis 1 affirms that God created mankind as male and female in His own image, Genesis 2 elaborates on how the two sexes were created and on the relationship between them. God first created man from the dust and breathed into him the breath of life (Gen 2:7). He stationed man in the Garden of Eden to develop it and guard it (Gen 2:15). He instructed man to eat of every tree except of the tree of knowledge of good and evil (Gen 2:16-17).

God paraded the animals before Adam for him to name (Gen 2:19, 20). This task entailed more than slapping an arbitrary label on each beast. It required considering the characteristics of each animal so that its name was appropriate to its particular nature. From this exercise Adam discovered that there was no creature that shared *his* nature (Gen 2:20). God, who even before He brought the animals to Adam had evidently already planned to create a "helper fit for him" (v. 18), now proceeded to create the woman from Adam's rib (Gen 2:21-22). Adam greeted Eve with rhapsodic relief, acknowledging her as part of his own flesh and calling her "Wo man" because she was taken out of Man (Gen 2:23).

In her equality with himself, Adam perceived Eve not as a threat but as a partner capable of fulfilling his inner longing. God blessed the blissful union, saying, "Therefore a man leaves his father and mother and cleaves to his wife, and they become one flesh" (Gen 2:24). The creation account closes with a reminder of the perfection in which Adam and Eve first came together: "And the man and his wife were both naked and they were not ashamed" (Gen 2:25). They felt no shame because they had nothing to hide. They lived together in perfect integrity and harmony.

Although the narrative focuses on the sameness of nature and the partnership between man and woman, within that equality and partnership there exists a clear sense of the woman's submission to man. We use the term "submission" here not with negative connotations of oppression, denigration, or inferiority, but in the positive sense of depending upon another person for direction and protection and to ensure unity and harmony.

Four main elements of the narrative suggest a distinction between the headship role of man and the helper role of woman: (1) the priority of man's creation (Gen 2:7, 22), (2) the manner of the woman's creation out of man (Gen 2:21-22), (3) the woman's having been created to be man's "helper" (Gen 2:18-20), and (4) man's naming of the woman both before and after the Fall (Gen 2:23; 3:20). Our *Women in Ministry* author examines each of these elements but contends that none of them support the headship-submission distinctions between the man and the woman. Is this right? Let us analyze the arguments.

1. The Priority of Man's Creation

Man Created First. Does the fact that Adam was made first reflect God's plan that man should serve in a leadership role in the home and the church? The answer offered in the chapter we are considering is No! It says, "A careful examination of the literary structure of Genesis reveals that such a conclusion does not follow."[7] It argues that the entire account of Genesis 2 "is cast in the form of an *inclusio* or 'ring construction,' in which the creation of man at the beginning of the narrative and that of woman at the end correspond to each other in importance. . . . The movement in Genesis 2, if anything, is not from superior to inferior, but from incompleteness to completeness. Woman is created as the climax, the culmination of the story. She is the crowning work of Creation."[8]

The fundamental problem with this interpretation is that it ignores details of the narrative as well as the meaning the Bible itself attaches to the priority of Adam's creation. To say, for example, that "the movement in Genesis 2, if anything, is not from superior to inferior, but from incompleteness to completeness," ignores first of all that the point at issue in our discussions is not superiority versus inferiority (I know of no scholar today who argues that man was created superior to woman), but equality versus functional distinction. Superiority is a non-issue.

Further, role distinctions don't imply inferiority! There are three Beings in the Godhead who are equal in glory and in being but who differ in function. The

Father leads, the Son submits to Him, and the Spirit submits to both. These role distinctions do not negate the fact that the three Persons are fully equal in divinity, power, and glory. The Son submits to the Father, but not because He is inferior, a kind of junior God. The ranking within the Trinity is part of the sublime "equal yet different" paradox that serves as a paradigm for male-female relationships.

The narrative does indeed suggest that the creation of woman is "the climax and culmination of the story" because in her, man found *at last* the "helper fit for him" (Gen 2:20). This is evident by Adam's explanation: "This *at last* is bone of my bones and flesh of my flesh; she shall be called Woman, because she was taken out of Man" (Gen 2:23). The movement of the narrative is indeed "from incompleteness to completeness," but it is Adam who experiences the process of becoming complete as a result of Eve's creation, and not the other way around. But the woman's creation as the climax and culmination of the narrative does not necessarily imply that there are no functional distinctions between man and woman, for we have already noted that at least in the process of producing children there are very clear distinctions.

Paul's Interpretation of the Order of Creation. Paul's interpretation of the creation of man and woman is the most decisive line of evidence that discredits the attempt to deny headship significance in the priority of Adam's creation. It is unfortunate that our *Women in Ministry* author interprets the critical passages in Genesis 1 to 3 in isolation without taking into account the inspired commentary provided by Paul. Doing this is typical of higher criticism, but not of responsible Seventh-day Adventist scholarship nor of the author's work in other areas.

We should note that later in his chapter the author briefly discusses what Paul says about headship and submission, but he makes no attempt to explain Paul's appeal to the order of Eve's creation. Instead, he merely argues that such passages refer to the role of women in the home and not in the church. But even the editor of the symposium appears not to be persuaded. She observes, "The text [1 Tim 2:11] seems to be discussing attitudes in worship rather than marriage relationship."[9]

Paul appeals to the order of the creation of Adam and Eve to justify his injunction that a woman should not be permitted "to teach or have authority over a man" (1 Tim 2:12 NIV). He writes, "For Adam was formed first, then Eve; and Adam was not the one deceived; it was the woman who was deceived and became a sinner" (1 Tim 2:13-14 NIV). In the Greek, the order of Adam and Eve's creation is strongly marked by "*protos,* first" Adam and "*eita,* then" Eve.

The logic of this passage (1 Tim 2:13-14) and of the parallel one in 1 Corinthians 11:8-9, where Paul speaks of the manner of the woman's creation out of man and not vice versa, is abundantly clear. Paul saw in the priority of Adam's creation and in the manner of Eve's creation a clear indication of the headship role God intended man to exercise in the home and in the church. The fact that the woman was created after man, out of man, and as his helper, meant to Paul that God intends the woman to fulfill a submissive role in relation to man. In the church, this role is violated if a woman teaches in a headship position or exercises authority over a man.

By rooting the headship-submission principle in the order of creation rather than in the consequences of the Fall, Paul shows that he views such a principle as a creational design and not the product of the curse. Contrary to *Women in Ministry's* argument that headship and submission are the consequences of the Fall, Paul grounds such a principle in the pre-Fall order of creation described in Genesis 2.

The local circumstances of the Christian congregations in Ephesus and Corinth may have provided the *context* of Paul's injunction, but they do not provide the *reason.* Paul's reason is *creational, not cultural.* This is a most important consideration, one that makes Paul's injunction relevant for us today. It is unfortunate that pro-ordinationists choose to ignore the *creational reason* given by Paul for not permitting a woman to teach in the church as the head of the congregation.

The Meaning of "First-Born." To some it may appear arbitrary and irrational that headship should be assigned on the basis of priority of creation. From a biblical standpoint, however, the arbitrariness and irrationality disappear, because the priority of creation represents not an accident but a divine design, intended to typify the leadership role man was created to fulfill. This typological understanding is reflected in the meaning that both the Old and New Testaments attach to primogeniture (being the firstborn). The firstborn son inherited not only a "double portion" of his father's goods, but also the responsibility of acting as the leader of worship upon his father's death.

Paul uses the typological meaning of the firstborn also to refer to Christ in Colossians 1:15-18: "He is the image of the invisible God, the first born of all creation; for in him all things were created. . . . He is the head of the body, the church; he is the beginning, the firstborn from the dead, that in everything he might be preeminent." The rich imagery of this passage presents Christ as (1) the Image of God, (2) the Firstborn, (3) the Source of Creation, (4) the Head of the church. All of these are drawn together to establish the preeminent authority of Christ over everything.

This use of the "firstborn" typology to express the headship and authority of Christ suggests that Paul attached the same meaning to Adam's being "first formed." In light of the Old Testament background, Paul saw in the priority of Adam's formation a type of the headship God called man to fulfill, and thus, a reason why men, rather than women, should teach in a headship, authoritative position in the church.

2. The Manner of the Woman's Creation out of Man

Genesis 2 suggests the principle of headship and submission not only by the order of creation of Adam and Eve, but also by the manner of their creation. God created man first and then made woman out of his rib (Gen 2:21-22). He did not make Adam and Eve from the ground at the same time and for one another without distinction. Neither did God create the woman first and then man *from* the woman and *for* the woman. God could just as easily have created the woman first and made man out of Eve's rib, but He did not. Why? Most likely because that would have obscured the distinction between the male-headship and the female-submission roles that God wanted to make clear.

Our *Women in Ministry* author rejects the possibility that the woman's derivation from Adam implies submission. He argues that "derivation does not imply submission. Adam also was 'derived' from the ground (v. 7), but certainly we are not to conclude that the ground was his superior. Again, woman is *not* Adam's rib. The raw material, not woman, was taken out of man, just as the raw material of man was 'taken' (Gen 3:19, 23) out of the ground. . . . As the man was asleep while God created woman, man had no active part in the creation of woman that might allow him to claim to be her superior or head."[10]

These arguments are based on invalid reasoning. First of all, they ignore the biblical distinction between Adam and the ground from which he was formed. The ground could never be Adam's superior because it is inanimate matter given to man to cultivate. To compare Adam with the ground is worse than comparing apples with oranges, because there is no similarity of nature and function between the two.

Second, the fact that Adam was asleep when God created woman is irrelevant, because male headship is not based on Adam's part in Eve's creation but on God's assigned roles revealed in the order and manner of the first couple's creation.

Third, the different ways God created man and woman are closely related to the different tasks they are called to fulfill. This point is well expressed by Werner Neuer: "The man is formed from the soil, whose cultivation is entrusted to him by God (Gen 2:15; 3:17), while the woman is created quite differently, out of man's rib, to be his helper. This is her God-given task in life (Gen 2:18). The appointed tasks of the sexes are as basically different as the ways in which they were created by God. Their different modes of creation are intimately related to their tasks in life. It is worth noting that Genesis 2 and 3 in their own language make clear the very different world-outlooks of the sexes. . . . While the man has an immediate relationship to the world of things, the woman is primarily directed to the world of persons (i.e., in the first instance to her husband)."[11]

Lastly, the notion that "man had no active part in the creation of woman that might allow him to claim to be her superior or head" again reflects the subtle and deceptive assumption that headship implies superiority—a concept that is foreign to the Bible and to the issue of women's ordination.

Equality and Oneness. We cannot know all the reasons why God created the woman from Adam's body instead of making her as a separate creation from the dust like Adam. However, three possible reasons stand out. First, creating the woman from man's rib suggests the sameness of nature between man and woman. Adam could acknowledge that the woman was bone of his bone and flesh of his flesh (Gen 2:23). Her creation from his rib suggests that "she was not to control him as the head, nor to be trampled under his feet as an inferior, but to stand by his side as an equal, to be loved and protected by him."[12]

Second, the human race, including the first woman, derives from the same source, Adam, who is the head and representative of humanity (Rom 5:12; 1 Cor 15:22).

Third, woman's creation from man establishes the basis for the one-flesh principle in marriage (Gen 2:24; 1 Cor 7:4), a principle that rests on a real biological and historical foundation.

Paul's Interpretation of the Manner of Creation. The decisive line of evidence that undermines our author's interpretation of Genesis 2:21-22 is the inspired Scripture's own interpretation of the passage.

In 1 Corinthians 11:8 Paul defends his call for women to respect the headship of man by appealing to the manner of the woman's creation: "For man was not made from woman, but woman from man." For Paul the *order* and *manner* of the creation of Adam and Eve are the theological foundation of the headship-submission principle. In biblical thought origin and authority are interrelated (see Col 1:15-18). A child must respect the authority of his parents because he derives from them. In Adam's historical situation Eve derived from him in the sense that God formed her from his body. Thus, Adam was her "source" to whom she owed due respect.

This line of reasoning, though present in Hebrew thought, is not explicit in Genesis 2. What is explicit there is that God entrusted Adam with certain responsibilities. He named first the animals (Gen 2:19-20) and then the woman herself, both before and after the Fall (Gen 2:23; 3:20). By this act Adam exercised the leadership role assigned him by God. Man was also instructed by God regarding the forbidden tree and was apparently held responsible for passing on the information to his wife (Gen 2:16-17). After the Fall, God held man accountable for the original transgression (Gen 3:9). In light of these facts, Paul's terse remark that the woman was taken "out of" the man represents a faithful interpretation of Genesis 2 and a legitimate theological reason for the apostle to call upon women to respect the headship role of men.

3. The Woman Created to Be Man's "Helper"

Genesis 2 further suggests the principle of headship and submission by the central role of man in the account of the woman's creation. God created man first and provided him with a garden, an occupation, and finally a wife to be "a helper (*'ezer*) fit for him" (Gen 2:18). Though the word "helper" suggests the woman's supportive role, our author rejects this interpretation. Instead, he argues that the Hebrew word *'ezer* (helper) does not imply submission because "The Hebrew Bible most frequently employs *'ezer* to describe a superior helper—God Himself as the 'helper' of Israel. This is a relational term describing a beneficial relationship, but in itself does not specify position or rank, either superiority or inferiority."[13]

It is true that the word "helper" in itself, whether in Hebrew or in English, does not necessarily imply submission. But the meaning of a word cannot be determined without consideration of its context. In this case the word occurs within the phrase which says that God created woman to be a helper fit for man. "If one human being is created to be the helper of another human being," as George W. Knight rightly notes, "the one who receives such a helper has a certain authority over the helper."[14] This does not mean that woman exists solely for the sake of helping man, but rather that she is a helper who corresponds to man because she is of the same nature.

The Old Testament does portray God as our Helper (Ps 10:14; 54:4; 22:11). This only serves to prove that the helper role is a glorious one, worthy even of God Himself. But this fact does not exclude submission, because the very nature of a helping role presupposes submission. Whenever God undertakes to help us, in a certain sense He subordinates Himself to us. But this does not "undo" His deity in helping us. To help us Christ emptied Himself and assumed a servant role, but this did not make Him any less God. The difference, however, between the helping role of God or of Christ and that of the woman is that while God assumes the role of Helper to meet human needs, Eve was created specifically to function as a helper suitable for Adam.

Corresponding Helper. The author seeks support for his interpretation in the adjoining word *keʻnegdo,* usually translated as "fit for him" or "suitable for him." He writes: "The word *neged* conveys the idea of "in front of" or "counterpart," and a literal translation of *keʻnegdo* is thus 'like his counterpart, corresponding to him.' Used with *'ezer* [helper], the term indicates no less than equality: Eve is Adam's 'benefactor-helper,' one who in position is 'corresponding to him,' 'his counterpart, his complement.'"[15]

The attempt to transform the word *neged* which denotes "in front of" or "counterpart," into a "benefactor-helper" role for Eve, is ingenious but is based on invalid reasoning. What Raymond Ortlund correctly observes in regard to alleged superiority applies also to the allegation of equality: "If *neged* means 'superior to [or equal, in our case]', then what are we to make of, say, Psalm 119:168? 'All my ways are before (*neged*) you.' Is the psalmist saying 'All my ways are superior [or equal] to you Lord'? Not only is that an unbiblical notion, [but] the whole burden of Psalm 119 is the excellency and authority of the law over the psalmist. The *neged* element in *keʻnegdo* merely conveys the idea of direct proximity or anteposition. The woman, therefore, is a helper corresponding to the man."[16]

The woman's creation *from* man and *for* him ("a helper fit for him," Gen 2:18) suggests a functional dependency and submission. As Gerhard von Rad points out, Genesis describes the woman not in romantic terms as a companion to man, but in pragmatic terms as a "helper" to him.[17] Bible writers speak of human relationships with a certain practicality.

Like many others, our author rejects the notion of a functional submission of woman to man in Genesis 2. He argues that in Eden before the Fall there was a perfect 50-50 partnership between husband and wife. He sees God as having introduced the notion of the headship of man and the submission of woman as part of the curse. This raises an important moral question to be examined later: Why would God establish role distinctions after the Fall if He knew such distinctions to be (as feminists claim) morally wrong? And, we might add, why did God assign the headship role to man rather than to the woman (Gen 3:16)?

This view, which finds no submission before the Fall, stems from a negative evaluation of all forms of submission and especially that of woman to man. This conviction has led our author and others to interpret all the Scriptural references to submission as reflecting the post-Fall condition. The strongest objection to this view is that submission, as we have seen, is present in Genesis 2, that is, before the Fall (described in Gen 3). We have seen that Paul calls upon women to be submissive to the headship role of man, not on the basis of the curse but on the basis of the order and manner of God's creation.

Paul's Interpretation of "Helper Role." The decisive factor against *Women in Ministry's* interpretation of the phrase "helper fit for him" (Gen 2:18) is Paul's allusion to this text in 1 Corinthians 11:9: "Neither was man created for woman, but woman for man." Paul makes this statement in the context of his admonition that women should respect male headship in the church by covering their heads according to the custom of the time. The head covering was a *custom* (1 Cor 11:13-15) subservient to the *principle* of male headship (1 Cor 11:3). While the principle is permanent, its application will vary in different cultures.

Significantly, Paul alludes to Genesis 2:18 to buttress his admonition to women to respect male headship, but he does so without using the phrase "helper fit for him." Instead he gives his own interpretation of this phrase, namely, that woman was created for man and not the other way around. There is no doubt in Paul's mind as to the meaning of "helper fit for him." He did not have to dissect *kʿnegdo* in order to come up with an interpretation. The apostle states unequivocally the plain meaning of the phrase "helper fit for him," namely, that woman was created for the sake of man. If woman was created for man's sake, that is, to help him in the tasks God gave him, then it follows that her helping role is a submissive one.

To avoid possible misunderstandings, we must note that Genesis 2:18 and Paul's interpretation of it in 1 Corinthians 11:9 do not say that woman was made to be man's slave or plaything; they say rather that she was made to meet man's need for a fitting companion and fellow-worker. When men view their wives as less than God-given helpers, they are unfaithful not only to the teaching of Genesis but also to the example of Christ's servant headship, which is the model for husband-wife relationships (Eph 5:23-30).

The foregoing considerations show the fundamental importance Paul attached to the order and manner of the creation of Adam and Eve as found in Genesis 2. For Paul, the creational order constitutes the theological basis requiring that women not serve in a headship role in the church. Such a role would not accord with the submissive, helping role God envisaged for woman at creation. To reject Paul's interpretation of Genesis 2 means to reject the internal witness of the Bible.

4. Man Names the Woman both Before and After the Fall

Genesis 2 indicates the principle of headship and submission still further by the fact that God entrusted man with naming not only the animals (Gen 2:19-20), but also the woman herself, both before and after the Fall (Gen 2:23; 3:20). In the Bible, name-giving often indicates authority. God exercises this prerogative by naming things He created and by later giving new names to such people as Abraham and Jacob (Gen 17:5; 35:10).

Giving a name is more than labeling. It is, as Gerhard von Rad puts it, "an act of appropriate ordering, by which man intellectually objectifies the creatures for himself."[18] God entrusted man with the responsibility of naming the animals to help him comprehend their characteristics and the environment surrounding him. Naming expressed an assessment of each creature's character (Gen 2:19).

"God was not waiting to see what sounds Adam would associate with each animal," James Hurley observes. "The prerogative of assigning them names reflects control. He was allowing his vicegerent to express his understanding of and to exercise his rule over the animals by assigning them names. Adam does so, and demonstrates his control: 'whatever the man called each living creature, that was its name' (Gen 2:19)"[19] In naming the animals Adam fulfills part of his commission to subdue the earth (Gen 2:18), which consists not only in transforming it physically, but also in comprehending it intellectually. It is significant that Adam, not Eve, is entrusted with naming the animal kingdom. This was to enable man not only to comprehend his environment, but to lead him to realize his need for a "helper fit for him" (Gen 2:18).

When Adam discovered that there was no animal suitable to be his companion, God proceeded to fashion a woman from his own body. In his reaction to the creation of woman, Adam revealed not only his joyful astonishment but also his intellectual understanding of the nature of male and female:

"This at last is bone of my bones
and flesh of my flesh;
she shall be called Woman,
because she was taken out of man" (Gen 2:23).

Note that God does not introduce the woman to man, nor does she introduce herself. Adam himself grasps the new situation. In designating her "Woman" Adam defines her identity in relationship to himself. He interprets her as feminine, unlike himself and yet his counterpart. He sees her as part of his own flesh. He defines the woman not only for his own understanding of her but also for her self-understanding. Adam's defining of the woman is in keeping with the headship responsibility God entrusted to him.

"Adam's sovereign act [of naming the woman] not only arose out of his own sense of headship, it also made his headship clear to Eve. She found her own identity in relation to the man as his equal and helper *by the man's definition*. Both Adam and Eve understood the paradox of their relationship [equal and yet different] from the start."[20] Adam's responsibility to serve as God's subordinate ruler continues after the Fall. In Genesis

3:20, Adam assigns the woman a new name which reflects God's promise that, despite their transgression, the woman would bring forth children to continue the race (Gen 3:15-16). "The man called his wife's name Eve [*Hawwah*, life-giving], because she was the mother of all living" (Gen 3:20).

There is no indication that Adam's assigning of a personal name to the woman after the Fall was any different from what he did originally in giving her a class name after her creation. In both instances the man exercised his headship responsibilities. By the first name, "woman—*'ishshah*," Adam defined the woman's *nature* as "taken out of man" (Gen 2:23); by the second name "Eve—*Hawwah*," Adam defined her *function* as "the mother of the living" (Gen 3:20). Both naming acts were in keeping with Adam's headship responsibilities.

The Author's Interpretation. Rejecting this interpretation, our author argues that although "assigning names in Scripture often does signify authority over the one named, . . . such is not the case in Genesis 2:23."[21] The first reason he gives is that "the word 'woman' (*'ishshah*) is not a personal name but a generic identification. This is verified in verse 24, which indicates that a man is to cleave to his *'ishshah* ('wife') and further substantiated in Genesis 3:20, which explicitly records man's naming of Eve only after the Fall."[22]

This argument has three major problems. First, while indeed the word "woman" is not a personal name but a "generic identification," this does not diminish the responsible role of Adam in giving her a class name. Such a name was designed to define who she was in relationship to himself at the moment of her creation. By giving Eve a class name Adam fulfilled the role assigned him by God to name all the living creatures according to their characteristics. We do not know what language was spoken in Eden. In Hebrew the name for woman, *'ishshah*, sounds very much like the name for man, *'ish*. A pun of sorts may have been intended.

The reason given for assigning Eve such a class name is "because she was taken out of man" (Gen 2:23). This explanation suggests that Adam called Eve *'ishshah*, woman, because he realized that she was indeed his own kind, from his own body.

Second, while Genesis 2:24 "indicates that a man is to cleave to his *'ishshah* ('wife')," this does not minimize the headship role of man. The function of this text is to affirm man's responsibility to form a committed marital relationship. This commitment involves *leaving* father and mother and *cleaving* to his wife. In both instances it is man who is called upon to take the initiative and responsibility to form a committed marital union. The use of the "generic" class name *'ishshah* (wife/woman), rather than a personal name, reflects the general principle stated in the text that man is to cleave to his wife.

Lastly, Adam's assigning the personal name "Eve" to his wife after the Fall (Gen 3:20) only serves to reconfirm his headship role. After Eve's creation, Adam gave her a *class name* to define her identity in relationship to himself. After the Fall, Adam gave her the *personal name* "Eve" to define her role as "the mother of the living" (Gen 3:20). In both instances Adam acts in keeping with his headship responsibilities by defining the woman's nature and function.

The second reason the author gives for rejecting any headship role in man's naming of the woman in Genesis 2:23 is his claim that this text "contains a pairing of 'divine passives,' indicating that the designation of 'woman' comes *from God,* not man. Just as woman 'was taken out of man' *by God,* with which man had nothing to do, so she 'shall be called woman,' a designation originating in God and not man."[23]

Assuming for the sake of argument that the designation of "woman" originates from God and not from man, does this negate the headship role of man? Hardly so! Why? Because Adam would then be using a term coined by God Himself to define the woman's derivation from himself. In this case, Adam exercised his authority by using a divinely coined term to define the woman's relationship to himself. However one looks at it, Adam is involved in naming Eve before and after the Fall, simply because this is part of his God-assigned headship role.

Are Submission and Equality Contradictory? Most feminists today view the principle of equality in nature and submission in function, which is present in Genesis 2, as a contradiction in terms. For example, Scanzoni and Hardesty write, "Many Christians thus speak of a wife's being equal to her husband in personhood, but subordinate in function. However, this is just playing word games and is a contradiction in terms. Equality and subordination are contradictions."[24]

The claim that equality and subordination are an unacceptable contradiction fails to recognize that such an apparent contradiction exists in our Savior Himself. On the one hand Christ says, "I and the Father are one" (John 10:30) and "He who has seen me has seen the Father" (John 14:9), and on the other hand He states, "I can do nothing on my own authority; . . . I seek not my own will but the will of him who sent me" (John 5:30) and "the Father is greater than I" (John 14:28). Christ is fully God (John 1:1; Col 1:15-20) and yet "the head of Christ is God" (1 Cor 11:3; cf. 15:28).

The submission in Genesis 2 is similar to the one that exists in the Godhead between Father and Son. In fact, Paul appeals to the latter model to explain in what sense a husband is the head of a wife, namely, as God is the head of Christ (1 Cor 11:3). This is a unique kind of submission that makes one person out of two. Man is called to be the head of a one-flesh relationship. Submission in Scripture does not connote subservience, as commonly understood, but willing response and loving assistance.

Susan T. Foh aptly remarks, "We know only the arbitrariness, the domination, the arrogance that even the best boss/underling relationship has. But in Eden, it was different. It really was. The man and the woman knew each other as equals, both in the image of God, and thus each with a personal relationship to God. Neither doubted the worth of the other nor of him/herself. Each was to perform his/her task in a different way, the man as the head and the woman as his helper. They operated as truly one flesh, one person. In one body does the rib rebel against or envy the head?"[25]

PART III – GENESIS 3: SIN AND SUBORDINATION

1. Distortion of Creation

The first two chapters of Genesis present God's creation as He intended it to be. We have seen that God built male headship (not male domination) and female submission into the glorious pre-Fall order of creation. The third chapter of Genesis describes the disruption and distortion of creation brought about by the Fall. Our purpose here is to analyze briefly how the Fall affected the relationship between man and woman.

Genesis 3 is a crucial chapter for understanding what went wrong with God's original perfect creation. If human life started out in Edenic bliss, how do we account for the pain, sorrow, conflicts, and death that afflict mankind today? Genesis 3 explains their origin and gives us hope for God's provision of redemption and ultimate restoration.

Much of the chapter consists of what might be called a trial, in which God interrogates Adam and Eve, establishes their guilt, and pronounces punishment over the serpent, the ground, the woman, and the man. Of special interest for our study is the judgment pronounced upon the woman in Genesis 3:16. This judgment has two aspects. The first relates to childbearing and the second to her relation to her husband. Childbearing, part of the pre-Fall divine design for filling the earth (Gen 1:28), was now to become a painful process (Gen 3:16). The husband-wife relationship would also experience a painful distortion: "Your desire shall be for your husband, and he shall rule over you" (Gen 3:16).

The Author's Interpretation. Our author finds in this passage the beginning of the submission of woman to man which he believes did not exist before the Fall. He maintains that it was only "after the Fall, according to Genesis 3:16, that the husband was given a servant headship role to preserve the harmony of the home, while at the same time the model of equal partnership was still set forth as the ideal. This post-Fall prescription of husband headship and wife submission was limited to the husband-wife relationship. In the divine revelation throughout the rest of the Old Testament and the New Testament witness, servant headship and voluntary submission on the part of husband and wife, respectively, are affirmed, but these are *never* broadened to the covenant community in such a way as to prohibit women from taking positions of leadership, including headship positions over men."[26]

So far we have examined the author's thesis by focusing on his interpretation of Genesis 1 and 2. We have found his attempts to negate the presence of male headship and female submission in these two chapters to be unsuccessful. A close study of significant details of these texts in the light of Paul's interpretation of the same passages has shown that the principle of male headship and female submission is rooted and grounded in the very order and manner of Adam and Eve's creation.

At this juncture we need to analyze the *Women in Ministry* chapter's interpretation of Genesis 3:16. We intend to address two questions: (1) Does Genesis 3 mark the origin of male headship and female submission, as our author claims? Or does it allow for the possibility of a painful distortion of an already existing headship-submission principle? (2) Is male headship restricted to the home, as the author contends, or does it extend also to the community of faith in such a way as to exclude women from serving in headship positions over men? We shall attempt to answer these questions by considering first the role of Adam and Eve in the Fall and then the divine judgments passed on them.

The Nature of the Temptation. In the first five verses of Genesis 3, Satan, masquerading as a serpent, plants seeds of doubt in Eve's mind which lead her to question the limitation God had placed on them regarding the tree of the knowledge of good and evil. The serpent pretended to disclose an important secret to Eve, namely, that by partaking of the forbidden fruit she would reach her full potential and become divine. Eve succumbed to the deception. Genesis describes in a matter-of-fact way the actual acts of Adam and Eve: "She took of the fruit thereof, and did eat, and gave also unto her husband with her; and he did eat" (Gen 3:6 KJV).

What happened has significant implications. The text clearly indicates that Eve played the leading role in taking the fruit, eating it, and giving it to her husband, who enters the scene at a later time. The latter is suggested by the prepositional phrase "with her" (*immah*) which, as H. C. Leupold points out, "strongly suggests that at the outset, when temptation began, Adam was not with Eve but had only joined her at this time."[27] Ellen White states even more plausibly that Adam was not at the tree during the temptation at all, but that Eve, after eating the forbidden fruit, went in search of Adam and brought some to him.[28]

Note that Adam did not take the fruit from the tree but received it from his wife, who played the leading role in the Fall. Adam willingly let his wife take the lead. Apparently, as Ellen White indicates, Eve "was flattered [by the serpent] with the hope of entering a higher sphere than that which God had assigned to her"[29] at her husband's side. She usurped Adam's headship, and instead of being his helper to live as God intended, she led him into sin.

A careful reading of Genesis 3 suggests that the original sin of Adam and Eve was largely due to role reversal. The Fall did not originate male headship and female submission, as our author contends, but actually resulted from a failure to respect these roles. Adam failed to exercise his spiritual leadership by protecting Eve from the serpent's deception, and, on her part, Eve failed to respect her submissive role by staying by her husband's side. The tragic consequences of the first sex role reversal carry a solemn warning for Christians today who are told that role interchangeability is a sign of human emancipation.

Why Is Adam Responsible for Mankind's Sin? If our author's contention is correct that "before the Fall there was full equality with no headship-submission in the relationship between Adam and Eve (Gen 2:24),"[30] then why didn't God summon Adam and Eve to account together for their transgression? After all, Eve had played the leading role. Why did God call out *only to Adam,* "Where are you" (Gen

3:9)? Why does Genesis 3:7 say that it was only after *Adam* ate of the forbidden fruit that the eyes of *both* were opened? Why does Paul hold Adam responsible for the entrance of sin into this world when he writes, "Sin came into the world through one man" (Rom 5:12)? Why didn't he say "sin came into the world through one woman" or "through the first couple"? Why is Christ portrayed as the second Adam and not the second Eve? The answer to these questions is simple: God had appointed Adam to serve in a headship role. He bore primary responsibility for failing to exercise his spiritual leadership at the time of the temptation. Consequently, as the head of Eve and of the human family, his transgression brought sin and death to fallen humanity.

In both Genesis 2 and 3, Adam is addressed as the one to whom God had entrusted the responsibility of spiritual leadership. Adam received the divine instructions not to eat of the tree of knowledge (Gen 2:16-17); consequently, he was in a special way responsible for instructing Eve so that neither of them would transgress God's command. The great fault of Adam in the Fall was his failure to exercise his role of spiritual leadership. Instead of leading his wife into obedience to God's command, he allowed his wife to lead him into disobedience.

The leadership position that God assigned to Adam made him especially responsible for the transgression of the divine commandment. Werner Neuer rightly observes that "the leadership position of the man intended by God in Genesis 2 precludes ascribing to Eve the chief guilt for the Fall, as has happened time and again in the Judaeo-Christian tradition. His seduction by Eve offers no excuse for Adam, for he was pledged on the basis of his spiritual responsibility to correct his wife and to prevent the disobedience initiated by her from turning into joint rebellion against God."[31] Because of his failure to exercise his spiritual headship role at the time of Eve's temptation, Adam is fittingly viewed in the Bible as the head of fallen humanity. If this interpretation is correct, as the text strongly suggests, then *Women in Ministry*'s contention that male headship is a post-Fall phenomenon is clearly incorrect.

The Curse on the Serpent. After interrogating the first human couple, God states the consequences of their actions to the serpent, the woman, and the man. These consequences have been generally referred to as "curses." The curse upon the serpent affects not only the serpent as an animal (Gen 3:14) but also the relation between Satan and mankind, characterized by an "enmity" and hostility which will eventually end at the destruction of Satan himself (Gen 3:15). God's merciful promise to defeat our enemy through the victorious Offspring of the woman is our only hope for a glorious destiny.

The Judgment Upon the Woman. The divine judgment upon the woman is of central concern for our study, because it deals directly with the impact of the Fall upon the husband-wife relationship. The judgment upon the woman has two aspects. The first relates to her role as a mother and the second to her role as a wife. As a mother she will still be able to bear children, but God decrees that she will suffer in childbirth: "I will greatly multiply your pain in childbearing; in pain you shall bring forth children" (Gen 3:16). Childbearing, which was part of the pre-Fall divine design for the filling of the earth (Gen 1:28), will now become a painful process.

As a wife, the woman will suffer in relation to her husband. "Your desire shall be for your husband, and he shall rule over you" (Gen 3:16). This divine judgment represents a measure-for-measure response to Eve's attempt to usurp her husband's headship. The meaning of the first phrase appears to be, as Leupold puts it, "She who sought to strive apart from man and to act independently from him in the temptation, [now] finds a continual attraction for him to be her unavoidable lot."[32] Feminists may try to banish a woman's attraction for man, but it is there to stay. This is not necessarily a punitive element. The meaning of the word "desire" (Hebrew *t'shuqah*) is illuminated by its occurrence in Song of Solomon, where the Shulamite bride joyfully exclaims, "I am my beloved's, and his *desire* is for me" (Song 7:10).

The second phrase, "he shall rule over you," has been the subject of numerous interpretations. Our *Women in Ministry* chapter acknowledges that the "word *mashal* [to rule] in this form in verse 16*d* means 'to rule' (and not 'to be like') and definitely implies subjection."[33] The meaning appears to be that as the woman sought to rule man by taking control in her own hands and leading him into temptation, now her penalty is that she will be ruled by her husband. This does not mean that God gives a license to man to exercise despotic rulership. The author rightly points out that the Hebrew word for "to rule," *mashal*, is used in many passages "in the sense of servant leadership, to 'comfort, protect, care for, love.'"[34] The Old Testament uses *mashal* in a positive sense to describe God's rulership (Is 40:10; Ps 22:28) and the future rulership of the Messiah (Mic 5:2).

When a man rules in the spirit of Christ, such rule is not harsh or domineering and "may be regarded as a blessing in preserving the harmony and union of the relationship."[35] But where sin prevails, then such a husband's rulership may become a miserable domination. God ordained that man should exercise godly headship, not ungodly domination.

The phrase, "he shall rule over you," represents God's rejection of the woman's attempt to take on the leadership role at the time of the Fall and His summons to the woman to return to her creation submission to man. The story of the Fall shows how the woman endangered herself and her husband by her bid to dominate. God's judgments upon the woman represent the divine remedy to maintain the intended order of the sexes as it appears in Genesis 2. The divinely intended submission of women has nothing to do with male domination and oppression of women. It is a beneficial arrangement designed to protect men and women from the destructive powers of evil.

Not all the elements of the divine judgment are punitive. God's declaration that the woman will bear children is not punitive; only the pains of birth are punishments for the Fall. Similarly, her desire for a man is not necessarily punitive, because the same is said about man before the Fall: the man leaves his parents in order to cleave to his wife (Gen 2:24). The punitive aspects of Genesis 3:16 do not imply that all aspects of subordination must be seen as punishment.

Summing up, we can say that the wording of Genesis 3:16 does not warrant our author's conclusion that the relationship between man and woman has been fundamentally altered by the Fall. George W. Knight cogently points out that "Genesis 3 presumes the reality of childbearing (Gen 1:28), in which the woman will now experience the effects of the Fall and sin (Gen 3:16). It presumes the reality of work (Gen 1:28; 2:15), in which the man will now experience the effect of the Fall and sin (Gen 3:17ff.). And it presumes the reality of the role relationship between wife and husband established by God's creation order in Genesis 2:18ff., a relationship that will now experience the effects of the Fall and sin (Gen 3:16). 'He shall rule over you' expresses the effect of sin corrupting the relationship of husband (the head) and wife. Just as childbearing and work were established before the Fall and were corrupted by it, so this relationship existed before the Fall and was corrupted by it. Neither childbearing, nor work, nor the role relationship of wife and husband is being introduced in Genesis 3; all are previously existing realities that have been affected by the Fall."[36]

The Judgment Upon Man. The divine punishment for Adam's disobedience contains three significant points worthy of consideration. First, man's relationship to the ground is distorted: "Cursed is the ground because of you; in toil you shall eat of it all the days of your life; thorns and thistles it shall bring forth to you; . . . In the sweat of your face you shall eat bread . . ." (Gen 3:17-19). Work is not the punitive element, just as childbearing was not Eve's punishment. The punitive element is the pain in cultivating the ground in the sweat of one's brow.

The second important point is God's rationale for inflicting the punishment. The first reason God gave for inflicting the punishment was not "Because you have eaten of the tree which I commanded you," but *"Because you have listened to the voice of your wife,* and have eaten of the tree of which I commanded you" (Gen 3:17). The point here is obvious. Adam sinned first of all because he listened to the voice of his wife rather than to the command of God. By so doing, he abdicated his headship. Second, and as a result of the first, Adam sinned by transgressing the simple and plain command God had given him (Gen 2:17).

Note that God issued a formal indictment only before sentencing Adam, and not before sentencing Eve. The reason is that Adam was the head and thus ultimately responsible for the disobedience of both. God did not place the blame on both as if both shared equal responsibility. God says: "Because *you* have listened to the voice of your wife . . . cursed is the ground because of *you"* (Gen 3:17). The *"you"* refers exclusively to Adam, because he had been entrusted with the responsibility to serve as the spiritual and moral leader.

A third point to note is that God told *only Adam* that he would die: "till you return to the ground, for out of it you were taken; *you* are dust, and to dust *you* shall return" (Gen 3:19). Eve died too, of course, but God pronounced the death sentence on Adam alone, because he was the head, and the death sentence upon him included Eve and all members of the human family that he represented.

Paul's Use of Genesis 3. In our study of Genesis 1 and 2 we noted that Paul faithfully appealed to the implication of these chapters to support his teaching that women ought not "to teach or to have authority over men" (1 Tim 2:12). We must now turn our attention to Paul's use of Genesis 3. His main reference to Genesis 3 is found in 1 Timothy 2:14: "And Adam was not deceived, but the woman was deceived and became a transgressor." This is the second of the two reasons Paul gives to support his teaching. The first reason is the priority of Adam's formation (1 Tim 2:13).

This second reason, based on Eve's deception, has produced many dangerous interpretations. Some have assumed that this verse teaches that women are disqualified to act as leaders in the church because they are more gullible than men. Paul "may have in mind the greater aptitude of the weaker sex to be led astray."[37] A variation of this interpretation is that women "are inferior in their gifts so far as the teaching office is concerned."[38]

These interpretations are wrong because nowhere does Scripture suggest that women are more prone to err than men or that their teaching gifts are inferior. If the latter were true, how could Paul admonish women to teach their children and other women (Titus 2:3-5; 2 Tim 3:15)? How could he praise women fellow-workers for their roles in the missionary outreach of the church (Rom 16:1, 3, 12; Phil 4:3)?

To understand the meaning of 1 Timothy 2:14 we must note that this verse is linked to the preceding one by the conjunction "and" (*kai*), which Paul often uses as an explanatory connective (see 1 Tim 4:4; 5:4-5). In this case the connective "and" suggests that the typological meaning of Adam's having been formed first, as mentioned in verse 13, is connected with the typological meaning of Eve's deception, mentioned in verse 14.

Apparently Paul is saying that both Adam's formation and Eve's deception typologically represent woman's subordination to man. As we have noted, Paul's first reason for his teaching appeals to the order of creation and the second reason to the Fall. The second reason shows what happens when the order of creation is disregarded. When Eve asserted her independence from Adam she was deceived.

The *Seventh-day Adventist Bible Commentary* supports this interpretation, "The apostle's second argument for the submissiveness of women is that when Eve tried to assert leadership she was beguiled."[39] In a similar vein George W. Knight writes: "In 1 Timothy 2:14 Paul also refers to the Fall after citing the creation order . . . to show the dire consequences of reversing the creation order on this most historic and significant occasion."[40]

Conclusion
Our study of the first three chapters of Genesis has shown that the principle of male headship and female submission was established by God at creation and not, as *Women in Ministry* contends, after the Fall. We have found that Genesis 1 simply affirms that man and woman are equally created in the image of God but are sexually

different. By twice calling the human race "man" (Gen 1:26-27), God whispers male headship already in Genesis 1, though it is explained in chapter two.

Genesis 2 clarifies the equality and gender distinctions of Genesis 1. Man and woman are equal in nature, because they share the same human flesh and bone and have the same spiritual value before God. Yet they are different in function, because woman is to be submissive to man. The latter is indicated by the following four elements of the narrative: (1) the priority of man's creation (Gen 2:7, 22), (2) the manner of the woman's creation out of man (Gen 2:21-22), (3) the woman's creation to be man's helper (Gen 2:18-20), and (4) man's naming of the woman both before and after the Fall (Gen 2:23; 3:20). The headship of man is implied also in chapter 3 where God calls upon the man to answer for the pair's transgression and indicts the man (not the woman) for failing to fulfill his headship role by listening to the voice of his wife rather than to His command.

Genesis 3 describes the distortion of the creation order brought about by the Fall. This distortion affected not only the serpent, the land, work, and childbearing, but also the submission of woman to man. Sinful man would now take advantage of his headship to dominate and oppress his wife. Contrary to our author's view, the curse on the woman marked not the institution of submission but rather its distortion into oppressive domination.

Paul attaches fundamental importance to the teachings of the first three chapters of Genesis. We found that he appeals to the pre-Fall order and manner of creation as the basis for the submission of woman to the leadership of man, both in marriage and in the church. Paul's appeal to the order of creation is in line with Christ's teaching that calls for a restoration of the creational relationship (Matt 19:8) by the members of His kingdom. The function of redemption is not to redefine creation but to restore it, so that wives may learn godly submission and husbands may learn godly headship.

Paul bases his teaching concerning the role of women in the church not on the consequences of the Fall described in Genesis 3, but on the pre-Fall order of creation presented in Genesis 1 and 2. The foundation of his teaching is not the divine judgments pronounced at the Fall but God's original purpose manifested in the order and manner of human creation. It is unfortunate that in his interpretation of Genesis 1, 2, and 3, our author consistently ignores Paul's appeals to these chapters to support his teachings in regard to male-female role distinctions in the home and in the church. Ignoring the internal witness of the Bible can give rise to private interpretations.

Genesis 1-3 deals primarily with husband-wife relations, but the underlying principle of equality and submission has broader implications for the roles of men and women within the community of faith. This will become evident in the next two sections, where we examine the ministry of women in both Old and New Testaments. We shall see that though women ministered to God's people in a variety of vital religious roles, including that of prophet, there are no indications in Scripture that they were ever ordained to serve as priests in the Old Testament or as pastors, elders, or bishops in the New Testament. The reason is to be found, not in the patriarchal mentality of Bible times but in the recognition of the headship role which God appointed man as the "firstborn" of the human family, to be fulfilled in the home and in public worship. The Bible implies this principle in the creation story of Genesis 2 and upholds it in both the Old and New Testaments.

PART IV – HEADSHIP, SUBMISSION, AND EQUALITY IN THE OLD TESTAMENT

Husband-Wife Relationships. The author's fundamental thesis is that the principle of male headship and female submission originated at the Fall (Gen 3:16) and was designed to govern *only* the husband-wife relationship and not male-female roles in the religious life of God's people. To prove the validity of this thesis he endeavors to show in the second half of his chapter that in both the Old and New Testaments the principle of headship and submission applies to the home but not to the religious community of faith. Since elsewhere I have dealt at length with the ministry of women in the Old and New Testaments, here I will limit my comments to a few basic observations.[41]

The author finds in the Old Testament ample "evidence for the husband headship principle in marriage," but he emphasizes that "such headship does not override the basic equality between marriage partners, nor does it imply the husband's ownership, oppression, domination, or authoritative control over the wife."[42] On this point we are in perfect agreement. God never intended that husband headship should be a means of domination or oppression but a responsibility of service. A survey of the evidence in this area is unnecessary because there is no disagreement.

The area of disagreement centers on the role of women in the religious life of ancient Israel and of the New Testament church. Our author maintains that "while the headship principle of Genesis 3:16 clearly functions to regulate the Old Testament husband-wife relationship, this principle is not widened into the covenant community in such a way as to cause the rejection of women leaders on the basis of gender—even women leaders exercising headship over men."[43]

Does a Prophetess Exercise a Headship Role? Deborah is the author's major example to support his contention that women served in headship roles over men in the Old Testament covenant community. He writes, "I note particularly the leadership role of Deborah the prophetess and judge (Judges 4-5). Deborah clearly exercised headship functions over men as the recognized political leader of the nation, the military leader of Israel on an equal footing with the male general Barak, and a judge to whom men and women turned for legal counsel and divine instruction. There is no indication in the text that such female leadership over men in the covenant community was looked upon as unusual or was opposed to the divine will for women."[44]

In examining Deborah's role in ancient Israel, we first note that she is introduced to us in Scripture as a "prophetess" who judged the people under a palm tree and not as a military leader. "Now Deborah, a prophetess, the wife of Lappidoth, was judging Israel at that time. She used to sit under the palm of Deborah between Ramah and Bethel in the hill country of Ephraim; and the people of Israel came up to her for judgment" (Jud 4:4-5).

Did Deborah as a prophetess exercise a headship role over men in ancient Israel? The answer is No! Why? Because the role of a prophet or prophetess is that of a messenger, not a leader. A prophet exercises no authority of his own but communicates the messages and decisions of the One who has sent him.

The careers of the Old Testament prophets make it clear that they did not exercise headship. They often rebuked the leaders who did have the headship, trying to persuade them to change their evil course and turn to God. All too often their efforts were rejected. Some of them, such as Micaiah (1 Kings 22) and Jeremiah (Jer 38), were imprisoned because their messages displeased the rulers. Isaiah is said to have been sawn in two at the order of the king. Jesus recognized and lamented how the prophets had been treated: "O Jerusalem, Jerusalem, killing the prophets and stoning those who are sent to you!" (Matt 23:37). Clearly the prophets did not exercise headship in Israel. Their messages had great power and moral authority, because they came from God; but the prophetic role entailed no headship. Even when the country's leaders obeyed God's word conveyed through the prophets, the prophetic role was never that of head. The relationship between prophets and leaders (heads) in the best of times is illustrated in Ezra 5:1, 2: "Now the prophets, Haggai and Zechariah the son of Iddo, prophesied to the Jews who were in Judah and Jerusalem, in the name of the God of Israel who was over them. Then Zerubbabel the son of Shealtiel and Jeshua the son of Jozadak arose and began to rebuild the house of God which is in Jerusalem; and with them were the prophets of God, *helping them*" (emphasis mine).

What is true of the male prophet is no less true of the female prophetess. Her role was not that of head but of messenger. The Bible sees the prophetess in a supportive and complementary role which does not negate male headship. Paul clarifies this point in 1 Corinthians 11:2-16, where he defends the right of women to pray and prophesy in the church because the gifts of the Spirit are given to the church without regard to sexual differences (Joel 2:28; 1 Cor 12:7-11). Note, however, that Paul opposes the behavior of those women who disregarded their subordinate position by praying and giving prophetic exhortations to the congregation with their heads uncovered like the men.

Paul opposes this practice because "any woman who prays or prophesies with her head unveiled dishonors her head—it is the same as if her head were shaven" (1 Cor 11:5). The "head" being dishonored is her husband, for Paul states in verse 3 that "the head of a woman is her husband." Why would it dishonor her husband for a woman to pray and prophesy in public with her head uncovered? Simply because the head covering, whatever its nature, was seen in that culture as the sign of her being under the "head" or authority of a man (cf. 1 Cor 11:10). Thus, the removal of such a sign constituted a repudiation of her husband's authority or headship, which a woman was called to respect, not only in the home but also in the church.

Did Deborah Exercise a Headship Role? The implications for our study are clear. Since the prophetic role did not involve headship, prophesying by a woman, such as Deborah, did not violate the principle of male headship, as long as she did it in a proper manner and demeanor that did not negate male headship. There are several indications that Deborah respected the principle of male headship explained by Paul in 1 Corinthians 11:2-16.

First, Deborah's role as a judge was unique, for, contrary to our author's assertion, she is the only judge in Judges who did not serve as a military leader. Instead of leading an army into battle like other judges, as the Lord's messenger she received instruction from Him to summon Barak to lead an army of ten thousand men into battle against Sisera, the general of Jabin, king of Canaan, who was oppressing Israel (Jud 4:6-7). It is significant that Deborah did not assume the headship role of an army general; she conveyed God's call to Barak to serve in that capacity.

Second, in a discreet way Deborah rebuked Barak for his unwillingness to go to battle without her (Jud 4:8). Because of his reluctance, Deborah warned Barak that "the Lord will sell Sisera into the hand of a woman" (Jud 4:9). But the woman who earned the glory by killing Sisera while he slept in her tent was not Deborah but Jael, the wife of Heber the Kenite (Jud 4:17-22).

Third, perhaps to avoid any possible misunderstanding about their role within their culture, the prophetic ministries of Deborah and Huldah (2 Kings 22:14-20) differ significantly from those of male prophets, such as Isaiah, Jeremiah, and Ezekiel. Male prophets exercised their prophetic ministry in a public manner, being commissioned to proclaim the word of the Lord before the people and the king himself (Is 6:9; 7:3; 58:1; Jer 1:10; 2:2; 7:2; Ezek 2:3; 6:2). For example, the Lord said to Isaiah, "Cry aloud and spare not, lift up your voice like a trumpet; declare to my people their transgression, and to the house of Jacob their sins" (Is 58:1). Similarly, to Jeremiah the Lord said, "Stand in the gate of the Lord's house, and proclaim there this word, and say, Hear the word of the Lord, all of you men of Judah who enter these gates to worship the Lord" (Jer 7:2).

The prophetic ministry of Deborah was substantially different from this. She did not go out and publicly proclaim the word of the Lord. Instead, individuals came to consult her privately under the palm tree where she sat: "She used to sit under the palm of Deborah . . . and the people of Israel came up to her for judgment" (Jud 4:5). Presumably she came to be known as a godly woman through whom God communicated His will. People came to trust her judgment in resolving their disputes. Though it would not have been out of place for Deborah as a prophetess to proclaim God's word publicly, she did not exercise her prophetic ministry in a public forum like the Old Testament male prophets. Even when she spoke to Barak she talked to him privately (Jud 4:6, 14). And the song of praise was sung by Deborah and Barak together (Jud 5:1), which suggests equality rather than headship. More telling still is the fact that she is praised as a "mother in Israel" (Jud 5:7). It is evident that she was perceived to be primarily a *spiritual mother,* not as filling the traditional role of an elder or judge or prophet.

Similarly, Huldah (2 Kings 22:14-20) did not proclaim God's word publicly, though it would not be wrong for a prophetess to do so since the prophetic role does not entail headship. Huldah, however, explained the word of the Lord privately to the messengers sent to her by King Josiah (2 Kings 22:15), giving no occasion to anyone to misinterpret her adherence to the womanly role. Miriam's prophetic ministry also avoided misinterpretation, for she ministered only to women. "Then Miriam, the prophetess, the sister of Aaron, took a timbrel in her hand; and *all the women went out after her* with timbrels and dancing. And Miriam sang to *them*" (Ex 15:20-21, emphasis mine).

The preceding considerations suggest that the ministry of Deborah as a judge was unusual, even unique. It is possible that the Lord used her at a critical time of apostasy, when the spiritual leadership of men was lacking. We are told that "the people of Israel again did what was evil in the sight of the Lord . . . and the Lord sold them into the hand of Jabin king of Canaan" (Jud 4:1-2). The exceptional calling of a woman like Deborah at a time of crisis can hardly be used to establish the general principle of women serving in a headship role over men in the covenant community. As if anticipating the current debate, Calvin makes a pertinent comment regarding Deborah: "If any one brings forward, by way of objection, Deborah (Jud 4:4) and others of the same class, of whom we read they were at one time appointed by the command of God to govern the people, the answer is easy. Extraordinary acts done by God do not overturn the ordinary rules of government, by which He intended that we should be bound."[45]

To sum up, women who fulfilled a prophetic ministry in the Old Testament did not exercise a headship role, nor did their male counterparts. In the New Testament, women prophesied publicly before the congregation, but their demeanor (head covering) had to show respect for male headship.

Note that prophetic speaking in the Corinthian congregations was understood in the broad sense of communicating a message of exhortation from God. We may conclude that this ministry did not involve assuming the leadership role of the church for at least two reasons. First, Paul suggests that the prophetic ministry of "upbuilding and encouragement and consolation" (1 Cor 14:3) was open to all: "For you can all prophesy one by one" (1 Cor 14:31). This by itself indicates that the prophetic role did not convey leadership or headship on the one who exercised it. Second, as we have seen, the prophetic role was that of a messenger, not of a leader or head. The prophets often had to convey the messages of God to the leaders, but they did not have headship power to implement the instructions in those messages.

In light of the above considerations, we conclude that the prophetic ministry of women in both the Old and New Testaments was not seen as exercising headship over men but as respecting the leadership role of men in the community of faith, even when the prophetic ministry involved bringing messages of rebuke or correction from God.

No Women Priestesses in the Old Testament. Regrettably, in his discussion of the role of women in the covenant community of ancient Israel, our author does not address the crucial question as to why women served as prophetesses but not as priestesses. An examination of this question could have provided a much-needed corrective to his claim that women exercised headship positions over men in the religious life of ancient Israel. The absence of priestesses shows otherwise. The reason women were precluded from ministering as priestesses is that priests served as representatives of God to the people. Their headship role could not legitimately be fulfilled by a woman. This fact alone constitutes a serious challenge to the author's thesis.

Another author addressed the question, "Why not a woman priest in Israel?" in chapter 2 of the same symposium, *Women in Ministry.* Since our first author frequently refers to this scholar, we will briefly consider the two basic reasons our second author gives for the exclusion of women from the priesthood. The first is historical and the second is theological. His historical reason is that priestesses in the ancient Near East "were often associated with sacred prostitution." Thus for him, the absence of priestesses in ancient Israel "is to be understood as a reaction to pagan syncretism and sexual perversion."[46]

This popular argument falls short on at least two counts. First, the fact that some of the pagan priestesses served as prostitutes cannot be a valid reason for God to exclude Israelite women from serving as exemplary priestesses at the sanctuary. A legitimate practice cannot be prohibited because of its perversion. The sons of Eli "lay with the women who served at the entrance to the tent of meeting" (1 Sam 2:22), but there is no indication that these prostitutions resulted in the abolition of male priesthood or of the ministry of women at the entrance of the sanctuary. If the argument were valid, then not even men should have functioned as priests because of the danger of male prostitution, which the Bible views as more abominable than female prostitution, calling male cult prostitutes "dogs" (Deut 23:18; Rev 22:15).

Second, there are indications that many, if not most, of the pagan priestesses in the ancient world lived chaste and devoted lives. Some of the Babylonian priestesses lived in cloisters.[47] The women priests who officiated, for example, at the temples of Vesta, Apollo, Athena, Polias, and Dionysius, as well as in the various mystery religions, were in most cases either celibate or very continent in their lifestyles. This shows that the argument regarding the danger of "sacred prostitution" does not hold water.[48]

Why Couldn't Women Offer Sacrifices? The theological reason the second author gives for the exclusion of women from the priesthood is "because of the sacrificial function, the only priestly act denied to women."[49] Women could not offer priestly sacrifices, he writes, because of "the incompatibility of the sacrifice, normally associated with death and sin, and the physiological nature of the woman traditionally associated in the Bible with life and messianic pregnancy."[50]

The notion that women were precluded from the sacrificial function of the priesthood because physiologically their nature is "associated in the Bible with life and messianic pregnancy," sounds more like an ingenious rabbinical speculation than a biblical reason. Nowhere does the Bible suggest such a reason.

Our second author seeks support for his view in the command, "You shall not boil a kid in its mother's milk" (Ex 23:19), but it doesn't fit. First, the primary reason for this injunction is generally recognized to be God's concern to prevent the Israelites from adopting a common Canaanite ritual practice. Second, boiling a kid in its mother's milk was not the same as a woman's offering an animal sacrifice. The former was prohibited, he speculates, "because it would be incongruous to associate the milk of the mother, carrier of life to the kid, with the death of the very kid."[51] But this hardly applies to a woman sacrificing an animal, because she would not be sacrificing her own offspring. In fact, sacrificing an animal would not have contradicted a woman's capacity to give life, because God promised to restore life through the death of the offspring of the woman (Gen 3:15). Typologically speaking, a woman could have offered sacrifices more fittingly than a man, because the animal she would sacrifice could represent her Messianic offspring, who would be sacrificed for the salvation of His people.

The Representative Role of a Priest. The true reason for the exclusion of women from the priesthood is to be found in the unique biblical view of the priest as representative of God to the people. This second author himself acknowledges this to be the "essential concept underlying the priesthood," namely, that "the priest was considered as God's representative."[52] He also correctly points out that in both the Old and New Testaments "the Messiah is consistently identified as a priest."[53] It was because of this headship role of a priest as representative of God and of the Messiah to come that women were excluded from the priesthood.

The priesthood developed through several stages in the Old Testament. During patriarchal times the head of the household or of the tribe fulfilled the priestly function of representing his household to God. Thus Noah (Gen 8:20), Abraham (Gen 22:13), Jacob (Gen 35:3), and Job (Job 1:5) each served as the representative priest of his family. With the establishment of the theocracy at Sinai and the erection of the tabernacle, God appointed the tribe of Levi to serve as priests in place of *the firstborn or head of each family.* "Behold, I have taken the Levites from among the people of Israel instead of every *firstborn* that opens the womb among the people of Israel. The Levites shall be mine, for all the *firstborn* are mine" (Num 3:12-13). We noted earlier that the notion of the firstborn derives from Adam, the first created, and is even applied to Christ, "the firstborn of all creation" (Col 1:15). The firstborn was the head of the family, and the priests served as the spiritual heads of Israel.

While God called all the people of Israel, male and female, to be "a kingdom of priests and a holy nation" (Ex 19:5-6; cf. Is 61:6), after the Sinai apostasy the

Levites were chosen to serve as the representative heads of the whole nation because of their allegiance to God (Ex 32:26-29). When the priests ministered they acted as the representatives of God to the people.

Because of this representative role which the priests fulfilled as heads of the household of Israel, women were excluded from the priesthood. A woman could minister as a prophet, because a prophet was primarily a communicator of God's will and God communicates His will through men and women, irrespective of gender. But a woman could not function as a priest, because a priest was appointed to act as the representative of the people to God and of God to the people. As James B. Hurley correctly observes, "The Mosaic provision [for an exclusively male priesthood] stands in a historical continuum and continues the practice of having representative males serve to officiate in public worship functions."[54]

"The fact that most pagan religions of the time did have priestesses, as well as priests," notes John Meyendorff, "shows that a male priesthood was the sign of a specifically biblical, i.e. Jewish and Christian, identity."[55] This unique, counter-cultural Jewish and Christian practice stems not from the religious genius of either Judaism or Christianity but from divine revelation which at creation established a functional headship role for man to fulfill in the home and in the household of faith.

Did God Dress Eve as a Priestess? The second author's most imaginative attempt to find "biblical" support for a priestly role for women in the Old Testament is his interpretation of the garment of skins God made for Adam and Eve (Gen 3:21). "God chose animal skin. This specification not only implies the killing of an animal, the first sacrifice in history, but by the same token, confirms the identification of Adam and Eve as priests, for the skin of the atonement sacrifice was specifically set apart for the officiating priests (Lev 7:8). By bestowing on Adam and Eve the skin of the sin offering, a gift reserved for priests, the Genesis story implicitly recognizes Eve as priest alongside Adam."[56]

This claim that "Adam and Eve were, indeed, dressed as priests" cannot be supported biblically. The Bible gives no indication that priests wore garments made from the skins of the animals they sacrificed. The priests wore fine linen garments (Ex 28:29), which were often called garments of "salvation" (2 Chron 6:41; Ps 132:16) because they typified the purity and salvation that God offered through the ministry of the priests. No such typological significance is attached to any skin garment in the Bible. We are on much firmer ground if we interpret the text at its face value as meaning, to use the words of Ellen G. White, that "the Lord mercifully provided them with a garment of skins as a protection from the extremes of heat and cold."[57] While the slaying of animals for man's needs may suggest the idea of sacrifice, the text *per se*, as Leupold points out, "does not teach that, nor is it an allegory conveying a lesson to that effect. The meaning is what the letter of the statement says—no more."[58]

Had God dressed Eve as a priest at the time of the Fall, it would be surprising that we do not find a single clear example of a "female priest" in the Bible. The reason is not cultural but theological, namely, the biblical teaching that only men could serve in the headship roles of priest in the Old Testament and of apostles, elders, and pastors in the New Testament.

Conclusion. Women played a most vital role both in the private and public religious life of ancient Israel. As full members of the covenant community, women participated in studying the law and teaching it to their children (Prov 1:8; Deut 31:12; Neh 8:2), in offering prayers and vows to God (1 Sam 1:10; Gen 25:22; 30:6, 22; 21:6-7), in ministering at the entrance of the sanctuary (1 Sam 2:22), in singing, and in the prophetic ministry of exhortation and guidance (Ezra 2:65; 1 Chron 25:5-6; Jud 4:4-6; 2 Kings 22:13-14).

But, in spite of the first author's attempts to prove the contrary, the religious roles of women in ancient Israel were different from those of men. Women served in accordance with the principles of equality of being and submission of function that are implicit in the creation story. The principle of male headship in the home and in public worship is recognized even by Clarence J. Vos, an Evangelical feminist, who writes: "It was not her [the woman's] task to lead the family or tribe in worship; normally this was done by the patriarch or the eldest male member. That a male was appointed to this function no doubt rested on the idea that the male was considered the 'firstborn' of the human family—a motif discernible in the creation story of Genesis 2."[59]

PART V – HEADSHIP, SUBMISSION, AND EQUALITY IN THE NEW TESTAMENT

In the final section of his chapter, our first author endeavors to prove that the New Testament is consistent with the Old Testament in applying the principle of headship and submission only to husband-wife relationships and not to the role of women in the church. To prove his thesis he attempts to show that *"all* of the New Testament passages regarding headship and 'submission' between men and women are limited to the marriage relationship" "and not men and women in general."[60]

For the sake of brevity I will comment only on the three Pauline passages relevant to our discussion on the role of women in the church (1 Cor 11:2-16; 14:34-36; 1 Tim 2:8-15), addressing the fundamental question, Are Paul's admonitions regarding women's behavior in the church meant for wives only or for women in general?[61]

1. Headship and Headcovering: 1 Corinthians 11:2-16

In 1 Corinthians 11:2-16 Paul discusses the appropriate headdress for men and women during a worship service. The basic rule for church order that Paul gives in this passage is that in worship services men should leave their heads uncovered while women should have their heads covered. It seems probable that Paul was responding to a report received about some Corinthian women who were either refusing to cover their heads or who were questioning the practice. Possibly some women saw the abandoning of their head coverings as an expression of their liberty and equality in Christ.

The importance of this passage lies not so much in what Paul says about head coverings as in the significance that he attaches to head coverings as a symbol of the role distinctions that men and women must preserve at church. For Paul, these distinctions are not grounded on cultural conventions but on the principle of male headship and female submission established by God at creation. To support this principle, in 1 Corinthians 11:8-9 the apostle appeals not to the story of the Fall in Genesis 3 but to the manner of the creation of Eve out of man and for man in Genesis 2. If the submission of women were regarded as a consequence of the Fall, as our author contends, then the headcovering would have been a shameful sign of guilt. But Paul sees it as a sign of honor for women (1 Cor 11:7, 15), because in Paul's culture it represented obedience to the submissive role that God assigned to women.

Modern readers find it difficult to comprehend why Paul should place so much importance on such a trivial matter as headcovering. The key to understanding why this custom was important for Paul is found in the opening verse of the section: "But I want you to understand that the head of every man is Christ, the head of a woman is her husband, and the head of Christ is God" (1 Cor 11:3). Paul is concerned that the principle of male headship and female submission be outwardly respected in the church through the custom of women covering their heads.

What matters to Paul is not the headgear itself but respect for the distinction between the sexes which the headgear expressed in that particular culture. By laying aside their headgear, the Corinthian women were rebelling against their divinely-intended submission. What to some appears as a petty fight over a trivial matter of women's head covering was in reality an important theological battle against women who wanted to obliterate role distinctions set in place by God Himself at creation.

Seen in its proper light, this passage speaks volumes to our culture today, where the feminist movement is promoting role interchangeability, the obliteration of sexual role distinctions in all realms of life. Ultimately, this effort results in the breaking down of the fundamental structure established by God for the well-being of the home, the church, and society.

Wives or Women? On the basis of still another author's analysis of 1 Corinthians 11 in Chapter 15 of the same symposium, *Women in Ministry*,[62] our author argues that the passage affirms male headship *only* in marital relationships and *not* over women in general. "The context in 1 Corinthians is one of wives submitting to the headship of their own husbands, and not the headship of men over women in general."[63] The main support for this conclusion is two Greek words, *gyne* and *aner*, which can be translated either as man and woman or as husband and wife. "The context of 1 Corinthians 11 clearly favors the translation 'husband' and 'wife.'"[64]

As we noted at the beginning, Seventh-day Adventists opposed to women's ordination do not hold to "the headship of men over women in general." In offering a choice only between this general headship and headship confined to the marriage relation, the author presents a false dichotomy. Taken together, the writings of Paul do not assert the subordination of all females to all males but the subordination of females under their proper heads. In the home, the proper head is the husband or father, as our author affirms. Paul's counsel in Ephesians 5:22, 23 is evidence for this view: "Wives, be subject to your husbands . . . . For the husband is the head of the wife." In the church family, the proper head is not all males but the appointed male leadership of the elder or elders, who serve in the role of father to the entire church, both male and female (see 1 Tim 3:2-5).

The author is correct when he says that the statement, "the head of a woman is her husband" (1 Cor 11:3, RSV) most likely refers to the husband-wife relationship. In fact, Paul uses the same words in Ephesians 5:23 when speaking exclusively of the headship of the husband over his wife. In spite of this evidence, four considerations give us reason to believe that the passage has a broader application that includes also the relationships and behaviors of men and women in the church.

First, verses 4 and 5 speak inclusively of "every man" and "every woman" respectively. The qualifying word *pas,* "every," suggests that the regulation about head coverings applies to all men and women and not just to husbands and wives.

Second, verses 7-9 appeal to the manner of the creation of Eve out of Adam as a basis for the regulation given. This theological reason suggests that Paul is thinking of all men and women rather than of husbands and wives exclusively.

Third, "verses 11-12 speak of the mutual interdependence of the sexes in the process of procreation. If only husband and wife were meant, these verses would be illogical, for the husband does not come into being through the wife nor is the wife the source of the husband. Verses 13-16 argue from nature, which would give greater support that men and women in general are being discussed rather than just husbands and wives."[65]

Fourth, the ambiguity which is caused by the double meaning of *gyne,* namely, wife and woman, can be clarified when we bear in mind that for Paul the husband-wife relationship in marriage is the paradigm for the man-woman relationship in the church. For Paul, the submissive role of a married woman is a model for women in general, and by the same token the headship role of a married man is a model for men in general. This important point will be elaborated shortly. This means that although 1 Corinthians 11 focuses on husbands and wives, the principle of headship and submission is applicable to the broader relations of men and women in the church. In Paul's view, men should behave properly like men, regardless of their marital status; likewise women, regardless of whether they are married or not, should behave in ways that befit women. It is not a matter of all men exercising headship over all women, but of each person respecting his or her God-given role.

We would conclude with Fritz Zerbst that "the Apostle had husbands and wives in mind when he wrote this passage. However, Paul in this passage at the same time speaks also generally of man and woman. In order to understand Paul we must bear in mind that the relationship between the sexes always has its center in marriage."[66]

2. Women Speaking in the Church: 1 Corinthians 14:33-36

In 1 Corinthians 14:33b-36 Paul gives brief instruction regarding the role of women in church somewhat similar to the advice found in 1 Timothy 2:9-15. The passage reads as follows: "As in all the churches of the saints, the women should keep silence in the churches. For they are not permitted to speak, but should be subordinate, as even the law says. If there is anything they desire to know, let them ask their husbands at home. For it is shameful for a woman to speak in church. What! Did the word of God originate with you, or are you the only ones it has reached?" (1 Cor 14:33b-36).

This passage occurs in the context of the discussion of how to maintain order in the worship assemblies. Beginning with verse 26, Paul gives specific instructions on how speaking in tongues and prophesying should be regulated in the church, so that good order might prevail. It is in this context that Paul gives his instruction regarding the silence of women in the assembly. This instruction has been the subject of considerable controversy, especially because it appears to stand in stark contrast to 1 Corinthians 11:5, where Paul assumes that women may pray and prophesy in the church.

Does 1 Corinthians 14:34 Contradict 1 Corinthians 11:5? The apparent contradiction between the two passages can be resolved by recognizing that Paul's concern in both situations is for women to respect their submissive role. In 1 Corinthians 11:5 respect for male headship entailed that women comply with the head-covering custom of the time when they prayed and prophesied in the church. In 1 Corinthians 14:34 respect for male headship entailed that women comply with the custom of the time by refraining from asking questions publicly of their husbands or church leaders.[67]

To appreciate the consistency of Paul's teaching about women's speaking and being silent in the church, it is important to distinguish between the permanent headship-submission principle and its cultural, time-bound application. Wearing a head covering and refraining from asking questions in the assembly were customary ways in Paul's time for women to show submission to their husbands and church leaders. Thus, "not asking questions in the assembly" was a *custom* subservient to the *principle* that "[women] should be subordinate" (1 Cor 14:34). While the principle is permanent, its application is culturally conditioned. Yet in every culture the principle is to be expressed in the home and in the church through appropriate customs.

Paul seeks to maintain an authority structure in the home and in the church, where men are called to exercise responsible and sacrificial leadership, and where women respond supportively. Repeatedly the apostle emphasizes the importance of respecting the headship-submission principle. "The head of a woman is her husband" (1 Cor 11:3). "Wives, be subject to your husbands, as to the Lord" (Eph

5:22; cf. Col 3:18). "Let a woman learn in silence with all submissiveness. I permit no woman to teach or to have authority over men" (1 Tim 2:11-12). "Train the young women . . . to be submissive to their husbands" (Titus 2:4-5).

In light of the headship-submission principle, it is understandable why Paul in 1 Corinthians 14:33b-34 would deny to women an authoritative speech function, such as questioning their husbands or church leaders in the church. To allow these things would have undermined the above principle. On the other hand, in 1 Corinthians 11:5, Paul readily allowed women who had proper demeanor to pray and prophesy in the church, because these activities did not involve assuming a position of authority over men.

Wives or Women? To defend his thesis that the principles of headship and submission apply only to the home and not to the church, our author endeavors to prove again that "Paul is not addressing women in general in these verses, but certain Corinthian *wives,* since the same Greek word *gyne* can mean either 'woman' or 'wife,' depending upon the context. This becomes obvious in light of verse 35, in which reference is made to the husbands of these women: 'And if they want to learn something, let them ask their own husbands at home.'"[68] This restrictive interpretation overlooks some major considerations.

First, we already noted in our discussion of 1 Corinthians 11:3 that for Paul the husband-wife relationship is the paradigm for the man-woman relationship in general. Married women, who made up the majority of women in the congregation, served as a model for women in general. Stephen B. Clark illustrates this point with a fitting analogy: "If Paul had forbidden children to speak in public as an expression of their subordination to their parents, no one would hesitate to apply the rule to orphans as well as to children with parents. The parent-child relationship would be the normal case, but the rule would also apply to children with surrogate parents. Similarly, unmarried women would be expected to adhere to a rule for married women."[69]

Second, it is difficult to see why *only* married women would be singled out and required to be silent, especially since in 1 Corinthians 11 married women with a proper demeanor are permitted to speak. In much of the ancient world marriage meant an *improvement* in the freedom and status of women. Thus we have reason to believe that Paul and his readers would reason that if married women were enjoined to be silent, how much more the single ones?

Third, in 1 Corinthians 12 to 14 Paul assumes that all the members of the church, men and women, participate in worship. "When you come together, each one has a hymn, a lesson, a revelation, a tongue, or an interpretation. Let all these things be done for edification" (1 Cor 14:26). If each member is encouraged to participate in worship, why would married women be excluded?

Fourth, we should note that Paul's ruling concerning women in the church in 1 Corinthians 14 is given in the context of a chapter dealing with spiritual gifts which are given to all, irrespective of marital status. This makes it hard to believe that Paul would exclude married women from exercising their spiritual gifts. Paul's concern is not to exclude the participation of married women from the worship service, but to ensure that all women exercise their spiritual gifts in accordance with God's law. "They should be subordinate, as even the law says" (1 Cor 14:34). The "law" to which Paul refers is presumably the headship-submission principle which he grounds in the order of creation (1 Cor 11:79; 1 Tim 2:13-14). This principle, as we have seen, applies to the behaviors of men and women in the church and not exclusively to the relationship between husbands and wives.

Fifth, are we really supposed to think, to use the words of Donald A. Carson, a highly respected Evangelical scholar, "that Christian women enjoyed full freedom and perfect egalitarianism in function in the church as long as they were single, and then from the day of their marriage onward became silent for fear of offending the husband to whom they were to submit? These considerations effectively dismiss those interpretations that admit that Paul insists on certain role distinctions between the sexes but limit such distinctions to the home, denying that they have any bearing on the church."[70]

3. Women and Leadership in the Church: 1 Timothy 2:9-15

From the earliest days of the New Testament church, most Christians have believed on the basis of 1 Timothy 2:11-15 that the New Testament places certain restrictions on the ministry of women in the church. It is not surprising that in the contemporary debate over the role of women in the church, this passage more than any other has polarized interpreters. The passage says, "Let a woman learn in silence with all submissiveness. I permit no woman to teach or to have authority over men; she is to keep silent. For Adam was formed first, then Eve; and Adam was not deceived, but the woman was deceived and became a transgressor. Yet woman will be saved through bearing children, if she continues in faith and love and holiness, with modesty."

The significance of this passage lies in the fact that it specifically addresses the question of the role of women within the church by stating unequivocally: "I permit no woman to teach or to have authority over men; she is to keep silent." It is not surprising that this passage has been examined at great length by evangelicals who oppose or limit the full participation of women in the ministry of the church, as well as by those who support it.

In light of the immediate and wider context of the pastoral epistles,[71] Paul's intent is not to prohibit women from participating in the general teaching ministry of the church ("they [women] are to teach what is good," Titus 2:3), but rather to restrain women from aspiring to the restricted teaching role of the leader of the congregation. The reason for Paul's ruling is that the exercise of a headship function by a woman is incompatible with the submissive role which God at the creation assigned to women in the home and in the church.

Paul's teachings regarding the role of women in the church appear to have been occasioned by false teachers who sowed dissension (1 Tim 1:4-6; 6:4-5; cf.

2 Tim 2:14, 16-17, 23-24) by teaching abstinence from certain foods, from marriage, and probably from sex altogether (1 Tim 4:1-3). These false teachers had persuaded many women to follow them in their ascetic program (1 Tim 5:15; 2 Tim 3:6-7). Apparently they were encouraging women to discard their submissive role in favor of a more egalitarian status with men. This is suggested by their encouragement to abstain from marriage (1 Tim 4:3), which indicates they probably denigrated traditional female roles. Paul's counsel in 1 Timothy 5:14 to young widows "to marry, bear children, rule their household" may also reflect his effort to counteract these false teachers by affirming traditional female roles in order to "give the enemy no occasion to revile us" (1 Tim 5:14).

The situation in Ephesus is remarkably similar to that of Corinth. In both metropolitan cities, church members appear to have been influenced by false teachers who promoted the removal of role distinctions between men and women. Most likely it was the need to counteract these false teachings that occasioned Paul's teaching about the roles of men and women in church ministry.

Contemporary Relevance. Paul's teachings on the role of women are relevant today, because in some ways the contemporary emancipation of women may closely reflect that of his time.[72] If, as numerous scholars argue, Paul's opponents in the pastoral epistles included "women [who] were in the forefront of the libertarian trend"[73] as evidenced by their extravagant dress, the "forsaking of domestic roles such as raising children in order to assume such a prominent role in congregational life—as teaching,"[74] then Paul was addressing a situation strikingly similar to the one existing today.

The existence of a "women's liberation" movement in early Christianity is implied not only by Paul's strictness (1 Tim 2:11-12; 5:13; 2 Tim 3:6; 1 Cor 11:5-10; 14:34), but also by such post-New Testament documents as the fictional *Acts of Paul* (about A.D. 185). In this book, Paul commissions a woman, Thecla, to be a preacher and teacher of the word of God. "Go and teach the word of God," he says. Thecla obeys by going away to Iconium, where she "went into the house of Onesiphorus . . . and taught the oracles of God."[75]

The attempt of this apocryphal document to present Paul, not as forbidding but as commissioning a woman to be an official teacher of the Word of God in the church, offers an additional indication of the possible existence of a feminist movement in Paul's time.[76] If such a movement existed at that time, then Paul's instruction on the role of women in the church would be particularly relevant to our time, when the feminist movement is gaining strength within the church.

Wives or Women? To defend his thesis that male headship applies only to the home and not to the church, the author interprets 1 Timothy 2:8-15 like the previous two Pauline passages. In his view, this passage also applies only to "the relationship of husbands and wives and not men and women in general."[77] His arguments are similar to those already examined. For example, his first argument is that when *"gyne* and *aner* are found paired in close proximity, the reference is consistently to wife and husband and not women and men in general."[78] He has used this argument with the two previous passages. The rest of his arguments are designed to buttress his contention that Paul's ruling applies exclusively to husband-wife relationships.

Surprisingly, his arguments apparently did not persuade the very editor of the symposium, despite the fact that she argues for the same egalitarian view. She correctly observes, "The text itself seems to be discussing attitudes in worship rather than the marriage relationship."[79] She recognizes that the purpose of 1 Timothy is not to instruct Timothy on how husbands and wives should relate to one another but on "how one ought to behave in the household of God, which is the church of the living God, the pillar and bulwark of the truth" (1 Tim 3:14-15).

Our author's attempt to differentiate between wives and women on the basis of the dual meaning of *gyne* is a legitimate academic exercise but is totally foreign to Paul's thought. For the apostle the role of a wife in the home serves as a paradigm for the role of women in the church because, after all, the church is an extended spiritual family, the household of God. To this fundamental biblical concept we shall return shortly.

Had Paul intended to confine his prohibition in verse 12 only to the relationship of a wife to her husband, then he likely would have used a definite article or a possessive pronoun with *man:* "I do not permit a woman to teach or to have authority over *her* man." This is how the apostle expressed himself when writing specifically about husband-wife relationships: "Wives, be subject to *your* (Greek *idiois*) husbands" (Eph 5:22; Col 3:18). But such a possessive pronoun is absent from 1 Timothy 2:12.

The context is abundantly clear. Paul addresses men and women in general as members of the church and not just husbands and wives, as he does in Ephesians 5:22-23 and Colossians 3:18-19. The apostle calls upon *all* men, not just husbands, to lift up holy hands in prayer (1 Tim 2:8). He summons *all* women, not just wives, to dress modestly (1 Tim 2:9). Similarly Paul prohibits *all* women, not just wives, to teach authoritatively as the head of the congregation (1 Tim 2:12). This teaching may not be popular, but it has the merit of being true to Scripture.

4. Excursus: The Church as a Family

Time and again throughout this study we have noted that our author differentiates between the roles of husband and wife in the home and of men and women in the church. Such a distinction presupposes that the church functions more like a service organization than like a family. In a service organization, roles are assigned on the basis of competence, irrespective of gender. In a family, however, it is different. Certain basic roles are determined by gender. A man is called to serve as a father and a woman as a mother. What is true for the home is equally true for the church. The reason is simple. In the Bible the church is seen not as a service organization but as an extended spiritual family, patterned after the natural family.

The Bible uses the family model to explain the respective roles of men and women within the church. Just as husbands and fathers ought to exercise godly leadership within the home, so upright and mature men ought to be appointed as spiritual fathers of the church, the household of God (1 Tim 3:1-5). Similarly, just as wives and mothers ought to nurture and train the children, so caring and mature women are to serve as spiritual mothers in the church (1 Tim 5:9-16; Titus 2:3-5). It is noteworthy that Deborah is praised in the Bible for having served God's people as "a mother in Israel" (Jud 5:7) rather than as judge. Just as in the case of marriage there is a certain distinction between the roles of father and mother, so in the church there is a certain distinction between the spiritual roles of men and women.

New Testament View of the Church as a Family. The New Testament teaches in various ways that the church is an extended spiritual family and not merely a service organization. By accepting Jesus Christ as their Savior, believers "receive adoption as sons" (Gal 4:5). As adopted children they call God "Abba! Father!" (Gal 4:6) and relate to one another as "brother and sister" (James 2:14-15; 1 Cor 8:11; 1 Thess 4:6; Rom 12:1). Within this spiritual family Christ Himself is called "the firstborn among many brethren" (Rom 8:29). Believers are called "sons of God" and "children of God," in contrast to unbelievers, who are outside God's family (1 John 5:1-5). To be a child of God means to have intimate fellowship with God the Father (Rom 8:15) and with Jesus Christ our elder brother (Rom 8:29).

The pastor-elder functions as a spiritual father within the church family because of his role in bringing new converts into the church and nurturing them subsequently. For example, Paul refers to the Corinthian believers as his children and to himself as their father. "I do not write this to make you ashamed, but to admonish you as my beloved children. . . . For I became your father in Christ Jesus through the gospel" (1 Cor 4:14, 16; cf. Eph 5:1; Gal 3:26). Furthermore, he refers to church members as "beloved children" (Eph 5:1), "sons and daughters" (2 Cor 6:18), "brethren" (1 Cor 1:10, 11, 26; 2:1), "sisters" (Rom 16:1; 1 Cor 7:15), all terms indicative of a family relationship.

This understanding of the church as an extended family of believers, led by elders who function as spiritual fathers and shepherds, explains why women were not appointed as elders or pastors, namely because their role was seen as being that of mothers and not fathers.

Paul develops the theme of the church as the family or household of God especially in his first letter to Timothy. He calls Timothy his "son" (1 Tim 1:2, 18) and advises him to treat older men like "a father; younger men like brothers, older women like mothers, younger women like sisters, in all purity" (1 Tim 5:1-2). He also reminds Timothy that a church leader must be a respectable family man, with the tried virtues of fatherhood. "The saying is sure: If anyone aspires to the office of bishop, he desires a noble task. Now a bishop must be above reproach, the husband of one wife, temperate, sensible, dignified, hospitable, an apt teacher, no drunkard, not violent but gentle, not quarrelsome, and no lover of money. He must manage his own household well, keeping his children submissive and respectful in every way; for if a man does not know how to manage his own household, how can he care for God's church?" (1 Tim 3:1-5).

The analogy between the church and the family is not an incidental illustration but the basis for defining leadership roles in the church. In effect, Paul is saying that a fundamental criterion for appointing a man to serve as church leader is a track record of being a good father. Why? Because the same skills and spiritual headship needed for a father to manage well "one's own house" are also required for overseeing the church family.

Women as Spiritual Fathers? The analogy between the church and the family helps us understand why the Bible precludes appointing a woman to serve as the representative spiritual father and shepherd of a congregation. The reason is not that women are less capable than men of piety, zeal, learning, leadership, preaching, or whatever else it takes to serve as a pastor, but simply because such a role is perceived in the New Testament as being that of a spiritual father and not of a spiritual mother. The New Testament emphasizes the importance of respecting the functional role distinctions of men and women established by God at creation. These role distinctions, we have noted, do not imply superiority or inferiority, but reflect a divine design and concern for well-ordered and harmonious relations within the home and the church.

Men and women were created *not superior* and *inferior,* but rather *different from* and *complementary to* one another. What God made woman to *be* and what He intends her to *do* make her different from but not inferior to man. This difference is reflected in the different roles men and women are called to fulfill in life. The woman is to be wife and mother, while the man is to be husband and father. As a father, a man is called to be the caring head and guardian of a home. This divinely established role in the natural family must be reflected in the church, because the church is the extended family of God. This means that to appoint a woman to serve as elder or pastor is analogous to assigning her the role of fatherhood in the family.

The Danger of the Partnership Paradigm. The biblical model of different yet complementary roles for men and women in the home and in the church may well be a scandal to liberal and evangelical feminists bent on promoting the egalitarian, partnership paradigm. Nonetheless, Christians committed to the authority and wisdom of the Scriptures cannot ignore or reject a most fundamental biblical principle. Blurring or eliminating the role distinctions God assigned to men and women in the home and in the church is not only contrary to His creational design but also accelerates the breakdown of the family, church structure, and society.

Donald G. Bloesch, a well-known evangelical theologian inclined toward the ordination of women, acknowledges that "it cannot be denied that the women's liberation movement, for all its solid gains, has done much to blur the distinctions between the sexes and that many women who have entered the ministry appear committed to the eradication of these distinctions."[80] This trend, as Bloesch ob-serves, "is in no small way responsible for accelerating divorce and the breakdown of the family."[81] Feminist ideologies are generally opposed to the sanctity of the family and to the worthiness of the call to motherhood. The reason is that such ideologies, as Michael Novak keenly observes, "thrive best where individuals stand innocent of the concrete demands of loyalty, responsibility, and common sense into which family life densely thrusts them."[82]

To realize freedom from the constraints of motherhood, some Evangelical femi-nists, like their liberal counterparts, denigrate the role of woman as homemaker and advocate abortion on demand. Donald Bloesch warns that "the fact that some clergywomen today in the mainline Protestant denominations are championing the cause of lesbianism (and a few are even practicing a lesbian life-style) should give the church pause in its rush to promote women's liberation."[83] Such things ought likewise to give us pause in the rush to promote women's ordination, one facet of the women's liberation movement.

The Danger of Role Reversals. Another important consideration is the nega-tive impact of role reversal when a woman serves in the headship role of elder or pastor in the church. If male headship in the church is replaced by that of a woman, male headship in the family will be imperiled. The headship of a husband in his family can hardly remain unaffected if a woman or his own wife serves as the head of the congregation to which he belongs. What impact will this role reversal also have on the families of the congregations? Will it not at least tempt some women in the congregation to arrogate to themselves a position of headship in the family similar to the headship exercised in the church by their female pastor?

Consideration must also be given to the impact of the role modeling a female pastor can have on the children of divided families who have no father figure in their homes. To these children the pastor sometimes becomes the only positive father role model in their lives. A female pastor would deprive these children of an appropriate father role model.

Even more crucial is the negative impact that role reversal can have in our apprehension of God as our heavenly Father. Vern Poythress perceptively remarks that "the absence of godly, fatherly leadership within the church makes the affir-mation of the Fatherhood of God closer to an abstraction. God's Fatherhood is, of course, illustrated preeminently in the great deeds of the history of redemption that embody His fatherly rule, care, and discipline. But we are richer in our under-standing of God because most of us have enjoyed having a human father, and we are richer still if we can see the fatherly care and rule of God embodied at a practical level in the older men of the church (Titus 2:2) and especially in the overseers."[84]

C. S. Lewis rightly warns that "we have no authority to take the living and seminal figures which God has painted on the canvas of our nature and shift them about as if they were mere geometrical figures."[85] The sexual role distinctions, Lewis notes, go beyond physical appearance. They serve "to symbolize the hidden things of

God."[86] Lewis warns that when we are in the church, "we are dealing with male and female not merely as facts of nature but as the live and awful shadows of realities utterly beyond our control and largely beyond our direct knowledge."[87]

Lewis means that the male role of father in the home and of the pastor as spiritual father in the household of faith (1 Cor 4:15) points to a much greater reality, "largely beyond our direct knowledge," namely, that of the heavenly Father, the original and ultimate "Father" of the home, the church, and the human family. Paul clearly expresses this connection in Ephesians 3:14-15. "For this reason I kneel before the Father, from whom all fatherhood (*patria*) in heaven and on earth derives its name" (NIV margin). The text suggests that all earthly fathers, whether biological fathers in the home or spiritual fathers in the church, reflect the image of the heavenly "Father," albeit in a human, creaturely way.

It is in no way derogatory to the female sex to affirm that an elder or pastor exercises fatherhood and not motherhood for God's family, because as E. L. Mascall observes, "his office is a participation in God's own relationship to his people and God is our Father in heaven and not our Mother."[88] The female sex has its own distinctive dignity and function, but it cannot represent the Fatherhood of God to His people, a dominant theme in both Old and New Testaments. The reason is simple. The sexual and symbolic role of a woman is that of mother and not of father. To change the nature of the symbol means to distort the apprehension of the reality to which the symbol points. To put it simply, a woman who stands for motherhood cannot appropriately represent the Fatherhood of God in the home or in the extended family of faith, the church.

Conclusion

The objective of our study has been to examine *Women in Ministry*'s fundamental thesis that the role distinctions of husband-headship and wife-submission originated as a result of the Fall (Gen 3:16) and apply exclusively to the home. Consequently, he contends, in the church women can serve even in headship positions over men.

Our study has shown that the author's thesis, though ingeniously defended, does not do justice to the biblical witness. We have found that the principles of male headship and female submission are rooted in the order of creation and apply not only in the home but also in the church. The Fall marks not the institution of the wife's submission but its distortion into oppressive domination.

Respect for the principles of male headship and female submission is evident in both the Old and the New Testament. Women served with distinction in ancient Israel and in the New Testament church in various vital ministries, yet they were never ordained to function as priests, elders, or pastors. The reasons were not socio-cultural but theological, namely, the recognition that God created man to serve in a servant-headship role in the home and in the community of faith.

The nature of this investigation has required that considerable attention be given to headship and submission in the man-woman relationship because of *Women in Ministry*'s attempt to restrict it to the home. The study of this important principle should not be seen as an end in itself, but rather as an exploration of a divine plan designed to ensure unity in diversity. "For just as the body is one and has many members, and all the members of the body, though many, are one body, so it is with Christ. For by one Spirit we were all baptized into one body" (1 Cor 12:12-13). The reason why God gave different gifts and functions to men and women is not that we may argue about who is the greatest in the kingdom, but that men and women, as joint heirs of the gift of eternal life, may use their different gifts to build up the body of Christ and bring human beings with their many differences into a saving relationship with Jesus Christ. In willingly following the divine plan, we will find our greatest strength and harmony both in our homes and in the church.

Endnotes

1. Nancy Vyhmeister, ed., *Women in Ministry* (Berrien Springs, Mich., 1998), p. 257.
2. Ibid., p. 434.
3. Richard M. Davidson, "Headship, Submission, and Equality in Scripture," *Women in Ministry*, ed. Nancy Vyhmeister (Berrien Springs, Mich., 1998), p. 259.
4. Ibid., p. 284.
5. Ibid., p. 260.
6. Ibid.
7. Richard M. Davidson (note 3), p. 261.
8. Ibid.
9. Nancy Vyhmeister (note 1), p. 342.
10. Richard M. Davidson (note 3), p. 262.
11. Werner Neuer, *Man and Woman in Christian Perspective* (Wheaton, Ill., 1991), p. 70.
12. Ellen G. White, *Patriarchs and Prophets*, p. 46.
13. Richard M. Davidson (note 3), p. 262.
14. George W. Knight III, *The Role Relationship of Men and Women* (Chicago, 1985), p. 31.
15. Richard M. Davidson (note 3), p. 262.
16. Raymond C. Ortlund, "Male-Female Equality and Male Headship," in *Recovering Biblical Manhood and Womanhood: A Response to Evangelical Feminism*, eds. John Piper and Wayne Grudem (Wheaton, Ill., 1991), pp. 103-104.
17. Gerhard von Rad, *Genesis*, trans. J. H. Marks (Philadelphia, 1961), p. 80.
18. Ibid.
19. James B. Hurley, *Man and Woman in Biblical Perspective* (Grand Rapids, 1981), p. 211.
20. Raymond C. Ortlund (note 16), p. 103.
21. Richard M. Davidson (note 3), p. 263.
22. Ibid.
23. Ibid.
24. Letha Scanzoni and Nancy Hardesty, *All We're Meant to Be: A Biblical Approach to Women's Liberation* (Waco, Tex., 1974), p. 28; cf. Paul K. Jewett (n. 35), p. 110.
25. Susan T. Foh, *Women and the Word of God* (Phillipsburg, N. J., 1979), p. 62.
26. Richard M. Davidson (note 3), p. 284.
27. H. C. Leupold, *Exposition of Genesis* (Grand Rapids, Mich., 1950), p. 153.
28. *Patriarchs and Prophets*, p. 56. The story makes the most sense if, as Ellen White says, Adam was not with Eve at the tree. Had he been at the tree, how could one account for his silence

during Eve's dialog with the serpent? Eve's giving some of the fruit to her husband "with her," then, takes place when she finds him and persuades him also to eat.

29. Ibid., p. 59.
30. Richard M. Davidson (note 3), p. 284.
31. Werner Neuer (note 11), p. 76.
32. H. C. Leupold (note 27), p. 172.
33. Richard M. Davidson (note 3), p. 267.
34. Ibid., p. 268.
35. Ibid., p. 269, citing *Patriarchs and Prophets*, p. 59.
36. George W. Knight III (note 14), p. 31.
37. Donald Guthrie, *The Pastoral Epistles: an Introduction and Commentary* (Grand Rapids, Mich., 1957), p. 77. See also H. P. Liddon, *Explanatory Analysis of St. Paul's First Epistle to Timothy* (Minneapolis, 1978), p. 19.
38. Paul K. Jewett, *Man as Male and Female* (Grand Rapids, Mich., 1975), p. 60.
39. *The Seventh-day Adventist Bible Commentary* (Washington, D. C., 1957), vol. 7, p. 296.
40. George W. Knight III (note 14), p. 32. The same view is expressed by Douglas J. Moo: "In vv. 13-14, then, Paul substantiates his teaching in vv. 11-12 by arguing that the created order establishes a relationship of subordination of woman to man, which order, if bypassed, leads to disaster" ("1 Timothy 2:11-15: Meaning and Significance," *Trinity Journal* 1/1 [1980]: 70).
41. For a fuller discussion, see chapters 1 and 2 of my book *Women in the Church: a Biblical Study on the Role of Women in the Church* (Berrien Springs, Mich., 1987).
42. Richard M. Davidson (note 2), pp. 270-271.
43. Ibid., p. 273.
44. Ibid., p. 272.
45. John Calvin, *Commentaries on the Epistles to Timothy, Titus, and Philemon* (Grand Rapids, Mich., 1979), p. 67.
46. Jacques B. Doukhan, "Women Priests in Israel: A Case for their Absence," *Women in Ministry,* ed. Nancy Vyhmeister (Berrien Springs, Mich., 1998), p. 38.
47. G. R. Driver and J. C. Miles, *The Babylonian Laws* (Oxford, 1952), pp. 359-360.
48. For documentation and discussion, see Elisabeth Meier Tetlow, *Women and Ministry in the New Testament: Called to Serve* (Lanham, Md., 1980), pp. 7-20.
49. Jacques B. Doukhan (note 46), p. 38.
50. Ibid.
51. Ibid., p. 33.
52. Ibid., p. 34.
53. Ibid., p. 35.
54. James B. Hurley, *Man and Woman in Biblical Perspective* (Grand Rapids, Mich., 1981), p. 52.
55. John Meyendorff, "The Orthodox Churches," in *The Ordination of Women: Pro and Con,* ed. Michael P. Hamilton and Nancy S. Montgomery (New York, 1975), p. 130.
56. Jacques B. Doukhan (note 46), p. 37.
57. *Patriarchs and Prophets,* p. 61.
58. H. C. Leupold (note 27), p. 179.
59. Clarence J. Vos, *Woman in Old Testament Worship* (Delft, England, 1968), p. 207.
60. Richard M. Davidson (note 3), pp. 281, 280, emphasis his.
61. A lengthy analysis of these texts is available in my book *Women in the Church* (note 41), chapter 6.
62. W. Larry Richards, "How Does a Woman Prophesy and Keep Silence at the Same Time? (1 Corinthians 11 and 14)," *Women in Ministry,* ed. Nancy Vyhmeister (Berrien Springs, Mich., 1998), pp. 313-333.
63. Richard M. Davidson (note 3), p. 275.

64. Ibid.

65. Ralph H. Alexander, "An Exegetical Presentation on 1 Corinthians 11:2-16 and 1 Timothy 2:8-15," Paper presented at the Seminar on Women in Ministry, Western Baptist Seminary, November 1976, pp. 5-6.

66. Fritz Zerbst, *The Office of Woman in the Church* (St. Louis, Mo., 1955), p. 33.

67. For a fuller discussion of this issue, see my *Women in the Church* (note 41), pp. 164-173.

68. Richard M. Davidson (note 3), p. 276, emphasis his.

69. Stephen B. Clark, *Man and Woman in Christ* (Ann Arbor, Mich., 1980), p. 187.

70. Donald A. Carson, "'Silent in the Churches:' On the Role of Women in 1 Corinthians 14:33b-36," in *Recovering Biblical Manhood and Womanhood: A Response to Evangelical Feminism,* eds. John Piper and Wayne Grudem (Wheaton, Ill., 1991), p. 151.

71. For a fuller examination of 1 Timothy 2:11-15, see chapter 6 of my book *Women in the Church* (note 41); in the present treatment I am stating only my conclusions.

72. For information on the improved social status of women in the Roman world in New Testament times, see Mary Lefkowitz and Maureen Fant, *Women in Greece and Rome* (Toronto, 1977); J. P. V. D. Balsolon, *Roman Women* (London, 1962).

73. Philip B. Payne, "Libertarian Women in Ephesus: A Response to Douglas J. Moo's Article: '1 Timothy 2:11-15: Meaning and Significance,'" *Trinity Journal* 2 (1981), p. 190; see also David M. Scholer, "1 Timothy 2:9-15 and the Place of Women in the Church's Ministry" in *Women, Authority and the Bible,* ed. Alvera Mickelsen (Downers Grove, Ill., 1986), pp. 195-205; Catherine Clark Kroeger, "1 Timothy 2:12—A Classicist's View," in *Women, Authority and the Bible,* ed. Alvera Mickelsen (Downers Grove, Ill., 1986), pp. 226-232.

74. See Carroll D. Osburn, "*Authenteo* (1 Timothy 2:12)," *Restoration Quarterly* 25 (1983), p. 11.

75. *Acts of Paul* 41, 42, in *New Testament Apocrypha,* eds. Edgar Hennecke and Wilhelm Schneemelcher (Philadelphia, 1965), vol. 2, p. 364; Tertullian challenges the use that some made of Thecla's example to defend the right of women to teach and to baptize, by pointing out that the presbyter who fabricated the story was convicted and removed from office (*On Baptism* 17).

76. The suggestion is made by Martin Dibelius and Hans Conzelmann, *The Pastoral Epistles, Hermeneia* (Philadelphia, 1972), p. 48.

77. Richard M. Davidson (note 3), p. 280.

78. Ibid., p. 279

79. Nancy Vyhmeister (note 1), p. 342.

80. Donald G. Bloesch, *Is the Bible Sexist?* (Westchester, Ill., 1982), p. 56.

81. Ibid.

82. Michael Novak, "Man and Woman He Made Them," *Communio* 8 (Spring 1981), p. 248.

83. Donald G. Bloesch (note 79), p. 56.

84. Vern Sheridan Poythress, "The Church as Family: Why Male Leadership in the Family Requires Male Leadership in the Church," in *Recovering Biblical Manhood and Womanhood: A Response to Evangelical Feminism,* eds. John Piper and Wayne Grudem (Wheaton, Ill., 1991), pp. 245-246.

85. C. S. Lewis, "Priestesses in the Church," in *God in the Dock,* ed. Walter Hooper (Grand Rapids, Mich., 1970), p. 238.

86. Ibid.

87. Cited in W. Andrew Hoffecker and John Timmerman, "Watchmen in the City: C. S. Lewis's View of Male and Female," *The Cresset* 41/4 (February, 1978): 18.

88. E. L. Mascall, "Women and the Priesthood of the Church," in *Why Not? Priesthood and the Ministry of Women,* eds. Michael Bruce and G. E. Duffield (Appleford, England, 1972), pp. 111-112.

Chapter 5

The Priesthood of All Believers

P. Gerard Damsteegt

~~~~~~~~~

In the prologue of *Women in Ministry* the authors welcome any response and invite those who disagree with their findings to dialogue.[1] This gracious invitation I have gladly accepted. In the quest for truth a frank exchange of thoughts is very important. If others have discovered new light on the role of women in the church, we certainly should be willing to accept it.

Women in Ministry is divided into four parts. The first part is entitled "Ministry in the Bible." It "explores the theological meaning of the different forms of priesthood and ministry among God's people throughout the Bible."[2] In this section the authors set forth their understanding of the biblical basis for ordaining women as ministers, making it one of the most significant parts of the book. It deserves careful consideration.

In this chapter and the three that follow, I will evaluate the four chapters of "Ministry in the Bible" in the light of the inspired writings and the time-honored principles of Bible interpretation used by Seventh-day Adventists. The following questions will receive careful consideration: Is each author's conclusion in favor of women's ordination based solely on the Bible (*Sola Scriptura*)—the vital principle at the foundation of the Protestant Reformation and the Advent movement? Does the author in *Women in Ministry* follow that book's own stated principle that "the whole of the Bible message must be taken into account"[3] in interpreting the Scriptures? Does the author avoid using some of the methods employed by higher

---

P. Gerard Damsteegt, Dr. Theol., *is Associate Professor of Church History, Seventh-day Adventist Theological Seminary, Andrews University.*

criticism (historical-critical method) in determining the meaning of a biblical text or practice? Are the inspired writings of Ellen G. White used accurately, and are the author's conclusions in harmony with these writings?

If all these questions can be answered positively, we should be willing to accept an author's conclusions as new light. If the arguments do not meet the above criteria, those authors may need to rethink their positions and adjust their arguments to be in harmony with the testimony of the whole Bible.

Sola Scriptura and the Writings of Ellen G. White

Some may question the need for comparing the conclusions of the authors with the writings of Ellen G. White when we stress the importance of the *Sola Scriptura* principle. Does this practice not undermine our claim that we judge all things by the Bible and the Bible only?

The phrase "the Bible and the Bible only" as the basis of our faith and practice found expression with Ellen White and the Seventh-day Adventist pioneers many times. However, each time Mrs. White used this phrase she contrasted the teachings of Scripture with the traditions of men which are not in harmony with the Word of God. Nowhere in her writings do we find her contrasting this phrase with the testimonies and messages God gave to her.[4]

Furthermore, the Bible itself predicts that in the time of the end the Spirit of prophecy will be manifested among God's people. This revival of the prophetic gift took place under the divine inspiration of the Holy Spirit. The Bible calls these end-time revelations the "testimony of Jesus" (Rev 12:17) which is equated with the "spirit of prophecy" (Rev 19:10). This unique phenomenon is one of the characteristics of God's remnant that is called to prepare the world for the return of Christ. In accepting the testimony of the Bible, we Seventh-day Adventists also accept the prophetic gift that this Bible said would appear in the time of the end to guide God's people.

Accepting this gift is in no way contrary to the claim that we have committed ourselves to follow "the Bible and the Bible only." James White affirmed the harmony between the Scriptures and the manifestation of the Spirit of prophecy in the writings of Ellen White. He wrote, "The position that the Bible, and the Bible alone, is the rule of faith and duty, does not shut out the gifts which God set in the church. To reject them is shutting out that part of the Bible which presents them."[5]

In her first book Ellen White explains the intimate relation of her writings to the Bible, stating "I recommend to you, dear reader, the Word of God as the rule of your faith and practice. By that Word we are to be judged. God has, in that Word, promised to give visions in the *'last days';* not for a new rule of faith, but for the comfort of His people, and to correct those who err from Bible truth.[6]

Seventh-day Adventists have found that Ellen White's writings are in full harmony with the Scriptures, leading people to a better understanding of the Bible and displaying the matchless love of Jesus as our Savior. These writings which reveal the testimony of Jesus in the time of the end came about as a result of the same divine inspiration as that of the Bible writers.

As Ellen White's writings are in complete agreement with the Bible, we have no reservations in using them for evaluating the conclusions of *Women in Ministry.* As we look at these four chapters from *Women in Ministry* in turn, we will evaluate each of them by the Bible and then in the light of the writings of Ellen G. White.

The Priesthood of All Believers

In this chapter I will discuss the first chapter of *Women in Ministry* dealing with ministry in the Bible, which focuses on the priesthood of all believers.[7] The author, a systematic theologian, discusses the priesthood first in the Old Testament, then the New. He concludes his study by implying that the priesthood of all believers demands the ordination of women as ministers.

The author mentions that throughout the Old Testament, males functioned as priests, but in the New Testament a radical change took place. "A new priesthood is unfolded in the New Testament, that of all believers. The Christian church is a fellowship of believer priests."[8] This view of the church, he asserts, "no longer poses roadblocks to women serving in any ministry. It in fact demands a partnership of men and women in all expressions of the ordained ministry."[9]

To remove any doubt about the correctness of this view, he asks, "Did Paul ever indicate that some gifts are bestowed upon men and others upon women? Is there any attempt on his part, or on Peter's, to distinguish between gift and role, between the Spirit gifting and the exercise of ministry by one particular gender?" He answers with an emphatic denial, stating that "in the Christian church distinctions of race, social position, economic status, and gender are no longer valid considerations in ordering the church's ministry. We are all ministers within Christ's fellowship."[10]

It is clear, therefore, that the author believes that the New Testament concept of the priesthood of all believers has eliminated the distinctions in roles between men and women in the proclamation of the gospel. To him, not roles, but spiritual gifts determine who qualifies for the various positions in gospel ministry, including the office of elder and minister. These gifts have nothing to do with whether one is a man or a woman.

We will now examine whether the New Testament indeed presents such a radical change in the church's leadership structure as to demand that nearly two thousand years later the remnant church must begin to ordain women as ministers in finishing the gospel commission.

The Old Testament Priesthood

Ever since sin entered into the world there have been priests. "In the beginning the head of each family was considered ruler and priest of his own household."[11] This headship role was fulfilled by a man who had the leadership responsibility in his family. "Every man was the priest of his own household."[12]

This patriarchal order continued until the time of the Exodus when God delivered His chosen people Israel from slavery in Egypt. At that time the Lord sanctified the first-born males for His service (Ex 13:1, 2, 12). Then He brought Israel to mount Sinai where He instituted a covenant with His people based on the sanctuary services. God here covenanted with Israel that they were to be a "kingdom of priests" (Ex 19:5, 6).

Did this covenant allow every Israelite to function as a priest in the sanctuary services? Not at all. The responsibility to officiate as priest was at first limited to the first-born (Num 3:12, 8:1-18), but after the golden calf idolatry it was assigned to the males of the family of Aaron of the tribe of Levi (Ex 28:1, 41, 43; Num 3:10). Yet Israel continued to be a "kingdom of priests" even though not every person officiated as a priest, because those who performed as priests represented the families and the nation.

In this "kingdom of priests," leadership responsibilities were divided among the priests, elders, rulers, prophets, and later on judges and kings. The priests led out in the religious matters, performing the sanctuary services and providing religious teaching. The elders, males occupying positions of leadership, assisted with governing the nation (Ex 24:1, 9, 14; Num 11:16; Neh 13:29), along with rulers who were responsible for groups of thousands, hundreds and tens (Deut 1:15). Then there were the prophets, both male and female, specially called by God as messengers to speak His word, counsels, warnings, and judgments. Later, judges and kings were chosen to lead the whole nation.

Despite these various leading roles, the nation of Israel remained a "kingdom of priests" because of the covenant God had made with His people. The covenant continued to be relevant throughout the Old Testament era (Jud 2:30; 1 Kings 19:14; 2 Kings 17:15, 35, 36; Neh 13;19).

During the 4000-year history of the Old Testament, despite times of great apostasy, God was directing and guiding His people. Under His wise leadership men were designated as the leaders in religious and political affairs, with the exception of the roles of prophet and judge, which could be occupied by God-fearing women as well as men.

The New Testament Priesthood

The death of Jesus Christ abolished the sacrificial system with its sanctuary services in the Jerusalem temple and the work of the priests (Dan 9:27). Israel's continued rejection of Christ's sacrifice for humanity and its determined persecution of His followers ended the nation's special covenant relationship in A.D. 34, at the conclusion of the prophetic seventy week period. At that time the Lord took away His kingdom from them and established the covenant with a new nation, called spiritual Israel (Mt 22:33-44). This spiritual kingdom no longer had the offices of priest, high priest, or king, for Christ had become their Priest, High Priest, and King.

After the crucifixion, however, God's covenant promise under the Old Testament continued to be valid, but now its blessings were bestowed on spiritual Israel. Peter emphasized this by stating that the *new believers* were a "royal priesthood, a holy nation" (1 Peter 2:9).

What kind of priesthood and spiritual nation did God establish after the cross? First, the Scriptures announce that Jesus Christ, our Lord, is our Priest (Heb 5:6; 7:11, 15; 8:4) instead of the Levitical priesthood. He is our High Priest (Heb 2:17; 3:1; 4:14, 15; 9:11), representing us before the Father. Instead of an earthly priest interceding for us, there is now one Mediator, Jesus Christ, who pleads our cases. In the judgment He determines whether our names will remain in the book of life or will be blotted out (Rev 3:5). He ministers not in an earthly sanctuary but in a sanctuary in heaven. There, in the presence of His Father, He applies His blood shed at Calvary as the Lamb of God for our sins, presenting His precious righteousness for repentant sinners.

Second, the New Testament calls God's people a royal priesthood and a holy nation. The new believers represent their Lord Jesus Christ and function as priests by delivering the gospel message to all the world. This new priesthood is to lead people to the heavenly High Priest through the gospel.

To enable His people to fulfill the great commission, Christ promised to give special gifts to this royal priesthood—to every member of His church—so believers could flourish in their divinely-assigned roles. Some would receive the gift of wisdom, others gifts of faith, healing, working of miracles, prophecy, discerning of spirits, languages, helps, or administration (1 Cor 12:8-10, 28). Others would receive gifts of ministry, exhortation, leadership, liberality, or mercy (Rom 12:6-8). As a result of these divine gifts some were to be "apostles, some prophets, some evangelists, and some pastors and teachers" (Eph 4:11).

But this was not all Christ did. He also provided a plan for a most efficient model of organization to protect the church against heresies, prevent confusion, and integrate the various gifts He has given church members to make the church into a powerful, well-organized army to invade the kingdom of Satan. This New Testament model of leadership continues to use the Old Testament office of elder but gives it a more spiritual character.

This biblical leadership model, designating only men as the elders or ministers, is the issue some are questioning. Determined efforts are being made to eliminate it. The author of the chapter we are considering wants us to believe that now all role distinctions between male and female in the gospel ministry are abolished. Is his assertion correct?

Harmony between Gifts and Roles in the Gospel Proclamation

If God saw fit to have the Old Testament kingdom of priests operate on the basis of the unique roles He assigned to men and women, why would not the New Testament priesthood of all believers continue to honor role distinctions between male and female in the operation of His church? Is there anything wrong in utilizing differences in roles or functions for accomplishing the great commission Christ gave His church?

Does the priesthood of all believers mean that since Christ's death on the cross all role differences between male and female have been abolished? Not according to the New Testament! Our author points out that Peter did not make a distinction between gifts and roles.[13] But *Paul* certainly did make that distinction. On more than one occasion Paul clearly stipulated that the office of an elder or minister in God's church is to be occupied by men with special qualifications.

Did Paul contradict Peter? Paul's letters, like Peter's, teach that spiritual gifts are given to each member of the church. But in other letters, when addressing a leadership conflict, Paul specifically stresses the importance of maintaining role distinctions between male and female in the leadership of the church.

Paul reveals God's plan of how to organize and operate the church in the most efficient manner. Under the inspiration of the Holy Spirit he presents an organizational model that continues to use the role distinctions between male and female that have been guiding God's people since the beginning.

In interpreting the Bible it is important to keep in mind that Scripture forms a unity, revealing a harmony of all its teachings. Peter and Paul were in harmony with each other, but the kind of counsel they gave depended on the specific situation they faced. Unfortunately, the *Women in Ministry* chapter we are considering does not seem to recognize that the different situations the apostles dealt with reveal the harmony and unity in the gospel ministry between the operation of spiritual gifts and gender distinctions between men and women. While God bestows spiritual gifts on every believer, He also assigns the office of an elder or minister to men.

The elders and ministers, under Christ as the Head and Shepherd of the church, function as undershepherds overseeing the operation of the church. In this office they are responsible to see that the spiritual gifts of the believers are most efficiently used. As leaders "they should arrange matters so that every member of the church shall have a part to act, that none may lead an aimless life, but that all may accomplish what they can according to their several ability."[14]

In evaluating the author's arguments we notice that he does not follow *Women in Ministry's* own recommendation that Scripture is an "intrinsic unity" and that "the whole of the Bible message must be taken into account."[15] In studying the *whole biblical counsel* one discovers that, when the New Testament affirms the priesthood of all believers, it also recognizes that God uses the spiritual gifts of all His people as well as the unique characteristics of the sexes in carrying out the gospel commission. When one perceives that God created men and women with complementary natures, one can appreciate that such a delegation of responsibilities in the gospel ministry not only makes good sense but is the best way to finish the remnant's mission.

Biblical Foundations of Church Leadership Roles

When Paul was faced with a leadership conflict, under the inspiration of the Holy Spirit he spelled out how Christians "ought to conduct" themselves within the church (1 Tim 3:15).

Paul warns that he cannot permit a woman "to usurp authority" over a man (1 Tim 2:13, KJV). He supports his admonition with two biblical events that took place at the very beginning of the human family. First, he appeals to God's order in creating the human race. Then he points to the order of transgression at the fall.

Paul's first reason for male leadership in the church is that "Adam was formed first, then Eve" (1 Tim 2:13). God's order in the way He created men and women is not without significance. After creating Adam, God taught him the importance of implicit obedience, forbidding him to eat from the tree of the knowledge of good and evil upon the penalty of death. In naming the animals Adam discovered that "there was not found an help meet for him" (Gen 2:20, KJV). Now Adam became aware that he was created to be a "social being" who "without companionship" would fail to achieve "perfect happiness."[16]

So God made a "help meet for him" (Gen 2:18, KJV). Here we get a glimpse of the role of the woman. She functions as Adam's companion and provides support by assisting him in the execution of his responsibilities. In this role she did not function as an inferior but was to be treated as an equal without doing away with Adam's unique role.

We see the special relationship between the sexes in the way God created the woman. She was formed from Adam's rib (Gen 2:21), indicating that she was "not to control him as the head, nor to be trampled under his feet as an inferior, but to stand by his side as an equal, to be loved and protected by him."[17] The difference in physical features between them accentuated Adam's role as protector. Ellen White observed that "Eve was not quite as tall as Adam. Her head reached a little above his shoulders."[18]

After Eve's creation Adam fulfilled his role as protector and leader. As God had instructed him at the very beginning not to eat of the tree of the knowledge of good and evil (Gen 2:16, 17), it would only be natural that Adam in his role as protector would instruct Eve that safety was in obeying God's command.

The New Testament's second reason that God chose male leadership comes from the fall and is connected to the transgression order. "Adam was not deceived, but the woman being deceived, fell into transgression" (1 Tim 2:14). The woman, the first to leave her God-appointed sphere and leading the way into transgression, could again be accepted by God by taking her original God-assigned supportive role (1 Tim 2:15).

Ellen White gives further insight into the reason why Eve left her God-ordained sphere. Said she, "Eve had been perfectly happy by her husband's side in her Eden home; but, like restless modern Eves, she was flattered with the hope of entering a higher sphere than that which God had assigned her. In attempting to rise above her original position, she fell far below it."[19]

Eve's experience has been repeated by many others not willing to recognize God's plan in the distinct role differences between men and women. Tragically, the result of discarding God's plan will be the same. Mrs. White wrote, "A similar result will be reached by all who are unwilling to take up cheerfully their life duties in accordance with God's plan. In their efforts to reach positions for which He has not fitted them, many are leaving vacant the place where they might be a blessing. In their desire for a higher sphere, many have sacrificed true womanly dignity and nobility of character, and have left undone the very work that Heaven appointed them."[20]

The experience of the Fall affirms Adam's role as leader. After Eve had sinned, he realized his failure as her protector. "He mourned that he had *permitted* Eve to wander from his side."[21] Further, God recognized Adam's leadership responsibilities. Although Eve sinned first, the Creator held Adam accountable. After the couple had eaten of the forbidden fruit, God called Adam, not Eve, to accountability as leader (Gen 3:9-11).

Third, the New Testament shows that Adam, not Eve, was responsible for the entrance of sin and death into the world. "Through one man sin entered the world, and death through sin, and thus death spread to all men" (Rom 5:12). Had Adam remained faithful, God could have created another companion for him. But he lacked "faith in his merciful and benevolent Creator" and he failed to think that God, "who had created Eve to be his companion, could supply her place."[22] When Adam followed Eve's pathway into disobedience, the floodgates of suffering and death were opened. The damage was irreversible, bringing the human race under Satan's dominion.

Qualifications of an Elder or Minister

Having clearly pointed out that it is not God's plan for women to have the leadership authority of the church, Paul tells us who would qualify for this position: an elder or minister who is responsible to oversee the operations of the church.

In his letters, Paul presents two lists of qualifications for elders or ministers. One list is addressed to Timothy, who is to appoint the leadership in the church of Ephesus, and the other is addressed to Titus, who is to select leaders in the church in Crete. Both lists state that the leadership position of elder or minister is assigned to men, not women. Scripture plainly states that an elder must be a husband of one wife (1 Tim 3:2; Titus 1:6).

Before making any recommendations regarding women's ordination, the author whose chapter we have been considering should have explained why the New Testament teaching that a man is to occupy the office of an elder is no longer valid. This he did not do, because he felt that the New Testament priesthood of all believers had made role distinctions between men and women irrelevant. The New Testament, however, continues to uphold the role distinctions between men and women in church leadership.

The author is also completely silent about how the New Testament distinguishes between gifts and functions or roles. According to the Bible, some leadership roles in God's church are gender specific. The New Testament requires that the one who aspires to the office of an elder must first be successful in the leadership of his home before he qualifies to administer the church (1 Tim 3:5; Titus 1:6). The Bible assigns the leadership role in the home church to the husband as priest and head of the home.

Does this mean that women cannot lead out in a church office? Certainly not. A woman with the gift of leadership or administration can be a great blessing in the various departments of the church. However, when it comes to the office of elder or minister whose task it is to oversee and guide the total operation of the church, a woman does not meet the biblical qualifications.

The reason is plain: God's plan for humanity was that men, not women, were to be the head of the home. Consequently, women were not to develop the kind of leadership experience associated with that role. The woman's role in the home is to be her husband's companion and support so that he will be a successful leader and develop the kind of experience that prepares him to lead and serve others, perhaps even in the office of an elder or minister. Her task is not insignificant; it is of vital importance for the stability and happiness of the home and for his success as a leader. Without her dedicated and supportive role, no man would qualify as a church elder or minister.

The qualifications for the office of an elder do not consist simply of administrative and organizational gifts. The Bible requires proven leadership in the home— a miniature church—before one qualifies for a larger sphere of influence in the local church. This means that not just any man should be appointed as elder or minister. Only a man who successfully demonstrates his spiritual leadership over the little flock in the home should be elected to lead a larger flock of believers. Strife and disharmony in the home would disqualify him from functioning as church leader.

Ellen G. White fully affirmed the requirements in 1 Timothy 3 and Titus 1 for elders and ministers. She believed strongly in distinct roles for men and women, as the Bible teaches.

Commenting on the importance of home influences on the church, Ellen G. White said, "Every family is a church, over which the parents preside. . . . When the father and mother as priest and teacher of the family take their position fully on the side of Christ, a good influence will be exerted in the home. . . . No man can bring into the church an influence that he does not exert in his home life and in his business relations."[23]

The home is the place where men and women learn how to behave in church. Mrs. White points out that "the home is a school where all may learn how they are to act in the church. . . . Let there be peace in the home, and there will be peace in the church. This precious experience brought into the church will be the means of creating a kindly affection one for another. Quarrels will cease. True Christian courtesy will be seen among church members. The world will take knowledge of them that they have been with Jesus and have learned of Him. What an impression the church would make upon the world if all the members would live Christian lives!"[24]

What are the dynamics that operate in the home church? It is important that the family structure reflect the role models that God has designed for it and not those superimposed by the general practice of society. The priesthood of all believers does not negate the father's function as priest of his home church. As priest, he conducts the daily morning and evening worships by presenting spiritual sacrifices, laying "upon the altar of God the morning and evening sacrifice, while the wife and children unite in prayer and praise. In such a household Jesus will love to tarry."[25]

We see the importance of the father's leadership role highlighted in the name "husband." Mrs. White wrote, "The meaning of 'husband' is *house band*. All members of the family center in the father. He is the lawmaker, illustrating in his own manly bearing the sterner virtues, energy, integrity, honesty, patience, courage, diligence, and practical usefulness."[26] His performance as priest and lawmaker of the home either qualifies or disqualifies him for the office of elder or minister.

Clearly then, the death of Christ at Calvary and the establishment of a New Testament priesthood of all believers did not do away with the distinct roles for which the Lord created men and women. On the contrary, God uses these distinctive roles to His glory in the finishing of the gospel commission. Any departure from His plan brings confusion into God's work and delays the proclamation of the last message of mercy.

Conclusion

The Scriptures as well as the writings of Ellen G. White reveal that God has given men and women their own roles that are necessary in the proclamation of the gospel. In the New Testament, God brings about a new nation—spiritual Israel—characterized by the priesthood of all believers. The leadership of spiritual Israel is in the hands of Jesus Christ. To assist His people, He has promised to give them special gifts in carrying out the gospel commission. Within this general priesthood He recognizes that men and women are by nature different and He utilizes these differences for the growth and prosperity of His church.

These distinctions become clear in His recognition of the home as a model church. The father of the home is to function as priest of his household, supported by his wife and children. As priest he is to lead out in worships and is responsible for the spiritual tone and for establishing and implementing just laws in the home that help the family government function successfully. This unique experience qualifies him for leadership in the church. In this light we can understand the New Testament requirement that only those who are successful in home leadership are eligible for being set aside as elders or ministers by the laying on of hands.

In my conversation with the author of the chapter we are considering, he mentioned that he limited himself to the subject of the priesthood of all believers and its implications for women's ordination. He felt that it was the responsibility of others to deal with the specific New Testament requirements for elders and ministers. To him, from the viewpoint of the priesthood of all believers, there were no obstacles to women's ordination. This position is understandable in the light of *Women in Ministry*'s assumption that "church organization is not spelled out in the Bible."[27]

One can only regret that the author did not see the relevance of addressing the biblical qualifications for elders and ministers. This omission explains why he could quickly move from the discussion of the priesthood of all believers to the subject of women's ordination without devoting attention to what the Bible teaches regarding the distinct roles the Lord has assigned men and women in the home as well as in the church.

This approach is clearly flawed. The chapter's recommendations conflict with the New Testament church leadership model. Its assertion that the priesthood of all believers "demands partnership of men and women in all expressions of the ordained ministry"[28] is unsound because it is not based on the whole message of Scripture.

Examining the appropriateness of women's ordination in light of the whole Bible does indeed require investigating the biblical view of the priesthood of all believers. However, one must then also determine what passages of Scripture are relevant to the subject of women's ordination. Finally, the researcher needs to put the two together, making a study of these texts in connection with the priesthood of all believers. This involves asking how the priesthood of believers relates to the specific requirements for the office of an elder or minister, the relations between gifts and gender roles, the position of the man as the priest of the home, the consequences of the fall, and the nature of the equality and submission of the woman.

Only after a discussion of these subjects can one draw conclusions whether women's ordination is biblical or not. If these subjects are beyond the scope of the assignment, one ought to refrain from endorsing the ordination of women until after having seen the results of a complete investigation into all its aspects in the light of the priesthood of all believers.

By not dealing with these issues so relevant to women's ordination, the chapter under consideration has not provided the evidence that women's ordination is in harmony with the Bible. No doctrine can be called biblical unless it is studied in the light of the whole testimony of Scripture. The chapter's findings, therefore, do not meet the criteria for new light which we have outlined at the beginning of this chapter. Consequently, the concept of the priesthood of all believers cannot be used as a sound biblical basis to establish the legitimacy of women's ordination.

Endnotes

[Except as noted, Scripture quotations in this chapter are from the New King James Version.]

1. Nancy Vyhmeister, "Prologue," *Women in Ministry*, p. 5.
2. Ibid., p. 7.
3. Ibid., p. 3.

4. See Arthur L. White, "The Position of 'the Bible, and the Bible Only' and the Relationship of This To the Writings of Ellen G. White." Washington, D. C.: Ellen G. White Estate, 1971.
5. James White, *Review and Herald,* October 5, 1854.
6. Ellen G. White, *Early Writings,* p. 78.
7. Raoul Dederen, "The Priesthood of All Believers," *Women in Ministry,* pp. 9-27.
8. Dederen, *Women in Ministry,* p. 23.
9. Ibid.
10. Ibid.
11. Ellen G. White, *The Story of Redemption,* p. 50.
12. Ellen G. White, *Patriarchs and Prophets,* p. 350.
13. Dederen, *Women in Ministry,* p. 23.
14. Ellen G. White, *Christian Service,* p. 62. See also Ellen G. White, "A Message to Church Officers About the Youth," *Review and Herald,* September 17, 1914, p. 18.
15. Vyhmeister, *Women in Ministry,* p. 3.
16. *Patriarchs and Prophets,* p. 46.
17. Ibid.
18. *The Story of Redemption,* p. 21. See also *Patriarchs and Prophets,* p. 45.
19. *Patriarchs and Prophets,* p. 59.
20. Ibid.
21. Ibid., p. 56, emphasis mine.
22. *The Story of Redemption,* p. 36. See also *Patriarchs and Prophets,* p. 56.
23. Ellen G. White, *Child Guidance,* p. 549.
24. Ibid.
25. *Patriarchs and Prophets,* p. 144; *Child Guidance,* pp. 521, 522.
26. Ellen G. White, *Testimonies for the Church,* 2:701.
27. Nancy Vyhmeister, "Prologue," *Women in Ministry,* p. 3.
28. Dederen, *Women in Ministry,* p. 23.

Chapter 6

Eve, a Priest in Eden?

P. Gerard Damsteegt

~

Chapter 2 of *Women in Ministry* tries to explain why there are no women priests in Israel. Its author, an Old Testament scholar, maintains that the absence of female priests in ancient Israel cannot be used as an argument against women's ordination.[1]

The author states that he approaches the Bible through "exegetical research." This, he explains, means that he "will not move from *a priori* definitions or from theological positions" but will seek an answer to his question "by listening to the biblical word in regard to its historical and theological contexts as it describes and signifies the institution of priesthood."[2] In other words, he tries to be as objective as possible.

He gives two reasons for the absence of women priests in Israel: First, a reaction against the ancient Near Eastern culture where priestesses were often associated with sacred prostitution; second, the nature of priestly work in sacrificing animals, thus associating the priests with death and sin. Such priestly labor, he explains, was incompatible with the physiological nature of the woman, traditionally connected with "life and messianic pregnancy."[3]

The author asserts that "had it not been for these two factors . . . women might well have been priests in Israel."[4] He adds that "this assumption is further supported by the Bible—implicitly in the messianic view of the priest as transcending the contingencies of birth (gender, class, race) and explicitly in the

P. Gerard Damsteegt, Dr.Theol., *is Associate Professor of Church History, Seventh-day Adventist Theological Seminary, Andrews University.*

recognition of women in the priesthood both in the Garden of Eden and in the redeemed community [in heaven]."[5]

For evidence of a woman's call to priesthood in Eden, he refers to Genesis 3:21: "The Lord God made tunics of skin, and clothed them." The evidence, he suggests, is two-fold. First there is the act of clothing Adam and Eve: "The rare occasions when God dressed humans in the Old Testament always concerned the dressing of priests." He says that the verb form describing the act of dressing is a "very technical term normally used for the dressing of priests."[6] The second evidence he finds in the word *tunic:* "The word for tunic is the same that designates the priestly garment." This means, he says, that "Adam and Eve were, indeed, dressed as priests."[7]

From this study he concludes that the "biblical identification of woman as priest in Eden and the redeemed community complements biblical approval of women's anointing as prophet and judge. In this context, and in reflection upon ordination to pastoral ministry, there is no case for women's exclusion."[8]

Can Pagan Customs Be Used to Explain Bible Worship Practices?

The author's suggestion that temple prostitution by pagan priestesses was one reason why there were no women priests in the Old Testament is not derived from the Bible. He bases his conclusions on certain scholars' interpretations of the customs and practices of pagan cultures. This method of explaining Bible worship practices by pagan customs is commonly used by non-Adventist higher critics. Adventists, however, traditionally have allowed the Bible itself establish the reasons for its worship practices. I would not call the author a higher critic, but his approach to Scripture in this instance reveals an element of the higher-critical method.

Mrs. White strongly warned believers against the use of higher criticism because it destroys faith in Scripture, undermines it as a divine revelation, and takes away its uplifting power. She wrote, "The work of 'higher criticism' in dissecting, conjecturing, reconstructing, is destroying faith in the Bible as a divine revelation; it is robbing God's word of power to control, uplift, and inspire human lives."[9] She saw this method of interpreting the Bible as Satan's tool, stating that "today by the pleasing sentiments of higher criticism . . . the enemy of righteousness is seeking to lead souls into forbidden paths."[10] Its influence in destroying faith in the Bible, she said, was similar to the destructive effects the rabbinical traditions had on the Scriptures in Christ's day.[11]

Scholarly opinion is divided as to the reasons for the absence of women priests in Israel. Conclusions on this subject depend on the methods scholars use. Commentators who base their conclusions only on the Bible fail to see temple prostitution as a reason for the absence of female priests. Our author, however, has allowed non-biblical practices to determine his interpretations.

When we confine ourselves to the Bible we find another reason for the absence of female priests in Israel. It becomes clear that after sin, God's plan stipulated that priests were to be specific males. By contrast, pagan nations showed no interest in following in God's order.

Creative Interpretation and Imagination

The argument that Eve was a priest in Eden is indeed creative, but it is not based on the Bible. Does Scripture support the claim that Genesis 3:21 uses a "technical term" for the act of clothing a priest? When one takes a Hebrew concordance and looks up references to the verb for clothing or dressing a person (*labash* in the Hiphil form, *yalbish*), it becomes clear that there is nothing special or technical about the verbal form "clothed" in Genesis 3:21 that restricts it exclusively to the priesthood, even when God is the one doing the act of clothing. Job 10:11 (RSV) says, "Thou didst *clothe* me with skin and flesh," referring to God's involvement in Job's birth, not to any divine appointment to priesthood. Later in the book, God asks Job, "Do you give the horse his might? Do you *clothe* his neck with strength?" (Job 39:19, RSV), implying, figuratively of course, that God does this for the horse. In Isaiah 22:21, God says that He will *clothe* Eliakim with the robe of Shebna, the steward of Hezekiah's house—definitely not a priestly dressing (see other non-priestly uses in Isa 50:3 and 61:10). And the same form is used in Proverbs 23:21 (RSV): "For the drunkard and the glutton will come to poverty, and drowsiness will *clothe* a man with rags." This verb form is commonly used for various acts of clothing.[12]

The claim that God dressed both Adam and Eve in priestly garments is also not supported by the Scriptures. The Hebrew word for "tunic" or "coat" in Genesis 3:21 (*k'tonet*) is indeed "the same that designates the priestly garment," but it is not at all limited to priestly clothing. A concordance will quickly show that the very same word is used to describe Joseph's coat, Tamar's garment, Hushai's coat, and the Shulamite's coat, none of which were priestly (Gen 37:3, 23, 31-33; 2 Sam 13:18, 19; 15:32; Song of Songs 5:3).[13] Thus the author's argument comes from an incorrect interpretation of the text and has no biblical basis.

The clothing God gave was not to confirm Adam and Eve as priests but expressed His special care for the couple in the light of the dramatic changes that sin brought to creation. A garment of fig leaves simply would not do. They needed something much more durable and protective against climate changes and to cover their nakedness. Ellen White vividly depicted the changed conditions the couple had to face. "In humility and unutterable sadness they bade farewell to their beautiful home and went forth to dwell upon the earth, where rested the curse of sin. The atmosphere, once so mild and uniform in temperature, was now subject to marked changes, and the Lord mercifully provided them with a garment of skins as a protection from the extremes of heat and cold."[14]

To further support his view of Eve as a priest, the author assumes that the animal skins with which God clothed Adam and Eve were taken from the animal that was used for "the first sacrifice in history," "the sin offering."[15] This assumption also is not supported by the Bible. Fortunately, inspiration has given us a clearer insight into the circumstances of the first sacrifice in full harmony with Scripture.

The sequence in Genesis 3 shows that first the couple was clothed by God, and then they were driven out of Eden. Ellen G. White tells us that at the gates, outside of Eden, Adam was to come to worship God. It was not God but Adam who killed the first sacrificial animal for a sin offering. It was then that Adam, and not Eve, began his role as priest of the family, taking the life of the animal which was offered for the first sin of the first family.[16]

In describing the first sin offering after the expulsion from Eden, Ellen White wrote, "When Adam, according to God's special directions, made an offering for sin, it was to him a most painful ceremony. His hand must be raised to take life, which God alone could give, and make an offering for sin. It was the first time he had witnessed death. As he looked upon the bleeding victim, writhing in the agonies of death, he was to look forward by faith to the Son of God, whom the victim prefigured, who was to die man's sacrifice."[17] There is not the slightest biblical support for the author's conclusion that "by bestowing on Adam and Eve the skin of the sin offering, a gift strictly reserved to priests, the Genesis story implicitly recognizes Eve as priest alongside Adam."[18]

A close reading of the Scriptures reveals why there has always been a male priesthood among God's people. The reason is to be found in the Old Testament practice of the consecration of the first-born male (Ex 13:2, 12). This first-born male was a type of God's gift of His first-born Son as Savior, Mediator and Priest to humanity. Only a male priesthood could function in this typical manner because Jesus was a male.

Ellen White explained: "The dedication of the first-born had its origin in the earliest times. God had promised to give the First-born of heaven to save the sinner. This gift was to be acknowledged in every household by the consecration of the first-born son. He was to be devoted to the priesthood, as a representative of Christ among men."[19]

Conclusion

The first weakness of the chapter we are considering is that the author does not arrive at his conclusions through the "Bible and the Bible only," using the Bible to interpret itself. The suggestion that female prostitute priestesses in pagan cultures were a reason why Israel had no female priests is not based on Scripture but on non-biblical sources. This interpretation is not in harmony with inspiration.

On the contrary, the pagan female priestesses were a perversion of God's original plan for worship. First, God gave the true pattern through a male priesthood which was to be a type of God's first-born. It was Satan who introduced perversions among the nations to distort God's plan for humanity.

The chapter's second weakness is that it does not follow the principle which *Women in Ministry* itself advocates: to take into account the whole Bible. Instead, the chapter makes a selective use of texts, citing only those which the author claims support his thesis. He should have consulted the whole Bible before concluding that the Bible supports women's ordination. The author feels a burden to assist the church by looking at the Bible from an "ecclesiological perspective,"[20] yet he takes no note of texts that are intimately connected with church leadership such as those dealing with the impact of sin on the relationship between male and female (Gen 3:16), the significance of Adam as the first-born and Eve as the first transgressor (1 Tim 2:12-14), and the qualifications for elders and ministers in 1 Timothy 3:1-7 and Titus 1: 5-9. These passages strongly contradict the author's conclusions. Neglecting to compare Scripture with Scripture in the context of the whole Bible undermines the soundness of the chapter's conclusions. Though not justifying the author's methods, one reason for this neglect could be his acceptance of *Women in Ministry*'s incorrect assumption that "church organization is not spelled out in the Bible."[21]

His final conclusion that the Bible does not exclude women from ordination as ministers does not have the support of the Scriptures. First, he has not demonstrated that the Bible identified Eve as priest in Eden. Second, he has not produced any evidence that women were *anointed* as prophet and judge. Some—but not all—men who served in those capacities were anointed to their office, but the Bible provides no indication that an anointing took place in appointing women to these positions. It seems that God called these women to various positions without the process of anointing. Furthermore, no woman in the Bible was ever called to the public office as priest of God.

In summary, this chapter falls well short of establishing a biblical basis for women's ordination. Although the author stresses that he approached the Bible from an exegetical perspective, the above facts show that his conclusions are not supported by the Bible. Instead, his research reveals an absence of the use of the time-honored practice among the Protestant Reformers and Adventist pioneers to build conclusions on the Bible and the Bible only regarding biblical teachings and practices.

Endnotes

[Except as noted, Scripture quotations in this chapter are from the New King James Version.]
1. Jacques B. Doukhan, "Women Priests in Israel: A Case for Their Absence," *Women in Ministry*, pp. 29-43.
2. Ibid., p. 30.
3. Ibid., p. 38.
4. Ibid.
5. Ibid., pp. 38, 39.
6. Ibid., p. 36.
7. Ibid.
8. Ibid., p. 39.
9. Ellen G. White, *Education*, p. 227.
10. Ellen G. White, *The Acts of the Apostles*, p. 474.

11. Ellen G. White, *The Ministry of Healing,* p. 142.
12. See, for instance, George V. Wigram, *The Englishman's Hebrew and Chaldee Concordance of the Old Testament* . . . , 5th ed. (Grand Rapids, Mich.: Zondervan, 1970), p. 638.
13. Ibid., p. 623.
14. Ellen G. White, *Patriarchs and Prophets,* p. 61.
15. Doukhan, *Women in Ministry,* pp. 36, 37.
16. *Patriarchs and Prophets,* pp. 61, 62, 68. See also Ellen G. White, *The Story of Redemption,* p. 50.
17. *The Story of Redemption,* p. 50.
18. Doukhan, *Women in Ministry,* p. 37.
19. Ellen G. White, *The Desire of Ages,* p. 51.
20. Doukhan, *Women in Ministry,* p. 29.
21. Nancy Vyhmeister, "Prologue," *Women in Ministry,* p. 3.

Chapter 7

Shapes of Ministry in the New Testament

P. Gerard Damsteegt

~

The author of chapter three in *Women in Ministry*, a professor of New Testament and Christian Origins, provides an overview of the forms of ministry that existed in the New Testament and early church.[1] The purpose of the chapter is to warn against "structural fundamentalism" on church organization which, he explained, is "the idea that one pattern of church organization and ministry was laid down once and for all time."[2]

The author tries to prove his point by asserting that the Bible does not provide us with a specific organizational pattern for the church. Instead, he argues that there were two types of ministry. One type he calls a charismatic ministry, to which persons were called by Christ or His Spirit. The other type he designates as an appointive ministry, to which persons were appointed by the church. Its organizational structure developed from a one-level appointed ministry to two levels, and later on to three levels of ministry.[3]

The seven men appointed in Acts 6 to "serve tables" the author sees as an example of a one-level appointed ministry. He calls these men "elders."[4] Sometime later, he says, a clear distinction emerged between elders and deacons, indicating a two-level ministry. It was not until the beginning of the second century, under church father Ignatius in Asia, that a three-level ministry developed, consisting of bishops, elders, and deacons.[5]

Further evidence of the changing pattern of church organization, the author argues, was that the church's leadership included women. The "small and

P. Gerard Damsteegt, Dr. Theol., *is Associate Professor of Church History, Seventh-day Adventist Theological Seminary, Andrews University.*

exclusive circle" of charismatic ministry of the twelve male apostles developed "to an ever-expanding circle" which ultimately included Junia, a woman apostle.[6] The appointive ministry included Phoebe, a woman minister.[7] From this he concludes that Scripture does not forbid women from being ordained as elders and ministers "if 'ordination' simply means credentialing."[8]

1. A Charismatic and an Appointive Ministry in the New Testament?

The author suggests that it will be "convenient to distinguish between two types of ministry" in the New Testament, "based on the mode of reception." The first he designates a "charismatic ministry." This ministry is composed of people who have been called by Christ or the Holy Spirit, "since it was marked by the bestowal of a spiritual gift." The second is the "appointive ministry," which is made up of persons "appointed by the church."[9]

Although the author admits that "this distinction was not always a sharp one,"[10] he finds it a convenient way to explain his view of women's involvement in the leadership of the church. Junia was appointed by God as an apostle, representing the charismatic ministry. Phoebe was appointed by the church as a minister and represented the appointive ministry.[11] Let us examine this theory in the light of Scripture.

Are People Called by God or the Church? Is a ministry where people are chosen by God different from a ministry where people are chosen by the church? The New Testament origins of the Christian church may be traced to the time when Christ, the true Head of the church, called the twelve apostles and ordained them to preach the gospel and heal the sick (Mk 3:13-19; Luke 6:12-16). Mrs. White stated that at this time the "first step was taken in the organization of the church."[12] As the twelve patriarchs were the representatives of ancient Israel, "so the twelve apostles stand as representatives of the gospel church."[13] This scene reveals a very close relation between Christ and His church. At this time He called the apostles to form with Him the nucleus of the Christian church.

The next time an apostle was chosen occurred after the death of Judas. The 120 disciples prayed earnestly to the Lord for insight into who should be chosen to fill the vacancy left by Judas. Under the guidance of the Holy Spirit, Matthias was selected to replace Judas as an apostle (Acts 1:21-26). Here we observe the close connection between the Spirit and the church in selecting a person to fill a vacancy in the apostolic office. It is important to notice the participation of the church in the selecting process. The disciples selected the names of the candidates for the apostolic office and, under the guidance of the Holy Spirit, drew the right person.

A few years later, on the Damascus road, Saul the persecutor was confronted with a divine revelation of Jesus Christ who chose him to become His special witness. Mrs. White noted that his conversion experience revealed "important principles" regarding how God works through His church.[14] From this experience one learns that although Christ had selected Saul as a "chosen vessel" (Acts 9:15), "the Lord did not at once tell him of the work that had been assigned him."[15] He placed him in connection with His church to learn the truth and God's plan for his life. "Christ had performed the work of revelation and conviction; and now the penitent was in a condition to learn from those whom God had ordained to teach His truth."[16]

It is clear, therefore, that in choosing His special messengers and bestowing special gifts on them, God does not bypass the authority of His organized church. Rather, He uses the church to confirm His work. Again one observes the intimate relationship between God's calling a person and the confirmation of this call by the church.

Several years later, speaking through certain prophets and teachers of the church of Antioch, the Holy Spirit chose Saul, also named Paul, and Barnabas to preach the gospel to the inhabitants of Asia Minor. Yet again we notice the role the church plays in setting these disciples apart for service. After fasting and prayer, the leaders of the church ordained them by the laying on of hands and sent them forth (Acts 13:1-3). During this missionary journey both were called apostles. Paul dated "the beginning of his apostleship in the Christian church" to the time of his formal ordination to the gospel ministry.[17]

In the calling of Paul and Barnabas, we see that although they were chosen by the Holy Spirit for a unique ministry, "the Lord works through appointed agencies in His organized church."[18] It is through His church that God affirms His appointments to office and confirms whatever gifts that He has bestowed upon individuals in harmony with the Scriptures. In the official ordination of Paul and Barnabas, the church confirmed their divine call and mission. Mrs. White remarked that "God has made His church on earth a channel of light, and through it He communicates His purposes and His will."[19]

Even when God selected some to be apostles, this gift operated in harmony with the organized church, not independent of it. Like Paul and Barnabas, Timothy also received the laying on of hands by the ministers of the church (1 Tim 4:14).

Similarly, a closer look at the appointive ministry reveals an intimate interaction between the Holy Spirit and the church. The first appointment of officers took place in Jerusalem when the church chose and ordained seven deacons. This was not done by the church only, but in cooperation with the Holy Spirit. The Bible mentioned that these seven men were "full of the Holy Spirit" (Acts 6:3). In describing the implementation of a new organizational structure for the church, Mrs. White said that "the apostles were led by the Holy Spirit."[20] Again one notices the unity between the Holy Spirit and church leadership in the operation of the church.

Later on Paul set forth more clearly the relation between spiritual gifts and their relation to the church. Instead of two distinct ministries operating in the church, he revealed that the ministry of believers with special spiritual gifts was to function within the appointive ministry structure, especially when everyone who has repented and has been baptized has received "the gift of the Holy Spirit" (Acts 2:38). The metaphor of the church as a body with many members is a perfect illustration of the unity of ministries in the church (1 Corinthians 12:12-27) instead of the operation of two distinct types of ministries, a charismatic or gift-based ministry and an appointive ministry.

Mrs. White commented that "every member was exhorted to act well his part. Each was to make a wise use of the talents entrusted to him. Some were endowed by the Holy Spirit with special gifts—'first apostles, secondarily prophets, thirdly teachers, after that miracles, then gifts of healings, helps, governments, diversities of tongues.' 1 Corinthians 12:28. But all these classes of workers were to labor in harmony."[21]

To distinguish between a charismatic ministry and an appointive ministry, therefore, seems artificial and difficult to justify in the overall pattern of the New Testament ministry. In the so-called charismatic ministry, persons are called by the Lord while the church confirms the calls. In the appointive ministry persons are called by the church under the guidance of the Holy Spirit. Trying to determine God's part and the church's part is rather difficult because both work intimately together.

2. Was Junia a Female Apostle in the Charismatic Ministry?

In discussing the charismatic ministry in the New Testament, the author argues that it included a female apostle. This view he bases on Paul's recommendation to the believers in Rome. Here Paul wrote: "Salute Andronicus and Junia, my kinsmen, and my fellowprisoners, who are of note among the apostles, who also were in Christ before me" (Romans 16:7, KJV). The author asserts that the text reveals Junia as a female apostle.

Whether the person was a woman (Junia) or a man (Junias) has been debated for many years. *The Seventh-day Adventist Bible Commentary* mentions that the proper name "may be the name of either a man or a woman."[22] The *Seventh-day Adventist Bible Dictionary* favors Junias instead of Junia because "the context suggests that he was a man, hence should be called by the masculine name Junias, as in the RSV."[23] It points out, however, that because the list in Romans 16 mentions several households (Rom 16:3, 13, 15) some commentators believe that "the Christian referred to was the wife of Andronicus, hence should be called by the feminine name Junia."[24]

The author of the chapter in *Women in Ministry* mentions that this name is "commonly taken to be Junias," a masculine name, and admits that it is "impossible to determine on the basis of grammar alone whether the name should be Junias or Junia."[25] However, from a computer search of available non-biblical Greek and Latin sources he is convinced that the text refers to "a female apostle named Junia."[26]

Was Junia a Woman? In evaluating this question one finds that there are only three references to the name Junia or Junias in the non-biblical Greek

literature that were included on the CD-ROM database our author used. The first
reference is by a pagan writer Plutarch (ca. A.D. 50-ca. 120), the second is by
Epiphanius (A.D. 315-403), and the third by Chrysostom (A.D. 347-407). These
last two writers were church fathers. Plutarch refers to a woman, Junia, the wife of
Cassius and sister of Brutus. Chrysostom refers to Rom 16:7 and speaks of Junia as
a woman. Epiphanius, however, mentions that Junias was a man who became
bishop of Apameia of Syria.[27] It seems that the evidence of these Greek sources is
inconclusive in determining whether this person is a man or a woman.

What is the author's reason for discarding the possibility of the masculine
name Junias in the Greek literature? He suggests that the Epiphanius source is
"spurious" and "can be characterized as a late attempt to masculinize what had
originally been feminine."[28] He provides no evidence, however, why it should be
considered spurious or for the assertion that Junia was indeed changed to Junias by
a later copyist.[29]

The author also cites Latin sources which use this name. The Latin pagan
sources he has access to all refer to women. Among Christians, the first writer to
comment on Rom 16:7 is Origen, whose commentary on Romans is only available in a Latin translation. Origen has two references to this person. The first
reference mentions Junia, a woman, the second Junias, a man.[30] Here we see that
the Latin sources also are not conclusive.

How does the author explain this discrepancy in Origen's writings in favor of
Junia? He assumes that the masculine name Junias "was probably introduced by later
copyists. In the light of medieval tendencies to change Junia to Junias, we may apply
the textual critical rule that the more difficult reading is to be preferred and conclude
that the version which was more offensive to the sensibilities of later copyists is probably the original one."[31] Based on these assumptions, the author expresses confidence
that the text refers to "a female apostle named Junia."[32]

Does this settle the issue? I do not think so. The author's method, using non-
biblical sources to determine the meaning of the biblical text, should be avoided
because of its speculative nature, especially in determining what is genuine and
what is spurious. The contradictory witness of the church historical documents
seems to indicate that we may never know the truth in this case.

Conflicting scholarly opinions mean that a person should think twice before
arguing in a discussion on women's ordination that Junia was a woman, realizing
that at this time there is no absolute certainty that she was a woman.

Was Junia an Apostle? Even if we assume that Junia was a woman, the next
question we have to answer is whether Paul indicated that she was an apostle. In
his letter to the Romans he wrote that Andronicus and Junia "are of note among
the apostles" (Romans 16:7, KJV). What does this phrase mean?

Commentators are divided on this issue. Some think that Andronicus and
Junia were apostles, while others interpret the text as a statement that they had a
high reputation among the apostles. *The Seventh-day Adventist Bible Commentary*

states that "the meaning may be either that they were well known by the apostles or that they themselves were distinguished apostles."[33]

When Ellen White discussed the leadership of the Jerusalem council (Acts 15) that decided theological matters, she mentioned that it was "'the apostles and elders,' *men* of influence and judgment,"[34] who decided the major theological issues. This indicates that there were no women apostles and elders or ministers at this time.

The view that Junia was a female apostle appeared first in the writings of the Catholic church father Chrysostom in the 4th century A.D.[35] However, before recommending this ancient commentator in support of an interpretation of Scripture, one may recall that this church father also interpreted the phrase "on the first day of the week" (1 Cor 16:2) as the Lord's day and a day of rest.[36]

The author admits that the phrase "among the apostles" (Greek *en tois apostolois*) is "somewhat ambiguous" but adds that it is "more probable" that Andronicus and Junia were apostles. His major reason is that it is "the most natural way to take the Greek."[37] It seems that one could conclude that the person is an apostle, but again one cannot be absolutely sure.

If we assume that Andronicus and Junia were apostles, we may ask where in the church organization would they function? Here it will be helpful to look at the word "apostle." In the Bible this word is not always used with the same meaning. At the beginning of the New Testament church the word was confined to the twelve apostles. As eyewitnesses of the ministry, death, and resurrection, and trained by Jesus Himself, they had a unique role in the leading the church in the spreading of the Gospel.

After the death of Judas Iscariot the apostles were looking for someone to take his place so that the number twelve would be maintained. Not just anyone could fill this place. Peter specified the person to be selected had to be an eyewitness of the ministry and resurrection of Jesus (Acts 1:21, 22). Two candidates were presented, but only one was chosen to fill the vacancy. These twelve continued to fulfill a special role in the proclamation of the Gospel.

During His ministry Jesus pointed out that the twelve would have a unique role to play in the judgment. When Peter inquired about their reward, Jesus said, "Verily I say unto you, That ye which have followed me, in the regeneration when the Son of man shall sit in the throne of his glory, ye also shall sit upon twelve thrones, judging the twelve tribes of Israel" (Matt 19:27, 28, KJV). In the last book of the Bible, the unique place of the twelve apostles is again highlighted in the description of the twelve foundations of the New Jerusalem, which will have on them "the names of the twelve apostles of the Lamb" (Rev 21:14, KJV).

The term "apostles," however, did not remain limited to the twelve. There were others who were called apostles, though they had not been eyewitnesses of Jesus' earthly life and resurrection. Here we think of Paul, who included himself along with the twelve apostles because he had seen the risen Lord by special revelation, was taught by Him, and was called by God to be an apostle of Jesus Christ to the Gentiles (Rom 11:13; 1 Cor 1:1; Gal 1:1, 12).

Then there were others who were closely connected to the apostles but who could not claim to be eyewitnesses of the resurrection of Jesus Christ, yet who were also called apostles. Among them were Barnabas, Apollos, Titus, Epaphroditus, and Silvanus (Acts 14:14, 4; 1 Cor 4:6, 9; 2 Cor 8:23; Phil 2:25; 1 Thess 1:1; 2:6).

For these persons, the word "apostle" had a broader meaning than belonging to the circle of the twelve. The word embraced the meaning of "messenger" or "those sent on an itinerant ministry." They were sent by the various churches to proclaim the Gospel and to raise up new churches. If Andronicus and Junia were indeed apostles, they might fall into this category, serving as missionaries.

No matter how we interpret their role, it is important to keep in mind that the Bible does not mention anything about their specific activities or responsibilities. Any statement on their work and responsibilities is guesswork. This lack of information means that any appeal to Junia as an apostle does not qualify as an argument in support of the ordination of women to the office of a minister.

3. No Specific Church Organizational Structure in the New Testament?

In explaining the appointive ministry, the author argues that the New Testament reveals no specific model of church organization that we should follow today. He bases his position on the theory that the early church organization developed from a one-level ministry seen in the election of the seven men in the Jerusalem church, who could be called interchangeably elders or deacons, to that of a two-level ministry of elders and deacons mentioned in Paul's later letters. This ministry came to include female ministers. Early in the second century this structure expanded to a three-level ministry of bishops, elders and deacons.

A One-level Model of Ministry? The author's argument for a one-level ministry postulates that at first the seven men appointed in Acts 6 were elders. This view he bases on a number of assumptions:[38]

First, the claim that the seven men were "deacons" is based on concepts and distinctions that have developed later. "Mrs. White simply calls them 'officers.'"[39] Acts 6 does not mention the title "deacon," nor does the entire book of Acts. It does, however, mention the title "elder."

Second, the first time the word "elders" appears is in Acts 11:30. Here, Paul and Barnabas deliver the famine relief for the believers in Judea to the elders, whom the author assumes to be the officers appointed in Acts 6. He infers that "the kind of work for which the seven were appointed in Acts 6 is said to be done by elders in Acts 11:30."

Third, the appointment of elders in Acts 14:23 "resembles somewhat" that of the appointment of the officers in Acts 6. Fourth, Acts 15 mentions only two offices in Jerusalem—apostles and elders.

Based on these assertions, the author concludes "that the church at this early stage knew of only one appointive ministry, which Luke designated 'elder.'"

Obviously this new view conflicts with an earlier Adventist view that the seven were "deacons." The author tries to harmonize these views by supposing that the Jerusalem church in Acts 6 had a one-level ministry which united the offices of elder and deacon into one person.

He suggests that "we recognize that to begin with there was only one appointive ministry that could be called either *diakonos* (suggested by *diakonein* in Acts 6:2), a word describing function, or *presbyteros*, a word describing dignity."[40] In his view, at this early stage there was only a one-level ministry where each of the seven elected officers could be called "interchangeably either deacon or elder,"[41] depending on whether one wants to emphasize their function or their dignity.

Can the Seven Men be Called "Elders"? This question should be answered with a firm "no" because the author's assumptions are not supported by the evidence.

First, there is no sufficient reason to conclude that the seven were not deacons simply because the title "deacon" does not appear in the book of Acts. In Acts 6 the church instituted a division of labor. The apostles decided to dedicate themselves exclusively to "prayer and to the ministry of the word" (Acts 6:4) while the seven were to take care to "serve tables" (Acts 6:2). Here the Greek word "serve" is *diakonein,* which is associated with the word *diakonos,* from which our word "deacon" comes. It is therefore quite natural to designate those who "serve tables" as "deacons" to distinguish them from those whose work focuses on ministering the Word.[42]

Second, there is no proof that the elders in Acts 11:30 who received relief funds are the same persons who distributed it, such as the seven men in chapter 6 did. This is simply an assumption. In the execution of this relief effort, it seems only natural that funds from outside of Judea should be sent to the elders in charge. These elders, as the overseers of the church, would be responsible for allocating the finances to the deacons in charge of distributing to the needy. Furthermore, the Bible mentions that the funds were to assist the believers in Judea and not just to those in Jerusalem (Acts 11:29). This makes it even more imperative to hand over the funds to the elders to make sure that the whole area of Judea would reap the benefit.

Third, just because selection for both offices followed a similar procedure— the apostles prayed when they appointed elders in every church (Acts 14:23) and when they appointed the seven (Acts 6:6)—this does not mean the seven were elders. Again, to say that they were elders is only an assumption, without evidence. Close comparison between these two appointment services reveals a marked difference. During the selection of the elders, in addition to praying, they fasted (Acts 14:32). As the elders occupy the highest office in the local church it seems only appropriate to fast in addition to simply praying. Fasting is not mentioned in connection with the appointment of deacons (Acts 6:6). This difference may well indicate that these two services pertained to an ordination of different officers.

Fourth, the fact that Acts 15 mentions only the offices of apostles and elders, but omits deacons, does not mean that there were no deacons. The Jerusalem council was held to deal with doctrinal issues. These issues were to be settled by the apostles and elders in charge of the spiritual leadership of the church, not by deacons. This may explain why deacons were not mentioned.

Fifth, the suggestion that Mrs. White called the seven simply "officers" is incorrect. In discussing the appointment of the seven, several times she called them "deacons."[43] When I discussed this point with the author, he mentioned that he already had discovered this mistake. However, he still felt that this did not at all invalidate his contention that the seven were elders.

The above evaluation reveals that the author's theory that the church at this early stage knew only of "one appointive ministry, which Luke designated 'elder'"[44] is incorrect. The concept of a one-level ministry is based on invalid assumptions and interpreting texts out of their contexts.

The absence of solid biblical evidence invalidates the theory that "in the earliest period, what can be said of 'deacon' also applies to 'elder.'"[45] The two-fold ministry of elder-bishop and deacon mentioned in various places of the New Testament is *not* a later "branching out from one original ministry that could at first be called interchangeably either deacon or elder."[46]

These incorrect assumptions therefore invalidate his arguments against the long-standing Seventh-day Adventist position. The New Testament indeed provides God's people with a model of church organization and leadership that is still valid today and has been confirmed in the writings of Ellen White.

Apostolic Church: A Two-Level Ministry of Servant Leadership. In order to understand the events of Acts 6, it is helpful see how the verb "to serve" (Greek *diakoneo*) is used in the gospels.

This verb describes the work or service of slaves, the work of Jesus' disciples, and that of Jesus Himself. It is used for a slave serving the master (Luke 17:8), Martha serving Jesus and His disciples (Luke 10:40), and Jesus serving the saints after the second advent (Luke 12:37). Luke used this verb to describe the nature of Jesus' ministry and that of His disciples (Luke 22:25, 26). This usage shows that service or ministry is the work of Christ's followers till He returns. Service is the nature of the work of the church and its members in fulfilling the gospel commission. With this in mind, we can return to Acts 6.

The Book of Acts more fully reveals the meaning of service as the New Testament church was being established. The apostles became overwhelmed by the demands of the fast-growing church in Jerusalem. To cope with the challenges, the apostles divided their mission of service or ministry into two major areas. Seven men were chosen to "serve tables" while the apostles confined themselves "to prayer and the ministry of the word" (Acts 6:2, 4). Both "the seven" and the apostles were involved in serving or ministering, but the manner of their involvement differed significantly. What each of these two areas of service entailed has been the subject of much speculation. Ellen G. White's commentary on these events, however, is very enlightening. It harmonizes with Scripture, and attention to it might prevent one from unwarranted speculations about the apostolic church's organization.

Mrs. White saw the appointment of "the seven" as an important step in the organization of the Christian church. Addressing the situation in Acts 6, she noted that as a result of the rapid growth of the church the Hellenists complained that their widows were neglected in the daily distribution of assistance. To remove all occasion for discontent, under the guidance of the Holy Spirit the apostles began "to outline a plan for the better organization of all the working forces of the church."[47]

What was this plan of church organization? It was to establish a division of labor between those serving as the spiritual leaders and those taking care of the specialized lines of work and the finances of the church. Now the apostles decided that it was necessary to focus on the proclamation of the gospel and to delegate to others their involvement in areas of church life not directly related to this ministry. The apostles felt the time had come "when the spiritual leaders having the oversight of the church should be relieved from the task of distributing to the poor and from similar burdens, so that they might be free to carry forward the work of preaching the gospel."[48] They said, "Wherefore, brethren, look ye out among you seven men of honest report, full of the Holy Ghost and wisdom, whom we may appoint over this business [of serving tables]. But we will give ourselves continually to prayer, and to the ministry of the word" (Acts 6:3-4, KJV). The church accepted this advice and ordained the seven as deacons. Mrs. White wrote that "by prayer and the laying on of hands, seven chosen men were solemnly set apart for their duties as *deacons.*"[49] This action was an "important step in the perfecting of gospel order in the church."[50]

The designation "deacons" for these men perfectly fits the description of their work, to "serve tables." To them, Ellen White wrote, was delegated "the oversight of special lines of work" which included looking after the "individual needs" and the "general financial needs of the church."[51] They were "ordained for the special work of looking after the needs of the poor."[52] Their work, however, did not exclude them from "teaching the faith." They "were fully qualified to instruct others in the truth, and they engaged in the work with great earnestness and success."[53]

Far from seeing the appointment of the seven in Acts 6 as only the first phase—a one-level ministry—of an evolving church organization, Mrs. White considered the Jerusalem church's leadership structure a model whose impact extended throughout the history of the Christian church. She testified that "the organization of the church at Jerusalem was to serve as a model for the organization of churches in every other place where messengers of truth should win converts to the gospel."[54]

After the stoning of deacon Stephen, the first great persecution of the Christian church began, and believers were scattered throughout the regions of Judea and Samaria (Acts 8:1). From this time onward the gospel was carried beyond the confines of Jerusalem. Wherever the apostles took this gospel, the new communities were organized according to the model of the Jerusalem church.

In harmony with this plan, the apostles appointed elders as spiritual leaders in every church (Acts 14:23, Titus 1:5). This practice makes it obvious that when the apostles left Jerusalem to preach the gospel throughout the world, they appointed elders in Jerusalem to continue the leadership instead of leaving a vacuum in the major center of the church. This explains the presence of elders in the Jerusalem church several years later (Acts 11:30). It was to those elders that Barnabas and Saul handed their relief for the believers in Judea.

In a letter to Timothy, the apostle Paul confirmed the effectiveness of this early division of labor in the Jerusalem church. He carefully spelled out the qualifications for those serving as spiritual leaders (elders) as well as those attending to the other church affairs (deacons) (1 Tim 3:1-13). In a similar manner Paul instructed Titus to establish order in the churches by appointing to the office of elder or bishop men who had met the qualifications (Titus 1:5-9).

As both apostles and elders or bishops form the spiritual leadership of the church, what was the significant distinction between them? One of the major differences was that the apostles were itinerant spiritual leaders while the elders or bishops were the local spiritual leaders. The apostles traveled from church to church, planted new churches, and oversaw the operation of a number of churches. Elders or bishops were connected to their local church and had no authority over other churches. Yet both apostles and elders worked closely together in giving leadership to the church.

This close cooperation can be seen in a major controversy over whether Gentiles had to be circumcised or not. A council was called together in Jerusalem to settle the conflict. The participants who were to decide the issue were the spiritual leaders of the churches—the apostles and elders (Acts 15:2, 6).

The close relationship between the leadership roles of the apostles and elders is seen in the word used to describe the office of an apostle and that of an elder. After the death of Judas the apostles were looking for a suitable replacement. The nature of the type of work he was to fulfill becomes clear from Peter's appeal, "Let another take his office" (Acts 1:20). The Greek word translated in some versions as "office" is *episkope,* referring to the role of "overseer." This is the reason why the King James Version rendered the word as "bishoprick." It is clear that from the very beginning the apostles served as overseers of the church. After the organizational model of the Jerusalem church was used to organize newly established churches, Paul described the elder as "a bishop" (Greek *episkopos*) (Titus 1:5, 7). In counsel to Timothy, Paul described the same position as the "office of a bishop" (*episkope*), which in this context refers to the role of having the oversight of the church (1 Tim 3:1, KJV). When Paul addressed the elders of the church in Ephesus, he again called them "overseers" whose task it was "to shepherd the church of God," because in the near future all kind of heresies would come into the church to destroy it (Acts 20:28, 29). This indicates that an important part of the role of the elders is to fortify the faith of the church members through the ministry of the Word. Paul gave Titus similar counsel, that an elder must hold fast "the faithful word as he has been taught, that he may be able, by sound doctrine, both to exhort and convict those who contradict" (Titus 1:9). Again we see the close parallel between the apostles and elders in their ministry and leadership roles.

Peter alluded to the close relationship between apostles and elders when, in addressing elders, he called himself "also an elder" (1 Peter 5:1). This confirms that an apostle was also an elder, one whose responsibility was not confined to a local church but who supervised and counseled various churches. Paul demonstrated this kind of leadership when he revisited the churches he had established.

In giving instruction to Timothy and Titus regarding the organization of the newly established churches, the apostle Paul called on them to implement the Jerusalem model of ministry by appointing spiritual leaders (elders) and deacons (1 Tim 3 and Titus 1). He carefully spelled out the qualifications for service in these offices. Those who met these requirements were to be ordained to serve in their respective offices.

The early Adventist pioneers adopted this New Testament model of church leadership, and it functioned successfully throughout the history of the Advent movement. In the early years of the movement, Mrs. White called upon believers to accept the leadership of the elders. Said she, "Elders, local and traveling, are appointed by the church and by the Lord to oversee the church, to reprove, exhort, and rebuke the unruly and to comfort the feebleminded. There is no higher tribunal upon earth than the church of God. And if the members of the church will not submit to the decision of the church, and will not be counseled and advised by it, they cannot be helped. If one and then another think they know best and choose their own judgment instead of the judgment of the church, what kind of a church would we have? What would be the use of a church if each one is permitted to choose his own course of action? Everything would be in the greatest confusion; there would be no harmony, no union."[55] Today we might associate "traveling elders" with ministers appointed as conference officials, union and division leaders, and the General Conference officers.

Ellen G. White's Description of the New Testament Ministry. In her narration of the history of the New Testament church, we notice that Ellen White designated the apostles and elders as the spiritual leaders involved in the oversight of the church. These she also called "ministers."

At first there were the twelve apostles. Later she referred to Paul as an apostle, as she also did with his travel companions, Barnabas and Silas. When Paul and Barnabas were ordained, the laying on of hands was performed by *"the ministers"* of the church in Antioch.[56]

Ellen White indicated that in the days of the apostles it was *"the ministers"* who performed the laying on of hands ceremony. After citing Paul's warning not to lay hands on a person too quickly, she said that the *"ministers of God* did not dare to rely upon their own judgment in selecting or accepting men to take the solemn and sacred position of mouthpiece for God. They selected the men whom their judgment would accept, and then they placed them before the Lord to see if He would accept them to go forth as His representatives."[57] The word "ministers" here refers to all leaders who qualify to ordain others and includes apostles and elders/ministers.

After returning from their first missionary trip, Paul and Barnabas united with "the ministers and lay members" in Antioch for evangelistic work.[58]

Soon after this, a crisis occurred which gives insight into the way the church settled conflicts. The orderly organization of the church played a key role in handling crises, as Ellen White pointed out. Said she, "The order that was maintained in the early Christian church made it possible for them to move forward solidly as a well-disciplined army clad with the armor of God. The companies of believers, though scattered over a large territory, were all members of one body; all moved in concert and in harmony with one another."[59] When conflicts erupted in a local church, these problems "were not permitted to create a division in the church."[60] The church implemented an effective conflict resolution strategy that delegated the problems to the spiritual leadership for a solution. Divisive issues "were referred to a general council of the entire body of believers, made up of appointed delegates from the various local churches, with the *apostles and elders* in positions of leading responsibility."[61] In this way, Mrs. White said, "the efforts of Satan to attack the church in isolated places were met by concerted action on the part of all, and the plans of the enemy to disrupt and destroy were thwarted."[62]

The crisis that arose in Antioch involved some Jewish Christians belonging to the party of the Pharisees who taught that it was still necessary to keep all the Mosaic laws in order to be saved. Paul and others, however, preached that Christ's death had abolished the law of ceremonies. This issue soon led to a widespread controversy in the church. In response, church leadership called a general council to settle the controversy. We notice that the spiritual leadership plays a crucial role in resolving this conflict. Mrs. White remarked, "The entire body of Christians was not called to vote upon the question. The 'apostles and elders,' men of influence and judgment, framed and issued the decree, which was thereupon generally accepted by the Christian churches."[63]

Ellen White noted that "the apostles and elders" were *men* of influence. This seems to indicate that there were no women apostles and elders or ministers at this time.

When Paul traveled with Silas on his second missionary journey, both were called "apostles." Wherever they led people to Christ they organized a new church. Describing their work in Thessalonica, Ellen White wrote that they appointed officers "to act as ministers and deacons."[64] This leadership was responsible to keep order in the church. This particular church urgently needed order because some persons came in with fanatical ideas and doctrines, causing disturbance. Although the Thessalonian church was properly organized, "there were some, self-willed and impetuous, who refused to be subordinate to those who held positions of authority in the church. They claimed not only the right of private judgment, but that of publicly urging their views upon the church." To establish order in the church, Paul emphasized the need of accepting the appointed leadership by showing "the respect and deference due to those who had been chosen to occupy positions of authority in the church."[65]

Although he was an apostle, Paul frequently called himself a minister, even as he referred to those with whom he worked as ministers. When believers in Corinth began to favor one worker over another, Paul tried to impress on them that a discussion "regarding the relative merits of different ministers was not in the order of God, but was the result of cherishing the attributes of the natural heart."[66] Paul told them that both he and Apollos were "but ministers."[67]

When Paul returned to the churches he had established, he chose from them men to train for the gospel ministry. Said Ellen White, "This feature of Paul's work contains an important lesson for ministers today. The apostle made it a part of his work to educate young men for the office of the ministry. He took them with him on his missionary journeys, and thus they gained an experience that later enabled them to fill positions of responsibility."[68]

Mrs. White's description of the New Testament church reveals that the twofold division of labor in the Jerusalem church between the spiritual leaders and deacons in Acts 6 continued throughout the apostolic era. At first the spiritual leaders were the apostles. When the apostles appointed other spiritual leaders these persons were called "elders" or "ministers," equating the office of an elder with that of a minister. In Ellen White's writings there is no evidence that at any time she used the office of a "deacon" as a synonym for the office of an "elder" or "minister."

4. A Three-level Model of Ministry?

I have said little about the author's three-level model of ministry because it falls outside of the time frame of Scripture. Still, it may be helpful to examine briefly the known history of this organizational structure.

In the New Testament, the terms "elder" and "bishop" were used interchangeably (Titus 1:5, 7; 1 Tim 3:1, 2), *elder* indicating the title and dignity of the office, and *bishop* revealing the officer's function as "overseer" (Acts 20:17, 28). Churches at that time were ruled by a council of elders. All this changed, however, at the beginning of the second century with an early Christian writer, Ignatius, later claimed by the papacy as a forefather of their own system.

Ignatius is the first representative of a new form of church government called "the episcopate." His writings reveal that at this time the presiding elder had taken on the title of bishop. In the new church structure, the bishop stood at the center of church life, with the other elders, the deacons, and the laity subject to his authority.

Ignatius described the relationship of the believers to the bishop in the following terms. "We should look upon the bishop even as we would look upon the Lord Himself, standing as he does, before the Lord."[69] "See that ye all follow the bishop, even as Christ Jesus does the Father. . . . Let no man do anything connected with the Church without the bishop."[70] "And say I, Honour thou God indeed, as the Author and Lord of all things, but the bishop as the high-priest, who bears the image of God. . . . Nor is there anyone in the Church greater than the bishop, who ministers as a priest to God for the salvation of the whole world. . . . He who honours the bishop shall be honoured of God, even as he that dishonours him shall be punished by God."[71]

This three-level ministry is a departure from the biblical model because it makes the bishop the head and center of the local congregation. This model of ministry has been described as the first phase of the episcopacy—a rulership of the church by the bishops. In time, this type of church organization came to its full fruition in the papacy. It was not until the rise of Protestantism that believers tried to recover the New Testament model of church leadership, a model also adopted by the Adventist pioneers.

Mrs. White strongly cautioned against minister-centered churches. In a warning to church leadership, she said, "Do not, my ministering brethren, allow yourselves to be kept at home to serve tables; and do not hover around the churches, preaching to those who are already fully established in the faith."[72] Instead, she urged, focus the church's attention on the real source of power. "Teach the people to have light in themselves, and not to depend upon the ministers. They should have Christ as their helper, and should educate themselves to help one another," so that the minister can be free to enter new fields.[73]

The vitality of the believers' life must not depend on ministers. In no uncertain terms Mrs. White stressed that "we must not encourage the people to depend upon ministerial labor in order to preserve spiritual life. Everyone who has received the truth must go to God for his individual self, and decide to live by every word that proceedeth out of the mouth of God. Those who have embraced the third angel's message must not make man their trust, and depend upon the ministers to make their experience for them."[74]

Having shown that both the one-level and the three-level models of ministry have no support in Scriptures, we find only one model remaining that portrays the New Testament church. This is the two-level ministry which I have discussed and which has been so clearly explained by Mrs. White. This is the model of church organization that the Lord has recommended for His church.

5. Was Phoebe a Female Minister?

Our New Testament scholar asserts that Paul highly recommended to the church of Rome a "female minister" of the church of Cenchrea, called Phoebe (Rom 16:1). He surmises that by the beginning of the second century there could have been "many" female ministers.[75] In time, however, "women came to be squeezed out of the ministry."[76] He sees Phoebe today as an example of holding open "the door for women to ministry."[77]

The basis on which the author justifies seeing Phoebe as a minister is his theory regarding the development of the earliest forms of organization in the Christian church. As we have already discussed, this theory assumes that during the earliest period of the church there was no distinction between an elder and a deacon. "What can be said of 'deacon' also applies to 'elder.' Both were ministries which, in the beginning, were one, and they remained one in many places for several decades."[78] When dealing with this early period, the author refers to both deacons and elders as *ministers*. Thus he calls Phoebe, a *diakonos*, a "female minister."[79]

When commenting on the work of the seven and discussing the verb "serve" (Greek *diakonein* [Acts 6:2]), the noun "servant" or "deacon" (Greek *diakonos*) and its usage in Acts 1:25 as "service" or "ministry" (from the Greek *diakonia*), he explains that these words mean "respectively, to serve, a servant, and service. Equally satisfactory synonyms are to minister, a minister, and ministry."[80] Similarly, in discussing the role of elders (1 Pet 5:1-4), he equates the position of elder with that of a minister.[81]

Phoebe a Minister? In Romans 16:1-3, Paul made the following recommendation to the believers in Rome: "I commend unto you Phoebe our sister, which is a servant of the church which is at Cenchrea" (Romans 16:1-3, KJV). Here he described Phoebe's position as *diakonos,* a Greek word which may be translated "servant," "deacon-deaconess," or "minister." The translation "servant" appears in the KJV, NASB and NIV. The RSV has "deaconess." The plural of this Greek word appears in 1 Timothy 3:8 where it is translated as "deacons." This usage explains why Phoebe is often referred to as a deaconess. Our author, however, calls her a minister.

The practice of calling Phoebe a "minister" has no scriptural support. The theory that at the beginning the designations elder and deacon referred to the same office is flawed, as we have shown earlier. This should be especially clear when we understand Paul's position on the role of women in the church. It seems, therefore, in full harmony with all his writings to consider that Paul associates Phoebe, at most, with the office of deacon and not that of an elder.

Furthermore, the author's assumption that the word "minister" is an "equally satisfactory" synonym for servant or deacon is just not so. Scripture teaches that all believers are "servants" (John 12:26). All are to be involved in serving or ministering, yet not all are "ministers," occupying the office of elders or ministers as described in the Bible. Only those with the proper qualifications can be selected to this office and may properly be addressed with the title of "minister." To call Phoebe a minister, as if she occupied an office that is similar to that of a modern minister, is reading into the Bible text a concept that is not there. Today's ministerial office is an extension of the office of an elder, not that of a deacon.

The author suggests that there could very well have been many women ministers. Said he, "if there could be one female minister [Phoebe] there could as well be many."[82] This estimation he bases on some correspondence from the pagan Pliny the Younger, Roman governor of Bithynia, to emperor Trajan. In a letter written in about A.D. 108 Pliny provided one of the first accounts of the persecution of Christians, in which he described the torture of 'two maidservants who were called *ministrae.* "[83] Our author explains that the word *ministrae* is "the plural of the Latin word *ministra,* feminine form of minister. It is the exact equivalent of the Greek *diakonos* and the origin of the English word 'minister.'"[84]

Is this letter evidence that there were many female ministers at the beginning of the second century A.D.? What is the precise meaning of the word *ministrae?* Unfortunately, the author does not tell us what this word meant in the Roman world at that time. Standard translations of this letter translate the Latin word as "deaconesses." The Loeb Classical Library rendered the phrase in this letter containing the word *ministrae* as follows: "two female slaves, who were styled deaconesses."[85] From this we may conclude that these persecuted Christian slaves were deaconesses. To compare their position to elders or ministers as we know them lacks any evidence. Again, the author has based his reasoning on incorrect assumptions, not facts.

Ellen G. White's Reference to Phoebe. Mrs. White referred to Phoebe in an article that was written as an encouragement to workers. She encouraged women as well as ministers to dedicate themselves to gospel work. Phoebe and other women who worked with Paul are mentioned as examples of what women can do for the Lord. In this context Mrs. White wrote, "The Lord has a work for women as well as men to do. They can accomplish a good work for God, if they will learn first in the school of Christ the precious, all-important lesson of meekness. They must not only bear the name of Christ, but possess His spirit. They must walk even as He walked, purifying their souls from everything that defiles. Then they will be able to benefit others by presenting the all-sufficiency of Jesus."[86] Nothing in the article gives any indication that Phoebe was a minister or that she served as a minister.

6. May Women be Ordained as Ministers, Despite the Qualifications in 1 Timothy 3?

From his view of a constantly-evolving pattern of church organization and structure which included the presence of female leadership at the highest levels of the New Testament—Junia an apostle and Phoebe a minister—the author asserts that there is nothing to prevent a woman from being ordained as an elder or minister. "If 'ordination' simply means credentialing," he says, "Junia and Phoebe clearly had it, for Paul's commendations of them are explicable on no other grounds."[87]

The author seriously questions using the list of qualifications in 1 Timothy 3 and Titus 1 to oppose ordination of women to the office of elder or minister. Like the non-Seventh-day Adventist scholars he quotes, he finds this list "problematic."[88] He bases his arguments on the following assertions.

First, he says that "the same qualification is mentioned for both *episkopos* [elder] and *diakonos* [deacon], but Rom 16:1 proves incontrovertibly that the early church had female *diakonoi* [deacons]."[89] With the presence of female "deacons," the qualification that "the deacons be the husbands of one wife" (1 Tim 3:12,

KJV) should not be taken as a prohibition against female deacons. Similarly, he feels, believers should not use the requirement that a bishop or elder must be the "husband of one wife" (1 Tim 3:2; Titus 1:6) to prevent the appointment of female elders or ministers.

Second, he argues, one should consider the characteristics of the New Testament language in interpreting the phrase "husband of one wife." He says, "Greek is an Indo-European language that possesses grammatical gender, as do also the Semitic languages. In such languages, when one has a group of mixed gender in view, or a person who could be of either gender, one must perforce use the masculine."[90] If one does not read the Bible in this manner, he continues, one will encounter major problems. Note, for example, that the language of the last commandment of the Decalogue does not seem to forbid a woman to covet her neighbor's husband, and Jesus' warning not to look at a woman lustfully seems to leave a woman free to lust after a man. These passages, however, apply to both male and female. The phrase "husband of one wife," the author suggests, should be read in the same way because it "is in the same class,"[91] applying to both male and female.

Can a Woman Qualify for the Office of an Elder in Timothy and Titus? The argument that the New Testament Greek language allows the qualification that an elder or minister be "the husband of one wife" to apply also to women is incorrect. This reasoning conflicts with the context of the phrase in 1 Timothy 3:2 and Titus 1:6.

First, the word used here to refer to the man (Greek *aner*) signifies a male, not a generic "person," for which Greek had a different term (*anthropos*). When *aner* is used in close connection with "woman" (*gyne* in Greek), particularly when the word "woman" is qualified by a pronoun or an adjective (such as in this case, the word "one"), it specifically signifies a male who is a "husband." It does not mean a generic "spouse." Hence translators always render this phrase "husband of one wife."

The immediate context confirms this interpretation. Following the stipulation that an elder or minister must be "the husband of one wife," the text mentions that he must be "one who rules his own house well" (1 Tim 3:4), "having faithful children not accused of dissipation or insubordination" (Titus 1:6). It is the husband who, as head of the home, is responsible for keeping his family in good order. These two requirements reveal that it is God's design for men to be the spiritual leaders of the church. It also makes it clear that women do not fulfill the requirements for the office of an elder or minister.

Second, the author neglects the larger context of the list of requirements within 1 Timothy. This list follows immediately after Paul's reminder to the church that men and women have different roles. A woman is not "to usurp authority over the man" (1 Timothy 2:12, KJV) because of specific biblical reasons. First, because of God's order of creation: "For Adam was first formed, then Eve" (1 Tim 2:13).

Second, because of the order of transgression: "And Adam was not deceived, but the woman being deceived was in the transgression" (1 Timothy 2:14, KJV). Thus, immediately after having emphasized that the man is to be the spiritual leader, Paul specified what kind of man is to be appointed in the office of elder-minister to oversee the operation of the church (1 Tim 3:1-7).

Women in Ministry states that "understanding is enhanced by a study of the context of the passage."[92] If our author had followed this counsel, his conclusions might have been different. His focus on the phrase "husband of one wife" without adequately considering its context has led him to misinterpret the meaning of the list of biblical requirements for church leadership. Neglecting to take the immediate as well as the larger context of the passage into consideration has resulted in erroneous conclusions.

The Author's Interpretation Conflicts with Ellen G. White's. In determining the fitness of a person to lead a church, Mrs. White used the New Testament list of requirements for elders to evaluate their suitability to that office. She wrote to one leader that he did not qualify to lead the church because of his failure in the leadership of his family. She mentioned that the Lord drew her attention to the importance of following the specific Bible requirement in 1 Timothy 3:4, 5 that spiritual leaders must be successful in their family government.

"Bro. S., your family is proud. They know not the first principles of the third angel's message. They are in the downward road, and should be brought under a more saving influence. These influences affect you and make you weak. You have not ruled well your own house, and while you lack so much at home, you cannot be entrusted to dictate important and responsible matters in the church. *This scripture was presented before me; 'One that ruleth well his own house, having his children in subjection with all gravity; for if a man know not how to rule his own house, how shall he take care of the church of God?'"* [93]

This testimony affirms the continual validity of the Bible counsel that successful leadership in the home is an indispensable requirement for any candidate for the office of elder or minister. If, as Ellen White believed, these Bible requirements in 1 Timothy 3 and Titus 1 are still valid 1900 years after the death of Christ, what argument can make us conclude that these qualifications are no longer gender related? The author's contention that these New Testament qualifications cannot be used to oppose the ordination of women to the office of a minister is in direct conflict with Paul's instructions to Timothy and Titus as well as the counsel of Mrs. White.

Does ordination mean simply "credentialing," as the author seems to suggest?

Here the illumination the Lord provided through Ellen G. White is crucial in keeping the church from becoming confused by the abundance of human theories. Commenting on the ordination of Paul and Barnabas by the ministers of the church in Antioch, Mrs. White wrote that "their ordination was a public recognition of their divine appointment to bear to the Gentiles the glad tidings of the gospel."[94] They were now "invested with full ecclesiastical authority" which authorized them "not only to teach the truth, but to perform the rite of baptism and to organize churches."[95] To call ordination simply "credentialing" is far removed from the significance the Lord gives to it.

If in the 19th century Mrs. White continued to affirm the validity of the New Testament list of requirements, the author should have explained why these are no longer applicable for 21st-century believers. Instead, he tries to demonstrate that the Apostle Paul never intended these leadership requirements in 1 Timothy and Titus to designate only males.

In the final days of earth's history, Seventh-day Adventists ought to pay even more attention to the scriptural requirements for leadership. Commenting on the care with which the early believers chose to fill the vacancy among the twelve apostles due to the death of Judas (Acts 1:21-26), Mrs. White said toward the end of her life:

"From these scriptures we learn that the Lord has certain men to fill certain positions. God will teach His people to move carefully and to make wise choice of men who will not betray sacred trusts. If in Christ's day the believers needed to be guarded in their choice of men for positions of responsibility, we who are living in this time certainly need to move with great discretion. We are to present every case before God and in earnest prayer ask Him to choose for us.

"The Lord God of heaven has chosen experienced men to bear responsibilities in His cause. These men are to have special influence. . . . *The Lord has not given men or women liberty to advance ideas that will bring commonness into His work, removing the sacredness that should ever surround it.* God's work is to become increasingly sacred to His people. In every way we are to magnify the exalted character of the truth. Those who have been set as guardians of the work of God in our institutions are ever to make the will and way of God prominent. The health of the general work depends upon the faithfulness of the men appointed to carry out the will of God in the churches.[96]

The issue facing Seventh-day Adventists is obvious. To what authority should we listen? What interpretation is correct? It is for the believers and their leadership to decide which voice they will follow.

Today's Minister is an Extension of the Office of an Elder. Because the author freely uses the word "minister," it would be helpful to understand what the present position of a minister in the Seventh-day Adventist church is. The word "minister" has always been associated with the role of an elder.

During the early years of our church the believers "preferred to call their ordained ministers 'brother.'"[97] However, in the early 1850s, when the Adventist pioneers began to implement the Bible plan of church organization, the title "elder" was used by Seventh-day Adventists in North America to refer to an ordained minister. "In recent years the title of 'pastor' has been gradually replacing the title of 'elder.'"[98]

This development shows that today the title of minister as well as pastor is associated with the biblical role of the elder. However, while the local church elder is appointed by the local church and is accountable to that church, confining his authority to that church, ministers or pastors are accountable to the conference who employs them and assigns them to one or more churches. The minister's authority goes beyond the local church and extends over all the churches he is responsible for.

Throughout the history of the Seventh-day Adventist church, the biblical criteria for the office of an elder as listed in 1 Timothy 3 and Titus 1 have been the guidelines in the appointment of ministers or pastors. These requirements have included the stipulation that only men could occupy this position. Ever since the 1990 General Conference allowed women to function as ministers or pastors, church leaders have been trying in vain to find biblical support that would justify this practice and confirm it through ordination.

Now the author of the chapter in *Women in Ministry* has provided believers with an interpretation that seems to allow this practice to be in harmony with the Bible. Unfortunately, this interpretation came about as a result of neglecting the context of the biblical requirements for the office of an elder or minister. In spite of the author's scholarly efforts, there is no biblical support for women to function in the role of overseer of the church or to be ordained to such a role. Those who have gone ahead with ordaining women have gone against the explicit Bible requirements for the function of elders and ministers. The original Seventh-day Adventist practice of not ordaining women as elders and ministers continues to be fully supported by the Scriptures and the counsels of Mrs. White. It is time that our administrators take a hard look at the current practices in the light of inspiration.

Conclusion

We have pointed out that the distinction between charismatic ministry and appointive ministry is artificial in several respects and does not account for the true nature of the New Testament ministry. Furthermore, having shown that the one-level and the three-level models of ministry are not supported by Scripture, we find only one model remaining that explains ministry in the New Testament—the two-level ministry. This pattern of church organization harmonizes all the biblical components of ministry, and it accords with the writings of Ellen G. White.

We maintain that the author's theory does not properly explain the development of ministry in the New Testament. It imposes a model of church organization on the New Testament that leads readers to believe that the Lord has not revealed in Scripture any specific pattern of church organization that is still relevant for the remnant church.

Upon this theory the author bases his charge of "structural fundamentalism" against those who believe that the Bible reveals "one pattern of church organization and ministry" for God's church that is still valid for today.[99] It also seems that the author's theory forms the basis of *Women in Ministry's* view that "church organization is not spelled out in the Bible."[100] However, as the above evaluation has shown, the assumptions underlying the theory are incorrect, and therefore so are its conclusions about women ministers and "structural fundamentalism."

In contrast, both the Bible and the writings of Mrs. White reveal a consistent basic model of church organization that was first introduced in the Jerusalem church in Acts 6, revealing a two-fold structure of servant-leadership. This New Testament model consists of spiritual leaders who have the responsibility to preach and teach the gospel and oversee the spiritual well-being of the church, and deacons who are in charge of the temporal affairs of the church. The model has been recommended for implementation wherever the church expanded in the world. In this model the Bible delegates the spiritual leadership role of elders and ministers to men who meet the criteria spelled out in the New Testament.

Seventh-day Adventists followed this successful biblical model until the question of women's ordination came up. This issue has created great tension, confusion, and conflict in the local churches between those who are convicted that the biblical model should be maintained and those who feel that male leadership in the churches is not relevant today in the increasingly-egalitarian cultures in Western Europe, North America and Australia. This conflict that has divided many churches will never end until the General Conference, unions, and conferences take a firm stand affirming the biblical model for the remnant church and thus terminate the recent practice of ordaining women elders. This return to the biblical model will require a strong education process that focuses on Christ's model of leadership as the basis for the remnant church.

Failure to return to the biblical model will have grave consequences, for it brings into the leadership of the church elders who are not convinced that the New Testament leadership model mentioned in this chapter is still applicable today. If decision makers can so easily dispense with these clear biblical teachings, there is no assurance that they would not do away with other New Testament teachings, lifestyle practices, and standards. Indeed, we may already observe such change in the growing laxness regarding jewelry, music in worship, movie theater attendance, and health reform practices.

The success of the Seventh-day Adventist church in finishing the work assigned to her depends on her faithfulness to the Scriptures. This chapter has shown the continual importance of the Reformation platform and the foundation of the Advent movement—the principle that for "every doctrine and practice" there is no safety but to stand on the solid foundation of the Bible.[101]

Endnotes

[Except as noted, Scripture quotations in this chapter are from the New King James Version.]

1. Robert M. Johnston, "Shapes of Ministry in the New Testament and Early Church," *Women in Ministry*, pp. 45-58.
2. Ibid., p. 52.

3. In my dialogue with the author he suggested I could use the terms one-, two-, and three-level ministry to describe his developmental pattern of church organization.

4. Johnston, *Women in Ministry,* p. 51.

5. Ibid., pp. 48-53.

6. Ibid., p. 52.

7. Ibid., p. 51.

8. Ibid., p. 53.

9. Ibid., p. 45.

10. Ibid.

11. Ibid., p. 53.

12. Ellen G. White, *The Acts of the Apostles,* p. 18.

13. Ibid.

14. Ibid., p. 120.

15. Ibid.

16. Ibid., p. 121.

17. Ibid., p. 165.

18. Ibid., p. 162.

19. Ibid., p. 163.

20. Ibid., p. 89.

21. Ibid., p. 92.

22. Francis D. Nichol, ed., *The Seventh-day Adventist Bible Commentary,* Commentary Reference Series (Washington, D. C.: Review and Herald Publishing Association, 1957), 6:650.

23. Siegfried H. Horn, *Seventh-day Adventist Bible Dictionary,* Commentary Reference Series, revised ed. (Washington, D. C.: Review and Herald Publishing Association, 1979), article "Junias."

24. Ibid.

25. Johnston, *Women in Ministry,* p. 47

26. Ibid.

27. Ibid., p. 55, note 12; John Piper and Wayne Grudem, *Recovering Biblical Manhood & Womanhood: A Response to Evangelical Feminism* (Wheaton, Ill.: Crossway Books, 1991), pp. 79, 80.

28. Johnston, *Women in Ministry,* p. 55, note 12.

29. The dating of the early church literature has been a subject of disagreement among scholars for centuries. The same can be said of the determination whether a source is genuine or spurious. There were even sharp disagreements in the early church. One writing could be considered on the same level as the New Testament Scriptures in certain localities while in other regions it was perceived as spurious. The Epistle of Barnabas is a good example of this.

30. Ibid., p. 56, note 13; *Recovering Biblical Manhood & Womanhood,* p. 80.

31. Johnston, *Women in Ministry,* p. 56, note 13.

32. Ibid., p. 47.

33. *The Seventh-day Adventist Bible Commentary,* 6:650.

34. *The Acts of the Apostles,* p. 196, emphasis mine. The Jerusalem Council took place about A.D. 49, approximately 16 years after the deacons were first appointed.

35. Chrysostom, *Homily 31 on Romans,* Nicene and Post Nicene Fathers, 1st series, 11:555. His reference is cited by Johnston, *Women in Ministry,* p. 56, note 13.

36. Chrysostom, *Homily 43 on 1 Corinthians,* Nicene and Post Nicene Fathers, 1st series, 12:258, 259.

37. Johnston, *Women in Ministry,* pp. 54, 55, note 11.

38. Except as otherwise noted, see Johnson, *Women in Ministry,* p. 49, for the assumptions and their conclusion.

39. The chapter in Mrs. White's book *The Acts of the Apostles* dealing with the appointment of the seven is called "The Seven Deacons." Chapter titles, the author mentioned, are

"mostly the work of the editors. The word 'deacon' does not occur in the text itself. Mrs. White simply calls them 'officers'" (Johnston, *Women in Ministry*, p. 57, footnote 19). Contrary to this statement, we find that Mrs. White used the word "deacons" several times in her chapter.

40. Johnston, *Women in Ministry*, p. 49.
41. Ibid., p. 51.
42. It is true that in Acts 1:25 the word *diakonia* is applied to the work of the apostles, but in Acts 6 the word is used to indicate the distinct nature of the work of the seven in contrast to the work of the apostles. We must also keep in mind that the work of the apostles as well as the seven involves service, which explains the use of the word in Acts 1:25. Yet the work of the apostles is of a different nature from the work of the seven. This difference in work justifies calling the seven "deacons."
43. *The Acts of the Apostles,* pp. 89-91, 97.
44. Johnston, *Women in Ministry*, p. 49.
45. Ibid., p. 51.
46. Ibid.
47. *The Acts of the Apostles,* p. 89
48. Ibid.
49. Ibid., emphasis mine.
50. Ibid., pp. 88, 89.
51. Ibid., p. 89.
52. Ibid., p. 90.
53. Ibid.
54. Ibid., p. 91.
55. Ellen G. White, *Manuscript Releases,* 5:296.
56. *The Acts of the Apostles,* p. 162.
57. Ellen G. White, *Testimonies for the Church,* 4:406, emphasis mine. She added, "No less than this should be done now."
58. *The Acts of the Apostles,* p. 188.
59. Ibid., pp. 95, 96.
60. Ibid., p. 96.
61. Ibid., emphasis mine.
62. Ibid.
63. Ibid., p. 196.
64. Ibid., p. 261.
65. Ibid., pp. 261, 262.
66. Ibid., p. 274.
67. Ibid., quoting 1 Corinthians 3:5, KJV.
68. Ibid., pp. 367, 368.
69. Ignatius, *Epistle of Ignatius to the Ephesians,* Ante-Nicene Fathers, 1:51.
70. Ignatius, *Epistle of Ignatius to the Smyrnaeans,* Ante-Nicene Fathers, 1:89.
71. Ignatius, *Epistle of Ignatius to the Smyrnaeans,* Ante-Nicene Fathers, 1:90.
72. Ellen G. White, *Historical Sketches,* p. 139.
73. Ibid.
74. Ellen G. White, *The Home Missionary,* December 1, 1894.
75. Johnston, *Women in Ministry*, p. 51.
76. Ibid., p. 53.
77. Ibid.
78. Ibid., p. 51.
79. Ibid.
80. Ibid., p. 49.

81. Ibid., p. 52.
82. Ibid., p. 51.
83. Ibid.
84. Ibid., p. 58, note 36.
85. Pliny, the Younger, *Letters,* Book X, chapter xcvi, trans. by William Melmoth, rev. by W. M. L. Hutchinson, vol. 2, Loeb Classical Library (New York: Macmillan Co., 1931-35), p. 405. See also Pliny, the Younger, *The Letters of the Younger Pliny,* trans. with an introd. by Betty Radice. (Baltimore, Md.: Penguin Books, 1963), p. 294.
86. Ellen G. White, "Words of Encouragement to Workers," *North Pacific Union Gleaner,* 2/3 (December 4, 1907).
87. Johnston, *Women in Ministry,* p. 53.
88. Ibid., p. 50.
89. Ibid.
90. Ibid.
91. Ibid., p. 51.
92. Nancy J. Vyhmeister, "Prologue," *Women in Ministry,* p. 3.
93. Ellen G. White, Letter to E. W. Shortridge, *Review and Herald,* Supplement, August 19, 1862, emphasis mine.
94. *The Acts of the Apostles,* p. 161.
95. Ibid.
96. *Testimonies for the Church,* 9:264, emphasis mine.
97. *Seventh-day Adventist Encyclopedia,* rev. ed., Commentary Reference Series (Washington, D. C.: Review and Herald Publishing Association, 1976), article "Elder."
98. Ibid.
99. Johnston, *Women in Ministry,* p. 52.
100. Vyhmeister, *Women in Ministry,* p. 3.
101. *The Ellen White 1888 Materials,* p. 44.

Chapter 8

The Laying on of Hands

P. Gerard Damsteegt

The fourth chapter of *Women in Ministry* dealing with ministry in the Bible concentrates on the laying on of hands.[1] The author of the chapter presents a thorough study of the biblical meaning of laying on of hands. In view of a common notion that the laying on of hands is nothing more than a gesture, the author shows from the Old and New Testaments the important symbolic meaning of the laying on of hands and demonstrates that it is central to the ordination service.

The intended result of the hands-laying, he points out, had to do with "obedience." The man who received the laying on of hands "was to obey the voice of God in his leadership," while the people "were to obey him."[2]

In his conclusion, the author discusses the connection between the laying on of hands and ordination to the ministry. Here he raises the question whether women should receive the laying on of hands. His immediate reply is, "Most definitely. The withholding of the laying on of hands may well be a refusal to recognize heaven's call and the individual's appropriately positive response."[3] "Furthermore," he adds, "to place a woman in the position of pastor or elder is to affirm that she is indeed called by God to ministry. Without the laying on of hands, she lacks an important biblical authorization to fulfill her responsibilities. Laying on of hands identifies her before the congregation as its minister, sets her apart from the congregation, empowers her to be a representative of the congregation, and appoints her to office."[4] He ends his appeal by asserting, "If the gesture is important at all, it should be equally important to pastors of both genders."[5]

P. Gerard Damsteegt, Dr. Theol., *is Associate Professor of Church History, Seventh-day Adventist Theological Seminary, Andrews University.*

The Laying on of Hands and the Office of an Elder or Minister

The author has limited his study of the laying on of hands only to the act itself and its significance. But the act of laying on of hands in ordination is part of the process of setting someone apart to a certain mission or office. The author does not discuss whether it is biblical to appoint a woman to the office of an elder or minister. He simply takes it for granted that it is biblical. Unfortunately, one cannot simply assume that this is correct, as the present volume shows. This means that, despite its helpful information about the laying on of hands, the author's study is not useful in determining whether women may legitimately officiate as ministers.

One does not get the whole biblical picture of the laying on of hands in ordination until one studies the matter in the light of *officiation,* which is the act of setting apart a person to a specific office. This is the area where current disagreements on women's ordination to the office of elder and minister come to a head. Therefore, any study of laying on of hands in ordination must take into consideration the crucial question: "Ordination to what office or function?" Studies and research neglecting to address this point cannot claim to reveal the biblical meaning of the laying on of hands for the issues now facing the church.

The author's chapter, therefore, is only a partial study that provides partial answers. He needed to address the question of what the biblical roles or functions of men and women mean for the laying on of hands. Although the chapter brings out some meaningful thoughts on the action of the laying on of hands, the fact that it does not deal with the legitimacy of appointing women to the New Testament offices of church leadership that are set aside for qualified men (1 Tim 3:1-7 and Titus 1:5-9) leads to serious errors of judgment.

Again we see the unfortunate results when an author makes a selective use of Scripture on a particular topic. By contrast, Adventists have always advocated withholding judgment and conclusions until all texts that have any bearing on a particular subject have been consulted. Before making a strong recommendation for women's ordination, the author should have explained how the passages in 1 Timothy 3 and Titus 1 that are publicly read during the laying on of hands ceremony for elders and ministers can be applied to women.

The Meaning of the Laying on of Hands

Much has been written on the meaning of ordination and the laying on of hands. Some have suggested that ordination bestows on a person special spiritual gifts and powers originally only given to the apostles, while others see ordination simply as an act affirming persons in the work they are already involved in. It will be helpful to investigate what Ellen White has said on this subject.

Mrs. White illustrated the meaning and importance of ordination when she discussed the ordination of Paul and Barnabas. Before their ordination both men "had already received their commission from God Himself."[6] Their work had been abundantly blessed. Yet they had not yet been "formally ordained to the gospel ministry."[7] Now they had reached a point in their Christian experience when God was to give them further responsibilities, in the execution of which "they would need every advantage that could be obtained through the agency of the church."[8]

With fasting and prayer and laying on of hands by the "ministers" of the church of Antioch, Paul and Barnabas were "solemnly dedicated to God."[9] By this action the ministers "asked God to bestow His blessings upon the chosen apostles in their devotion to the specific work to which they had been appointed."[10]

The result of this action were far-reaching. Now "they were authorized by the church, not only to teach the truth, but to perform the rite of baptism and to organize churches, being invested with full ecclesiastical authority."[11] This act of ordination, Mrs. White said, was "a public recognition of their divine appointment."[12]

Did this ordination ceremony bestow special virtues on Paul and Barnabas? Mrs. White stated that "there is no record indicating that any virtue was imparted by the mere act of laying on of hands."[13] She explained that "the ceremony of the laying on of hands added no new grace or virtual qualification. It was an acknowledged form of designation to an appointed office and a recognition of one's authority in that office. By it the seal of the church was set upon the work of God."[14]

The understanding that ordination, setting one apart by the laying on of hands, is the church's recognition of individuals to perform certain functions for the church suggests that, within the guidelines set by Scripture, both men and women may be set apart by the laying on of hands to perform certain functions. With this understanding, Ellen White had no difficulty in recommending that women be set apart by the laying on of hands. She wrote about the part-time work of some laywomen:

"Women who are willing to consecrate some of their time to the service of the Lord should be appointed to visit the sick, look after the young, and minister to the necessities of the poor. They should be set apart to this work by prayer and laying on of hands. In some cases they will need to counsel with the church officers or the minister; but if they are devoted women, maintaining a vital connection with God, they will be a power for good in the church."[15]

Since, through an act of consecration ("the laying on of hands"), both male and female can be authoritatively appointed or commissioned to perform certain specific functions, the debate over women's ordination is not whether women can or cannot be ordained in this sense. Both men and women may be commissioned to do certain assigned tasks on behalf of the church.

The key issue to be addressed is whether, among the varied ministries of the church, women may legitimately be appointed or commissioned through ordination to perform the leadership functions of elders or ministers. Can the church ordain a woman to the leadership office of elder or minister and be in harmony with Scripture?

"Women Elders" and "Women Ministers"?

When it comes to selecting church elders and ministers, Mrs. White specifically stated the necessity of following the Bible requirements and not to rush *men* into the office of elder or minister (1 Tim 5:22). The candidates for this office must have proven that they are mature and fully qualified. She urged that the "Bible rule" should be followed in the ordination process so that it is clear that the men selected to be ordained are fit for this office.

Commenting on the selection of church leaders, she said: "Set in order the things that are wanting, and ordain elders in every city, as I had appointed thee: if any be blameless, the husband of one wife, having faithful children not accused of riot or unruly. For a bishop must be blameless, as the steward of God." (Titus 1:5-7) She stressed, "It would be well for all our ministers to give heed to these words and not to hurry men into office without due consideration and much prayer that God would designate by His Holy Spirit whom He will accept." She continued:

"Said the inspired apostle: 'Lay hands suddenly on no man.' [1 Tim 5:22] In some of our churches the work of organizing and of ordaining elders has been premature; *the Bible rule* has been disregarded, and consequently grievous trouble has been brought upon the church. There should not be so great haste in electing leaders as to ordain men who are in no way fitted for the responsible work—men who need to be converted, elevated, ennobled, and refined before they can serve the cause of God in any capacity.

"The gospel net gathers both good and bad. It takes time for character to be developed; there must be time to learn what men really are. The family of the one suggested for office should be considered. *Are they in subjection? Can the man rule his own house with honor?* What character have his children? Will they do honor to the father's influence? If he has no tact, wisdom, or power of godliness at home in managing his own family, it is safe to conclude that the same defects will be carried into the church, and the same unsanctified management will be seen there. It will be far better to criticize the man before he is put into office than afterward, better to pray and counsel before taking the decisive step than to labor to correct the consequences of a wrong move."[16]

It is clear that Ellen White considered vitally important the quality of family leadership of the man to be ordained as church elder or minister. Failure of the man as a successful head of his family would disqualify him for church leadership. A woman could not qualify for elder or minister because she is not called to rule her family.

Conclusion

The author needed to take into consideration that a study of the laying on of hands is not complete without addressing the question, Ordination to what office or role? However, in the light of *Women in Ministry*'s assumption that "church organization is not spelled out in the Bible"[17] one might understand why he does not feel a burden to discuss this point.

The author's assertion that the Bible approves the laying on of hands for women as well as men cannot be used as evidence that women must be ordained as ministers. If the Bible assigns the office of an elder or minister to men, what right do church administrators have to appoint women to that office, as our author suggests?

According to the Bible requirements for church leadership, only those with successful leadership experience in their families qualify for the laying on of hands for ordination to the office of elder and minister. For women to be ordained to this office by the laying on of hands violates the clear Bible requirements. In spite of this, the author argues that "placing a woman in the position of pastor or elder is to affirm that she is indeed called by God to ministry."[18] This call, he stresses, needs to be affirmed with laying on of hands, because without it "she lacks an important biblical authority to fulfill her responsibilities. Laying on of hands identifies her before the congregation as its minister . . . and appoints her to office."[19] The legitimacy of placing women in such an office is the point that needs to be proved. Our author, however, appears to assume it.

In response, we say that since women do not meet the qualifications for the position of elder and minister, they should not be put into this office. It is unbiblical to appoint, ordain, or commission them as elders or ministers. It is doubly unbiblical to conduct the laying on of hands ceremony for those women already placed in the office of elder or minister because the laying on of hands is a sign of investing these women with biblical authority to function in an office of leadership that the Bible assigns to men! It is difficult to understand how anyone who claims to follow the Bible could participate in such a service that is contrary to the Bible, expecting God to bless.

If the Seventh-day Adventist church continues to appoint women as elders and ministers, the confusion that already exists among its members will increase. An immediate moratorium on the ordination of women as elders is the first step administrators ought to take to return the church to the only firm foundation for Seventh-day Adventists as God's prophetic remnant, who claim to follow the Bible and the Bible only for all their teachings and practices.

Endnotes

[Except as noted, Scripture quotations in this chapter are from the New King James Version.]

1. Keith Mattingly, "Laying on of Hands in Ordination: A Biblical Study," *Women in Ministry,* pp. 59-74.
2. Ibid., p. 71.
3. Ibid.
4. Ibid., pp. 71, 72.
5. Ibid., p. 72.
6. Ellen G. White, *The Acts of the Apostles,* p. 161.
7. Ibid., p. 160.
8. Ibid.
9. Ibid., p. 161.

10. Ibid., p. 162.
11. Ibid., p. 161.
12. Ibid., p. 160.
13. Ibid., p. 162.
14. Ibid., pp. 161, 162
15. Ellen G. White, "The Duty of the Minister and the People," *Review and Herald,* July 9, 1895, emphasis mine.
16. Ellen G. White, *Testimonies for the Church,* 5:617, 618, emphasis mine.
17. Nancy Vyhmeister, "Prologue," *Women in Ministry,* p. 3.
18. Mattingly, *Women in Ministry,* p. 71.
19. Ibid., pp. 71, 72.

Chapter 9

Does Paul Really Forbid Women to Speak in Church?
A Closer Look at 1 Timothy 2:11-15

C. Raymond Holmes

"A woman should learn in quietness and full submission. I do not permit a woman to teach or to have authority over a man; she must be silent. For Adam was formed first, then Eve. And Adam was not the one deceived; it was the woman who was deceived and became a sinner. But women will be kept safe [saved] through childbirth, if they continue in faith, love and holiness with propriety." 1 Timothy 2:11-15 NIV

According to the Andrews University press release, October 22, 1998, announcing the publication of *Women in Ministry: Biblical and Historical Perspectives,* the book consists of a response to two questions posed by "Adventist church leaders": "May a woman be legitimately ordained to pastoral ministry?"[1] and "If so, on what grounds?"

In our collective search for answers to these fundamental questions the Word of God must be our guide rather than prevailing social opinion, the supposed offensiveness of male leadership in ministry, the giftedness of women to serve as pastors, or their sense of call to ministry. We serve a cause that transcends our own span of life, that transcends the way we personally feel about things. This cause represents values that need caring for and that may require vigorous defense from time to time. We must never allow ourselves to take positions which

C. Raymond Holmes, D.Min., *is Professor of Preaching and Worship, Emeritus, Seventh-day Adventist Theological Seminary, Andrews University.*

we do not really believe simply to soothe feelings or rid ourselves of a sense of threat or insecurity. To use an expression from Scripture, this is a time for the patience of the saints.

Some among us feel that we should not be discussing the issue of women's ordination at all because it is potentially divisive and might destroy the unity of the church. Others feel that we should be broad-minded and simply resolve the issue on the basis of human rights and gender equality. Still others feel that the issue distracts us from the mission of the church, and that we should simply drop it and get on with the business of evangelism. Some even hold that theological and doctrinal pluralism makes it impossible to arrive at any kind of resolution. But none of these arguments are satisfactory because, practically speaking, they constitute burying our collective heads in the sand of indifference to truth.

If we accept theological and doctrinal pluralism, there is no way to settle the issue of women in ministry. Indeed, any issue becomes nothing more than a power struggle to see which view has the most votes. But power struggles are not the way the business of the church should be carried on, a business that involves both proclaiming and guarding the truth.

The question of women in ministry is charged with emotion, making it difficult to stay focused on the issue itself. We are obligated, therefore, to keep before us our oneness in Christ and the fellowship we share in His church. We must recognize that in our fervor and zeal to express views which may differ, there is always the danger of causing hurt which is abhorrent to sincere advocates on either side. However, precisely because of its critical nature and implications, the issue obligates us all to a thorough study and discussion of the subject in the context of Christian love. There must be no lack of compassion. We must resist all expressions of an overweening righteousness. To disagree is one thing, but to do so without a credible alternative is to invite ridicule and astonishment.

Unfortunately, decisions have been made before the discussion phase has been completed and a consensus achieved, producing a desperate need to find theological justification for those actions. Something in human nature finds it difficult to face the possibility that actions may have been precipitous and that, in this case, we may have run ahead of the Holy Spirit.

Women who have ministry as a career goal tend to see ordination as the ultimate symbol of approval. Some of them testify to insensitivity, abuse, and cruelty by men, and therefore resent any interpretation of the Bible, no matter how sound, that denies this approval. Denial of their desire to be ordained is viewed as discriminatory, unjust, oppressive, an extension of male domination and abuse. Some see the denial of ordination as a human-rights issue, an attack on a minority, something to which American society has become very sensitive in the latter half of the twentieth century. Therefore, whatever is said or written in the discussion must reflect sensitivity to such feelings. Having said this, however, we must also note that the Seventh-day Adventist church holds the unswerving conviction that to obey what the Bible teaches is the way of happiness and blessing for every believer and is basic to the success of the church's mission.

Some among us believe that every office of ministry should be considered open to women. However, many others of us remain convinced that the male-headship argument is biblically valid, a position to which even *Women in Ministry* bears witness.[2] Furthermore, after many years of study and debate, we are still unconvinced that the so-called "progressive" interpretation of key Bible passages can be sustained. We see such interpretations as regressive, moving back, away from the historic interpretation. Partly because we are unwilling to ignore or leap over biblical evidence for purely social or cultural reasons, we have the impression that the view held by the Christian church for almost twenty centuries is being abandoned far too easily.

The reader must understand at the outset that we are not anti-women-in-ministry. On the contrary, we encourage qualified women to seek and prepare for positions in ministry. But we *are* concerned that such positions be supported by biblical authority. We believe that this is what the church-at-large desires, and we are bound by conscience to participate in the search for that authority.

The Text

There are a number of New Testament passages pertinent to the role of women in ministry, such as 1 Corinthians 11:3-10, 14:33b-38, Ephesians 5:22-24, 1 Timothy 2:11-15, and 1 Timothy 3:1-4.

None of these passages are problematic, obscure, or painfully puzzling. All are written in clear prose and do not contain typological, figurative, symbolic, or poetic language, which means that they are not difficult to understand. It does not take a scholar to interpret them. Any believer in the Bible's authority and divine inspiration can do it and be confident about conclusions. The Seventh-day Adventist church, since its inception, has held to the conviction that the responsibility for interpreting the Bible belongs to the whole church and not just to scholars. This is the philosophy behind Sabbath school classes, which are such powerful instruments in building faith, molding character, and motivating the mission of the church. The primary prerequisite for interpreting and understanding the Bible, for both layperson and scholar, is faith in the Bible as the inspired, infallible, and unerring Word of God.[3]

Concerning principles of interpretation (hermeneutics), Seventh-day Adventists have consistently held to the Reformation position that the Bible interprets itself and that it is to be interpreted literally unless the context clearly indicates otherwise.

In this chapter we will concentrate on 1 Timothy 2:11-15, asking how this passage in particular helps in the search for answers to the two questions posed in our first paragraph: "May a woman be legitimately ordained to pastoral ministry?" and "If so, on what grounds?"

As has been shown elsewhere in this book, several of the authors of *Women in Ministry* argue that the traditional interpretation of 1 Timothy 2 has not taken into account what is "now known" to be the "initial situation" that Paul was addressing in Ephesus. They speculate that the apostle's restriction on women "teaching and having authority over men" was due to the infiltration of the false teaching of the cult of the Mother Goddess, Artemis, and proto-gnostic doctrines in the Ephesian church. On this hypothesis, *Women in Ministry* argues that Paul's statement is not applicable today. In the opinion of the book's scholars, Paul did not allow women to "teach and have authority over men" because he sought to restrain "certain assertive women in the church" or "wives domineering over their husbands in worship settings" or even some "unlearned women" who at that time were "instigating violence" because "they had not learned sufficiently."[4]

Against this view, I am going to argue that 1 Timothy 2:11-15 is not as problematic as *Women in Ministry* would want readers to think. The passage can be understood literally, at face value, taking into account the general and immediate context, thus permitting the text to teach us principles which are universally applicable to the relationships of men and women and to the question of ordaining women to the headship role of elders or pastors.

The Context

In the immediate context, Paul establishes his apostolic authority (1 Tim 1:1, 12-17; 2:7) and warns against the teaching of "false doctrines" (1:3) which "promote controversies rather than God's work" (1:4). When he says, "I do not permit" (2:12), he is not expressing a personal opinion but is exercising his proper authority as an apostle. He appeals to the order of creation (2:13), basing what he says on God's revelation, not on any other source. His appeal is to a universal principle applied to a specific situation, and what he says is an apostolic command.

Chapter 1 indicates that the letter was written to assist young Timothy in the correction of false teachings that had crept into the church at Ephesus (1:3, 4, 6, 7)—and, by inference, to assist all pastors wherever similar teachings might appear down through the ages. Paul identifies two people by name, Hymenaeus and Alexander, as responsible for false teachings, and he boldly condemns them for what he terms their blasphemy (1:20). Already at the outset, and in light of this correction, it is sound interpretation to conclude that the ideas dealt with in chapter 2, verse 12—which is at the heart of the passage we are dealing with and most in dispute, namely, about women teaching men and/or exercising authority over men in public worship—are on the list of false teachings that Paul intends to see corrected.

Chapter 2 consists of instructions concerning public worship. In 2:1-10 Paul discusses prayers of intercession and thanksgiving that are to be offered and also the need for modest attire on the part of women in worship. He follows this counsel (in 2:11-15) with instruction that women are to give deference to male leadership in public worship.

Clearly and unmistakably, the context of chapter 2 is that of public assemblies for worship. Everything that Paul says in this passage must be understood in reference to public worship.

Thus 1 Timothy 2:11-15 (our main text), together with 1 Timothy 3:1-4—which clearly reserves the office of "overseer" (elder, pastor) to men—is a crucial passage concerning the role of women in ministry. Because it is one of the Pauline passages most passionately disputed by advocates of women's ordination, we sense the great importance of understanding it correctly. We certainly cannot ignore it in any serious attempt to find reliable answers to the questions posed above: "May a woman be legitimately ordained to pastoral ministry?" and "If so, on what grounds?"

Some people conclude that 1 Timothy 2:11-15 is irrelevant because it says nothing specifically about women in ministry or about their ordination or commissioning. But if a specific reference to ministry and ordination were a valid criterion for judging relevancy, then on what basis may proponents of women in ministry use Galatians 3:28 (which says that in Christ Jesus "there is neither male nor female") to support their position? But the questions that must be asked are, What contribution does our passage make to the broad issue of the role of women in public ministry? and What universal principles does it provide?

Observations

(1) Paul's use of the term "woman" does not refer only to one female, as some have suggested. The immediate context, in which Paul uses the plural "women," indicates that the reference is to all Christian women.

In 2:8 Paul addresses "men." In 2:9-10 he addresses "women." Then in 2:11-12 he switches to the singular term "woman." In verse 15 the plural form "women" is again used. Obviously "woman" is not a reference to a particular unnamed woman, but in the context refers to any woman among many women. Furthermore, this cannot be a reference to married women only, for instructions concerning them do not appear until 3:11, specifically referring to the wives of deacons. In order to deny that verses 11-15 apply to church life, one must limit the instructions on dress and adornment found in verses 8-10 to apply only to the home setting, a view no Bible-believing Seventh-day Adventist will support. We may conclude that 2:9-15 applies to all women in the church, whether single or married.

(2) First Timothy 2:11-15 does not prohibit women from learning, reassuring us that Paul appreciated a woman's intellectual ability. It does not follow, however, that because women have the requisite gifts of intelligence and ability to learn, they are eligible to exercise a teaching role over men in public worship.

(3) It is enlightening to discover the kind of teaching referred to in 1 Timothy 2:11-15. Other passages can help us. First Corinthians 12:28-29 tells us that "in the church" God has appointed teachers. Ephesians 4:11 tells us that Jesus gave

teachers to the church for the specific purpose of preparing "God's people for works of service, so that the body of Christ may be built up." Paul referred to his own appointment as "a teacher of the true faith to the Gentiles" (1 Tim 2:7). In 2 Timothy 3:16 Paul refers to the teaching function of the God-breathed (inspired) Scripture, "so that the man of God may be thoroughly equipped for every good work." Paul admonished young Timothy: "Devote yourself to the public reading of Scripture, to preaching and to teaching," roles which Timothy was authorized to perform "when the body of elders laid their hands" on him (1 Tim 4:13-14). Timothy was further admonished to watch his "doctrine closely" (4:16). The ones who are to benefit from this teaching ministry "are believers" (6:2). This teaching is to be done with "careful instruction" and involves "sound doctrine" (2 Tim 4:2-3). James 3:1 is a solemn warning to teachers within the body of Christ, the church, who "will be judged more strictly."

These are not references to teaching general knowledge, but specifically to the teaching of the gospel, the message and doctrine concerning Christ, that is entrusted to elders or pastors within the fellowship of the church. In the light of the wider context of Paul's pastoral epistles to Timothy and Titus, as well as the immediate context which links this form of teaching with exercising "authority over men," we may conclude that Paul is here prohibiting women from the kind of teaching done in the capacity of a leader of the church. In other words, the Apostle Paul is not forbidding all teaching to women, but only the kind of "teaching" in the church which gives women a position of authority over men.

(4) First Timothy 2:11-15 does not forbid women teaching women and children. After all, Timothy was taught by his mother and grandmother (2 Tim 1:5; 3:15). Titus 2:3-4 admonishes women to teach other women. In all candor we must note that Priscilla joined Aquila in explaining to Apollos "the way of God more adequately" (Acts 18:26), but her assistance was not given publicly during a gathering of the church for worship. Then there is the kind of teaching and exhortation that takes place among the members in the church, in which both men and women legitimately participate as they fellowship and socialize, conversing, sharing, and testifying (Col 3:1-17). Hebrews 10:25 says, "Let us not give up meeting together, as some are in the habit of doing, but let us encourage one another—and all the more as you see the Day approaching." Sabbath School classes help to fulfill this admonition.

(5) Though women are not prohibited from prophesying, the text prohibits them from teaching men in the specific situation of public worship. The counsel is consistent with 1 Corinthians 11:2-16, where Paul tells us that women who have the gift of prophecy must use it in ways that do not undermine male leadership. The context in 1 Corinthians 11 and 12 is also that of public worship. Evidently the gift of prophecy given to women can be exercised without violating the biblical principle of male headship or the prohibition against women teaching men. The prime example of this for Seventh-day Adventists is the ministry of Ellen G. White, who did not hesitate to use to the fullest the prophetic gift given her by God, but

without ordination and with no claim to leadership of the denomination (see *Testimonies for the Church*, 8:236-238).

(6) There has been a heated debate over the proper translation of the Greek word in 1 Timothy 2:12 rendered "authority" in the *New International Version* and in some other versions. Translations such as "engage in fertility practices," "instigate violence," and "originator of man" have been substituted. Such substitutions leap over the contextual evidence. It is the context that supports "authority," for it constitutes the specific application and meaning of "full submission." The *New International Version*'s "have authority" is a bit weak. The *King James Version*'s "usurp authority" is a bit strong. The *New American Standard*'s "exercise authority" best conveys the original meaning. The context clearly reveals that women are not prohibited from the exercise of authority in a setting that harmonizes with their distinct roles, such as women teaching women or children. They are prohibited only in the specific situation of public worship and in respect to men.

(7) Paul includes qualifiers. First, he says that "A woman should learn in quietness and full submission" (1 Tim 2:11). We cannot ignore the fact that the focus here is not on the learning itself—Paul takes it for granted that women legitimately should learn—but on the attitude the women bring to that learning. (In such a setting, verse 12 ["I do not permit a woman to teach or to have authority over a man; she must be silent"] does not prohibit women from teaching men only until they are properly educated, despite what some have claimed.) The word "quietness" in the *New International Version* is a good translation, because Paul does not mean to enforce absolute silence on these women learners. This is apparent by his choice, under inspiration, of the Greek term *en hesychia,* which means "peaceable and nonargumentative," implying respectful listening. Another Greek word was available, *sige,* had he wished to indicate total silence. The "quiet lives" of 1 Timothy 2:2 and the "quiet spirit" of 1 Peter 3:4 are certainly more realistic understandings than absolute silence. Whoever heard of an absolutely silent person! The same word is used in verse 12 where women are enjoined to "be in quietness," that is to say, to be peaceable and nonargumentative, rather than to teach or exercise authority over men in public worship.

Paul's second qualifier is that women must learn in "full [all] submission" (1 Tim 2:11). In context, this cannot refer to submission to God or to the congregation or to what is being taught. Verse 11 actually begins with "in quietness" in the original Greek, and verse 12 ends with "in quietness," like the covers of a book framing the contents. The two verses are closely linked and constitute a unit of thought in which women are encouraged to learn but prohibited from teaching men. They are to learn in "full submission" and not "exercise authority over men" in public worship. The use of the word "submission" with reference to husband-wife relationships in other passages, such as 1 Peter 3:1-7, is not compelling enough to assume that Paul uses it the same way here in 1 Timothy 2. The context of 1 Timothy 2 simply does not support such an assumption. First Peter 3 speaks specifically about husband-wife relationships; 1 Timothy 2 does not. Once again the immediate context, which focuses on public worship, helps us understand that the submission Paul requires is submission to the male leadership in public worship. He appeals to the order of creation, in which "Adam was formed first, then Eve" (1 Tim 2:13), as his authority. The submission of women to men is to be demonstrated by refraining from teaching or exercising authority over them in public worship.

Writing under the inspiration of the Holy Spirit, Paul recognizes the significance of the "Adam first, then Eve" sequence. It is much safer to trust the apostle Paul in this regard than to rely on the opinions of contemporary scholars. The reference to the creation of "Adam first, then Eve" is to a reality, a fact, that stands independent of any local or specific situation.

This does not mean that all women are to be in submission to all men at all times. Why not? Because not all men engage in authoritative teaching when the church assembles for worship. The only conclusion that does not ignore or leap over the context is that women are to learn in submission to those men who do engage in such teaching. In the worship life of the church, women, though equal with men, are to submit voluntarily to male leadership.

(8) How long would Paul's prohibition be valid? We must remember that as far as the Bible is concerned, principle always transcends occasion. While each of Paul's letters addresses specific situations, all of them appeal to principles that are transcendent. They cannot be dismissed as inapplicable to the life of the Christian community in subsequent ages. The principles governing the ministry in Timothy's time apply to the ministry of today. References to the "later times" (1 Tim 4:1) and the "coming age" (6:19) support the universal application of principles governing ministry and the roles of both men and women in that ministry. The general context indicates that the prohibition was not meant to be local and temporary, for a certain place and period, but universal for all time and all places. The whole of 1 Timothy consists of Paul's instructions for "the church of the living God" (3:15) through the ages to the "later times" (4:1). Dismissing the instructions of Paul in 1 Timothy 2:11-15 on the claim that they were directed only to a specific situation in Ephesus effectively destroys the intent of the entire letter.

Therefore, any idea that this text is applicable only to a specific situation in the Ephesian congregation, where Timothy was ministering, and not to any other period or place in the history of the Christian church, especially our own, is untenable, unacceptable, and must be rejected in the strongest terms. Otherwise we would have to conclude that the rest of 1 Timothy is not applicable to our time, together with all the rest of Paul's writings as well as Jesus' Sermon on the Mount. Ultimately, such reasoning would force the conclusion that the whole of Scripture is not applicable to any other time than when it was written—which would do violence to the truth that "all Scripture is inspired by God and profitable for teaching, for reproof, for correction, for training in righteousness; that the man of God may be adequate, equipped for every good work" (2 Tim 3:16-17 NASB). Scripture is for all time, all places, all situations. The teaching of the

New Testament cannot be limited to apostolic times; it is for "the church of Christ in all ages."[5] The interpretive principle is, "These messages were given, not for those that uttered the prophecies, but for us who are living amid the scenes of their fulfillment."[6]

(9) It is significant that 1 Timothy was not addressed to the church at Ephesus but to Timothy himself. Thus the occasion was not simply a specific problem in that congregation, but rather the need for the young evangelist-pastor to be instructed in the principles for ordering the life of a congregation. Timothy would minister elsewhere during his career and face similar situations. He could not change the principles from situation to situation, congregation to congregation, nation to nation, culture to culture, any more than we can. While times may change, there are permanent biblical principles governing the life of the Christian community wherever it is found.

(10) First Timothy 2:13 ("For Adam was formed first, then Eve") is central to Paul's argument. There are those who say that the prohibition against women teaching and so exercising authority over men in public worship is attributed to mankind's fall into sin and the subsequent curse (Genesis 3), which Jesus atoned for on the cross. By reason of the cross, they say, this prohibition along with all other consequences of the Fall is wiped away. But we must remember that Paul, the apostle of redemption, does not use Adam and Eve's sin to justify the prohibition. Rather, he rests it squarely on the creation of man and woman, "Adam first, then Eve," which preceded the Fall and involved no sin at all (Gen 2:4-25).

As mentioned above, 1 Timothy 2:11-15 is not complicated. It is plain that Paul bases his prohibition on the creation account, "Adam first, then Eve." Why does he do this? Because he wants to let us know that there is a significant difference between the roles of men and women in the worship life of the church. The fact that Adam came first in the order of creation is the reason why men are given the primary role of authoritative teaching in the church. That this makes Paul a male chauvinist who regarded women as inferior is utter nonsense. The idea that a distinction between the roles of men and women implies that women are of less worth than men is not biblical. On the contrary, the Bible teaches that men and women are of equal worth while at the same time having different roles.

The reference to Adam and Eve in verse 13 cannot be to their marital relationship, for the context does not support such a view. It is the God-designed sequence, "Adam first, then Eve," not the marital relationship, that the inspired apostle cites as the authoritative basis for his command. In light of this, the rendering of verses 11 and 12 offered by Charles B. Williams, and approvingly quoted in *Women in Ministry*—"A married woman must learn in quiet or perfect submission. I do not permit a married woman to practice teaching or domineering over a husband"—is neither a legitimate translation nor an acceptable interpretation.[7]

The gospel does not abolish Paul's instructions. To discover the proper role for women in ministry we must study the Gospels and all other relevant passages of

Scripture, just as we do with all doctrinal matters. The prohibition found in 1 Timothy 2:11-15 is not contrary to the gospel. The Bible teaches that though men and women are equal in Christ, they have been given different roles. What we must do then is establish the means, the polity, by which those differing roles are permitted to determine and shape the role of women in ministry.

(11) Verses 13 and 14 must be viewed as a unit. In verse 14 Paul wrote, "Adam was not the one deceived; it was the woman who was deceived and became a sinner." As difficult as it may be for all friends of women to accept, this sentence indicates that besides the order of creation, an additional reason for the prohibition against women teaching men in public worship is that Eve was deceived, not Adam. Observe that Paul never says women suffer deception more than men. Yet he twice says that Eve, the first woman and mother of all women, was deceived (1 Tim 2:14 and 2 Cor 11:3). In light of Paul's earlier assertion that the order of creation establishes the man as the head, this second reason strongly suggests the danger of deception any time women (and men) attempt to violate God's divine arrangement.

Note that by directing his temptation to Eve instead of Adam, who had been charged with the leadership responsibility concerning the dangers of the forbidden tree (Gen 2:16-17), Satan struck at the headship principle governing the functional relationships between men and women, and he succeeded in disrupting the harmony our first parents enjoyed while they lived out the principles enshrined in God's arrangement. Both of our parents were responsible for the Fall—Eve usurping Adam's headship, and Adam failing to exercise his responsibility to protect his wife and guide her to obey God.

When Satan tempted our first parents, his ultimate goal was to lead them into thinking that they could be "like God" (Gen 3:5). To do so, he approached Eve with the suggestion that she could attain a higher role than that which God had assigned her at creation. Thus, Eve took the first step in her desire to be like God when she usurped the man's headship role. Ellen G. White explains: "Eve had been perfectly happy by her husband's side in her Eden home; but, like restless modern Eves, she was flattered with the hope of entering a higher sphere than that which God had assigned her. In attempting to rise above her original position she fell far below it. A similar fate will be reached by all who are unwilling to take up cheerfully their life duties in accordance with God's plan. In their efforts to reach positions for which He has not fitted them, many are leaving vacant the place where they might be a blessing. In their desire for a higher sphere, many have sacrificed true womanly dignity and nobility of character and have left undone the very work that Heaven appointed them" (*Patriarchs and Prophets*, p. 59).

Thus, Paul's second reason for prohibiting women "from teaching and exercising authority over men" (i.e., "Eve was deceived") strongly underscores the danger of deception which arises whenever women attempt to violate God's creation arrangement of male headship. We must reiterate strongly that Paul's statement does not make women inferior to men, nor less intelligent or capable. It simply recognizes and illuminates a fact of creation: men and women are inherently different. God made them that way, and He likes them that way (Gen 1:31). Male and female have different weaknesses, generally speaking, as well as different strengths. Is it possible that, by virtue of their more caring and kindly natures, women aspiring to male headship roles are an easier target for deception? Is it possible that this is why Eve was the serpent's chosen target instead of Adam (Gen 3:1-4)?[8] Affirmative answers to these questions harmonize with the context. The charming gifts of sympathy and compassion given to women in abundance by God, and so desperately needed in an uncaring world, must be used by women in ministry in ways appropriate to their nature and role.

(12) "But women will be kept safe [saved] through childbirth, if they continue in faith, love and holiness with propriety" (1 Tim 2:15). This verse completes Paul's argument. He is not saying that women are saved on the basis of their having children, or because they go through the birth process. That would contradict everything he says elsewhere about salvation by grace through faith. Taking into account the whole context, the meaning of this concluding verse is obvious. The reference is to childbearing, a woman's primary role and most glorious calling. It illustrates the major difference between women and men. The verse ends with the qualifier, "if they continue in faith, love and holiness with propriety." Paul underscores the idea that the fulfillment of proper feminine roles in the church, combined with the virtues of faith, love, holiness, and propriety, is tangible proof of salvation.

A Word About Biblical Headship

Historically, Seventh-day Adventists have affirmed the validity of the biblical teaching of male headship—a theological concept which means that within the loving relationship of male-female equality and complementarity, God calls upon men to be heads of their homes (as husbands and fathers) and churches (as elders or pastors), and that He holds them accountable if they refuse to shoulder leadership responsibilities.[9] In recent times, however, some pro-ordination scholars have questioned the validity of the biblical doctrine of headship in the home and in the church.

One Adventist author writes: "Since 'headship' is often shorthand for hierarchy and control, and this type of hierarchy is directly linked to abuse, it is imperative for Christians to establish a biblical view of the relationship between women and men. Clearly any model that endorses abuse is questionable for any who take Jesus seriously, for He said: 'I am come that they might have life, and that they might have it more abundantly' (John 10:10 KJV), and 'Come unto me all ye that labour and are heavy laden, and I will give you rest' (Matt 11:28 KJV)."[10] The same author concludes that "there is no such thing as biblical 'headship.'"[11] Another Adventist author does not so radically reject headship, but confines headship and submission to the relationship of husbands and wives: "This post-Fall prescription of husband headship and wife submission was limited to the husband-wife relationship."[12]

However, 1 Corinthians 11:3, which refers to the relationship of men and women in public worship and *not* to the husband-wife relationship, presents us with an unmistakable order of headship: God, Christ, man, woman. The word translated "head" carries the meaning of "over" in the sense of a distinct position. God the Father occupies a distinct position over Christ, Christ over the man, and the man over the woman. Without some such order society would disintegrate, as would the organization of the church. Biblically speaking, headship was never intended to be dictatorial, but benevolent. First Corinthians 11:11-12 indicates that though men and women occupy distinct positions in the divine relational order, this does not grant them the right to abuse one another. The problem is never with the biblical view of the divine order, but with the people who distort it. Instead of trying to change what Scripture says, why not submit to God's revealed truth and preach it in such a way that people are changed?

Without a doubt we must have a biblical view of male-female relationships. We dare not cast aside the biblical teaching of male headship in home and church merely because some men have abused it. Should we stop eating good food because some of us eat too much of it and by doing so abuse ourselves? The Bible does not teach abusive but loving headship, sacrificial headship, the kind that is willing to die for the loved one. See Ephesians 5:24-28: "Now as the church submits to Christ, so also wives should submit to their husbands in everything. Husbands, love your wives, just as Christ loved the church and gave himself up for her and to present her to himself as a radiant church, without stain or wrinkle or any other blemish, but holy and blameless. In this same way, husbands ought to love their wives as their own bodies. He who loves his wife loves himself."

Of course, headship has the potential for abuse, but so does love when misunderstood. Women can abuse men by a manipulative use of submission and get almost anything they want from their men. Submission, too, must be Christlike.

Conclusion

Does 1 Timothy 2:11-15 help us find answers to the two fundamental questions: "May a woman be legitimately ordained [commissioned, appointed] to pastoral ministry?" and "If so, on what biblical basis?" Let us briefly review the salient information the passage presents.

1) The context indicates that the passage refers to the specific situation of the public gathering of believers for worship. 2) The reference is to all Christian women, not just to married women. 3) While the text does not prohibit women from learning, it prohibits them from teaching men and exercising authority over men in public worship in the role of the leader of the congregation, the church family. 4) The prohibition is universal, for all times and places. Paul stated his purpose in writing the epistle: "I am writing these instructions so that, if I am delayed, you will know how people ought to conduct themselves *in God's household, which is the church of the living God,* the pillar and foundation of the truth" (1 Tim 3:14, 15, emphasis mine). 5) The basis for the prohibition rests on

the order of creation, "Adam first, then Eve." 6) The text illuminates the differences in male and female roles. 7) Finally, the text is not confusing or problematic and can be understood by all.

The challenge facing the church today is not that of women preparing for ministry, but their proper training. Instead of preparing them for a role in ministry that would violate the instructions given in 1 Timothy 2:11-15 (and in other passages as well), why not prepare them for the role for which they are suited and to which God is calling them? That role is clarified for the Seventh-day Adventist church in the following counsel regarding specific ministry for women:

"There are women who should labor in the gospel ministry. In many respects they would do more good than the ministers who neglect to visit the flock of God."[13]

"The Lord has a work for women as well as for men. . . . The Saviour will reflect upon these self-sacrificing women the light of His countenance, and will give them a power that exceeds that of men. They can do *in families* a work that men cannot do, a work that reaches the inner life. They can come close to the hearts of those whom men cannot reach. Their labor is needed."[14]

"Those women who labor to teach souls to seek for the new birth in Christ Jesus, are doing a precious work. They consecrate themselves to God, and they are just as verily laborers for God as are their husbands. They can enter *families* to which ministers could find no access. They can listen to the sorrows of the depressed and oppressed. They can shed rays of light into discouraged souls. They can pray with them. They can open the Scriptures, and enlighten them from a 'Thus saith the Lord.'"[15]

"You are to do your duty to the women who labor in the gospel, whose work testifies that they are essential to carrying the truth into *families*. . . . The cause would suffer great loss without this kind of labor by women. Again and again the Lord has shown me that women teachers are just as greatly needed to do *the work to which He has appointed them as are men.*"[16]

Without question this counsel is based on biblical evidence and authority. Mrs. White was specific as to the nature of the ministry to which women are called by the Lord. It is a caring and compassionate ministry, once called "soul care," for which women are especially suited and qualified. It is ministry to families in their homes. It is a unique ministry, as important as the work of the minister but differing from it. For this specific ministry women must be trained.

Finally, we will not solve the present conflict over ordination by changing the subject or by substituting words like "commissioning" and "appointing" for "ordaining" in reference to the method by which the church sanctions its ministers. Any proposed solution must clearly accord with Scripture, which is our ultimate authority.

Does Paul really prohibit women from speaking in church? Wrong question! The right question is: Does Paul, in 1 Timothy 2:11-15, prohibit women from teaching and exercising authority over men in public worship assemblies as the

leader of the congregation? The answer, no matter how difficult it may be to accept, is Yes, he does. Our time and energy would be much better spent were we to
use them seeking to understand what Paul means by what he says, and in learning
how to apply it, than in trying to prove that he doesn't really say what he says.

Endnotes

1. Currently the words "commissioned" and "appointed" are often being used in place
   of "ordained."
2. See Samuele Bacchiocchi, *Women in the Church: A Biblical Study on the Role of Women in the
   Church* (Berrien Springs, Mich.: Biblical Perspectives, 1987); C. Raymond Holmes, *The
   Tip of an Iceberg* (Berrien Springs, Mich.: Adventists Affirm and Pointer Publications, 1994);
   and Samuel Koranteng-Pipim, *Searching the Scriptures: Women's Ordination and the Call to
   Biblical Fidelity* (Berrien Springs, Mich.: Berean Books, 1995). See also Samuel Koranteng-
   Pipim, *Receiving the Word: How New Approaches to the Bible Impact our Biblical Faith and
   Lifestyle* (Berrien Springs, Mich.: Berean Books, 1996), pp. 115-129; and *Adventists Affirm*
   1/1 (Spring 1987) (Appendix A in the current volume), 1/2 (Fall 1987), 9/1 (Spring 1995).
3. See Ellen G. White, *Selected Messages,* 1:17; *The Great Controversy,* p. vii; *The Ministry of
   Healing,* p. 462.
4. For documentation, see Samuel Koranteng-Pipim, "Are Those Things So?—Part I: An Evaluation of the Biblical Arguments of *Women in Ministry,*"in the current volume, pp. 179-218,
   especially the section on "Speculative Interpretations," pp. 191-195.
5. Ellen G. White, *The Great Controversy,* p. viii.
6. Ellen G. White, *Selected Messages,* 2:114.
7. Cited in *Women in Ministry* (Berrien Springs, Mich.: Andrews University Press, 1998),
   p. 278.
8. See Thomas R. Schreiner, "An Interpretation of 1 Timothy 2:9-15: A Dialogue with Scholarship" in *Women in the Church,* Andreas J. Köstenberger, Thomas R. Schreiner, H. Scott
   Baldwin, eds. (Grand Rapids, Mich.: Baker Books, 1995), pp. 144-146.
9. Unsigned editorial [J. H. Waggoner, resident editor], "Woman's Place in the Gospel," *The
   Signs of the Times,* Dec. 19, 1878, p. 38. Key portions of this editorial are reproduced on p.
   291 of this book. For a recent re-statement of the biblical teaching of headship, see *Seventh-
   day Adventists Believe . . . ,* pp. 303-305.
10. Sheryll Prinz-McMillan, "Who's in Charge of the Family?" in *The Welcome Table,* Patricia
    A. Habada and Rebecca Frost Brillhart, eds. (Langley Park, Md.: TEAMPress, 1995),
    p. 199.
11. Ibid., p. 216.
12. Richard M. Davidson, in *Women in Ministry,* p. 284.
13. Ellen G. White, *Evangelism,* p. 472.
14. Ibid., pp. 464-465, emphasis mine.
15. Ellen G. White Manuscript Release #330, in *Manuscript Releases,* 5:327, emphasis mine.
16. Ellen G. White, *Evangelism,* p. 493, emphasis mine.

Chapter 10

One Chilling Word

S. Lawrence Maxwell

[First published in ADVENTISTS AFFIRM, Spring 1995, pp. 38-41]

~

Why not ordain women to the Adventist ministry? Everyone knows that the women in our church are as good as the men; in character, many are better. Women have proved themselves capable in every other church position they have held. And in many cases it is *better* that a woman be the minister, especially when ministering to a woman; women are more understanding of women's needs.

So why not? Only male pride and selfishness block women from serving in the roles God wants them to fill. That must be right; I hear it all the time.

I could get quite enthusiastic about women's ordination except for one word I find in my Bible. To be frank with you, that one word totally chills my enthusiasm.

It is the name of a man. The word—the man—is Korah, perhaps more easily recognized when linked with his two equally ambitious friends, Dathan and Abiram.

It seems to me that every argument brought up to support or to oppose women's ordination today was present in Korah, Dathan, and Abiram's campaign to get themselves ordained. If I am right—that is, if the arguments are as similar as I think they are—ordaining women to the Adventist ministry could prove to be just as offensive to God as ordaining those three men would have been, with disastrous consequences to our church if we go ahead.

I confess that I find this prospect definitely chilling.

S. Lawrence Maxwell, *prior to retirement, edited SIGNS OF THE TIMES.*

Reasons Given Today

The reasons I have heard in support of women's ordination include:

1. *Insider dominance.* Long ago (I have heard it said) a small part of the denomination decided that only members of their group should be ordained. Since that group happened to be entirely male, men have ever since made sure that the powers and privileges associated with ordination are limited to men only.

2. *Dimensions of the priesthood.* Every member of the church is a priest. Peter wrote, "Ye are a chosen generation, a royal priesthood (1 Peter 2:9). Therefore, obviously, women are as eligible for ordination to the priesthood as are men.

3. *Experience proves eligibility.* By having served successfully in many lesser positions within the church structure, women have proved their ability and suitability for ordination and ought therefore to be advanced to the more-responsible positions currently limited to fully ordained males.

4. *God's call.* Over the last several years numerous Adventist women have publicly testified of their conviction that God has called them to the ordained ministry. This call, it is claimed, not only proves their suitability for the ministry but also God's desire that they be ordained.

5. *Preparation creates obligation.* Many Adventist women have already prepared themselves to fill positions as ordained ministers. The church is obligated to let them climax their preparation with ordination. This is especially true where church leadership has encouraged a woman with the promise that her preparation would lead to ordination.

6. *Danger of mutiny.* There is such a strong feeling among the laity in favor of women's ordination that leadership will have enormous difficulties controlling the rebellion that will break out if permission for ordination is not given soon.

So much for the reasons given in our day. A few more will emerge as we proceed. But let us look at the issues in Korah's day. See how similar they are!

Reasoning in Korah's Time

1. *Insider dominance.* Korah snarled at Moses and Aaron, "Ye take too much upon you: . . . wherefore then lift ye up yourselves above the congregation of the Lord?" (Num 16:3). Clearly, in Korah's view, Moses and Aaron had conspired to restrict the priesthood to Aaron's family, forever keeping administrative and priestly powers in their own hands.

2. *Dimensions of the priesthood.* Korah quoted from God's instruction to Moses at Mount Sinai, "Tell the children of Israel, . . . Ye shall be unto me a kingdom of priests, and an holy nation" (Ex 19:6). The whole nation were holy priests! Then why was the priesthood limited to one family? Clearly this was contrary to God's will!

3. *Experience proves eligibility.* The 250 men who presented themselves for ordination along with Korah, Dathan, and Abiram were experienced leaders in the congregation. They were recognized by their peers as "princes of the assembly, famous in the congregation, men of renown" (Num 16:2). Korah himself was a deacon. So of course it was appropriate to ordain them as priests.

4. *God's call.* Those 253 men would not have presented themselves for ordination if they had not been convinced that God had called them. The laity agreed. In the estimation of the congregation they were "people of the Lord" (Num 16:41).

5. *Preparation creates obligation.* Every one of the 253 had prepared for the priesthood. The censer was the sacred object in which a priest burned incense while interceding for sinners. Each one of the 253 had gone to the effort of providing himself with a censer and, probably, priestly clothing also. So they ought to have been allowed to be priests, considering all the effort and expense they had gone to to prepare.

6. *Danger of mutiny.* Korah and his party had tremendous backing. The congregation were convinced that Moses and Aaron had abused their authority. If the leaders did not approve the new ordination policy, the members were prepared to stone them.

God's Response

There really is a close resemblance between the reasoning of our day and the reasons given in Korah's, so it is interesting to examine God's response. What comes through very, very clearly is that God didn't buy Korah's arguments. He wasn't impressed at all, except negatively, but *negatively* He was very greatly impressed, so much so that He opened the ground under the three leaders and burned up their 250 cohorts.

Oh, but the church members were angry then! Talk about mutiny! Today's leaders who fear the wrath of the laity can point to the public reaction in Korah's day as evidence. Even after the demanding delegation was so dramatically destroyed, the Israelites were still sufficiently furious the next morning that they gathered against Moses and Aaron shouting, "Ye have killed the people of the Lord" (Num 16:41). Only the immediate intervention of a devastating plague saved the godly leaders' lives.

But do note that God did intervene to save Moses and Aaron. God was on the side of the leaders who refused to ordain Korah, Dathan, and Abiram in spite of their reasoning and the obvious support they had from the congregation. Because what happened in those days happened in order to teach us things we need to know about God, we can expect God to support leaders who resist women's ordination today.

"Whom I Shall Choose"

When the uprising had cooled somewhat, God moved forward to settle the question of ordination for all time. I find what He did next extremely significant. He told Moses to ask the leader of each of the twelve tribes for a rod. Each prince was to write his name on his rod, with Aaron's name on the rod for the tribe of Levi. Then these rods were to be placed before the Lord in the tabernacle overnight. God said, "The man's rod, whom I shall choose, shall blossom" (Num 17:2-4).

The key words in this whole experience, in my estimation, are those four: "Whom I shall choose."

Whom *I* shall choose. Whom *God* shall choose. What comes through to me as the most important lesson is that God chooses who shall be ordained, and that He has reserved this choice exclusively to Himself. It is not for us to choose who should be ordained. That is God's prerogative. Our reasons may sound marvelously persuasive. We may say, "It seemed good to us . . . ," but we do not make the choice. God does. In the days of Israel, God chose the family of Aaron. He did not choose the family of Korah or of Dathan or of Abiram or of any of the 250. When they tried to push their way into the priesthood, no matter how good their reasons sounded to themselves or to the members of the congregation, they were still not part of that group which God had chosen, and He rejected them.

The Missing Text

Can the proponents of women's ordination show from the Bible or from the Spirit of Prophecy any clear statement that God has chosen women for ordination? We have seen that Korah's six reasons justifying his ordination were insufficient. Because today's reasons supporting women's ordination are so similar to Korah's, we must conclude that they also are insufficient.

We do, on the other hand, find specific texts in the Bible saying that ordained ministers should be men. Correction: not just *should* be men, they *must* be men. See 1 Timothy 3:2: "A bishop then must be . . . the husband of one wife." Husbands are men. The Greek has "one-woman man," and the word used for man in this passage is *aner.* Paul might have used *anthropos,* the more generic word for "human" or "person," and if he had intended to say that bishops could be men or women he very likely might have. But he didn't. The word he used specifically distinguishes men from women. But do note that he did not say that just any man could be a bishop, even as in the Old Testament not just any son of Aaron could be a priest. The office has always been limited. The Christian leader Paul spoke of must be "blameless" and married, "vigilant, sober, of good behaviour," etc. There is a long list of requirements that eventually eliminates almost all men and leaves only a very few eligible. Do note that not only the women are ineligible. So are 99% of all men.

If the defenders of women's ordination could find even one text or Spirit of Prophecy statement which says that a minister must be a woman, whether married to one husband or not, what a difference it would make to this whole discussion! But in all the years that some have been asking for women's ordination, no one, not even the most zealous, has found such a text or statement. And when I think what happened to those men of old who set up their own criteria and said that they were fit when God had not said they were, then I feel a cold chill in my bones. Do we want what happened to Israel that day to happen to our church today? I don't.

To avoid her fate, Jesus said, "Remember Lot's wife." Perhaps, to avoid his fate, we should add, "Remember Korah."

Chapter 11

Are Those Things So?—Part I:
A Summary and Evaluation of Key Biblical Arguments of *Women in Ministry*

Samuel Koranteng-Pipim

~

Introduction

The Apostle Paul commended the Bereans for "receiving the word" and "searching the Scriptures" to see "whether those things were so" (Acts 17:11). Their example suggests that whenever influential scholars and leaders urge new beliefs and practices on the church, members who are committed to biblical fidelity should always ask, "Are those things so?"

The authors of *Women in Ministry,* the pro-ordination book from the Seventh-day Adventist Theological Seminary at Andrews University, have proposed a new understanding of Scripture which would result in the church adopting a new belief and practice. They have submitted their volume as a "resource tool for decision making," correctly recognizing that the ordination of women *as elders or pastors* is a theological issue.[1] As such, it is only through a correct understanding of Scripture—determining "whether those things were so"—that the church can legitimately depart from its 150-year-old practice of ordination.

One supporter of the book adds: "The ultimate purpose of *Women in Ministry* is to provide information for informed decision making, a clear indication that there is a decision to be made. In so doing, the book calls the church to do some

---

Samuel Koranteng-Pipim, Ph.D., *is Director of Public Campus Ministries for the Michigan Conference of Seventh-day Adventists.*

serious Bible study. If the basis of our decision is going to be in our interpretation of Scripture, we must do it well."[2]

The question before us is: Did the writers "do their work well"?

The editor of *Women in Ministry* states in the prologue: "We believe that the biblical, theological, and historical perspectives elaborated in this book affirm women in pastoral leadership."[3] The author of one of the chapters who describes the volume as "the official view of the Seminary and the position of virtually all of its faculty" thinks that this work by twenty Andrews University scholars will "demonstrate that the Seminary faculty stands for sound Biblical and historical scholarship on this contemporary and controversial issue."[4]

Similarly, some influential promoters of *Women in Ministry* are applauding it in Seventh-day Adventist publications as the product of "skillful exegesis of Scripture and careful examination of relevant E. G. White materials,"[5] a volume that presents "a powerful argument" and "an impressive array of evidence" for the ordination of women,[6] and one which "brings together a wealth of material and deserves to be taken seriously.[7]

To evaluate these claims, we must follow Paul's counsel to "prove all things [and] hold fast that which is good" (1 Thess 5:21). Like the Bereans, we must carefully examine *Women in Ministry* to see "whether those things were so."

Summary of This Analysis

Contrary to this chorus of claims by authors and reviewers, I am going to argue in this chapter and in its companion chapter later in the book that there is no evidence in the Bible, in the writings of Ellen G. White, or in the practice of the early Seventh-day Adventist church to support ordaining women as elders or pastors. Despite its authors' noble motives and laudable efforts, I will contend that *Women in Ministry* is constructed upon questionable assumptions and imaginative and speculative interpretations.

The editor alerts readers to this very possibility. She writes in the introduction, "The Seminary Ad Hoc Committee on Hermeneutics and Ordination prayerfully submits this book, not as the final answer to whether or not the Seventh-day Adventist Church should ordain its women in ministry, but rather as a resource tool for decision making. *While recognizing that good decisions are based on hard facts, we are also cognizant of the fact that at times clear evidence may be lacking, thus making necessary the use of sanctified judgment and imagination to resolve questions and issues.*"[8]

In evaluating the authors' "use of sanctified judgment and imagination to resolve questions and issues" regarding women's ordination as elders and pastors, my assessment of *Women in Ministry* will show that the book is based on: (1) ambiguity and vagueness, (2) straw-man arguments, (3) substantial leaps of logic, (4) arguments from silence, (5) speculative interpretations (6) questionable re-interpretations of the Bible, (7) distorted biblical reasoning, (8) misleading and erroneous claims regarding Adventist history, (9) a seriously flawed concept of "moral imperative," and (10) a fanciful view of the Holy Spirit's leading.[9] The first seven of these will appear in this chapter; the remaining three I will take up in the companion chapter later in the book. At the close of that chapter, I will conclude by mentioning the implications arising from the book's mistaken conclusions.

1. Ambiguity and Vagueness

Several of the chapters in *Women in Ministry* are written in such a way as to be unclear about the issues that divide us. Authors repeatedly avoid a clear statement of what is at issue (the ordination of women *as elders or pastors*) and use a phrase which may be intended to win more support (women in ministry or leadership). To illustrate this fuzziness, I will mention the use of expressions like "full equality," "equal partnership," and "women in leadership and public ministry."

(a) "Full Equality" and "Equal Partnership." One of the fundamental arguments underlying *Women in Ministry* is that at creation Adam and Eve were "fully equal," enjoying "total egalitarianism in marriage." According to the book's leading proponent of this view, prior to the Fall there was no role differentiation between male and female. Role distinctions came as the result of the Fall. Because today the relation between husband and wife, even in Christian homes, "does not quite approach total role interchangeableness," Christians should aspire to God's "ultimate ideal" of "full equality" in their homes. Thus, God's ideal for Christian homes "is still the partnership of equals that is set forth from the beginning."[10]

To speak of "full equality" as the ideal for today without coming to terms with the nature and extent of this equality leaves the reader to wonder just how far believers in this view are willing to go. Some, no doubt, will take it to mean a partnership of identical roles, and others will probably understand it to mean a partnership with different roles of equal value. Thus the phrase "full and equal" could be hailed by radical feminists who reject the Bible's teaching that because of God's creation arrangement, He calls upon men today to bear the primary headship responsibility as leaders in their homes (e.g., 1 Cor 11:3, 8, 9; Eph 5:23-33; cf. 1 Tim 2:12, 13).

Even more, just as radical feminists seek "full equality" by getting rid of *gender* or *sex roles* in marriage and in the church, so also does gay theology seek to bring about "equality" between homosexuals and heterosexuals by obliterating *sexual identity*. Radical feminists and pro-gay advocates can also endorse the "full equality" or "total role interchangeableness" concepts as validations of their claim that there were no gender-based role distinctions at creation.

As far as I know, none of the authors of *Women in Ministry* have endorsed radical feminist and gay theology. Yet this kind of fuzziness or this lack of clarity is a common prelude to liberalism's revisionist theologies. I suggest that we should not speak of "full equality," "equal partnership" or even "shared responsibilities" without stating unambiguously that to act as "equal and joint partners" does not mean to act identically. Individuals in a relationship can be equal and yet have different roles. They can act "jointly" and yet not act identically; they may "share" duties, but not bear the same responsibilities.[11]

This lack of clarity on "full equality" and "equal partnership" also overlooks the fact that Ellen G. White rejects the egalitarian model of "total role interchange-ability." Despite the abuse of God's creation arrangement for role relations in the home, she writes that "heaven's ideal of this sacred [marriage] relation" is one in which the man is the head of the home. This kind of relationship is "what God designed it should be" (*Thoughts from the Mount of Blessing*, pp. 64, 65). And because "the husband is the head of the family, as Christ is the head of the church," she writes, "any course which the wife may pursue to lessen his influence and lead him to come down from that dignified, responsible position is displeasing to God" (*Testimonies for the Church*, 1:307).

At a time of rampant divorces, sometimes because each party seeks to be the "head," we need to be clear on what we mean by "total role interchangeableness" as God's ideal for the home. And at a time of increasing homosexual demands for marital rights, we need to say unambiguously that men were not created equal with women personally or even physically *as candidates to be spouses of men*. Failure to do so will open a welcome door for those who seek to nullify the biblical case for divinely-instituted role differences and a monogamous heterosexual relationship. Proponents of gay theology within Adventism have not lost sight of this fact.[12]

What has been said about the vagueness of expressions like "full equality" and "joint leadership" also applies to using the expression "mutual submission" as though Ephesians 5:21 ("Submit to one another") means complete reciprocity ("wives submit to husbands and husbands submit to wives *as if there were no role distinctions among you.*")[13]

(b) "Women in Leadership" and "Women in Public Ministry." The book frequently refers to women serving in positions of "leadership" and "public ministry." For instance, it is claimed that in Bible times nothing barred women from holding "the highest offices of leadership, including authoritative teaching roles that constituted 'headship' over men," and that "in the late-nineteenth century, women were active in [the Seventh-day Adventist] church leadership and ministry," serving in "both leadership and ministerial positions in the early history of the Seventh-day Adventist denomination."[14] Or that "throughout both the Old and New Testaments women served not only in home and family administration but also in public and religious spheres. The roles of women in Scripture are varied and vigorous"; "the entire [biblical] canon can be seen to affirm women, whether in the home or in public ministry, or both."[15]

What, exactly, is meant by "leadership" or "public ministry"? These terms are often not clearly defined in *Women in Ministry*. If they mean positions of genuine, significant responsibility in the church, then the implication that women in churches today should likewise be given roles in which they can exercise their spiritual gifts in significant ways is not biblically objectionable. In fact, this is what Seventh-day Adventists historically have believed and practiced.

If, however, "leadership" and "public ministry" mean women served in positions of ultimate responsibility *as priests, apostles, and elders or pastors* in Bible times and as *elders or pastors* in early Seventh-day Adventist history, then, as we shall later show, the authors of *Women in Ministry* do not sufficiently substantiate their claim.

My point is this: the basic issue is not "women in ministry" (a non-issue), but "women *as ordained ministers-pastors;* not women "in leadership" or "public ministry," but women *as elders or pastors.* Broad, undefined terms can be misleading.

2. "Straw Man" Arguments

A straw man is a set of arguments a writer claims his opponent believes so that he can attack them and gain an easy victory. Typically, straw men are presented as unavoidable and unacceptable alternatives to the writers' position. Two examples in *Women in Ministry* grow out of the suggestion that anyone who rejects women's ordination 1) views "women as inferior to men," or 2) wants "all women to be in submission to all men."[16] Let's look at these straw men.

(a) **Male Superiority and Female Inferiority?** When *Women in Ministry* concludes that male headship (and female submission) "is part of God's plan for fallen human beings rather than an original mandate for the sinless world,"[17] it positions itself between liberal feminists (who reject any form of male headship and female submission before and after the Fall) and conservative opponents of women's ordination (who accept headship–submission, before and after the Fall).

Unlike liberal feminists, the authors of *Women in Ministry* believe in a "post-Fall" headship, a loving servant leadership of the husband.[18] (Conservatives opposed to women's ordination also hold to the same kind of loving servant headship, but they argue that headship was instituted by God at creation and reiterated at the Fall.[19]) *Women in Ministry* rejects headship *at creation,* arguing instead for "total egalitarianism"—an alleged divine ideal of "full equality" which is void of functional role differentiations between male and female.[20]

But in giving reasons for their rejection of headship before the Fall they resort to "straw man" arguments and misleading reasoning. For example, in the chapter that provides the exegetical and theological framework for the entire book, we read that "there is no hint of ontological or functional superiority-inferiority or headship-submission between male and female."[21] Does a belief in the biblical teaching of headship–submission before the Fall necessitate a belief in male superiority and female inferiority at creation? It doesn't, and to my knowledge, this view is not held by any credible Adventist scholar opposed to women's ordination.[22] The opponents I know believe that as human beings Adam and Eve were equal (that is, *ontologically,* neither one was superior or inferior to the other), but they were expected to do different things (that is, there was to be *functional role differentiation*).

The issue in the debate over women's ordination is not whether women were created equal to men (a non-issue), but rather whether God instituted a functional role differentiation between male and female when He created both of them equal. This is the real issue in the headship–submission debate. In my earlier work, *Searching the Scriptures,* I have offered several lines of evidence for headship before the Fall.[23]

Regrettably, the authors did not interact with the biblical evidence. They set up and knocked down straw-man arguments about superiority and inferiority. And having shown that Adam and Eve were created equal, neither superior to the other in worth (ontological equality), the writers give the false impression that they have proved that our first parents were created without prescribed role distinctions (functional role differentiations).

If no headship–submission existed at creation, these authors in *Women in Ministry* will need to explain, for example, why Adam (not Eve) is repeatedly held responsible for the entrance of sin and death into the world even though it was Eve who sinned first (Rom 5:12-21; 1 Cor 15:21-22). Note that in Genesis 3, God also approached Adam (not Eve) first after sin, suggesting the reality of male headship before the Fall.[24]

(b) "All Women Under All Men"? One writer in the book sees only three options in the discussion of women's relation to men: (1) Scripture instructs "all women to be under the authority of all men" (this is assumed to be the position of conservatives *opposed* to women's ordination); (2) "Women (when married) are [to be] under the headship of their husbands, but in the church men and women stand together in full equality under Christ" (the position of conservatives *for* women's ordination— the posture *Women in Ministry* wants to project); (3) or "the Apostle Paul contradicts himself on this issue in his various New Testament writings and thus should be ignored—or that his counsel is outdated in this modern era" (the liberal or radical feminist position from which the book wants to distance itself).[25]

Writers of *Women in Ministry* must be commended for going to great lengths in distancing themselves from radical feminist and liberal hermeneutics.[26] It is an error, however, to give the impression that view #1 is the position of conservatives opposed to women's ordination. To my knowledge, the conservative Adventist scholars opposed to women's ordination do not argue that "all women must be in submission to all men."[27] Neither do they claim that headship gives "any male preponderance over all females," nor that it gives "males the right to rule over women."[28]

What Adventist opponents of women's ordination hold is that biblical headship-leadership, in contrast to male domination, was instituted by God to govern the relationship of the man and woman, two spiritually-equal human beings, in both the home and the church. In this relation, it is the man who exercises primary responsibility for leading the home and church families in a God-glorifying direction (cf. 1 Cor 11:3; Eph 5:21-33), and God holds these men responsible when they abdicate their God-assigned responsibilities as husbands and elders or pastors.

In contrast to the view that "all women must be in submission to all men," Adventist opponents of women's ordination argue that in the home women must be in submission to *their own husbands,* and in the church they must be in submission to *the elders or pastors,* who are appointed by God to positions of headship.

This is why I say the authors created straw-man arguments when they attacked the shortcomings of ugly alternatives which are not held by their opponents (i.e, the suggestion that those who reject women's ordination want to "treat women as inferior to men," or view "all women to be in submission to all men"), thus giving the impression that there are no other credible alternatives when in truth there are.

3. Substantial Leaps of Logic

Several insightful and otherwise excellent chapters in *Women in Ministry* display substantial leaps of logic. In these instances the conclusions do not follow from the established premises. As examples of leaps of logic, I will discuss the claims about "the priesthood of all believers" and "slavery and women's ordination."

(a) **"Priesthood of All Believers."** A recurring claim in *Women in Ministry* is that the doctrine of "the priesthood of all believers" leads to an egalitarian (i.e., "equalitarian") model of the ordained ministry, in which gender plays no role. The author of the lead chapter writes:

"Males functioned as priests in the days of the biblical patriarchs as well as after God's covenant with Israel at Mount Sinai. With the move from Israel to the Christian church, however, a radical transformation occurred. A new priesthood is unfolded in the New Testament, that of all believers. The Christian church is a fellowship of believer priests. Such an ecclesiology, such an understanding of the nature and mission of the church, no longer poses roadblocks to women serving in any ministry. It in fact demands a partnership of men and women *in all expressions of the ordained ministry.* The recognition of the priesthood of all believers implies a church in which women and men work side by side in various functions and ministries, endowed with gifts distributed by the Holy Spirit according to his sovereign will (1 Cor 12:7-11)."[29]

The claim that women can also function "in all expressions of the ordained ministry" (including the headship roles of elders or pastors) does not follow. The priesthood of all believers is not about particular church functions of men and women. Christians are part of a priesthood because every believer has direct access to God through Christ without any need for other intermediaries (cf. Heb 10:19-22). The New Testament doctrine of the "priesthood of all believers" (1 Pet 2:5, 9-12) also recognizes that the church is a worshiping community (a *priestly* people called to offer "spiritual sacrifices" of praise and prayer) and also a witnessing community (a *missionary* people called to declare the "praises of him who called you out of darkness into his wonderful light"). Every church member—whether man or woman—has been called to the soul-winning ministry of the church.

It does not follow that every church member may perform an identical function in the church.[30] The Bible itself establishes what the qualities of an elder or pastor should be (1 Tim 3:1-7). Among other things, the elder or pastor must be "the husband of one wife," one who "rules well his own house" (vv. 2, 4, 5; Titus 1:6). This gender-based qualification cannot be legitimately fulfilled by a woman.[31]

Moreover, the apostle Peter makes it clear that the doctrine of "the priesthood of all believers" was not a new innovation "unfolded in the New Testament." Rather, it was based on an Old Testament concept (1 Pet 2:5, 9-12; cf. Ex 19:5-6). In the Old Testament, there was "the priesthood of all believers." God declared, "Ye shall be unto me a kingdom of priests, and an holy nation" (Ex 19:6). Yet, no women served as priests in the Old Testament. Not even all males served as priests, but only those from the tribe of Levi.[32] And whereas all priests were Levites, not all Levites were priests. Only the family of Aaron and his male descendants were assigned this responsibility (Ex 28:1, 41, 43; Num 3:10, 32; 20:28; 25:10-13).

If there was such a "radical transformation" of the Old Testament concept of "priesthood of all believers" as to demand "a partnership of men and women in all expressions of the ordained ministry," how is it that we cannot find a single unequivocal example of women serving as elders or overseers in the New Testament?

To claim, as many writers in *Women in Ministry* do, that the priesthood of all believers eliminates gender role distinctions requires a substantial leap of logic. It is not validated in the Old Testament or the New Testament. Pro-ordinationists can only sustain their reinterpretation of the concept by imposing on the Bible the feminist concept of "full equality," understood to mean the total obliteration of male-female role differentiation.

(b) Slavery and Women's Ordination. Another manifestation of a leap of logic is the claim that because the arguments of those opposed to women's ordination "parallel" those of nineteenth-century slave holders, and because slavery was later shown to be wrong, opposition to women's ordination must also be wrong.[33]

For example, one writer puts in two parallel columns the arguments of those who favored slavery and of those who favor limiting ordination to men. He thus shows that proponents of both positions argue that: (1) their position is based on a high view of Scripture; (2) their view is established on divine creation; (3) Jesus set the precedent (He used a slavery analogy in Luke 17; He ordained only males); (4) the apostles approved Jesus' precedent; (5) there is divine blessing for upholding it; (6) there exists a slippery-slope argument (if you abandon it, it will jeopardize a divine arrangement).[34]

It is puzzling that no committee member caught the fallacy in this kind of argument. Let me illustrate. Are we Adventists to suggest that because our arguments for the Sabbath parallel those used by slave holders (high view of Scripture, divine creation ordinance, the precedent set by Jesus and the apostles, etc.), our doctrine of the Sabbath must necessarily be wrong? Certainly not.

Thus, the fact that pro-slavery theologians argued their case in this manner does not make their case right. And the fact that anti-women's ordination scholars argue for the creation ordinance and the absence of Bible precedents does not make their case wrong. The rightness of a position should be judged on the merits of the issue, in the light of Scripture's witness.[35]

"The headship principle is different from slavery in two major ways: (1) the headship principle was a creation ordinance, while slavery was never instituted by God; and (2) as a pre-Fall creation ordinance, the headship principle is morally right and therefore morally binding on all God's people, irrespective of the place and time in which they live; but slavery, as a post-fall distortion of God's will for humanity, is morally offensive and cannot be justified under biblical Christianity. (The book of Philemon shows this.)"[36]

4. Arguments from Silence

These are instances in which the book's authors attempt to deduce some inferences from the silence of Scripture. Most of these deal with the "culture of the times" argument. Let me explain.

There is no record in the Bible of any ordination of women, such as priests in the Old Testament and apostles and elders or pastors in the New Testament. *Women in Ministry* argues that this lack of biblical precedent should be understood as a cultural accommodation to oppressive structures (race, gender, religion, etc.) in existence during Bible times. Thus, the authors claim, the failure of Jesus to ordain women as apostles and the New Testament church's failure to ordain women as elders and pastors were concessions that had to be made to accommodate the (supposedly) insensitive, male-chauvinistic or anti-women cultural practices of their times so as not to jeopardize their ministries prematurely.

In making this claim, proponents of women's ordination are simply arguing from silence. I will examine how *Women in Ministry* deals with the following examples: "Jesus and the ministry of women," "the apostolic church and women," "women leaders of the NT church," and "Junia as a female apostle." (The claim that Phoebe was a "female minister" will be taken up in a later section.)

(a) **Jesus and the Ministry of Women.** What does *Women in Ministry* have to say in response to the fact that Jesus did not ordain any woman among the twelve apostles? The authors offer two sets of arguments. First, "within the social restraints of his day, Paul and the early church (like Jesus) did not act precipitously."[37] Or as another writer states: "Custom here may have been so entrenched that Jesus simply stopped short of fully implementing a principle that he made explicit and emphatic [i.e., the inclusion of "women, Samaritans and Gentiles"]. . . . However, at this time this may have been an ideal awaiting its time of actualization."[38]

Second, they argue that if opponents to women's ordination insist that Jesus' example of ordaining no women apostles should be followed, by the same logic,

Gentiles should also be excluded from the category of apostles since Christ never ordained a Gentile. "While Jesus treated women and Gentiles in a way that was revolutionary for His day," argues one writer, "yet He did not ordain as one of His disciples either a Gentile or a woman. But this pattern was no more normative for the future roles of women in church leadership than for future roles of Gentiles."[39]

These arguments are flawed. With respect to the argument that the "entrenched custom" of those times would not have permitted Christ and the early church to have acted "precipitously," we must point out that such a view, in effect, charges our Lord Jesus Christ with insensitivity or false accommodation to the "injustice" women suffered in His day. How could this be, when Scripture teaches that Jesus never yielded to sin (Heb 4:15)? "Sin" surely includes the sin of gender injustice. The Gospels tell us that Jesus never hesitated to correct his culture when issues of right and wrong were at stake. His treatment of women also contrasted sharply with that of the rabbis of His day.[40]

On why Christ never ordained a Gentile, the Bible provides an answer. He chose twelve *Jewish* apostles because in God's divine wisdom, the church began among the Jews, and it was all Jewish at the beginning ("salvation is of the Jews" John 4:22; cf. Rom 3:1, 2; Acts 1:8). Seventh-day Adventists understand that the 70 weeks determined for the Jews (Dan 9:24ff) still had several years to run. There were no Gentile leaders in the church in Christ's day, but there were many qualified, spiritual women. The New Testament actually does report some Gentile apostles (2 Cor 1:19; 1 Thess 1:1; 2 Thess 1:1, Silvanus?), but not one female apostle (we'll look at Junia later). Thus, those who attempt to present a "Gentile" argument to counter the absence of women apostles among Christ's followers apparently fail to understand Christ's prophetic priority of beginning His mission with the house of Israel (cf. Matt 10:5-6).

If Jesus had wanted to demonstrate that women had full access to all leadership roles in the church, He could easily have chosen and ordained six men and their wives as apostles, since the wives of apostles frequently accompanied their husbands (1 Cor 9:5). But He did not. Christ could have chosen and ordained at least one of the women who were actively involved in His ministry, traveling to the places He was teaching, and supporting Him and His disciples with their own money (see Luke 8:1-3). But He did not. He could have ordained His own mother, since she already had heaven's certification as "highly favored" (Luke 1:28, 30). But He did not. He could have chosen and ordained Mary, just as He commissioned her to bear witness to His resurrection (Mark 16:9ff.; John 20:11ff.). But He did not. Christ could have ordained the Samaritan woman as an apostle, since she defied several "cultural" stigmas (a woman five times divorced, living unlawfully with a man, and a Samaritan) to become a powerful and successful evangelist (John 4). But He did not. Instead, after spending all night in prayer (Luke 6:12), Christ appointed twelve men as His apostles (Matt 10:2-4; Mark 3:13-19). Why?

Was it because He did not want to act "precipitously" in light of the "restraints of His day"? Was it because He lacked the courage to stand against gender injustice entrenched in His culture? Or was it because women were not capable or qualified? No. Jesus did not ordain even one woman as an apostle because He understood the headship principle He Himself had instituted at creation, and He submitted to its authority.

(b) **The Apostolic Church and Women.** One author in *Women in Ministry* writes: "While women may not have immediately received full and equal partnership with men in the ministry of the church, evidence of women in leadership roles in the early church is sufficient to demonstrate that they were not barred from positions of influence, leadership and even headship over men."[41]

Here is a paradox. How may women not "immediately" have "received full and equal partnership with men in the ministry" and yet at the same time exercise "leadership and even headship over men"? It can only be one or the other. Either they served as leaders (elders-pastors) or they did not. By inserting the word "immediately" without telling us how much time elapsed before women allegedly received the "equal partnership," is the writer attempting to marry biblical faith with feminist egalitarianism? The New Testament shows that women were actively involved in soul-winning ministry but never served in the headship roles of elder or pastor.

Contrary to the suggestion that women could not "immediately" receive "full and equal partnership with men in the ministry," the New Testament writers note the active role of women in gospel ministry. We read about the significant contributions of Mary, Martha, Joanna, Susanna (Luke 8:2, 3; Acts 1:14), Tabitha (Acts 9:36), Lydia, Phoebe, Lois, Eunice, Priscilla, Tryphena, Tryposa, Persis, Euodia, Syntyche, and Junia (Acts 16:14, 15; 18:26; 21:8, 9; Rom 16:1-4, 6, 7, 12; Phil 4:3). Yet these women were not ordained to the role of apostle, elder or pastor, not because of any "social restraints" against which the early believers chose not to act "precipitously," but because the New Testament church understood that the creation arrangement of headship precluded women from exercising the leadership function of apostle, elder, or pastor in the worshiping community.

(c) **Women Leaders of the New Testament Church?** The above section shows some of the inconsistencies in *Women in Ministry*. On one hand, the authors argue that social restraints precluded women from "equal partnership with men in ministry." Yet they proceed to argue that New Testament evidence suggests that some women actually exercised "positions of influence, leadership and even headship over men." As evidence, an impressive roster of women is listed: Phoebe, Junia, women at Philippi, Euodia and Syntyche, etc.[42]

One of the greatest weaknesses of the book is that while it helpfully provides an inventory of prominent women in the Bible (and in Seventh-day Adventist history), showing that women indeed functioned in spheres of genuine, significant responsibility in soul-winning ministry, *Women in Ministry* proves the exact opposite of what it sets out to demonstrate. Despite the significant ministry of these New Testament women, *not one of them is ever described as apostle, elder or bishop,* whether ordained or non-ordained (we'll look at Junia and Phoebe shortly).

How could the apostle Paul, having established his normative doctrine of headship (God's creational arrangement of functional role distinctions within the partnership of spiritual equals) proceed to violate it in his actual practice? Whenever in doubt, we should supplement our study of the *descriptive* components of the practice in Bible times (which mention women and the significant roles they played) with an analysis of the *prescriptive* teaching of Paul which formed the foundation of what he and the early church practiced. Otherwise, we may give the impression that Paul was merely operating with reference to culture rather than being guided by transcultural norms. But as passages such as Ephesians 5: 21ff., 1 Timothy 2:11ff., and 1 Corinthians 11 show, Paul did in fact establish general parameters (which he already found in the Old Testament creation accounts) for women's roles in the church.[43] In short, not only Paul's practice, but also the principles underlying the patterns of established churches should be part of the investigation. Paul's norms regarding women's roles in the church are foundational; questionable inferences about what may have been the case are not.

(d) Junia, A "Female Apostle"? Much is made in *Women in Ministry* about Junia being a "female apostle."[44] This claim is based on the apostle Paul's description of Andronicus and Junia as "my kinsmen, and my fellowprisoners, *who are of note among the apostles,* who also were in Christ before me" (Rom 16:7, KJV).

There are two problems in this text. First, does the name Junia have a feminine ending (proving Junia was a woman), or does it have a masculine ending (proving Junia was a man)? This is a grammatical problem arising from the Greek language. In Romans 16:7, the ending for the name of Junia in the Greek is *-an,* which would be the direct object (accusative) form both for men's names that end in *-as* (like Elias, Zacharias, Silas, Thomas, or Cephas) or women's names that end in *-a* (like Martha, Joanna, or Lydia). Therefore it is impossible to tell from the Greek ending alone whether the person described by the apostle Paul is Juni*as* (male) or Juni*a* (female). This explains the varied opinions among the church fathers. For example, whereas Origen (died A.D. 252) referred to the person as Junias, a man, Chrysostom (died A.D. 407) referred to this person as Junia, a woman. Church historian Epiphanius (died A.D. 403) sees the person as man. Thus, grammatically and historically, both genders are possible.

But let's assume that the person Paul refers to is a woman by the name Junia. Does Romans 16:7 require us to believe that Junia was a female apostle? This is the second problem confronting interpreters. The answer hinges on how one understands the phrase translated "among the apostles" (*en tois apostolois*). In the Greek the phrase is ambiguous. Does it mean that Andronicus and Junia were numbered among the apostles (as the NIV has it, "They are outstanding among the apostles,") or does it mean that their reputation was well known by the apostles (as the KJV puts it, they are "of note among the apostles")?

How do we resolve a problem in which both interpretations are allowed by the Greek? This is where one's hermeneutical principles of interpretation are revealed. The historic Adventist approach is to (1) interpret an obscure passage by a plain passage in Scripture, and (2) look for any applicable precedents in Scripture, noting that one Scripture will never contradict another.

On the basis of this "time-honored" Adventist approach, one should recognize five relevant facts: (1) Paul's doctrine of headship was established on the creation order (1 Tim 2; 1 Cor 11; Eph 5). (2) Jesus Himself ordained only males as apostles, pointing back to the Old Testament patriarchs as foundations of the "church in the wilderness" (Acts 7:38). (3) Every known apostle in the New Testament was a male—Paul and Barnabas (Acts 14:14, 4), Apollos (1 Cor 4:6, 9), Silvanus and Timothy (1 Thess 1:1; 2:6), Titus (2 Cor 8:23, Greek), Epaphroditus (Phil 2:25). (4) While women played significant roles in the early church's soulwinning ministry, none of them is known to have served as apostle, elder, or bishop. (5) The apostle Paul, who worked closely with these active women, taught that the headship function of elder or overseer could only be held by a person who, among other things, was the "husband of one wife" (1 Tim 3:2; Titus 1:6).

The above considerations lead me to the conclusion that the ambiguous phrase "among the apostles" (*en tois apostolois*) should be understood as "of note among the apostles" in the sense that Junia was well known by the apostles, not that she was numbered among them. No New Testament evidence supports the idea that the woman Junia mentioned in Romans 16:7 was an apostle, nor is there any New Testament evidence that the man Andronicus mentioned in the same text was an apostle. The most plausible and biblically-consistent understanding is that both Andronicus and Junia were well known and appreciated by the apostles as Christian converts prior to Paul's own conversion.[45]

Unlike the interpretation in *Women in Ministry*,[46] this interpretation does not violate clear and plain biblical teaching on headship, the example of Jesus Christ in appointing only males as apostles, and the fact that all the known apostles mentioned in the New Testament are males.

My conclusion is that Junia, even if a woman, could not have been an apostle. Any assertion that Junia was a "female apostle" is speculative and arguably false.

5. Speculative Interpretations

One of the most serious methodological problems in *Women in Ministry* is the frequency of speculations and conjectures. Biblical certainties are downgraded into probabilities and probabilities into possibilities. Then possibilities are upgraded into probabilities and probabilities into certainties. This sounds like hard criticism. But let us look at the effort to construct a religious or cultural background to Paul's statements in 1 Corinthians 11, 14, and 1 Timothy 2:11-15, passages which contain such statements as "the head of the woman is the man," "every woman that prayeth or prophesieth with her head uncovered dishonoreth her head," "neither was the man created for the woman; but the woman for the man," "let your women keep silence in the churches," and "I suffer not a woman to teach, nor to usurp authority over the man. . . . For Adam was first formed, then Eve."

(a) "Proto-Gnostic" Setting for 1 Corinthians and 1 Timothy? Instead of accepting Paul's argument from Genesis 2, that Adam was created first and Eve later, as the basis for his teaching that the man occupies a position of headship in the home and in the church, *Women in Ministry* ventures numerous guesses for "the real reason" behind Paul's statements. These arguments are often propped up with expressions like "perhaps," "seems to," "likely," "apparently," "could be," and "might be."

I find it ironic that one author, who had earlier used some convoluted reasoning of his own to argue for a "female apostle," sees the apostle Paul doing the same here. In this scholar's opinion, "Paul's reasoning at several points in 1 Corinthians 14 is rather convoluted and calls for sophisticated exegesis."[47] Thus, some authors of *Women in Ministry* employ such "sophisticated exegesis" in their discussion of the life setting of 1 Corinthians 11 and 14 and 1 Timothy 2.

For example, in arguing that "any attempt to understand this passage [1 Cor 11 and 14] requires that we first know what was going on in Corinth in the early-to-mid 50s A.D.," one author speculates that Paul was dealing with "incipient gnosticism" or "proto-gnosticism."[48] The editor of the book also sees "incipient gnosticism," together with "the pagan worship of the mother goddess" and Judaism, as the religious background of 1 Timothy 2.[49] Gnosticism, we should note, was a second-century heresy that taught a dualistic (spirit-matter) world view, arguing that matter was bad and spirit good. Consequently, Gnostics held, the Genesis creation account and any teaching that is based on it are flawed, since the Genesis account involves the creation of matter.[50]

On the basis of this alleged "proto-gnostic" background, the authors of *Women in Ministry* claim that Paul was dealing with false teaching introduced by "gnostic Christian" women in Corinth or Ephesus. The problem with this kind of interpretation is that it requires more source material than we have in order to be sure of the cultural surroundings at the time when Paul wrote.

The scholars of *Women in Ministry* see "incipient-" or "proto-gnosticism" as the background of Paul's writings (first century), yet they have to appeal to later sources (second- or third-century writings) to reconstruct the heresy they believe Paul is dealing with. This kind of methodology, called "anachronistic interpretation," is like Sunday keepers' attempts to interpret the meaning of the "Lord's day" in Revelation 1:10 (first-century writing) by the meaning the term assumed in the writings of early church fathers in the second or third centuries. We would make a similar methodological mistake if we were to define the word "gay" in Ellen White's writing by the meaning of the term today. Such methods are open to serious criticism.[51]

But even if we suppose that *Women in Ministry* is correct and Paul was opposing an early form of gnosticism, "there is then not the slightest occasion, just because the false teachers who are being opposed are Gnostics, to link them up with the great

Gnostic systems of the second century."[52] The appeals to Jewish parallels are also unpersuasive since these sources often postdate the New Testament writings.

(b) Speculative Interpretations of 1 Tim 2:11-15. Several of the authors of *Women in Ministry* argue that the traditional interpretation of 1 Timothy 2 has not taken into account what is "now known" to be "the initial situation" that Paul was addressing in Ephesus. Basing their positions partly on the "persuasive" work of a non-Adventist scholar, Sharon Gritz, the authors speculate that Paul's restriction on women's "teaching and having authority over men" (1 Tim 2:11ff) was due to the infiltration of the false teaching of the cult of the Mother Goddess, Artemis, in Ephesus.[53]

But our book's scholars differ on how the questionable claims and assumptions of Gritz's "Mother Goddess" hypothesis help them to understand 1 Timothy 2.[54] For example, one writer who finds the speculation "persuasive" concludes, "Paul's concern in 1 Tim 2:8-15 is not that women might have authority over men in the church but that *certain assertive women in the church* who had been influenced by false teachers would teach error. For this reason, he charges them to 'be silent.'"[55]

Another writer does not see the issue as a concern about "certain assertive women in church" but rather as "dealing with husband-wife relations" in worship settings. For him, Paul was "correcting a false syncretistic theology in Ephesus . . . [in which] *wives* were apparently domineering over their *husbands* in public church meetings."[56]

The editor of the book speculates in a different direction. Believing the religious background in Ephesus to be "the pagan worship of the mother goddess," Judaism, and "incipient gnosticism," she challenges the "husband-wife relation" theory.[57] She argues that "the text itself [1 Tim 2] seems to be discussing attitudes [of women] in worship rather than the marriage relationship."[58] In her opinion, "Paul could be saying that he was *currently* not permitting women to teach [and "instigate violence"], because of a number of reasons, or even that he was not permitting women to teach *until such a time as they had learned sufficiently.*"[59]

Believing such conflicting speculations to be the new light that has eluded the Christian church throughout its history, one of the *Women in Ministry* authors asks: "One wonders what might have been the case if the Timothy passage had thus been understood throughout the history of the church"![60]

Fortunately, Seventh-day Adventists and the wider Christian church did not have to wait for this explanation to understand 1 Tim 2. If it is true that Paul wrote his epistle to restrain "certain assertive women in the church" or "wives domineering over their husbands in worship settings" or even some "unlearned" women who at that time were "instigating violence" because "they had not learned sufficiently," why is Paul's prohibition directed to *all women?* Since Paul's prohibition applies to all women, those who believe in these new theories need to show that all (or *any*) Christian women at Ephesus were teaching these kinds of false theologies. Such evidence cannot be found.

What *is* taught in Scripture is that the people who were teaching false doctrine in Ephesus were not women, but men. Paul, for example, talks about Hymenaeus and Alexander (1 Tim 1:20) and Hymenaeus and Philetus (2 Tim 2:17-18), who were all men. Similarly Paul warns the Ephesian elders of men (*andres,* from *aner,* a male) who will arise "speaking perverse things, to draw away disciples after them" (Acts 20:30). These false teachers are men, not women. Until someone shows from Scripture that all the Christian women at Ephesus—or even any of them—were teaching false doctrine, proponents of this new interpretation have no factual basis for it.

It is clear that some of the Ephesian women were being influenced by the false teaching (1 Tim 5:11-15; 2 Tim 3:5-9), but they were not the purveyors. It is also clear from Scripture that women were gossiping at Ephesus (1 Tim 5:13), but gossiping is not the same as teaching false doctrine. We all may know people who gossip but who don't teach false doctrine. Again, it is true that there were pagan religions in Ephesus where *non-Christian* men and women did a number of things not done by Christians (Acts 19:21-41). But to say that they did such things after becoming Christians is speculation without evidence.

How can one say that Paul's prohibition was a temporary restraint on the women of Ephesus until "such a time as they had learned sufficiently"? The apostle Paul did not cite a lack of education, formal training, or teaching skills as the reason why women should not "teach or have authority over men" (1 Tim 2:12 RSV). On the contrary, Paul instructed older women to "teach what is good. Then they can train the younger women" (Titus 2:3, 4 NIV). He also commended the teaching that Eunice and Lois provided for Timothy (2 Tim 1:5; 3:14, 15). Evidently Priscilla was well educated and a capable teacher, since she "expounded to" Apollos, an "eloquent man" who was already "instructed in the way of the Lord" (Acts 18:24-26).

Significantly, Paul's epistle to Timothy—the very epistle which commands that women not be allowed to "teach or to have authority over men," and which restricts the pastoral role of overseer to men—was addressed to the church at Ephesus (1 Tim 1:3), the home church of Priscilla and Aquila. Prior to writing this epistle, Paul had already stayed at the home of Priscilla and Aquila in Corinth for eighteen months (Acts 18:2, 11). The couple later accompanied Paul to Ephesus (Acts 18:18-21). When Paul stayed in Ephesus for another three years, "teaching the whole counsel of God" (Acts 20:27, 31; cf. 1 Cor 16:19), it is likely that Priscilla was among those who received instruction from him.

Yet not even well-educated Priscilla, nor godly teachers Eunice and Lois, nor any other accomplished woman, was permitted to "teach or to have authority over men." The reason why women were forbidden to "teach or to have authority over men" was not inadequate education or a lack of ability to teach. Paul instead pointed to the creation order, stating that "Adam was formed first, then Eve" (1 Tim 2:13).[61] Adam carried the special right and responsibility of leadership which belonged to the "firstborn" in a family (cf. Col 1:15-18).[62]

The editor of *Women in Ministry* offers another idea to prop up the gnostic heresy hypothesis. She argues that Paul's use of the conjunction "for" (*gar*) in 1 Timothy 2:12-13 does not mean that Paul is about to give the reason why women should not "teach and exercise authority over men"; instead, she claims, he uses the term to introduce examples of what happens when women falsely teach men.[63] This explanation is creative, but not convincing.

It is not convincing because in other places in his letter to Timothy, when Paul gives a command, the word "for" (*gar*) that follows almost invariably states the *reason* for the command (see 1 Tim 4:7, 8, 16; 5:4, 11, 15, 18; 2 Tim 1:6, 7; 2:7, 16; 3:5, 6; 4:3, 5, 6, 9-11, 15). In the same way, when he gives the command to women not to "teach or exercise authority over men" (1 Tim 2:11-12), he gives reasons in verses 13-14 why they should not do so ("for [i.e. because] Adam was created first, then Eve"). If the reason for the prohibition was to cite "an example of what happens when false teaching [by women] is propounded and accepted," we should have expected Paul to prohibit all men and all women "to teach and exercise authority over men," for the same bad results follow when men teach falsely.

We therefore conclude: "The suggestion that women were prohibited from teaching because they were mainly responsible for the false teaching finds no substantiation in the text. Even if some women were spreading the heresy (which is uncertain but possible), an explanation is still needed for why Paul proscribes only women from teaching. Since men are specifically named as purveyors of the heresy, would it not make more sense if Paul forbade all false teaching by both men and women? A prohibition against women alone seems to be reasonable only if *all* the women in Ephesus were duped by the false teaching. This latter state of affairs is quite unlikely, and the probable presence of Priscilla in Ephesus (2 Tim. 4:19) also stands against it."[64]

Even if we agree for the sake of argument that Paul was responding to "certain women" or "all women" in Ephesus, such a response to a specific situation does not nullify the universal principle he employs ("Adam was formed first, then Eve") to address that unique situation. If we claim that apostolic letters written to address specific "initial situations" are not applicable to the church today, then the rest of the New Testament would not be applicable to us either, since all the books of the New Testament were addressed to particular communities facing special circumstances.

6. Questionable Re-Interpretations of the Bible

By "questionable re-interpretations" I mean interpretations that are unwarranted and contradict Scripture. I will consider how *Women in Ministry* addresses some key questions on the biblical doctrine of male headship and female submission in both the home and the church. I will also examine the claims that there were "women priests" in the Old Testament, and that the prophetesses Miriam, Deborah, and Huldah exercised "headship-leadership over men."

Key Questions on Headship. Unlike liberal or radical feminists, the authors of *Women in Ministry* accept the biblical teaching of headship in the home. But they insist that this headship was instituted after the Fall and does not apply in the church.[65] Creation headship would strike a fatal blow to the egalitarian concept of ministry. If headship existed before the Fall, with no role interchangeability, the whole enterprise in *Women in Ministry* collapses.

We will focus on three major issues: (a) When did headship begin—at creation or after the Fall? (b) What is the nature of headship—does it call for gender-role distinctions or does it nullify them? (c) What is the extent of headship—is it for the home only or does it also extend to the church? In addressing these questions we will show that the interpretations found in *Women in Ministry* contradict the Bible.

(a) When Was Headship Instituted: At Creation of After the Fall? According to the author of chapter 13 of *Women in Ministry,* Genesis 2:24 provides the "ultimate ideal" or the "divine ideal" for husband-wife relations. This Bible text says, "Therefore shall a man leave his father and his mother, and shall cleave unto his wife: and they shall be one flesh." The author repeatedly refers to this passage as revealing "God's original plan for total equality," "full equality with no headship/ submission," "equal partnership," and "total role interchangeableness."[66]

In essence, our scholar's study of the creation account of Genesis 2 leads him to deny headship (functional role distinctions) before the Fall. This "equal partnership" or "total role interchangeableness" that was allegedly instituted before the Fall was also to be the ideal after the Fall. He argues that Genesis 2:24 was "clearly written to indicate its applicability to the *post-Fall conditions.* God's ideal for the nature of sexual relationship after the Fall is still the same as it was for Adam and Eve in the beginning—to 'become one flesh.'"[67]

Observe that if we accept this kind of reasoning, we will also have to argue that New Testament passages (like Eph 5:22-33; Col 3:18, 19; 1 Pet 3:7; 1 Cor 11:3, 11, 12) which Adventists have historically understood as God's permanent arrangement for male-female role relations in the home are merely non-ideal accommodations exacted by the Bible writers; Christians who seek to reach the assumed egalitarian ideal may justifiably repudiate the biblical teaching of male headship/leadership and female submission/supporting role. More importantly, however, the author's denial of creation headship, postponing its origin to the "post-Fall conditions," contradicts Paul's explicit use of Genesis 2:24 in Ephesians 5.

Although our scholar correctly recognizes Ephesians 5:21-33 as "the fundamental New Testament passage dealing with husband-wife relations,"[68] he does not take into account the use the inspired apostle himself makes of the verse from Genesis 2. In Ephesians 5, Paul makes it clear that he bases his teaching of headship on the nature of Christ's relation to the church, which he sees revealed as "mystery" in Genesis 2:24 and, thus, in creation itself. From this "mystery" he establishes a pattern of relationship between the husband as head (on the analogy of

Christ) and derives the appropriateness of the husband's headship/leadership and the wife's submission/supporting role.

Paul's quotation of Genesis 2:24 in Ephesians 5:31, therefore, indicates that the headship-submission principle in the home ("husbands, love your wives" and "wives, submit to your husbands"), which Christ modeled for us, was established at creation, prior to the Fall. Thus, *Women in Ministry*'s claim that there was no headship before the Fall is directly negated by the apostle Paul's statement in Ephesians 5—"the fundamental New Testament passage dealing with husband-wife relations."

(b) Nature of Headship: Does It Nullify Gender Roles? *Women in Ministry* also argues that at creation, there was "total role interchangeableness," so that there were no functional role distinctions before the Fall. This assertion contradicts the Bible's own self-interpretation.

Not only does Paul ground his headship doctrine in Genesis 2, but he also sees male-female role distinctions in the creation account. The inspired apostle's reason given in 1 Timothy 2:13 for not permitting a woman to "teach or have authority over man"—"for Adam was formed first, then Eve"—reflects his understanding of the creation account in Genesis 2:4-25, where we find the narrative of Adam being formed before Eve. The apostle's use of the word "form" (*plasso*, cf. Gen 2:7, 8, 15, 19) instead of "make" (*poieo*, cf. Gen 1:26, 27) also indicates that the reference in 1 Timothy 2 is to Genesis 2, where we find that God "formed man of the dust of the ground" (v. 7). Thus, the apostle Paul understands the order in which Adam and Eve were created as having implications for role differences between male and female (cf. 1 Cor 11:3, 8-11).

"If God indeed fashioned Eve later than Adam, for a purpose for which another male human being was not suited, then it is not difficult to argue that, in principle, there are things for which the woman may be suited for which the man is not, and vice versa. This observation appears to provide some substantiation for the kinds of functional distinctions between men and women in the Creator's purpose that have traditionally been held."[69]

As noted earlier, Ellen G. White rejected the egalitarian model of "total role interchangeability." Despite the abuse of God's creation arrangement for role relations in the home, she wrote that "heaven's ideal of this sacred [marriage] relation" is one in which the man is the constituted head of the home. This kind of relationship is "what God designed it should be."[70] And because "the husband is the head of the family, as Christ is the head of the church," she wrote, "any course which the wife may pursue to lessen his influence and lead him to come down from that dignified, responsible position is displeasing to God" (*Testimonies for the Church*, 1:307).

Thus, not only does Paul see Genesis 2 as an institution of the headship principle, but also his use of the passage in Ephesians 5 ("husbands love your wives, wives submit to your husbands") and 1 Timothy 2 ("I do not permit a woman to teach or have authority over man, for Adam was formed first, then Eve") indicates that headship calls for gender role distinctions. Therefore, the concept of "total egalitarianism" or "total role interchangeableness" as God's original plan for the home directly contradicts the inspired apostle as well as conflicting with Ellen G. White.

(c) **Extent of Headship: Home, Not Church?** *Women in Ministry* also argues that while the headship principle (erroneously believed to have originated at the Fall) is relevant today, the principle is only valid for the *home* situation and not for the *church* family. There are at least three major reasons against this view.

First, the Bible teaches that the church is not just another social institution; it is a worshiping community—a group of people who relate to God through a faith relationship in Christ. Thus the church, in both Old and New Testaments, exists whenever and wherever "two or three have gathered in my [Christ's] name" (Matt 18:20). Rightly understood, the worshiping household is a miniature model of the church. Even before Jesus Christ established the New Testament church (Matt 16:18, 19), the church was already in existence in Old Testament times. Israel, with its priests and ceremonial system of worship, was "the church in the wilderness" (Acts 7:38). But long before the Exodus brought Israel the opportunity to be "a kingdom of priests, and an holy nation" (Ex 19:6), the church existed in the homes, wherever "two or three . . . gathered in my name."[71]

The numerous Bible references to the church as the family of God[72] suggest that the relationship of male and female in the church—"the household of God" (1 Tim 3:15 RSV)—is to be *modeled after the home family,* of which the Eden home was the prototype (Eph 5:22, 23; Col 3:18; 1 Pet 3:1-7; 1 Cor 11:3, 7-9; 14:34, 35; 1 Tim 2:11-3:5). The frequent correspondence between home and church found in Scripture (e.g., Acts 2:46; 5:42; 1 Cor 14:34, 35; cf. Phil 4:22) finds an echo in John Chrysostom's statement that "a household is a little church" and "a church is a large household."[73]

Second, the Bible makes the success of male headship in the home a necessary qualification for one to be elder or overseer in the church. Thus, since only males can legitimately be heads of their homes (as husbands and fathers), according to Scripture, they alone can serve in the headship office of the church (as elders or overseers). For example, the pastoral epistles of Paul to Timothy and Titus, the very books which describe the qualities of an elder-pastor, view the church as the family of God, thus establishing the family structure as the model for church structure: "If a man does not know how to manage his own household, how can he care for God's church?" (1 Tim 3:4, 5 RSV; cf. Titus 1:6). This is why the Bible teaches that the elder or overseer must be "the husband of one wife" (1 Tim 3:2; Titus 1:6).

Third, it is logically and practically inconsistent to propose that God made the husband the spiritual head at home (a smaller family unit) and his wife the spiritual head of the church (a larger family unit). The "total egalitarian" model would create serious conflicts and confusion, yet God is not the author of confusion. Therefore, He is not the author of the idea that women should be the spiritual heads in the church.

The description of the church as "the household of God" (1 Tim 3:15; Eph 2:19) and the patterning of church authority after the headship arrangement in the home reveal the high estimation God places on the home family.[74] Is it possible that those who wish to drive a wedge between the patterns of authority in the church and in the home do not understand the true nature of male headship and the complementary female supportive role?

One thing is undeniable. The egalitarian interpretations of the Genesis 2 creation account, positing "total role interchangeableness" or "full equality with no headship-submission" as God's divine ideal for the family, contradict the apostle Paul's own interpretation of the Genesis passage. Are those who propose that women should be ordained as elders or pastors better interpreters of Scripture than the inspired apostle?

(d) Women Priests in the Old Testament? I was astonished by one suggestion in *Women in Ministry* that women actually served as priests in the Old Testament. The reason given to support the suggestion amazed me even more! The suggestion is that in the Garden of Eden God ordained Eve as a priest alongside Adam. The author of this idea argues:

"Adam and Eve were, indeed, dressed as priests, with one difference, however: instead of the fine linen that characterizes the priestly garment (Ex 28:39), God chose animal skin. This specification not only implies the killing of an animal, the first sacrifice in history, but by the same token, confirms the identification of Adam and Eve as priests, for the skin of the atonement sacrifice was specifically set apart for the officiating priests (Lev 7:8). By bestowing on Adam and Eve the skin of the sin offering, a gift strictly reserved to priests, the Genesis story implicitly recognizes Eve as priest alongside Adam."[75]

Thus our scholar reads Genesis through the lenses of pro-women's ordination and discovers Eve as a "female priest"! In the concluding paragraph of his chapter in *Women in Ministry*, he states: "Thus biblical identification of woman as priest in Eden and the redeemed community ["priesthood of all believers"] complements biblical approval of women's anointing as prophet and judge. In this context, and in reflection upon ordination to pastoral ministry, there is no case for women's exclusion."[76]

If the clothing of Adam and Eve with animal skin meant that they were dressed as priests, does this mean that God congratulated them for sinning?

It is puzzling that this chapter was agreed upon by the Ad Hoc Committee that developed *Women in Ministry*. Perhaps it illustrates where the logic of the "egalitarian" model leads those seeking a biblical justification to ordain women as elders or pastors.[77] Since other chapters in the present volume challenge the biblical basis for this unbelievable claim,[78] I will concentrate more on the author's cultural arguments.

It seems that our scholar does not accept the biblical explanation that the headship principle instituted at creation is the reason why there is no evidence of female priests in the Old Testament. He has manufactured two reasons—namely God's "reaction to pagan syncretism and sexual perversions" and "the incompatibility of the sacrifice [women performing sacrifices in Israel], normally associated with death and sin, and the physiological nature of the woman traditionally associated in the Bible with life and messianic pregnancy"! In other words, "had it not been for these two factors, ancient Near Eastern cults and more decisively the sacrifices, women might well have been priests in Israel."[79]

It is encouraging that at least one writer, the lead author in *Women in Ministry*, offers a gentle corrective to the speculative "female priest" theory when he observes that "males functioned as priests in the days of the biblical patriarchs as well as after God's covenant with Israel at Mount Sinai."[80] Indeed, the Bible teaches that *only* males served in the headship role of priest in the Old Testament. Prior to Sinai, the head of each household (male) and firstborn sons (males) performed this role.[81] At Sinai, however, this responsibility was assigned "as a gift to Aaron and his sons" (Num 8:19; cf. Num 3:9-13, 32, 45; 25:10-13). Ellen G. White summarized it this way:

"In the earliest times every man [male] was the priest of his own household. In the days of Abraham the priesthood was regarded as the birthright of the eldest son [male]. Now, instead of the first-born of all Israel, the Lord accepted the tribe of Levi for the work of the sanctuary. . . . The priesthood, however, was restricted to the family of Aaron. Aaron and his sons alone [males] were permitted to minister before the Lord" (*Patriarchs and Prophets*, p. 350).

The absence of female priests in the Old Testament was not due to the culture of those times, since the ancient Near Eastern cultures would have allowed female priests, as was the case in the surrounding Canaanite religions. Also, the reason why Israelite women were prohibited from serving as priests was not that God did not want them to engage in the kind of immorality that the pagan priestesses engaged in (i.e., God's prohibition was not in "reaction to pagan syncretism and sexual perversions"). Such an argument, besides lacking basis in Scripture, implies that women are more prone to idolatry and sexual immorality than men—a sexist argument which is unproven. Finally, the absence of female priests in the Old Testament was not due to "the physiological nature of the woman traditionally associated in the Bible with life and messianic pregnancy," since it takes both men and women to give birth to human life, and since the anticipated "messianic pregnancy" that resulted in the "virgin birth" of Christ greatly limited the physical involvement of both earthly parents.

The reason for the absence of women priests in the Old Testament can best be explained by God's special divine arrangement at the beginning. The headship principle, instituted by God at creation and reiterated after the Fall, is the only biblically and theologically consistent explanation for why there were no women priests in ancient Israel. The questionable re-interpretations we have been considering contradict this teaching of Scripture.

(e) **The Case of Miriam, Deborah, and Huldah.** A brief response must also be made to the claim in *Women in Ministry* that women such as Eve, Sarah, Hagar, Shiphrah and Puah, Jochebed, Miriam, Ruth, Deborah, Hannah, the Shunammite woman, and Huldah occupied headship/leadership positions in the Old Testament. Of these, Miriam the prophetess-musician (Ex 15:20), Deborah, "a prophetess . . . [who] was judging [NIV "leading"] Israel at that time" (Judges 4:4), and Huldah, the prophetess to whom Josiah the king and Hilkiah the high priest looked for spiritual guidance (2 Kings 22), are often cited as exceptional "women leaders exercising headship over men."[82]

On the above assumption, it is claimed that women today should be ordained as elders or pastors. In making this claim, however, *Women in Ministry* seems to confuse the issue of women exercising the leadership authority of elders or pastors with the legitimacy of women filling the messenger role of prophets. It also overlooks the fact that under the Old Testament theocracy, Israel was a nation governed by God and His law. In the Old Testament system, the leaders who were selected—prophets, priests, judges and kings—differed in how they were chosen and in the extent of their respective authority. The leadership role of *prophet* (likewise *judge*) was not an elected office. God Himself chose and authoritatively commissioned (ordained) prophets (and judges) as His mouthpiece; they were not elected by the people as leaders to exercise administrative or executive authority. Thus, kings (and judges) and priests were all to be subject to the authority of God, whose prophets delivered His messages.

Similarly, in both the Old and New Testaments, God chose and commissioned (ordained) prophets without regard to gender (e.g., Miriam, Deborah, Huldah). On the other hand, the Bible teaches that elders and pastors are to be chosen and commissioned (ordained) by the church within guidelines stipulated in Scripture. One such criterion for the office of elder or pastor is that the one chosen must be "the husband of one wife" (1 Tim 3:2; Titus 1:6), an expression whose Greek construction emphasizes that the elder or pastor must be the kind of man who loves only one woman as his wife.

Elders and pastors (the Bible makes no distinction in their office) are to be subject to the authority of God's messages coming through His chosen prophets. As leaders of the church, elders and pastors are given administrative and leadership responsibility and authority that prophets are not. Church leaders are responsible to God for their reception of the prophetic message, but they are not under the administrative authority of the prophets.

We may see this difference clearly both in Scripture and in the experience of Ellen G. White. Elijah could give King Ahab God's message, but he did not have executive authority to make the king obey or to countermand Ahab's orders to have Elijah arrested (1 Kings 17:1-3, 18:7-10). Jeremiah proclaimed God's judgments with divine authority, for which he was imprisoned by priest, princes, and king (Jer 20:1, 2; 37:11-38:10). They had authority different from his. Even Deborah's authority as "prophetess [who was] judging Israel" illustrates how God-fearing women are to exercise their unique gifts and leadership in the context of the biblical teaching of headship.[83]

In Seventh-day Adventist history, the closest parallel to the prophetic authority and unique leadership of Deborah is Ellen G. White. Though she never claimed to be a leader of the church, she did exercise her role as a messenger of the Lord. In the early 1870s, Mrs. White had authority to communicate God's plan for Seventh-day Adventist education, but she did not have authority to make the leaders follow it in founding Battle Creek College. Prophetic authority is not the same thing as the administrative responsibility of the chosen leadership. Mrs. White herself refused to be called the leader of the Seventh-day Adventist church, referring to herself as "a messenger with a message": "No one has ever heard me claim the position of leader of the denomination. . . . I am not to appear before the people as holding any other position than that of a messenger with a message" (*Testimonies for the Church*, 8:236-237).

Our conclusion is that Miriam, Huldah and Deborah (like Ellen G. White) were prophets. But their authority as prophets should not be confused with exercising headship authority in the home (as husbands) and in the church (as elders or pastors). We can only do so by resorting to questionable re-interpretations of biblical teaching. *Women in Ministry,* therefore, misleads readers when it compares the headship authority of the elected leadership office in the church (elders or pastors) with the prophetic authority of the non-elected office of prophets and prophetesses.

7. Distorted Biblical Reasoning

Occasionally, *Women in Ministry* resorts to convoluted and sophisticated explanations to bolster an untenable position. As an example of this, we shall look at the claim that Phoebe was a "female minister."

(a) **Phoebe: A "Female Minister"?** In Romans 16:1-2, the apostle Paul writes: "I commend unto you Phebe our sister, which is a servant [*diakonos*] of the church which is at Cenchrea: That ye receive her in the Lord, as becometh saints, and that ye assist her in whatsoever business she hath need of you: for she hath been a succourer of many, and of myself also" (KJV).

Based on the above description of Phoebe as a *diakonos* ("servant," KJV, NIV, NASB; or "deaconess," RSV), one of the authors of *Women in Ministry* claims that Phoebe functioned "as Paul's emissary, as did Titus and Timothy" and that her designation as "deacon" "does not imply the modern 'deaconess' but rather the same position as that of the church leaders designated in 1 Tim 3:8-10."[84] Another author maintains that Phoebe is an example of New Testament "women in church leadership-headship roles."[85]

These writers do not offer any biblical proof for their assertions. They build their cases on the "able" studies provided by another *Women in Ministry* writer who concludes that Phoebe was a "female minister," and that "if there could be one female minister there could as well be many."[86]

However, a careful study of the evidence presented by the book's leading proponent of the "female minister" theory indicates that it involves a convoluted handling of
the biblical data and that it contradicts Ellen White's understanding. The following
points capture the essential thrust of *Women in Ministry*'s arguments:

(1) The term *diakonos,* used for Phoebe in Romans 16:1, comes from the same
root word (*diakonein*) used for the appointive ministry of the seven men in
Acts 6.[87]

(2) But this office of *diakonos* assigned to the seven men of Acts 6 is *not* that of
deacons as "has often been assumed," even in Ellen G. White's book *The
Acts of the Apostles*.[88]

(3) Instead, the kind of work for which the seven men of Acts were appointed is
the same as "elder," the only appointive ministry originally known in the
apostolic church.[89]

(4) Only later did the one appointive ministry of *diakonos* (now re-defined by
the author to mean "elder" or "minister") divide into two levels of "elder"
and "deacon."[90] The alleged later "distinction between deacon and elder/
bishop is hardened in the pastoral epistles, especially in 1 Tim 3:1-13."[91]

(5) Phoebe occupied "the same position as the deacons of 1 Timothy 3," which
our author claims was originally the same office as that of elder, or possibly
that of apostle.[92]

(6) Therefore, the designation of Phoebe as *diakonos* in Romans 16:1 "proves
incontrovertibly that the early church had female *diakonia*"—i.e., female
ministers. And "if there could be one female minister [Phoebe] there could
as well be many."[93]

In responding to this interpretation, we will briefly discuss the meaning of the
term *diakonos.* We will note how Ellen G. White understood the function of the
seven men of Acts 6 and what bearing it has on the "female minister" theory.

(b) **Meaning of "Diakonos."** In the New Testament the term *diakonos,* like the
related terms *diakonia* and *diakoneo,* has both a broad and a narrow meaning. In its
broad sense it conveys the idea of a "ministry" or "service" carried out on behalf of
the church. Thus, services like preparation of a meal (Luke 10:40), serving a meal
(Luke 22:27), providing financial and material support (Luke 8:1-3), the employment of any spiritual gift (1 Cor 12:5; 1 Pet 4:10), doing the work of a "deacon" by
taking care of the needy (Acts 6:1-4), and providing spiritual oversight and leadership for the churches by serving as an elder (1 Tim 4:6) or apostle (Acts 1:25) are all
termed "ministry" (*diakonia*). Because in this broad usage anything a person does to
advance the work of the church is a ministry, the one who labors in this manner is a
"minister" or "servant" (*diakonos*) of the Lord.[94]

In its narrow and technical usage, *diakonos* refers to the office of a "deacon"
which among other things can only be occupied by one who is a "husband of one
wife" (1 Tim 3:8-13; Phil 1:1). This deacon office, first occupied by the seven
men of Acts 6, involved ministering to the poor, needy, and sick. But "although

deacons were to care for the temporal affairs of the church, they were also to be actively involved in evangelistic work (Acts 6:8; 8:5-13, 26-40)."[95]

Whether we apply the broad meaning or the narrow one, calling Phoebe a *diakonos* does not prove she was an apostle or a female minister.[96] Indeed, Paul explains why he calls her a deacon—because she is a "succourer [helper] of many" (Rom 16:2). As for the seven deacons, they certainly were not apostles; they were elected specifically to do work the apostles felt unable to do at that time. Until recently, Seventh-day Adventists have upheld the view that Romans 16:1-2 refers to Phoebe's valuable ministry of care and hospitality for church members. To change from this well-established view surely needs better evidence than what *Women in Ministry* provides.[97]

Ellen G. White presents Phoebe not as a "female minister," but rather as an example of how we should "care for the interests of our brethren and sisters." Referring to Romans 16:1, 2, she states, "Phebe entertained the apostle, and she was in a marked manner an entertainer of strangers who needed care. Her example should be followed by the churches of today" (*Testimonies for the Church,* 6:343, 344).

(c) **Ellen White on "the Seven Men" of Acts 6.** The "female minister" theory proposal in *Women in Ministry* can only be sustained by proving that the seven men of Acts 6 were elders and not deacons. The leading proponent of this theory is wrong when he argues that because the title of chapter 9 ("The Seven Deacons") in Ellen White's *The Acts of the Apostles* may be the work of editors, it therefore does not show that she believed the seven men of Acts 6 were deacons.[98]

During her lifetime, all editorial work on her books was submitted to Ellen G. White for approval before a book was published. We can safely conclude that she approved the chapter heading in *The Acts of the Apostles,* chapter 9. Also, contrary to what *Women in Ministry* says, in that very chapter (p. 91) Mrs. White does indeed refer to the seven men as "deacons" (not ministers or elders). Furthermore, elsewhere in the book she describes Philip as "one of the seven deacons" (p. 106); she also refers to Stephen as "the foremost of the seven deacons" (*Lift Him Up,* p. 104). To claim that Acts 6 is describing seven elders and not seven deacons is to interpret the Bible differently from the way Ellen White interprets it. And to assert, as our author does, that Mrs. White describes these men only as "officers" and not "deacons" in the text is simply wrong.

(d) **The History of the Appointive Ministry.** Is there a biblical basis on which to speculate that the original appointive ministry in the New Testament church was that of elder, and that this office was later divided into two levels (elders and deacons) so that in the pastoral epistles the distinction between the two was "hardened"?

As *Women in Ministry* notes, the first leaders of the church were the twelve apostles specially chosen by Christ Himself (Matt 10:1-4; Mark 3:13-19; Luke 6:12-16). Like the twelve patriarchs or the leaders of the tribes of Israel, these twelve male apostles constituted the original ministry. We find that to them was entrusted the responsibility of general spiritual leadership of the churches, serving as overseers (*episkope*, "office," a cognate of *episkopos* [bishop or elder], is applied to the apostolate in Acts 1:20) and ministering to believers' needs (*diakonia*, "ministry," is their work in Acts 1:25; cf. the cognate *diakonos*, "deacon," "one who ministers").

But as the gospel work prospered, it was practically impossible for the apostles alone to perform all the functions of spiritual leadership and at the same time minister to members' physical needs. Led by the Holy Spirit, the original ministry of the twelve apostles was expanded to include chosen deacons (*diakonos*) and elders (*presbyteros*) or bishops/overseers (*episkopos*).[99]

Were the offices of elders and deacons really one office originally, later split into those two? *Women in Ministry* offers slim evidence for this, which we have reproduced in note 90 and will merely comment on here. (1) According to the leading proponent of the "female minister" theory, "The kind of work for which the seven were appointed in Acts 6 is said to be done by the elders in Acts 11:30." But the Bible text does not say this. It records only that the relief money for Judea was delivered to the elders, not that the elders personally conducted the distribution, as the seven did in Acts 6. As the representatives of the believers, the elders would be the appropriate ones to receive the gifts from the distant churches, regardless of who did the actual distribution. (2) The argument that the elders' method of appointment "resembles somewhat" the method for the seven appointed in Acts 6 is a weak basis for claiming that they were the same. Such partial resemblance does not indicate that the offices were identical. (3) Finally, our author argues that because Acts 15 mentions only the offices of apostle and elder in Jerusalem, the office of deacon was not in place by the time of the Jerusalem council. But this is an argument from silence regarding deacons. The kinds of decisions spoken of in Acts 15 may well have been considered the responsibility of the apostles and elders, and not the deacons, to make.

The three points above, together with the denial that Acts 6 instituted the office of deacon, are the bases upon which our *Women in Ministry* scholar constructs his theoretical history of the appointive ministry. But as we have shown, it does not follow from these points that "we must conclude" that the church had only one office of elder at the early stage and that this one office was later split into two (elder and deacon). The New Testament writers and Ellen G. White affirm that the apostles instituted the office of deacon at a very early stage in the history of the Christian church. And each of the deacons mentioned in Acts 6 was a male.

Inasmuch as the New Testament offices of apostles, elders, and deacons were a continuation and extension of the headship and leadership roles instituted at creation (and exercised by male priests in the Old Testament, and male apostles at the time of Christ), the spiritual qualification for these offices included gender specifications ("the husband of one wife," 1 Tim 3:2, 12; Titus 1:6). Though our author claims that this gender specification actually was generic,[100] such a claim overlooks the fact that in two passages in Acts where qualifications are set forth, one for apostle (Acts 1:21) and the other for the deacon office under consideration (Acts 6:3), the text uses the Greek word *aner,* a male, instead of the generic *anthropos,* a person. The term *anthropos* could have been used here without grammatical difficulty if a person of either gender had been intended.

In light of the above facts from Scripture, the speculations about Phoebe in *Women in Ministry* cannot be sustained. Contrary to the authors' claims, Phoebe, being a "sister," could not have occupied "the same position as that of the church leaders designated in 1 Tim 3:8-10." Neither could she have been an example of New Testament "women in church leadership-headship roles."

(e) Phoebe's Commendation: A Ministerial Credential? The authors of *Women in Ministry* argue that Paul's commendation of Phoebe (as "a servant of the church") and his request on her behalf ("receive her in the Lord, as becometh saints") imply that Phoebe functioned "as Paul's emissary, as did Titus and Timothy,"[101] or that this commendation is a kind of ministerial credential for Phoebe. Writes the leading proponent of the "female minister" theory:

"Paul requests that she [Phoebe] be given the same kind of reception as his other representatives, the same kind of support and respect that Paul enjoins for Titus and the other *apostoloi* [apostles] (Titus in 2 Cor 8:24; Timothy in 1 Cor 16:10). Such a letter of commendation was the only kind of credential that the early church could offer. If there could be one female minister there could as well be many."[102]

The argument suffers from at least two serious interpretive fallacies. First, it disregards the context, namely Paul's commendations of and personal greetings to several individuals in Romans 16. Second, it is an instance of a procedure known technically as "illegitimate totality transfer," which supposes that the meaning of a word (e.g. *diakonos*) or expression (e.g., Paul's commendation) in a given context is much broader than the context allows. In this way the sense of a word (e.g., *diakonos*) or expression (commendation or request) and its reference (particular individuals, e.g., Phoebe, Titus, Timothy) are linked in an unwarranted fashion, giving the impression that the given word or expression means the same thing in any conceivable context.

Context really is the key for understanding the meaning of a word. While *diakonos* was indeed a church office, the most common meaning of the word was "servant." When the apostles call themselves *diakonos,* the translation as "minister" misses the point—they were specifying that, like Christ, they led by *serving.* They were not identifying themselves as "deacons" or "ministers." Any reference to the *office* of deacon can be determined only from the *context.* The Bible's stated fact of Phoebe's devoted service to the church, making herself the servant of all, does not mean that she held the office of "deacon." The context does not suggest that Paul is talking about a church office.

A fair reading of the New Testament shows all church office names were derived from common functions. Serving, then, did not make one a deacon; being elderly did not make one an elder; being sent (*apostolos*) did not make one an apostle like the Twelve; and being an *aggelos* (messenger) did not make one an angel, though the Greek words are the same. The context is crucial to a proper understanding of a word's meaning.

In light of our discussion in the preceding pages, the assertion that Phoebe functioned as "Paul's emissary, as did Titus and Timothy" and that Paul's letter was a "kind of credential" for one of many "female ministers" can be dismissed as a convoluted interpretation. On the contrary, when Paul commended Phoebe as "a servant [*diakonos*] of the church . . . [and] succourer of many, and of myself also" (Rom 16:1-2), he was speaking of her valuable personal ministry to members of the church as well as to himself.

We must conclude that Phoebe was not a female minister. Hence there is no basis for the statement, "if there could be one female minister there could as well be many." From the evidence given us in the New Testament, there weren't *any*.[103]

These are some of the areas in which Seventh-day Adventists should carefully examine the assertions *Women in Ministry* makes regarding the interpretation of key Bible passages. Like the Bereans, we must ask, "Are those things so?" and be prepared truly to *search* the Scriptures to find out.

In "Are Those Things So?—Part II" later in this volume I will examine how *Women in Ministry* handles certain historical, ethical, and theological issues, and I will offer my conclusions regarding the book and the choices facing the Seventh-day Adventist church today.

Endnotes

1. Nancy Vyhmeister, "Prologue," *Women in Ministry: Biblical and Historical Perspectives,* ed. Nancy Vyhmeister (Berrien Springs, Mich.: Andrews University Press, 1998), p. 5.
2. See, Beverly Beem, "What If . . . Women in Ministry?" *Focus* [Andrews University alumni magazine], Winter 1999, p. 31.
3. Vyhmeister, "Prologue," *Women in Ministry,* p. 5. Hereafter, the book *Women in Ministry* will be abbreviated as *WIM.*
4. Roger L. Dudley, "[Letter to the Editor Regarding] *Women in Ministry,*" *Adventist Today,* January-February 1999, p. 6.
5. Calvin Rock, "Review of *Women in Ministry,*" *Adventist Review,* April 15, 1999, p. 29.
6. Beverly Beem, see note 2.
7. Fritz Guy, "Review of *Women in Ministry,*" *Ministry,* January 1999, p. 29.
8. Vyhmeister, "Prologue," *WIM,* p. 5. Another writes that the silence of the Bible on the ordination of women is an invitation "to careful study, prayer for guidance, and use of sanctified reason" (see Staples, "A Theological Understanding of Ordination," *WIM,* p. 151). On the proper role of reason in theology, see Frank M. Hasel, "Theology and the Role of Reason," *Journal of the Adventist Theological Society* 4/2 (1993), pp. 172-198.
9. Space constraints will not allow me to address every flaw I see in *Women in Ministry.* In the following pages I will highlight only a few of the book's biblical, theological, and historical arguments that trouble me.

10. Richard M. Davidson, "Headship, Submission, and Equality in Scripture," *WIM*, p. 275. Denying that God made man the head of the home at creation, Davidson argues that God's original plan for the home was "total equality in marriage" (p. 267) or "total egalitarianism in the marriage relationship" (p. 269) or "headship among equals" (p. 270), expressions understood to mean the absence of role differentiation before the Fall (pp. 264, 267, 269). Though he believes that "headship" was instituted *after the Fall*, it is his view that God's original plan of "total egalitarianism in the marriage relationship" is still the same in the post-Fall situation "as it was for Adam and Eve in the beginning" (p. 269). In other words, today, as at the beginning, there should be no "ontological or functional" role distinctions. Rather, Christians should aspire for the "ideal" of "full equality" in their homes (p. 284; cf. p. 275). Cf. Peter M. van Bemmelen, "Equality, Headship, and Submission in the Writings of Ellen G. White," *WIM*, pp. 297-311, who also speaks about an "original equality" in which Eve "fully shared in Adam's headship" (pp. 308, 298).

11. A friend of mine recently stated, "I know of a pastor who once commented that everyone in the world is willing to love God with all their heart and love their neighbor as themselves— so long as each individual person is allowed to pour into the words 'love,' 'God,' and 'neighbor' whatever definition they want! But God does not allow this. He defines for us what these terms mean. The same is true for 'full equality,' etc." (Jarrod Williamson to Samuel Koranteng-Pipim, correspondence dated June 22, 1999).

12. For example, speaking at the annual meeting of North American Seventh-day Adventist college and university Bible teachers in San Francisco, California, in 1992, Ron Lawson, the "liaison" of the pro-homosexual group Kinship, correctly remarked that the push for women's ordination, when successful, will eventually open the door for the church to embrace homosexuality, since both causes are waging a similar battle against "discrimination" and since both share the same basic view of total obliteration of gender-role distinctions. The experience of other Christian denominations which have jettisoned the Bible's teaching on sexual role differentiation for an "egalitarian" model confirms Lawson's observation that an open attitude toward homosexuality inescapably follows once that step is taken. For a discussion of how Seventh-day Adventists' attitudes are changing with respect to the question of homosexuality, see my "Born A Gay and Born Again?: Adventism's Changing Attitude to Homosexuality" (1999), to be published in a future issue of the *Journal of the Adventist Theological Society.*

13. For the other side of this issue see Wayne Grudem, "The Myth of 'Mutual Submission,'" *CBMW News*, October 1996, pp. 1, 3, 4; cf. John Piper and Wayne Grudem, eds., *50 Crucial Questions About Manhood and Womanhood* (Wheaton, Ill.: Council on Biblical Manhood and Womanhood, 1992), pp. 13-15; see especially p. 13 note 4. Cf. C. Mervyn Maxwell, "Let's Be Serious," *Adventists Affirm* 3/2 (Fall 1989), pp. 25, 26.

14. Richard M. Davidson, "Headship, Submission, and Equality in Scripture," *WIM*, p. 282; Vyhmeister, "Epilogue," *WIM*, p. 434; Roger L. Dudley, "The Ordination of Women in Light of the Character of God," *WIM*, p. 399.

15. Jo Ann Davidson, "Women in Scripture," *WIM*, pp. 159, 179.

16. Ibid., p. 175.

17. Vyhmeister, "Epilogue," *WIM*, p. 434; cf. Richard M. Davidson, "Headship, Submission, and Equality in Scripture," *WIM*, pp. 259-295; van Bemmelen, "Equality, Headship, and Submission in the Writings of Ellen G. White," *WIM*, pp. 297-311.

18. Writes Richard M. Davidson: "The nature of the husband's headship is paralleled to that of Christ, who 'loved the church and gave Himself for it' ([Eph 5] v. 25). The husband's 'headship' is thus a loving servant leadership. It means 'head servant, or taking the lead in serving,' not an authoritarian rule. It consists of the husband's loving his wife as his own body, nourishing and cherishing her, as Christ does the church (vv. 28-29)" (Davidson, "Headship, Submission, and Equality in Scripture," *WIM*, p. 275). On the basis of Eph 5:33, our author underscores the headship-submission relationship as "love (of the

husband for his wife) and respect (of the wife for her husband)"; it is a kind of "mutual submission," though "this does not quite approach total role interchangeableness in the marriage relation." It "works itself out in different ways involving an ordering of relationships, and exhortations according to gender" (ibid., p. 275).

19. This is a summary of my view: "The headship principle was instituted by God at creation, reiterated after the Fall, and upheld as a model of male-female Christian relationships in the home and church. In other words, the male headship role and the female supporting role describe the relationship for which men and women were fitted by nature, unfitted by sin, and refitted by grace. This relationship was formed at creation, deformed by the fall, and re-formed (i.e., transformed for its original purpose) by the gospel" (Samuel Koranteng-Pipim, *Searching the Scriptures*, pp. 49-50).

20. Richard M. Davidson, "Headship, Submission, and Equality in Scripture," *WIM*, pp. 269, 284; cf. Vyhmeister, "Epilogue," *WIM*, p. 434; van Bemmelen, "Equality, Headship and Submission in Ellen G. White," *WIM*, pp. 297-311.

21. Richard M. Davidson, "Headship, Submission, and Equality in Scripture," *WIM*, p. 260.

22. Richard M. Davidson summarizes the arguments of those who believe in headship before the Fall as follows: "(a) man is created first and woman last ([Gen] 2:7, 22), *and the first is superior and the last is subordinate or inferior;* (b) woman is formed *for the sake of man*—to be his 'helpmate' or *assistant to cure man's loneliness* (vss. 18-20); (c) woman comes out of man (vss. 21-22), *which implies a derivative and subordinate position;* (d) woman is created from man's rib (vss. 21-22), *which indicates her dependence upon him for life;* and (e) the man names the woman (v. 23), *which indicates his power and authority over her*" (Richard M. Davidson, "Headship, Submission, and Equality in Scripture," *WIM*, pp. 260-261, emphasis added; cf. his "The Theology of Sexuality in the Beginning: Genesis 1-2," *Andrews University Seminary Studies* 26/1 [1988]:14). To my knowledge, no credible Adventist scholar opposing women's ordination uses the above reasons in support of headship before the Fall. It is regrettable that our author goes to great lengths to challenge what is really a non-issue in the Adventist debate over the biblical legitimacy of women's ordination. In fact, in my earlier work, I specifically challenged such reasons as views not held by any Seventh-day Adventist scholar who has written against women's ordination (see my *Searching the Scriptures* (1995), p. 54 note 3. Our position on the headship principle is *not* the same as these summarized views. I have argued that Genesis 1-2 teaches an ontological equality between the sexes; consequently, no inferiority or superiority exists within the complementary relationship of man and woman (*Searching the Scriptures*, pp. 26-27, 31-32, 45-47; cf. *Receiving the Word*, p. 120).

23. (1) God expressed His intended arrangement for the family relationship by creating Adam first, then Eve. Therefore, Paul writes, "I do not permit a woman to teach or to have authority over a man; she must be silent. *For Adam was formed first, then Eve*" (1 Tim 2:12, 13 NIV). (2) God gave to Adam the directions for the first pair regarding custody of the garden and the dangers of the forbidden tree (Gen 2:16, 17). This charge to Adam called him to spiritual leadership. (3) God instructed that in marriage it is the man who must act, leaving dependence on father and mother to be united with his wife (Gen 2:24; Matt 19:4, 5), and that in the marriage relationship the woman's role is to complement the man's in his duties (Gen 2:18, 23, 24). In this instruction, God charged the man with the responsibility of lovingly providing for and protecting the woman (cf. Eph 5:25, 28-31; 1 Pet 3:7; 1 Tim 3:4; Titus 1:6). (4) Although Eve first disobeyed, it was only after Adam had joined in the rebellion that the eyes of *both* of them were opened (Gen 3:4-7). More significantly, after the Fall God first addressed *Adam*, holding him accountable for eating the forbidden fruit: "Where art thou? . . . Hast thou eaten of the tree . . . ?" (Gen 3:9-12; cf. 3:17: *"Because thou hast hearkened unto the voice of thy wife,* and hast eaten of the tree. . ."). It appears inexplicable for God, who in His omniscience already knew what had happened, to act in this way if Adam had not been given headship in the Eden relationship. (5) Despite the fact that the woman initiated the rebellion,

it is *Adam,* not Eve, nor even both of them, who is blamed for our Fall (Rom 5:12-21; 1 Cor 15:21, 22), which suggests that as the spiritual head in the partnership of their equal relationship, Adam was the representative of the family. See *Searching the Scriptures,* pp. 46, 47.

24. For a detailed discussion, see Werner Neuer, *Man and Woman in Christian Perspective,* translated by Gordon J. Wenham (Wheaton, Ill.: Crossway Books, 1991), pp. 59-81; cf. *Women in the Church: Scriptural Principles and Ecclesial Practice,* A Report of the Commission on Theology and Church Relations of the Lutheran Church Missouri Synod (n.p.: 1985), pp. 18-28.

25. Jo Ann Davidson, "Women in Scripture," *WIM,* p. 158.

26. See, for example, Jo Ann Davidson, "Women in Scripture," *WIM,* pp. 157-169; cf. Vyhmeister, "Epilogue," *WIM,* pp. 2-4, "Proper Church Behavior in 1 Timothy 2:8-15," *WIM,* p. 335.

27. Jo Ann Davidson, "Women in Scripture," *WIM,* p. 179; cf. pp. 175, 158.

28. Vyhmeister, "Epilogue," *WIM,* p. 434; see also her "Proper Church Behavior in 1 Timothy 2:8-15," *WIM,* p. 350.

29. Raoul Dederen, "The Priesthood of All Believers," *WIM,* p. 23, emphasis mine; cf. J. H. Denis Fortin, "Ordination in the Writings of Ellen G. White," *WIM,* pp. 116-118, 128, 129 and Jerry Moon, "Ellen G. White on Women in Ministry," *WIM,* p. 203.

30. "This new order, the priesthood of all believers," according to *Seventh-day Adventists Believe . . . ,* p. 143, "means that each church member has a responsibility to minister to others in the name of God, and can communicate directly with Him without any human intermediary. It emphasizes the interdependence of church members, as well as their independence. This priesthood makes no qualitative distinction between clergy and laity, *although it leaves room for a difference in function between these roles"* (emphasis mine).

31. The phrase "husband of one wife" is a call to *monogamous fidelity*—that is to say, an elder must be "faithful to his one wife." The word *aner* (translated "man" or "husband" in the English translations) means a *male* of the human race. Therefore, the Greek phrase, *mias* [of one] *gynaikos* [woman] *andra* [man] (1 Tim 3:2; Titus 1:6), literally translates as a "man of one woman," or "one-woman man," meaning "a *male* of one woman." When used of the marriage relation it may be translated "husband of one wife" (KJV) or "husband of but one wife" (NIV). Because in this passage the words for "man" and "woman" do not have the definite article, the construction in the Greek emphasizes character or nature. Thus, "one can translate, 'one-wife sort of a husband,' or 'a one-woman sort of a man.' . . . Since character is emphasized by the Greek construction, the bishop should be a man who loves only one woman as his wife." (See Kenneth S. Wuest, *The Pastoral Epistles in the Greek New Testament for the English Reader* [Grand Rapids, Mich.: Eerdmans, 1952], p. 53.) Also, because the word "one" (*mias*) is positioned at the beginning of the phrase in the Greek, it appears to emphasize this *monogamous* relationship. Thus, the phrase "husband of one wife" is calling for *monogamous fidelity*—that is to say, an elder must be "faithful to his one wife" (NEB). For an excellent summary of the various interpretations of this text, see Ronald A. G. du Preez, *Polygamy in the Bible with Implications for Seventh-day Adventist Missiology* (D.Min. project dissertation, Andrews University, 1993), pp. 266-277.

32. Dederen has pointed out that there were a few non-Levites who, on occasion, performed priestly functions: Gideon (Judg 6:24-26); Manoah of Dan (Judg 13:19); Samuel (1 Sam 7:9); David (2 Sam 6:13-17); Elijah (1 Kgs 18:23, 37, 38) (see Dederen, "The Priesthood of All Believers," *WIM,* p. 11). A careful study of these specific instances may offer some biblically-consistent explanations. For example, since Samuel was Elkanah's son, he too was a Levite (1 Chron 6:27, 28, 33, 34; cf. *Patriarchs and Prophets,* p. 569). On David's apparent offer of sacrifices, it appears from 1 Chronicles 15ff. and *Patriarchs and Prophets,* pp. 706, 707, that David did not offer the sacrifices himself but simply paid for and directed them. It is in this sense that he is credited with offering the sacrifices. Regarding Elijah, we have no evidence from Scripture about whether or not he was not a Levite. Without other information, we may

have to assume that he was a Levite living in Gilead (1 Kings 17:1). With respect to Gideon, Ellen White makes it clear that though God in this one instance specifically directed him to offer the sacrifice, it was wrong for Gideon to have "concluded he had been appointed to officiate as a priest" (*Patriarchs and Prophets*, p. 547; cf. p. 555); the same may apply to Manoah of Dan (Judg 13:19). In any event, even if it can be shown that the above Old Testament characters were all non-Levites and that they actually performed priestly functions, these exceptions only prove the validity of an established rule that only Levites could serve as priests. The phenomenon of "exceptions" to the normal order must always be recognized. But when those exceptions were initiated by humans instead of by God, there were disastrous consequences. See, for example, Korah (Num 16:3-7); Saul (1 Sam 13:8-14); Jeroboam (1 Kings 12:31-13:5; 13:33, 34); Uzzah (2 Chron 26:16-21).

33. Walter B. T. Douglas, "The Distance and the Difference: Reflections on Issues of Slavery and Women's Ordination in Adventism," *WIM*, pp. 379-398; cf. Vyhmeister, "Epilogue," *WIM*, pp. 434, 435.

34. Douglas credits Richard M. Davidson for his comparison of pro-slavery and anti-women's ordination arguments, *WIM*, pp. 394, 395; see especially note 44 on p. 398.

35. To balance *WIM*'s discussion of "the hermeneutical problem of slavery," see Robert W. Yarbrough, "The Hermeneutics of 1 Timothy 2:9-15," in *Women in the Church: A Fresh Analysis of 1 Timothy 2:9-15*, eds. Andreas J. Köstenberger, Thomas R. Schreiner, and H. Scott Baldwin (Grand Rapids, Mich.: Baker, 1995), pp. 185-190; George W. Knight III, *The Role Relationship of Men and Women: New Testament Teaching* (Chicago, Ill.: Moody Press, 1985), pp. 7-15.

36. See my *Searching the Scriptures*, p. 62.

37. Richard M. Davidson, "Headship, Submission, and Equality in Scripture," *WIM*, pp. 281, 282.

38. Jo Ann Davidson, "Women in Scripture," *WIM*, p. 176. Davidson is citing Evelyn and Frank Stagg's response to her questions: "Why did Jesus select twelve male apostles? . . . Why only *Jewish* men?"

39. Richard M. Davidson, "Headship, Submission, and Equality in Scripture," *WIM*, p. 294 note 111.

40. Stephen B. Clark perceptively writes: "We can contrast Jesus with the rabbis as seen in the Talmud and Midrash. Jesus does not behave the same way. Women come to him and he helps them directly. He heals them (Mk. 5:25-34). On occasion he touches them (Mt. 8:14-15). He talks to them individually, regularly in private and sometimes in public (Jn. 11:17-44). On one occasion he even talks to a woman when both of them were unaccompanied (Jn 4:7-24). He teaches women along with the men (Lk 10:38-42). When he teaches, he speaks of women and uses womanly tasks as illustrations. On occasion, he makes use of two parables to illustrate the same point, one drawn from the activities of men, the other from the activities of women (Lk. 15:3-10). He never shows disrespect to women, nor does he ever speak about women in a disparaging way. He relates in a brotherly fashion to women whom he knows. He has some women traveling with him to serve him (Lk. 8:1-3). Finally, he calls women 'daughters of Abraham' (Lk. 13:16), explicitly according them a spiritual status like that accorded to men. One might add that after his resurrection Jesus appears to women first and lets them carry the news to the men (Jn. 20:11-19; Mt. 28:9-10)" (Clark, *Man and Woman in Christ: An Examination of the Roles of Men and Women in Light of Scripture and the Social Sciences* [Ann Arbor, Mich.: Servant Books, 1980], pp. 241, 242).

41. Richard M. Davidson, "Headship, Submission, and Equality in Scripture," *WIM*, p. 282.

42. Ibid. Davidson points to the work of Jo Ann Davidson and Robert M. Johnston for support.

43. Refer to Samuele Bacchiocchi's detailed critique of Richard M. Davidson's chapter beginning on p. 65 of this volume.

44. Robert M. Johnston, "Ministry in the New Testament and Early Church," *WIM,* p. 47; cf. Richard M. Davidson, "Headship, Submission, and Equality in Scripture," *WIM,* pp. 282, 294 note 113; Jo Ann Davidson, "Women in Scripture," *WIM,* p. 177; Vyhmeister, "Epilogue," *WIM,* p. 434.

45. We can only refer to them as apostles in the general usage of the word *apostolos,* meaning a "sent one." In this sense, both Andronicus and Junia could be conceived as missionaries— dedicated individuals engaged in the soul-winning ministry of the early church.

46. Robert M. Johnston lays the foundation for the speculative interpretation that Junia was a "female apostle." While acknowledging that the phrase in Romans 16:7 ("among the apostles") is ambiguous, Johnston believes that it is "more probable" to take it to mean Junia was "numbered among the apostles." He gives the following interesting reasons: "(1) It is the most natural way to take the Greek; (2) Ancient commentaries, when not ambiguous, such as that of Chrysostom, understood it that way . . . ; (3) Paul, who was always anxious to defend his apostleship, would not have spoken of the apostolic opinion in such a way as to seem not to include himself; (4) The first option [i.e., Junia being "well known by the apostles"] is not usually taken when the person in question is thought to be a man named Junias" (Johnston, "Ministry in the New Testament and Early Church," pp. 54, 55 note 11). Readers should understand that the above weak reasons are the sole basis for the belief by the authors of *Women in Ministry* that Junia was a "female apostle"!

47. Ibid., p. 56 note 14.

48. W. Larry Richards, "How Does A Woman Prophesy and Keep Silence at the Same Time? (1 Corinthians 11 and 14)," *WIM,* p. 315.

49. Vyhmeister, "Proper Church Behavior in 1 Timothy 2:8-15," *WIM,* pp. 338-340.

50. On Gnosticism and its late sources, see Edwin M. Yamauchi, *Pre-Christian Gnosticism: A Survey of the Proposed Evidences,* second edition (Grand Rapids, Mich.: Baker Book House, 1983).

51. Responding to a similar hypothesis by Richard and Catherine Kroeger that in 1 Timothy 2:11ff Paul was correcting the "proto-gnostic" heresies in the Ephesian church, Thomas R. Schreiner wrote, "The lack of historical rigor, if I can say this kindly, is nothing less than astonishing. They have clearly not grasped how one should apply the historical method in discerning the nature of false teaching in the Pauline letters." "An Interpretation of 1 Timothy 2:9-15: A Dialogue with Scholarship," in *Women in the Church: A Fresh Analysis of 1 Timothy 2:9-15,* eds. Andreas J. Köstenberger, Thomas R. Schreiner, and H. Scott Baldwin (Grand Rapids, Mich.: Baker, 1995), pp. 109, 110.

52. Werner G. Kümmel, *Introduction to the New Testament,* 17th ed. (Nashville, Tenn.: Abingdon, 1975), p. 379.

53. Jo Ann Davidson, "Women in Scripture," *WIM,* p. 178; Richard M. Davidson, "Headship, Submission, and Equality in Scripture," *WIM,* pp. 280, 294 note 108; cf. Vyhmeister, "Proper Church Behavior in 1 Timothy 2:8-18," *WIM,* pp. 338-340, 351 note 4. Cf. Sharon Hodgin Gritz, *Paul, Women Teachers, and the Mother Goddess at Ephesus: A Study of 1 Timothy 2:9-15 in Light of the Religious and Cultural Milieu of the First Century* (Lanham, Md.: University Press of America, 1991). On the basis of Gritz's work Jo Ann Davidson lists the "major tenets" of this Mother Goddess worship as the belief that "a female goddess gave birth to the world, that Eve was created before Adam, and that to achieve highest exaltation woman must achieve independence from all males and from child-bearing. Sharon Gritz suggests that such false teaching was endangering the faith of the new Christian converts in Ephesus. And Paul was likely counseling Timothy how to deal with such radical departure from the Christian faith" (Jo Ann Davidson, p. 178; cf. Richard M. Davidson, p. 280). In building their work on Gritz, some *Women in Ministry* authors are apparently not aware that Gritz's claims and assumptions "are a thorough misrepresentation of ancient Ephesus and of Artemis Ephesia" (see S. M. Baugh's "A Foreign World: Ephesus in the First Century," in *Women in the Church: A Fresh Analysis of 1 Timothy 2:9-15,* eds. Andreas

J. Köstenberger, Thomas R. Schreiner, and H. Scott Baldwin [Grand Rapids, Mich.: Baker, 1995], p. 50). For more on this, see next note.

54. "The central weakness of Gritz's work," argues one knowledgeable scholar, "is that she nowhere provides any kind of in-depth argument for the influence of the Artemis cult in 1 Timothy. She records the presence of such a cult in Ephesus and then simply assumes that it functions as the background to the letter [of Paul to Timothy]. To say that sexual impurity (1 Tim. 5:11-14) and greed (1 Tim. 6:3-5) are signs of the Artemis cult is scarcely persuasive! Many religious and nonreligious movements are plagued with these problems. Gritz needs to show that the devotion to myths and genealogies (1 Tim. 1:3-4), the Jewish law (1 Tim. 1:6-11), asceticism (1 Tim. 4:3-4), and knowledge (1 Tim. 6:20-21) indicate that the problem was specifically with the Artemis cult" (Thomas R. Schreiner, "An Interpretation of 1 Timothy 2:9-15: A Dialogue with Scholarship," in *Women in the Church: A Fresh Analysis of 1 Timothy 2:9-15,* eds. Andreas J. Köstenberger, Thomas R. Schreiner, and H. Scott Baldwin [Grand Rapids, Mich.: Baker, 1995], p. 110).

55. Jo Ann Davidson, "Women in Scripture," *WIM,* p. 178, emphasis supplied, citing Thomas C. Geer, Jr., "Admonitions to Women in 1 Tim 2:8-15," *Essays on Women in Earliest Christianity,* ed. C. D. Osburn (Joplin: College Press, 1993), 1:281-302.

56. Richard M. Davidson, "Headship, Submission, and Equality in Scripture," *WIM,* pp. 283, 280, emphasis supplied.

57. According to Vyhmeister, three main religious currents interacted to form the background of 1 Timothy—(1) pagan worship of the mother goddess in Ephesus (Artemis or Diana), (2) Judaism, and (3) "incipient gnosticism." She concludes: "From this mixed environment came the women in the Ephesian congregations. Those from pagan backgrounds would need to learn that the excesses of Artemis worship, along with its ascetic or sensual practices, were inappropriate for Christian women." On the other hand, those from a Jewish background would need encouragement "to study, learn, and serve in the Christian community" (Vyhmeister, "Proper Church Behavior in 1 Timothy 2:8-15," *WIM,* p. 340).

58. Ibid., pp. 342, 353 note 50; cf. p. 352 note 31.

59. Ibid., p. 344, emphasis added. Vyhmeister interprets the word translated "authority" (*authentein*) in Paul's statement, "I do not permit women to teach or have authority" to mean "taking independent action, assuming responsibility, or even . . . instigating violence" (p. 345). She offers this creative interpretation for 1 Tim 2:11-12: "Paul does not want women to teach at this time, certainly not until they have learned in quietness, submitting to the teaching of the gospel. Neither does he want them to take upon themselves the responsibility for violence or independent action of any kind. They should emulate Eve, who in the next verse is presented as responsible for the fall of the human race" (p. 346).

60. Jo Ann Davidson, "Women in Scripture," *WIM,* p. 178.

61. For an alternative to the speculations in *Women in Ministry,* see C. Raymond Holmes's "Does Paul Really Prohibit Women from Speaking in Church?" beginning on pp. 161 in the current volume.

62. Paul's description of Christ in Colossians 1:15-18 RSV as "the first-born of all creation," "the head of the body, the church" suggests His pre-eminent authority. His headship and authority are tied in with His being the "first-born." Paul's use of "first-born" language to express the headship and authority of Christ suggests that he attached the same meaning to Adam's being "first formed." If this is the case, it indicates that Paul saw in the priority of Adam's creation the establishment of his right and responsibility as the head of the first home, the first church. This may explain why Adam is presented as the one who brought death into the world, and Christ, the second Adam, as the One who brought life (Rom 5:12-21).

63. Vyhmeister, "Proper Church Behavior in 1 Timothy 2:8-15," *WIM,* pp. 346, 347.

64. Thomas R. Schreiner, "An Interpretation of 1 Timothy 2:9-12: A Dialogue with Scholarship," in *Women in the Church: A Fresh Analysis of 1 Timothy 2:9-15,* eds. Andreas

J. Köstenberger, Thomas R. Schreiner, and H. Scott Baldwin (Grand Rapids, Mich.: Baker, 1995), p. 112.

65. This position is best articulated by a leading conservative among the Seminary scholars. Writes Richard M. Davidson: "The nature of the husband's headship is paralleled to that of Christ, who 'loved the church and gave Himself for it' ([Eph 5] v. 25). The husband's 'headship' is thus a loving servant leadership. It means 'head servant, or taking the lead in serving,' not an authoritarian rule. It consists of the husband's loving his wife as his own body, nourishing and cherishing her, as Christ does the church (vv. 28-29)." On the basis of Ephesians 5:33, our author underscores the headship-submission relationship as "love (of the husband for his wife) and respect (of the wife for her husband)"; it is a kind of "mutual submission," though "this does not quite approach total role interchangeableness in the marriage relation." It "works itself out in different ways involving an ordering of relationships, and exhortations according to gender" (Richard M. Davidson, "Headship, Submission, and Equality in Scripture," *WIM*, p. 275).

66. Ibid., pp. 269, 271, 275, 280, 281, 284.

67. Ibid., p. 269, emphasis mine. Again he writes: "But just as the equal partnership was described in Gen 2:24 as the divine ideal for *after the Fall* as well as before, so the New Testament counsel calls husbands and wives to a love partnership of mutual submission" (ibid., pp. 280, 281).

68. Ibid., p. 274.

69. Harold O. J. Brown, "The New Testament Against Itself: 1 Timothy 2:9-15 and the 'Breakthrough' of Galatians 3:28," in *Women in the Church: A Fresh Analysis of 1 Timothy 2:9-15*, p. 202. For more on this, see Samuele Bacchiocchi's evaluation of Davidson's chapter, beginning on pp. 65 of the current book.

70. Ellen G. White writes: "In both the Old and the New Testament the marriage relation is employed to represent the tender and sacred union that exists between Christ and His people, the redeemed ones whom He has purchased at the cost of Calvary. . . . [Quoting Isaiah 54:4, 5; Jeremiah 3:14, and Song of Solomon 2:16; 5:10; 4:7.] In later times Paul the apostle, writing to the Ephesian Christians, declares that *the Lord has constituted the husband the head of the wife,* to be her protector, the house-band, binding the members of the family together, even as Christ is the head of the church and the Saviour of the mystical body. . . . [Quoting Ephesians 5:24-28]. The grace of Christ, and this alone, can make this institution what God designed it should be—an agent for the blessing and uplifting of humanity. And thus the families of earth, in their unity and peace and love, may represent the family of heaven. Now, as in Christ's day, the condition of society presents a sad comment upon *heaven's ideal of this sacred relation.* Yet even for those who have found bitterness and disappointment where they had hoped for companionship and joy, the gospel of Christ offers a solace" (*Thoughts from the Mount of Blessing,* pp. 64, 65, emphasis mine).

71. "God had a church when Adam and Eve and Abel accepted and hailed with joy the good news that Jesus was their Redeemer. These realized as fully then as we realize now the promise of the presence of God in their midst. Wherever Enoch found one or two who were willing to hear the message he had for them, Jesus joined with them in their worship of God. In Enoch's day there were some among the wicked inhabitants of earth who believed. The Lord never yet has left His faithful few without His presence nor the world without a witness" (Ellen G. White, *The Upward Look,* p. 228).

72. For the various expressions used in the Bible to refer to the church as God's family, see Vern Poythress, "The Church as Family: Why Male Leadership in the Family Requires Male Leadership in the Church," in *Recovering Biblical Manhood and Womanhood: A Response to Evangelical Feminism,* eds. John Piper and Wayne Grudem (Wheaton, Ill.: Crossway, 1991), pp. 233-236.

73. Chrysostom (A.D. 347-407), *Homily XX on Ephesians,* cited by Stephen B. Clark, *Man and Woman in Christ* (Ann Arbor, Mich.: Servant Books, 1980), p. 134.

74. "In the home the foundation is laid for the prosperity of the church. The influences that rule in the home life are carried into the church life; therefore, church duties should first begin in the home" (Ellen G. White, *My Life Today*, p. 284). "Every family in the home life should be a church, a beautiful symbol of the church of God in heaven" (*Child Guidance*, p. 480). Not only is authority in the church patterned after the home, but the home government is patterned after the church. Ellen G. White wrote, "The rules and regulations of the home life must be in strict accordance with a 'Thus saith the Lord.' The rules God has given for the government of His church are the rules parents are to follow in the church in the home. It is God's design that there shall be perfect order in the families on earth, preparatory to their union with the family in heaven. Upon the discipline and training received in the home depends the usefulness of men and women in the church and in the world" (*Signs of the Times*, Sept. 25, 1901).

75. Jacques B. Doukhan, "Women Priests in Israel: A Case for their Absence," *WIM*, pp. 36, 37.

76. Ibid., p. 39.

77. Apparently, this questionable interpretation of Genesis that is included in *Women in Ministry* is not challenged by members of the Ad Hoc Committee as long as there is "agreement on the big picture" of ordination (borrowing the words of the editor; see Vyhmeister, "Prologue," *WIM*, p. 4).

78. P. Gerard Damsteegt has offered a more thorough response to Doukhan's "female priest" concept in his contribution to this volume (see pp. 123-128). See also Samuele Bacchiocchi's comments in this volume (pp. 65-110).

79. Doukhan, "Women Priests in Israel: A Case for their Absence," *WIM*, p. 38; cf. pp. 33, 34.

80. Raoul Dederen, "The Priesthood of All Believers," *WIM*, p. 23. Though Dederen does not believe in "female priests" in the Old Testament, yet as we have shown in an earlier section he goes on to argue mistakenly that a "radical transformation occurred" so that a new "priesthood of all believers" is unfolded in the New Testament which allows women to function "in all expressions of the ordained ministry." Cf. Denis Fortin, "Ordination in the Writings of Ellen G. White," *WIM*, p. 116; Vyhmeister, "Epilogue," *WIM*, p. 433.

81. Thus, prior to Sinai, Noah (Gen 8:20), Abraham (Gen 22:13), Jacob (Gen 35:3) and Job (Job 1:5) performed the headship role of priest of the family. At the time of the Exodus, God claimed all firstborn males as His own (Ex 13:1, 2, 13). Later, because of their faithfulness during the time of the golden-calf apostasy, males from the tribe of Levi took the place of the firstborn males or heads of each family (Num 3:5-13; 8:14-19).

82. See, for example, Richard M. Davidson, "Headship, Submission, and Equality in Scripture," *WIM*, pp. 272, 273; cf. Vyhmeister, "Epilogue," *WIM*, p. 434, and Jo Ann Davidson, "Women in Scripture," *WIM*, pp. 161-172.

83. The unique leadership of Deborah as prophet and judge in Israel is probably the best model of how women can exercise their leadership gifts in the absence of capable men (Judges 4:4ff.). However, whereas other judges led Israel into victory in battles, God told Deborah that Barak was to do this (vv. 6-7). Apparently she was the only judge in the book of Judges who had no military function. Also, Deborah does not assert leadership for herself, but she gives priority to a man—even though the man was reluctant to go to battle without her (v. 8). Deborah rebuked Barak's failure to exercise his God-appointed leadership; he is told that the glory that day would go to a woman—not Deborah, but Jael (vv. 9, 17-25.). Thomas R. Schreiner therefore concludes that Deborah's "attitude and demeanor were such that she was not asserting her leadership. Instead, she handed over the leadership, contrary to the pattern of all the judges, to a man" (see Schreiner, "The Valuable Ministries of Women in the Context of Male Leadership: A Survey of Old and New Testament Examples and Teaching," in John Piper and Wayne Grudem, eds., *Recovering Biblical Manhood and Womanhood*, p. 216).

84. Jo Ann Davidson, "Women in Scripture," *WIM*, p. 177.

85. Richard M. Davidson, "Headship, Submission, and Equality in Scripture," *WIM*, p. 282; cf. Vyhmeister, "Epilogue," *WIM*, p. 434.

86. Robert M. Johnston, "Ministry in the New Testament and Early Church," *WIM*, p. 51. Jo Ann Davidson points readers to Robert Johnston's work in *Women in Ministry*, where the latter "studies this significant detail" about Phoebe's role as a *diakonos* (Jo Ann Davidson, p. 185 note 78). Similarly, Richard M. Davidson writes: "Examples of women in church leadership/headship roles have been ably presented in Robert Johnston's and Jo Ann Davidson's chapters (chaps. 3 and 9). Deacons included the woman Phoebe (Rom 16:1) and probably the women referred to in 1 Tim 3:11" (Richard M. Davidson, *WIM*, p. 282).

87. Robert M. Johnston argues that the appointive ministry "could be called either *diakonos* (suggested by *diakonein* in Acts 6:2), a word describing function, or *presbyteros*, a word describing dignity" (Johnston, "Ministry in the New Testament and Early Church," *WIM*, p. 49).

88. Johnston is aware that the office of the seven men in Acts 6 is referred to as "deacon" in the chapter heading of Ellen G. White's *The Acts of the Apostles* (chapter 9 of that book is titled "The Seven Deacons," pp. 87-96). But he counters: "It is to be noted, however, that the chapter titles are mostly the work of the editors. The term 'deacon' does not occur in the text itself. Mrs. White simply calls them 'officers' (89)." See Johnston, "Ministry in the New Testament and Early Church," *WIM*, pp. 49, 57 note 19. Note, however, that in *The Acts of the Apostles*, pp. 91, 106, Ellen G. White does refer to the seven as "deacons."

89. Johnston argues that "at least in the earliest period, what can be said of 'deacon' also applies to 'elder.' Both were ministries which in the beginning were one, and they likely remained one in many places for several decades. Even in the pastoral epistles, Timothy is called *diakonos* (which the RSV translates 'minister') in 1 Tim 4:6, though he had a charismatic gift that was somehow associated with prophetic designation and the laying on of hands (1:18, 4:14)" (Johnston, *WIM*, p. 51).

90. Johnston concludes: "To begin with there was only one appointive ministry that could be called either *diakonos* (suggested by *diakonein* in Acts 6:2), a word describing function, or *presbyteros* [elder], a word describing dignity. Only later did this one ministry divide into two levels, and the two terms came to be used to designate the two levels of ministry" (Johnston, "Ministry in the New Testament and Early Church," *WIM*, p. 49). Explaining the basis of his conclusion, Johnston writes: "The kind of work for which the seven were appointed in Acts 6 is said to be done by the elders in Acts 11:30. Their method of appointment in the churches, reported in 14:23, resembles somewhat that of Acts 6. In Acts 15 we hear of only two offices in Jerusalem, those of apostle and elder. We must conclude that the church at this early stage knew of only one appointive ministry, which Luke designated 'elder'" (ibid., p. 49).

91. Ibid., p. 50.

92. Ibid., p. 51. Our author reasons this way: "Paul requests that she [Phoebe] be given the same kind of reception as his other representatives, the same kind of support and respect that Paul enjoins for Titus and the other *apostoloi* [apostles] (Titus in 2 Cor 8:24; Timothy in 1 Cor 16:10). Such a letter of commendation was the only kind of credential that the early church could offer. If there could be one female minister there could as well be many" (Johnston, p. 51; cf. ibid., p. 49)

93. Ibid., pp. 50, 51. Believing that he has "proved" that Phoebe was a "female minister" and speculating that there "could as well be many" female ministers, this scholar transforms his speculations into the following assertion of certainty: "That there were women in the appointive ministry implies something about that ministry that logically should have remained true even after it began to be differentiated into two and then three levels, just as the qualities of a piece of clay remain the same even when it is divided in two. But at some unknown point in history it ceased to be true, and women were squeezed out, at least from certain levels" (Johnston, *WIM*, p. 52).

94. Cf. Matt 20:26; 23:11; Mark 9:35; 10:43; John 12:26; Rom 13:4; 15:8; 1 Cor. 3:5; 2 Cor. 3:6; 6:4; 11:23; Gal 2:17; Eph 3:7; 6:21; Col 1:23, 25; 4:7.

95. *Seventh-day Adventists Believe . . . : A Biblical Exposition of 27 Fundamental Doctrines* (Silver Spring, Md.: Ministerial Association, 1988), p. 148.

96. The question confronting Bible students is this: Since in the Greek, the word *diakonos* can be either male or female in gender, depending on the context, when Paul referred to Phoebe as *diakonos,* was he using this term in the broad and general sense to suggest Phoebe's *activity* of caring for the needy of the church (she was a "succourer of many" [Rom 16:2])? Or was the apostle using the term *diakonos* in the narrow and technical sense to suggest that Phoebe held the male *office* of deacon (1 Tim 3:8-13), the same position held by the seven men of Acts 6?

97. Because she is described as a "sister" (Rom 16:1), she could not have served in the male office of a "deacon" without contradicting the gender requirement in 1 Tim 3:12 (a deacon must be the "husband of one wife"). Her ministry as "succourer" (KJV) or "helper" (RSV) (i.e., her "great help to many people" [NIV]), however, parallels what we designate today as the position of "deaconess." By describing Phoebe as a *diakonos,* Paul was simply speaking of her valuable ministry to church members as well as to himself. One respected scholar has captured the Adventist understanding: "Though the word for 'servant' [*diakonos*] is the same as is used for [the office of] deacon . . . it is also used to denote the person performing any type of ministry. If Phoebe ministered to the saints, as is evident from [Rom 16] verse 2, then she would be a servant of the church and there is neither need nor warrant to suppose that she occupied or exercised what amounted to an ecclesiastical office comparable to that of the diaconate. The services performed were similar to those devolving upon deacons. Their ministry is one of mercy to the poor, the sick, and the desolate. This is an area in which women likewise exercise their functions and graces. But there is no more warrant to posit an *office* than in the case of the widows who, prior to their becoming the charge of the church, must have borne the features mentioned in 1 Timothy 5:9, 10." See John Murray, *The Epistle to the Romans,* 2 vols., *The New International Commentary on the New Testament* (Grand Rapids, Mich.: Eerdmans, 1965), 2:226. Even if (for the sake of argument) we assume that the term *diakonos* in Romans 16:1 reflects its narrow and technical usage (i.e., to the male office of "deacon") and not its broad and general usage (i.e., the work of "ministry" on behalf of the church), the office of deacon is not the same as that of a "church leader"—either as elder or apostle, as is the case with Titus and Timothy. The authors of *Women in Ministry* who seek to discover an example of "women in church leadership/headship roles" in Romans 16:1 require the use of very powerful egalitarian lenses.

98. Johnston, "Ministry in the New Testament," *WIM,* p. 57 note 19.

99. According to the Bible (1) those who are permitted to perform the oversight-leadership functions of the ministerial office are elders or pastors; and (2) the New Testament makes no essential distinction between the two offices. The Greek terms for elder or presbyter (*presbyteros*) and overseer or bishop (*episkopos*) are used interchangeably in the New Testament (Acts 20:17, 28; Titus 1:5-7; 1 Pet 5:1-3). The same qualifications are required for both (1 Tim 3:1-7; Titus 1:5-9). Both perform the same work of shepherding the flock (Acts 20:17, 28; 1 Pet 5:1-4; 1 Thess 5:12). Thus we may conclude that since presbyters (elders) and bishops (overseers) are known by the same names and are required to possess the same qualifications, and since they do actually discharge the same oversight duties, the two terms refer to the same office of shepherding the flock. The book of 1 Peter brings all the terms together: pastor (shepherd), elder (presbyter), and bishop (overseer). "For ye were as sheep going astray; but are now returned unto the Shepherd (*poimen,* = pastor) and Bishop (*episkopos,* overseer) of your souls" (1 Pet 2:25). "The elders (*presbyteros*) which are among you I exhort, who am also an elder . . . : Feed (*poimano,* to tend as a shepherd) the flock of God, taking the oversight (*episkopeo*) thereof. . . . And when the chief Shepherd (*archipoimen*) shall appear, ye shall receive a crown of glory that fadeth not away" (1 Pet 5:1-4). The *elders* are commissioned to stand as *overseers,* functioning as *pastors/shepherds* to the flock.

100. Johnston, "Ministry in the New Testament and Early Church," *WIM*, pp. 50, 51.

101. Jo Ann Davidson, "Women in Scripture," *WIM*, p. 177.

102. Johnston, "Ministry in the New Testament and Early Church," *WIM*, p. 51.

103. *Seventh-day Adventists Believe . . .* , p. 150 note 10 correctly observes that because in New Testament times the term *diakonos* had a broad meaning, "it was still employed to describe all who served the church in any capacity. Paul, though an apostle, frequently described himself (see 1 Cor. 3:5; 2 Cor. 3:6; 6:4; 11:23; Eph 3:7; Col. 1:23) and Timothy . . . (see 1 Tim. 4:6), as *diakonoi* (plural of *diakonos*). (*Seventh-day Adventist Bible Commentary*, rev. ed., 7:300). In these instances it has been translated as 'ministers' or 'servants' instead of 'deacons.'"

Chapter 12

Testimony:
He Led Me All the Way

Mercedes H. Dyer

~

"God never leads His children otherwise than they would choose to be led, if they could see the end from the beginning" (*The Desire of Ages,* p. 224).

As I contemplate the way God has directed the events in my life, I humbly praise Him for His wonderful love and continual guidance.

In many instances, what I could not know at the time is clearly visible from my current perspective. Nothing has happened to me by chance. Even my birth in Argentina had special meaning thirty years later.

When my father died in 1925, leaving my mother with five small children under ten years of age, my grandfather planned to take us all to Brazil to do self-supporting work, he to start a sanitarium and my mother to start a school. She was graduating from the normal course at Emmanuel Missionary College that summer. Grandfather with his son Harvey left for Brazil with many of our belongings. We were to follow with Grandmother after graduation.

When we received a telegram that Grandfather was ill, we took Grandmother to nearby Niles, Michigan, to catch the train for Miami to sail to Brazil. I can still see her with one foot on the train step, when over the loudspeaker a message called her name. Grandfather had died. Uncle Herald pulled the trunk from the platform, and Grandmother never got on the train.

We returned to Berrien Springs, where all five of us children received our education. Mother organized us into a working family, and from childhood we

Mercedes H. Dyer, Ph.D., *is Professor of Educational Psychology and Counseling, Emerita, Andrews University.*

cleared the land, tilled the soil, cared for the cows and chickens, did laundry for the community, sold vegetables and milk, and earned our living and our tuition.

Even the work program in the Berrien Book Bindery was part of God's plan. During my senior year in college, my boss taught a class in bookbinding and asked me to take it so I would have the credit on my record. He was not a college graduate and I would be. I might need to teach bookbinding some day, he said.

After two summers of graduate work at Michigan State University, I was preparing to return to Michigan State when I was strongly impressed with the words, "Go instead to the University of Michigan! Some day you may need a degree from the University of Michigan." I did not question the impression. When I finished the M.A. thesis at the University of Michigan three years later, I asked my advisor what I should do next.

He said, "Fill out the form for your degree, and you will get the diploma in the mail."

"But I received the diploma last summer!" I said. (I had never told anyone; and in spite of having it, I struggled for a year to write the thesis.)

My advisor's face turned ashen. He said, "We never make a mistake. You must have had more credits than you need."

"Yes," I said, "I have 12 credits from Michigan State University, but the University of Michigan accepts no more than 6 credits from any school."

"Well," said my adviser, "with your M.A. thesis completed, you are ready to begin your doctorate degree."

In 1946 not many Seventh-day Adventist faculty members held M.A. degrees, let alone Ph.Ds. I had no intention of going on for a doctorate. I was happy to be dean of girls at Shenandoah Valley Academy.

Someone from the General Conference visited me and told me that I was being considered for dean of women at River Plate College in Argentina, where I was born. One day my principal called me in and told me he had a call for me to go to Argentina, but he said, "You can't go; we need you here. Our dean of boys will stay on next year and this is the first time in eight years that the same dean of girls and dean of boys will continue to work together. If the General Conference can wait another year, maybe you can go then."

River Plate College was willing to wait a year. When I arrived in 1947, Dr. Rhys, the dean of the college, took my credentials to the Argentine Minister of Education to be certified. The old gentleman said, "Her degree is an American degree, and we do not accept American degrees." Dr. Rhys insisted that the degree was from the University of Michigan. But all the gentleman said was, "Let her take another degree here in Argentina."

Dr. Rhys insisted that my degree was not from some small foreign college but from the prestigious University of Michigan. At length the Minister of Education asked, "Where is the University of Michigan?" His mind was beginning to recall that he had once visited a school in Ann Arbor, Michigan. "The University of Michigan is located in Ann Arbor, Michigan," said Dr. Rhys with growing confidence. "Well, if her degree is from Ann Arbor, we'll accept it," said the government man.

Now I knew why that voice had told me years before to attend the University of Michigan.

River Plate College wanted me to teach English—and bookbinding! God knew all along that only an Argentine-born citizen would be needed at that time in that place, and He had provided and prepared the person for His needs.

Incidentally, the gentleman at the Department of Education died a couple of months later.

In the course of time, I came to understand why I had supposed that I needed to write an M.A. thesis even after I had received my M.A. diploma. My professor had started me on a doctoral degree—which I proceeded to complete after returning to the States.

The opportunities at Columbia Union College and at Andrews University have shown me over and over that when we put God first and do not question "why," our lives are abundantly blessed. God has taken me to countries around the world and even provided a ticket for my husband to accompany me to Australia.

It was not a happenstance that the plane was full when I was on the way to Bermuda to give lectures. The steward came on the plane repeatedly and asked for passengers to give up their seats for international passengers. The offers started with vouchers of $100. After about 45 minutes, I was strongly impressed that the plane would not leave until I got off. The offers had gone for vouchers of $350, $500, $750. Several had accepted. Finally, $1000 was offered with the promise of two meal tickets and a guaranteed flight on the next plane. Yet no one was moving. I knew my assignment was not until the next day and I could well use the time studying in the airport, so I got off. The plane left.

The following year my assignment was for Australia but I did not want to go alone. When I found out the price of the ticket, I told my husband Fred that I had his ticket. But the voucher was for another airline which did not have flights to Australia. As the time approached, I visited the ticket office again and casually asked if my airline had a flight to Australia. To our surprise, they had just listed a flight for Australia!

Throughout the years I have witnessed changes and have seen the emphasis on positive-thinking programs, women's programs, the push for equality, better pay, recognition and status struggles. Yet as we study the life of Jesus, He never asked for rank or salary.

He looked to His Father and studied the prophets who had foretold His work. He lived to do His Father's will and to honor Him. He asks us to follow Him, to deny self and take up our cross and follow Him.

"Those who are true to their calling as messengers for God will not seek honor for themselves. Love for self will be swallowed up in love for Christ. No rivalry will mar the precious cause of the gospel. They will recognize that it is their work to proclaim, as did John the Baptist, 'Behold the Lamb of God, which taketh away the sin of the world.' John 1:29. They will lift up Jesus, and with Him humanity will be lifted up" (*The Desire of Ages,* pp. 179, 180).

The Bible clearly defines the role of pastors and deacons. It clearly emphasizes the role of women as helpers submissive to their husbands. Throughout the Bible and the writings of Ellen G. White, we are directed to follow God rather than our own will. It is not the spirit of Christ or of heaven to exert our own will. It is the desire of the authors of this book that Jesus be honored and that by following His example, His messengers will be humble servants not seeking their own ways but doing the will of their Master.

Part III
Historical and Theological Issues

⌣

Chapter 13

A Very Surprising (and Interesting) History

C. Mervyn Maxwell
[First published in ADVENTISTS AFFIRM, Fall 1998, pp. 18-22]

~

As you read this story, do remember that administrators are human, like the rest of us, and need our prayers. Remember too that the money they attempted to save at a crucial point in this story was God's tithe; it was not their own money.

It is a story which shows how the NAD [North American Division] leadership came to the position that (a) ordination is merely a matter of church policy, not of sacred obligation, and (b) commissioning is equivalent to ordination.

In order to move meaningfully into the story, it is needful for us, for a few moments, to flash back a couple of hundred years.

Development of the Parsonage Allowance

When America was young, many churches provided rent-free residences for their pastors. These residences were known as parsonages (or as manses, vicarages, and so on). Because they belonged to their respective churches, the law stipulated that these parsonages (or whatever they were called) were tax free. Thus the custom arose under which ministers lived in houses that were both rent free and tax free. As times changed, more and more churches began paying their pastors a "parsonage allowance," allowing the men to find their own housing at church expense. Because this new custom was a modification of the older custom, the churches persuaded the government to treat the parsonage allowance as tax free.

Not being required to pay income tax on income used for rent, mortgage, and utilities is obviously a plus for pastors, but because most pastors have been

---

The late Dr. C. Mervyn Maxwell *was Professor of Church History, Emeritus, Andrews University.*

underpaid, few people have seemed to be jealous. Indeed, the advantage has been considerably undercut with the growth of social security since 1950. The American government requires employers to pay one half of the social-security (pension) tax of their regular employees, leaving employees with the burden of paying only the other half. Ministers, however, by some quirk of the law, are considered "self-employed" and are thus required to meet their entire social-security obligation. Even so, most ministers in America pay somewhat lower taxes than other people do who have similar incomes.

The Complaint of the IRS

Now, in 1965 the United States tax people (the Internal Revenue Service, or IRS) began to complain that young Seventh-day Adventist ministers who had been designated "licensed ministers" and hadn't yet been ordained were not really ministers and so were not eligible for the parsonage allowance.

But if the licensed ministers were to be classed legally as ordinary employees rather than as self-employed persons (like ministers), the church would have to pay half of their social-security obligation. With about 850 licensed ministers at the time, the total cost to the church in the United States loomed large.

For twelve years denominational leadership stalled the IRS, hiring lawyers to persuade the government to change its mind so the church could save all this offering money. Eventually, when it became evident even to the lawyers that the IRS was not going to change its mind and was, in fact, about to seize conference properties in lieu of taxes and penalties, the leaders asked the IRS what they could do to convince the government that licensed ministers really were ministers (and so were eligible for the parsonage allowance and self-employed status).

The IRS answered that if the denomination voted that licensed ministers were authorized to perform weddings, the IRS would be satisfied. So the denominational leadership voted (1976) that in the NAD licensed ministers were empowered to do what they had never before been empowered to do, namely, to perform weddings and baptisms, provided only that they were ordained as local elders and that their conference committees approved.

This decision to make licensed ministers virtually equal to fully ordained ones was not voted without protest. In particular, some of the General Conference treasurers, the men most particularly concerned about finances, argued that it was wrong to reduce the value of ordination merely in order to save money, even to save offering money. Speaking for himself and for some of his associates, Robert Osborn, an assistant General Conference treasurer, wrote earnestly to the NAD leadership: "There is a definite detected feeling that it is hardly becoming to alter our attitude toward our licensed ministers for tax considerations in a particular country [the USA]."

But the response of top leadership was that "the difference between the functions of the licensed and ordained ministry is not a moral or theological issue, but a matter of church policy," and that "the process by which the church trains its ministers obviously is not a matter of theology nor doctrine, but one of methodology, policy."

In this way, for the sake of saving money, the denomination deprived ordination of much of its distinctiveness. No longer did the General Conference look on ordination as a calling whose nature was determined by Scripture and the Spirit of Prophecy. No longer was the work of the ordained minister a matter for theological study; instead, it was a matter for committee action and administrative policy. And this view appears to be reflected in the NAD's official position today in regard to the role of women.

Enter the Term, "Commissioned"

Now it is of significance that when the IRS said (in 1978) that it would accept a licensed minister as equivalent to an ordained minister, it used a word that had little meaning in our denomination at the time. The IRS said that if the person were allowed to perform marriages, it would accept the person as equivalent to an ordained minister whether the person had been licensed, ordained, or *commissioned*. Here was a new word, "commissioned." As we shall see, it was pregnant with meaning for the future.

Through the years many treasurers, departmental directors/secretaries, and institutional managers had been given ministerial licenses and later ordained. These licensees were individuals, mostly men, who had manifested what might be called specialized ministries, but though they were scarcely ministers in the ordinary sense, some of them at least were considered eligible for the parsonage allowance. But in the mid-1970s a reaction against this practice set in. At the very time when the General Conference and the NAD were defining ordination as merely a policy item, many Seventh-day Adventists at all levels were complaining that ordaining treasurers and departmental directors/secretaries and institutional managers just so they could get the parsonage allowance was wrong and seriously diluted the grand significance of ordination to the gospel ministry. Thus many officers who might in previous years have qualified for the parsonage allowance found themselves no longer eligible.

Then someone came up with a novel type of recognition; what about "commissioning" such people, calling them "commissioned ministers," and giving them the right to perform weddings and baptisms? The IRS had promised that it would let such people receive the parsonage allowance. Further, if such men were not ordained, the church members would stop complaining.

And so it was formally voted, and at least some treasurers, departmental directors/secretaries, and institutional managers again found themselves privileged when the American income-tax time came around on April 15 each year. Bible workers also began to be commissioned for the first time, and people felt it was right that these hard-working gospel workers should receive special recognition. Then came the idea of commissioning church-school teachers, not as ministers but as "commissioned teachers," and again people felt it was right to recognize these often unsung champions.

The Commissioning of Women Pastors

It had long been understood that granting a person a ministerial license implied that unless something went seriously amiss, the person within a few years would be ordained to the gospel ministry; in other words, persons granted ministerial licenses were considered to be "on the path toward ordination" (or, more popularly, "on track for ordination"). The few women who had been granted ministerial licenses over the years had not been viewed as "on the path toward ordination" for the reason that the church was following the obvious Bible instruction that elders should be men.

In 1975 the practice of granting ministerial licenses to women was discontinued, but at the same time the annual council of the General Conference voted that—if great caution were exercised—selected women might be ordained as local elders. You should know that this surprising turn of events came about at the insistent urging of a relatively small group of articulate promoters.

Two years later (1977), women were allowed to serve as "associates in pastoral care." The language was chosen carefully. Women were not to be known as "assistant pastors." Many leaders were uneasy about allowing women to serve as pastors.

The Battle Heats Up

In 1984 a young woman elder serving as a pastor in the Potomac conference baptized someone with the backing of her local conference but without authorization from the *Church Manual.* In 1985 the annual council of the General Conference forbade any more baptisms by women elders—but in 1986 the Southeastern California Conference voted to let women baptize anyway. The General Conference promised to work harder on ordaining women to the gospel ministry and persuaded Southeastern California to back away. The California conference did back away for a while, but in doing so it stepped up the rhetoric. We now began to hear terms like "discrimination," "gender inclusiveness," "affirmative action," and "justice!" Many Adventists felt aggrieved that the language of politics and radical feminism was invading our church.

A Difficult Choice

In 1989, in preparation for the 1990 Indianapolis General Conference session, leadership thrust upon a large study group called the "Women's Commission" the choice of voting Yes or No on a double-barreled recommendation. This recommendation, which was to be sent on to the annual council of the General Conference for further action, offered that (1) women could not now be ordained as ministers but that (2) if they met certain specifications, they could perform essentially all the functions of an ordained minister in their local churches.

Many members of the women's commission regarded the choice as unfair, for in order to vote Yes on (1) not allowing women to be ordained as ministers, it was unavoidable to vote Yes also on (2) allowing women to function essentially like ordained ministers. Most of the people on the women's commission voted Yes, which meant *both* that women could not become ordained ministers but that they could behave almost like ordained ministers in divisions that wanted them to. This recommendation went to the annual council and from there to the 1990 General Conference.

The two provisions were divided up for the 1990 Indianapolis General Conference, and the vote on Wednesday went overwhelmingly against ordaining women ministers. When the other matter came up on Thursday, many overseas delegates, feeling that the big vote was in the past, were out of their places, apparently sightseeing and shopping. The main argument offered by NAD speakers was addressed to those overseas delegates who were present. It was this: Yesterday we voted with you for what you wanted; we ask you to vote with us today, taking into account America's cultural needs. There was no appeal to Scripture. This time the vote went in favor, although by a considerably smaller margin than on Wednesday.

We all know that five years later the question of ordaining women as ministers was brought up again, though in a different fashion. This time the North American Division asked for the right to ordain women ministers to the gospel ministry *within its own territory.* Four speakers were appointed by the NAD to persuade people to vote Yes, and only one speaker was appointed to persuade them to vote No. The "No" speaker presented a strong, well-organized Bible study, and, as we have already reminded ourselves, the delegates voted 1481 to 673 that No, North America should not be authorized to go its own way.

The Push Continues

Within weeks after this vote was taken, the Sligo church, located only a few miles from General Conference headquarters, ordained some women pastors, and a little later, the La Sierra University church followed suit.

As we have observed elsewhere, within three months the NAD appointed a commission to seek ways to enlarge the scope of women as pastors. At about the same time, the idea arose of conducting "commissioning services" for women pastors.

The Commissioning Service

Thus far, the conference treasurers, departmental directors/secretaries, and institutional managers who had been granted "commissioned" status had merely received notification in the mail.

Suddenly, such privacy seemed inadequate. Urgent voices insisted that the appointment of women to commissioned-minister status should be made more public, more like, well, more like an ordination service. Thus the "commissioning service" was developed, complete with prayers, Scripture readings, a sermon, a charge, *and the laying on of hands,* all expanded to fill perhaps a whole hour at a large gathering, like a camp meeting.

Conclusion

In this way a process that began with a plan to reduce income taxes (a) produced the concept that ordination is merely a matter of church policy, and (b) developed into the concept that commissioned women ministers are equivalent to ordained male ministers.

When they learn about it, many Seventh-day Adventists consider it a very surprising (and interesting—and saddening) history.

[EDITOR'S NOTE: At the close of this article as originally published in ADVENTISTS AFFIRM, a note from the editorial board indicated that factual material had "been derived from phone calls to administrators at all levels of the church, from materials written by Bert Haloviak, Kit Watts, and Samuel Koranteng-Pipim, from additional research, and from the experience of the editors."]

Chapter 14

Great Flying Leaps:
The Use of Ellen G. White's Writings in *Women in Ministry*

Larry Kirkpatrick

The use of the writings of Ellen G. White in the book Women in Ministry *often suggests wishful thinking instead of sound analysis.*

I was present at a meeting of pastors and other church workers held at La Sierra University in late 1995, a few months after the Utrecht General Conference session rejected the request of the North American Division to allow divisions to decide for themselves whether to ordain women as pastors. There I heard my colleagues share their professional opinion that what was needed was a change in the way most Seventh-day Adventist members think, a re-education in the way they interpret the Bible, a distinct change in *their* hermeneutics. Dissatisfaction and dismay seemed to be the common feeling toward the supposedly hardheaded, ignorant parishioners in the pews. According to many of my fellow pastors, many Adventists were too caught up in a "fundamentalist" reading of the Bible and were unaware of their narrow, legalistic, ingrown biases and spiritual immaturity. What was needed, we were told, was a good dose of enlightenment which, it was said, "the seminary is working on." The consensus was that the manner in which ordinary Adventists interpreted Scripture was in need of a carefully orchestrated readjustment. When the scholars provided this "help," the church would finally move forward. The solution envisioned was *your* re-education.

Larry Kirkpatrick, *a pastor in the Nevada-Utah Conference, was an M.Div. student at the Seventh-day Adventist Theological Seminary, Andrews University, at the time of this chapter's writing.*

I did not agree. Not long afterward, I was sent to the Seminary. There, one day, *Women in Ministry* was introduced at a special chapel service. I secured my copy and over the next several weeks read and considered its arguments and assertions. I have to admit that reading *Women in Ministry* has had an impact upon my viewpoint. My conviction has grown clearer that the ordination of women to positions of pastoral ministry identical to those of men is unbiblical and also insupportable by the writings of Ellen G. White.

Since others contributing to *Prove All Things* have undertaken to address other aspects of *Women in Ministry*, this chapter will address the use of Ellen G. White's writings in the book. We will consider some of the "great flying leaps" that the authors of *Women in Ministry* have found themselves compelled to make in their attempt to support women's ordination from the writings of Ellen White.

Among the 20 chapters which constitute *Women in Ministry*, four of them— fully one-fifth—give significant consideration to Ellen White's counsel. In spite of this, her writings do not ring out prominently. In order to make her sound as though she were saying what the authors wish she had said, her writings had to be used with great selectivity, and elaborate explanatory constructs had to be devised. Although I am convinced that the authors have done their work in earnest, we must look closely at their conclusions. If the church should swallow their ideas without chewing, Adventism itself would be revised. A wholly different approach to Scripture would shift our perception of every doctrine and erect an ideological structure alien to Adventism.

Ordination in the Writings of Ellen G. White

Chapter seven of *Women in Ministry*, "Ordination in the Writings of Ellen G. White," attempts to reconstruct Ellen White's thinking on ordination in general and then apply it to the present-day issue of women's ordination.[1] In the process, the fundamental sense in which the church is understood to operate takes an alarming turn.

One issue that marks the thinking of those in favor of women's ordination is their perception of the church's degree of autonomy. Does heaven simply rubber-stamp whatever the church decides, or is the church's relationship with heaven better understood as a seeking to discover God's will through the inspired sources He has made available to it? If the rubber-stamp view is correct, then the church is left with virtual autonomy to decide what to do about issues such as women's ordination. But if the second view is right, then the church should invest its energies, not in thinking up its own solutions apart from inspiration, but in discovering heaven's solutions through the inspired writings. The line dividing these two churchly self-perceptions is sharp and black, and the hallways of history demonstrate the tendency of each.

In the chapter we here discuss, its author holds that Ellen White's understanding of ordination is best described under two headings: through an evaluation of God's purpose for the church, and by the priesthood of all believers. The author highlights what he sees as Ellen White's emphasis on the "pragmatic," "adaptable," and "practical" attitude of the church in carrying out its work.[2] But such heightened emphasis on the pragmatic could mislead us. It could lead us to the conclusion that heaven is almost indifferent to how the church functions. In contrast to this idea, Mrs. White repeatedly pointed to the necessity of order. In speaking about the early days when the battle was fought to move from pragmatism to organization, she noted that "The first-day Adventists were opposed to organization, and most of the Seventh-day Adventists entertained the same ideas. We sought the Lord with earnest prayer that we might understand His will, and light was given by His Spirit that there must be order and thorough discipline in the church—that organization was essential. System and order are manifest in all the works of God throughout the universe. Order is the law of heaven, and it should be the law of God's people on the earth."[3]

Indeed, when the great controversy began, it was the adversary who suggested that an adaptation in heaven's order be made.[4] The motive? To "preserve harmony" and to "remove dissatisfaction."[5] Yet there was nothing wrong with heaven's order. The difficulty was in the minds of the rebel angels.

The author of the chapter under discussion sees the New Testament church's "creation of new ministries"[6] in the appointment of the first seven deacons as evidence of the church's adaptability. He suggests that the early structure of the church failed to provide for new ordained ministries. Yet Mrs. White discusses the ordination of the first apostles by Christ in terms very similar to our present understanding.[7] It is difficult to see where there was a lack of provision for ordained workers in the New Testament church. The further "perfecting" of gospel order mentioned in Mrs. White's writings[8] does not portray a church that was pulling a brand new ministry out of thin air, then demanding a divine "yes" response. Instead, her description of this "further perfecting" illustrates how God guided the early church *into* heaven's revealed order. The apostles were not a free-wheeling band of merry pragmatists, but a prayerful and responsive group of listeners seeking heaven's guidance.

What proponents of women's ordination have identified as the church's pragmatic adaptability is better understood as heaven's use of situations to further reveal God's plan for the optimum organization of the church. The "adaptability" of the apostles was actually their willingness to interact with heaven and respond in harmony with the organizational plan revealed by God. This area of understanding becomes especially important when a misunderstanding of it is used to propose that if she were alive today, Ellen White's response to the issue of women's ordination would be founded on pragmatism. Rather, perhaps the reason that her responses seem so pragmatic and common-sense to us is that they were founded upon her Scripturally-informed life. Her day-to-day living carved out a habit of consistent, positive response to God's will. Assertions that the New Testament church or the early Adventist church functioned in a pragmatic manner need to be carefully reconsidered.

The trouble with the adaptive view is that it is used to give the church *carte blanche* in its approach to the Bible. Once it has been determined that the church can adapt to situations according to its own authority, apart from Scripture, all controls given in inspired writings are neutralized. The church may then pragmatically define its own theological workspace, its own boundaries. The standard, "to the law and to the testimony: if they speak not according to this word, it is because there is no light in them" (Isa 8:20), is removed, and the church places itself where there are no effective controls by which the Holy Spirit can protect it from itself. In essence, the church can decide whatever it wants, and heaven is thought to be under obligation to stamp the decision "approved."

One is startled to recall a passage in Peter Geiermann's *The Convert's Catechism of Catholic Doctrine:* "Q. *Why do we observe Sunday instead of Saturday?* A. We observe Sunday instead of Saturday because the Catholic Church transferred the solemnity from Saturday to Sunday."

By contrast, the Adventist pioneers consistently found the authoritative basis for their beliefs not in councils, creeds, theology, theologians, or academicians, but in the Word of God. They operated under hermeneutics in which *heaven* defined the workspace and the Scriptures were given full weight. If these had not been their principles, it is unlikely that our spiritual ancestors would have accepted the seventh-day Sabbath. The authority of Scripture is our only real foundation for observing the Sabbath. If the authority of Scripture is undermined in any way by the church, the church strips itself of its own authority, for its authority is derived from Scripture.[9]

The author of the chapter suggests that James White moved from holding the view that what is not made explicit in Scripture is forbidden, to his holding the view that what is not made explicit in Scripture is *not* forbidden. But in commenting on this method of approaching Scripture, Ellen White makes the following observation:

"The English reformers, while renouncing the doctrines of Romanism, had retained many of its forms. Thus though the authority and the creed of Rome were rejected, not a few of her customs and ceremonies were incorporated into the worship of the Church of England. It was claimed that these things were not matters of conscience; that though they were not commanded in Scripture, and hence were nonessential, yet not being forbidden, they were not intrinsically evil. Their observance tended to narrow the gulf which separated the reformed churches from Rome, and it was urged that they would promote the acceptance of the Protestant faith by Romanists."[10]

But in the paragraph that followed Mrs. White went on to make this point: "The very beginning of the great apostasy was in seeking to supplement the authority of God by that of the church. Rome began by enjoining what God had not forbidden, and she ended by forbidding what He had explicitly enjoined."[11]

The author of the chapter "Ordination in the Writings of Ellen G. White" leans on another scholar's doctoral dissertation.[12] However, there is little evidence that either James or Ellen White ever moved to the position suggested in it.

Ordination Formal and Informal

It is not difficult to gather from Ellen G. White's writings her understanding of ordination. In *The Acts of the Apostles* she discusses the ordination of Paul and Barnabas: "God foresaw the difficulties that His servants would be called to meet, and, in order that their work should be above challenge, He instructed the church by revelation to set them apart publicly to the work of the ministry. Their ordination was a public recognition of their divine appointment to bear to the Gentiles the glad tidings of the gospel."[13]

No magical power accompanies ordination.[14] And yet Paul considered the event of his "formal ordination"[15] or "sacred appointment"[16] "as marking the beginning of a new and important epoch in his lifework."[17] We thus suggest that "formal ordination," as Ellen White uses the phrase, has reference to ordination in the sense of recognition by God's visible church that the one ordained operates under God's sanction. In a general sense, all believers are called and ordained to work for the salvation of others; but ordination to the congregational leadership role of pastoral ministry is specifically reserved to those meeting the Scriptural requirements, including 1 Timothy 3:2 and Titus 1:6, that an elder be "the husband of one wife."

The idea that Paul and Barnabas were "already ordained" suggests the spectre of an unfortunate grey zone, in which individuals affirm in their own mind that they are ordained as well as called. Such would almost inevitably perceive themselves as waiting in line for the slowly-grinding wheels of an inept and unjust church to confirm their call. But it is heaven that affirms the call through His church, not the one waiting to be ordained who affirms it to oneself. The hazard here is the shift from recognition by a community of faith to self-recognition by the individual; thus perceived, God's church becomes a ponderous bureaucracy standing in the way of service, rather than the facilitator of recognition by the body. The shift is from recognition through the church to obligatory affirmation by the church. The author has misunderstood Ellen White.

The Priesthood of All Believers

Women in Ministry repeatedly implies that the doctrine of the priesthood of all believers in some way provides a hermeneutical highway supporting the ordination of women.[18] When the author of "Ordination in the Writings of Ellen G. White" discusses the priesthood of believers, he notes several Ellen G. White statements insisting that all who become church members are to be actively involved in working for the salvation of others. Mrs. White persistently warns against leaving this work to "only ordained ministers."[19] She even states that "All who are ordained unto the life of Christ are ordained to work for the salvation of their fellow men."[20] These statements make clear that there is a sense in which every Christian is a minister for God, and every Christian is ordained by God. However, the context of these repeated statements makes clear her double concern: that ordained pastors not hinder the ministry of church members, and that church members not sit idly on the sidelines while much work remains to be finished! Mrs. White never minimizes the work of pastoral ministry. She wants leadership to be carried forward efficiently and looks hopefully for the active participation of the whole body of the church in soul-winning. But where in Ellen G. White's writings do we find a formal ordination ceremony required for anyone to work for others? Nowhere.

In the fifth volume of *Testimonies for the Church,* pages 617-621, we find some of Ellen White's most specific statements regarding the selection of leaders for God's church. Here there is no mention of the priesthood of all believers, but we do find specific biblical guidelines such as Titus 1:5-6 and 1 Timothy 5:22 receiving primary attention. Again, the compilation on pages 437-445 of *Gospel Workers* makes no mention, not even implicitly, of the priesthood of all believers in this connection; but we do discover a concern for the kind of men to be chosen for service in the gospel ministry. Ellen White was plain when she discussed leadership and when she discussed the priesthood of believers. The readers of *Women in Ministry* should ponder why Ellen White never blended pastoral leadership with the priesthood of believers as the Seminary's book does.

The reason why Ellen White did not blend these two teachings may be that she saw clearly the distinction between the general believer's commission and the specific office of leadership. All are priests, but not all are pastors. All are to work for the salvation of others, but not all are to lead in the work of salvation for others. When these doctrines are blended together in an attempt to sustain the present drive for women's ordination, confusion is inevitable. What about children? Are children priests? Yes! Then does it logically follow that children should be ordained and function in the headship role of pastor? A great flying leap takes us to unexpected places, doesn't it?

Upon their baptism, believers are recipients of the great commission to work for the salvation of others. Specific ordination to the leadership role of pastoral ministry is to a position called in the Greek *episkopos,* a role scripturally reserved to males. The general "ordination" which all receive to work for the salvation of others and which flows from one's initial baptism does not negate the exercise of headship and submission in congregation or family. Christians are not called into a mob but into a church. It is a church operating under system and order—not *our* system and order, but heaven's. The "priesthood of all believers" argument for women's ordination is vague and ill-conceived.

The author says that Ellen White favored women as laborers in the gospel ministry. But what does he mean by this? He appears to believe that God was leading the church toward women's ordination in the role of pastoral ministry and administrative leadership.[21] On what basis? Precisely upon the basis of the church's "adaptability." Having read the chapter several times now, I still have difficulty gathering anything concrete from the reference to the priesthood of all believers. Unfortunately, it seems that this author has misunderstood Ellen White's teaching in several ways. This results in a misguided ecclesiology suggesting that the church is its own theological master. This result in particular opens the door for the subjective interpretive methods that are used to justify the ordination of women to headship roles denied them by Scripture. It is the diving board from which to make great flying leaps.

A Power that Exceeds that of Men: Ellen G. White on Women in Ministry

We now direct our attention to an entirely different chapter from *Women in Ministry*. In "'A Power that Exceeds That of Men': Ellen G. White on Women in Ministry," a different writer has examined the evidence and taken an interesting tack.[22] Highlighting Mrs. White's counsel concerning ministry options optimized for women, he presents positive insights into special opportunities uniquely tailored to women. Here, there is no press for any one-size-fits-all plan that would ignore gender-role differentiation. An exhaustive evaluation of Ellen White's thought concerning women in ministry shows that she repeatedly emphasized the value of team ministry by husband and wife.[23] This article also calls attention to the concept of specialized ministries. Having considered the evidence in this chapter, it is apparent to me that substantial benefit would accrue to God's church if Ellen White's counsel regarding women in ministry were taken more seriously. But a concept that would warp heaven's arrangement, insisting that women function in roles identical to men's, would effectively hinder the church's service to Him.

In this chapter the author is clearer generally than others in the book when considering Ellen White statements that have been presented as evidence in favor of the ordination of women. For example, the author presents the counsel given by Ellen White to Mrs. S. M. I. Henry when she became a Seventh-day Adventist. What was this counsel? To go forward and not let others "prescribe the precise way in which she should work." The chapter's author here notes that Sister White's counsel to Mrs. Henry "does not primarily concern participation in the organized church, but in a parachurch women's organization [the Woman's Christian Temperance Union, or WCTU]."[24] Whereas some authors leave the reader unaware that the women mentioned who were laboring in gospel ministry were pastors' wives giving Bible studies,[25] this author identifies the exact situation.

One weakness in this chapter is the emphasis placed upon Ellen White's statement that "It is not always men who are best adapted to the successful management of a church."[26] The author concludes from the passage that "the primary determinant of fitness for church leadership is not gender, but character."[27] But the same document that he has quoted from points out that the man in question, a brother Johnson, although a church member, was unconverted, besides being controlling and dictatorial.[28] Perhaps a more accurate conclusion would be that *conversion* is a crucial prerequisite for church leadership. An interesting parallel exists with some of Ellen White's counsel regarding family worship. To one dilatory father, she wrote the following:

"You have not zealously performed your duty to your children. You have not devoted sufficient time to family prayer, and you have not required the presence of the entire household. The meaning of 'husband' is *house band*. All members of the family center in the father. He is the lawmaker, illustrating in his own manly bearing the sterner virtues, energy, integrity, honesty, patience, courage, diligence, and practical usefulness. The father is in one sense the priest of the household, laying upon the altar of God the morning and evening sacrifice. The wife and children should be encouraged to unite in this offering and also to engage in the song of praise. Morning and evening the father, as priest of the household, should confess to God the sins committed by himself and his children through the day. Those sins which have come to his knowledge, and also those which are secret, of which God's eye alone has taken cognizance, should be confessed. This rule of action, zealously carried out by the father when he is present, or by the mother when he is absent, will result in blessings to the family."[29]

Here we see that primary responsibility for spiritual leadership in the family rests upon the father, but that the mother is also involved, exercising spiritual leadership in the father's absence. Clear preference is given to the father. The mother's role is one of support.

The author of this chapter correctly suggests that the Ellen G. White writings support specialized ministries.[30] He makes no call for the ordination of women on the same basis as for men. He does not suggest that Mrs. White's writings support the ordination of women to pastoral ministry in the sense of the contemporary pastoral leadership role, but he does find that she would approve of an ordination/ consecration service in connection with specialized local ministries.[31] Mention of the specialized nature of women's leadership in ministry is utterly lacking in the other chapters composing the book. Here is an article that does not take a great flying leap. Its author appears to have looked before leaping, and conspicuously avoided many of the pitfalls of other contributors to *Women in Ministry*.

Equality, Headship, and Submission in the Writings of Ellen G. White

Turning our attention to another chapter, we now consider "Equality, Headship, and Submission in the Writings of Ellen G. White." The contributors to *Women in Ministry* offer sometimes contradictory solutions in their attempt to solve the considerable problem of getting Ellen White to "fit" their theology of women's ordination. One example of this is the issue of headship before the Fall. In one solution, the book proposes that Adam and Eve "fully shared" in headship before the Fall.[32] This novel position could be called "initial co-headship." Other contributors to the book suggest that Ellen White understood that before the Fall there was no explicit headship.[33] But do either of these solutions mesh with the writings of Mrs. White?

The evidence presented in support of the initial co-headship view is that Adam and Eve were created equal, of the same nature, and that they were to "have no interest independent of each other," and were made so that "in all things she should be his equal."[34] Another evidence suggested is that God initially gave dominion to Adam and Eve together, and that this dominion was shared.[35] But this solution is too clever. The author has introduced a substantial distortion of the new human social structure, before sin had even entered into the world.

This strange proposal leaves the first human family with *two heads and no body.* If both were heads, then who or what were they head over? The animals? No, the Bible says they were to exercise *dominion* over the animals. To exercise headship over the animals would logically include animals in the body; yet animals are not made in God's image, only people are. The author does not discuss animals in relation to headship. But a head that is connected to no body has no headship. This theory leaves the reader in a logical trap. Paul would ask, "And if they were all one member, where were the body?" (1 Cor 12:19).

Eve was made "of the same nature"[36] as Adam. She was made to be Adam's equal "in all things." Yet sameness of nature and equality in all things does not require uniformity in roles. The very fact of their complementary individuality is strong evidence that heaven designed that they fill specialized roles. Indeed, the same document from which the author draws the quotation that "in all things she should be his equal" repeatedly points the reader back to Eve's misguided aspirations from before the Fall, in order to warn modern Eves against receiving the same temptation![37] If God wanted absolute sameness He could have simply photocopied Adam on the spot.

As we already noted, another contributor to the book holds that there simply was *no* headship before the Fall. One of the main Ellen White statements applying directly to the results of the Fall is presented as if proving that headship only came at the point of the Fall.[38] Using this quotation, the author affirms that the husband's rule over his wife "grows out of the results of sin."[39] But this is incorrect. As we will note below, the pre-Fall gender-differentiated role of "protector" assigned uniquely to the male of that holy pair has been ignored. In contrast to the mutually exclusive theories presented in *Women in Ministry,* Ellen White holds a third view that cannot be harmonized with either.

That the divine plan from before the Fall included unique roles for each one of the Edenic pair is clear in the writings of Ellen G. White. She wrote plainly that Eve was to be loved by Adam "and protected by him."[40] The husbandly role of "protector" repeatedly recurs when Mrs. White writes regarding marital relations.[41] James White saw himself in this role.[42] Adam is presented not only as "protector," but also as "the father and representative of the whole human family."[43] Had Ellen White meant that this applied to Eve as well, she could easily have said so. We needn't force the idea of role interchangeability into the statement that Eve "was his second self."[44] The "second self" statement occurs when Ellen White points out that Eve was "a part of man, bone of his bone, and flesh of his flesh,"[45] a truth both *before* and *after* the Fall. Adam's role as "protector," emanating from the period before the Fall, is echoed in similar statements.

Not only was Adam to function as Eve's protector, but he was "to maintain the principles of the heavenly family."[46] The maintenance of God's arrangement as it was before the Fall "would have brought peace and happiness. But the law that none 'liveth to himself' (Romans 14:7) Satan was determined to oppose. He desired to live for self. He sought to make himself a center of influence. It was this that had incited rebellion in heaven, and it was man's acceptance of this principle that brought sin on earth."[47]

It was while Eve was operating independently from her husband that disaster entered. Ellen White points out that Eve was at fault in not staying with her husband.[48] She also points out that when Eve approached Adam, he immediately understood that the situation was a ploy of the enemy about whom they had been warned.[49] Adam was saddened because he had not adequately maintained his protective headship role.[50] Had they been together, the ensuing 6000 years likely would have been altogether different for humankind.

When had the male been designated head of the human family structure? "In the beginning, the head of each family was considered ruler and priest of his own household. Afterward, as the race multiplied upon the earth, men of divine appointment performed this solemn worship of sacrifice for the people."[51] What was Ellen White's understanding? Not that Adam and Eve shared initial co-headship, nor that neither was head before the Fall, but simply that Adam was the head of his family.

It seems apparent that the authors of *Women in Ministry* are driven to solutions that require great flying leaps of logic that leave them scattered all over the board. It is no cutting-edge hermeneutical system that takes them to their conclusions but instead a subset of fragmentary and sometimes mutually exclusive notions.

Ellen White and Women's Rights

In "Ellen White and Women's Rights," another writer addresses herself to a significant statement by Ellen White in which she wrote that "those who feel called out to join the movement in favor of woman's rights and the so-called dress reform might as well sever all connection with the third angel's message."[52] The author's conclusion?

"In the end, the woman's movement was secular, driven by political activities, and continually searching for ways to capture the support of public opinion. The focus of Ellen White was spiritual, driven by holy living and reform that advanced personal and corporate holiness. She wanted a religious, not political, reform movement."[53]

With this we agree. But the author's conclusion that "it seems likely she [Mrs. White] would support women's ordination"[54] appears strained. How does she get there? On the basis of a great flying leap.[55]

The author takes up the passage and works through it phrase by phrase in an endeavor to derive "principles" from her study. But has she blended in any biases of her own? Although Ellen White insisted that "the spirit which attends the one [women's rights movement] cannot be in harmony with the other [the third angel's message],"[56] the author contends that "because today's ordination issue is not associated with secular, political, religious, or social reform movements such as those in the nineteenth century, this principle does not relate as it did when Ellen White wrote."[57] Instead, she has turned Mrs. White's statement around to its opposite meaning, to the point that she can assert "it seems likely she would support women's ordination."[58] How could Mrs. White support women's ordination unless the spirit which attends the one were indeed in harmony with the other?

Today's ordination issue is very much associated with secular, political, religious, and social reform agendas. Its first field of battle was the secular and the political turmoil of the nineteen seventies. It entered Christendom through denominations and religious structures that, a century and a half earlier, had willfully rejected the third angel's message. These bodies have continued to experience biblical disorientation. A certain element within contemporary Christendom has now absorbed these old issues and taken them up as their own cause. Where have we gotten the bug as a church? Not even from the world, but as an echo from the interest in women's ordination that is current in the fallen churches.

Another plank in the author's discussion is Ellen White's statement that "the Scriptures are plain upon the relations and rights of men and women."[59] The author follows with a detailed search of the Ellen G. White CD-ROM for the word "rights." While the results are interesting, she has inadvertently sidestepped a number of significant statements by Ellen White showing instances of Mrs. White's actual understanding of what she considered to be the plain teaching of Scripture. Let's consider some of Ellen White's own applications of the fact that "the Scriptures are plain upon the relations and rights of men and women":

"In early times the father was the ruler and priest of his own family, and he exercised authority over his children, even after they had families of their own. His descendants were taught to look up to him as their head, in both religious and secular matters. This patriarchal system of government Abraham endeavored to perpetuate, as it tended to preserve the knowledge of God."[60]

This reference makes plain the headship function of the male. This headship was not restricted merely to the immediate family, or just to the secular sphere, but encompassed also the religious sphere. Furthermore, this "patriarchal system of government" tended to preserve the knowledge of God.

"The Lord has constituted the husband the head of the wife to be her protector; he is the house-band of the family, binding the members together, even as Christ is the head of the church and the Saviour of the mystical body. Let every husband who claims to love God carefully study the requirements of God in his position."[61]

Here headship is again linked with protection. When the male fulfills the headship role, he acts as a family binder. He is carefully to study the requirements of God in his position. Immediately after this statement, Mrs. White observed that "Christ's authority is exercised in wisdom, in all kindness and gentleness; so let the husband exercise his power and imitate the great Head of the church."[62]

"The husband is the head of the family, as Christ is the head of the church; and any course which the wife may pursue to lessen his influence and lead him to come down from that dignified, responsible position, is displeasing to God. It is the duty of the wife to yield her wishes and will to her husband. Both should be yielding, but the Word of God gives preference to the judgment of the husband. And it will not detract from the dignity of the wife to yield to him whom she has chosen to be her counselor, adviser, and protector. The husband should maintain his position in his family with all meekness, yet with decision."[63]

Here once more we find the husband in the headship role, the partner uniquely foremost in filling the "protector" role. A careful balancing act is evident here between the wife's duty to yield and a husband's filling his role with meekness yet decision. A relationship is indicated in which "both should be yielding," and there is a beautiful sharing between the married couple. No indignity is incurred by a wife who yields to the one whom she has chosen to fill the husbandly role.

"How can husband and wife divide the interests of their home life and still keep a loving, firm hold upon each other? They should have a united interest in all that concerns their homemaking, and the wife, if a Christian, will have her interest with her husband as his companion; for the husband is to stand as the head of the household."[64]

When Mrs. White mentions that "the wife, if a Christian, will have her interest with her husband," she reminds us that being a wedded couple is not about each party's seeking their rights. Instead, each party will have his or her interest with the spouse. There is to be a "united interest" in all that concerns "their" homemaking. Homemaking is not an exclusively feminine task. The male, in filling his headship role, also contributes to homemaking. After all, "he is the houseband of the family, binding the members together."[65]

"The husband and father is the head of the household."[66]

In the above and many of the other citations that we have considered, Ellen White frequently links fatherhood with headship. An examination shows that often Ellen White has mentioned the children of the household in connection with the father's role. It seems that Mrs. White had no problem applying her understanding that "the Scriptures are plain upon the relations and rights of men and women."

Two letters to a pastor's wife over the space of some years further demonstrate Ellen White's specific application of the scriptural principles we have been considering. John and Mary Loughborough worked steadily to advance the third angel's message through the years. Even so, the household was occasionally the scene of domestic imperfections. Unfortunately, the manner in which Mary related to her husband was becoming a matter of comment, and Mrs. White wrote to her to suggest a personal adjustment:

"You have sought to please your friends altogether too much, and if you would have eternal life you must cut loose from relatives and acquaintances and not seek to please them, but have your eye single to the glory of God, and serve Him with your whole heart. This will not wean you from your husband at all, but will draw you closer to him, and cause you to leave father, mother, sisters and brothers and friends and cleave to your husband, and love him better than anyone on earth, and make his wishes your wishes. And you can live in harmony and happiness. . . . God has given the man the preference, he is the head, and the wife is to obey the husband, and the husband is not to be bitter against the wife, but love her as his own body. Dear sister, I saw that you were not half given up to God, not half consecrated to Him. Your will was not swallowed up in the will of God. And you must get ready, fitted and prepared for Christ's coming, or you will come short, be weighed in the balance and found wanting. You must be more devoted to God, more in earnest about your soul's salvation and eternal interest. I saw that if you would labor with your husband for God, you would not lose your reward. That is, labor to have him free and not lay a feather in his way, but cheer, encourage, and hold him up by your prayers."[67]

Seven years later, we again find counsel in this vein offered to Mary:

"Dear Mary, let your influence tell for God. You must take a position to exert an influence over others to bring them up in spirituality. You must guard yourself against following the influence of those around you. If others are light and trifling, be grave yourself. And, Mary, suffer me a little upon this point.

"I wish in all sisterly and motherly kindness to kindly warn you upon another point. I have often noticed before others a manner you have in speaking to John in rather a dictating manner, the tone of your voice sounding impatient. Mary, others notice this and have spoken of it to me. It hurts your influence.

"We women must remember that God has placed us subject to the husband. He is the head and our judgment and views and reasonings must agree with his if possible. If not, the preference in God's Word is given to the husband where it is not a matter of conscience. We must yield to the head. I have said more perhaps upon this point than necessary. Please watch this point.

"I am not reproving you, remember, but merely cautioning you. Never talk to John as though he were a little boy. You reverence him and others will take an elevated position, Mary, and you will elevate others.

"Seek to be spiritually minded. We are doing work for eternity. Mary, be an example. We love you as one of our children and I wish so much that you and John may prosper. Be of good courage. Trust in the Lord at all times. He will be your stronghold and your deliverer."[68]

These personal letters give clear insight into Ellen White's perception of how the "rights and relations" between men and women, presented so plainly to her in Scripture, were to be applied. One senses here no preoccupation with rights but with the simple translation of Scriptural principles into practical godliness.

In contrast to Ellen White, the author devotes fully a third of her chapter to the issue of "rights."[69] Could it be that her intense focus upon this aspect has led to a misguided analysis? Ellen White seems more concerned about humility than rights:

"A study of women's work in connection with the cause of God in Old Testament times will teach us lessons that will enable us to meet emergencies in the work today. We may not be brought into such a critical and prominent place as were the people of God in the time of Esther; but often converted women can act an important part in more humble positions."[70]

Clearly, the end-time emphasis of God's people will not be upon women's rights, but upon the third angel's message.

The author later adds that "the women's rights movement as a movement, not the favoring of women's rights, was the problem."[71] Of course, Ellen White was not against the legitimate rights of women, but she was focused upon giving the last message of mercy to the world. The very idea of Mrs. White's following in the wake of a disoriented secular movement seems far-fetched. A Mrs. Graves once approached Ellen White, insisting that she enter into the issue of woman's suffrage.[72] But in a letter to her husband James, Mrs. White wrote that her work "was of another character."[73] Indeed it was.

The conclusions[74] presented in "Ellen White and Women's Rights" are, unfortunately, an example of the logical leaps made in *Women in Ministry*. Although much of the information in the author's article is accurate and helpful, her theories appear to be overly imaginative.

Is women's ordination truly, as it has been painted in this book and in "Ellen White and Women's Rights," a matter of "rights" and "hierarchy?"[75] No. It is a matter of what God says is right in a divinely ordered system of perpetual equality between men and women with pre-Fall role differentiation.

Will failure to ordain women in our contemporary western culture reduce our influence in soul-winning as the author contends?[76] No. Rather, a failure to adhere to heaven's plan as revealed in Scripture would reduce our influence. It would make evident that we had effectively discarded the emphasis on the authority of the Bible that has characterized the Advent movement since its inception.

Would women's ordination somehow cause us to reach more people than we are reaching now?[77] No. Instead, when women take advantage of their innately heightened effectiveness in certain specialized ministries, we will see this potentiality realized.

Would the ordination of women provide more workers for the field?[78] No. Ordination neither adds nor subtracts workers from the field.

The relentless push for women's ordination only brings increased polarization within the church. It would be well to ponder how deep this polarization caused by forcing women's ordination upon the church can become before the pain becomes unbearable for some members. The "thinking" of Adventism is much more than the sum of its institutional centers, or of a certain class of "theological elites" to whom we are persistently being encouraged to turn for guidance. Too often, it is *they* who are out of touch with the thinking of Adventism as a whole.

The pro-women's-ordination subculture within the church says that, not they, but *we* need to be reeducated in Bible interpretation. In this they are simply wrong; wrong in making women's ordination a litmus test of Adventist political correctness; wrong in using the reputation of the Seminary or the *Adventist Review* for propaganda purposes; wrong for making a bold attempt to replace the sound hermeneutic that this church is founded upon. Fortunately, we can turn to the Bible and to the writings of Ellen G. White and find very sound inspired guidance. Let us draw close to the documents that heaven has provided and step back from revisionism and imaginative speculation.

Reading through the reasoning presented by many of the contributors to *Women in Ministry* is like watching a theological train wreck occur in slow motion. As inevitably as night follows day, surrendering to the subjective reorientation of Scripture presented in *Women in Ministry* would leave us without any substantial foundation for presenting the third angel's message to a world already awash in its own philosophical emptiness.

The New Hermeneutic

Before closing this chapter, it may be helpful to take a moment to distill the methods of interpretation used in *Women in Ministry* into the readily graspable core of its hermeneutical system. For although the hermeneutical method of the book is really more of a subjective quagmire than a minutely defined system, there is a shape that can be seen moving under the dark waters.

There seems to be a consistent pattern of:

A. Using inspired writings selectively.
B. Building interpretive constructs above plain Scripture.
C. Introducing subjective systems of interpretation, which tend toward enshrining a subset of the scholarly elite as the final arbiters of truth.
D. Using interpretations of selected passages as canon-within-a-canon controls (similar to but different from A).
E. Permitting the current wave of group-think to act as a correcting override.

If we accept the principles of interpretation that are showcased in *Women in Ministry,* we may not be quoting either Scripture or Ellen White thirty years from now. Instead, we will have turned our attention "to bishops, to pastors, to professors of theology"[79] as our guides. What this book, which some hope will function "determinatively" in the future of this discussion,[80] effectively does is to provide an implicit system by which the authoritative use of Scripture is replaced with an amorphous machine. This machine is actually a subjective philosophical black-box designed to generate whatever outcome is desired by its user, while characterizing the results as being conservative and biblical. It works as follows:

1. Consider various texts one by one, often providing reasonably sound explanations. Here, one can create the illusion of being "conservative," "scriptural," "biblical," etc. Texts are introduced and may provide the appearance of authoritative biblical justification for the teaching to be presented.

2. When these texts are compiled, and the impression is given that the outcome is "biblical," they may then be used to construct an overarching idea that is one step removed from Scripture and is outside of it. Several of these ideas may be

layered together. This is the "black box." Its legs are not the Scriptures that have been considered, but the "principles" represented as having been "derived" from them. In the end, Scripture need not be used authoritatively and reason can be the truly determinative element.

3. Next, an assertion may be made, based upon the "principles" or "ideas" previously derived. This is the arbitrary output of the system. Yet what comes out needn't sound arbitrary if a very reasonable or scriptural-sounding representation can be made. If presented well, the outcome can shift the foundation from Scripture to what human reason has said about Scripture. In this way, the system can affirm whatever is desired. Surround the discussion with Scriptures, leap the ideological chasm from A to B, and if no one catches on, the mental transaction has been made.

4. Finish by reemphasizing Scripture, thus solidifying the impression that the whole production has been the product of a diligent and scholarly study of the Bible.

5. This system can be reused at will. It may be made to support an almost infinite number of ideas either scriptural or unscriptural, because by means of "interpretation," it makes an end-run around the authority of Scripture. It is a shortcut on a long road that leads to places where the Seventh-day Adventist movement must not go.

It may be asked, just how does this differ from the use of Scripture among our pioneer Adventists? This indeed is the right question to ask. The documents of our history are still available for all to study for themselves. The answer is not hard to come by. The Adventist pioneers interpreted Scripture by Scripture. They saw nothing to gain by lingering in this world and proceeding from a stance of hearing God's Word only selectively. They treated the Bible as it was and is in reality: the voice of God to the soul.[81] Perhaps this is why we are told that "The most humble and devoted in the churches were usually the first to receive the message. Those who studied the Bible for themselves could not but see the unscriptural character of the popular views of prophecy; and wherever the people were not controlled by the influence of the clergy, wherever they would search the word of God for themselves, the advent doctrine needed only to be compared with the Scriptures to establish its divine authority."[82]

But what about us? What if we permit the meaning of our faith to be reworked in an unduly imaginative manner by theological experts?[83] Will our Bible-based Adventist heritage of Seventh-day Adventism be placed in jeopardy? Do we realize that the Bible could effectively be removed from the common member in the pew? that there could come a time when little meaningful difference exists between a theologian and a magician? Instead of casting a spell, the theologian may invoke an arcane, private knowledge as his final appeal. This is where reliance upon theological finesse and academic panache risks taking us. It means the use of a philosophical system effectively (a) to negate the need to respond in conformity to God's will through real life change, and (b) to negate the past experience of God's people. If present trends continue to prevail, we could become such a different people from the early Adventists that our real links to that past are severed, and we could flounder as every other movement eventually has. It must not happen.

Conclusion

The manner in which the contributors in *Women in Ministry* generally have used the writings of Ellen G. White is hermeneutically unsound. Quotations and references have been gathered up and "principles" supposedly consistent with them have been constructed which in some cases exactly contradict Mrs. White. Unfortunately, all of the good intentions of the authors cannot change the misguided nature of their conclusions.

This brings us back to the attitudes expressed by my fellow ministers at the beginning of this chapter. Are great flying leaps the theological solution that the church has really been waiting for? Is *Women in Ministry* a triumph for God's people, providing at long last "help from the seminary?" Or is it more a case of self-disclosure to the church? Have a group of well-meaning but misguided scholars disclosed much more than they had intended? Is it safe to adopt their methods of interpretation? Finally, can we hear the concern of our brothers and sisters around the world who tremble to see how far we in North America have departed from the spirit and interpretive methods of the original Advent movement?

The church today stands upon the verge of a great flying leap.

Don't jump.

Endnotes

1. This section reviews J. H. Denis Fortin's chapter, "Ordination in the Writings of Ellen G. White," in *Women in Ministry,* ed. Nancy Vyhmeister (Berrien Springs, Mich.: Andrews University Press, 1998), pp. 115-133.
2. Fortin, pp. 116, 119-123, 125, 127-129.
3. *Testimonies to Ministers,* p. 26.
4. *The Great Controversy,* p. 498.
5. Ibid.
6. Fortin, pp. 119-122.
7. *The Desire of Ages,* pp. 290-297.
8. *The Acts of the Apostles,* pp. 89, 91-92.
9. *The Great Controversy,* p. 93.
10. Ibid., p. 289.
11. Ibid., pp. 289-290.
12. Andrew Mustard, *James White and SDA Organization: Historical Development, 1844-1881* (Berrien Springs, Mich.: Andrews University Press, 1987), cited in footnotes 31-33 in *Women in Ministry,* p. 131.
13. *The Acts of the Apostles,* p. 161.
14. Ibid., p. 162.

15. Ibid., p. 164.
16. *Sketches From the Life of Paul,* p. 43.
17. *The Acts of the Apostles,* p. 164.
18. This idea is liberally sprinkled throughout the book. Note for example, beyond the discussion that follows, Raoul Dederen's "The Priesthood of All Believers," pp. 9-27.
19. Ellen G. White, "The Great Commission; a Call to Service," *Review and Herald,* March 24, 1910, p. 1.
20. Ellen G. White, "Our Work," *Signs of the Times,* August 25, 1898, p. 2.
21. Fortin, p. 128.
22. This section reviews Jerry Moon's "'A Power That Exceeds That of Men': Ellen G. White on Women in Ministry," in *Women in Ministry,* pp. 187-209.
23. Moon, pp. 190, 193.
24. Ibid., p. 196.
25. Fortin, pp. 127, 128.
26. Moon, p. 200; Ellen G. White, *Manuscript Releases,* 19:56.
27. Ibid.
28. Ellen G. White Letter 33, 1879, in *Manuscript Releases,* 19:55-61.
29. *Testimonies for the Church,* 2:701.
30. Moon, pp. 193-200.
31. Moon, pp. 202, 204.
32. Peter van Bemmelen, "Equality, Headship, and Submission in the Writings of Ellen G. White," *Women in Ministry,* p. 298.
33. Richard Davidson, "Headship, Submission, and Equality in Scripture," *Women in Ministry,* pp. 264, 267.
34. van Bemmelen, p. 298.
35. Ibid.
36. *Patriarchs and Prophets,* p. 46.
37. "She was perfectly happy in her Eden home by her husband's side; but, like restless modern Eves, she was flattered that there was a higher sphere than that which God had assigned her. But in attempting to climb higher than her original position, she fell far below it." *Testimonies for the Church,* 3:483. "A neglect on the part of woman to follow God's plan in her creation, an effort to reach for important positions which He has not qualified her to fill, leaves vacant the position that she could fill to acceptance. In getting out of her sphere, she loses true womanly dignity and nobility." Ibid., p. 484.
38. Davidson, pp. 267-268 quoting *Patriarchs and Prophets,* pp. 58-59.
39. Davidson, p. 269.
40. *Patriarchs and Prophets,* p. 46.
41. See Ellen G. White's *Testimonies for the Church,* 1:105, 307-308; *Testimonies on Sexual Behavior and Divorce,* p. 117; *Thoughts From the Mount of Blessing,* p. 64; *Review and Herald,* December 10, 1908; *Manuscript Releases,* 4:217, 13:83, etc.
42. See Arthur L. White, *Ellen G. White: The Early Years* (Hagerstown, Md.: Review and Herald Publishing Association, 1981), pp. 110-111.
43. *Patriarchs and Prophets,* p. 48.
44. van Bemmelen, p. 298.
45. *Patriarchs and Prophets,* p. 46.
46. *Counsels to Parents, Teachers, and Students,* p. 33.
47. Ibid.
48. "The angels had cautioned Eve to beware of separating herself from her husband while occupied in their daily labor in the garden; with him she would be in less danger from temptation than if she were alone." *Patriarchs and Prophets,* p. 53.
49. Ibid., p. 56.
50. "He mourned that he had permitted Eve to wander from his side." Ibid.

51. *The Spirit of Prophecy,* 1:53-54.
52. *Testimonies for the Church,* 1:421.
53. Alicia Worley, *Women in Ministry,* p. 372.
54. Ibid., p. 369.
55. This section discusses Alicia Worley's "Ellen White and Women's Rights," in *Women in Ministry,* pp. 355-376.
56. *Testimonies for the Church,* 1:421.
57. Worley, p. 368.
58. Ibid., p. 369.
59. *Testimonies for the Church,* 1:421.
60. *Patriarchs and Prophets,* p. 141.
61. *The Adventist Home,* p. 215.
62. Ibid.
63. *Testimonies for the Church,* 1:307-308.
64. *The Adventist Home,* p. 119.
65. Ibid., p. 215.
66. Ibid., p. 211.
67. Ellen G. White, Letter 6, 1854. In *Manuscript Releases,* 10:20.
68. Ellen G. White, Letter 5, 1861. In *Manuscript Releases,* 6:126.
69. Worley, pp. 359-365.
70. Ellen G. White, *Special Testimonies,* Series B, p. 2. Also in *Seventh-day Adventist Bible Commentary,* 3:1140.
71. Worley, p. 371.
72. Ibid., p. 372, citing *Manuscript Releases,* 10:69.
73. Ellen G. White, Letter 40a, 1874. In *Manuscript Releases,* 10:69.
74. Worley, p. 370-372.
75. Ibid., p. 355.
76. Ibid., p. 370.
77. Ibid.
78. Ibid.
79. *The Great Controversy,* p. 595.
80. Calvin Rock, "Review of *Women in Ministry,*" *Adventist Review,* April 15, 1999, p. 29.
81. "Study God's word prayerfully. That word presents before you, in the law of God and the life of Christ, the great principles of holiness, without which 'no man shall see the Lord.' Hebrews 12:14. It convinces of sin; it plainly reveals the way of salvation. Give heed to it as the voice of God speaking to your soul." *Steps to Christ,* p. 35.
82. *The Great Controversy,* p. 372.
83. Nancy Vyhmeister, "Prologue," in *Women in Ministry,* p. 5, prepares the way for the book's "use of sanctified judgment and imagination to resolve questions and issues."

Chapter 15

Spiritualism and Women:
Then and Now

Laurel Damsteegt

~

Those who feel called out to join the movement in favor of woman's rights and the so-called dress reform, might as well sever all connection with the third angel's message. The spirit which attends the one cannot be in harmony with the other. The Scriptures are plain upon the relations and rights of men and women. Spiritualists have, to quite an extent, adopted this singular mode of dress. Seventh-day Adventists, who believe in the restoration of the gifts, are often branded as spiritualists. Let them adopt this costume and their influence is dead.

Ellen G. White, *Testimonies for the Church*, vol. 1, p. 421

The author of chapter 17 of *Women in Ministry*, "Ellen White and Women's Rights,"[1] makes a study of the above passage, mostly to show that it has nothing to do with the ongoing struggle within the Seventh-day Adventist church to ordain women to the gospel ministry.

This *Women in Ministry* author admits that spiritualism was connected with the Woman's Rights Movement of the 19th century, but says spiritualism declined at the end of that century. Therefore, she feels that Mrs. White's warning in the passage above does not apply to the ordination question our church faces today. Through a discussion of editorial changes and a full-blown study on "rights," she seeks to make this passage of "none effect."

Laurel Damsteegt, M.Div., M.S.P.H., *in addition to family responsibilities, works with her husband in producing materials about the history of God's people since Bible times.*

This chapter will seek to show that spiritualism was not only a part of the earlier women's movement, but it is a vital part of this movement today. Instead of spiritualism fading out, as the *Women in Ministry* chapter indicates, it has crescendoed into the New Age movement and is very much a part of the whole feminist movement and, indeed, our very culture. Spiritualism deals not only with the obvious—rappings, necromancy, and divination—it has very much to do with a philosophy carefully delineated in *The Great Controversy.* There we are told that this insidious, pervasive movement will be instrumental in setting aside the authority of Scripture to bring about the joining of hands of all Christendom to bring on the final movements.[2]

Women's ordination is but a small step in the feminist agenda. To believe that ordination itself is the *only* issue for women in the Seventh-day Adventist church is surely naive. Ordination, the laying on of hands that would give an ecclesiastical blessing for a woman to function fully as a minister of the gospel of the Seventh-day Adventist church, adds little to what she already does or can do. But ordination is necessary as a vital stepping stone in the feminist agenda for a robust total "equality" of position. The recent document, "The President's Commission on Women in Ministry—Report," tells just a bit of what is on the agenda for the Seventh-day Adventist woman, pushing reluctant Adventists to put women in line not only for pastorates but also for conference and union leadership and even the presidency of the General Conference.[3]

Women in Ministry differs from other Adventist publications pushing for women's ordination in that its authors present themselves as theologically conservative. Their conservative approach makes ordination of women appear innocuous. It seems that an attempt has been made to disassociate women's ordination from feminism and even from liberal Adventism.

If the issue were just over sending out fine Christian women to evangelize and win souls, no one would have a problem. But the issue is not women doing God's work with heart and soul. The issue is who is behind the agenda to bring feminist perspectives into the Seventh-day Adventist church. The prince of the powers of darkness has poisoned even the most beautiful and powerful avenues of reaching people.

Bound up in this "simple" issue are such important considerations as the foundations of our faith. If we interpret Scripture to allow women to oversee, or to "usurp authority over the man" (1 Tim. 2:12), we are going directly contrary to Scripture. Just how important is this changing of the meaning of Scripture? Suppose we were to change the name or being of God from our Heavenly Father, which the Bible calls Him, to Mother or Light, as many in the feminist movement urge, would we not create a new idolatry? If we deem man and woman the same, as many feminists promote, do we not open the door to androgyny, great perversion, and wickedness? If we discard the biblical roles that distinguish men and women, do we not insult the Creator who crafted us differently for His glory?

Feminism has seeped into every fiber of the current generation. It is not something most are even aware of, because education has been thoroughly revamped by feminism. It seeks to change attitudes even in kindergarten and throughout school.[4] Most people living in this culture don't even realize how much feminism has affected them.

I can understand that some proponents of women's ordination might feel resentful when ideas expressed in *Women in Ministry* are compared to radical feminism. But feminism is a continuum. All feminism has the same roots and leans in the same direction—variations are just matters of degree. Yesterday's radical feminism has become today's norm. Furthermore, feminism transcends denominational distinctions, which is one reason why we face it within our church. To quote Mary A. Kassian,

"In spite of their political, sociological, or theological nuances, feminists all adhere to a common presupposition. It is this common presupposition that has shaped and dictated the progression of feminism's philosophical development. Moreover, in the Church, feminism transcends denominational distinctions. The denominational ties of Roman Catholic, Baptist, United Church, Methodist, Episcopalian, Presbyterian, Anglican, and Jew are all superseded by the common bond of feminism. . . .The major consideration was only that women's concerns were being pursued within the context of established Judeo-Christian institutions."[5]

Unfortunately, some proponents of women's ordination do not realize what is behind the scenes. They are totally Christian and kindly naive, yet they are totally deceived about the issues involved here. Supporting this feminist agenda item is dangerous because it is part of a much larger picture, one that we have been warned against. "Those who feel called out to join the movement in favor of woman's rights and the so-called dress reform, might as well sever all connection with the third angel's message."

Woman's Rights and Spiritualism

In 1975 I wrote a research paper entitled "Attending Spirits" that showed how the women's rights movement of the 1900s was directly linked to spiritualism.[6] I tediously paged through early Adventist periodicals up through 1881[7] (we never dreamed of CD-ROM searches in those days) to get a feel for the feminist concerns and issues that surrounded the now-well-known statement (*Testimonies for the Church* 1:421) quoted at the beginning of this chapter.

I puzzled over how women's rights could be considered spiritualistic. I pored over the periodicals looking for clues.

Then I discovered an important lead. In the September 26, 1871, *Review and Herald,* Uriah Smith published a most insightful article, "Victoria C. Woodhull."[8] This opened the whole issue for me. In an account of spiritualistic mediums of that day, he told how the career of Mrs. Woodhull was "planned and executed thus far wholly by the spirits."[9]

I had not previously heard of Victoria C. Woodhull. Now I began digging into the histories and found that she was a renowned spiritualist who, because of direct spirit-leading, became one of the foremost women's rights activists of her time.

Finding out about Victoria C. Woodhull opened up for me a whole study on spiritualism in the women's rights movement. My conclusions, drawn in 1975, were that there was legitimate concern enough for Adventists to distance themselves from the women's rights movement: "SDA publications were quick to link Mrs. Woodhull's gross immorality first to spiritualism and then to the surge for equality, or woman's rights. In the final analysis one could get the idea that early Adventists considered such rights to be a facet of Spiritualism."[10]

Imagine my amazement in reviewing current secular literature to find newly published evidence supporting this early study! In the last three years four major works have come out about Victoria C. Woodhull and spiritualism.[11] Some devotee has even made an extensive web site listing a complete bibliography of books, videos, articles, and reviews about Victoria C. Woodhull![12]

While other women's rights activists such as Elizabeth Cady Stanton and Susan B. Anthony had struggled vainly to make an impact on society, Woodhull, at the direct leading of the spirits, proclaimed herself a candidate for President of the United States and was granted a hearing before the Judiciary Committee of the Joint Houses of Congress! She drew up "The Woodhull Memorial," a document dealing with woman's suffrage, and presented it to the joint committee. Astonished women's rights advocates couldn't believe her inroads and welcomed her into their inner circle (for a while, anyway).

But fascinated as I was by these assertions, I was astonished when I came to understand the strong spiritualist trends among many of the other women's rights activists in the early post-civil war years. Spiritualism was a "new" religious movement dominated by women.[13] Its two strong attractions were "rebellion against death [espousing necromancy] and rebellion against authority."[14] Spiritualist women were among the first to speak in "promiscuous assemblies" (gatherings of both sexes), giving special messages said to be from the spirits of such men as Socrates and Benjamin Franklin. "Not surprisingly, the rights of women were very much on the minds of these great thinkers."[15]

"At a time when no churches ordained women and many forbade them to speak aloud in church, Spiritualist women had equal authority, equal opportunities, and equal numbers in religious leadership."[16] "Spiritualism validated the female authoritative voice and permitted women an active professional and spiritual role largely denied them elsewhere."[17]

"Spiritualism and woman's rights drew from the same well: Both were responses to the control, subjugation, and repression of women by church and state. Both believed in universal suffrage—the equality of all human beings. For women—sheltered, repressed, powerless—the line between divine inspiration, the courage of one's convictions, and spirit guidance became blurred. Not all woman's rights advocates became Spiritualists, but spiritualism embraced woman's rights."[18]

I have been shocked to note how many of the leading personalities in the women's rights movement actually consulted the dead or had spiritualistic philosophies. Among them were Harriet Beecher Stowe,[19] Isabella Beecher Hooker,[20] Horace and Mary Greeley,[21] and even Henry Ward Beecher, the powerful preacher.[22]

Susan B. Anthony wrote, "Oh dear, dear! If the spirits would only just make me a trance medium and put the rights into my mouth. You can't think how earnestly I have prayed to be made a speaking medium for a whole week. If they would only come to me thus, I'd give them a hearty welcome."[23]

Elizabeth Cady Stanton heard spirit raps and "miraculously" wrote the Declaration of Rights and Sentiments on the famous McClintock "spirit table."[24] Later, her very detailed instructions for her funeral included being dressed in ordinary clothes, and that "common sense women should conduct the services." The mahogany McClintock spirit table was placed at the head of her coffin.[25] This table, now famous, is presently housed at the Smithsonian as a symbol of early feminism and its spiritualistic connection.

Victoria C. Woodhull claimed that the "Woodhull Memorial" she presented to Congress was conceived by the spirits as she dictated it to someone while she was in a trance.[26]

Even "conservative" women's rights leaders were spiritualists. Harriet Beecher Stowe (who had no use for Woodhull) regularly "contacted" her dead son. Spiritualists claim that *Uncle Tom's Cabin* was dictated to her by the spirits.[27]

These persons not only had the philosophy, they also followed the lifestyle and had dealings with the spirits that clearly define them as spiritualists. Amazing.

Bound up in this woman, Victoria C. Woodhull, and the women's rights movement were tenets of spiritualism waiting to be revealed.

Spiritualism seeks to equalize the roles of women and men under the guise of "love"; it makes marriage look foolish and tears down Christianity by voiding scriptural authority.

Spiritualism Seeks to Destroy God's Protective Gift of Marriage

When Victoria Woodhull and her sister, Tennie C. Claflin, came to public notice, they were mediums and stock brokers on Wall Street and published a small weekly newspaper. Beautiful, totally immoral, and assertive, these women scandalized the papers with their blatant sexual openness. Driven by the spirits to lead a "social revolution," they delighted in publicizing the immoral behavior of the famous people of their time to support their sexual revolution, which was totally against marriage and the biblical roles of women. These sisters tried to show how people doing evil things could still be viewed as "good."

Henry Ward Beecher, probably the most famous preacher of that era, taught a gospel of love to his huge church.[28] Victoria C. Woodhull came to know many of the naughty details of his liaisons, and she blackmailed him. She wanted him to "come out" and support her sexual revolution. He would have nothing to do with her, so she published one of his sordid stories.

Woodhull felt that *doing* evil was not "evil," but *being hypocritical* about it was. Being a "good person" does not mean being righteous, she said; a "good person" can do very evil things.

This is a significant tenet of spiritualism, that there is no difference between good and evil, that morality is not really all that important. Ellen White focused on this aspect of spiritualism:

"Love is dwelt upon as the chief attribute of God, but it is degraded to a weak sentimentalism, making little distinction between good and evil. God's justice, His denunciations of sin, the requirements of His holy law, are all kept out of sight. The people are taught to regard the Decalogue as a dead letter. Pleasing, bewitching fables captivate the senses and lead men to reject the Bible as the foundation of their faith."[29]

Woodhull and Claflin (under the inspiration of the spirits) and a few of the more radical women's rights advocates understood what their conservative sisters could not. Religion and marriage were the two institutions obstructing the way of "true" social equality. Christianity, very fundamental and biblical in those days, taught the headship of men in the home and church according to the writings of Paul. To these women activists, marriage bound the woman and kept her from reaching her full potential. How could she find freedom when she had no "choice?"

Shocking to the Victorian mentality of the last century were Woodhull's vulgar remarks:

"If I want sexual intercourse with one hundred men I shall have it . . . and this sexual intercourse business may as well be discussed now, and discussed until you are so familiar with your sexual organs that a reference to them will no longer make the blush mount to your face any more than a reference to any other part of your body. . . . I do not propose to have any blush on my face for any act of my life. My life has been my own. I have nothing to apologize for."[30]

Woodhull and Claflin taught that woman should be free to truly love whomever and whenever she pleased (like the men). In a talk entitled "The Scarecrows of Sexual Freedom," Woodhull denounced a "loveless and indissoluble marriage" as "legalized prostitution."

"They say I have come to break up the family. I say amen to that with all my heart. . . . In a perfected sexuality shall continuous life be found. . . . *Such to me, my brothers and sisters, is the sublime mission of Spiritualism, to be outwrought through the sexual emancipation of woman, and her return to self ownership, and to individualized existence.*"[31]

In one of her speeches, Mrs. Woodhull announced that she had "declared relentless warfare against marriage, and ha[d] sworn to wage it 'until the last vestige of this remnant of savagery shall be wiped from the otherwise fair face of present civilization.'"[32]

So far, I have shown that spiritualism was deeply involved in the feminist movement in the nineteenth century. *Women in Ministry* acknowledges this. But *Women in Ministry* says spiritualism has no part in the feminist movement today—and therefore Mrs. White's warning, quoted at the beginning of the chapter, does not apply to the ordination question our church faces today. Let's take a look at modern feminism.

Modern Feminism

Current literature depicts Woodhull as a prototype of modern feminists and of the whole feminist movement that has saturated our culture. "Victoria never stopped believing that the spirits had brought her into the world to lead a 'social revolution.' She said that from her birth, and even before, she had been marked for this fate."[33]

Despite the fact that she was far more radical than others in her day and that ultimately she became an icon that for years blackened the women's rights movement, feminists today are grateful for her lead. "Woodhull rejected the 19th century definition of women's role. Women must 'own themselves,' she said. In her life and views she was more than a century before her time."[34] Gloria Steinem, one of today's leading feminists, urges women to "catch the spirit of the real Victoria Woodhull."[35]

Today her spiritualistic philosophy permeates our culture. Sex education and the X-rated media have created a society that never blushes over any type of immorality. A president can be "good" while doing evil deeds; more and more people cohabit[36] because they "love" each other; single-parent families are on the increase. An ever-growing number of persons who do get married divorce.

The practical outworking of the Woodhull and Claflin morality has affected our church. Instead of being a sacred covenant, marriage sometimes becomes a temporary alliance. The divorce rate climbs. Children are left to single-parent homes. Some members give themselves permission to sin on the basis that God loves us so much He doesn't care even if we make an intentional, premeditated "mistake." Despite all the marriage classes and counseling available today, the Adventist home is in jeopardy.

Feminism has gone far beyond even the most blatant imaginings of Victoria Woodhull and Elizabeth Cady Stanton. Whereas Elizabeth Cady Stanton took the first steps in breaking down male-female distinctions in dress by donning (for a while) the bloomer costume,[37] and Victoria Woodhull broke down the reserve in speaking openly about sexuality, *gender* issues hadn't even been dreamed of.

Today, as we are beginning to see the full implications of *gender,* perhaps we can better understand the reason for God's distinctions in roles and dress.[38] Note how the United Nations agency in charge of research on women is seeking to recast gender. Their statement below shows how a person is not necessarily born with a specific gender; gender develops socially, politically, or economically:

"Gender is a concept that refers to a system of roles and relationships between women and men that are determined not by biology but the social, political, and economic context. One's biological sex is a natural given; gender is constructed. . . . Gender can be seen as the *'process by which individuals who are born into biological categories of male or female become the social categories of women and men through the acquisition of locally defined attributes of masculinity and femininity.'"*[39]

We still often believe the term "gender" is the same as what used to be "sex" on a demographic form. Not so, the feminists tell us. Gender includes far more than "male" and "female." One radical feminist calls for a "reversion of an unobstructed *pansexuality.*"[40] Such can include male and female, but also homosexual, lesbian, bisexual, and transgender.[41]

"Young women openly enter into intimate relationships with both genders that are more than just experiments. They resist being described as straight or gay—or even bisexual, which some think suggests promiscuity and one-night stands. Instead they use words like *fluid* and *omnisexual.*"[42]

"'Family,' too, has been redefined so the term 'could refer to two roommates.'"[43]

Is the feminist movement something Adventists want to be identified with, or did Mrs. White have a reason for saying that any who feel called to join it might as well leave the church?

Spiritualism Has No Use for Christianity and the Scriptures

In the 19th century, a higher-critical method of interpreting Scripture was making inroads into Christianity. Scholars interpreted the Bible in new and creative ways, and many "errors" were "discovered." Many matters long accepted as settled suddenly were unsettled.

Higher criticism maintains that one cannot read Scripture and believe that God gave it *as it reads.* Rather, one must come to understand that the Bible was written by many authors who expressed the "myths" and situations of their own culture.

"Scholarship" breathed doubt into the Word. Skeptical scholars suggested that many of the stories were not *really* true, though their authors may have truly believed them. Creation, authorship, miracles, Bible stories, all came under attack. Historical-critical methodology was, and still is, fond of dwelling on the "errors" and "discrepancies" in Scripture. Instead of building faith, historical criticism places doubt, distrust and disillusionment in the hearts and minds of readers.

In short, higher critics viewed the Bible as a *man*-made book that recorded *man's* experience. All who believed that God Himself was the Author of infallible Scripture were derided as "fundamentalists."

Leaders of the women's rights movement found those criticisms very much to their liking. These leaders were soon in the forefront of the discussion of Scripture. Just as today there are moderates and radicals in attitudes and views towards Scripture, so also back then.

Moderate Feminism and Scripture. An example of moderate feminism was Miss Frances E. Willard, President of the Woman's Christian Temperance Union. She had such a positive impact on the women's movement that she is remembered today by a statue in the Capitol Building of the United States.

Miss Willard and another woman were elected by local Methodist boards to serve as delegates to a Methodist General Conference. The church leaders refused to seat them. Willard became so angry that she wrote *Woman in the Pulpit,* a book promoting the ordination of women. But ordination of women was not achieved in her church in her day. (Most interestingly, a colleague, Mrs. S. M. I. Henry, a national evangelist of the W.C.T.U. and a close friend and fellow worker of Miss Frances Willard, disagreed with her on the ordination issue. Mrs. S. M. I. Henry later became a Seventh-day Adventist and was largely responsible for beginning a "Woman's Work" within the Adventist church. Mrs. Henry believed in the plain reading of the Scriptures. This is why she accepted the Sabbath and why she did not believe in the ordination of women, though she very strongly believed in women becoming involved in gospel work.)[44]

Moderates such as Frances E. Willard, predecessors of today's "biblical feminists," maintained that tradition is built on man's Scriptural misinterpretation, that there is a better way of reading controverted passages. Literalism is the culprit, not the Bible itself.[45] Moderates would have you compare passages. They would sincerely uphold Scripture as the Word of God but point a finger at man, who has made it seem oppressive. Said Miss Willard:

"I think that men have read their own selfish theories into the Book, that theologians have not in the past sufficiently recognized the progressive quality of its revelation, nor adequately discriminated between its records as history and its principles of ethics of religion, nor have they until recently perceived that it is not in any sense a scientific treatise; but I believe that the Bible comes to us from God, and that it is a sufficient rule of faith and of practice. . . . To me the Bible is the dear and sacred home book which makes a hallowed motherhood possible because it raises woman up, and with her lifts toward heaven the world."[46]

Miss Willard was a contemporary of Mrs. White and spoke strongly about ordaining women to the gospel ministry. Isn't it interesting that, in contrast to Frances Willard, who interpreted Scripture to mean it was necessary, Ellen White never once mentioned ordaining women to a pulpit ministry? Nor was Ellen G. White ever called Elder White or Pastor Ellen. She always called herself Sister White.

As a special messenger from the Lord, she gave plenty of messages advocating that women work for the Lord with all their hearts and souls. Indeed, the Bible and Mrs. White call for participation of women in the soul-winning ministry. And women who work in soul-winning lines are to be paid fairly; Mrs. White repeatedly calls for remuneration to wives of ministers who work alongside their husbands,[47] a fact which Adventists on both sides of the women's issue affirm.[48] But Mrs. White had no special vision or counsel showing women as pastors or having hands laid on them for that role, advocating women's ordination. She was not even ordained herself.[49]

Radical Feminists and Scripture. Radicals of the 19th century, on the other hand, looked at the Bible itself as the problem. Donna Behnke, who discusses the issue of inspiration and early feminism in a Ph.D. dissertation, cites Elizabeth Cady Stanton's views on Scripture as an example of the higher-critical methodology being used in Stanton's day. "She not only used higher criticism and rejected biblical liter-alism, but also refused to believe the Bible itself was inspired. . . . No amount of rationalizing could erase the fact that the Bible taught principles adverse to women."[50]

Mrs. Stanton edited *The Woman's Bible* that compiled all the passages of the Bible relative to women with essays authored by various individuals about each "problem text." "The first step in the elevation of women under all systems of religion is to convince them that the great Spirit of the Universe is in no way responsible for any of these absurdities. . . . *The Woman's Bible* comes to the ordi-nary reader like a real benediction. It tells her the good Lord did not write the Book; that the garden scene is a fable; that she is in no way responsible for the laws of the Universe."[51]

Stanton was radical and endured much opposition from churchmen and other more conservative feminists who believed that women were elevated by Scripture. But she was by no means alone in her fight. Another author maintained that "what-ever progress woman has made in any department of effort, she has accomplished independently of, and in opposition to, the so-called inspired and infallible 'Word of God,' and that this book has been of more injury to her than has any other which has ever been written in the history of the world."[52]

In one especially heated women's rights convention, in Philadelphia in 1854, the role of revelation came to the fore. Many views were aired. One spokesman, a Rev. Grew, maintained that "unless women were prepared to discredit the entire Bible from beginning to end, . . . they would have to acquiesce and admit that it taught their subjection."[53]

In the heated discussion William Lloyd Garrison, "author, anti-slavery speaker, and pioneer 'liberator' who also became an ardent pioneer spiritualist,"[54] arose and bluntly stated the view of inspiration held by radical women's rights advocates as well as spiritualists:

"Why go to the Bible? What question was ever settled by the Bible? What question of theology or any other department? None that I ever heard of! With this same version of the Bible, and the same ability to read it, we find that it has filled all Christendom with theological confusion. All are Ishmaelites; each man's hand against his neighbor.

"The human mind is greater than any book, the mind sits in judgment on every book. If there be truth in the book, we take it; if error, we discard it. Why refer to the Bible? In this country, the Bible has been used to support slavery and capital punishment; while in the old countries, it has been quoted to sustain all manner of tyranny and persecution. All reforms are anti-Bible. We must look at all things rationally. We find women endowed with certain capacities, and it is of no importance if any book denies her such capacities."[55]

The Woman's Bible sought to explain away the plain Word of God using myths and allegories and culture—higher-critical methodology. Ursula Bright boldly de-clared of the Bible:

"It is a grand volume, a masterpiece composed of clever, ingenious fables, containing great verities; but it reveals the latter only to those who, like the Initiates, have a key to its inner meaning; a tale sublime in its morality and didactics truly—still a tale and an allegory; a repertory of invented personages in its older Jewish portions, and of dark sayings and parables in its later additions, and thus quite misleading to any one ignorant of its esotericism. . . .

"Slowly we see a light breaking. When the dawn comes we shall have a revision of the Bible on very different lines from any yet attempted. In the meantime may we not ask, Is there any curse or crime which has not appealed to the Bible for support? Polygamy, capital punishment, slavery and war have all done so. Why not the subjection of women? Let us hold fast that which is good in the Bible and the rest will modify itself in the future, as it has done in the past, to the needs of humanity and the advance of knowledge."[56]

In the nineteenth century, rationalism and the effects of the Enlightenment were prominent in intellectual circles. Josephine Henry explicitly revealed the end of the rational approach.

"The by-paths of ecclesiastical history are fetid with the records of crimes against women; and the 'half has never been told.' And what of the history which Christianity is making today? . . . Answer, ye mental dwarfs and moral monstrosities, and tell what the Holy Bible has done for you. . . .

"When Reason reigns and Science lights the way, a countless host of women will move in majesty down the coming centuries. A voice will cry, 'Who are these?' and the answer will ring out: 'these are the mothers of the coming race, who have locked the door of the Temple of Faith and thrown the key away; "these are they which came out of great tribulation and washed their robes and made them white in the" fountain of knowledge.'"[57]

Was this blatant, blasphemous hatred for inspiration as it reads just in the feminism of the past? Oh no! If anything, today's feminism has gone far beyond this and reinterpreted all of the Bible in various and radical ways.

Feminist Theology

Today's feminists go well beyond the view of earlier women's rights' views of biblical inspiration. In 1968, Mary Daly in *The Church and the Second Sex* argued that the Bible authors were merely men of their times who could never be "free of the prejudices of their epochs."[58] Therefore, women of the church have just as much right to direct current theology as Paul did in Scripture, to act as prophets, and to guide the church in a new direction.[59]

As modern feminist theology has developed, the Bible is viewed not so much as a timeless Book that applies to all peoples in all times to *shape* all culture, but a Book to be picked apart and subjected to acceptance or rejection relative to their own culture or situation.[60]

According to one published report, Elizabeth Schüssler Fiorenza argues that "feminists must employ a 'hermeneutics of suspicion'—that is, they must systematically assume that the Bible's male authors and interpreters deliberately covered up the role of women in early Christianity. . . . The wider implication of the Schüssler Fiorenza work is that the biblical texts cannot be authoritative Scriptures for women until they are critically reinterpreted from women's experiences of oppression. And what is true for the Bible holds for every other dimension of the Christian religion."[61]

Through such methods the Bible is rewritten and Christianity redesigned to better fit women. Schüssler Fiorenza states, "Women today not only rewrite biblical stories about women, but also reformulate patriarchal prayers and create feminist rituals celebrating our ancestors. We rediscover in story and poetry, in drama and liturgy, in song and dance, our biblical foresisters' sufferings and victories. . . . In ever new images and symbols we seek to rename the God of the Bible and the significance of Jesus. . . . We not only spin tales about the voyages of Prisca, the missionary, or about Junia, the apostle, but also dance Sarah's circle and experience prophetic enthusiasm. We sing litanies of praise to our foresisters and pray laments of mourning for the lost stories of our foremothers."[62]

Even biblical feminists (believers in both the Bible and feminism) like Hardesty and Scanzoni, who in the 1970s wrote *A Biblical Approach to Women's Liberation,* "altered traditional hermeneutics to present the thesis that equality between men and women was to be reflected by the obliteration of sex roles in Church and marriage . . . known as the egalitarian position. Egalitarians prided themselves in being both feminist and Biblical."[63]

"Biblical feminists chose Galatians 3:28, 'In Christ there is neither male nor female . . . ,' as the crux around which to interpret Scripture. Notwithstanding that the context of this verse dealt with who could become a Christian and on what basis—and not with male/female roles." This crux became the measuring stick by which all other Scripture was to be measured. "Biblical feminists decided that *equality* meant monolithic, undifferentiated role-interchangeability. Rather than gleaning their definition of equality from the Bible, Biblical feminists adopted the feminist definition of equality that was current in contemporary North American society. They chose 'equality' as their *crux interpretum* and then demanded that all Biblical interpretation support their predetermined, feminist definition."[64]

If some Scripture did not suit their fancy, they would label it "unauthentic or incorrect" or creatively seek for new meanings of Greek words like *kephale* (head)[65] and then argue that these new definitions altered the meaning of the text. "Finally, passages that could not be discounted in any of these ways were handled by labeling them 'cultural' and hence inapplicable to the contemporary Church."[66]

However, feminists have a way of "evolving." "Conservative Biblical feminism is no longer advanced by those who initiated it. Writers such as Scanzoni, Hardesty, and Mollenkott have left evangelicalism to join liberal religious feminism."[67] In order to embrace both the Bible and concerns of the women's movement they ended up compromising the Bible.

As Phyllis Trible, a very liberal feminist, once said, "A feminist who loves the Bible produces, in the thinking of many, an oxymoron. Perhaps clever as rhetoric, the description offers no possibility for existential integrity. After all, if no man can serve two masters, no woman can serve two authorities, a master called scripture and a mistress called feminism."[68]

Our only hope is to seek a simple, childlike interpretation of Scripture. Carsten Johnsen once defined spiritualistic interpretation of Scripture as "an insisting ego-centric desire to spiritualize away the tangible reality of God's living Word, ignore its simple message, distort and reject its plain command."[69] He showed how Kellogg's pantheism, which Ellen G. White rebuked, spiritualized away the plain, simple, real Word of God. This was called the alpha of apostasy. The omega, which is to be much worse, was still to come.

Potentially Ambiguous

The author of the chapter "Ellen White and Women's Rights" goes to some effort to define Ellen White's meaning of "rights," but soft-pedals the issue of the spiritualistic roots of the women's rights movement. According to her, the statement in the first volume of *Testimonies for the Church*, page 421, "one of the few on women's rights, is one of the most direct, yet it is potentially ambiguous and misunderstood."[70]

Remember, this is the passage we began with: "Those who feel called out to join the movement in favor of women's rights . . . might as well sever all connection with the third angel's message. The spirit which attends the one cannot be in harmony with the other."

In order to come to a so-called "better" understanding of what this passage means, the author uses questions, projections, underlying issues, and an analysis of the principles to make an otherwise plain paragraph obscure, subtle and ambiguous. If one doesn't agree with the prophet, speculating about her grammar and context can muddy the water sufficiently to make room for softer interpretations.

In essence, here is the problem that the author raises with this powerful passage. The quotation came out of a testimony, first published in 1864, called "The Cause in the East." When it was republished in the first volume of the *Testimonies*, "slight editorial changes occurred—mostly in the 1880s—between Ellen White's statement in the original and that published in *Testimonies to the Church*, 1:421. White wrote, 'the relations and rights of *women* and men,' while the editors corrected to 'of *men* and women' [her italics] probably to conform to common usage. If Ellen White was intentionally referring to women first, why might she have wished to emphasize women's rights over men's? Perhaps she believed women's rights were more endangered. Support for this possibility is suggested by her writing far more about the need for women to protect their personal boundaries, to develop themselves, to be sensitive to their call to service, and to see their coequal roles in the home than about men's needs in these areas."[71]

Any time there are "editorial changes" one has to ask, Who made them and why? In the statement quoted above, the *Women in Ministry* author presupposes that the first edition of the testimony represented the real Ellen White; the second, that of the "editors."

Here a higher-critical methodology is subtly being used on Ellen White.[72] Observe how much speculation has entered into this analysis. Note all the tentative, suggestive words: "probably," "if," "might have," "perhaps," "possibility," "suggested." The plain fact is that the paragraph was changed under Ellen White's supervision by her own editors, Marian Davis and Mary White, who edited everything she wrote during that period. The passage was not edited secretly or postmortem.[73] Mrs. White had another thirty-five years to protest the changes if she didn't agree with them. Editors attempted to clarify, not change, any sense that was originally intended. In discussing the editorial changes, the preface to the volume noted:

"Some grammatical and rhetorical changes also have been made for the sake of strength and clearness. In making these changes great care has been taken to preserve every idea, and in no case have either words or sentences been omitted unless as above indicated, to avoid unnecessary repetition."[74]

Sister White intended to speak about the rights and relations of women and men, or men and women; either way means the same thing, because she wasn't stressing the rights of one over the other but the *relation* between the two.

The *Women in Ministry* author continues with the chapter's analysis:

"Another change is perhaps more significant. The original wording was 'Those who feel called out to join *the Woman's Rights Movement*,' but this was replaced with 'Those who feel called out to join the *movement in favor of woman's rights*' [her italics]. The modification communicates a subtle but significant change in focus from the specific movement called the Woman's Rights Movement to the larger context of anyone favoring women's rights. Thus the specificity that *may* have been intended is removed in favor of a more general application."[75]

Here the author implies that there was a motive behind the "editor's" change from *the* Woman's Right's Movement to "anyone favoring women's rights." She felt Ellen White was specifying only the Woman's Rights Movement and did not mean the broader issue of standing up for one's rights. By contrast, however, we have detailed how the Woman's Rights advocates were truly spiritualistic. We have also detailed how their daughters today carry on and have extended their notions and philosophies more extensively. Feminism has not left Spiritualism behind in deed (morality), philosophy (existentialism), theology (feminist theology), or mysticism (New Age and goddess rituals).

The next pages of the *Women in Ministry* chapter give an excellent study on "rights" in Ellen White's writings. Essentially, the author cites examples of Ellen White's views of such relationships as government and citizen, church leadership and member, parent and child, and husband and wife. In each scenario the author shows how those in authority have the responsibility of guarding the interests and individuality of those under them. She also tactfully shares how those abused "are to allow the denial of their rights in a spirit of humble submission." Those who are violated should patiently "bear the violation of their rights."[76] If defrauded, rather than take the grievance to the courts of justice one should rather "suffer loss and wrong."[77] She concludes that "Christians need not contend for their rights because 'God will deal with the one who violates these rights. . . . An account is kept of all these matters, and for all the Lord declares that He will avenge.'"[78]

As good as the analysis of Ellen White's use of rights is, one is left asking, "So, how does understanding rights in all these various situations change the plain meaning of our *Testimonies* passage?" Ellen White surely connected the women's rights movement or feminism to spiritualism. God never tells us to fight for our rights but to surrender, submit, be humble, be poor in spirit, show self-abnegation and self-denial. In a famous passage Mrs. White tells us that dissatisfaction with one's "sphere" was a cause of Eve's sin and compares Eve to women who are dissatisfied with their roles.

"Eve had been perfectly happy by her husband's side in her Eden home; but, like restless modern Eves, she was flattered with the hope of entering a higher sphere than that which God had assigned her. In attempting to rise above her original position, she fell far below it. A similar result will be reached by all who are unwilling to take up cheerfully their life duties in accordance with God's plan. In their efforts to reach positions for which He has not fitted them, many are leaving vacant the place where they might be a blessing. In their desire for a higher sphere, many have sacrificed true womanly dignity and nobility of character, and have left undone the very work that Heaven appointed them."[79]

Some of the most important sentences of this *Women in Ministry* chapter do not have endnotes. This is especially true whenever the author discusses ordination. Suddenly the endnotes become very sparse. In an otherwise heavily-referenced article, one can't help but wish this next sentence had been supported by an endnote: "Because today's ordination issue is not associated with secular, political, religious, or social reform movements such as those in the nineteenth century, this principle does not relate as it did when Ellen White wrote."[80]

Has the author read the current scene correctly? It seems to me that women's ordination is very much a cultural expectation and is very much urged by modern feminism. It is *not* disassociated from the religious and secular movements of our day. It is a part of their stream.

Here's another key sentence that I wish had been supported by evidence: "Because Ellen White makes it clear that women have a right to accept a call from God to ministry, and all persons should receive equal remuneration and recognition for equal work performed, it seems likely she would support women's ordination."[81]

Our *Women in Ministry* author has not made it clear that Ellen White says that God calls women to an ordained ministry. Perhaps the editor might have cross-referenced these positive assertions with other authors who did attempt to show this within the book.

Spiritualism Was Not Only "Back Then"

The *Women in Ministry* chapter we have been considering, "Ellen White and Women's Rights," seems to indicate that spiritualism waned. It says:

"Ellen White's wise advice to avoid any association with spiritualism was soon validated. After exerting significant force on religious thinking and various women's reform movements in the 1850s and early 1960s [*sic*], spiritualism fell into disrepute and scandal in the 1870s. Spiritualists continued to fight for the radical reforms of the 1850s even after many women's rights leaders distanced themselves from spiritualism because its ideas of 'free love' were not helping the cause. Thereafter women's rights leaders more narrowly focused on suffrage, which was achieved by the Nineteenth Amendment in 1920.[82]

But was this the end of the alliance between spiritualism and feminism? No! I have already given some evidence. Here is more. Karen Linsey has written that spiritualism is even more involved than formerly.

"The Feminist spirituality movement began to emerge in the mid-1970s and has become one of the largest submovements within feminism. [It is] amorphous, blending radical feminism, pacifism, witchcraft, Eastern mysticism, goddess worship, animism, psychic healing and a variety of practices normally associated with the occult."[83]

Within feminism today there is a whole neo-pagan revival which harks back to the goddesses of Greece and Rome, a renewal of interest in the Craft (witchcraft), and the New Age revival of ritual and its blending of the earth and environment with religion. Margot Adler writes,

"I have begun to see a resurgence of women returning to the Goddess, seeing themselves as Her daughters, finding Pagan-equality, self-identification, and individual strength for women. Paganism has been for all practical purposes, anti-establishment spirituality. Feminists and Pagans are both coming from the same source without realizing it, and heading toward the same goal without realizing it, and the two are now beginning to interlace."[84]

Note the spiritualistic doctrine embedded in the following quotation from the program notes of the feminist 1998 Re-Imagining Revival, a convention attended by 900 feminists from major Protestant denominations. "I found God in myself and I loved her, I loved her fiercely." Another, attributed to the late liberal Paul Tillich, has echoes of Victoria C. Woodhull: "No sexuality is unclean in the context of the sacred. In the heart and soul of the deities, we are all loved, and it doesn't matter who (you) are sleeping with."[85]

Compare these statements with the following passages from *The Great Controversy:* "Spiritualism teaches 'that man is the creature of progression; that it is his destiny from his birth to progress, even to eternity, toward the God-head.' And again: 'Each mind will judge itself and not another.' 'The judgment will be right, because it is the judgment of self. . . . The throne is within you.' Said a spiritualistic teacher, as the 'spiritual consciousness' awoke within him: 'My fellow-men, all were unfallen demigods.' And another declares, 'Any just and perfect being is Christ.'"[86] And another: "And to complete his work, he declares, through the spirits that 'true knowledge places man above all law;' that 'whatever is, is right;' that 'God doth not condemn;' and that *'all* sins which are committed are innocent.'"[87]

Seventh-day Adventists must wake up and become sensitive to the inroads of spiritualism at the end of time. True, spiritualism does not always assume its medium-spirit-rapping guise, so some may *think* it has diminished. Once again we can thank Mrs. White for warning us about this change.

"It is true that spiritualism is now changing its form and, veiling some of its more objectionable features, is assuming a Christian guise. But its utterances from the platform and the press have been before the public for many years, and in these its real character stands revealed. These teachings cannot be denied or hidden. . . . While it formerly denounced Christ and the Bible, it now *professes* to accept both. But the Bible is interpreted in a manner that is pleasing to the unrenewed heart, while its solemn and vital truths are made of no effect."[88]

Spiritualism has broken out of its denominational castings to be absorbed by psychology, philosophy, and Eastern religions that have spawned the popular New Age Movement. It is preached from every theater and TV in the world because it has become our culture.[89]

Mrs. White had an important vision about the destiny of spiritualism.

"I saw the rapidity with which this delusion was spreading. A train of cars was shown me, going with the speed of lightning. The angel bade me look carefully. I fixed my eyes upon the train. It seemed that the whole world was on board. Then he showed me the conductor, a fair, stately person, whom all the passengers looked up to and reverenced. I was perplexed and asked my attending angel who it was. He said, 'It is Satan. He is the conductor, in the form of an angel of light. He has taken the world captive. They are given over to strong delusions, to believe a lie that they may be damned. . . .'

"He who is the father of lies, blinds and deceives the world by sending forth his angels to speak for the apostles, and to make it appear that they contradict what they wrote by the dictation of the Holy Ghost when on earth. These lying angels make the apostles to corrupt their own teachings and to declare them to be adulterated. By so doing, Satan delights to throw professed Christians and all the world into uncertainty about the Word of God. That holy Book cuts directly across his track and thwarts his plans; therefore he leads men to doubt the divine origin of the Bible."[90]

Conclusion

I was interested to note that some parts of chapter 17 in *Women in Ministry* concurred with my earlier estimates of spiritualism in the women's rights movement.[91] However, the rest of the chapter tries to prove that the women's rights movement of the 19th century has nothing to do with the present thrust to ordain women to the gospel ministry. Here we differ.

As I mentioned earlier, in 1975 I wrote a research paper entitled, "Attending Spirits," showing how the women's rights movement of the 1900s was directly linked to spiritualism. I would like to conclude my present response to chapter 17 of *Women in Ministry* with the same conclusion I made in 1975: "that the radical feminists were far beyond their time; modern Liberation [feminism] has encompassed most of their thought and has moved on. Further study in basic tenets of current Women's Liberation and a comparative study to the [Women's] Rights of the 1860's and '70s which was considered to be spiritualism, might prove that the undercurrents of these Movements are analogous, so that the principle of 1T 421 is still most valid."[92]

"Those who feel called out to join the movement in favor of woman's rights and the so-called dress reform, might as well sever all connection with the third angel's message."

I wouldn't dare to be so blunt. Ellen White said it.

Endnotes

1. Alicia Worley, "Ellen White and Women's Rights," *Women in Ministry* (Berrien Springs, Mich.: Andrews University Press, 1998), pp. 355-376.
2. Ellen G. White, *The Great Controversy* (Mountain View, Calif.: Pacific Press Publishing Association, 1950), p. 588. Note the philosophy outlined as being spiritualism in Chapter 34, "Can Our Dead Speak to Us?" (in other versions known as "Spiritualism") and the safeguard recommended on p. 559. See also J. H. Waggoner, *The Nature and Tendency of Modern Spiritualism* (Battle Creek: Steam Press of the Seventh-day Adventist Publishing Association, 1877).
3. "The President's Commission on Women in Ministry—Report," in *Adventists Affirm* 12/3 (Fall 1998): 13. See pp. 399-404 of this volume.
4. Dale O'Leary, *The Gender Agenda: Redefining Equality* (Lafayette, La.: Vital Issues Press, 1997), p. 31.
5. Mary A. Kassian, *The Feminist Gospel* (Wheaton, Ill.: Crossway Books, 1992), p. xi.
6. Unpublished manuscript by Laurel Ann Nelson, "Attending Spirits," Spring, 1975.
7. *Advent Review and Sabbath Herald,* vols. 15-53, 1860-1881; *The Health Reformer,* vols. 1-13, 1866-1878; and *Signs of the Times,* vols. 1-6, 1874-1880.
8. Uriah Smith, "Victoria C. Woodhull," *Review and Herald,* September 26, 1871, p. 116.
9. Ibid.
10. Laurel Nelson, "Attending Spirits," p. 60.
11. Lois Beachy Underhill, *The Woman Who Ran for President: The Many Lives of Victoria Woodhull* (Bridgehampton, N. Y.: Bridge Works Publishing Co., 1995); Barbara Goldsmith, *Other Powers: The Age of Suffrage, Spiritualism, and the Scandalous Victoria Woodhull* (New York, N. Y.: Harper Perennial, 1998); Ann Braude, *Radical Spirits: Spiritualism and Women's Rights in Nineteenth-Century America* (Boston, Mass.: Beacon, 1989); Mary Gabriel, *Notorious Victoria* (Chapel Hill, N. C.: Algonquin Books of Chapel Hill, 1998).
12. http://members.tripod.com/~Victoria_Woodhull.
13. Goldsmith, p. 27.
14. Braude, p. 2.
15. Goldsmith, p. 35.
16. Braude, p. 3.
17. Alex Owen, *The Darkened Room: Women, Power and Spiritualism in Late Victorian England* (Philadelphia, Pa.: University of Pennsylvania Press, 1990), p. 6.

18. Goldsmith, p. 49.
19. Ibid., p. 267.
20. Ibid., p. 251.
21. Ibid., p. 58.
22. Ibid., p. 36.
23. Ibid., pp. 38, 39, 48, 435.
24. This particular table belonged to spiritualists Thomas and Mary Ann McClintock. The beginnings of its fame are described: "The tilt-top table with three legs was a common fixture in many parlors but now, according to those present, a remarkable occurrence took place. As members of the group presented their ideas, the table began to vibrate with raps of approval from the spirits. As word of this phenomenon spread, the McClintocks' table became famous as the first 'spirit table.' Soon it was believed that certain tables served as catalysts to transmit the thoughts of the spirits." Goldsmith, p. 32. Later it was found that spirits could produce "automatic writing."
25. Goldsmith, p. 435.
26. Ibid., p. 248.
27. Ibid., p. 267. *Centennial Book of Modern Spiritualism in America,* p. 250.
28. Ibid., p. 36; pp. 85, 86.
29. *The Great Controversy,* p. 558.
30. Underhill, p. 254.
31. Page Smith, *Daughters of the Promised Land* (Boston: Little Brown and Company), p. 152, emphasis mine.
32. J. H. Waggoner, "Present Standing of Spiritualism," *Review and Herald,* November 18, 1873, p. 178.
33. Goldsmith, p. 7.
34. http://members.tripod.com/~Victoria_Woodhull/
35. Underhill, xvii.
36. "Self-ownership" is a very important facet of cohabitors. "It may resemble a marriage, but both partners are highly aware it is far more than the lack of a 'piece of paper' that separates them from married couples. Each member of the pair places greater value on his own autonomy than on the durability of the relationship." Mona Charen, "Before you decide on moving in. . . ", *Washington Times,* March 26, 1999.
37. For more on the dress reform aspects of this issue see my paper, "Attending Spirits," pp. 44-58. A copy of it is at the Ellen G. White Estate Branch Office, Andrews University.
38. "I saw that God's order has been reversed, and His special directions disregarded, by those who adopt the American costume. I was referred to Deuteronomy 22:5: 'The woman shall not wear that which pertaineth unto a man, neither shall a man put on a woman's garment: for all that do so are abomination unto the Lord thy God.' God would not have His people adopt the so-called reform dress. It is immodest apparel, wholly unfitted for the modest, humble followers of Christ.

"There is an increasing tendency to have women in their dress and appearance as near like the other sex as possible, and to fashion their dress very much like that of men, but God pronounces it abomination. 'In like manner also, that women adorn themselves in modest apparel, with shamefacedness and sobriety.' 1 Tim. 2:9." Ellen G. White, *Testimonies for the Church,* 1:421.
39. "Gender Concepts in Development Planning: Basic Approach" (INSTRAW, 1995), p. 11, in O'Leary, p. 120.
40. O'Leary, p. 107.
41. Ibid., pp. 86-93.
42. Wendy Bounds, "Dating Games Today Break Traditional Gender Roles," *Wall Street Journal,* April 26, 1995), p. B-1 in O'Leary, p. 38. There is a campus-based faith organization that "works to enhance the spiritual lives of gay, lesbian, bisexual and transgender individu-

als at the University of Minnesota. We are sponsored by the United Methodist Church, Lutheran Campus Ministries, University Episcopal Center and University Baptist Church." "Gay, Lesbian, Bisexual, Transgender, Faith Advocate Group," *The Christian News,* May 31, 1999, p. 15.

43. O'Leary, p. 24.
44. For more information see Laurel Damsteegt, "S.M.I. Henry: Pioneer in Women's Ministry," *Adventists Affirm,* 9/1 (Spring, 1995): 18.
45. Donna Alberta Behnke, *Created in God's Image: Religious Issues in the Woman's Rights Movement of the Nineteenth Century* (Evanston, Ill.: Ph.D. Dissertation, Northwestern University, June 1975), p. 129.
46. Frances E. Willard in *The Woman's Bible,* Part II (New York: European Publishing Company, 1898), pp. 201-202.
47. In the Spring of 1977 I had the opportunity of doing extensive research on the minister-wife team of Stephen and Hetty Haskell. In Chapter 9 of that paper I thoroughly discuss Ellen White's views of remuneration to women. (See "Humble Giants," by Laurel Damsteegt [nee Nelson], pp. 74-80. "Humble Giants" is at the Ellen G. White Estate Branch Office, Andrews University.) In essence, women are to be recognized separately from their husbands and each receive wages. The most complete manuscript of Ellen White's views on women and wages is Manuscript 43a, 1898 (Manuscript Release #330), found in *Manuscript Releases,* 5:323-327.
48. See Laurel Damsteegt, "Shall Women Minister?" *Adventists Affirm,* 9/1 (Spring 1995): 4.
49. See William Fagal's discussion on Ellen White's view of ordination in "Did Ellen White Support the Ordination of Women?" *Ministry,* February 1989, pp. 6-9. Reprinted in this volume, beginning on page 279.
50. Behnke, p. 135.
51. Elizabeth Cady Stanton's letter to the editor of *The Critic* in support of *The Woman's Bible,* in *Up From the Pedestal* (Chicago, Ill.: Quadrangle, 1968), p. 119. Cited in Behnke, p. 136.
52. "E.M." in *The Woman's Bible,* Part II, p. 203.
53. Behnke, p. 95.
54. *Centennial Book of Modern Spiritualism,* p. 107.
55. Behnke, p. 96.
56. Ursula Bright, *The Woman's Bible,* Part II, pp. 188, 189.
57. Josephine K. Henry, *The Woman's Bible,* Part II, p. 198.
58. Mary Daly, *The Church and the Second Sex* (Boston, Mass.: Beacon Press, 1968), pp. 74-75.
59. Ibid., p. 185.
60. Mary A. Kassian, *The Feminist Gospel* (Wheaton, Ill.: Crossway Books, 1992), p. 90.
61. Pamela Abramson, Mark Starr, Patricia King, "Feminism and the Churches," *Newsweek,* Feb. 13, 1989, p. 61.
62. Elizabeth Schüssler Fiorenza, "Emerging Issues in Feminist Biblical Interpretation," *Christian Feminism: Visions of a New Humanity,* ed. Judith L. Weidman (San Francisco: Harper & Row, 1984), p. 53.
63. Kassian, p. 206.
64. Ibid., pp. 208, 209.
65. Kassian's footnote on p. 277: "Berkeley and Alvera Mickelsen, Philip Payne, Gilbert Bilezikian and Catherine Kroeger have recently argued that 'kephale,' the Greek word for 'head,' means 'source' and therefore does not contain any implications for authority or an authority structure. For a detailed discussion regarding the meaning of kephale and an interaction with their theory, refer to 'The Meaning of *Kepahale* (Head): A Response to Recent Studies,' by Wayne Grudem, published in *Recovering Biblical Manhood & Womanhood,* eds. John Piper and Wayne Grudem (Wheaton, Ill.: Crossway Books, 1991), pp. 425-468."
66. Kassian, p. 211.
67. Ibid., p. 216.

68. Phyllis Trible, quoted in Kassian, p. 109.

69. Carsten Johnsen, *The Mystic "Omega" of End-Time Crisis* (Sisteron, France: n.d.), p. 43.

70. Worley, p. 355.

71. Ibid., p. 356.

72. For how some Adventists are using the higher-critical approach to studying Ellen White, see an example in Jan Daffern's, "The Masculinization of Ellen White," *Ponderings*, 2/3 (March, April 1989): 23.

73. For the full story and concerns about the editing of the *Testimonies* see Ron Graybill, "Visions and Revisions, Part II: Editing the Testimonies," *Ministry*, April, 1994, p. 9.

74. Publishers, "Preface to Third Edition," *Testimonies for the Church* (Battle Creek: Review and Herald, 1885), page iii.

75. Worley, pp. 356, 357, emphasis hers.

76. Ibid., p. 365.

77. Ibid., p. 365.

78. Ibid., p. 365.

79. *Patriarchs and Prophets*, p. 59.

80. Worley, p. 368.

81. Ibid., p. 369

82. Ibid., p. 367.

83. Karen Linsey, MS, quoted by Allan Turner in "Wimmin, Wiccans, and Goddess Worship," http://allanturner.com/ss09.html.

84. Margot Adler, *Drawing Down the Moon: Witches, Druids, Goddess-Worshippers, and Other Pagans in America Today* (Boston: Beacon Press, 1970), p. 177.

85. "Feminists Exchanging Truth for a Lie," *Christian News*, October 19, 1998, p. 21. See also, "Earthquake in the Mainline, *Christianity Today*, November 14, 1994, pp. 39-43 about the 1993 Re-Imagining Colloquium. Even though the colloquium represented mainline churches (Presbyterian Church [U.S.A.] [PCUSA], the United Methodist Church, the Evangelical Lutheran Church in America [ELCA], the American Baptist Convention [ABC], the United Church of Christ, and four religious communities of Roman Catholics), *Christianity Today* minces no words: "What other language besides 'heresy' is appropriate where the Incarnation and Trinity were derided, where Scripture was contradicted, and where a goddess named Sophia was actively promoted" (ibid., p. 39).

86. *The Great Controversy*, p. 554.

87. Ibid., p. 555, emphasis original.

88. Ibid., pp. 557-558, emphasis original.

89. For more explicit coverage of how spiritualism has affected our current culture, see Laurel Damsteegt's article, "Doctrine of Devils," *Adventists Affirm*, 11/1 (Spring, 1997): 41-52.

90. *Early Writings*, pp. 263, 264.

91. Worley, p. 366.

92. L. Damsteegt (nee Nelson), "Attending Spirits," p. 62.

Chapter 16

Ellen G. White and Women in Ministry

William Fagal

~

[The following was published as a two-part article in *Ministry* magazine,
December 1988 and February 1989]

Part I: Did Ellen White Call for Ordaining Women?

What was Mrs. White's stance in regard to the ordination of women? Her
prophetic role and her involvement in the founding and nurturing of the Seventh-
day Adventist Church make this a question of interest to Adventists today. In
recent years some have proposed that we may find support in Mrs. White's writings for ordaining women as pastors or elders. This study examines the main passages that people are using in support of women's ordination to see what those
passages actually teach.

The "Ordination" Statement

In 1895 Ellen White wrote the following: "Women who are willing to consecrate some of their time to the service of the Lord should be appointed to visit the
sick, look after the young, and minister to the necessities of the poor. They should
be set apart to this work by prayer and laying on of hands. In some cases they will
need to counsel with the church officers or the minister; but if they are devoted
women, maintaining a vital connection with God, they will be a power for good in
the church. This is another means of strengthening and building up the church.
We need to branch out more in our methods of labor. Not a hand should be
bound, not a soul discouraged, not a voice should be hushed; let every individual

---

William Fagal is the Director of the Ellen G. White Estate Branch Office, Andrews University.

labor, privately or publicly, to help forward this grand work. Place the burdens upon men and women of the church, that they may grow by reason of the exercise, and thus become effective agents in the hand of the Lord for the enlightenment of those who sit in darkness."[1]

Careful reading of this statement reveals that:

1. This ministry is part-time. "Women who are willing to consecrate some of their time . . ." Therefore from the start it does not seem to be referring to pastoral ministry.

2. The work is something other than that which the church was already doing. "This is another means of strengthening and building up the church. We need to branch out more in our methods of labor."

3. Since "in some cases they will need to counsel with the church officers[2] or the minister," she does not equate them with the minister, nor does she regard them as the officers whose responsibility it is to lead the local congregation.

Was Mrs. White here calling for an ordained woman ministry? If one uses the term *ministry* in its broad sense of service, yes. But she has clearly distinguished this ministry from that of the pastor or the leading church officers.

Further, the article from which the statement comes is entitled "The Duty of the Minister and the People." It calls for involvement of the laity in the work of the church. Its purpose is not to change the structure of the pastoral ministry, but rather to change its emphasis from a focus on the minister's work to one in which the laity is active and motivated.

Ordination of Women Physicians

Since Mrs. White said that women should train as physicians,[3] and in another statement calls for a "setting apart" of physicians who are engaged in missionary work and soul winning, some have felt that the two statements together indicate that she felt that women should be ordained. The statement about physicians reads as follows:

"The work of the true medical missionary is largely a spiritual work. It includes prayer and the laying on of hands; he therefore should be as sacredly set apart for his work as is the minister of the gospel. Those who are selected to act the part of missionary physicians are to be set apart as such. This will strengthen them against the temptation to withdraw from the sanitarium work to engage in private practice."[4]

Does Ellen White here call for physicians to be ordained as ministers? She could have said so much more directly: "He therefore should be set apart as a minister." But instead, she said the physician is to be "as sacredly set apart . . . as is the minister." He is "to be set apart as such." As what? As a missionary physician. That is made even clearer by the motivation for doing it—"to strengthen [him] against the temptation to withdraw from the sanitarium work to engage in private practice." Ordaining physicians as ministers would not be likely to have a bearing on that, but ordaining them as missionary physicians would.

When studying Mrs. White's calls for ordination, one must not fail to consider the positions those calls concerned. Neither of the above statements supports the assertion that she called for women to be included in the ordained pastoral or church elder ministry.

Women in the Gospel Ministry

Ellen White said clearly, "There are women who should labor in the gospel ministry. In many respects they would do more good than the ministers who neglect to visit the flock of God."[5] Women who do such labor, especially full-time, were to be paid fairly from the tithe for their work. "The tithe should go to those who labor in word and doctrine, be they men or women."[6] She added, "Seventh-day Adventists are not in any way to belittle woman's work."[7]

Some believe that Mrs. White thus called for elimination of any role distinction between men and women in the ministry of the Adventist Church. The fairness she urged in the treatment of women workers, they say, should be understood to include ordination to the gospel ministry irrespective of gender.

Yet Mrs. White did not make that connection. Her statement, "There are women who should labor in the gospel ministry," comes from a manuscript whose opening paragraph says: "The ministers are paid for their work, and this is well. And if the Lord gives the wife as well as the husband the burden of labor, and if she devotes her time and her strength to visiting from family to family, opening the Scriptures to them, although the hands of ordination have not been laid upon her, she is accomplishing a work that is in the line of ministry. Should her labors be counted as nought, and her husband's salary be no more than that of the servant of God whose wife does not give herself to the work, but remains at home to care for her family?"[8]

The subject under discussion is the pay of ministers' wives, and the kind of work they are doing is described as visiting homes and opening the Scriptures to the families. Further, rather than seeing ordination as a remedy to the injustice regarding pay, Mrs. White dismisses it as irrelevant to the issue. Her point is simply that those ministers' wives who function as what we would call Bible instructors are "accomplishing a work that is in the line of ministry," and they should be paid for it.

It is in this setting that Mrs. White's statement "There are women who should labor in the gospel ministry" appears. The sentence that follows it underscores the nature of the work she envisioned for these women: "In many respects they would do more good than the ministers who neglect to visit the flock of God." Immediately she adds, "Husband and wife may unite in this work, and when it is possible, they should. The way is open for consecrated women."[9]

So it seems that she was not calling for women to function in the same roles as do men, but rather to have a complementary ministry that focuses on personal work. She noted that women were not ordained, but gave no hint that that practice should change—though she called in strong terms for reform in pay practices:

"The Lord has settled it. You are to do your duty to the women who labor in the gospel, whose work testifies that they are essential to carry the truth into families."[10] She even thought of setting up a fund from her own tithe money to pay certain ministers' wives who were giving their whole time to giving Bible studies and working with families, but who were not being paid.[11]

Women as Pastors to the Flock

In the above statement about women who should labor in the gospel ministry, she describes that labor as we would the work of a Bible instructor. She associated this work with care for (visiting) "the flock of God." This statement may provide a key to understanding more clearly a statement published a short time later in an article entitled, "The Canvasser a Gospel Worker":

"All who desire an opportunity for true ministry, and who will give themselves unreservedly to God, will find in the canvassing work opportunities to speak upon many things pertaining to the future, immortal life. The experience thus gained will be of the greatest value to those who are fitting themselves for the ministry. It is the accompaniment of the Holy Spirit of God that prepares workers, both men and women, to become pastors to the flock of God."[12] The remainder of the paragraph describes the character-building benefits of engaging in the canvassing work.

Was Ellen White here calling for women to be appointed pastors of churches, and therefore perhaps even to be ordained to that ministry? There are several indications that she was not.

First of all, when Ellen White wrote about ordained church pastors, she typically referred to them as *ministers* rather than *pastors*. In cases in which she used the term *pastor* she seems to have done so with a specialized meaning in mind, using the term to refer to a person doing personal labor in the nurture of the flock, rather than a particular church office or position.

For example, she wrote about an Elder H who told "the poor sheep that he would rather be horsewhipped than visit. He neglected personal labor, therefore pastoral work was not done in the church and its borders. . . . Had the preacher done the work of a pastor, a much larger number would now be rejoicing in the truth."[13]

Speaking of ministers who devote excessive time to reading and writing, she said: "The duties of a pastor are often shamelessly neglected because the minister lacks strength to sacrifice his personal inclinations for seclusion and study. The pastor should visit from house to house among his flock, teaching, conversing, and praying with each family, and looking out for the welfare of their souls."[14]

She again expressed her concern for personal care for the flock this way: "Responsibilities must be laid upon the members of the church. The missionary spirit should be awakened as never before, and workers should be appointed as needed, who will act as pastors to the flock, putting forth personal effort to bring the church up to that condition where spiritual life and activity will be seen in all her borders."[15]

In each instance here the concept of *pastor* is associated with the function of personal work for the flock of God, even when it is done by members of the church other than the minister. One who visits families, who teaches and prays with them, who shows personal care and interest, is doing pastoral work.

If Mrs. White intended to open the regular pastoral ministry to women, we might well expect her to give strong emphasis to the point rather than simply mentioning it as an aside in an article focusing on the canvassing work. In the same volume of *Testimonies* we find an article entitled, "Women to Be Gospel Workers."[16] Its focus also is on personal work in families and with other women, with no mention of the workers being ordained ministers.

The same volume also includes a chapter entitled "Young Men in the Ministry,"[17] in which, after saying that "the Lord calls for more ministers to labor in His vineyard," she adds, "God calls for you, young men. He calls for whole armies of young men."[18] The whole chapter is a call for men to enter the ministry, with no mention of women doing so. The same sort of gender-specific call for the ministry of men also appears in the chapter "The Need of Educational Reform."[19] It seems only natural to expect these articles to urge women also to join the ranks of ministers if Mrs. White believed that women canvassers were preparing for ordination.

It seems that Mrs. White did not envision men and women doing the same work of ministry. Rather, she called for women especially to undertake a personal ministry of visitation and instruction in the home.[20] Such a work was necessary, important work, and was "in the line of ministry,"[21] though often neglected by the men. The work of these women would complement rather than duplicate the regular ministry of the men. And there is no call for ordination connected with it.

Women Engaged in the Ministry

Some have thought the following passage calls for women to serve as ministers in the same capacity as men: "Young men and young women who should be engaged in the ministry, in Bible work, and in the canvassing work should not be bound down to mechanical employment."[22] The context is a call for our institutions to train young people for evangelistic work.

One could argue that in this statement Mrs. White is urging both young men and young women to go into all three lines of labor. But that is not necessarily the case. The statement may be understood simply as urging young people to go into whichever line of evangelistic work that is suitable to them, without trying to specify what is appropriate to each gender. The burden of the message is not to change church policy to make room for women to serve in the same capacities as men, but rather to encourage the employment of both men and women in soul-winning work.

"Woman Ministry"

"Address the crowd whenever you can."[23] This injunction, published in *Evangelism* in a section the compilers entitled "Women in Public Ministry," was directed to Mrs. S. M. I. Henry, who had been granted a ministerial license the previous year. Some have taken it as Mrs. White's encouragement for women to seek a preaching ministry, which today is equated with being an ordained minister of the church.

But in this injunction Ellen White is not promoting the employment of women as ministers in the usual sense of the term. The statement is in a letter from Mrs. White, published in Mrs. Henry's column in the *Review,* expressing a concern for the women of the church to be instructed in how to be servants of Jesus.[24] Earlier paragraphs make it plain that Mrs. White was encouraging Mrs. Henry to minister to and address groups of women:

"If we can arrange, as you are now working, to have regularly organized companies intelligently instructed in regard to the part they should act as servants of the Master, our churches will have life and vitality such as have been so long needed.

"Christ our Saviour appreciated the excellency of the soul. Our sisters have generally a very hard time, with their increasing families and their unappreciated trials. I have so longed for women who could be educators to help them to arise from their discouragement, and to feel that they could do a work for the Lord."[25]

Mrs. Henry spoke to Adventist and non-Adventist groups throughout the United States and Canada, presenting her plan for "woman ministry," which stressed the role of the mother in the moral education of society. Her work was the first approach the Adventist Church made to training parents and helping them with their problems.[26]

When Ellen White herself published the material she had written to Mrs. Henry, she did not publish the entire letter, but reworked portions of it for general use. She published it in *Testimonies,* under the title "Women to Be Gospel Workers."[27] And she left out the section containing the words "address the crowd whenever you can."

Conclusion

Mrs. White called for greater involvement of women in the work of the church. She encouraged a greater diversity of methods of labor, and she wanted women to see what great things they could accomplish for the Master. But she had no concern with today's social agenda. Her statements neither support ordination for women nor explicitly forbid it. None of her writings deal directly with this issue. It appears to me that she envisioned women fulfilling a role complementary to that of men, without concern for ordination as pastors or elders. God would bless their efforts.

"Women may take their places in the work at this crisis, and the Lord will work through them. If they are imbued with a sense of their duty, and labor under the influence of the Spirit of God, they will have just the self-possession required for this time. The Saviour will reflect upon these self-sacrificing women the light of His countenance, and this will give them a power which will exceed that of men. They can do in families a work that men cannot do, a work that reaches the inner life. They can come close to the hearts of those whom men cannot reach. Their labor is needed."[28]

Part II: Did Ellen White Support the Ordination of Women?

What does Adventist history show us about Ellen White and the ordination question? If she simply did not address the matter as an issue in her writings, and therefore neither endorsed nor explicitly forbade ordination of women, can we perhaps discover her attitude by studying her actions? This article will examine claims made on the basis of certain historical documents and events in an effort to see whether these can show that she supported ordaining women as pastors or elders. Some key statements by Mrs. White on women's role in gospel work will be presented at the end.

Was Ellen White Herself Ordained?

There is no record of Ellen White ever having been ordained by human hands. Yet from 1871 until her death she was granted ministerial credentials by various organizations of the church. The certificate that was used read "Ordained Minister." Several of her credential certificates from the mid 1880s are still in our possession. On the one from 1885 the word *ordained* is neatly struck out. On the 1887 certificate, the next one we have, it is not.

Had she been ordained in the interim? Some have argued that she had. But the question is settled definitely by her own hand. In 1909 she filled out a "Biographical Information Blank" for the General Conference records. On the blank for Item 19, which asks, "If ordained, state when, where, and by whom," she simply inscribed an X. This is the same response she made to Item 26, which asked, "If remarried, give date, and to whom." In this way she indicated that she had never remarried, nor had she ever been ordained. She was not denying that God had chosen and equipped her, but she indicated that there had never been an ordination ceremony carried out for her.[29]

Why then do some of her credentials say "ordained minister"? The fact that "ordained" was sometimes crossed out highlights the awkwardness of giving credentials to a prophet. The church has no such special category of credentials. So it utilized what it had, giving its highest credentials without performing an ordination ceremony. In actuality, the prophet needed no human credentials. She functioned for more than 25 years prior to 1871 without any.

Licensing of Women Ministers

A number of women received ministerial licenses from the Seventh-day Adventist Church during the late 1800s and early 1900s. Most of these were the wives of ordained ministers, and most of them apparently were engaged in personal labor similar to that of a Bible instructor today. Some notable exceptions are Minnie Sype, Lulu Wightman, and apparently Ellen Lane, who functioned effectively as public evangelists. But to date I have seen no evidence that women served as the leaders of churches. Further research may shed more light on this matter.

Some have suggested recently that the circumstances surrounding the licensing of women as ministers in the Seventh-day Adventist Church comprise a mandate for ordaining women today. The argument, in brief, is this:

The year 1878 saw two important events: the church first licensed women as ministers, and the church first called for an examination to be made of candidates for license, since it was understood that licensing would put women on the path to ordination. Ellen White took an active part in examining the qualifications of candidates for license, some of whom presumably were female. And shortly after the church began licensing women, it considered ordaining them. Though the proposal was not adopted, Mrs. White did not oppose it or warn against it. Rather, she later called for ordaining women to church ministries and paying them from the tithe.

Several inaccuracies appear in this scenario. First, Ellen Lane was first licensed not in 1878, but three years earlier in 1875, at the same time that Sister Roby Tuttle was licensed.[30] Further, these were not the first women to receive the ministerial license. That honor seems to belong to Sarah A. H. Lindsey, who received a license from the New York and Pennsylvania Conference on August 9, 1871.[31] The licensing of these women therefore cannot demonstrate that the church at that time assumed licensing of women would lead to ordination. The policy calling for an examination prior to licensing anyone came seven years after the first woman was licensed, and the question of ordaining women would not be considered until 1881, 10 years after their first licensing.

Second, there is no absolute evidence that Ellen White took active part in the examination of candidates, male or female, for license. The assertion that she did is based on two pieces of evidence: (1) Mrs. White attended certain conference sessions at which women were granted the ministerial license,[32] and (2) she wrote the following comment about her stay at a camp meeting in Oregon—"I was unable to sit up yesterday, for with much writing, reining myself up to meet different ones who put in requests for license, speaking in public, and showing the unfitness of different ones to attempt to teach others the truth, it was too much for my strength."[33]

The statement does not say that she took part in examinations or, as has been claimed, that she recommended that some of the candidates not receive licenses. It merely lists things she had been doing and makes no connection between "meeting" license applicants and "showing the unfitness" of certain unnamed individuals to teach the truth. The lack of connection between those two elements is shown by the fact that they are separated by another item on the list—"speaking in public." And there is not a hint here that any of the candidates for license are female.

If Mrs. White's "showing the unfitness of different ones to attempt to teach others the truth" was not in the context of an examination for a license, then what *was* it about? A possible clue occurs later in the same paragraph, where she describes her sermon of the night before: "I here brought in genuine sanctification and the spurious article which is so common."[34] Was she counteracting false doctrine that was already being taught there, and showing the unfitness of those who were already teaching it? We don't know for certain. But it goes beyond the facts to assert that Mrs. White here said that she recommended that certain applicants not receive licenses.

The third inaccuracy in the scenario lies in the claim that the church considered ordaining women shortly after it began licensing them, indicating that licensing was understood to put them on the ordination track. We have already shown above that rather than three years (1878-1881), which would correspond roughly to today's typical time between licensing and ordination in the Adventist ministry, it was 10 years after the church started licensing women that it first considered ordaining them. And the events of that consideration need some further explication.

The Committee on Resolutions at the 1881 General Conference session introduced the following for consideration:

"*Resolved,* That females possessing the necessary qualifications to fill that position, may, with perfect propriety, be set apart by ordination to the work of the Christian ministry."[35]

After discussion in which eight delegates spoke to the issue, the resolution was referred to the General Conference Committee.[36] Referral to committee is a way to provide for more careful study of something on which the whole body is uncertain. It has also functioned at times as a means of dealing with something that will not pass, without having to vote it down. Though General Conference sessions were held yearly until 1889 (when they became biennial), neither the committee nor anyone else ever reintroduced the matter until recent years. Apparently the idea of ordaining women had little support in the church at that time. But did Ellen White support it?

Ellen White's Silence

Mrs. White was not present at the 1881 General Conference session. She likely read the report of the resolutions in the *Review* a few weeks later or heard about them from her son W. C. White, but we have no record of her making any comment one way or the other on the matter. This is harder to explain from the position that she favored ordination than from the position that she opposed it. Proponents of ordination today deny that her silence lent approval to the handling of the matter. They say that her silence must at least be viewed as permissive in light of her encouragement to women to participate in the work of the church and her responsibility to warn the church against error.

Ellen White's silence, by itself, neither promotes nor precludes ordination for women. But if she favored it, why didn't she speak out when the church veered away from ordaining women? She may simply have felt that the issue was not important. Or if she felt that the church should not ordain women, she may have made no comment on the resolution simply because none was necessary. No corrective was needed, because the church was not about to begin ordaining women.

She took a similar course at first in relation to the pantheism crisis a few years later. In connection with this crisis, which came to a head with the publication of Dr. John Harvey Kellogg's book *Living Temple,* she wrote that:

"About the time that *Living Temple* was published, there passed before me, in the night season, representations indicating that some danger was approaching, and that I must prepare for it by writing out the things God had revealed to me regarding the foundation principles of our faith. A copy of *Living Temple* was sent me, but it remained in my library, unread. From the light given me by the Lord, I knew that some of the sentiments advocated in the book did not bear the endorsement of God, and that they were a snare that the enemy had prepared for the last days. I thought that this would surely be discerned, and that it would not be necessary for me to say anything about it."[37]

Had the church leaders discerned the danger of the concepts in *Living Temple* and moved against it, evidently Mrs. White would have said nothing. Yet her silence would not have been permissive in regard to pantheism. Only when it was clear that the error was gaining ground did she speak out.

Charged to Protest Injustice and Equity

If denying ordination to women were (as some today claim) arbitrary, unjust, and oppressive, we could expect Ellen White to speak out. She stated, "I was charged not to neglect or pass by those who were being wronged. I was specially charged to protest against any arbitrary or overbearing action toward the ministers of the gospel by those having official authority. Disagreeable though the duty may be, I am to reprove the oppressor, and plead for justice. I am to present the necessity of maintaining justice and equity in all our institutions."[38]

The women who might have been affected by the 1881 resolution were licensed as ministers of the gospel, but church officials did not see fit to permit their ordination. Mrs. White spoke strongly in favor of the women workers being paid and paid fairly, even from the tithe;[39] she spoke about the importance of supporting aged ministers;[40] she protested against unfair treatment of Black ministers;[41] but she had nothing to say when the General Conference declined to ordain licensed women ministers. Evidently she did not see this as "arbitrary," "overbearing," or a matter of "justice and equity."

Again, one must be careful not to claim too much on the basis of silence. Yet Mrs. White's silence on the ordination issue should make one slow to claim that she gave her support or influence to the cause of bringing women into the ordained pastoral ministry.

The final claim of the scenario we have been examining is that Ellen White called for women to be ordained and for them to be paid from the tithe. We have already examined the passages that are used to say that Mrs. White called for women to be ordained to the gospel ministry (see Part I, "Did Ellen White Call for Ordaining Women?"), and we have found that they do not make such a call. Yet we must recognize that Mrs. White did call for women to be involved in an active personal ministry, and that she envisioned paying from the tithe the women workers who gave themselves whole-souled to this work, "although the hands of ordination have not been laid"[42] upon them. But there is no basis in her writings nor in Adventist history for saying that Mrs. White supported ordination of women to the gospel ministry.

Mrs. White's View

What then was Mrs. White's view of the ministry of women? Though there are no indications that she called for women to serve as ordained elders or pastors, she presents a broad view of service for women in God's work. She saw women as able to do a great work for Christ in personal contacts, bringing the message for this hour into homes and families. And she recognized and cited important contributions they could make in various leadership responsibilities in the church as well.

For instance, she called for training to be offered for women in our schools. Speaking of Avondale, the newly opened school in Australia, she said, "The Lord designs that the school should also be a place where a training may be gained in women's work." After enumerating certain domestic and educational training to be included, she added, "They are to be qualified to take any post that may be offered—superintendents, Sabbath school teachers, Bible workers. They must be prepared to teach day schools for children."[43]

She described the important mission women could fulfill: "Wonderful is the mission of the wives and mothers and the younger women workers. If they will, they can exert an influence for good to all around them. By modesty in dress and circumspect deportment, they may bear witness to the truth in its simplicity. They may let their light so shine before all, that others will see their good works and glorify their Father which is in heaven. A truly converted woman will exert a powerful transforming influence for good. Connected with her husband, she may aid him in his work, and become the means of encouragement and blessing to him. When the will and way are brought into subjection to the Spirit of God, there is no limit to the good that can be accomplished."[44]

While Mrs. White emphasizes a husband-wife ministry here, single women ("the younger women workers") are also included. The type of work is not designated, but would surely include the various lines of work that we have noted before. She says that with modesty and propriety, with the will and way brought into subjection to God, women may let their light shine and may exert a limitless influence for good.

Personal Ministry

In *Testimonies,* volume 6, Ellen White published an article called "Women to Be Gospel Workers." Presumably it represents fairly what her view of women as gospel workers really entailed. In it she stressed the importance of personal work for others, then went on to write of the work that women are to do, after first speaking of what they are to be. "The Lord has a work for women as well as men to do. They may accomplish a good work for God if they will first learn in the school of Christ the precious, all-important lesson of meekness. They must not only bear the name of Christ, but possess His Spirit. They must walk even as He walked, purifying their souls from everything that defiles. Then they will be able to benefit others by presenting the all-sufficiency of Jesus.

"Women may take their places in the work at this crisis, and the Lord will work through them. If they are imbued with a sense of their duty, and labor under the influence of the Spirit of God, they will have just the self-possession required for this time. The Saviour will reflect upon these self-sacrificing women the light of His countenance, and this will give them a power which will exceed that of men. They can do in families a work that men cannot do, a work that reaches the inner life. They can come close to the hearts of those whom men cannot reach. Their labor is needed.

"A direct necessity is being met by the work of women who have given themselves to the Lord and are reaching out to help a needy, sin-stricken people. Personal evangelistic work is to be done. The women who take up this work carry the gospel to the homes of the people in the highways and the byways. They read and explain the word to families, praying with them, caring for the sick, relieving their temporal necessities. They present before families and individuals the purifying, transforming influence of the truth."[45]

So the core of her burden for women was that they do personal work with women and families. If done in the right spirit, under the influence of Christ, "the light of His countenance . . . will give them a power which will exceed that of men. . . . Their labor is needed."

This need is still with us today. Though some urge this need as a reason that women should be ordained, Mrs. White envisioned women performing this ministry without reference to their serving as ordained elders or pastors. She said that such ministry is capable, when rightly done, of exhibiting a power greater than that of men. It is noble work, needed work. In defining women's work in this way, she has in no way belittled it.[46]

Such statements appear in many places in Mrs. White's writings.[47] Her view is consistent: without calling for ordination of women as pastors or elders, she urged a vigorous participation of women especially in personal ministry.

Ellen White's view of women's ministry requires no change in church structure or polity, yet its implementation would revolutionize the church's practice. There would be a great increase in personal work being done, both by paid full- and part-time workers and by volunteer laborers. If the work were done in the spirit of Jesus, the women would show a power greater than that of the men. There would be an explosion in the numbers of people won to Christ and His truth through the gentle, appealing ministry of women. There would be healing in the home relationships, as godly women workers challenged men to reflect the self-sacrificing headship of Christ in their own relationship with their wives, and women to honor that headship as they would the headship of Christ. Families would be strengthened, and the church would make a start on the road to showing a world filled with hurting and broken families what a difference the practice of the Lordship of Jesus really makes.

Endnotes

1. *Review and Herald,* July 9, 1895, p. 434.
2. The assertion, advanced by some, that "church officers" here refers to conference officials is unlikely in view of Ellen White's use twice in this article of the term "conference officers" to refer to this group and her corresponding single use of "officers of the church" to refer to the local church leaders. She seems to have been able to avoid ambiguity on this point.
3. See, for instance, *Medical Ministry,* p. 140.
4. *Evangelism,* p. 546 (Manuscript 5, 1908).
5. Ibid., p. 472.
6. Ibid., p. 492 (see also p. 491 for fairness in pay).
7. Ibid., pp. 492, 493.
8. Manuscript 43a, 1898. She protests such practices through much of the manuscript. More of what she says here may be seen in *Evangelism,* pp. 492, 493, though the material is credited to other, later books and manuscripts of Mrs. White.
9. Ibid. (Manuscript Release #330 [*Manuscript Releases,* 5:323]).
10. Ibid.
11. Ellen G. White letter 137, 1898 (Manuscript Release #959), pp. 1, 2 [*Manuscript Releases,* 12:160, 161].
12. *Testimonies for the Church,* 6:322.
13. "Experiences in Australia," p. 53, written in Adelaide, Australia, Oct. 11, 1892 (Manuscript Release #763, pp. 5, 6 [*Manuscript Releases,* 9:343, 344]).
14. *Gospel Workers,* p. 337.
15. *Testimonies for the Church,* 5:723.
16. Ibid., 6:114-118.
17. Ibid., pp. 411-416.
18. Ibid., p. 411.
19. Ibid., pp. 126-140.
20. We are reminded again of the statement quoted earlier: "There are women who should labor in the gospel ministry. In many respects they would do more good than the ministers who neglect to *visit the flock of God"* (*Evangelism,* p. 472, italics supplied).
21. Manuscript 43a, 1898 (Manuscript Release #267, p. 1 [*Manuscript Releases,* 5:29]).
22. *Testimonies for the Church,* 8:229, 230.
23. *Evangelism,* p. 473.
24. *Review and Herald,* May 9, 1899, p. 293.
25. Ibid.
26. *SDA Encyclopedia* (Washington, D.C.: Review and Herald, 1976), pp. 581, 582.
27. *Testimonies for the Church,* 6:114-116.
28. Ibid., pp. 117, 188.
29. Arthur L. White, "Ellen G. White the Person," *Spectrum* 4, No. 2 (Spring 1972): p. 8. The Biographical Information blank is on file at the White Estate office in Washington, D.C. A photocopy is in Document File 701 at the White Estate Branch Office, Andrews University.
30. *Review and Herald,* Aug. 26, 1875, p. 63.
31. Ibid., Sept. 12, 1871, p. 102.
32. Ibid., June 12, 1879, p. 190.

33. Letter 32a, 1880.
34. Ibid. This was evidently a problem affecting the church at large, for in the next year Mrs. White published an 82-page pamphlet entitled *Bible Sanctification: A Contrast of the True and False Theories* (Battle Creek, Mich.: Steam Press, 1881). This was an edited version of a series of 10 articles published in the *Review and Herald* between January 18 and May 3, 1881. Their appearance in pamphlet form in the same year of their publication in the *Review* indicates the importance they held for the church. *Bible Sanctification* was later republished as *The Sanctified Life*.
35. *Review and Herald,* Dec. 20, 1881, p. 392.
36. Ibid.
37. *Selected Messages,* 1:202, 203.
38. Review and Herald, July 26, 1906, p. 8 (also in *Selected Messages,* 1:33).
39. *Evangelism,* p. 492; see also p. 491 concerning fairness in pay.
40. Ibid.
41. *Testimonies for the Church,* 9:223.
42. Manuscript 43a, 1898 (also in *Gospel Workers,* p. 452).
43. *Evangelism,* p. 475 (Letter 3, 1898).
44. Ibid., pp. 467, 468 (Manuscript 91, 1908).
45. *Testimonies for the Church,* 6:117, 118.
46. She cautioned others concerning that danger: "Seventh-day Adventists are not in any way to belittle woman's work" (*Evangelism,* pp. 492, 493).
47. See, for example, *Christian Service,* pp. 27-29; *Evangelism,* pp. 459-461, 464-478, 491-493; *Gospel Workers,* pp. 452, 453; *Welfare Ministry,* pp. 143-166; and *Counsels on Health.* She also calls for women to become involved in medical missionary work, some as doctors and nurses, and others as nonprofessionals.

Chapter 17

Are Those Things So?—Part II:
A Summary and Evaluation of Key Historical and Theological Arguments of *Women in Ministry*

Samuel Koranteng-Pipim

~

In an earlier chapter, "Are Those Things So?—Part I," we examined some of the biblical arguments of *Women in Ministry,* organized under seven categories. The current chapter will take up the remaining three categories of concern which we mentioned in the introduction to the other chapter. In keeping with the other chapters in this section of *Prove All Things,* the focus here will be on *Women in Ministry*'s handling of historical and theological matters. We will take up numbering them where the list in the earlier chapter left off.

8. Misleading and Erroneous Claims Regarding Seventh-day Adventist History

There are instances in which *Women in Ministry* is "factually challenged." We must remember that the members of the Seminary Ad Hoc Committee had been asked to come up with a basis in the Bible or Ellen G. White's writings on which to support the ordination of women as elders or pastors. There is no such basis in either source; so the committee manufactured one. This may sound like harsh criticism, so let me show you what I mean.

Samuel Koranteng-Pipim, Ph.D., *is Director of Public Campus Ministries for the Michigan Conference of Seventh-day Adventists.*

Here are five "facts" that I say the committee "manufactured." See what you think. (a) There were women ministers (preferred term "leaders") in the early Seventh-day Adventist church (at least prior to 1915); (b) our pioneers wrote strongly in support of women ministers; (c) the early Seventh-day Adventist church voted at the 1881 General Conference session to ordain women; (d) Ellen G. White called for women's ordination in an 1895 statement; (e) Ellen G. White herself was ordained.

I will show that, in making the above claims, the authors of *Women in Ministry* make a use of historical sources that is characterized by misunderstanding, a serious inflation of the evidence, and an uncritical reliance on revisionist histories of the early Seventh-day Adventist church offered by feminists and liberal pro-ordinationists.

(a) **Did Early Seventh-day Adventist Women Function as Ministers?** In early Seventh-day Adventist history women played major roles in the publishing and editorial work, home missionary work, the work of Sabbath schools, church finances and administration, frontier missions and evangelism, and medical and educational work. Those women who labored as full-time workers were issued the denomination's ministerial *license* but not the ministerial *credentials* reserved for ordained ministers—indicating that they were not authorized to perform the distinctive functions of ordained ministers.[1]

In *Women in Ministry,* however, some of the authors have left the erroneous impression that because early Adventist women labored faithfully and successfully in the soul-winning ministry, and because they were issued ministerial *licenses,* these women performed the functions of the *ordained* ministry.[2] On this inaccurate basis, they join other revisionist historians in concluding that today the "ordination of women to full gospel ministry is called for by both the historical heritage of the Seventh-day Adventist Church and by the guidance of God through the ministry of Ellen G. White."[3]

Contrary to such creative reinterpretation, the Adventist women of the past typically understood that while they had been called to do the work of soul-winning, and while it was biblically legitimate for them to preach, teach, counsel, minister to the needy, do missionary work, serve as Bible workers, etc., the Scriptures prohibited them from exercising the headship responsibility of elder or pastor. These dedicated Adventist women did not view their non-ordination as elders or pastors to be a quenching of their spiritual gifts or as an arbitrary restriction on the countless functions they could perform in gospel ministry. As they labored faithfully within the biblical guidelines of what is appropriate for men and women, the dedicated women of old discovered joy in God's ideal for complementary male-female roles in the church.[4]

In early Adventist records, full-time workers carrying ordained ministers' *credentials* were listed as "Ministers," while the term "Licentiates" was used for unordained workers (men and some women) with ministerial *licenses.* Not until

1942 would the *Yearbook* of the church employ the terms "Ordained Ministers" and "Licensed Ministers" for these two categories of church workers. Both the early and later distinctions between the two groups of workers ensured that unordained laborers in the soul-winning ministry would not be confused with ordained ministers. One author, whom *Women in Ministry* quotes on other matters, noted that by the turn of the century, when about 15% of church employees were women in various roles, "the church classified *none of them* as ministers except Mrs. White"[5] (a reference to her ordained minister credentials; see discussion below). Indeed, we have yet to see any of these women referred to as "ministers" in the writings of Mrs. White or the other pioneers. There is, therefore, no valid justification for some contemporary writers to suggest or to create the impression that women listed as "licentiates" or even occasionally as "licensed ministers" performed the functions of ordained ministers or were generally thought of as "woman ministers."[6] Nor does the history of those days support the idea that women today seeking to do full-time work in gospel ministry must be ordained as elders or pastors. The facts from the "historical heritage of the Seventh-day Adventist Church" do not support such a conclusion.[7]

(b) Did our Adventist Pioneers Endorse Women as Ministers? Under the heading of "Defense of women in ministry," a chapter in *Women in Ministry* devotes two pages to citations from the *Review and Herald* and other sources which, the author claims, show the pioneers to be "so passionate in defense of 'women preachers.'"[8] By "women preachers," our author seems to want readers to understand "women as pastors." But in fact, most of the articles address a different issue. While none of the pioneers endorses women pastors or elders, they all uphold the right or propriety of women to speak in the church or in other public places.

For example, our *Women in Ministry* author cites a January 7, 1858 *Review and Herald* article by James White, claiming that he "spoke favorably . . . on women's role in the church." It quotes how he dealt with an objection: "Some have excluded females from a share in this work, because it says, 'your young men shall see visions' . . . ." Actually, though, the article is not about "women's role in the church" but about "Unity and Gifts of the Church," specifically addressing the gift of prophecy. It does not mention women as pastors or elders. It has only one paragraph that our author could quote, but he omitted its first sentence, where James White indicates that the role he was referring to was *prophecy*. The paragraph actually begins this way: "Under the influence of the Holy Spirit both sons and daughters will prophesy. Some have excluded females from a share in this work, because it says, 'your young men shall see visions.'" By omitting the first sentence and applying the remainder of the paragraph to a topic James White was not discussing—"women in ministry" and "women preachers"—the author has misled the reader regarding James White's actual concern.

Likewise J. N. Andrews's *Review and Herald* article (January 2, 1879) which the author cites was not addressing whether women could be ministers or could preach. His title, which our author did not give, was "May Women Speak in Meet-ing?" Andrews's opening sentence shows his real concern: "There are two principal passages cited to prove that women should not take *any part* in speaking in reli-gious meetings" (emphasis mine). Andrews's article did not specifically mention preaching. His purpose was to show that women may freely bear their testimony or take other speaking parts in meeting.

The author next cites a James White article (*Review and Herald*, May 29, 1879) as stating that "Joel's message that 'sons and daughters' would prophesy indicated the participation of women in preaching." In fact, James White never mentioned preaching in the article, and his only comment about Joel's message is that "women receive the same inspiration from God as men." On women's role in the church, he said, "But what does Paul mean by saying, 'Let your women keep silence in the churches'? Certainly he does not mean that women should take no part in those religious services where he would have both men and women take part in prayer and in prophesying, or teaching the word of God to the people." Having women as ministers was not James White's concern.

The author claims that others through the years defended the sisters and their "prominent roles in the work of God." He cites the example of G. C. Tenney, whose article appeared in the *Review and Herald*, May 24, 1892. The author claims Tenney "defended women who labored publicly in the gospel," an undefined ex-pression which leaves the reader to think of women serving as gospel ministers. But in fact, as Uriah Smith's introduction to the article indicates, Tenney was deal-ing with "the question whether women should take any public part in the worship of God." Where our author says that Tenney "rested his case" by stating that God is no respecter of persons, male or female, Tenney actually was defending women's bearing their testimony, not serving as ministers. The sentence before the one quoted in *Women in Ministry* reads, "But it would be a gross libel on this valiant servant of Christ [Paul] to impute to him the purpose to silence the testimony of the most devoted servants of the cross." Nowhere in his article does Tenney ever mention "preachers" or "preaching," which *Women in Ministry* seems to equate with "pastors" or "pastoring." He speaks only of women participating in the work of the gospel and being able to speak aloud in the meetings of the church.

The chapter quotes Ellen G. White recounting how, prior to her addressing a congregation for more than an hour, S. N. Haskell had been called upon to answer a question from a Campbellite objector who quoted "certain texts prohibiting wom-en from speaking in public." According to Mrs. White, Haskell briefly answered the objection and "very clearly expressed the meaning of the apostle's words" (*Manu-script Releases*, 10:70). Interestingly enough, even here the words "preaching" and "preacher" are not used. As in the other cases, the issue seems to have been just what Mrs. White said it was: the propriety of women "speaking in public."

Only one of the six exhibits found in this section of *Women in Ministry* even mentions women preaching. It is the article by J. A. Mowatt, under the title "Women as Preachers and Lecturers." It was reprinted from an Irish newspaper; evidently it was not written by a Seventh-day Adventist. *Women in Ministry* quotes in full Uriah Smith's introduction to the article. Alert readers will note how Smith qualifies his endorsement of the article. After noting that Mowatt applies the prophecy of Joel to "female preaching," Smith shifts the point: "while it must embrace public speaking *of some kind* [emphasis mine], this we think is but half of its meaning." Smith declines to comment on the work of the non-Adventist female preachers and lecturers whom Mowatt commends so glowingly. His interest, he says, is in the argument that women have the *right* to do such activities.

All of the exhibits, then, contend that women are not required to be silent in public or in the meetings of the church. Only one of them, from a non-Adventist, offers an explicit endorsement of women preachers. Far from being "so passionate in defense of 'women preachers,'" the Adventist sources seem uninterested in that specific aspect of the matter. They are concerned with the right of *all* women to participate in the services of the church, to testify for the Lord, and to have an active part in the work of saving souls.

Given our author's interest in determining the pioneers' views on women as pastors, it is unfortunate that he has overlooked a significant *Signs of the Times* editorial in 1878 which addresses the issue explicitly. J. H. Waggoner, the magazine's resident editor and the author of a treatise on church organization and order, is the presumed author of the unsigned editorial "Women's Place in the Gospel." After defending, as others had done, the right of women to speak in meeting, Waggoner specifically addressed whether Scripture allowed women to serve as pastors or elders. He wrote, "The divine arrangement, even from the beginning, is this, that the man is the head of the woman. Every relation is disregarded or abused in this lawless age. But the Scriptures always maintain this order in the family relation. 'For the husband is the head of the wife, even as Christ is the head of the church.' Eph. 5:23. Man is entitled to certain privileges which are not given to woman; and he is subjected to some duties and burdens from which the woman is exempt. A woman may pray, prophesy, exhort, and comfort the church, but *she cannot occupy the position of a pastor or a ruling elder.* This would be looked upon as usurping authority over the man, which is here [1 Tim 2:12] prohibited" (emphasis mine).

Waggoner's editorial conclusion revealed how this position harmonized with that of the other pioneers we have cited: "Neither do the words of Paul confine the labors of women to the act of prophesying alone. He refers to prayers, and also speaks of certain women who 'labored in the Lord,' an expression which could only refer to the work of the gospel. He also, in remarking on the work of the prophets, speaks of edification, exhortation, and comfort. This 'labor in the Lord,' with prayer, comprises all the duties of public worship. Not all the duties of *business meetings,* which were probably conducted by men, or all the duties of *ruling elders,* and *pastors,* compare 1 Tim. 5:17, with 2:12, but all that pertain to exercises purely religious. We sincerely believe that, according to the Scriptures, women, as a right may, and as duty ought to, engage in these exercises" (*The Signs of the Times,* December 19, 1878, p. 320, emphasis his). Waggoner's 1878 statement supports the idea that the women licentiates of his time were not serving in the role of pastor or elder.

The views of those opposing ordination of women in the Seventh-day Adventist church today correspond to those of our pioneers. They believe that women may serve the Lord in many ways, both personal and public, even including preaching. It is the headship role of pastor or elder which they believe Scripture restricts to qualified men.

Women in Ministry's attempts to promote ordination of women by misrepresenting the views of our pioneers should concern all fair-minded Seventh-day Adventists.

(c) Did the 1881 General Conference Session Vote to Ordain Women? The 1881 General Conference session considered a resolution to permit ordaining women to the gospel ministry (*Review and Herald,* Dec. 20, 1881, p. 392). The minutes clearly show that instead of approving the resolution (as some today have claimed), the delegates referred it to the General Conference Committee, where it died. Neither Ellen G. White nor the other pioneers brought it up again. The issue did not resurface until recent decades.

Some authors in *Women in Ministry* make the oft-repeated claim that at the 1881 General Conference session, the church voted to ordain its women. Recycling this myth, one of the authors referred to the comments of a current General Conference vice-president who served as chairman of the July 5, 1995, Utrecht business meeting session which considered the ordination question. Our author writes:

"The [SDA] church has often considered the issue of ordaining women, and has, at times, come amazingly close to doing so. . . . The church, at the General Conference session of 1881, had voted that women might, 'with perfect propriety, be set apart for ordination to the work of the Christian ministry.' The action was then referred to the General Conference Committee. After that, as [the current General Conference vice-president] has so eloquently explained, 'Nothing happened.' Nearly 90 years later in 1968, leadership in Finland officially requested that women be ordained to the gospel ministry."[9]

This author apparently didn't know what really happened to the 1881 General Conference session "vote" for women's ordination, but another author suggests that the resolution was "voted" but was either later killed or ignored by a three-member committee consisting of George I. Butler, Stephen Haskell, and Uriah Smith. He cites the 1881 "resolution" (from *Review and Herald,* December 20, 1881, p. 392) thus:

> *Resolved,* That females possessing the necessary qualifications to fill that position, may, with perfect propriety, be set apart by ordination to the work of the Christian ministry.
>
> This was discussed . . . and referred to the General Conference Committee.

Speculating on why "nothing happened," this author suggests: "These brethren [Butler, Haskell, and Smith] seem to have been uncertain at the time whether women could be ordained 'with perfect propriety.' There is no record of further discussion or implementation of the resolution voted. However, . . . [quoting another scholar] 'the fact that this could be at least discussed on the floor of a G. C. Session indicates an open-mindedness on the part of the delegates toward the subject.' It also clearly demonstrates the open-mindedness toward women serving in the gospel ministry during this time period in the Adventist Church's history."[10]

What many readers of *Women in Ministry* may not know is that there is no need to speculate on what happened regarding woman's ordination in 1881. What actually happened is recorded in the *Review and Herald*. The 1881 General Conference session *never* approved the resolution, and therefore the referral to a committee was not for the purpose of implementing the resolution. Here are the facts.

1. In the nineteenth century, items were brought to the General Conference session as "resolutions," in the appropriate debating form: "Resolved that . . . ." To untrained modern ears, this sounds like the decision (i.e., the resolution of the matter), when in fact it was only the *starting point* for discussion of the proposal.

2. Once a resolution was presented, it would be debated from the floor, after which it could either be voted on ("Approved" or "Rejected") or handled in some other way appropriate to parliamentary procedure. For example, (a) sometimes a motion was made and passed that the resolution (the issue being discussed) be "tabled," which meant that the members would stop deliberating on it then and take it up at a later time; (b) the delegates could vote to "refer to committee," which meant that they would not take the matter up again until the designated committee had considered it and returned it with a recommendation, after which it could be debated again and a decision reached on it (a process illustrated by another resolution appearing on the same page of minutes); (c) in some cases, referral to committee (then and today) is a polite way of killing a motion—handing it off to another group that is not expected to do anything with it.

These then are the facts regarding the 1881 resolution:

(1) An item was brought to the floor proposing that women be ordained.

(2) After discussion, the resolution was not "approved," as was almost every other resolution on that page, but was "referred to the General Conference Committee," who never sent it back to that session or to any subsequent General Conference session.

(3) In order for an item to be "referred to [any] committee," those present at the session had to vote in favor of referring it to committee. Referral does not happen just because one person calls for it.

(4) The fact that the "resolution" (i.e., the proposal brought to the floor) was "referred to the General Conference Committee" means that the 1881 General Conference delegates *did not accept* the women's ordination proposal!

(5) Therefore, contrary to some widely-held assertions, the 1881 General Conference session actually *declined* to approve the proposal to ordain women! For whatever their reasons (we are not told in the minutes of the

session), the delegates referred the matter to the General Conference Committee and let it die there. No one brought it to the General Conference delegates again until 1990 (North American Division request at Indianapolis) and 1995 (North American Division request at Utrecht).

(6) The minutes of the meeting, published in the *Review and Herald,* reveal that prior to the matter being "referred to committee," it was discussed by at least eight of the delegates.[11] After that discussion came the decision to refer to committee. Thus, contrary to some pro-ordination scholars (not writers in *Women in Ministry*), the "resolution" *was* entertained on the floor. And having discussed it, the delegates voted that it be "referred to the General Conference Committee."

(7) If the 1881 resolution was referred to the committee to be *implemented,* as *Women in Ministry* alleges, one wonders why at the next General Conference session no one questioned the failure of the committee to implement it. General Conference sessions were held yearly until 1889, after which they were held every two years. One also wonders why Ellen G. White failed to speak out against this alleged "injustice" against women when a group of three committee men supposedly refused to act upon a General Conference decision. The silence of subsequent General Conference sessions and Ellen G. White is additional evidence showing that in 1881, the church *never approved* the resolution on women's ordination.

Why did the General Conference in 1881 turn away from women's ordination? Was it because the delegates were not bold enough, or "open-minded" enough, or even prudent enough to act "with perfect propriety" to ordain women who were "serving as gospel ministers"?[12]

For answer, it is best to read the *published* theological position of the leading Seventh-day Adventist pioneers (e.g., through the editorials by resident editors of the *Review* and *Signs*—Uriah Smith, J. H. Waggoner, James White, J. N. Andrews) on their view on the question of women serving in the headship roles of elder or pastor. When we do, we discover that, for them, because of God's "divine arrangement, even from the beginning," women could not serve in the headship roles as husbands in their homes or as elders or pastors in the church. To do so, according to our Adventist pioneers, would be to disregard and abuse God's divine arrangement.[13]

(d) Did Ellen G. White's 1895 Statement Call for Women's Ordination?

Women in Ministry takes a statement by Ellen White out of its context and misuses it to argue for ordaining women as elders or pastors.[14] This is the actual statement:

"Women who are willing to consecrate some of their time to the service of the Lord should be appointed to visit the sick, look after the young, and minister to the necessities of the poor. *They should be set apart to this work by prayer and laying on of hands.* In some cases they will need to counsel with the church officers or the minister; but if they are devoted women, maintaining a vital connection with God, they will be a power for good in the church."[15]

On the basis of this statement, one writer in *Women in Ministry* laments: "If only Ellen White's 1895 landmark statement had come fourteen years sooner [in 1881]!" He apparently believes that this "landmark statement" would have encouraged the General Conference committee brethren who were wondering about the question of "perfect propriety" in implementing the alleged 1881 vote to ordain women "who were serving in the gospel ministry."[16]

But evidence that Ellen G. White's 1895 statement is not applicable to the ordination of women *as pastors or elders* may be found within the passage itself.

> (1) This is a part-time ministry, not a calling to a lifework. "Women who are willing to consecrate some of their time . . . ."

> (2) The work is not that of a minister or a church officer. "In some cases they will need to counsel with the church officers or the minister." Evidently this work is not that of an elder or pastor.

> (3) It was a ministry different from what we were already doing. The portion quoted here is followed immediately by, "This is another means of strengthening and building up the church. We need to branch out more in our methods of labor."

> (4) The statement appears in an article entitled, "The Duty of the Minister and the People," which called upon ministers to allow and encourage church members to use their talents for the Lord. The last sentence of the quoted paragraph reflects this thrust: "Place the burdens upon men and women of the church, that they may grow by reason of the exercise, and thus become effective agents in the hand of the Lord for the enlightenment of those who sit in darkness."

Thus the statement and its context clearly indicate that these women were being dedicated to a specific *lay* ministry, not the ministry of elders or pastors.[17]

This, however, is not the only statement from Mrs. White addressing laying on of hands for women. We could wish that *Women in Ministry* had cited the only known statement in which Mrs. White specifically spoke of ordination for women. Here it is: "Some matters have been presented to me in regard to the laborers who are seeking to do all in their power to win souls to Jesus Christ. . . . The ministers are paid for their work, and this is well. And if the Lord gives the wife as well as the husband the burden of labor, and if she devotes her time and her strength to visiting from family to family, opening the Scriptures to them, *although the hands of ordination have not been laid upon her,* she is accomplishing a work that is in the line of ministry. Should her labors be counted as nought, and her husband's salary be no more than that of the servant of God whose wife does not give herself to the work, but remains at home to care for her family?" (*Manuscript Releases,* 5:323, emphasis mine).[18] Here, in the opening paragraph of her message, Mrs. White honors the ministry of women and calls for full-time workers to be paid appropriately, but she dismisses the lack of ordination as irrelevant. In this paragraph and elsewhere in her manuscript she highlights the arena in which women could make an especially significant contribution: personal work with women and families. Such work did not require ordination.

When did she write this way about ordination for women? In 1898, three years after *Women in Ministry* says she called for women to be ordained!

(e) **Was Ellen G. White Ordained?** The implication that Mrs. White was ordained involves a serious inflation of the evidence. It rests on the fact that she was issued ministerial *credentials,* the same as those which were given to ordained men.[19] Because Ellen White's ministerial credentials have given rise to some unfortunate misstatements by those seeking her support for women's ordination, I digress briefly to illustrate how this misinformation became institutionalized.

One source is the 1995 pro-ordination book *The Welcome Table.* Having reproduced two of Ellen White's credentials (dated 1885 and 1887), an author comments on p. 308 of that book:

"Notice her [Ellen G. White's] credentials dated Dec. 6, 1885, where the word *ordained* has been crossed out. However, that is not the case in credentials issued December 27, 1887."

By this comment, readers of the book are left with the erroneous impression that although Ellen White was not ordained in 1885, by 1887 the church's position had evolved to the point of ordaining her. (Some proponents of women's ordination go so far as to suggest that even though the Seventh-day Adventist church has today rejected women's ordination, as allegedly in the [1885] case of Ellen G. White, one day the church will see the light and ordain its women, even as the church allegedly did [in 1887] after "denying" Ellen G. White her rightful ordination in 1885!) But "are those things so?"

The above statement is a half-truth; the other half is "manufactured." The full truth, as we have already noted, is that a number of dedicated women who worked for the church in the late 1800s and early 1900s were issued *licenses* (not ministerial *credentials* that are given to ordained pastors). Ellen White was the only woman ever to be issued ministerial credentials by the Seventh-day Adventist church; she received them from 1871 until her death in 1915. At least *three,* not two, of her ministerial credential certificates from the 1880s are still in the possession of the Ellen G. White Estate. These are dated 1883, 1885, and 1887.

On one of the certificates (dated 1885) the word "ordained" is neatly crossed out, but on the other two it is not. Does this mean that Ellen White was "ordained" in 1883, "unordained" in 1885 and "re-ordained" in 1887? Obviously not. Rather, the crossing out of "ordained" in 1885 highlights the awkwardness of giving credentials to a prophet. No such special category of credentials from the church exists. So the church utilized what it had, giving its highest credentials without an ordination ceremony having been carried out. In actuality, the prophet needed no human credentials. She had functioned for more than twenty-five years (prior to 1871) without any.[20]

Although Ellen G. White was the only woman known to have been issued Seventh-day Adventist ministerial *credentials,* she was never ordained. Mrs. White herself makes this clear.

In 1909, six years before her death, she personally filled out a "Biographical Information Blank" for the General Conference records. In response to the request on Item 26, which asks, "If remarried, give date, and to whom," she wrote an "X," indicating that she had never remarried. Earlier, Item 19 had asked, "If ordained, state when, where, and by whom." Here she also wrote an "X," meaning that she had never been ordained. She was not denying that God had chosen her and commissioned her as His messenger, but she was responding to the obvious intent of the question, indicating that there had never been an ordination ceremony carried out for her.[21]

This clear and unambiguous statement of Ellen White herself should put to rest the unfounded impression left by *Women in Ministry* that the church's issuance of a ministerial credential to Ellen White is an indication that she was ordained.

If any woman was so spiritually gifted as to qualify for ordination *as elder or pastor,* it was Ellen G. White. If any woman was so effective in her ministry as a teacher, preacher, and soul-winner as to qualify for ordination *as elder or pastor,* it was Ellen White. If any Adventist was so "justice-inspired," "sensitive" and "caring" (and with demonstrable evidence of other fruits of the Spirit) as to qualify for ordination *as elder or pastor,* it was Ellen G. White. If any Adventist was so prolific an author and so gifted a leader as to qualify for ordination *as elder or pastor,* it was Ellen G. White. And if any woman could legitimately claim the title of *Elder or Pastor,* it was Ellen White.

But during her later years, Mrs. White was known mostly as "Sister White" and affectionately as "Mother White." She was never known as "Elder White" or "Pastor Ellen." Every church member knew that "Elder White" was either her husband, James, or her son, W. C. White.

Could it really be that we are ethically and theologically more enlightened than Ellen G. White? Or is it perhaps that we do not view the Bible as she did? Whatever our response is, this much can be said: The claim or implication by some advocates of women's ordination that Ellen White was ordained is clearly wrong.

Summary. Throughout our history, Seventh-day Adventist women labored faithfully in the ministry as teachers, preachers, missionaries, Bible workers, etc., and made a vital contribution to the mission of the church, all *without ordination.* Far from providing a case for ordination, the nine women mentioned in the *Women in Ministry* chapter we have been considering illustrate what women may accomplish without it. They are by no means alone. The Bible workers, as an example, offered valuable service in the ministry; they were an important part of the evangelistic team because they often knew more about the people being baptized and joining the church than the minister did; and the minister welcomed their wisdom and judgment. But none of these women was ever ordained. If these women, who were well-versed in Scripture, had been asked if they wanted to be ordained as elders or pastors, most would likely have exclaimed, "Oh, no! It isn't biblical!" I say this because it continues to be the attitude of thousands of dedicated Adventist women around the world today.

In light of these facts of Adventist history—such as that Ellen G. White was never ordained, she never called for women to be ordained as elders or pastors, and none of our dedicated Seventh-day Adventist women of the past was ever ordained as elder or pastor—I again ask those who support women's ordination, just as I would ask those who support the attempted change of the Sabbath from Saturday to Sunday: "Since the testimonies of Scripture indicate that God the Father *did not* do it; the Old Testament is clear that the patriarchs, prophets and kings *never did* do it; the gospels reveal that Jesus, the Desire of Ages, *would not* do it; the epistles and the acts of the apostles declare that the commissioned apostles *could not* do it; Ellen White, with a prophetic vision of the great controversy between Christ and Satan, *dared not* do it, should we who live at the turn of another millennium do it?"[22]

What then shall we say in response to these manufactured "facts" in *Women in Ministry?* Simply this: It would have been better to tell the facts as they are, for then *Women in Ministry* would have been what the Ad Hoc Committee wanted it to be, a reliable guide to church members trying to make the right decision regarding the ordination of women as elders or pastors.[23] Even if there was no intent to mislead, neither the church nor her Lord are well served by "scholarly research" which distorts the history it purports to tell.

9. A Seriously Flawed Concept of "Moral Imperative"

For the Christian, there is a moral imperative always to trust and obey biblical truth. If, however, the Christian is compelled to believe and practice error, that imperative is not moral; it is coercion. In the light of our evaluation of the biblical and historical arguments for women's ordination, we are now better prepared to judge whether there is a "moral imperative" for women's ordination, as claimed in *Women in Ministry.*

As we have shown in our analysis and critique, the two-year investigation by the "Ad Hoc Committee on Hermeneutics and Ordination" produced neither a hermeneutic nor a theology of ordination superior to what the Adventist church historically has upheld. The book's title is misleading, in that the real goal of the book seems not to be "women in ministry" (which the Adventist church has never opposed), but rather the ordaining of women as elders and pastors. The arguments put forth to justify the ideology of women's ordination are biblically and historically deficient; if employed in other areas, they could easily be used to undermine the relevance of many other biblical teachings.

Since the biblical and historical arguments underlying *Women in Ministry* are seriously flawed, the book's "moral imperative" argument, its concepts of "equality," "women's rights," "justice," "fairness," and "character of God," and its appeals to the "Holy Spirit's leading" to meet "the needs of a growing church" cannot be sustained as ethically credible bases for ordaining women *as elders or pastors*.[24]

In fact, what has taken place in the Seventh-day Adventist church over the past two or three decades suggests that the so-called "moral imperative" argument could easily be used to coerce those who refuse to surrender to this unbiblical ideology of ordaining women. Let me explain.

When church leaders initially agreed that women *could* be ordained as elders, it was with the understanding that there would be liberty of conscience for those who could not accept the practice either because of biblical reasons or because their cultures were thought to prevent them from moving in that direction. In many places, however, this "could be" policy for women's ordination has already developed into an understanding that women *should* be ordained. With the questionable "moral imperative" argument being proposed in *Women in Ministry*, we are coming into a phase that says women *must* be ordained, not only as local elders but also as pastors.

In other words, if the "moral imperative" argument is accepted, the ideological legislation which was originally permissive will become compulsory! Those who are found to be in disagreement with the ordination of women and who believe for biblical reasons that they cannot participate in such ordinations or allow women to be ordained will be looked upon as out of harmony with church policy and possibly considered unfit for employment in areas where the ideology has become entrenched. This serious situation will inevitably take away the right of individual conscience.

Whenever error is legislated as a "moral imperative," such legislation inevitably leads to the persecution of those standing for truth. Already in certain places where the "moral imperative" argument has been embraced it is very difficult for Adventists who oppose women's ordination to be hired or retained. The policy is usually unwritten, but those familiar with several situations can testify to the intolerant attitude toward, and sometimes the *a priori* exclusion of, those who uphold the long-established Adventist position—a position which, by the way, is embraced by an overwhelming majority of the world church, as demonstrated through official General Conference session votes.

The only moral imperative the church should embrace is that which is founded on truth. The Christian's obligation to such an imperative is to trust and obey it, regardless of intimidation and persecution from those who demand compliance with error.

10. A Fanciful View of Holy Spirit's "Leading"

In a final effort to support their "biblical, historical, and ethical" arguments for ordaining women as elders or pastors, *Women in Ministry*'s authors appeal to a mistaken understanding of the Holy Spirit's "leading." They urge the Seventh-day Adventist church to listen to the voice of the Holy Spirit as He calls upon us today to change our patterns of ministry in response to the pragmatic needs of a growing church. Writes the editor in her summation chapter: "If circumcision, based on divine [Old Testament] mandate, could be changed [by the apostles, elders, and believers, together with the Holy Spirit, at the Jerusalem Council of Acts 15], how much more could patterns of ministry [ordaining women as elders and pastors], which lack a clear 'Thus says the Lord,' be modified to suit the needs of a growing church?"[25]

By this innovative argument, the *Women in Ministry* authors add their voices to those within our ranks who also are invoking the name of the Spirit to justify their questionable re-interpretations of Scripture.[26] But can we make Scripture mean anything we desire, and then give the Holy Spirit the credit? Christians must always seek the Spirit's guidance to understand Scripture. But should they invoke the Spirit to circumvent the Bible's explicit teaching on male-female roles in both the home and the church or to invent some new theories to justify certain egalitarian ideologies, as *Women in Ministry* seeks to do?

Bible-believing Seventh-day Adventists have always insisted that those who seek to live under the authority of the Spirit must be willing to bow before the teachings of the Word—the Spirit's authoritative textbook. "To the law and to the testimony: if they speak not according to this word, it is because there is no light in them" (Isa 8:20; cf. Gal 1:8, 9). "The Spirit was not given—nor can it ever be bestowed—to supersede the Bible; for the Scriptures explicitly state that the word of God is the standard by which all teaching and experience must be tested" (*The Great Controversy*, p. vii).

As we have attempted to show in these two chapters, besides the misleading and erroneous claims regarding early Seventh-day Adventist beliefs and practice and the seriously flawed concept of "moral imperative," *Women in Ministry's* arguments for ordaining women as elders or pastors are based on questionable re-interpretations of Scripture. Hence, following the kind of Spirit's "leading" proposed by the book will spawn in the church an uncontrollable subjectivism in which interpreters select only the Scriptures pleasing to them and which fit their fanciful interpretations. This is a sure recipe for contradictory doctrinal views in the church (theological pluralism).

Moreover, because the Holy Spirit does not leave us to wander aimlessly without a sure compass, unless our interpretations are in harmony with the Bible, what we may assume to be the Spirit's voice could actually be echoes from the loud noises within our cultures. Thus, the so-called Holy Spirit's "leading" would be nothing more than promptings from our unrenewed human experiences or feelings. Ellen G. White explained why faith must be established on the Word of God, not on one's subjective experience or feeling:

"Genuine faith is founded on the Scriptures; but Satan uses so many devices to wrest the Scriptures and bring in error, that great care is needed if one would know what they really do teach. It is one of the great delusions of this time to dwell much upon feeling, and to claim honesty while ignoring the plain utterances of the word of God because that word does not coincide with feeling. . . . Feeling may be chaff, but the word of God is the wheat. And 'what,' says the prophet, 'is the chaff to the wheat?'" (*Review and Herald,* November 25, 1884).

In short, *Women in Ministry*'s "new light" of ordaining women as elders or pastors is foreign to the Bible writers and the studious Bible-believing Seventh-day Adventist pioneers, including Ellen G. White. Since this "new light" contradicts biblical teaching on gender-role differentiation, the authors' attempt to claim the Holy Spirit's "leading" should be dismissed as a fanciful effort to make scholarly ingenuity seem more important than fidelity to the Bible's text and context. The following statement by Mrs. White, referring to the distinctive truths of Seventh-day Adventists, is also appropriate in this regard:

"When the power of God testifies as to what is truth, that truth is to stand forever as the truth. No after suppositions contrary to the light God has given are to be entertained. Men will arise with interpretations of Scripture which are to them truth, but which are not truth. The truth for this time God has given us as a foundation for our faith. One will arise, and still another, with new light, which contradicts the light that God has given under the demonstration of His Holy Spirit. . . . We are not to receive the words of those who come with a message that contradicts the special points of our faith" (*Selected Messages,* 1:161).

Conclusion: Moving Beyond Ideology

For more than 100 years the Adventist position on the ordained ministry claimed the support of Scripture as expressed in the teaching and practice of the Adventist pioneers, including Ellen G. White. By the 1970s, however, this established position began to be reversed in favor of ordaining women as elders and pastors.

This new trend was created by the converging interests of feminism, liberalism, church leaders' desire to enjoy United States tax law benefits to ministers, questionable church policy revisions and *Church Manual* alterations allowing women to serve as elders, calculated attempts by some influential North American churches unilaterally to ordain women as pastors, the silence of leadership to this defiance of two General Conference session votes against women's ordination, the strategy of the North American Division's "President's Commission on Women in Ministry" to obviate the 1995 Utrecht vote, and now, the book *Women in Ministry* by the Seminary Ad Hoc Committee, in response to the request by certain North American Division leaders for the pro-ordination scholars of the Seminary to "*do something about it [Utrecht]."*

Our Assessment of *Women in Ministry.* *Women in Ministry* offers the best arguments that Adventist proponents of women's ordination can find to present to a Bible-believing conservative Seventh-day Adventist church. How do we assess the biblical and historical research provided by our pro-ordination authors? Does the book's "new light" offer a sound theological basis to depart from nearly 150 years of Seventh-day Adventist belief and practice? Can this work be used legitimately at a future time to overturn the General Conference session decisions at Indianapolis (1990) and Utrecht (1995)?[27]

As we noted in Part I, a supporter of the book correctly states, "If the basis of our decision is going to be in our interpretation of Scripture, *we must do it well.*"[28] The simple question we must ask, therefore, is: Did the twenty authors of *Women in Ministry* do their job well?

The editor of the book believes they did.[29] An author of one of the chapters (a member of the Ad Hoc Committee who seeks to make *Women in Ministry* "the official view of the Seminary and the position of virtually all of its faculty") thinks that this work will "demonstrate that the Seminary faculty stands for sound Biblical and historical scholarship on this contemporary and controversial issue."[30]

We also noted how some influential promoters of the book are applauding it as the product of "skillful exegesis of Scripture and careful examination of relevant E. G. White materials,"[31] a volume that presents "a powerful argument" and "an impressive array of evidence" for the ordination of women,[32] and one which "brings together a wealth of material and deserves to be taken seriously."[33]

With all due respect, we disagree with these "opinions of learned men" (*The Great Controversy,* p. 595). Heeding the Bible's command to "prove all things; [and] hold fast that which is good" (1 Thess 5:19-21), and accepting the invitation from the book's editor for responses by those who may disagree with their findings, we examined the above claims. Our analysis and evaluation in these two chapters and the contributions of other chapters in *Prove All Things* call into serious question what the authors and promoters are saying.

Contrary to their claims, *Women in Ministry,* like its forerunner *The Welcome Table,* does not present a cogent and defensible way to neutralize the witness of the Bible and the historical precedent of early Seventh-day Adventism. As I have attempted to show in this two-part evaluation, *Women in Ministry* is built largely on: (1) ambiguity and vagueness, (2) straw-man arguments, (3) substantial leaps of logic, (4) arguments from silence, (5) speculative interpretations, (6) questionable re-interpretations of the Bible, (7) distorted biblical reasoning, (8) misleading and erroneous claims regarding Adventist history, (9) a seriously flawed concept of "moral imperative," and (10) a fanciful view of the "Holy Spirit's leading."[34]

The editor of *Women in Ministry* may have had these shortcomings in mind when she stated in her prologue that "at times clear evidence may be lacking, thus making necessary the use of sanctified judgment and imagination to resolve questions and issues" associated with women's ordination as elders and pastors.[35] Given the fact that there is no clear evidence in Scripture for ordaining women, we can now understand why the authors of *Women in Ministry* often resorted to "sanctified judgment and imagination," and why the committee needed two long years of "animated" discussions, writing, re-writing, editing, and cross-referencing to produce their 438-page volume. Ellen G. White's observation is pertinent:

"Numberless words need not be put upon paper to justify what speaks for itself and shines in its clearness. *Truth is straight, plain, clear, and stands out boldly in its own defense; but it is not so with error. It is so winding and twisting that it needs a multitude of words to explain it in its crooked form"* (*Early Writings*, p. 96, emphasis mine).

Despite the good intentions and best efforts of the authors of *Women in Ministry*, their book falls short of its goal. It does not provide a sound biblical and historical basis for resolving "this contemporary and controversial issue." Perhaps a future work by some other proponents may be able to make a more judicious use of biblical and historical data to provide the much-desired justification for women's ordination. But I doubt it, because the basis for women's ordination as elders or pastors simply doesn't exist, either in the Bible or in the writings of Mrs. White.

Perhaps here is where the Seminary Ad Hoc Committee has provided its greatest service. After two years of hard work and prayer, they have produced a 438-page book that reveals, when carefully examined and tested, that there is no support in either the Bible or the Mrs. White's writings for ordaining women as elders and pastors. Those of us who have for a long time cautioned against this practice gratefully respond, "Thank you, Ad Hoc Committee."

Some Important Implications. To the extent that my conclusions about the book are valid, I would say the following:

1. Acting upon any advice that is contrary to Scripture ultimately leads to disobedience of God's Word in general. "The very beginning of the great apostasy was in seeking to supplement the authority of God by that of the church. Rome began by enjoining what God had not forbidden, and she ended by forbidding what He had explicitly enjoined" (*The Great Controversy*, pp. 289, 290).

"True faith consists in doing just what God has enjoined, not manufacturing things He has not enjoined" (*That I May Know Him*, p. 226).

2. No one can disobey God's Word without experiencing destructive consequences. Because our Lord is merciful and patient, not willing that any should perish, the consequences of our disobedience are often slow in coming. But consequences always follow. Thus, the legislation of any secular ideology instead of the proclamation of sound theology will surely have consequences.

Already the worldwide church is harvesting some of the baneful results of the push to ordain women as elders and pastors. For example, there are tensions and divisions in churches where the ideology of women's ordination is being forced upon loyal members; strained relationships and broken homes where the erroneous doctrine of "total egalitarianism" or "total role interchangeableness" has been accepted; mistrust in and loss of credibility by church scholars and leaders who are perceived as pushing upon the church an alien agenda; disillusionment among dedicated women in ministry, who are made to believe that the church is quenching their desire to be part of the soul-winning work or is discriminating against them; vilification of scholars and leaders who have courageously stood up against women's ordination; erosion of confidence in the Bible and the writings of Mrs. White as dependable sources of answers to today's perplexing questions; and the unwitting laying of a theological foundation for pro-homosexual theology, when we reject God's creation order of gender or sex roles in marriage and in the church.

3. These consequences will continue as long as we do not renounce our errors and embrace God's truth: "The teachings and restrictions of God's Word are not welcome to the proud, sin-loving heart, and those who are unwilling to obey its requirements are ready to doubt its authority" (*Steps to Christ*, p. 111).

Instead of being faithful to the inspired writings of Moses, David, Isaiah, Matthew, Peter or Paul, those set on their own ways would rather cling to the opinions of their self-appointed experts—be they pastors, professors, parents, or personal acquaintances. In so doing they forget the warning by Ellen G. White: "Satan is constantly endeavoring to attract attention to man in the place of God. He leads the people to look to bishops, to pastors, to professors of theology, as their guides, instead of searching the Scriptures to learn their duty for themselves. Then, by controlling the minds of these leaders, he can influence the multitudes according to his will" (*The Great Controversy*, p. 595).

4. We can, however, avert these destructive consequences by turning away from our errors. In view of the biblical teaching that only qualified men may legitimately serve in the headship role of elders or pastors, we can take the following specific steps:

(a) *Church Leaders* should call for an immediate moratorium on ordaining women *as elders* and also initiate proceedings to rescind the biblically-compromising 1975 Spring Council and 1984 Annual Council actions that permitted women to be ordained as *elders,* actions that have brought the church to the straits we are in now;

(b) *Church scholars and editors* should renounce ideological proclivities, temptations, or pressures to justify or promote the divisive and unbiblical practice of ordaining women;

(c) *Women ordained as elders* should willingly and courageously give up that office, bringing their practice into line with the Bible (Acts 17:30-31);

(d) *Women laboring in the ministry* should serve in accordance with God's biblically-prescribed will, resisting ideological attempts to transform "women's ministry" into "feminists' ministry";

(e) *Church members* should respectfully, but courageously, demand a plain "thus saith the Lord" whenever and wherever vocal groups, scholars, leaders, pastors, or even committees urge them to ordain or accept women as elders or as pastors; insisting upon a prayerful, unbiased, and biblically sound investigation of the issue is both a right and a duty of every church member.

Retracing our erroneous steps, as evidence of genuine repentance, may be uncomfortable, humiliating, even costly. But what is more costly than what it cost Jesus to save us? Loyalty to Christ may cost us our pride, but it will surely give us a free conscience.

"God does not require us to give up anything that it is for our best interest to retain. In all that He does, He has the well-being of His children in view. Would that all who have not chosen Christ might realize that he has something vastly better to offer them than they are seeking for themselves. Man is doing the greatest injury and injustice to his own soul when he thinks and acts contrary to the will of God. No real joy can be found in the path forbidden by Him who knows what is best, and who plans for the good of His creatures. The path of transgression is the path of misery and destruction" (*Steps to Christ,* p. 46).

The Choice We Face. In presenting their book to the worldwide Seventh-day Adventist church, the twenty scholars of *Women in Ministry* stated: "We hope and pray that this volume may assist individuals, leaders, and the community of faith at large in deciding how to deal with the issue of ordination and, more specifically, the relationship of ordination to women."[36]

If the "biblical, theological, and historical perspectives" elaborated in *Women in Ministry* are all that these professors can present to the church, then the decision on "how to deal with the issue" of women's ordination *as elders or pastors* is not a difficult one to make. Their well-publicized and widely distributed volume offers compelling evidence against the practice. It is one more proof that the campaign waged during the past two or three decades by a few influential scholars and leaders to impose women's ordination on the church is a tragic mistake.

In light of this fact, we must ask: What should be our individual and collective responses to the teaching of Scripture regarding the ordination of women to the headship office of elder or pastor? Should we go beyond the legitimate role of women in ministry by ordaining them as elders or pastors?[37] Should we risk the displeasure of God by doing what seems right in our own eyes? Or should we seek a scriptural basis for empowering women for ministry and bring an end to the present "divisiveness and disunity," "embarrassment," and "dishonor upon this church that we love"?[38]

Worthy Examples. Our Lord Jesus Christ, the church's Head and the true "Shepherd and Bishop of our souls," has set us an example that we should follow (1 Pet 2:21, 25). In the face of the ultimate test of obedience, He could say, "Not my will, but thine, be done," a decision that was immediately rewarded with help from heaven (Luke 22:42, 43).

His own mother, Mary, also leaves us an example of complete submission to the will of God. In becoming the Messiah's mother before she was married, she faced circumstances that would bring her abuse and derision; yet she said, "I am the Lord's servant. May it be to me as you have said" (Luke 1:38 NIV). Later, though she was highly "favored of the Lord" and a faithful disciple of Christ (Luke 1:28, 30; Acts 1:14), in the upper room she submitted to the biblical guidelines for the choice of a male apostle to be added to the eleven (Acts 1:20-26).[39] Mary speaks to all of us—women and men—on this issue of women's ordination, as well as on every other issue, when she says, "Whatsoever he [Christ] saith unto you, do it" (John 2:5).

Finally, the apostle Paul leaves us an example of total surrender of our aims and ambitions to the cross of Christ. If, like him, we all—men and women, church leaders and members, professors and students—also reckon ourselves as "crucified with Christ" and seek to live by the principle, "Not I but Christ" (Gal 2:20), our spirit will be like his. When we are called upon to make decisions of costly discipleship, the kind suggested when we seek to do God's will on the role of women in the soul-winning ministry, the spirit of Paul must always be ours:

Paul "had no ambitions [for himself]—and so had nothing to be jealous about. He had no reputation—and so had nothing to fight about. He had no possessions—and therefore had nothing to worry about. He had no 'rights'—so therefore he could not suffer wrong. He was already broken—so no one could break him. He was 'dead'—so none could kill him. He was less than the least—so who could humble him? He had suffered the loss of all things—so none could defraud him."[40]

May this spirit of faithful, obedient surrender to Christ and His Word inspire us not only to resist attempts at legitimizing and legislating cultural *ideology*, but also to trust and obey the sound *theology* from God's Word.

> *1. When we walk with the Lord,*
> *In the light of His Word,*
> *What a glory He sheds on our way!*
> *While we do His good will,*
> *He abides with us still,*
> *And with all who will trust and obey.*
>
> ***Chorus:***
> *Trust and obey,*
> *For there's no other way*
> *To be happy in Jesus,*
> *But to trust and obey.*
>
> *2. Not a shadow can rise,*
> *Not a cloud in the skies,*
> *But His smile quickly drives it away;*
> *Not a doubt nor a fear,*
> *Not a sigh nor a tear,*
> *Can abide while we trust and obey.*
>
> *3. Not a burden we bear,*
> *Not a sorrow we share,*
> *But our toil He doth richly repay;*
> *Not a grief nor a loss,*
> *Not a frown nor a cross,*
> *But is blest if we trust and obey.*

4. *But we never can prove*
The delights of His love,
Until all on the altar we lay,
For the favor He shows,
And the joy He bestows,
Are for them who will trust and obey.

5. *Then in fellowship sweet*
We will sit at His feet,
Or we'll walk by His side in the way;
What He says we will do,
Where He sends we will go,
Never fear, only trust and obey.

Endnotes

1. See Kit Watts, "Ellen White's Contemporaries: Significant Women in the Early Church," in *A Woman's Place: Seventh-day Adventist Women in Church and Society,* ed. Rosa T. Banks (Hagerstown, Md.: Review and Herald Publishing Assn., 1992), pp. 41-74; Laurel Damsteegt, "S. M. I. Henry: Pioneer in Women's Ministry," *Adventists Affirm* 9/1 (Spring 1995), pp. 17-19, 46. The spirit of the early Adventist women is also reflected in the soul-winning ministries of women in Africa and many other parts of the world. See, for example, J. J. Nortey, "The Bible, Our Surest Guide," *Adventists Affirm* 9/1 (Spring 1995), pp. 47-49, 67; cf. Terri Saelee, "Women of the Spirit," *Adventists Affirm* 9/2 (Fall 1995), pp. 60-63. But contrary to revisionist interpretations of Adventist history, none of these roles required women to be ordained as elders or pastors (see William Fagal, "Ellen White and the Role of Women in the Church," available from the Ellen G. White Estate, and adapted as chapter 10 in Samuele Bacchiocchi's *Women in the Church* (Berrien Springs, Mich.: Biblical Perspectives, 1987). A summary version of Fagal's work is found in his "Did Ellen White Call for Ordaining Women?" *Ministry,* December 1988, pp. 8-11, and "Did Ellen White Support the Ordination of Women?" *Ministry,* February 1989, pp. 6-9, together reproduced as chapter 16 of this book; cf. Samuel Koranteng-Pipim, *Searching the Scriptures,* pp. 70-83, where we discuss "Restless Eves" and "Reckless Adams."
2. See, for example, Michael Bernoi, "Nineteenth-Century Women in Ministry," *WIM,* pp. 220-229; Randal R. Wisbey, "SDA Women in Ministry, 1970-1998," *WIM,* p. 235. A more restrained position is found in Jerry Moon's "'A Power that Exceeds that of Men': Ellen G. White on Women in Ministry," *WIM,* pp. 190-204.
3. Bert Haloviak, "The Adventist Heritage Calls for Ordination of Women," *Spectrum* 16/3 (August 1985), p. 52. More examples of such revisionist interpretation of Seventh-day Adventist history can be found in some pro-ordination works, which leave readers with the wrong impression that the issuance of ministerial licenses to dedicated Adventist women of the past implied that they labored as ordained ministers. See, for example, Josephine Benton, *Called by God: Stories of Seventh-day Adventist Women Ministers* (Smithsburg, Md.: Blackberry Hill Publishers, 1990). Cf. the following chapters in *The Welcome Table:* Bert Haloviak, "A Place at the Table: Women and the Early Years," pp. 27-44; idem, "Ellen G. White Statements Regarding Ministry," pp. 301-308; and Kit Watts, "Moving Away from the Table: A Survey of Historical Factors Affecting Women Leaders," pp. 45-59; cf. "Selected List of 150 Adventist Women in Ministry, 1844-1994," Appendix 6. A careful review of the source references in some of the chapters of *Women in Ministry* shows that their authors followed too closely the trail left by the revisionist

interpreters of Adventist history of ordination (see, for example, Bernoi, *WIM*, p. 233 notes 74 and 78; Wisbey, *WIM*, p. 252 notes 1, 2, 4).

4. For a helpful corrective to the historical revisionism of some on the issue of ordination, refer to the careful work by William Fagal in this volume (see pp. 273-286); cf. Samuel Koranteng-Pipim, *Searching the Scriptures*, pp. 70-83, on "Restless Eves" and "Reckless Adams."

5. John G. Beach, *Notable Women of Spirit: the Historical Role of Women in the Seventh-day Adventist Church* (Nashville, Tenn.: Southern Publishing Association, 1976), p. 55, emphasis mine.

6. Of the nine notable "women in Adventist ministry" which Michael Bernoi profiles (*WIM*, pp. 225-229), only four were licentiates for significant periods of time: Ellen Lane, Sarah A. Lindsey, Hetty Hurd Haskell, and Lulu Wightman, who all gave substantial full-time work to evangelism, whether private or public. The other five women vary from the general picture *Women in Ministry* would like to draw. S. M. I. Henry held a license for about three years while she advocated a "woman ministry" which encouraged women to work for the Lord where they were; female pastors were not a part of her program. Margaret Caro was licensed in 1894 and from 1897 to 1900 (we have not found record yet of her licensing in 1895 and 1896). During this whole time she seems to have continued her dental practice, using the proceeds to help educate young people for the Lord. I found no record of licensing of any kind—not even a missionary license—for Minerva Jane Chapman. But look at her achievements! L. Flora Plummer was licensed in 1893, but in the year before that and the year after she was given a missionary license; I have yet to find another year in which she was a licentiate. This means that during the time she was secretary and, according to *Women in Ministry*, acting president of the Iowa Conference (a claim I could not verify because the references were erroneous), she was not even carrying a ministerial license but was a licensed missionary! This makes the author's claim for her sound inflated: "Of all the women who *labored in the gospel ministry* while Ellen White was still alive, Flora Plummer was perhaps the most notable" (emphasis mine). Finally, Anna Knight was a licensed missionary, not a licensed minister, contrary to what one might assume from her listing among the "women in Adventist ministry." (The above information is drawn from the church's *Yearbooks* and from the *General Conference Bulletin* Index, which extends only through 1915.) So all of these truly notable women serve as examples of what women may indeed do in the line of ministry. But *Women in Ministry* seems to want us to think of them as examples of woman ministers from our history and to consider how we have fallen away from our "roots." The conclusion is inescapable: all nine women cited by Bernoi were certainly part of the Adventist soul-winning ministry; but none of them was a minister as we use the term today.

7. One example of where *Women in Ministry* fosters a confusion between the duties of ordained ministers and licentiates is found on pp. 225-226, where the author claims that Sarah A. Lindsey's "1872 license permitted her to preach, hold evangelistic meetings, and *lead out in church business and committee sessions*" (emphasis mine). He offers no evidence for the latter point, which may be no more than his assumption. Several pieces of evidence suggest a conclusion different from his. An expression used for licentiates in some conference session minutes at that time indicates a more limited authorization: candidates were "granted license to improve their gift in preaching as the way may open" (see, for example, *Review and Herald* 35/14 [March 22, 1870]: 110). In 1879, in an article our author quotes on another point, James White wrote his understanding that 1 Cor. 14:34, 35 applied to women keeping silence in the *business meetings* of the church (ibid. 53/22 [May 29, 1879]: 172). And, as we will show at the end of the next subsection, J. H. Waggoner mentioned "business meetings" as an area where the scriptural restrictions likely applied. Beyond this one matter, the chapter shows an unwise dependence on feminist secondary sources, which are often unreliable. We cite a few examples from the same two pages of *Women in Ministry*. Ellen Lane was not licensed by the Michigan Conference in 1868, as claimed. The minutes

show that the licentiates that year were "Wm. C. Gage, James G. Sterling, and Uriah Smith" (ibid. 31/23 [May 12, 1868]: 357). Though she was indeed licensed in 1878, as the chapter states, she was actually first licensed in 1875 (ibid. 46/8 [August 26, 1875]: 63). Further, she was not the first woman licentiate among Seventh-day Adventists, a distinction which apparently belongs to Sarah A. H. Lindsey. The chapter also mentions Mrs. Lindsey, as we noted above, but it dates her licensing to 1872, though she is known to have been licensed in 1871 (ibid. 38/13 [September 12, 1871]: 102). After citing her licensing, the chapter mentions that in one series of meetings she preached twenty-three times on the second advent, but it fails to note that this series took place in early 1869, three years before the author's date for her licensing (ibid. 33/25 [June 15, 1869]: 200). Thus in fact her example serves to demonstrate that lack of ordination or even licensing need not stand in the way of a woman who wants to serve God. See Michael Bernoi, "Nineteenth-Century Women in Adventist Ministry Against the Backdrop of Their Times," *WIM*, pp. 225, 226.

8. See Michael Bernoi, "Nineteenth-Century Women in Adventist Ministry Against the Backdrop of Their Times," *WIM*, pp. 211-229. The portions referenced here are from pp. 222-224.

9. Randal R. Wisbey, "SDA Women in Ministry, 1970-1998," *WIM*, p. 235. Wisbey is currently the president of Canadian University College. He is quoting Calvin Rock, who served as the chairman of the Utrecht business meeting that considered the North American Division request to ordain its women. Cf. "Thirteenth Business Meeting," *Adventist Review*, July 7, 1995, p. 23.

10. Bernoi, "Nineteenth-Century Women in Adventist Ministry Against the Backdrop of Their Times," *WIM*, p. 224. The scholar he quotes is Roger W. Coon, former associate director of the Ellen G. White Estate, now retired. Dr. Coon's document says that the resolution was "introduced" and "referred to committee," but it never claims the resolution was voted.

11. The minutes of the 1881 General Conference session state that the resolution "was discussed by J. O. Corliss, A. C. Bourdeau, E. R. Jones, D. H. Lamson, W. H. Littlejohn, A. S. Hutchins, D. M. Canright, and J. N. Loughborough, and referred to the General Conference Committee" (*Review and Herald*, December 20, 1881).

12. Cf. Wisbey, *WIM*, p. 235; Bernoi, *WIM*, p. 224. A visit to the endnotes of the Seminary scholars reveals their reliance on the pro-ordination authors who also wrote for *The Welcome Table*. There was no reason why these *Women in Ministry* authors should have missed the facts on this matter. The information was readily available in published works by those opposing women's ordination (see, for example, Samuele Bacchiocchi's *Women in the Church* [1987] and my *Searching the Scriptures* [1995] and *Receiving the Word* [1996]). More fundamentally, the primary sources—the minutes themselves—are easily obtained at Andrews University, and their pattern of recording actions is clear and consistent.

13. For example, see the editorial in the December 19, 1878 *Signs of the Times* which summarized the understanding of the Adventist pioneers on the headship responsibility of the man in both the home and the church. I have already quoted the key points in this chapter, on p. 291. Cf. Uriah Smith, "Let Your Women Keep Silence in the Churches," *Review and Herald*, June 26, 1866, p. 28.

14. Bernoi, "Nineteenth-Century Women in Adventist Ministry," *WIM*, pp. 224, 225; cf. J. H. Denis Fortin, "Ordination in the Writings of Ellen G. White," *WIM*, pp. 127, 128. Cf. Rose Otis, "Ministering to the Whole Church," *Elder's Digest*, Number Nine, p. 15. *Elder's Digest* is published by the General Conference Ministerial Association. A more nuanced discussion of Ellen White's 1895 statement is provided by Jerry Moon, "'A Power That Exceeds That of Men': Ellen G. White on Women in Ministry," *WIM*, pp. 201, 202.

15. Ellen G. White, *Review and Herald*, July 9, 1895, p. 434, emphasis mine.

16. Bernoi, "Nineteenth-Century Women in Adventist Ministry," *WIM*, p. 224. Observe that this kind of "historical research" is built on the following questionable assumptions and speculations: (1) "women were serving as gospel workers" [understood as elders or pastors];

(2) the 1881 General Conference session voted to ordain women as pastors; (3) a 3-member male committee failed to implement the alleged 1881 General Conference session vote because they were wondering about the question of "perfect propriety"; (4) it took Ellen G. White 14 long years to speak to the "correctness" of women's ordination.

17. This fact is acknowledged by Jerry Moon, "'A Power That Exceeds That of Men': Ellen G. White on Women in Ministry," *WIM*, p. 201. For more on this matter, see William Fagal's reprinted articles in this present volume, pp. 273-286.

18. Though no mention of this statement appears in Bernoi's chapter, two other chapters do mention it. One of them gives only a brief summary of the statement and omits the specific reference to ordination (J. H. Denis Fortin, "Ordination in the Writing of Ellen G. White," *WIM*, p. 127), while the other provides a helpful and much more thorough study of the manuscript in question (Jerry Moon, "'A Power That Exceeds That of Men': Ellen G. White on Women in Ministry," *WIM*, pp. 192-194). The chapter does not quote the reference to ordination as a part of that discussion, but it does quote it later, in the chapter's last sentence.

19. Michael Bernoi notes, "For a number of years both she [Hetty Hurd Haskell] and Ellen White were listed together in the *Yearbook* as ministers credentialed by the General Conference, Ellen White as ordained and Mrs. Haskell as licensed" (Bernoi, "Nineteenth-Century Women in Adventist Ministry," *WIM*, p. 227). Given this way without further explanation, such a statement will mislead many into assuming that Mrs. White was ordained.

20. For more on this, see William Fagal's "Ellen G. White and Women in Ministry," in the present volume, pp. 273-286.

21. A copy of her Biographical Information Blank may be found in Document File 701 at the Ellen G. White Estate Branch Office, James White Library, Andrews University. Arthur L. White published the information regarding these matters in the introduction to his article, "Ellen G. White the Person," *Spectrum* 4/2 (Spring, 1972), p. 8.

22. See my *Searching the Scriptures* (1995), p. 65.

23. Instead of recycling misinformation, half-truths, and errors, we must honestly and accurately state the facts regarding the position and practice of our pioneers on women's ordination. Having done so, we may then be at liberty to: (1) debate the rightness or wrongness of their action or (2) decide either to follow their theological understanding and practice or chart our own course. It is irresponsible, however, to attempt to inject our biases and self-interests into a historical fact or re-interpret it in order to push our ideological agenda to "do something about Utrecht."

24. Wisbey, "SDA Women in Ministry: 1970-1998," *WIM*, p. 251; Douglas, "The Distance and the Difference: Reflections on Issues of Slavery and Women's Ordination," *WIM*, p. 394; Alicia Worley, "Ellen White and Women's Rights," *WIM*, pp. 367-370; Dudley, "The Ordination of Women in Light of the Character of God," *WIM*, p. 413-415; Vhymeister, "Epilogue," *WIM*, p. 436.

25. Nancy Vyhmeister, "Epilogue," *WIM*, p. 436. Serious Bible students will challenge *Women in Ministry*'s editor's claim that the Jerusalem Council arbitrarily "changed" the Old Testament mandate regarding circumcision and that this alleged "change of opinion" came after there was "agreement of apostles, elders, and believers, together with the Holy Spirit, on the new instructions" (ibid.). Rather than being an arbitrary act motivated by some pragmatic needs in the apostolic church, the Jerusalem Council's decision was in harmony with, and anticipated by, the Old Testament itself. God Himself instituted circumcision in the Old Testament as an outward expression of an inner heart transformation. The inspired writers of the New Testament simply made explicit what the Old Testament had been teaching all along (see, for example, Deut 10:16; 30:6; Jer 4:4; 9:25; Rom 2:25-29; Col 2:11-13).

26. In my *In the Spirit of Truth* (Berrien Springs, Mich.: Berean Books, 1997), I have briefly addressed a proposal similar to the one presently offered by the authors of *Women in Ministry*. Readers interested in a detailed treatment of the Holy Spirit's role in Bible interpreta-

tion may want to consult my Ph.D. dissertation, "The Role of the Holy Spirit in Biblical Interpretation: A Study in the Writings of James I. Packer" (Andrews University, 1998). This 410-page work explores how the relationship between the Spirit and the inspired Word has been understood by major theological figures and movements since the sixteenth century Reformation and culminating in the works of one of contemporary Evangelicalism's most widely respected theologians.

27. Earlier in our discussion of the expected use of the book, we pointed to the prologue of the volume, where the authors submit their work to the church "as a resource tool for decision making," a euphemistic expression for the overturning of the previous General Conference session decisions. An admiring reviewer of the book adds, "The ultimate purpose of *Women in Ministry* is to provide information for informed decision making, a clear indication that there is a decision to be made. In so doing, the book calls the church to do some serious Bible study. If the basis of our decision is going to be in our interpretation of Scripture, we must do it well." See Beverly Beem, "What If . . . Women in Ministry?" *Focus,* Winter 1999, p. 31.

28. Ibid.

29. Vyhmeister, "Prologue," *WIM,* p. 5; idem, "Epilogue," *WIM,* p. 436. In a letter accompanying *Women in Ministry*'s wide distribution to church leaders around the world, the authors express the belief that they have provided the church with "carefully researched information" that will "foster dialogue."

30. Roger L. Dudley, "[Letter to the Editor Regarding] *Women in Ministry,*" *Adventist Today,* January-February 1999, p. 6.

31. Calvin Rock, "Review of *Women in Ministry,*" *Adventist Review,* April 15, 1999, p. 29. In his glowing review, Rock offers "special kudos" to the Seminary Ad Hoc Committee for "providing a deeply spiritual, highly reasoned, consistently logical approach to the issue of women's ordination." In his opinion the book provides "incisive arguments" for those who believe in women's ordination, and "a thoughtful, thorough treatment" of the major aspects of the women's ordination question (ibid).

32. Beverly Beem, "What If . . . Women in Ministry?" *Focus,* Winter 1999, p. 31.

33. Fritz Guy, "Review of *Women in Ministry,*" *Ministry,* January 1999, p. 29.

34. Therefore, Seventh-day Adventists who wish to believe in women's ordination should do so on the basis of better evidence and methods superior to those found in *Women in Ministry.* And the attempt to put the Seminary's imprimatur on a work that is patently biased and arguably defective in biblical and historical scholarship holds the potential of damaging the credibility of the Seminary as a place of sound teaching. Similarly, the attempt to legislate women's ordination as a "moral imperative" could lead to and institutionalize intolerance and persecution of those who uphold the biblical teaching of role relationships in the church. In my opinion, it is a tragic mistake for the Seventh-day Adventist Theological Seminary to have financed the publication of this book, when the same work could have been published independently by the pro-ordination scholars. In this respect, the Seminary has set an unfortunate precedent by opening its door to those who may be seeking ways to commandeer the name and resources of our church's leading theological institution for their own ideological agendas.

35. Vyhmeister, "Prologue," *WIM,* p. 5.

36. Ibid.

37. In an earlier work, I have articulated the legitimate role of women in ministry thus: "Notwithstanding male leadership in the church, (i) the fact that men and women are equal, having a complementary relationship between them, and (ii) the fact that Scripture calls women to labor in ministry suggest that: The Seventh-day Adventist church should make provision that will encourage a greater participation of women in ministry. This may include stronger support for their training at the Seminary, adequate and fair remuneration of women for their labor and, in some cases (such as in team ministries),

their being authoritatively commissioned for roles and duties that are not in violation of biblical teaching. Of the many lines of ministry, women could be encouraged to participate in the study, teaching and preaching of the gospel in personal and public evangelism; to be involved in ministries of prayer, visitation, counseling, writing and singing; to labor as literature evangelists, health evangelists, to raise new churches, and to minister to the needy; to serve in positions of responsibility that do not require ordination *as elders or pastors,* serving as colleagues in partnership with ordained men at the various levels of the church organization; to teach in our institutions and seminaries; and above all, to minister to their children at home. But I do not believe that the Bible and Spirit of Prophecy permit women to be ordained elders or pastors" (see my *Searching the Scriptures,* pp. 88, 89).

38. Alfred C. McClure, "NAD President Speaks on Women's Ordination," *Adventist Review,* February 1995, pp. 14, 15.

39. For more on this, see my *Searching the Scriptures,* pp. 56-58.

40. Leonard Ravenhill, *Why Revival Tarries* (Minneapolis: Bethany Fellowship, 1959), p. 173, cited in Stephen F. Olford, *Not I, But Christ* (Wheaton, Ill.: Crossway Books, 1995), pp. 55, 56.

Chapter 18

Testimony:
Neither Muslim nor Feminist Any Longer

Shakeela Bennett

~

I was baptized into the Seventh-day Adventist church through the straight testimony, the plain unadulterated truth. I marveled at the grace that was shown me and prayed that it would not be in vain. I needed God to strengthen me, not only in a life of obedience to Him but also with a spirit of grace toward others. My life was significantly changed by the principles I found in the Word of God, and in addition I enjoyed being in the presence of a people who stood for truth with no compromises and no excuses. Following the will of God was my top priority.

I had grown up in the Muslim religion, which meant that as a female there were not many doors open for me. I was limited even in my participation at the mosque, where the men did the praying. Women did the cooking and serving, and I had to keep my head, arms, and legs covered at all times. I couldn't understand why God had created me as a woman and yet seemed to hold it against me because I was one. "Who needs a God like this?" I would ask myself. I eventually walked away from Islam.

Because my father had abandoned me and my ex-husband was abusive, in my estimation men did not have much value. I was always considered a very independent person, and I prided myself on that. When I discovered the women's movement it seemed like *"The Blessing from Above."* It convinced me that there must be a God, one that fit comfortably into my way of thinking. Freedom at last! Women

Shakeela Bennett *is a wife, mother, and home-school teacher, who also assists her husband in running his computer business.*

had taken a back seat long enough. We needed the opportunity to show what we were made of. It was said, "Anything a man can do, a woman can do better"—and I was out to prove it.

It was an uphill battle, but I liked uphill battles; they made me stronger. I encouraged my friends. "Walk!" I said. "You don't have to stay where you are if you're not happy; you are capable of making your own way. Our generation should count our blessings. We don't have to put up with things our moms had to." I truly felt that men needed us women more than we needed them. They used to be the sole breadwinners, but now that they no longer were, what purpose did they fill?

I remember the day my boss walked into my office and was offended by a poster on my wall. It said, *"When God made man, She was only joking."* He asked me politely to take it down, and I not so politely pointed out his male chauvinism. This man never once claimed to be a Christian, but there were certain boundaries he felt one should not cross. Disown God if you must, but mock Him not. I resented having to take down my poster and felt that "my rights as a woman" were being violated. I chalked it up to male stupidity and hypersensitivity.

Then I Met Jesus

Then I met Jesus, there on the cross. What I saw brought me to my knees, for you see, when you are in the presence of Jesus, you are unable to stand on your feet. I saw a love unfathomable. Oh, yes, I would undoubtedly have laid down my life for my children, but if they turned their backs on me, would I still have done so? Jesus did. Before I was even born He did it. Knowing that I would spend most of my life not appreciating what He did for me, He did it anyway.

And then there was the Father who had to stand by, watching His Son being tortured and ridiculed, watching as huge metal spikes were driven through His hands and feet, and who *chose* to do nothing about it. Why? For me; that's why. Could I stand by and watch my child go through this and do nothing? No, I couldn't.

Let's not forget the Holy Spirit. His presence at Calvary converted many, among them the thief on the cross. Even while the Son was in agony and facing death, He continued to work fervently, to seize the opportunity of the moment to lift a man's mind to the Son of God and ultimately to God the Father.

Each time I visit Calvary I come away comforted. Each time I go there I meet Him the Father, Him the Son, and Him the Holy Spirit—and I think back to my poster in the office and my "I am woman, hear me roar" mentality. What blasphemy! But I know that God has forgiven me my ignorance. I know, too, that He has given me an appreciation for the woman I am, the woman He created me to be.

Become a Pastor?

In my new-found love for the Lord, I toyed with the idea of becoming a pastor, but I noticed the lack of opportunities for women in this career choice. This led me to search the Scriptures and Mrs. White's writings for answers. Through this search God showed me that He had imparted the gift of ministry to me, but it was not to be in the minister's position, even though I might have the qualifications.

Although there was no mention in Scripture of God's choosing women as priests, I felt sure that I would find accommodation for this career choice in the writings of Ellen G. White. Despite my confidence, however, I could find no such justification. One passage is representative of many I could cite: "The primary object of our college was to afford *young men* an opportunity to study *for the ministry* and to prepare young persons of *both sexes* to become workers in the *various branches of the cause*" (*Testimonies for the Church*, 5:60, emphasis mine). I felt that Mrs. White's distinction between "young men" and her reference to "young persons of both sexes" was not accidental.

I clearly saw the Godhead as all males, the disciples that Jesus Himself called as all males, the apostles as all males. I grew from the experience and concluded that I do not need to be the head. Even being a toe has its blessings. Being a toe doesn't make me a lesser person but a unique part of the body.

I have never before been as contented and fulfilled as I am today. I thoroughly enjoy the challenges of being a wife, a mother, a homeschool teacher, a homemaker, a nurse, an advisor, a nurturer, and my husband's home-based business associate, to mention only a few of them. My husband and my younger son, who is now sixteen, both appreciate my contributions to their lives as a stay-at-home wife and mother. I am blessed by being given the opportunity to minister to them in these ways.

Many women today feel unfulfilled in their God-given role, even as I did at one time. Reflecting back on this feeling, I realize that in my case it was due to "social peer pressure," the pressure to be superwoman. To be considered an accomplished and respected woman, one would have to be able to work outside the home, raise the kids, clean the house, cook the meals, make time for a husband (if there were one), and at the same time keep oneself looking stunning. If a woman could not follow these rules, or chose not to, she was considered illiterate, if not downright ignorant. Until I met my Lord, I bought into this line of thinking. In the words of Ellen G. White, I was a "restless modern Eve":

"Eve had been perfectly happy by her husband's side in her Eden home; but, like restless modern Eves, she was flattered with the hope of entering a higher sphere than that which God had assigned her. In attempting to rise above her original position, she fell far below it. A similar result will be reached by all who are unwilling to take up cheerfully their life duties in accordance with God's plan. In their efforts to reach positions for which He has not fitted them, many are leaving vacant the place where they might be a blessing. In their desire for a higher sphere, many have sacrificed true womanly dignity and nobility of character, and have left undone the very work that Heaven appointed them" (*Patriarchs and Prophets*, p. 59).

This statement does not condemn a woman's aspirations for self-improvement or a better life. Rather, it calls for all to seek to live according to God's plan.

Appeal

I would like to entreat other women to find contentment in their roles as wives, mothers, missionaries, evangelists, and in any other positions that God has bestowed upon them for the uplifting of souls. Let us leave the shepherding to the men, as Christ has ordained it to be. Our Lord Jesus Christ, the Chief Shepherd, the High Priest, the Head of the Church, knows what is best for us. Aaron and his sons were chosen as priests, not Miriam; the sons of Levi, too, not his daughters; twelve male disciples, not six of each gender to establish equality. If we as women were called to be shepherds, then Jesus would have made it known when He was here. He cared not about being politically correct, and when faced with controversial subjects, He went by the Book!

I would like to see pastors recognize the qualifications of the women in their congregations to fulfill specific roles within the church body. At the same time, I would like to see more women in the churches recognize the gifts that God has placed within their grasp and use them for the uplifting of souls and the building up of the church.

After experiencing life as a secular feminist and now as a Christian woman, I feel I have a lot to offer my church without aspiring to a role that I am not ordained by God to have. As I have spent more time with God and His Word, He has shown me my unique qualities as a woman. He has affirmed me—and this is all the affirmation I need!

Part IV

Ordination and
Women in Ministry

Chapter 19

My Daughters' Ordinations

Wellesley Muir

~

Seven a.m., and the phone was ringing. I was eating breakfast, but the voice on the other end was urgent. "It's Gladys," I told my wife.

"Daddy, what shall I do?"

"Do about what?"

"Daddy, the college church is asking me to serve as an elder. What do you think about ordaining women?"

My quick-off-the-cuff answer was, "I'm against it."

"Why?" she wanted to know.

"I really haven't thought about it. We're back in the States after serving 21 years overseas where ordaining women is not an option. I'm heavily involved in a church building program right now and haven't stayed on top of current issues. This is something I need to study."

A feeling of pride filled my heart. The college church had recognized my daughter as a spiritual leader! I said, "Gladys, you need to pray and study this out for yourself. Since they asked you to serve, go ahead if that's what God leads you to do. I can't make the decision for you."

I hung up—and then it hit me. *You've really let your daughter down! She has questions, and you gave no Bible reasons "for" or "against."* I remembered that we were overseas when our mission president returned from a trip to the States and announced, "It's been voted for ministerial interns to baptize." My instant reaction had been, "Isn't that kind of like having sex before marriage?" Up to that time, only ordained ministers had been authorized to baptize. It troubled me that it was

---

Wellesley Muir *is a pastor and missionary, now living in California.*

the tax authorities and not the Bible that had led to such a decision. But, occupied with the pressures of raising money and building a church, I swept the ordination matter from my mind.

My teenage daughter figured church leaders knew what they were doing and accepted ordination. Taking it all very seriously, she bought a black dress to wear in the pulpit.

My older daughter, Gail, working on a master's degree at an Adventist university, didn't bother to ask her parents' opinion on women's ordination. She simply wrote home saying she had been ordained as an elder.

All of our family, along with a new son-in-law, attended the 1990 General Conference session at Indianapolis, though we were not delegates. My ordained daughters seemed pleased when the session voted 1173 to 377 not to ordain women ministers. It was obvious they had been searching Scripture and making decisions on their own. They said, "Amen!" when Paul Wangai's mother from Africa stood up and said, "God called women to evangelize, not baptize."

The next day, I watched their distraught expressions when, while many delegates were absent, a vote was taken approving a document making it possible for women ordained as local elders to do just about everything an ordained minister does, including baptizing and marrying.

By 1995 my wife and I were serving in Thailand. We traveled to Utrecht, again joining our family there. I served as a delegate from the Asia Pacific Division. Two Seminary professors made presentations. One, *against* ordaining women, appealed powerfully to the Bible for authority. The other, *for* women's ordination, was not biblically convincing.

My daughters told me they felt God led when the session voted 1481 to 673 not to let the North American Division go its own way. Their reaction: "What we really need to do now in order to be consistent is to take an action annulling all previous actions permitting the ordination of women as local church elders."

My daughters said that! I didn't. They did. I am so proud of them!

Today my younger daughter is a full-time missionary on an island in the Asia Pacific Division. She looks back on her ordination at a college church and says, "There were no Bible reasons. It was a politically-correct thing. The leaders wanted to be 'cool.'" She did not accept her latest invitation to be an elder.

My older daughter and her husband are full-time missionaries in West Africa. Recalling her ordination, she says, "They wanted to make a 'statement.' There was nothing spiritual about my ordination. It was all political." Soon after becoming a local church elder, she got "turned off" (her words) when she was sent to an elders' retreat and one woman elder, a featured speaker, spent two hours telling all the reasons why it is all right to drink wine.

After moving away from the university my daughter was again asked to serve as an elder, but desiring to be a woman of the Word, she declined. Later she decided to return her ordination certificate to the church that had issued it.

My daughters! Did I tell you I'm proud of them? Wow!

Chapter 20

Dream On!
Young Single Women and the Ministry

Carolyn Stuyvesant

~

Let me make a simple statement of fact. I did not ask, or even hint, that I would like to write this. I even turned down the invitation—flat. This writing business is high-risk stuff. And when the content is personal, the risk multiplies somewhat in the fashion of the points on the Richter scale.

But then I got to thinking about Adventist women—young women—those who have never been married and, yes, perhaps wanted to be married more than anything else other than to receive eternal salvation. This is not a chapter for men. Or married women. Or single moms. Or elderly people. All of you may move on to the next chapter, please.

Now to you young single women, I admit that after refusing the invitation to write this, I later phoned back and agreed to produce a chapter if it could be for young single women. Even this is extremely high risk. But I seek refuge in the fact that I've always been single and for some reason I've lived longer than you have. It's true, things—some things—are different now from when I was young, but . . . .

That Sabbath Afternoon

It was a cold, spring Sabbath afternoon. Half a dozen of us senior nursing students were curled up in easy chairs and on a sofa in the home of the nursing school director. She had filled us with rice, walnut patties, vegetables and cake. Now we relaxed as we watched raindrops slide down the window panes. I don't know now how it happened, but it did. Some girl set off a verbal spark that got our hostess

Carolyn Stuyvesant, M.S., M.Div., *is a returned missionary and a writer.*

talking about decades of past experiences. She had always been single. We knew she had spent years overseas, and we had heard whispers that she had been confined for a year—maybe two—in a treacherous internment camp during World War II.

We girls were all single, and all of us deeply hoped we wouldn't always be. That afternoon, somehow with no previous discussion, it seemed as if we were all headed in the same direction: Had this woman planned—wanted to be single? How had she managed isolation, loneliness, and all that attends singleness both at home and overseas? How had she become so lovable, so human, so understanding of humanity all around the world?

Our questions were quite subtle—we didn't come at her with an agenda, but we finally brought her around to telling us a two-hour story of her experiences in the internment camp. Obviously it was not the place anyone would choose for a summer's vacation. She had a refrain which she voiced every few paragraphs: "But God was with me," or, "God showed me what to do." There was a special sort of light in her blue eyes as she spoke those words softly, gently. Yes, she had wanted to be married, to rock her own babies. Yes, there had been a lover, then there wasn't. (Her eyes glistened at that point in the story.) Thirty years had gone by since there suddenly wasn't. At some point she took a white index card from her Bible and handed it to me with the comment, "This has given me much courage and comfort for many years." I read the lines to the others.

"Jesus does not call on us to follow Him, and then forsake us. If we surrender our lives to His service, we can never be placed in a position for which God has not made provision. Whatever may be our situation, we have a Guide to direct our way; whatever our perplexities, we have a sure Counselor; whatever our sorrow, bereavement, or loneliness, we have a sympathizing Friend. If in our ignorance we make mistakes, Christ does not leave us. His voice, clear and distinct, is heard, saying, 'I am the way, the truth, and the life.' 'He shall deliver the needy when he crieth; the poor also, and him that hath no helper.'

"'Thou wilt keep him in perfect peace, whose mind is stayed on Thee: because he trusteth in Thee.' The arm of Omnipotence is outstretched to lead us onward and still onward. Go forward, the Lord says; I will send you help. It is for My name's glory that you ask; and you shall receive. Those who are watching for your failure shall yet see My word triumph gloriously. 'All things, whatsoever ye shall ask in prayer, believing, ye shall receive'" (Gospel Workers, p. 263).

When I finished reading she said seriously, "It is not necessary for any young woman to be married to experience this. It's an experience that has nothing to do with being married or not being married. Through the years I have come to the conclusion that if a woman can fully accept this and practice it, it will be more rewarding than marriage would be without it."

We talked on until dark. Then we left. While I had been listening I had been thinking of my dreams—to be married, go to Congo, have four children and be a lifelong missionary. Surely nothing could be wrong with that—maybe two children rather than four. That wouldn't matter too much. I could go elsewhere in Africa with a little protest, but single? Never!

When the Protest Was Over

Now looking back I can see that God waited until I quit protesting because of singleness, and then He immediately sent me to the mountains of Ethiopia (rather than to the rainforests of Congo). His choice was more right than mine for one who is highly allergic to mold and pollen. The call had been placed for me to teach missionaries' children, then to nurse when another teacher arrived. (I carried licenses for both teaching and nursing.)

As the next ten years unfolded I worked as teacher and nurse in several places. My sister and brother-in-law, along with their two young sons, arrived a few months after I did to work in the same area where I was. I wonder at God's kind providence in this, for the mission committee had no idea we were even related until near time for my departure. When I had agreed to go, we all thought they would soon be on their way to Asia!

A few months after their arrival in Ethiopa I helped deliver their baby girl and later taught their two boys to read and a few other things. How I prize those years! Yet life *is* mysterious!

From Planting to Harvest

Now after this prelude we'll get down to my assignment. It's something like this: Show how God has helped you, a single woman, in ministry.

I like to think that as one who is older, I have an advantage in that I have lived long enough to see some results from seed-sowing. In this age, when a bank computer takes six seconds longer than usual to respond, we get uneasy. But I have learned that it often takes many years to see results of mission work. Probably more frequently we will not know until Jesus comes.

When I first went to Ethiopia, I was asked among other things to be public relations secretary for the Addis Ababa church. What could this mean? Then I thought: What's more public than a library? I made a list of 15 libraries in the city. Then I wrote to my parents to ask them to solicit funds to place ten different titles of Ellen G. White books and 5 of "missionary" books in each library. God, in His typical way, inspired people to give. Sometime later we delivered all the books to all the libraries. Occasionally I did a spot-check on the cards. Rarely had books been signed out.

Eleven years later, after returning home, I received word from a missionary who said that a university student had "chanced" upon one of those Ellen G. White books and was subsequently baptized. (Our mission stamp appeared in all the books.)

Later, while working in a mission hospital 500 miles north, I gave Bibles to Orthodox priests who at times walked a hundred miles for treatment. It was a thrill to send Bibles to their churches in areas where no one had ever seen a Bible. (Most churches had one or two gospels in the ancient, nearly dead language of

Ge'ez, but rarely if ever the entire Bible, and certainly not in the contemporary language of Amharic.) I often wondered what happened to these Bibles.

A number of years after I returned home, a furloughing missionary told me of a young man living in a large city. He had become an alcoholic and was unable to hold a job. Feeling that he must earn a living he travelled far to the north, opened a bar and house of prostitution, and continued drinking. His parents, disgraced by his conduct, pleaded that he close his business, which he did. In desperation he took a small amount of food and some fiction and headed out to the desert toward Sudan. He slept under bushes, ate his food, and read his fiction, hoping someway to overcome his alcoholism.

When his food was gone he begged. When his reading material was finished he walked to an Orthodox church and asked the priests for books. They said they had none to spare. Suddenly a priest handed him a black volume and said, "Here, take this unclean heretics' book." (Any religious book not in Ge'ez was considered unclean by most of the traditional priests of the countryside.) The young man took the Bible and returned to his "home" in the bushes. There he read it until he found Jesus and the salvation that He gives. He overcame his desire for alcohol and, seeing our stamp in the Bible, walked about 100 miles to our hospital in the mountains. There he was advised to go to Addis Ababa and take Bible studies, which he did. He was later baptized.

And speaking of harvesting—some harvests come very unexpectedly. A few years ago I received a beautiful thank you letter from a young man in Kenya. He explained that when he was living in Ethiopia and about age seven, as I recall, he had been given a sweater by a student at the nearby academy. (I had given this academy student some clothes to give to poor children in the nearby village.) This student had received the sweater. It was just enough to get him to school for the first time in his life. He posed the question: Where would I be if you hadn't sent that sweater? My sister and I distributed thousands of pounds of clothes, but no recipient was more grateful than this student, I'm sure. I imagine that he wore it as a shirt. Now, 16 years later, he was graduating from college in another country. I doubt I've ever seen him. How did he remember my name, let alone find my address? Such a small thing! Who gave me the sweater when I came home on furlough? I have no idea. The angels know. Someday the donor will receive a big thank you.

I am continually astonished at what a network of people and events God seems to require to bring children to Himself. No one can honestly say, "I brought this person to Christ." Donors, publishers, transportation agents and many more are almost always involved in bringing even one soul to Christ. And there are the ever-present angels and the Holy Spirit. No single woman is ever alone in soul-winning.

A Different Kind of Family

The second summer that I was in Ethiopia I was asked to relieve a furloughing nurse in the south. Through some strange leadings of the Lord I was brought to a village where a seven-year-old boy lived who weighed about 30 pounds and had never walked. At this time he was sick—near death. His mother had died more than five years before, and since then he had been fed very little. By all counts this kind of starvation would result in irreversible physical and mental damage. About that time my sister's family and I were moving north for a year. We decided to take this boy with us. On our way we stopped at a small hotel for the night. The child and I occupied the same room. I was so apprehensive I couldn't sleep—and he, poor child, was more so than I. Picking him up in my arms I went out at midnight for a walk by a sparkling lake where fluttering birds also were yet awake in the moonlight. I can still feel his little limp bony form in my arms, his legs dangling, and his head on my shoulder. I sang him songs he couldn't understand as I rocked him while we walked. He did not know English, nor I his language.

We had him for nine months, then sent him to some kind people where he could attend school when he was able and where he could frequently see his father who loved him dearly and was grateful for our help. It was very slow-going, but he completed academy and a teacher-training course. For many years he has taught elementary grades. The past three years he has been the principal of a large, new six-grade school, has helped to build a church nearby, and is a church elder. He is married and has two children. O Child, you are probably the closest to being a child of mine that I have ever had. You were small and required much love and nurturing from us all. You are God's gift to me and an honor to your family! What a host of medical personnel, family, teachers and friends share in your achievements! I wonder—might you have died had God not sent this single nurse to Africa to find you?

Nor is the single life all success and roses. Where is our boy—now a grown man, if indeed he is alive, who came with us to attend school and to translate for us to the small one? Is he alive? Some say he is. Even real parents sometimes lose children. Lord, if he is still living . . . .

And we have more boys and girls who are now grown, and most have families of their own. Recently six of them and their families, along with my sister's family and me, went on a wonderful camping trip. What thrilling days they were in Africa when these and even more had come home at Christmas! But this trip was a pleasant reminder. One of our "children" is now the director of the library in an Adventist college. Amazingly, the library is only about one block from the house where we six students spent that memorable Sabbath afternoon thirty-eight years ago! (I had nothing to do with arranging this.) The words spoken seriously, gently, almost echo down that street, "Girls, you can safely go if God calls you, and you will someday be glad you went. You might even thank Him for sending you single."

When I think of all our children, I'm glad I went. These young people helped to fill a chasm within me. They are a wonderfully loyal lot who saved me, I am sure, from my foreign stupidity more times than I know or would care to admit. Still today when I pick up the phone and hear, "Aunty Carolyn" spoken by one of our *lijjoch* (children), I'm so glad I went, even single. I believe that it is accurate to say that four of them and two parents are Seventh-day Adventists because of what we did for them. But then their teachers and pastors—and certainly their real parents—deserve the greater portion of the credit. And there were those who sacrificed to provide tuition. But I—I believe that other than their real parents, of course, I have perhaps reaped the largest part of the joy and deep satisfaction.

Educating a flock of children is no small feat, especially when they reach college years. It was imperative that they learn to help themselves as much as possible. They had already worked at the academy and for us.

We decided to send one to college in Australia. I had been almost a failure at three summers of canvassing when I was in school. But I was determined to teach this young man to sell books. We purchased the first Adventist Arabic volumes ever to be sold in Ethiopia. This student, his brother, and I headed for the Red Sea area where there were many Moslems. In three days we sold our entire supply of hundreds of Arabic, Amharic, and English books in a place that had about been written off as hopeless by the publishing department. The student went to Australia, and the following three summers found him canvassing. The first summer he was the second-highest in sales of all the students in the Division. The following two summers he had the highest number of sales.

I have learned that one of the greatest joys in life is to teach and inspire young or old and then discover that they far exceed my abilities in that area and others. Spare me from being the principal of a 350-student six-grade elementary school! Spare me from selling books except in a limited way, sometimes. I'd be lost in counseling many hundreds of refugees, as another of our "children" does. Launching young people is wonderful work when God supplies the wisdom and the power.

Pastor in My Place

In my academy and college years—and even earlier—I wished God had made me to be a man so I could be an ordained minister. Had I been a man I'm quite sure that is what I would have chosen to be. But as a woman, I've never had the slightest desire to be ordained as a minister. Since I am a woman I decided that the best thing to do would be to become a minister's wife. But God had another idea. I have come to realize that apparently He had numerous tasks for me as a single woman to do that required someone with a broad education and not too many home tasks to occupy every minute of spare time. In Ethiopia I longed for one—just one—of our children to become an ordained minister. But my choice was not theirs.

Then God brought him—an Ethiopian Orthodox priest. We had Bible studies for about a year. Generally the translator was an Ethiopian pastor from whom I learned much. The priest took voluminous notes and was baptized soon after I left Ethiopia. His wife and children are also members. (Ethiopian Orthodox priests are required to be married.) For years he was an evangelist, but the last eight years, perhaps, he has been the only pastor in a nine-church district with 8000 members under his care. He baptizes about 300 new converts every year. When I think of how we came in contact and the many hours of intense study it took, I believe that only a single woman would have had the time. And where did I get the time? I paid the stipend for a very fine volunteer nurse to work in my place for the last five months of my stay in Ethiopia. In this way I was free to give numerous Bible studies and distribute Scriptures—which would be a book-length story if it were written.

Blessed Is the Single Woman

Big things are not usually born big—not even elephants. Often small circumstances are not recognized as part of a big plan. I didn't realize what was developing. All I can say is that as I was flying one day over vast, almost inaccessible, but well-inhabited terrain I was nearly overwhelmed at the magnitude of the unfinished, yes, *unstarted* work in Ethiopia. Millions had never seen a Bible. The literacy rate was five to ten per cent.

Through a series of events and a lot of sleepless but prayerful nights a single woman volunteer, who lived with me at the time, and I decided to give out gospels. The Bible Society printed these colorful books with one gospel per pamphlet. They included the 231-letter alphabet, so that a person who learned it well would be able to read, since Amharic is a phonetic language. Some years before, I had taught the entire alphabet to an adult who worked for me in my house. It was a thrill to watch her read her Bible fluently though I knew almost no Amharic and couldn't read a sentence. The idea of thousands of people across the mountains learning to read Scripture excited me.

We purchased tens of thousands of gospels. By dropping them from the mission plane, hauling them in pickups and Land Rovers, sending them with pilots, carrying them on donkeys and mules and by foot—by using every advantage we had—some Adventist students, some Orthodox priest students, my friend, a few others, and I distributed 239,000 gospels and 3,489 Bibles—a total of 19 tons—and all of this in less than two years. We placed Bibles in 160 Orthodox churches and gave a few to schools and government officials. The priests took multiples of 30 gospels, sometimes less, to use as textbooks for reading classes. Each church usually had several priests, some as many as 60 or 80. Often they were the only ones who could read. Copies of the alphabet were generally not available where we were distributing. Books were not obtainable. What joy—inexpressible joy—people's faces showed when they received these Scriptures!

We not only went to churches, but to large open-air markets where thousands of people came one day a week. Some of these were three days' walk from the mission. Sometimes our "children" would distribute 5,000 gospels in a day. One Sunday the mission pilot flew my volunteer friend and 3,000 gospels to a bandit-infested area four or five days' walk away. In that district they circled churches scattered over the mountains and dropped their books near the churchyards. (The gospels were stapled individually into plastic bags.)

Yet it required securing government permits each time we went. The name of each person involved had to appear along with the signature of the local governor and two other men as well as a stamp and seal. It included a statement that only Bibles and Bible portions could be distributed and no preaching or teaching was allowed.

Even with a permit it could be dangerous to distribute. Prejudice ran high in many areas. Some of our "children"—actually teenagers—distributed thousands of these carried by donkeys as they themselves walked for days. There were some incidents, but the Lord delivered us from them all. I personally went by foot and bus many times.

Flying in the mission plane to a group of hewn-stone churches was the most challenging. At Christmas thousands of pilgrims came, mostly by foot, to this remote area. It was very dangerous to do what we wanted. The church ruled. Yet we felt God was leading.

We flew in 23,000 gospels and 500 Bibles to the nearby airport just before Christmas. Five men and I spent a week there. They slept at one end of an empty clinic-hospital complex and I at the other end. No one would go unless I went. I sensed the danger but felt that God wanted the work done. Space does not allow a recital. It is enough for you to know that within a week all the gospels were distributed peacefully, and priests from 393 churches received Bibles as well. We allowed only one priest from a given church to take a Bible. Many government workers and teachers also got Bibles.

The 393 priests lined up in orderly fashion. Each signed his name and wrote the name of his church and district. Then he accepted with deep gratitude a Bible and a small book of Romans. The list of these names is one of the most precious things I own. Only three days before, we had been commanded by a committee of 13 religious leaders to take all our books back! I have seen the walls of Jericho fall. Less than two years before, I had flown over the Semien Mountains and wept as I saw these remote, inaccessible villages perched on hundreds of peaks. Later as we studied the signature list, comparing it with maps and district names, we discovered that every one of those areas would have several Bibles—and some even more. Not many, but perhaps enough with the Holy Spirit's guidance. Old-time Adventists told me that no Adventists had attempted to work in this area since the early 1930s because several had been beaten, stoned, and imprisoned.

The pastor and I visited a man who was the highest church official in that area in an attempt to get cooperation. He was much more friendly and appreciative than many. But tension ran high that week. After the distribution was over we were visiting again. I asked this dignified gentleman who was sitting in his clerical robes, "It is my understanding that no one has ever been allowed to distribute Bibles here in this area. How is it that we have been allowed this time?" "Please tell her it is because she is unmarried. She is a holy woman. We would not allow this if a man were the leader, or a married woman. This is true in many places where you have been working. If a man were to come as the leader we would expect a political motive. But women are not in politics. And she is holy. That is most important."

The translator explained to me that this man really considered me to be a nun because of my conduct and the fact that I had never been married. Nuns have great liberty in spiritual leadership, though women are never allowed to be priests.

I think I concealed both my surprise and pleasure at this answer to the question which many Adventists had been voicing.

Out in the fresh air, as we walked with no one in hearing distance, I almost exploded. "Pastor, do you mean that it is because I'm a single woman leading in this that these people are allowing it?"

"Yes," he said, "a number of priests have said so."

Early the next morning I went up a lonely mountainside. Looking up to the brilliant blue sky I shouted, "O God, I'm single! Single! Single! Thank you for seeing to it that I'm single! And for bringing me here single! Oh, what a God you are!" Even now I feel chills rippling up my spine.

But what we accomplished numerically on that trip and many others was trivia alongside what an Ethiopian scholar did by God's help in an adjoining province where no Protestant missionaries were allowed and no Bibles could be sold or distributed. Providentially this gentleman and I met. God had chosen him 50 years before to do the work of distributing Bibles in his home province. With the highest degree offered in the Orthodox system, and with parents who were high-ranking in the church, he was now the man of the hour. He had been impressed by God that this was the time to begin distributing Scriptures.

He came to me to ask for Bibles. I had none to give him, but I shared tens of thousands of gospels. Still he wanted Bibles and I wanted him to have them. No Protestant would dare to go to his province to give Bibles or gospels. I had flown over this rugged, mountainous countryside and had concluded that the only way we could provide Scriptures was to drop them by airplane. Already I was praying for money. And here was a man who knew every church—about 3000 of them, every trail and every mountain. He wanted 20,000 Bibles.

I took him to our church on the compound and showed him the gospels that people were stamping and asked if he wanted some. The next day he returned. Yes, indeed he wanted some. He began hauling them in his little VW to his house. After a while he asked where we got our money. I told him that we prayed for it, and God sent it because He wants people to know His Word. He was dumbfounded.

"You *pray* for money? He *hears* you? Your prayers don't come out of a book? I've never seen prayers like that in our books!"

"We don't pray from a book. We tell God what we need and ask Him to send it if He sees it is best."

"I want you to teach me how to pray. I must have Bibles to give my people."

We went into the church auditorium where I explained more about prayer. Then we knelt. I prayed. Then he prayed. He was amazed at the whole idea.

In the four years that followed he, along with a remarkable network of helpers he had gathered, distributed 24,000 Bibles, 1.5 million gospels, and 600,000 New Testaments—about 150 tons—in this province where Amharic Scriptures had never before been allowed. It was a massive literacy program that even appealed to the

Communists who soon began to take over the country. Later they made life terribly difficult for Bible believers, but the distribution was completed before that.

Only eight months before this scholar first came, I had been riding with some friends one Sunday along the only paved road in that province. It was miles from any town. All the country people were in church. No one was around. Suddenly we had a flat tire. As I got out of the car I noticed two women far away gathering cow dung for fuel. People aren't supposed to gather cow dung on Sunday. Slowly they moved toward us. A couple of us took some forbidden gospels to them and explained what they were and that the alphabet was in them. "They are free," spoke my translator. "You may take them home to your children. They can learn to read."

As those ladies stood there looking at the Books in their hands, their lips began to quiver. Tears rolled down their cheeks. One choked out the words, "How did you know our poverty?" And the other echoed, "How did you know?" (How could we help but know as we looked at patches on patches on rags.)

We waited for more. "You see," they both sobbed at once, "just yesterday we each sent our son to the priest to learn to read. They came home and said, 'The priest told us we must each bring 5 cents (2.5 cents U.S.) for an alphabet.' But we don't have 5 cents. It's been many years since we saw 5 cents in our houses. Our boys cannot go to school. We don't have the money!"

Their words were all mixed up with their tears. They wiped their faces with their muddy hands, and warm, loving, smiles broke through. They continued their story. "We have been praying ever since yesterday for 5 cents each to buy the alphabet. God has heard our prayers. But how did *you* know our poverty? Did *God* tell you?"

That was July 1, 1973. Early in February 1974 the scholar began his herculean task of distributing to the province. Tens of thousands learned to read, and their first stories were of Jesus!

The Rest of the Story (Part of It)

It was the fall semester of my sophomore year in college. My adviser had assured me that one of the requirements for an elementary education major was physical geography. It wasn't my first love until we reached the section on rainforest—then the Ituri Forest in Congo, Central Africa. The more I studied, the more I dreamed. Not only did I dream of a minister-husband and four children while I worked a lifetime in Congo, but I would write stories for African children and get Sabbath school lessons translated. Who knows what else? I'll always wonder how many of the dreams and how much of the intense desire was inspired by God and how much originated in my own imagination.

As the years went by in Ethiopia I almost forgot Congo—then called Zaire—until I was on vacation in Rwanda and collecting African stories for the *Storytime in Africa* books I was writing. Standing on a hill one day and looking across Lake Kivu, I was informed that just across the water was Zaire. Zaire! My heart began to pound!

Later I asked a missionary—could we go to Zaire by Land Rover? We crossed the border and drove about 15 miles along a road that led to Customs, some of it in wonderfully dense, dark forest. Then we returned to Rwanda. God had let me see this dreamed-of land. And once later from a jet we chanced to traverse the Ituri Forest at about 35,000 feet. It was awesome—all of it! I'm glad for the little that I saw. But I had long since learned that wet country was not for me. God had chosen the highlands of Ethiopia rather than "the white man's grave." I had let go of those Congo dreams. My sister and I worked with translators to produce the Amharic children's Sabbath school lessons which are still being published, and a children's songbook in Amharic. The five-volume set of *Storytime* was finally published about 20 years after it was begun—and in English. Actually they were completed long after I had returned to the U.S. To date well over 250,000 copies have been sold, some in abridged versions in four languages. Just last year all 5 volumes were published in French in Togo.

In the U.S. once more (something that required a tremendous amount of adjustment), I was busy with many things. Then one day late in 1990 it happened. I learned of a missionary couple—he a minister I had known but briefly—who had spent many years in Zaire, much of it in the jungles. They had begun their work perhaps ten years before I had, and they were the parents of *four* children!

On a sad day the young, grief-stricken parents had laid their beautiful, blonde three-year-old girl to rest in the jungle. Later an African couple, missionaries from Rwanda, laid their baby girl to rest beside her. Two little girls sleep in a deep forest waiting for Jesus to come.

The parents of the blonde were now working in another area of Africa but still had a deep interest in Zaire. The father expressed a strong desire to have children's books—and others—for the people of eastern Zaire. They needed children's Sabbath school lessons and storybooks in their own Swahili.

You know, I suddenly came alive! He knew publishers and had been a press manager himself. In fact, he had supervised the printing of the first five-volume sets of *Storytime in Africa* ever produced. His wife had been a typesetter for years. Moreover, he knew a woman, a wife and mother of three who had also been a typesetter. They *lived* in Zaire! She wanted most of all to develop children's materials, and also books for adults. And there was a missionary couple who had come home who were working on translating a book and typesetting it.

My job was to stay in Southern California and find money to keep everybody happy as they worked on a colossal, previously-unplanned, book production. I soon discovered that my experience in Ethiopia was an immense blessing. I had learned more easily to recognize God's leading and to know something of His intense longing to have children, millions of them!—of His indescribable desire to have them, to have His own people cooperate with Him, and much more.

We were amazed at how fast funds flowed in, and we were sometimes disheartened at the slow process of book making. But in eight years' time our team, with the help of many others, produced 18,000 hymnals in three languages, 15,000 sets of Bible studies in each of two languages, 32,000 *Steps to Christ* in yet another language, 5,000 bound copies of the 3-year cycle of the children's Sabbath school lessons for teachers' use, 15,000 copies of *From Here to Forever,* and 7,000 copies of the 5-volume set of *Forever Stories,* which are bound in one volume.

Very close to my heart is the special 10,000-copy Swahili edition of *Storytime in Africa,* which I renamed "Waiting for Jesus" in memory of the two little girls sleeping in the forest. Since few people there have Bibles, in this edition we added many precious Bible passages which children can understand. We also added 15 children's songs at the back of the book.

It was a thrill to learn that R.E.A.C.H. purchased 3,000 copies of these books to give as Christmas presents to each student in their schools. Can you imagine my feelings that Christmas? No!

With the money from those 3,000 to add to other funds it was possible to produce the *Forever Stories,* 3,000 copies of which were purchased and given to R.E.A.C.H. students. The Quiet Hour donated funds for Bibles and evangelism.

The war had begun in Rwanda before the project was finished in Zaire. Hostilities had spread to Zaire before all the books were distributed. But to date nearly all the books have been given out or sold, and the rest are in process. The missionaries had to evacuate. God had put our team together just in time. The missionary mother who had been in Zaire also produced many helps for Sabbath school and elementary school teachers.

What a gathering it will be when we reach heaven. I can hardly wait!

Dream On! To the young unmarried women at the start of a new century, I say, Dream on! And dream BIG! But let God have you *and* your dreams. You will never be sorry.

> *"Sing, O barren woman,*
> *you who never bore a child;*
> *burst into song, shout for joy,*
> *you who were never in labor,*
> *because more are the children of the desolate woman*
> *than of her who has a husband,"*
> *says the Lord.*
> Isaiah 54:1 NIV
>
> *O my Strength, I sing praise to you;*
> *You, O God, are my fortress, my loving God.*
> Psalm 59:17 NIV

AUTHOR'S NOTE: It was Dr. C. Mervyn Maxwell who asked me on July 9, 1999 to write this chapter. He and his wife have been good friends of mine for 25 years, beginning when I first attended the Andrews University Seminary in pursuit of an M.Div. degree. They were always intensely interested in my projects and prayed many prayers for various aspects of them and for me.

Although he did not believe that women should be ordained to the gospel ministry, yet Dr. Maxwell treated women with deep respect and helpfulness. He had a way of inspiring them to work for the Lord. After outlining some of what he wanted me to write, he burst out with, "Carolyn, we need testimonies of what God has done for us! God wants us to speak up for Him! You have much you need to tell!"

After agreeing to write this, I never had another opportunity to talk with him. I sense a terrible loss and will miss him deeply.

"How painful it is to the Lord when one of his people dies!" Psalm 116:15 TEV

Thank God, the resurrection is soon to come!

Chapter 21

Why All the Fuss?

Wellesley Muir

~

Paul says, ". . . there is neither male nor female; for you are all one in Christ" (Gal 3:28, NKJV). So why all the fuss about ordaining women? It's simple. The Bible provides as much evidence for keeping Sunday as for ordaining women. It's true, not a single text says, "You shall not keep Sunday." So how much fuss do you think there would be if leading Adventists said, "Let's keep Sunday"?

In his *Dies Domini*, Section 12, Pope John Paul II quotes Genesis 2:3: "God blessed the seventh day and made it holy." Eleven lines later in the same document he says: "Sunday is the day of rest because it is the day 'blessed' by God and 'made holy' by him." Wait a minute! Did God bless both Sabbath and Sunday? We need to pray for the pope.

Not a single Bible verse says, "You shall not ordain women!" Inspired by God, Paul writes clearly: "If a man desires the position of a bishop, he desires a good work. A bishop then must be blameless, the husband of one wife, . . . one who rules his own house well, having his children in submission" (1 Tim 3:1, 2, 4 NKJV).

Feminist pressures ask us to revise the Scripture to say, "If a woman desires the position of a bishop, she desires a good work. A bishop then must be blameless, the wife of one husband, . . . one who rules her own house well, having her children in submission." Does God ask both men and women to rule their homes? "Therefore as the church is subject to Christ, so let the wives be to their own husbands in everything. Husbands, love your wives as Christ also loved the church

---

Wellesley Muir *is a pastor and missionary, now living in California.*

and gave Himself for it." (Eph 5:24, 25 NKJV). We need to pray for our church, our leaders and our homes.

The Creator of the universe instituted the Sabbath and the family at the very beginning of earth's history. Jesus chose to make man the head of the family. It's His decision for church leadership to model His plan for families. The breakdown of the family is the world's greatest problem. God calls the last-day church to build strong, loving, disciplined families.

Does this mean that God has no place for women to serve in His church? Absolutely not! God has given women the most important position on the planet— that of being mothers. But doesn't God want to use women in finishing His work on earth? Yes, Yes, and Yes!

No man in the remnant church has accomplished more for God's work than Ellen G. White. She wrote: "But God will have a people upon the earth to maintain the Bible, and the Bible only, as the standard of all doctrines and the basis of all reforms. . . . *Before accepting any doctrine or precept, we should demand a plain 'Thus saith the Lord' in its support"* (*The Great Controversy,* p. 595, emphasis supplied). Let's look at the words omitted by the ellipsis in the preceding statement. "The opinions of learned men, the deductions of science, the creeds or decisions of ecclesiastical councils, as numerous and discordant as are the churches which they represent, the voice of the majority—not one nor all of these should be regarded as evidence for or against any point of religious faith."

In the paragraph preceding our quote, Ellen White tells how Paul looked down to the last days and declared, "The time will come when they will not endure sound doctrine" (2 Tim 4:3 KJV). Then she says, "That time has fully come" (*The Great Controversy,* p. 595). On the same page she adds, "Satan . . . leads the people to look to bishops, to pastors, to professors of theology, as their guides, instead of searching the Scriptures to learn their duty for themselves."

A Cultural Issue?

Isn't all this just a matter of culture? Isn't John Paul II right to suggest that we take Sabbath and find its fulfillment in Sunday? Sunday, after all, is wrapped up in the culture of our times. Wasn't the Roman Church right when it decided to take the popular pagan day of the sun and make it the Christian Sabbath? Isn't it time for Seventh-day Adventists to be sensitive to the culture of our times and give women positions that God reserved for men? Books with feminist ideals have been sold in our college and university bookstores for many years. Can't we get their message?

If culture is the issue, God missed a perfect opportunity. At the time of the Exodus, Egyptian culture dictated that it was proper for a woman to become a pharaoh. The Lord could have avoided all the trouble of having Miriam watch over her baby brother in a basket on the Nile and followed the culture of the times by making her Israel's leader, a position which she later coveted.

God's attitude on culture comes to us in clear language. "According to the doings of the land of Egypt, where you dwelt, you shall not do: and according to the doings of the land of Canaan, where I am bringing you, you shall not do; nor shall you walk in their ordinances" (Lev 18:3). It is not the feminist agenda, but the will of Jesus, we must seek. God is getting us ready for the culture of heaven. He wants us to be part of His family. Christ—not a goddess, as "discovered" by some women pastors in other denominations—is the head of His church.

Bible reasons should be enough justification for obeying God, but we can also find some practical reasons for not ordaining or commissioning women. First, the women's issue affects our own church's unity. If we are honest, we must admit that ordaining women is a divisive issue in the Seventh-day Adventist church, even in North America. Jesus never commanded his followers to ordain women, but He did call upon them to live together in harmony.

Impact on Outreach

What is more, the women's issue affects our church's outreach. With a billion Roman Catholics in the world, more Catholic Christians choose to leave Babylon and join the remnant church than any other group. The great majority believe in the biblical teaching of male leadership, and there is no scriptural reason to offend them by ordaining women pastors. Many Protestant groups also believe it is unbiblical. Among them are the Southern Baptists, the largest Protestant denomination in North America. Other large groups in the world who may be offended by women pastors include Buddhists, Muslims, and Hindus.

The impact of this issue on our evangelism was brought home to me forcefully and personally. While serving as a pastor in Bakersfield, California, I received a call from an attorney. "I'm looking for a church that follows all the Bible," he said.

My response: "You've found the right church."

He questioned, "Does your church ordain women elders?"

Even though my own church had no women elders, I had to admit my daughters had been ordained in Adventist churches. Although I visited him several times after that, he continued to be offended by a practice not authorized by Scripture, and he turned away from the Adventist church. Jesus has very strong words for anyone who offends others. "It would be better for him if a millstone were hung around his neck, and he were thrown into the sea, than that he should offend one of these little ones" (Luke 17:2, NKJV).

Because of our family's 23 years of mission service, we have contact with a lot of overseas leaders and know first hand that many are offended by what is going on in North America. Whether we call it "ordain" or "commission," it's all the same when we lay hands on a candidate and give them the full authority of the gospel minister. Even the government tax people agreed.

To commission women and say, "We uphold the General Conference action not to ordain," is about as true as President Clinton saying, "I did not have an affair with that woman." Commissioning women while ordaining men will not satisfy many. One woman says, "We dream of achieving full recognition as equals in ministry" (*Pacific Union Recorder*, Dec. 7, 1998, p. 10).

We cannot afford to be a stumbling block to the rest of the world. Our over-seas brothers and sisters expect the best example from North America. We've gone pretty far, but God will forgive us, just as He forgave my daughters for sincerely accepting a non-biblical ordination. And I pray God will forgive me for sidestep-ping the issue when my daughter first asked me about ordination for women.

Delegates at the 1990 and 1995 General Conference sessions, our church's highest authority, made decisions regarding women as ordained ministers based on Bible principles. We in North America need to demonstrate leadership to the world field. We need to recommend to the next General Conference session that, based on the Word of God, all previous actions to ordain women as local church elders be annulled.

We must get on our knees, review the plain instructions in the Word and ask, Is Jesus truly leading North America to ignore the decision of two General Conference sessions and promote a book, *Women in Ministry,* which endorses women's ordina-tion? Is the Holy Spirit truly guiding the North American Division to recommend to the General Conference session in 2000 that every use of "ordained minister" in our *Church Manual* be revised to read "ordained/commissioned minister?"

Jesus calls women and men, pastors, educators, medical workers and adminis-trators to be ready to stand with Him on the sea of glass in heaven soon. He gives my daughters, my wife, and me—all of us—one great task: "the gospel to all the world." The little lady who died in 1915 is right, "God will have a people on earth to maintain the Bible, and the Bible only, as the standard of all doctrines and the basis of all reforms" (*The Great Controversy,* p. 595).

Why all the fuss? Shall our church follow popular fashions or maintain the Bible as our standard? That's a question worth fussing about.

Chapter 22

The Larger Issues

Jay Gallimore

Before sharing my thoughts on this sensitive subject, it is important to give a little history. Having a close-up seat from which to watch the church wrestle over the question of whether to ordain women has been a learning experience. When it became obvious that this item was going to be voted on at a General Conference session for the second time, we knew the questions in our own field would intensify.

In the midst of all the debate, our real concern was how to keep our conference's mission in focus. We decided that we would answer questions regarding the process and endeavor to be fair to the other view if our own opinion were asked. Like most other conferences, ours took no official position. Our officers wrote no articles or sent out any books on either side. While my personal position was known, we did our best to be officially neutral. However, in some conferences, administrators led their fields to take official positions supporting the ordination of women. Some even published their positions all over the North American Division and beyond. Instead, we told our colleagues in ministry that regardless of which view they took, they were appreciated by us.

To this day I have friends—including ministers and scholars—on both sides whom I admire and appreciate. The two scholars who presented the opposing sides of the women's ordination issue at the last General Conference session have addressed our ministerial meetings (though not on this issue), and we would be pleased to have them again. Even though there was discussion and interest in the topic in our field, we are grateful to the Lord that the issue did not become the center of attention. Our main mission is the proclamation of the three angels'

Jay Gallimore *is President of the Michigan Conference of Seventh-day Adventists.*

messages, not who should be ordained. Besides, the decision was to be made at the General Conference session, not in the local field. I say this not to detract from the importance of the issue but to keep it in perspective.

From my viewpoint as a church administrator, I would like to focus on three aspects of our recent experience regarding ordination for women. First, some observations about the importance and pitfalls of the process we adopt to address divisive issues. Second, what I saw happen as the church addressed *this* divisive issue. Third, what I believe are important considerations as the church moves on from here. In exploring these, I hope to call attention to what I think are the larger issues which all too often are overlooked in our desire to achieve our objectives. I pray that these may help us evaluate what we have done so far and steer a better course in the future.

1. Process: How We Handle Divisive Issues

There is no question that the church will be faced with divisive issues. But the real challenge it faces is how to process them. The way we address this will predict our ability to stay together and complete our mission. Acts 15 reveals that the early church solved disputable matters by sending delegates to a general council. They were assisted in their decisions by the prophetic gift. They dealt, for instance, with whether Christians should eat food offered to idols. It was a touchy issue. Yet in His messages to the seven churches, Jesus affirmed the Jerusalem council's position by condemning strongly those who continued to eat food offered to idols.

Ellen G. White clearly advised us that when representatives are gathered from all over the world and a fair process is in place, the decisions of the world church are to be respected. "God has ordained," she wrote, "that the representatives of His church from all parts of the earth, when assembled in a General Conference, shall have authority" (*Testimonies for the Church,* 9:261).

This statement assumes that the church delegates understand that Scripture stands over the church. Deliberations must come under the guidance of the Bible. This is the *"moral imperative"* for any church that puts its trust in the Bible as the Word of God. The clear statements of God's Word are not disputable matters. Nevertheless, in disputable matters and policy issues, the majority decisions are to be respected. Otherwise, we could not maintain our unity. We are held together by policy, not personality.

Cultural War. When the North American Division began to process the question of whether to ordain women to the gospel ministry, we knew this was going to be tense. There was, and is, a cultural war going on in the western world, and the church has not escaped it. Through the years Christianity has greatly improved the position of women in the world. Overcoming a great deal of sinful culture, the Bible has restored correct concepts concerning the noble calling that the Creator gave to women. Building on the gains of Protestant Christianity, the secular feminist movement determined to make further improvements. Unfortunately, it chose a fundamental position that would challenge the very fabric of western civilization. It demanded, for women and men, an *identical* role and function. This has embroiled western culture in a never-ending dispute.

Here is the weakness of the feminist viewpoint. It demands that equality be defined by function. But how can two opposite genders, with a different physical and emotional creation, function *identically* in all aspects of life? This presents a great dilemma, not only to society, but to Bible-believing Christians. The Bible supports the equality of women and men in a context of cooperation, while the feminist movement supports equality in a context of competition. In the western cultural war the feminists played this card. Anyone opposed to women's assuming *identical* and *competitive* roles to those of men in *all* areas of life and society was to be considered a bigot or worse. In this context the western cultural war spilled over into the North American Division and into the world church. Anytime culture and the Bible clash, this question will arise: Will we be faithful to the Bible or try to adapt the Bible to what is perceived as modern culture? Will we risk being misunderstood and even scorned in order to stay true to the Scriptures?

This cultural war is still going on. The Christian Reformed Church, headquartered in Grand Rapids, Michigan, has experienced similar conflict. It is one of the great Reformation churches from Holland that planted itself solidly on western shores. In many areas it shares a common biblical conservative approach with Adventists. Christian Reformed Church delegates voted to ordain women but failed to give the action the required confirmation at their next annual meeting. Still later, through some clever parliamentary maneuvering, proponents of ordaining women got their council to declare inoperative the portions of their governing principles which limited ordination to men, even while allowing those portions to remain unchanged! Subsequent ordinations have caused division among believers, pastors, and congregations. Not only have ministers and congregations left their communion but the church's fellowship with certain other Reformed groups has been threatened.

Despite these battles, in North America there remain many churches with millions of members which do not ordain women. Most of these churches are known to take the Bible seriously. These events remind us of how important it is to preserve the integrity of the Seventh-day Adventist movement as a church which seeks to ground all its beliefs and practices on the Word of God.

Our Challenge. In addressing this issue, our North American Division faced a challenge not easily resolved. The real solution lay in setting up a process that made the Scriptures the final arbitrator and guide. Laying aside all preconceived ideas and appealing unitedly to the Bible has always been our strength and glory as a church. To keep our feet on solid ground, we must be committed to submitting collectively to the Holy Spirit's leading through the body. However, if we do not consult the Spirit of God and we ignore the Word He inspired, what can we expect? He does not force Himself on us. Neither will He be taken for granted. When He has made available the resources of inspiration, He longs for us to use them.

2. Reality: How We Handled This Issue

Unfortunately, we in the North American Division chose a political route toward a solution. It pains me to say that at our year-end meetings, where the decisions were made, never once did we use any kind of process to consult the Bible or the Spirit of Prophecy on this issue. Of course there were devotions and prayers. But I am talking about a focused process of collectively searching the Bible and the Spirit of Prophecy on an issue to see if there is "any light from the Lord." On one occasion, when a North American Division assistant was asked to relay a request for a normal parliamentary procedure, the request was refused with the comment, "We've got to win this one." While it is doubtful that the request would have made any difference, the incident revealed our political mind-set. Of course, a year-end meeting must handle a lot of business and policy issues. Setting up a Bible search process on every issue would be impractical. But when a change as major as this is proposed, we need to re-think our method of decision-making in light of the Bible. In short, we need the Lord's guidance.

Nothing in what I am saying should be understood as critical of the "brethren." I *am* one. The leaders and delegates to a year-end meeting are my brothers and sisters in Christ and in the third angel's message. They can count on my care and support. This is not a finger-pointing exercise. I must confess that at year-end, no suggestion came from my lips to adopt a different process. But to review and think constructively about how to do things better should never be viewed as non-supportive. The North American Division has many fine accomplishments to commend. We are writing about just one issue.

We church leaders, from the local church to the General Conference, need our hands held up. We need affirmation, encouragement and prayer. Leadership is not an easy path, and there are many pressures. This is also why we must give those around us the freedom to tell us some things we may not want to hear. What a blessing Jethro was to Moses! I tell my own colleagues they can help me best by telling me the truth.

All of us must learn from the past or we will be condemned to repeat it. We grow when we thoughtfully review both our successes and mistakes. There is in my heart—and I believe in many others—a deep longing for the Lord's leadership in all things. We must remember that His leadership does not come automatically. We must seek it with all of our mind, heart and soul.

Interesting Developments. When in a different form the ordination issue was slated to come before a General Conference session for the second time (at Utrecht in 1995), some very interesting developments took place. At the North American Division presidents' meeting in Pine Springs, California, we were asked to sign a statement of support for women's ordination. This was to be published and used at the General Conference session to persuade the delegates to vote Yes. An uneasy silence came over the room. Someone noted that signing or not signing such a document would automatically put everyone in a difficult position at home. One president who had personally favored ordaining women told how he had returned home to find stiff opposition among his lay people. Another president gave a similar testimony. The result was that no one signed the document, and it was withdrawn.

Later, at the General Conference session, all the political and persuasive weight our Division could muster was put into the effort. The North American Division president ably presented the case for his Division's request. His speech was supported by another presentation by the Division's former president. Then the delegates were given the pro and con by two capable scholars. For the first time the Bible evidence was laid out, allowing the church to determine on which side lay the weight of Scripture. Though the issue had been presented as a policy matter, whether to allow divisions to decide for themselves about ordination, most delegates knew that they were really voting on the biblical legitimacy of women's ordination. How could the world church make so fundamental a change unless it could find biblical support? How could it allow itself to be divided on something so essential to its unity and function? So as it had done five years earlier, the world church gave an emphatic No. However, the following events brought sadness to more than one heart.

Instead of accepting the decision of the body graciously, a noticeable portion of North America's delegation did not show up at the next business session. Then a special meeting was called for the North American delegates. Many of the speeches surprised me with their unhappiness. Clearly the majority of the Division's delegates had invested enormous amounts of emotional energy in this issue. Before Utrecht there had been talk about winning. It was rumored that the leaders in other fields that had voted against the motion five years earlier were moving away from their previous opposition. For a while, expectations were high that the vote would at least be close. In addition, the request for ordaining women came from the financially-powerful North American Division. Some voices quietly warned that if the other divisions did not go along, the funding from North America for the world church might be reduced. This was not a small thing for the overseas divisions to weigh.

When it became clear that the world church was nowhere near approving ordination for women, some of the North American delegates wanted to turn toward isolationism. During the above-mentioned meeting, one speech, made by a west coast professional woman, even suggested weakening our bond to the world church into a loose-knit association. This would allow the North American Division to do what it wanted. To his credit, the division president responded that we would continue to be part of and supportive of the world church. Though feelings ran strong among some delegates, in my opinion the North American Division delegates and home field would have rejected the idea of separation or a weakened relationship.

In the midst of all this unhappiness, a delegate from California addressed the group. This talented young woman in her twenties spoke with words and tones that reflected a nobility of character and a walk with Jesus. In light of the charged atmosphere, I could hardly believe my ears as she appealed to the delegates to trust the Lord in this matter. She quoted some beautiful soothing statements from Ellen White. As she spoke, I said to myself, "Jesus is speaking to the delegates of the North American Division in the person of this young Adventist woman." As she pointed us to the Savior and asked for patience, faith, and submission, you could sense the anger and defiance melting away. It is a moment I will never forget. When she sat down, a conference president stood up and tried to belittle her words, but his speech seemed so out of place. The meeting soon finished and the North American delegation was back in their delegate section doing business.

"Ordinations." Much of the pro-ordination activity had centered around several of our educational centers. It is not surprising that some would attempt to defy the world church by organizing an ordination for the women pastors of a few of these institutional churches. At one of these places, one of the women pastors refused to participate. Even though she strongly supported the pro-ordination position, she wished neither to defy the world church nor bring disunity among God's people. What a noble response!

Of course none of these "ordinations" were legitimate or recognized. It is important to note that even though these ceremonies happened in conferences and unions whose leadership and committees were actively in favor of women's ordination, to their credit the conference and union committees never voted to authorize the "ordinations." Had a union conference taken this step, our unity in North America could have been shaken. But we must also note that virtually no North American Division voices spoke up publicly to call this what it was. The General Conference president online courageously called it rebellion. To my knowledge, though, no one was ever reprimanded for participating in these "ordinations."

Nevertheless, in spite of two General Conference session No votes on different aspects of the question, attempts continue by certain leaders to promote women's ordination. In the July 1999 North American Division issue of the *Adventist Review,* an article entitled "Why I Stay" said in the opening paragraph, "I wish my church could settle the issue of women's ordination (yes, I'm one of those people) and deal with a few other hot potatoes. And I often wonder why the church allows its fundamentalist fringe to set so much of its agenda." Really! Two thirds of the delegates to the world church hardly fit the "fundamentalist fringe" label. I was assured in a letter from the *Review* that the author was just listing his concerns. The paragraph is reproduced in the endnote so readers can draw their own conclusions.[1] Attitudes like this, printed in our leading papers, do not strengthen our unity. Further, major publications and news releases often feature women who have been appointed senior pastors of churches. Does this really fit the spirit of the action at Utrecht?

Education Needed? After the Utrecht vote, we heard a lot of statements about the need to educate the rest of the world church. Some made a major point about our responsibility to help the church understand how to interpret the Bible. Considerable effort has been and is being expended in this area. The March 1999 issue of *Ministry* gave the higher-critical method some real promotion. If this method were adopted, the church would no doubt discover that its biblical objections to ordaining women would be gone.

But our view of ordaining women is not the only thing that would change. Many of our basic truths would be lost. Over and over, as a church, we have rejected this method because the Bible itself rejects it. Believe me, there are far larger issues here than whom we ordain. If we want to know where this method will take us, we can just look at many of what used to be the great Protestant churches. Today they are losing members right and left. They struggle to find a consensus on anything. Their moral force in the world has been reduced to a yawn. Like Samson flirting with Delilah, once a church gets its hair cut by the higher-critical method, its power over the Philistines is gone. Why? Because the higher-critical method destroys people's faith in the Bible as the Book of truth.

Issue Never Decided? Some have tried to make a case that the issue of women's ordination has never been decided. They point out that never in recent years has the direct question of whether women may properly be ordained come to the General Conference in session. But this is begging the question. After all, the wording to be voted on was framed by the proponents of women's ordination. Cleverly, a straightforward statement of the issue was not put forward so that, if it lost, the door would be left open to try again. Yet, if the church had voted, for instance, to allow divisions to decide on their own, it would have been a Yes vote for women's ordination.

Both in 1990 and 1995, however, the debate itself centered on the real issue: Does the Bible support ordaining women to the gospel ministry? Even the two scholars mentioned earlier focused on this, not on the technically-worded ballot. If the vote had been Yes, tremendous pressures would have immediately been put on every conference to move this way. Demands for affirmative action in all areas of leadership would have followed. Would these moves have stopped at western borders? Not likely. Enormous division and stress might have been brought on the church worldwide. We would have become focused on social issues rather than the gospel commission given by the Savior.

Some have been under the false impression that the great majority in the North American Division was supporting this change. Such conclusions may be premature. Perhaps someday, even our Division may be grateful for the courage and wisdom of the world church. The Utrecht decision preserved harmony, not only in the world field, but for the most part in the North American Division itself.

Seminary Book. Then there is the recent publication of the book *Women In Ministry* by the Seminary. In a phone conversation, I asked a key leader in the Seminary why the Seminary had produced this book contrary to the position of the world church. He told me that North American Division administration had requested the Seminary professors to produce this book. He noted to me that it was sent out under Seminary letterhead, giving it official standing. Even though he told me it was printed with private funding, he did not back away from the fact that this was published with the influence of the Seminary behind it.

I asked why the Seminary, which is owned and supported by the world church, would publish a book undermining the position of the world church. At least, why wasn't another book also published in support of the church's position? He replied that they had asked two people who were opposed to sit on the committee, but they refused. As I see it, it is not surprising that they refused, because the committee of fifteen people which produced this book had a mission to produce a work supporting the ordination of women. He also noted that some people in other parts of the world had not heard the arguments which support the ordaining of women. This Seminary leader is a very fine man whom I appreciate. He has done and continues to do some excellent things for the Seminary. Yet we must ask those from the North American Division and the Seminary who were involved, What happened to the fairness and support that the world church deserves on this issue? Were emotions and personal agendas allowed to prevail over principle?

All have a right to share or publish their own viewpoints. If those in favor want to put together a private effort to publish their position, they should be able to do so without criticism for doing it. But when the Division and the Seminary leadership publish a book under the auspices of the Seventh-day Adventist Theological Seminary which opposes the position of the world church, then voices should ask for accountability. Whether on this issue or any other, the world church should be able to count on the loyalty of the institutions that serve it.

A Larger Issue. Here, then, is one of the larger issues. When the world church speaks and decides on an issue, will we as leaders and institutions support it? Isn't due process to be respected? Don't we as leaders have a sacred responsibility to support the church that is the body of Christ, even when it disagrees with our opinion? Will we trust the Lord to lead His church? Defective though it may be, this world church that keeps the commandments of God and the faith of Jesus is still the apple of the Father's eye. Money, education and power do not in themselves render us superior Christians. It is our Christlikeness, love, and humility that make our service valuable.

In North America we have been blessed with many resources, including financial. Those resources continue to be shared generously with the rest of the church. We must ever count such generosity as a privilege. May the time never come when we will yield to the temptation to use these blessings in a wrong way. We should humbly remember that the Lord who gave them can remove them.

3. Prospects: Where We Go from Here

Approach to Scripture. A great deal has been said about the need to use the "principle approach" to understanding the Bible. This new approach was supposed to be superior to what was scorned as the "proof text" method. Of course, anybody can string together a bunch of texts and make them say anything the person wants said. However, from William Miller onward, Adventists have always insisted that the context support the texts for the subject matter being studied. Time, place, and circumstances have also been given consideration. But in the end, we have insisted that we take the text as it reads and not try to spiritualize it into saying something else. Symbols, for instance, had to be obviously symbols.

In other words, we have used what I call the "common sense approach." Some would call it the Reformation method. We have always believed that a common person could read the Bible and understand it. Of course, we have also understood the application of principle. But principle application should not violate what the Bible actually says. For example, one of the major arguments often used against us by the first-day Christians is this: "The principle of the fourth commandment is to keep one day in seven holy. It doesn't matter which day, just so you keep one in seven. You Adventists are legalistic for insisting that the Sabbath has to be Saturday. God isn't interested in which day, just so we keep one." The danger here is obvious. If we change the way we approach the Bible and allow "principle" to contradict what Scripture says, then there is no limit to what the Bible can be made to say. In that respect, the "principle" people can end up in the same ditch as the "proof text" people.

If it had not been for what the Bible says, would the ordination issue have passed at the General Conference? I think so. And after the two presentations, pro and con, the proponents left Utrecht understanding clearly that unless they could diffuse what the Bible texts actually say, the possibility of this passing at some later time was not very good. That is why the Seminary produced the book.

The very first of our Fundamental Beliefs states that "The Holy Scriptures are the infallible revelation of His will. They are the standard of character, the test of experience, the authoritative revealer of doctrines, and the trustworthy record of God's acts in history." Doesn't it seem odd that a church with such a belief should have this debate over our own time-tested methods of biblical interpretation? Satan would like nothing better than to subvert the authority of Scripture in the Seventh-day Adventist church. If he were able to accomplish that, think of the consequences. Like a succulent piece of fruit left in the desert sun, we would dry up and blow away. Why, after all, do our members go to church on Saturday? Why are they willing to sacrifice prosperity and peace in order to keep the Sabbath holy? Why do they return tithes and offerings? Why do they abstain from pork? Why do they believe the dead are in the grave asleep? Why are they willing to go against the popular culture? There is only one answer. The Bible!

Careful About Culture. We need to be careful that we don't make culture the new golden calf of the remnant church. Of course there are many differences among all of our cultures, differences which are quite innocent. However, the gospel cuts across parts of every culture. No matter what our ethnic or national setting, we must be willing to subject our culture to the Bible and not the Bible to our culture. Otherwise, not only will our unity be destroyed but culture instead of the Bible will become the authority of our lives. We will end up with a culture that is merely influenced by the Bible instead of a culture that is shaped by the Bible. If we go down this slippery slope there will be no behavior, no matter how wrong, that cannot be justified in some future session. Very soon the church will have the same values as the culture around it. Unless the church can maintain its Bible foundation and vigorously call all cultures to repentance, it will lose both its power and its reason to exist.

Ordination to the gospel ministry is no mystery. Those ordained are to oversee the church and give leadership to it. So why should not women be given this opportunity? I confess that I do not understand all the reasons why God in Scripture has assigned that role to male leadership. Again and again I have had to test my own emotional feelings by the Bible's teaching. But Scripture seems too plain to simply dismiss this as culture. Neither can I explain why God insists on tithes and offerings, especially when the modern culture considers the system of 10% plus offerings to be a relic of the Old Testament. All I know is that we are blessed when we obey. God is not in the business of hurting His sons and daughters. He gave His only begotten Son so He could adopt us as His children. He loves us. We have every reason to trust Him, even if we don't understand all of His ways. We need to walk with humility before God and with each other.

Spiritual leadership in any area is not a call to arrogance or pride. It is a call to do justly, love mercy and walk humbly with our God. Leadership does not make one more valuable than other brothers and sisters. It does bring sober responsibilities. We have nothing to fear by doing things God's way, even if it seems out of step with modern values. He saw our day. He understands our culture. He knew the temptations we would face. Our trust in Him will not be disappointed. Our minds and lives must be held captive to the Word of God or we will be held captive to someone else.

Too often those who do not find biblical support for the ordination of women have been written off as backward male chauvinists who demean and belittle women. But I have yet to meet anyone opposed to the ordination of women who did not also believe that women should be involved in ministry. They support fairness and opportunity for women. Their wives and daughters are often well-educated professionals in their own right. Also there are many women in the North American Division, perhaps a majority, who do not support the ordination of women.

Cooperative Roles. It goes without saying that both women and men should be respected and treated as God's daughters and sons. Equality, fairness, appreciation, and respect should be the heart and soul of how we treat one another. Unfortunately, too many males have used their God-given leadership in the home and in the church to abuse rather than to bless and minister to females. This was never God's plan. Neither is it His plan for the gender roles to be identical in every respect. By nature and revelation God has assigned the genders some roles that are different yet cooperative. It would be foolish to replace one wrong with another. As my mother used to say, two wrongs don't make a right. All of us need to work together to implement His plan the way He wants it.

Our sisters in Christ should be part and parcel of our executive committees. Their voices should be given equal weight with those of their brothers. While their function may be different from that of overseeing the churches, this does not make them any less valuable.

Both men and women are equally needed in the great work of the church. Jesus called all of us to be His disciples. We must not exclude anyone. Nor are we to assign responsibilities contrary to His directions. It is His church; He makes the rules. Our sinful cultures have no right or place to judge those rules as inferior to their own morals. Our western cultures are full of the exploitation of women. Their feminine gifts are used to sell everything from tooth paste to cars. The pornography business is huge and vicious. The Miss America and Miss Universe contests present an unbiblical and perverted picture of women to the world. Never in the history of the world have so many women been so degraded while being told they are being lifted to a higher position. But none of us, whether male or female, can obtain a higher or better position than conformity to the will of God. Angels love to do His will, whether it is attending pitiful wrecks of humanity or conversing with the most intelligent beings of the unfallen worlds. Doing His will is their delight and joy.

Lessons from Our History. In the early part of the century we had many women involved in the gospel work. In those days our ministers, like the apostles, focused on raising up new churches and equipping the members for ministry. But as our ministers moved toward becoming "settled pastors" over churches, fewer opportunities were found for women to be involved. This is a financial reality. When the feminist movement hit, very few women were found spreading the three angels' messages full time and on the payroll.

I believe this has been a mistake. We need to rethink this "settled pastor" concept in light of the Bible and the writings of Mrs. White. A return to New Testament principles would create more opportunity for women to be involved in specialized ministry. In the meantime, while we need to be faithful to Scripture and the intent of the world church, we must continue to make opportunities for women to participate in ministry. However, rather than trying to find some way around the world church, we need to accept the voted position. Unfortunately, the movement to make the commissioned minister's credential identical to the ordained minister's credential is another attempt to circumvent the will of the world church.

What should we do? In harmony with the Bible and Mrs. White's counsel, the church should create a track in ministry, especially for women, which will put them in cooperative roles with the ordained ministry. If this were done wisely and well, it could be a great blessing to the church the world over.

Conclusion

In summary, the larger issues are these. Will we faithfully support our church when it has settled such a matter? Will we seek to involve women in ministry in a way that will be in harmony with the body of Christ and not antagonistic to it? Will we be faithful to the authority of the Bible? Will we use the method of interpretation that it recognizes? Will we set up processes at all church levels to seek diligently and fairly the counsel of Scripture and of Ellen G. White on major issues? Will we be willing to accept such counsel and follow it? Will we reject the political atmosphere of competition and human glory for an atmosphere of cooperation and self-sacrifice? And finally, will we walk humbly with Jesus and each other?

My appeal to myself and others in all areas of church leadership is this: Let us dedicate ourselves to finding processes that seek the Lord's wisdom in issues like this. Let us lay aside political processes that divide us. Let us together, in humility, seek to sit at the feet of Jesus and listen to Him through His Word. The church is not a congress or a parliament. The local church board meetings, the conference constituency meetings, and the year-end meetings are not to become political swimming pools. We are not politicians. We are the members of Christ's body. We are His disciples. We are ministers of the gospel, ordained and charged to "preach the Word." This is the church of the living God! As leaders, let us seek the Lord's help to create better ways to solve the problems we are dealing with. Let us renew our commitment to the authority of Scripture and the Spirit of Prophecy. The Lord loves us. If we seek Him with all of our heart, He will do "exceeding abundantly above all that we ask or think." He will bring a unity and harmony among us that will make angels stand in awe. If we let Him, He will lead His church.

Endnote

1. "Why I Stay," *Adventist Review,* July 1999. Here is the first paragraph of the article: "To be honest, at times I am frustrated with my church. Sometimes I feel it is somewhat out of tune with the times and the world I live in. Sometimes I get upset by its frequent failures to deal decisively with important issues. I wish my church could settle the issue of women's ordination (yes, I'm one of those people) and deal with a few other hot potatoes. And I often wonder why the church allows its fundamentalist fringe to set so much of its agenda. And yes, I need a double or triple portion of grace to interact with some people in the church."

Epilogue

Mercedes H. Dyer, Editor

~

Heeding the Bible's admonition to "prove all things" (1 Thess 5:21), and accepting *Women in Ministry*'s invitation to dialog, the authors in *Prove All Things* have examined the key claims of the Seminary's book, the best arguments that the church's pro-ordination scholars can offer. The Seminary book contains much helpful information, and we have no reason to believe that its authors brought to their work any but the best of motivations.

Our Findings

Even so, in *Prove All Things* we have shown that the central conclusions of the book *Women in Ministry* are lacking the needed biblical foundation. In some cases, Bible texts are used to support the desired conclusion while other texts on the subject, leading to a different conclusion, are overlooked. In other cases, questionable information from non-biblical sources is used to reinterpret or set aside the plain meaning of what the Bible says on the subject. In still other cases, conclusions are based on imaginative or creative reasoning which is not supported by the Bible. But we must take the Bible--all of it--for our guide, or our whole reason for existence is in jeopardy in the world. The Bible does not contradict itself. We take the Bible as the inspired and holy Word of God. By it we are to "prove all things; hold fast that which is good" (1 Thess 5:21).

Mercedes H. Dyer, Ph.D., *is Professor of Educational Psychology and Counseling, Emerita, Andrews University.*

We also found that *Women in Ministry* authors selected quotations from the writings of Ellen G. White and the Seventh-day Adventist pioneers to make it appear that they supported women in pastoral leadership roles, for which ordination would be an appropriate step. But the whole of Mrs. White's writings are very clear that the position of women is a supportive, helping, healing, teaching, caring, and submissive role. In her view, women have a ministry that is very important, in some cases exceeding that of men, but it is not in filling the headship position of elder or pastor in the church. Ellen White is very clear on this point. When her writings are searched as they may be, there can be no question where she stood on this issue. Likewise the pioneers spoke with one voice about the right and duty of women to speak in the church, to participate in the life of the church, and to evangelize and minister to people's needs outside of the church; but they did not endorse placing women in the leadership role of the congregation. They understood their stand to be the position taught in Scripture.

Among other points, *Prove All Things* has presented the case for the following biblical and historical understandings concerning the relationships between men and women in the church and the role of women in ministry, finding that:

• the Bible supports differences in roles for men and women while confirming their equality in value and salvation;

• the Bible indicates that role distinctions originated at Creation, not after the Fall;

• the Bible emphasizes that the husband is to be the spiritual leader in the home; it requires that only the man who trains his family in the Lord, demonstrating his godly and effective leadership there, may qualify for the leadership of the church;

• the Bible teaches that all who truly are followers of Christ are given "spiritual gifts" and are responsible to present Christ *in their appropriate roles* as part of the "priesthood of believers";

• the Bible does not present Eve as a priest ordained in Eden nor does it give evidence in either the Old or New Testaments that any women served as priests;

• the Bible offers no compelling evidence for the claims that Junia, Phoebe, or any other woman, served as an apostle or minister in the New Testament period;

• the Bible in its entirety is inspired by God, and thus Paul's instructions in 1 Corinthians 11 and 14, 1 Timothy 2 and 3, and Titus 1 are applicable today and cannot be written off as "culturally conditioned";

• the Holy Spirit inspired the Bible, which is the Word of God, and also the writings of Ellen G. White, as a lesser light. Our methods of studying these messages from God ought to be consistent with time-honored principles of interpretation, not influenced by higher criticism or its assumptions;

• Ellen G. White, who called herself a "messenger of the Lord," was never ordained as an elder or pastor nor did she call for the ordination of women to such a role in her 1895 statement;

• the biblical understanding of the Seventh-day Adventist pioneers, as expressed by editor J. H. Waggoner in *The Signs of the Times* (Dec. 19, 1878, p. 320), was that "a woman . . . cannot occupy the position of a pastor or ruling elder." Although women in early Adventism served in many and varied soul-winning endeavors and some were issued licenses, none are known to have served as elder or pastor;

• the General Conference of 1881 declined to approve the ordination of women to the pastoral ministry and sent the motion to a committee where the matter was dropped.

• spiritualism permeates our current society, exhibiting itself in many forms and with many groups, including modern feminism. Its very pervasiveness makes it difficult for us to recognize. Spiritualist viewpoints underlie many of feminism's goals and perspectives.

Our Concerns

Those of us involved with ADVENTISTS AFFIRM, the sponsor and publisher of *Prove All Things,* earnestly pray that our church's leadership will resist the temptation to compromise. The pressures of modern society for our leaders are enormous and frightening. The church cannot be neutral or please every group clamoring for its own agenda. We must hold to the Word of God. We must not depart from God's will expressed in His Word. We strongly believe that the Seventh-day Adventist movement has been divinely guided and is in a special way God's appointed means to finish His work on earth. We tremble as we witness pressures pushing in at every side. The adversary is working desperately, for he knows the time is short.

Our work is to preach the gospel to all the world because Jesus is coming soon. God has opened the floodgates of heaven with the resources of today's technology to reach even the hidden recesses of the hills and valleys of the world. His Word is being loudly proclaimed by evangelists and dedicated laymen who are sacrificing their lives to fulfill the gospel commission to all the world.

In light of the testimony of Scripture and the urgency of the hour in which we live, why spend time and resources to satisfy pride and self-fulfilling desires? Are we like the disciples of Christ asking "who will be the greatest" when the most stupendous event in history is upon us? Let us repent of our waywardness and seek the Lord with all humility and earnestness lest we be found wanting.

Our Appeal

What, then, shall the church do on the question of women in ministry? This is for our leadership, not for us at ADVENTISTS AFFIRM, to decide. We make no demands, issue no ultimatums. But we do not hesitate to state our beliefs and, in love and concern, to offer counsel. Five years ago in the *Adventist Review* (February 1995), our North American Division president described the church's situation as "untenable," ordaining women as elders but not as pastors. He confessed his difficulty at explaining the reason for this to those who inquired. He offered no theological justification for ordaining women elders, stating only that we had "crossed the theological bridge" when we began to do so. Inexplicably, he asserted that there could be "no turning back."

We ask, If we have embarked on a practice which violates the teaching of Scripture, why should we be reluctant to turn back? In our evangelism, we call people who have conscientiously kept Sunday all their lives to turn back when they see what the Bible actually teaches about the Sabbath, even if it should cost them their jobs, friends, and family. Are we unwilling to turn back when we find what Scripture actually teaches about the role of women in the church? Such change is not without pain and cost, but should these concerns prevent us from bringing our practice into line with the Bible? We see no end to the division and disunity on this issue which rack the church today, short of coming into harmony with the Word of God. Obedience to the Word is our only strength. Shall we be reluctant to take hold of it?

We believe that the church should take a strong, decided stand to obey God, following Him and Him only. We believe that the church should stop ordaining women locally and internationally, whether as elders or pastors, and that it should not place them in leadership roles which Scripture calls on men to fulfill. Only fully consecrated men who are doing God's will and who demonstrate their commitment by their lives should be ordained to the leadership of the church. It is time to trust God in faith and humility. May God help us to see clearly His will for His children and to walk willingly in it.

> "Trust and obey,
> For there's no other way
> To be happy in Jesus,
> But to trust and obey."

Appendices

Appendix A

Answers To Questions
About Women's Ordination
(First published in [ADVENTISTS] AFFIRM, Spring 1987)

Some Fundamental Questions

Why is the issue of the ordination of women as elders or pastors of such crucial importance for the Seventh-day Adventist church at this time?

What is at stake is the authority of the Bible for defining SDA beliefs and practices. The New Testament expresses its teaching on the role of women in the church in theological terms, basing it on interpretation of earlier Bible passages. It is presented as part of God's "law" and as "a command of the Lord" (1 Cor. 14:34, 37). If such a Biblical teaching is regarded as limited to the culture of Paul's time, the same could be said of Biblical teachings regarding creation, Sabbath keeping, clean and unclean meats, footwashing, tithing, etc. The authority of Scripture as a whole would thus be undermined and discredited. The issue is important enough that it is scheduled for consideration and resolution at the 1990 General Conference.

Is the authority of the Bible really such an important issue for Seventh-day Adventists?

What issue is more important to Seventh-day Adventists than the authority of the Bible? Our entire belief structure, our reason for existence and our mission to the world are based on the authority of the Bible.

What does the Bible teach regarding the role of women in the church?

The Bible presents women as full participants with men in the religious and social life of the church. In the fifth year of Jeremiah's prophetic ministry, the priests went to Huldah the prophetess for counsel (2 Kings 22:13-14). Women served as musicians and attendants at the tabernacle and temple (1 Sam. 2:22,

1 Chron. 25:5-6, Ps. 68:24-25). Women prayed aloud and prophesied in the church (1 Cor. 11:5). They labored side by side with Paul and other workers in the gospel (Phil. 4:3). In the closing chapter of Romans, Paul begins his greetings and commendations with women, and he includes several other women subsequently in the chapter (16:1-5, 6, 12, 13, 15). Widows (Acts 9:39) may have been an organized body for service in the New Testament church. But women did not serve as priests in the Old Testament (Ex. 28:1, Num. 3:1-13) nor did they serve in the leadership/teaching role of elder or pastor in the New Testament (1 Tim. 2:11-14; 3:1-7; Titus 1:5-9; 1 Cor. 14:33-36).

What does the New Testament actually say about women in elder-pastor leadership roles?

"I permit no woman to teach or to have authority over men; she is to keep silent" (1 Tim. 2:12). "If anyone aspires to the office of bishop, he desires a noble task. Now a bishop must be above reproach, the husband of one wife, . . . an apt teacher" (1 Tim. 3:1-2). "This is why I left you in Crete, that you might amend what was defective, and appoint elders in every town as I directed you, if any man is blameless, the husband of one wife. . ." (Titus 1:5-6). "As in all the churches of the saints, the women should keep silence in the churches. For they are not permitted to speak, but should be subordinate, as even the law says. . . . If any one thinks that he is a prophet, or spiritual, he should acknowledge that what I am writing to you is a command of the Lord" (1 Cor. 14:33-37). There are more New Testament directives on this subject than there are about tithing or footwashing or the Sabbath. These New Testament passages are examined in this issue.

Was the Biblical exclusion of women from elder-pastor roles a consequence of a prevailing patriarchal, "male-chauvinist" culture and mentality?

No. The culture of the time permitted women to serve as priests. Many religions included women in their priesthood. By contrast, the inspired writers of both the Old Testament and the New Testament maintained the role distinctions as assigned by God to men and women from the beginning.

Why should the Seventh-day Adventist church resist pressure from humanistic-feminist ideologies which are bent on eliminating role distinctions between men and women?

"Role-interchangeability," which eliminates role distinctions, should concern Seventh-day Adventists because we are committed to belief in the creation as it is presented in Scripture. Contrary to Christians who interpret the creation story as a poetic description of the evolutionary process, Adventists accept as factual the account of the six days of creation. Because we accept the *doctrine* of creation, we accept the *order* of creation. But if Adventists accept the humanistic notion that the roles of men and women are completely interchangeable, we will undermine our belief in the doctrine of creation, on which the Sabbath commandment is based. Also, in terms of day-today living, eliminating the clear role distinctions between men and women accelerates the breakdown of the family, leads to confusion of identity among children, and may contribute to acceptance of homosexuality as a legitimate lifestyle.

What has been the experience of churches that have ordained women as priests or pastors?

Some denominations have endured quarrels and divisions over appointing women ministers. For some this has involved forming new churches or even denominations. However, some other denominations feel that their new women ministers have been a real help to them.

So what shall we conclude from the experience of the various denominations? Seventh-day Adventists don't arrive at truth by asking, "Do Baptists get spiritual help from attending church on Sunday?" We don't ask, "Do Pentecostals feel close to God when they talk in tongues?" We don't ask if Catholics find it meaningful to have a Pope and a Virgin Mary.

Seventh-day Adventists ask, "What does the Bible say?" We believe God's *best* blessings fall on people who choose to obey His revealed will.

What is Ellen G. White's relationship to this issue? Was she ever ordained?

Ellen White was never ordained. After more than 25 years of her prophetic ministry, the church voted her the credentials of an ordained minister, but she indicated in 1909 (when she was in her eighties) that she had never been ordained (Arthur L. White, *Spectrum*, 4/2 [Spring, 1972]: 8). Nor did she ever exercise the special functions of an ordained minister, such as performing marriages, baptizing, and organizing local churches. As are all church members, she too was ordained of God to work for Him and was given a special work to do. But she was never ordained by human hands.

Didn't Ellen White have a position of authority in the church?

Her authority was in the messages God gave her rather than in any position the church gave her. She specifically rejected the idea of a leadership position in the church. "It is not right for you to suppose that I am striving to be first, striving for leadership. . . . I want it to be understood that I have no ambition to have the name of leader, or any other name that may be given me, except that of a messenger of God. I claim no other name or position" (Letter 320, 1905; Manuscript Release #340). "I am not to appear before the people as holding any other position than that of a messenger with a message" (*Testimonies for the Church*, vol. 8, p. 237).

Did Ellen White urge the church to ordain women?

To the gospel ministry and as elders? No. She urged that certain women who were "willing to consecrate some of their time to the service of the Lord should be appointed to visit the sick, look after the young, and minister to the necessities of the poor. They should be set apart to this work by prayer and laying on of hands"

(*Review and Herald,* July 9, 1895). It was "to this work," a personal work of visitation and mercy, that they were to be set apart. This is not the same as the role of church leadership entrusted to the pastor or elder.

Didn't Mrs. White encourage women to participate in the work of the church?

Yes, she did. Noting a "sphere" in which God had called and equipped women to work (see *Patriarchs and Prophets,* p. 59), she called for greater involvement. She urged women especially to engage in personal work for women and families. A clear example of this may be found in her article, "Women to Be Gospel Workers" (*Testimonies for the Church,* vol. 6, pp. 114-118). Among other things, she says there that women "can do in families a work that men cannot do, a work that reaches the inner life. They can come close to the hearts of those whom men cannot reach. Their labor is needed" (Ibid., pp. 117-118). "Sisters, God calls you to work in the harvest field and to help gather in the sheaves. . . . In the various lines of home missionary work the modest, intelligent woman may use her powers to the very highest account" (*Welfare Ministry,* p. 160).

Does Ellen White warn against seeking a role or "sphere" different from the one we're assigned by God?

Yes. Referring to Eve, she writes: "She was perfectly happy in her Eden home by her husband's side; but like restless modern Eves, she was flattered that there was a higher sphere than that which God had assigned her. But in attempting to climb higher than her original position, she fell far below it. This will most assuredly be the result with the Eves of the present generation if they neglect to cheerfully take up their daily duty in accordance with God's plan. . . .

"A neglect on the part of woman to follow God's plan in her creation, an effort to reach for important positions which He has not qualified her to fill, leaves vacant the position that she could fill to acceptance. In getting out of her sphere, she loses true womanly dignity and nobility" (*Testimonies for the Church,* vol. 3, pp. 483-484).

Because our women haven't been ordained, has our church undervalued their work and treated them unfairly?

Our church has not handled the pay and hiring issues fairly. Mrs. White protested such unfairness in her own time. But her remedy was not to ordain women, but to treat them justly, as we see in the following example: "And if the Lord gives the wife as well as the husband the burden of labor, and if she devotes her time and her strength to visiting from family to family, opening the Scriptures to them, *although the hands of ordination have not been laid upon her,* she is accomplishing a work that is in the line of ministry. Should her labors be counted as nought, and her husband's salary be no more than that of the servant of God whose wife does not give herself to the work, but remains at home to care for her family?" (Manuscript Release #330, emphasis supplied). Again, "This question [appropriate pay for women workers] is not for men to settle. The Lord has settled it. You are to do your duty to the women who labor in the gospel, whose work testifies that they are essential to carrying the truth into families" (*Evangelism,* p. 493).

Ordination of Women and the Old Testament
Were women excluded from the Israelite priesthood because of their frequent ritual impurity caused by menstrual flow?

This idea is widely held, but it lacks Biblical support. No Bible text gives any indication that their monthly seven-day ritual impurity (Lev. 15:19-24) was the basis for women's exclusion. In fact, men became ritually unclean more frequently than women did: not just once a month, but every time they had a natural or unnatural discharge of semen (Lev. 15:1-18). Women could have served at the temple on a rotating basis, like men, according to their ritual status (1 Chron. 24; Luke 1:5,9).

What is more, the Bible tells us that women did serve in a limited role at the tabernacle (Ex. 38:8, 1 Sam. 2:22). If ritual impurity were the factor keeping them from serving as priests, it would also have disqualified them from ministering at the entrance to the tabernacle.

Were women excluded from the priesthood to avoid the dangers of the Canaanite fertility cults and sacred prostitution?

No. Many pagan priestesses lived celibate, devoted lives. The fact that some pagan priestesses served as prostitutes cannot have been the reason God excluded devout Israelite women from serving with honor as priestesses at the sanctuary. The sons of Eli "lay with the women who served at the entrance of the tent of meeting" (1 Sam. 2:22), yet their mutual immorality resulted in abolition of neither the male priesthood nor the ministry of the women who served at the entrance to the sanctuary.

Furthermore, the danger of *male* cult prostitution was equally present in Old Testament times. Scripture condemns it as being equally, if not more, abominable than female prostitution (Deut. 23:18; Rev. 22:15). If the danger of prostitution were the reason for excluding women from the priesthood, men would not have been eligible either.

Why then were women included in prophetic, religious and social ministries in Old Testament times, but excluded from serving as priests?

One reason appears to be that the role of the priest was seen in the Bible as representing the head of the household. During patriarchal times the male head of the household or tribe functioned as the priest, representing his household to God (Gen. 8:20; 22:13; Job 1:5). Later God appointed the tribe of Levi as priests instead of the first-born son or head of each family (Num. 3:6-13). "The Levites shall be mine, for all the first-born are mine" (Num. 3:12-13).

A woman could minister as a prophet, communicating God's will, but a male was appointed to the priestly role because the male was viewed by Bible writers as the "first-born" of the human family (Gen. 2:7, 21-23) to whom God assigned the headship role in the home and in the church.

The New Testament continued this concept, appointing representative males as elders or pastors. The New Testament practice ran contrary to the culture of the time, since most pagan religions had priestesses as well as priests. The New Testament practice was based on the divine revelation in the Old Testament (see 1 Tim. 2:12-13), pointing to a headship role established at creation for man to fulfill at home and in the household of faith.

It was God's plan, of course, that every *individual* should be a "priest" in Old Testament times (Ex. 19:6) as in our own times (1 Pet. 2:9; Rev. 1:6)—but this was as individuals in our individual relationship to God, not as ordained priests representing the community.

Is the creation account of Gen. 1:1-2:4, where man and woman are presented as equals, more trustworthy than the account in Genesis 2:4b-25, where woman is subordinate to man?

Such a view pits the Bible against itself. There is no reason to assume that a contradiction exists between Genesis 1 and 2. The author of Genesis obviously saw the two accounts as complementary, not contradictory, or he would not have put them together.

When one recognizes the different purposes of chapters one and two, the apparent tension resolves. Chapter one portrays man and woman in relation to *God.* Here both are equal, for both are created in the image of God and both are subordinate to God. Chapter two portrays man and woman in relation to *one another,* and reveals a functional subordination of woman to man.

Jacques Doukhan, a professor of Old Testament at the SDA Theological Seminary, Andrews University, has shown in his doctoral dissertation that Genesis 1 and 2 are not contradictory but complementary. The principle of equality in being and subordination in function not only resolves the apparent tension between Genesis 1 and 2 but also explains why women are presented in the Bible as equal to men in personhood and yet subordinate to men in certain roles.

Are "equality in being" and "subordination in function" contradictory terms?

Not necessarily. Such a "contradiction" existed in our Saviour Himself. On the one hand Jesus could say, "I and the Father are one" (Jn. 10:30) and "He who has seen me has seen the Father" (Jn. 14:9), while on the other hand He could say, "I can do nothing on my own authority; . . . I seek not my own will but the will of him who sent me" (Jn. 5:30), and "the Father is greater than I" (Jn. 14:28).

The subordination of woman to man in the Bible is a subordination not of inferiority, but of unity. An equal accepts a subordinate role for the greater unity. In this relationship the head governs out of genuine love and respect and the subordi-

nate responds out of a desire to serve common goals. It is a similar kind of subordination to that which exists in the Godhead between the Father and the Son. In fact,
Paul appeals to this heavenly example to explain the way a husband is the head of his
wife, namely, as God is the head of Christ. "The head of a woman is her husband,
and the head of Christ is God" (1 Cor. 11:3). This is the unique kind of Christian
subordination which makes one person out of two equal persons.

**Wasn't Eve's subordination to Adam in Gen. 3:16 a part of the curse, which
Christ came to take away?**

In the Bible, neither blessings nor curses are arbitrary, but are directly determined by one's relationship to God's law. "Behold, I set before you this day a blessing
and a curse: the blessing, if you obey the commandments of the Lord your God, . .
. and the curse, if you do not obey the commandments of the Lord your God"
(Deut. 11:26-28). The same commands bring a blessing if followed, or a curse if
violated. The curse is the law's application to a rebellious heart. Christ takes away the
rebellion from the heart, so that we may realize the blessing of obedience.

What we often call a curse in Gen. 3:16, "Your desire shall be for your husband, and he shall rule over you," is part of a broader description of the results of
their rebellion on the man and woman's pre-fall functions. For example, God had
commanded them to "be fruitful and multiply." Now, after sin, Eve's part in that
function would be by pain and labor (Gen. 3:16). Likewise Adam had been placed
in the garden "to till it and keep it" (Gen. 2:15). But now, after sin, his efforts
would be laborious, the ground would bear thistles, and he would survive by "the
sweat of [his] face" (Gen. 3:17-19). The man and woman are not given new functions here, but sin's effect on their established functions is spelled out. In this
setting the "rule over" statement appears. What had been a natural and happy
leadership before the fall would now have to be asserted in conflict, as a result of
the spirit of rebellion and the desire for supremacy that sin has brought into the
human heart.

When Jesus quells the rebellion in the heart, He does not free woman from
the travail of giving birth nor man from the laboriousness of his toil. Indeed, they
may each find blessing there. Neither does Jesus change the structure of the man-
woman relationship. But He changes the quality of that relationship to reflect His
submission and self-sacrificing love. Under His lordship, and within this structure, He has provided for us to live happily together until He makes "all things
new," and "there shall be no more curse" (Rev. 21:5; 22:3).

**What evidence is there for a "structure" in the relationship of the man and
woman before the fall?**

These are some indications of God's design for man's leadership role in their
relationship: 1) Genesis 2 tells us that God made the woman *of* the man, to be a
helper fit *for* the man, and that God brought her *to* the man. This implies no
inferiority, but it does establish the structure of their relationship. 2) The warnings

about the tree of knowledge are given to the man before the creation of the woman (Gen. 2:15-17). Evidently he was responsible to convey to her the knowledge of God's will in this matter. 3) Adam names the woman (Gen. 2:23), an act indicating an authority over her.

Did Adam "rule over" Eve before the fall?

Not in the same way as after. God appointed him head, but before sin there was no disharmony that would have caused conflict. Though Adam was king in Eden, Eve was not his slave but his queen. He held her in the highest regard, and it was spontaneous and natural for her to be in harmony with him and with the will of God as revealed through him. She never conceived of this structure as involving subjection or self-denial, for there was no rebellious "self" to deny. Nor did she think of Adam as "ruling over" her, but as one through whom God had revealed to her her greatest privilege and pleasure, to glorify God through and with her husband, to whom she had been given as a helper. Law and authority remain virtually unrecognized when there is perfect and natural harmony of wills.

But with the entry of sin, lawlessness and a spirit of rebellion became a part of man's nature, and all of this changed. Before the fall the authority structure had been natural and even unrecognized. The woman's will was in harmony with the man's and both were fully under the lordship of the Creator. So it had been with the angels: "When Satan rebelled against the law of Jehovah, the thought that there was a law came to the angels almost as an awakening to something unthought of. In their ministry the angels are not as servants, but as sons. There is perfect unity between them and their Creator. Obedience is to them no drudgery. Love for God makes their service a joy" (*Thoughts from the Mount of Blessing*, p. 109).

Sin in the heart makes the law of God evident to us, because it is no longer natural for us to obey that law. Submission to God-ordained authority was a non-issue to woman prior to the fall and the consequent rebellion it created in her heart. But after the fall she became conscious of the law and its necessary new application to her in a sinful condition. "The law of God existed before the creation of man or else Adam could not have sinned. After the transgression of Adam the principles of the law were not changed, but were definitely arranged and expressed to meet man in his fallen condition" (*Selected Messages*, book 1, p. 230).

Does Mrs. White say that Eve was Adam's equal before the fall and that only after the fall was Adam to be her ruler?

Ellen White says both that Eve was Adam's equal before sin entered and that woman is man's equal today. But in her writings this equality doesn't give man and woman identical roles and neither does it deny the Biblical concept that in some respects woman is to be in subjection to man. *Testimonies for the Church*, vol. 3, p. 484, says that "when God created Eve, He designed that she should possess neither inferiority nor superiority to the man, but that in all things she should be his equal. . . . But after Eve's sin, as she was first in the transgression, the Lord told her that Adam should rule over her. She was to be in subjection to her husband, and this was a part of the curse."

This subjection is evidently *still* a part of God's plan. Ellen White also said, "We women must remember that God has placed us subject to the husband. . . . We must yield to the head" (Letter 5, 1861). "The husband is the head of the family, as Christ is the head of the church; and any course which the wife may pursue to lessen his influence and lead him to come down from that dignified, responsible position is displeasing to God" (*Testimonies for the Church*, vol. 1, p. 307). Indeed, when a woman honors that requirement of God, she helps her husband to develop into the responsible, loving man that God calls him to be.

But along with the on-going subjection there remains also something of the original equality. *The Adventist Home*, p. 231, says, "Woman should [today, now] fill the position which God originally designed for her, as her husband's equal."

However, never, at creation or at the present time, has equality implied that men and women have identical God-given roles. Two sentences after the Ellen White statement just quoted occurs this sentence: "We may safely say that the distinctive duties of woman are more sacred, more holy, than those of man."

In the Garden of Eden man and woman were assigned different duties to perform, but they also enjoyed perfect harmony. The man led kindly and the woman cooperated joyfully. Sin, however, made selfishness grow in human hearts, just as it made weeds grow in the ground. Eve's independence of her husband in the first sin would show up repeatedly as woman would seek repeatedly to circumvent man's leadership. Adam's original disregard for God's law would show up repeatedly as man attempted to dominate woman with unloving authoritarianism. Role distinctions would be marred by sin—and the gospel, when it came, would not obliterate these distinctions. Instead, the gospel would reinfuse the distinctive roles of "equal" men and women with the love and joyfulness which God had given them in Eden.

What are the implications of this for the issue of ordination of women to the headship positions in the church?

In our current situation, we must see what it means to follow the eternal principle of harmony with God-ordained authority. What is the leadership structure that God has given to the church in His Word? The apostle Paul outlines that structure in light of the creation and fall narratives of Genesis (1 Cor. 11:7-12, 14:34; 1 Tim. 2:12-14). He indicates that God has established the leadership of certain qualified men in the church (1 Tim. 3:1-7; Titus 1:5-9). The whole Great Controversy began with Lucifer over the issue of harmony with God-ordained authority. The church only perpetuates the sin problem when it tries to establish authority contrary to God's directions, no matter how desirable that may seem. In the very context of authority (here, appointing a king), Ellen White says, "That which the heart desires contrary to the will of God will in the end be found a curse rather than a blessing" (*Patriarchs and Prophets*, p. 606). On the other hand, when we set the heart willingly to obey God, even what seemed a curse to us will be seen to be a blessing. "The Lord your God turned the curse into a blessing for you, because the Lord your God loves you" (Deut. 23:5).

Can Joel 2:28, "Your sons and your daughters shall prophesy," settle the issue for us of men and women filling the same spiritual roles?

The New Testament, like the Old (Joel 2:28), provided for women to serve as prophets and to have visions and dreams. But neither the Old Testament nor the New permitted women to serve as ordained religious leaders of the congregation.

Ordination of Women and the New Testament

Jesus treated women in a revolutionary way—affirming their personhood, appreciating their intellectual and spiritual capacities, accepting some of them into His inner circle of traveling companions, and honoring them with the first announcement of His resurrection. Is this evidence that He intended to open the way for women to serve as pastors and elders?

Jesus did indeed treat women as persons of equal value to men. He admitted them into His fellowship. He took time to teach them the truths of the Kingdom of God. A woman was first with the story of the resurrection, and at least one woman (Mary) received the Holy Spirit with the others at Pentecost. Yet the fact remains that Christ called no woman to be part of the twelve apostles. Why would Jesus not have commissioned women to preach or teach publicly, if this had been His intention? Whatever the cultural situation may have been in Palestine (we have very little *contemporary* evidence of how women were treated there), such a move would have been quite acceptable in the larger harvest field, since the priestly role of women was readily accepted in the Gentile world, where the gospel was to be preached.

Jesus never dealt with the issue of a leadership role for women. But through the Holy Spirit He clarified that issue in the writings of the apostles. Those messages are as much the voice of Jesus as if He had spoken them while on earth. Jesus' own choice of twelve male apostles was consistent with the Old Testament headship role man was called to fulfill at home and in the community of faith. The same role structure was respected in the life and order of the apostolic church.

Some say that Paul, in contrast to Jesus, was an anti-feminist who viewed women as inferior and for this reason excluded them from leadership roles within the church.

Is this the same Paul who proclaimed, "There is neither male nor female; for you are all one in Christ Jesus" (Gal. 3:28)? In this well-known statement Paul affirmed the spiritual oneness in Christ of both men and women. In other places he commended a significant number of women for working intensively with him in the missionary outreach of the church. In fact, he may have worked more actively with women than Jesus did. A number of women were "fellow-workers" with Paul in his missionary outreach (Rom. 16:1-3, 6, 12, 13, 15; Phil. 4:2-3).

Ordination of Women and Paul

Does Paul's commendation of certain women as "fellow workers" (Rom. 16:3) and as those who have "worked hard" (Rom. 16:12; Phil 4:3) in gospel service imply that certain women served as congregational leaders in the apostolic church?

No. The same Paul who praised women for their outstanding contribution to the mission of the church also instructed women not "to teach" (1 Tim. 2:12) or "to speak" (1 Cor. 14:34) as representative leaders of the church. Thus, his insistence on different roles for men and women at home and in the church must be seen as an indication not of Paul's chauvinism but rather of his respect for the role distinctions established by God at creation.

His practice accorded with the rest of the apostolic church. In the New Testament church there were no women apostles, no women public evangelists, elders or pastors. No women engaged in public "teaching." No woman served as head or leader of a congregation. The reason is not that the culture was chauvinistic, but rather that the church faithfully respected the role distinctions assigned by God to men and women at creation.

Does Galatians 3:28 represent the great breakthrough in which Paul proclaimed the abolition of all differences between men and women, opening the way for women to be ordained as pastors or elders?

No, for this same Paul vigorously upheld role distinctions for men and women (1 Cor. 11:3-15; Eph. 5:22).

If Galatians 3:28 does not abolish all role distinctions among Christians, then what does this passage say?

The text asserts the basic truth that in Christ every person, Jew or Greek, slave or free, male or female, enjoys the status of being a son or daughter of God. This truth is made clear in the following verse which says, "If you are Christ's, then you are Abraham's offspring, heirs according to promise" (v. 29). This means that to be "one in Christ" is to share equally in the inheritance of eternal life.

The real issue in Galatians 3:28 is religious. The great concern of Jews and Christians of the first century was religious status, that is, the status of men and women before God.

By contrast, the primary concern of many people today, including many Christians, is social status, often focusing on the social equality of men and women. The prevailing perception among such people today is that we can only bring about true equality by abolishing all role distinctions between men and women, thus realizing what sociologists call "role interchangeability." Though popular, this view is a distortion, a perversion, of God's creation order. In the Bible equality does not mean role interchangeability. Christianity does not abolish the headship of the husband or the subordination of the wife; rather, it redefines these roles in terms of sacrificial love, servanthood and mutual respect.

Some say that Galatians 3:28 represents Paul's most mature thought while texts such as 1 Timothy 2:12-15 and 1 Corinthians 14:33-36 reflect his imma-ture thinking, still affected by his rabbinic training. Is this true?

To claim that Paul in his epistles was sometimes immature or inconsistent because of the influence of his rabbinic training undermines the authority of the Scriptures and assumes that an intelligent man like Paul was incoherent at times.

It makes more sense to believe that Paul saw no tension between oneness in Christ (Gal. 3:28) and the functional subordination of women in the church (1 Tim. 2:12-15; 1 Cor. 11:2-16; 14:33-35). This tension is not in Paul nor in the Bible, but in the minds of modern critics.

Since the message of Galatians 3:28 eventually led to the abolition of slave-free differences, should the same truth lead to the elimination of man-woman differences, opening the way for women to be ordained?

Three important observations discredit this popular argument. First, Paul com-pares the relationships among Jews and Greeks, slaves and free, and men and women in only one common area: the status distinction these created in one's relationship to God. He declares that everyone stands on a level before the cross.

Second, in other areas Paul recognized that the distinctions among the three relationships still existed. Being one in Christ did not change a Jew into a Gentile, a slave into a freeman, or a man into a woman; rather, it changed the way each of these related to the other.

Third, there is an important difference between Paul's view of the man-woman relationship and his view of the slave-freeman relationship. While Paul defends the subordination involved in the man-woman relationship by appealing to the order in which man and woman were created, he never teaches that slavery is a divine institution, a part of God's order of creation and should be perpetuated. On the contrary, he encourages the slave when offered the opportunity of emancipation to take advantage of it (1 Cor. 7:21), and he classifies slave-kidnapers among the "unholy and profane" (1 Tim. 1:9-10). While slavery is a temporary institution resulting from the fall, male-female differences are unchangeable biological dis-tinctions originating from creation.

If Paul allowed slavery, which we today condemn, can we say on the basis of "progressive revelation" that if he were alive today God would inspire him to change his mind on both the slavery issue and on women's ordination?

Paul did not endorse slavery, as we have shown above. On the contrary, the principles he laid down for modifying slavery led to the abolition of slavery in Christian countries.

God cannot contradict Himself. What He reveals is always truth; hence, what He reveals at one time is always in harmony with what He reveals at another time. Some people go so far as to say that under "progressive revelation" gay men can now be ordained as ministers. Such a conclusion cannot be justified, however, because the Bible clearly condemns homosexuality. Some say that under "progressive revelation" women can now be ordained as elders and ministers. But this conclusion also is unsound, for the Bible forbids their filling those roles. Revelation may be progressive but it is never contradictory.

Is it unfair or even immoral not to ordain women to the gospel ministry or eldership if they are qualified in every other respect than gender? Galatians 3:28 claims that in Christ "there is neither male nor female."

Some have tried to portray this as an issue of basic fairness or morality. But there is no Biblical command enjoining ordination for women, so a failure to ordain is not a violation of a Biblical injunction. On the contrary, there is a command in the New Testament that the church should not appoint women to the headship role of pastor/teacher, a role upon which ordination is normally conferred. Should we violate that injunction?

The principle set forth in Galatians 3:28 is that all Christians are of equal value in the eyes of Christ. To say that this puts us under moral obligation to ordain women is to fail to see the difference between worth and function. For all to have equal worth is not the same as all having identical function. The doctrine of spiritual gifts argues eloquently against equality of function.

Paul expresses it this way: "If the ear should say, 'Because I am not an eye, I do not belong to the body,' that would not make it any less a part of the body. If the whole body were an eye, where would be the hearing? . . . But as it is, God arranged the organs in the body, each one of them, as he chose" (1 Cor. 12:16-18). "But God has so composed the body, . . . that the members may have the same care for one another. . . . Now you are the body of Christ and individually members of it. And God has appointed in the church first apostles, second prophets, third teachers . . ." (1 Cor. 12:24-28). Not all have the same function, but all are equally needed and important to the body. This is how God has arranged it. Immoral? Unfair? No—His design. And His appointment of different ones to exercise the gifts does not override the instructions in His Word regarding their exercise.

Does Ellen White support the view that role distinctions between husband and wife have been done away in Christ?

No. On the contrary she writes: "The husband is the head of the family, as Christ is the head of the church; and any course which the wife may pursue to lessen his influence and lead him to come down from that dignified, responsible position is displeasing to God. It is the duty of the wife to yield her wishes and will to her husband. Both should be yielding, but the word of God gives preference to the judgment of the husband. And it will not detract from the dignity of the wife to yield to him whom she has chosen to be her counselor, adviser, and protector. The husband should maintain his position in his family with all meekness, yet with decision" (*Testimonies for the Church*, vol. 1, pp. 307-308).

Pauline Passages About the Role of Women

What is the significance of Paul's discussion about head covering in 1 Corinthians 11:2-16 for the discussion of the role of women in the church?

In spite of certain difficulties of interpretation, 1 Corinthians 11:2-16 provides one of the clearest statements on the fundamental significance of the role differences which must exist between men and women at home and in the church. The lengthy discussion about head coverings can mislead a person today into thinking that Paul majored in minors. In fact, the discussion on head coverings is only secondary to the fundamental principle Paul asserts about the headship of man ("the head of the woman is man," v. 3, NIV) and of the subordination of woman (vv. 5-10), which must be respected at home and in the church.

The principle was being challenged by emancipated Corinthian women who interpreted the freedom of the gospel as freedom from wearing a sign of submission to their husbands (head covering), especially at times of prayer and sharing in the church service. To counteract this trend, which would have resulted in the violation of role distinctions which God Himself had created, Paul emphasizes at length the importance of respecting the custom of head covering as a way of honoring the creation order.

What does Paul's instruction in 1 Corinthians 11:2-16 on head coverings mean for us today?

Paul urges respect for the head-covering custom because in his time it fittingly expressed sexual differentiation and role distinction. Applied to our culture, the principle means that if certain styles of hair and clothing are distinctively male or female, their gender association must be respected in order to maintain the clear distinction between the sexes enjoined in Scripture. This principle is particularly relevant today, when some promote the blurring of sexual differences (unisex), while others are adopting the dress and sometimes the behavior of the opposite sex.

Why does Paul say, "I permit no woman to teach or to have authority over men" in the church (1 Timothy 2:12)? Is it because women in his day were uneducated?

That is an assumption without support in the Bible. If lack of education had been the basis of Paul's prohibition, he would have prohibited both men and women to teach in the church if they were uneducated. But women as well as men could have been trained to become good teachers. Deaconesses and other female workers in apostolic teams must have received some training.

In fact, the situation in Ephesus may have been quite different from what is often supposed. Some of the women may have been more educated than many men, and so they may have felt justified to act as teacher-leaders of the congregation. Priscilla was well enough educated in the Christian faith to instruct an intellectual like Apollos, when he went to Ephesus (Acts 18:26). All of this suggests that the reason for Paul's instruction was not that women were uneducated.

Does 1 Timothy 2:12 really forbid all kinds of teaching and speaking by women in the church? If the Adventist church took Paul's statement literally, "I permit no woman to teach. . . she is to keep silent," following it would cripple us, since we use the talents of women so heavily in Sabbath School and in other teaching and speaking ministries.

The Bible is clear that in Paul's ministry women were not expected to be totally silent. They prayed, prophesied and exercised an appropriate teaching ministry (1 Cor. 11:5; Acts 18:26; Phil. 4:3; Rom. 16:12; Titus 2:3-4) which Paul encouraged. The nature of the teaching forbidden to women in 1 Timothy 2:12 is the authoritative teaching restricted to the pastor, the elder-overseer of the congregation. This conclusion is supported by the meaning of the parallelism ("or to have authority over men," v. 12) and by the use of the verb "to teach" and of the noun "teaching" in Paul's writings, especially in his letters to Timothy.

Paul's letters to Timothy present the teaching ministry as a governing function performed by Paul himself, by Timothy, or by other appointed elder-overseers of the congregation (1 Tim. 2:7; 3:2; 5:17; 2 Tim. 1:11; 2:2). Paul charges Timothy to "command and teach" (1 Tim. 4:11), "take heed to yourself and to your teaching" (4:16), "teach and urge these duties" (6:2), "preach the word. . . in teaching" (2 Tim. 4:2).

In light of the restrictive use of the words "to teach" and "teaching" in these letters, it is reasonable to conclude that the teaching forbidden to women is the authoritative teaching done by elder-overseers.

Why does Paul forbid women to teach as leaders of the congregation?

Because the women were not to occupy the headship role of authority over men. This role is inappropriate for women, not because they are any less intelligent or dedicated than men, but because of the order for men and women established by God at creation (1 Tim. 2:13; 1 Cor. 11:8).

Does Paul or any other New Testament writer ever portray women as teaching?

Yes. Paul uses the Greek word *kalodidaskalos*, "teacher of good things," to refer to what the aged women were to be in the instruction they gave to younger women (Titus 2:3, 4). On the other hand, the Greek verb used for the authoritative teaching role that Paul assigns to the elders is *didasko*, "to teach." The only place in the New Testament where *didasko* is an action of a woman is in Revelation 2:20, where the church at Thyatira is reprimanded because "you tolerate the woman Jezebel, who . . . is teaching."

Is it true that Paul's argument about the priority of Adam's creation ("For Adam was formed first, then Eve," 1 Tim. 2:13) is faulty because it is based on the wrong creation account (Genesis 2 instead of Genesis 1) and because it attaches significance to the fact that man was created before woman?

Accusing Paul of being "faulty" can have serious consequences. If we say that Paul made a mistake in interpreting the meaning of Genesis in respect to the role relations between men and women, how can we know he was not also in error in interpreting the meaning of the Second Advent, or the relationship between faith and works in the process of salvation?

Paul clearly stated the basis of his authority to those who challenged it: "If any one thinks that he is a prophet, or spiritual, he should acknowledge that what I am writing to you is a command of the Lord" (1 Cor. 14:37-38). Strikingly, Paul made this very claim in the context of his teaching about the role of women in the church. It behooves us to accept his interpretation.

Why does Paul appeal to Adam's being created before Eve to justify his injunction that women should not be permitted "to teach or to have authority over men" (1 Timothy 2:12)? Is it arbitrary to assign leadership on the basis of priority of creation?

Paul does not tell us why he reasons in this line. Often Scripture does not feel obligated to justify itself. But it seems likely that Paul saw in the priority of Adam's creation the symbol of the leadership role God intended man to fulfill at home and in the church. From a logical standpoint, it seems arbitrary to assign leadership on the basis of priority of creation. From a Biblical standpoint, however, the arbitrariness disappears because the priority of creation is not an accident but a divine design, intended to typify the leadership and headship role man was created to fulfill. Further, the significance attached to the priority of Adam's formation is reflected in the meaning which Scripture attaches to the "first born," a title used even with reference to Christ ("the first-born of all creation," Col. 1:15).

The sanctification of the seventh day provides another example. From a logical standpoint it seems arbitrary that God should choose to bless and sanctify the seventh day instead of the first day, since all days consist alike of 24 hours. From a Biblical standpoint, however, it is not arbitrary that God should choose the seventh day as a symbol of creation and as a type of re-creation and sanctification (Gen. 2:2-3; Ex. 31:13, 17; Ezek. 20:20).

Is it true that if Paul's argument about the priority of Adam's creation is valid, then the animals should rule mankind because animals were made before Adam was?

Of course not. Proponents of this argument fail to note that the Bible attaches no significance to the prior creation of the animals. Animals were created before mankind, but man does not derive from animals. On the other hand, Paul clearly associates the priority of Adam's formation with Eve's derivation out of man (1 Cor. 11:8-9).

It is amazing how we will argue even with Bible writers when they tell us something we don't want to hear.

What kind of speaking does Paul prohibit to women in 1 Corinthians 14:34 when he writes, "The women should keep silence in the churches. For they are not permitted to speak, but should be subordinate, as even the law says"?

Paul is not here prohibiting all kinds of speaking by women in church, since a few chapters earlier he speaks kindly of "any woman who prays or prophesies," provided only that she dresses modestly (1 Cor. 11:5). The key phrase that qualifies the kind of women's speaking Paul had in mind is, "but should be subordinate" (v. 34). This phrase suggests that the speech denied to women was speech that was seen as inappropriate to them as women or wives. Such speech may have included speaking up in the church as authoritative teachers of the congregation, or as critics of the prophets, elders or even their own husbands. It may also have included any form of questioning viewed as challenging church leadership. In other words, it probably included all forms of women's speech that reflected lack of subordination to their husbands and/or to the church leaders.

Does the Bible clearly teach that a church elder should be a man and not a woman?

Yes. In the lists of qualifications for an elder in 1 Timothy 3:1-7 and Titus 1:5-9, specific reference is made, among other things, to the fact that an elder must be a husband (Greek *aner*, man or husband) of one wife. The elder, then, is to be a married man loyal to his wife. Whether we like it or not, the specifications require males.

The very structure of the passage in 1 Timothy supports this conclusion. The qualifications for the office of elder (3:1-7) include being "an apt teacher." They follow immediately after the prohibition of women as teacher-elders (2:11-15). This placement of the qualifications for eldership (including fitness for teaching) immediately after the prohibition respecting women reveals explicitly that women should not be elders. Making them elders would cast them in a type of teaching role that Scripture specifically prohibits to them.

Does the New Testament distinguish between the office of elder and that of pastor?

No. The term "pastor" (Greek *poimen*) is used only once in the New Testament (Eph. 4:11) and it refers to leaders of the congregation better known elsewhere as elders, overseers or simply as leaders. Such leaders, however, were clearly seen as "pastor-shepherds," as indicated by the use of such picturesque expressions as to "shepherd the flock" in describing the work of elders (1 Pet. 5:1-2; Acts 20:17, 28; John 21:16).

In view of the fact that the term "pastor" is seen in the New Testament as descriptive of the shepherding function of elders, the present policy of the Seventh-day Adventist church to allow for the ordination of women as local elders but not as pastors is based on an artificial distinction between the two offices, a distinction which does not exist in the New Testament. Even the church's ordination practice underscores the Biblical unity of the two offices: we often read the same Bible passages for both ordinations.

Why not ordain women as local elders? Doing so wouldn't mean we would ordain women later as pastors, would it?

We have no right to approve a practice which Scripture forbids in principle. Further, the ordination of women as elders will be used as a lever to pressure the church into ordination of female pastors. Though many people now claim that the two issues are unrelated, they exhibit a strong sense of urgency to ordain women elders in as many churches as possible, before the General Conference Session in 1990. If widespread, the practice will be a power base from which to point out that Biblically there is no difference. Then the argument will be, Since we are already ordaining women as elders, how can we justify denying them ordination as pastors? Fidelity to God's Word is always best for God's church. It is our strength. Compromise on God's Word brings confusion and weakness.

But most of the people I know (many of them anyway) are in favor of ordaining women as elders or even pastors. Shouldn't this count for something?

Many, many Adventists as well as a large number of other Protestants oppose women's ordination. But popular opinion does not define Scriptural truth. Ellen White, in harmony with historic Protestantism, reminds us that "the Bible is its own expositor. Scripture is to be compared with Scripture" (*Education,* p. 190). Opinion polls, culture, and sociology may be interesting, but they must not be allowed to reinterpret the meaning of the Bible.

A Word of Counsel to Ponder

"God will have a people upon the earth to maintain the Bible, *and the Bible only,* as the standard of all doctrines and the basis of *all reforms.* The opinions of learned men, the deductions of science, the creeds or decisions of ecclesiastical councils, as numerous and discordant as are the churches which they represent, *the voice of the majority—not one nor all of these* should be regarded as evidence for or against any point of religious faith. Before accepting any doctrine or precept, we should demand a plain *'Thus saith the Lord'* in its support" (*The Great Controversy,* p. 595, emphasis supplied).

Appendix B

An Appeal to the World Field
Regarding the Ministry of Women
in the Church
(First Published in ADVENTISTS AFFIRM, Autumn 1989)

The editorial board of ADVENTISTS AFFIRM has prepared this document with the contributions and counsel of other Adventist scholars and church leaders who share the same concern over the implications of the current women's ordination movement for the authority of Scripture and the integrity of the Seventh-day Adventist message and mission. As individual churches are asked to make decisions on this issue, and as the 1990 General Conference approaches, we urge our members and leaders to consider carefully the steps they will take.

Concerns

1. We are deeply concerned over the **confusion and divisiveness** created in our churches by the effort to ordain women as local elders and eventually as pastors. Many Adventists from various parts of the world have expressed their agony in seeing their congregations pressured to ordain women as local elders.

2. We are deeply concerned by the **erosion of confidence in leadership** to which the effort for women's ordination contributes. Many earnest Adventists are beginning to question whether the church will follow Biblical principles. Independent ministries have arisen as a reaction to the perceived trend of cultural conformity within the church. This is one cause of the **weakening of the financial commitment to the church** on the part of an increasing number of Adventists, many of whom see in the women's ordination movement another indication of compromise with the world. The church gets strong pressure from all sides; adherence to Bible principle is our only safe course.

3. We are deeply concerned that the Commission on the Role of Women, which met in July of 1989, did not base its recommendations on **Biblical**

instruction regarding leadership and headship. It appealed instead to such social factors as "widespread lack of support . . . risk of disunity, dissension, and diversion from the mission of the church."

4. We are deeply concerned over the **contradiction apparent in the 1989 Annual Council's decision** not to ordain women to the gospel ministry and yet to authorize them to "perform essentially the ministerial functions of an ordained minister." Advocates of ordination complain that the action makes gender the only factor for excluding women from serving as full-fledged pastors. Others find the decision unacceptable because it enables women to function in the headship role of a pastor. Further, letting people (male or female) perform the functions of an ordained minister without being ordained downgrades ministerial ordination, making it appear superfluous.

5. We are deeply concerned over **claims that the Bible writers were heavily influenced by their culture** ("culturally conditioned"), leading them to exclude women from the office of elder or pastor. Such reasoning tends to limit the authority and application of Scripture to cultures of long ago, instead of allowing the Bible to guide all cultures in all places with full authority. The same reasoning is used by other Christians to negate the Bible teachings regarding Sabbath keeping, adornment, and footwashing, and could bring into question all the other distinctive beliefs of the Seventh-day Adventist church.

6. We are deeply concerned over the **effect on the Adventist witness to the world** of the unbiblical ordination of women. How can the Adventist church effectively witness to the many evangelical Christians whose churches have taken a clear Biblical stand on the role distinctions between men and women? Shall we tell our evangelical friends that what the Bible teaches on this subject is less authoritative than what it teaches about the Sabbath, even though Scripture presents both of them as part of God's order of creation?

7. We are deeply concerned over increasing promotion of **feminist interpretations which distort what the Bible says** about the sacrificial headship role of a caring husband and the willing helper role of an intelligent, loving wife, labeling such Scriptures "patriarchal" and "chauvinistic." Such interpretations tend to destroy the Bible's authority and undermine the Creator's ideal for stable, nurturing homes. We believe this is one factor that has contributed to the unraveling of marriages. In some Adventist churches, broken marriages outnumber those which have not experienced divorce.

8. We are deeply concerned over what we consider the **misinterpretation of the Jerusalem council's decision** regarding circumcision (Acts 15) as a basis for having different ordination practices in different parts of the world. The Jerusalem council faced a situation quite different from ours. The issue before them was whether Gentiles could be saved without circumcision. The leaders came to "one accord" (Acts 15:25) as the Holy Spirit guided them, not in explaining away Scripture as influenced by culture, but rather in understanding what Scripture taught

regarding the admission of the Gentiles into the church. The four prerequisites for the admission of the Gentiles were in fact based on the teaching of Moses (Lev 17-18), to whom church leaders appealed as their final authority: "For from early generations Moses has had in every city those who preach him, for he is read every sabbath in the synagogue" (Acts 15:21).

9. We are deeply concerned over the **appeal to civil laws** to justify the ordination of women as pastors. The claim that the Adventist church in North America must ordain women as pastors because "our [American] civil laws prohibit us from making gender differences in the various professions, including ministry" is misleading in two respects: (1) America respects the right of churches to maintain theologically-based role distinctions in ecclesiastical matters; (2) If the laws of men conflict with the Word of God, "we must obey God rather than men" (Acts 5:29). When Sunday laws are passed, shall we not see the appeal to civil law pressed upon us again?

10. We are deeply concerned over efforts to make the ordination of women a **"human rights issue."** It is a Biblical issue.

11. We are deeply concerned over **misinformation regarding support for women's ordination** in the North American Adventist church. Despite widespread publicity promoting women elders, for instance, recent figures show that over 80% of North American Adventist churches have not yet elected a woman elder. Surveys claiming to show support for ordaining women have not, we believe, reflected the feelings of the rank and file. In any event, *our theology and practice are not determined by survey but by Scripture.*

Affirmations

1. We affirm that **men and women are equal before God.** Both were created in the image of God (Gen 1:27), and both have been redeemed by Jesus Christ (Gal 3:28).

2. We affirm that Scripture teaches **difference in function** while maintaining equality of being. Man is called to exercise a caring, sacrificial headship in home and church, patterned after the headship of Christ (Eph 5:21, 25; 1 Cor 11:3). Woman is called willingly to accept and cooperate with the caring headship of man, not as a cultural custom, but as a divinely ordained principle ("as to the Lord" Eph 5:22; see 1 Cor 11:3; 1 Tim 2:12-13). God ordained these distinctions as part of the created order; they should be respected, not only in the home, but in the church as well.

3. We affirm that **1 Timothy 2:12-3:7 is authoritative today,** and cannot be confined to ancient Ephesus. "I permit no woman to teach or to have authority over men. . . . Now a bishop must be above reproach, the husband of one wife." Paul supports his teaching with an appeal, not to culture, but to Scripture, and specifically to creation: "For Adam was formed first, then Eve; and Adam was not deceived, but the woman was deceived and became a transgressor." To restrict

Paul's argument to the past or to limited situations today would make void his appeal to Scripture and deny his teaching authority.

4. We affirm that **role distinctions were assigned by God at creation before the fall** (Gen 2:18-23), and **remain as a part of redemption after the cross**. "For Adam was formed first, then Eve" (1 Tim 2:13); "the head of every man is Christ, the head of a woman is her husband, and the head of Christ is God" (1 Cor 11:3). The fall distorted the functional relationships between men and women, in both home and church. In place of a caring, sacrificial leadership, men may try either to dominate or to escape responsibility. In place of a noble cooperation, women may try to usurp man's leadership or adopt a servile submission. In so doing, both lose the blessings God intended for them.

5. We affirm that **redemption in Christ removes the distortions** of the appropriate functional relationships which resulted from the fall, and elevates the proper functional relationships:

—In the home, husbands should overcome their desires to dominate or be passive, learning instead to provide a caring, sacrificial leadership for their wives and children, seeking to encourage and enable them in every good thing. Similarly, wives should forsake any desire to resist their husbands' appropriate authority, learning instead to willingly and joyfully cooperate with their husbands' caring leadership, thus helping them to develop into the men God has called them to be.

—In the church, redemption gives to men and women an equal share in the blessings of salvation and equal grace to serve in accordance with their own God-ordained roles.

6. We affirm that both the **Old and New Testaments amply support the active participation of women** in the private and public religious life of God's people. In the Old Testament women participated in the study and teaching of the law (Neh 8:2; Prov 1:8; Deut 13:6-11), in offering prayers and vows to God (1 Sam 1:10; Num 30:9; Gen 25:22; 30:6, 22; 2 Kings 4:9-10, 20-37), in ministering "at the entrance to the tent of meeting" (1 Sam 2:22), in singing at the worship of the temple service (Ezra 2:65), and in engaging in the prophetic ministry of exhortation and guidance (2 Kings 22:14-20; 2 Chron 34:22-28). In the New Testament we find women fulfilling a vital role serving Jesus and the early church. They supported Jesus with their means (Luke 8:2-3), performed charitable social work (Acts 9:36), and distinguished themselves in fulfilling the mission of the church (Acts 16:14-15; 21:8-9; Rom 16:1-4, 12). Likewise, for more than 100 years the **Adventist church has incorporated women** into its ministry as Bible Instructors, who have helped to win thousands of people and been an important part of the pastoral team. Though it needs to do more, the church has utilized women's talents in this and many other vital ways. Thus we believe that women have appropriate functions in the work of God and the church.

7. We affirm that the **Bible precludes ordaining women** as priests in the Old Testament and as apostles/elders/pastors in the New Testament, because of **Scriptural and theological** rather than social and cultural reasons. The New Testament

explicitly appeals to the order and method of creation of Adam and Eve to explain why women should not exercise a headship teaching function within the church. See 1 Tim 2:13; 1 Cor 11:8. In these texts the order and manner of Adam and Eve's creation reveal God's design for man to function as the spiritual head of the home and church. (For more information, see the first issue of AFFIRM [Appendix A in this volume].)

8. We affirm that there exists a **distinct correlation between the headship role of a father in the home and that of an elder-pastor in the church.** "A bishop . . . must manage his own household well" (1 Tim 3:2-5). Ellen White upholds this correlation: "As the priest in the home, and as the ambassador of Christ in the church, he [the minister] should exemplify the character of Christ. . . . He who fails to be a faithful, discerning shepherd in the home, will surely fail of being a faithful shepherd to the flock of God in the church" (*Reflecting Christ*, p. 179). "The family of the one suggested for [the elder's] office should be considered. . . . If he has no tact, wisdom, or power of godliness at home in managing his own family, it is safe to conclude that the same defects will be carried into the church" (*Testimonies for the Church*, vol. 5, p. 618).

9. We affirm that there exists a **correlation between the role of an elder/pastor as spiritual father of the family of faith and the role of God as the Father of the human family.** Though God transcends sexual role distinctions, He has chosen to reveal Himself as our Father, as Jesus attested repeatedly. Apparently the reason is that the role of a father in the home and of an elder (older father figure, 1 Tim 5:1) or pastor in the household of faith (1 Cor 4:15) best represent the role that God Himself sustains towards us, His children (Eph 3:14-15). The unique symbolic role which an elder or pastor is called to fulfill, as representative of the heavenly Father, Shepherd, and Head of the church, cannot legitimately be fulfilled by a woman as pastor, because her Scriptural role is that of mother rather than father (1 Tim 5:2). To appoint a woman to serve in the headship role of elder/pastor is an adulteration of the pastor's representation of God. Attempts to support women's ordination by blurring this distinction through such means as prayers addressed to God as "our Father and Mother in heaven" are reminiscent of the paganism the Bible writers so strongly opposed.

10. We affirm that no new teaching or practice should be introduced into the Seventh-day Adventist church unless we have a **clear mandate from Scripture.** On this matter Ellen White's counsel is unmistakable: "The Bible must be our standard for *every doctrine and practice.* . . . It is the word of the living God that is to decide *all controversies*" (*The Ellen G. White 1888 Materials*, pp. 44-45, emphasis supplied). "God will have a people upon the earth to maintain the Bible, and the Bible only, as the standard of all doctrines and the basis of all reforms. The opinions of learned men, the deductions of science, the creeds or decisions of ecclesiastical councils, as numerous and discordant as are the churches which they represent, the voice of the majority—not one nor all of these should be regarded as evidence for or against any point of religious faith. *Before accepting any doctrine or*

precept, we should demand a plain 'Thus saith the Lord' in its support" (*The Great Controversy,* p. 595, emphasis supplied).

Appeal

What shall the church do?

1. The church is called to be faithful to the Word, taking the Bible as our standard for every doctrine and practice. Because we believe it would place women in the authority role that the Bible forbids, we urge the church not to yield to calls to ordain women, even if only in select parts of the world field. We need a church unified in fidelity to Scripture.

2. Because we believe that allowing women pastors to perform essentially all the functions of an ordained minister places them in the role that the Bible disallows, and also diminishes the meaning of ordination, we believe that this is more than a matter of policy, to be dealt with at the lower levels of church administration. It is a step that is filled with theological significance. By placing women in the pastoral authority role, it would direct us contrary to Scripture, even though it stops short of ordaining women to the pastoral ministry. Therefore this action of the 1989 Annual Council needs to be considered by the 1990 General Conference session, though the Annual Council's action did not place it on the agenda. Since the existing provisions of the *Church Manual* make no allowance for women to perform the functions of an ordained minister, we believe it is essential that the world church consider the matter and act on it. Only the world church in General Conference session can modify the *Church Manual.*

3. We have been distressed over the strife and division this issue has brought to the church. We believe that ordination of women to the role of elder has fostered an ongoing problem. Though it is always difficult to retrace our steps, we believe that we must be prepared to do so if our practice is out of harmony with Scripture. We appeal to our churches to consider the matter Biblically and bring an end to the ordination of women as local elders. We further appeal to the church leadership to give earnest consideration to rescinding the 1975 and 1984 actions permitting ordination of women as elders, actions that have brought us to the straits we are in now.

4. Some have been legitimately concerned about the apparent inequities between the way North America treats its unordained male and female pastors. For more than a decade the unordained male pastors have been able to perform the essential functions of an ordained minister; the recent Annual Council action extends this privilege to the female pastors. But this is not the only solution to the problem. The United States tax code problem which prompted the 1977 action no longer exists. Would it not be simpler to rescind our action and return to the practice the church had long maintained, and which it still follows in most of the world? This would provide one policy for the unity of the world church, remove the unequal treatment of unordained men and women serving

in their various pastoral roles, and restore something of the significance of ordination in North America.

5. Both Scripture and Ellen White attest that women are vital to the work of God on earth. We believe the church should give serious consideration to the development of programs at the college and seminary level designed to prepare women to serve in such functions as counseling, personal evangelism, Bible Instructors, personal ministry in the home, health educators, and outreach coordinators. Women so prepared should be employed in the work of the church. Conferences need to budget for a larger number of women to provide professional services to our congregations. The evangelistic challenge, as well as the increasing number of broken homes, single parents and emotionally abused children, demand more than ever the special services of women who have been trained in theological and counseling skills. "They can come close to the hearts of those whom men cannot reach. Their labor is needed" (*Testimonies for the Church*, vol. 6, pp. 117-118).

What can delegates to the 1990 General Conference session do?

They can give serious study to the issue prior to the session, and be prepared to speak and act with conviction to address the matter at Indianapolis.

What can church members do?

They can become informed on the issue themselves and encourage their churches to give study to the matter when the question comes up regarding their local church officers. They can also express their convictions to their conference, union, division and General Conference leaders, who will represent them in the councils of the church and at the 1990 General Conference session. This is both their right and duty. We believe our leaders have been hearing mainly from a small but vocal group on one side of this issue, and they need to know that there are many who will support them when they take their stand on the teaching of the Word, to restore a biblical gospel order in the church.

And we should all pray that God will lead us to follow Scripture and be true to Him.

Appendix C

An Appeal for a Biblical Stand on Women's Ordination

[A four-page document prepared for delegates to the Utrecht General Conference Session]

Dear Delegate to the 1995 General Conference Session:

At this GC session, you will be urged by selected administrators to vote that Divisions may independently choose to ordain women to the gospel ministry.

The initiative for this proposal has come from the North American Division (NAD) in response to pressure from a relatively small group of influential professionals.

You may be encouraged to learn that in spite of 20 years of campaigning, over 80% of churches in the NAD continue to recognize that ordaining women elders is not biblical and have not ordained them. Many NAD leaders and the vast majority of believers are *not* asking for the change.

Believing that the approval of this administrative request will seriously undermine the authority of Scripture and the unity of the Seventh-day Adventist message and witness, the editorial board of ADVENTISTS AFFIRM, along with other scholars and church leaders, have prepared this document for your prayerful consideration.

Two Bases for SDA Unity

The unity of the world-wide Seventh-day Adventist movement is one of the wonders of the world. We are unified because—

  (1) our doctrines are based exclusively on the Bible. We have demanded a "plain thus saith the Lord" for all our "teachings and practices" (see *The Great Controversy,* p. 595.)

We are united also because—

(2) under the inspired leadership of God's chosen messenger, we have developed a unique system of organization that binds us together in churches, Conferences, Unions, and Divisions.

Part of this unity, based on the Bible, is that our *Church Manual* affirms "the equality of the ordination of the entire ministry" (1990, p. 38). The *SDA Minister's Manual*, 1992, p. 79 says that "ordination to the ministry is the setting apart of the employee to a sacred calling, *not for one local field alone but for the world church.*"

Tragically, the NAD proposal involves a deep modification in both of these aspects of our unity.

Where Both Sides Agree

Both sides agree that—

1. Men and women are equal, equally created by God in His image and equally saved by the "precious blood" of Jesus (Genesis 1:26, 27; Galatians 3:28; 1 Peter 1:19).
2. Both men and women have been called to soul-winning ministry, to utilize their skills and spiritual gifts (Joel 2:28, 29; 1 Corinthians 12).
3. God has called women to public service in SDA history as well as in Bible times.
4. Men and women should receive equal pay for equal work.
5. Ordination is the church's appointment and commissioning of individuals for assigned services.

Where We Disagree

The two sides disagree over—

1. Whether the Bible *permits* women to be "appointed and commissioned" as *pastors and elders* or whether the Bible *prohibits* it.
2. Whether the matter is *merely cultural and administrative* and can be settled by vote, or whether it is a *biblical* and *theological* issue, on which God calls us to obedience.

Our disagreement is not as to whether women *can* serve as pastors/elders, but as to whether God *permits* them to.

Is the Bible Silent on the Question?

No, it is not silent. The Bible states specifically, in two different places (1 Timothy 3:2 and Titus 1:6), that a pastor/elder is to be **"the husband of one wife."**

How Sound Are the Arguments for Women's Ordination?

Q 1. Will ordaining women vastly increase the church's soul-winning personnel?

We think not! Hundreds of thousands of women are *already* serving the SDA movement as volunteers in such areas as Sabbath school, lay activities, and evangelism, and multiplied thousands are *already* serving as church employees. The number who would be added through ordination is relatively minute.

Almost all the women who have been ordained as local elders in the NAD over the past twenty years were *already active* before their ordination, either as church employees or as volunteers. Ordaining them as local elders has added scarcely a handful to the number of active workers, but it has added a great deal of tension to local congregations.

Around the world, our women have always been encouraged to preach, teach, evangelize, and serve in numerous other capacities in partnership with ordained men.

But then, *why "empower women for mission" if we depart from Scripture?* Our strength as a movement has been our fidelity to the Word. Remove this fidelity, and our mission will be gravely weakened.

Q 2. Will ordaining women provide "unity in diversity"?

Ordaining women has not promoted unity in the NAD! On the contrary, it has undermined confidence in the scriptural soundness of various denominational leaders. And it has been divisive. In certain places and publications, God-fearing teachers, ministers, and members who choose to follow the plain teaching of the Bible have been scornfully mocked as "naive," "fanatic," "literalist," and "fundamentalist." In some cases, lay members have been manhandled and verbally abused.

In every Division that might start ordaining women as pastors and elders, a similar thing would happen. Because people have Bibles and can read, sooner or later they would discover that Scripture assigns the primary spiritual leadership of home and church to men (Ephesians 5:22-28; 1 Corinthians 11:3) and says that a pastor/elder should be "the husband of one wife" (1 Timothy 3:2; Titus 1:6), one who "rules his own house well," because "if a man does not know how to rule his own house, how can he take care of the church of God?" (1 Timothy 3:4-5). This discovery of scriptural instruction inevitably divides congregations between those seeking to obey the Bible as it stands and those who choose to reinterpret it in harmony with local culture.

Bible unity is grounded in biblical truth (Eph 4:3, 13).

Q 3. Is women's ordination "present truth," "progressive revelation," and "Spirit leading"?

Jesus said, "Thy Word is truth" (John 17:17). Present "truth" becomes present *"error"* when it contradicts specific Bible teaching. The NAD request contradicts a specific Bible teaching found in two Bible passages (1 Timothy 3:2; Titus 1:6), both of which say that a pastor/elder is to be "the husband of one wife," something that a woman can never be.

The Holy Spirit is indeed active in His church, leading into all truth; but inasmuch as "it was the Spirit of God that inspired the Bible, IT IS IMPOSSIBLE THAT THE TEACHING OF THE SPIRIT SHOULD EVER BE CONTRARY TO THAT OF THE WORD" *(The Great Controversy*, p. vii, emphasis supplied).

"To the law and to the testimony: if they speak not according to this word, it is because there is *no light* in them" (Isaiah 8:20).

Q 4. Is the prohibition against ordination of women "not biblical" because North American Bible teachers are divided on the subject?

Tragically (we feel broken-hearted to admit it), not a few NAD Bible teachers question many biblical teachings, including the literal interpretation of Genesis 1-2, the importance of committed Sabbath keeping, the relative importance of polygamy and of homosexuality, the possibility of victorious living, the inspiration of Ellen G. White, and even the significance of those most characteristic doctrines, the sanctuary and 1844. Because our theologians are divided on these topics and some say they are "not biblical," are we to infer that the topics are really not biblical?

No, indeed! It is women's ordination that is not biblical.

Q 5. Does the Bible forbid women to preach and teach in church?

No, it doesn't. 1 Corinthians 11:2-16 shows that women may "speak and prophesy" in church provided only that they dress modestly (cf. Acts 18:26; Titus 2:3-5). Hebrews 10:25 says we should all be "exhorting one another, and so much the more as ye see the Day approaching,"

1 Timothy 2:12-14, however, forbids a woman to teach and have authority over a man in view of God's creation arrangement and woman's role in the fall: "For Adam was first formed, then Eve. And Adam was not deceived, but the woman being deceived was in the transgression." Hence, a pastor/elder is to be "the *husband* of one wife." The reasoning is not popular today, but it comes from our heavenly Father and is found in the New Testament.

Q 6. Are prophets and pastors/elders the same?

No! Prophets and pastors/elders are not the same.

The authority of a prophet lies in the *message* given directly by God. The authority of a pastor/elder lies in the *Bible* and in his *particular administrative position.*

E. G. White, though a prophetess, did not attempt to serve as an *administrative leader.* "No one has ever heard me claim the position of leader of the denomination. I have a work of great responsibility to do—to impart by pen and voice the *instruction* given me, not alone to Seventh-day Adventists, but to the world" (*Testimonies for the Church,* 8:236, 237).

God Himself, exclusively, chooses His prophets—selecting either men or women. By contrast, He has given His church discretion in choosing pastors/elders—provided they meet God's requirements, which include that the pastor/elder must be a man (1 Timothy 3:2; Titus 1:6).

Q 7. Was Ellen G. White an ordained elder?

To suggest that Ellen G. White was an ordained elder is to misrepresent the facts.

Mrs. White was issued ministerial credentials—the highest credentials our church had to offer—from 1871 until her death in 1915. Three of these credentials have been preserved. The second one (1885) has the word "ordained" neatly crossed out, but the earlier and later ones (1883 and 1887) do not have the word crossed out.

Are we, then, to conclude that she was an "ordained person" in 1883, "unordained" in 1885, and "reordained" in 1887? Of course not.

In 1909 she clarified the matter completely when she personally filled out the "Biographical Information Blank" for the General Conference. In response to the request "If remarried, give date, and to whom," she wrote an "X," indicating that, No, she had not remarried. When asked, "If ordained, state when, where, and by whom," she again wrote an "X," meaning that she had never been ordained.

During her later years, Mrs. White was known mostly as "Sister White" and affectionately as "Mother White." She was *never* known as "Elder White" (and certainly not as "Pastor Ellen"!).

Every church member knew that "Elder White" was either her husband, James White, or one of her two minister sons.

Q 8. Did E. G. White write in direct support of ordination of women as pastors/elders?

She did not.

However, a single statement of hers is sometimes misused in support of women's ordination.

The statement is not about ordaining pastors/elders but about consecrating part-time volunteers for work with children and the sick. It appears in an article on the duty of ministers to encourage work by lay members.

"Women who are willing to consecrate *some of their time* to the service of the Lord should be appointed to visit the sick, look after the young, and minister to the necessities of the poor. They should be set apart to this work by prayer and laying on of hands. In some cases they will need to *counsel with* the church officers or *the minister*" (Ellen G. White, *Review and Herald*, July 9, 1895, p. 434, emphasis supplied).

Over the 150-year history of our movement, some dozens of women have held "ministerial licenses," but this does not for a moment mean that they were ordained as pastors or elders! As dynamic members of evangelistic teams, many of these women served as Bible Instructors. Through their dedication and their thorough knowledge of the Bible, they won thousands and thousands of converts. Pastors and evangelists cherished them, for they were better acquainted with new converts than the ministers were.

If any of these women, who were well versed in the Scriptures, were asked if they wanted to be ordained, they would exclaim, "Oh, no! It isn't biblical!"

Here's something: Whereas pastors tend to spend much of their time in church administration and preparing routine sermons, Bible Instructors can spend all their time winning souls.

If we want to empower women for soul-winning, let's not make them pastors; let's train them to be Bible Instructors.

Q 9. Are we bound to follow previous SDA councils?

One of the arguments used by NAD leadership is that previous Annual Councils have endorsed women's ordination.

Notice the irony. The NAD leadership is not willing to revoke the decision of an Annual Council—Annual Councils are composed almost entirely of North Americans—but is urging us to revoke the decision of the General Conference of 1990, which in full session *overwhelmingly* voted *against* women's ordination to the pastoral ministry.

In any case, Ellen G. White said, "God will have a people upon the earth to maintain *the Bible, and the Bible only,* as the standard of all doctrines and the basis of all reforms. The *opinions of learned men,* the deductions of science, the creeds or *decisions of ecclesiastical councils,* . . . not one nor all of these should be regarded as evidence for or against any point of religious faith. Before accepting any doctrine or precept, we **should demand a plain 'Thus saith the Lord' in its support**" *(The Great Controversy,* p. 595, emphasis supplied).

Is It "Disloyalty" to Vote No to a Request by Church Leaders?

Not at all. At General Conference sessions leaders present their best arguments, but under God they look to you for guidance. Your loyalty to our leaders is best shown by encouraging them to uphold biblical teaching and not give in to cultural pressures.

Thus, you should vote your conviction, based on the Bible.

"The Bible must be our standard for every doctrine and practice. We must study it reverentially. We are to receive no man's opinion without comparing it with Scripture. Here is divine authority which is supreme in matters of faith. *It is the Word of the living God that is to decide all controversies*" *(The Ellen G. White 1888 Materials,* pp. 44-45, emphasis supplied).

What Should You Do?

Whereas the request of the NAD leadership to allow each Division to ordain women as pastors will, if approved,

(a) interrupt the worldwide unity we have enjoyed for 150 years,

(b) undermine our doctrinal unity, and

(c) repudiate Article 1 of our Fundamental Beliefs, which demands that we seek biblical authority for every doctrine and practice,

We appeal to you, dear delegate, to:

1. Respectfully and courteously stand your ground by the grace of God and vote NO to the unbiblical NAD proposal.

2. As you have opportunity, urge leadership to expand the training of women to fill the many roles which God calls them to fill other than as pastors/ elders, and to budget increased amounts for their salaries.

Seventh-day Adventists Choose to Stand on the Bible

Millions of Seventh-day Adventists around the world testify that they are Adventists today because the evangelist who brought the Message to them or to their parents based it entirely *on the Bible.*

Why do SDAs keep the seventh-day Sabbath? *Because the Bible says,* "Six days shalt thou labor and do all thy work, but the seventh day is the Sabbath of the Lord thy God. In it thou shalt not do any work" (Exodus 20:8-11).

Why do SDAs believe in the second advent of Christ? *Because the Bible says,* "If I go, I will come again" (John 14:1-3).

Why do SDAs pay tithe? *Because the Bible says,* "Bring ye all the tithes into the store house, that there may be meat in my house, saith the Lord" (Malachi 3:10-11).

Why do SDAs believe the investigative judgment began in 1844? *Because the Bible says,* "Unto 2300 days, then shall the sanctuary be cleansed" (Daniel 8:14).

Why do SDAs accept the Spirit of Prophecy? *Because the Bible says,* "Here are they that keep the commandments of God and have the testimony of Jesus" "which is the spirit of prophecy" (Revelation 12:17; 19:10).

So why do SDAs reject the ordination of women as pastors/elders?

Because the Bible says, in 1 Timothy 3:2, that an elder must be "THE HUSBAND OF ONE WIFE," and because the Bible says again in Titus 1:6 than an elder must be "THE HUSBAND OF ONE WIFE."

Furthermore, 1 Timothy 2 and 3 say that an elder must be one who "RULES HIS HOUSE WELL," because "if a man does not know how to rule his own house, how will he take care of the church of God?" and that in church a WOMAN must not have authority over men, "for Adam was created first then Eve" (compare Titus 1:6 and 1 Corinthians 14:34).

It is a matter of what the Bible says.

Appendix D

A Very Significant Development Regarding Women Pastors

[Published originally in ADVENTISTS AFFIRM 12/3 (Fall 1998), pp. 5-17.]

The North American Division has passed an action of such significance to the question of women pastors and to the Seventh-day Adventist movement as a whole that we think every Adventist will want to know about it.

This action appears designed to circumvent the 1990 General Conference (GC) decision opposing women's ordination to the ministry and the 1995 GC decision forbidding the North American Division (NAD) to go its own way in this matter. It seems intended to achieve this goal without risking a third vote on ordination by the General Conference in session.

The editors of ADVENTISTS AFFIRM greatly regret that even after two overwhelming decisions by the world church, some of our people continue to divide us over the controversial issue of women pastors. A relatively small group of articulate individuals is "pushing the Brethren" to adopt its pro-feminist agenda, at a time when many other issues, like congregationalism, evolution, divorce, homosexuality, rock-like music, and the denial of basic doctrines, are forcing their way into some of the major centers of our church in North America. We feel a great need for God's special people to pray for our leaders to be fully open to heaven's guidance.

This is the reason for this issue of ADVENTISTS AFFIRM.

Definitions and Background. The action in question was voted on at the NAD headquarters in Silver Spring, Maryland during the October 7-10, 1997 year-end meeting.

Some Definitions. For those of you who may appreciate some definitions, the "NAD" is the "North American Division of the General Conference of Seventh-day Adventists." It is one of 14 divisions of the General Conference around the world. The NAD covers the United States, Canada, and certain islands in the Atlantic and Pacific Oceans and consists of 58 conferences gathered into 9 union conferences. It counts about 850,000 members in an Adventist world population of some 10,000,000.

A "year-end meeting" is a gathering of the principal officers of a division and of its union and local conferences, along with selected laity and representatives of major institutions in the division. It is held in the autumn, after the General Conference annual council, and meets for the purpose of hearing reports and laying plans for the coming year. Most, though not all, of the actions voted on at a year-end meeting have been prepared in advance by committees and are accepted unanimously as a matter of routine, with little discussion at the time of the vote.

The action that we are considering here dealt with a document entitled, "President's Commission on Women in Ministry—Report," a copy of which is included in this issue of ADVENTISTS AFFIRM. (From here on we will refer to it as "the Document.") Apparently some, at least, of the top NAD administrators intended that the Document would merely be read at the year-end meeting and then laid aside; that is, they appear to have planned that it would merely be "received." But when the time came that the document was actually read at the meeting, urgent voices demanded that it be voted on as an official "recommendation." After a short discussion, the chair agreed to allow such a vote. In consequence, the Document was officially voted on under three heads. First, it was "received"; second, the recommendations which it contains were to be sent to appropriate committees; and third, those recommendations that would be approved by the committees were, so far as funds would allow, to be "implemented," that is, put into effect as official policy.

Already several of the recommendations appear to be undergoing implementation.

Unlike most proposals at year-end meetings, which are approved unanimously, this one was not. A substantial minority of the conference presidents and other officers present *voted against it.*

ADVENTISTS AFFIRM desires to congratulate all the officers who voted No and to encourage them to increase in their holy boldness.

At the 1990 Indianapolis session of the General Conference, the world field, by a vote of 1173 to 377, said that women were not to be ordained as Seventh-day Adventist ministers. At the 1995 Utrecht session of the General Conference, the world field, by a vote of 1481 to 673, said that the NAD should not go its own way and ordain women in its own territory, but that instead the whole church should hold together.

In the face of these overwhelming decisions, the Document intends to authorize women to serve as senior pastors, even as conference presidents and union-conference presidents, subject to their being "commissioned" but *without their needing to be ordained.*

Because of the significant nature of the Document, we are, as we mentioned above, including a copy of it for you to read for yourself. It begins on p. 13 [p. 399 of this book]. But because it is written in rather terse language, we are first introducing it with comments for those who may appreciate them. For easy cross reference, we'll follow the Document section by section. We suggest that you flip the pages back and forth so you can read them section by section while reading our comments.

COMMENTS ON THE DOCUMENT
Introduction

You will notice from the Document's own Introduction that the Document as a whole is the result of considerable forethought.

Two years before it was actually voted on and approved, NAD leadership announced that a commission was already in process of being appointed to expand the roles of women. (A "commission" as the term is used here is a special committee given a special assignment. It is very different from the "commissioning" discussed below.)

The special task assigned to this commission was to "recommend ways to expand the role of women in ministry" and to "affirm women in pastoral" ministry. This announcement about the formation of the commission was made at the 1995 NAD year-end meeting, which was held in Battle Creek, Michigan, on October 12-13. The Utrecht General Conference had voted on July 5 against having the NAD go its own way. This means that it was only three months later that the NAD set out to advance every aspect of pastoral ministry among women other than ordination itself. As we shall see, the commission's recommendations make ordination irrelevant. Under the commission's recommendations, we are offered a distinction without a difference.

The Introduction tells us that the make-up and function of the commission, that is, its "membership" and "terms of reference," were officially approved in February 1996 by the NAD Committee on Administration (NADCOA). The commission itself met in the spring and summer of the same year, 1996, and again in the spring of 1997, at which time it finalized its report for presentation at the October 7-10, 1997 NAD year-end meeting.

It appears that the Document represents a serious intention, an intention to find a way around the *spirit* of the Indianapolis and Utrecht decisions—without actually violating their *letter!*

I. Appointment of an Associate Ministerial Secretary

In its very first section, Section I, the Document recommends that the NAD move "with a sense of urgency" to appoint a woman as an associate ministerial secretary or even as the principal ministerial secretary. In a local conference, union conference, or (as in this case) a division, the ministerial secretary, often called the ministerial director, is the person who is most concerned with the effectiveness of all the ministers in the given territory.

If this recommendation is fully implemented, all the pastors, male and female, in North America will be guided by a woman pastor.

II. Needs to be Addressed by the Ministerial Association

The long Section II, consisting of 12 sub-sections, calls on the NAD Ministerial Association to engage energetically in encouraging women who are already pastors and in putting pressure on conferences to hire additional women pastors.

(The ministerial association in a local conference, union conference, or division is the department that fosters the work of ministers and which is headed up by the ministerial secretary or director.)

This section calls for "regular contacts" to be maintained between the NAD Ministerial Association and conference administrators, who are to be reminded on a "regular" basis "regarding the NAD's support for women in pastoral ministry and of policies that encourage the hiring of women pastors." Indeed, the NAD Ministerial Association is called on to engage in "active promotion of qualified women, seeking to match . . . candidates with openings."

This means that the NAD Ministerial Association is to identify churches known to be willing to have a woman pastor and to urge the conferences to place women there.

Conference officers who are willing to place women in churches are to be publicly praised; and if laymembers in a conference criticize the conference officers so that the officers are in danger of not being reelected at a forthcoming constituency meeting—that is, if they have put themselves "at risk"—the NAD Ministerial Association is to do whatever may be needed to let the laity know that the officers have the full endorsement of the NAD.

Here and in several other places, the Document anticipates opposition to the appointment of women pastors. This is significant in that it points up the fact that there is no groundswell among the NAD membership demanding women pastors or even local women elders. There isn't!

What about conference presidents who are not in favor of women pastors and are unwilling to pay their expenses to attend seminars designed only for women pastors? (Remember, conferences regularly conduct seminars for *all* their pastors. These female seminars would be extra, meetings from which male pastors would presumably be excluded.)

If any presidents choose not to pay expense money for their women pastors, the NAD Ministerial Association is to send expense money to the women directly.

Women pastors are to be invited by conferences to take major appointments at camp meetings and retreats. Subsection L calls for the "preparation and dissemination of educational materials in multiple media designed to raise awareness about women in pastoral ministry and the role of women in the church." This recommendation is further developed in Section X, below.

This Section II as a whole makes clear that the North American Division is committing itself fully and energetically to the employment of women as pastors in the same roles as men in spite of the overwhelming decisions against ordination of women made at the 1990 and 1995 General Conference sessions.

III. The Commissioning Service

Section III, which is very short—but which requires a rather lengthy explanation—summons the local conferences, union conferences, and the NAD itself to "promptly conduct commissioning services for those women who are eligible."

Commissioning services, what are they? The current *North American Division Working Policy*, pp. 147-148, defines "commissioning" as a procedure designed to recognize the service of individuals who are "not on the path to ordination as a minister of the Gospel."

But there is considerably more to be said about the subject before it can be properly evaluated, so we have decided to place it in a separate article immediately following the Document and beginning on p. 18 [pp. 225-230 in this book]. The article is titled, "A Very Surprising (and Interesting) History." For now, we shall proceed with our section-by-section commentary.

Section III in the Document recommends that "the NAD, and its union and local conferences, be encouraged to promptly conduct *commissioning services* for those women who are eligible."

IV. Ministerial Function of Commissioned Ministers
V. Working Policy Revisions

Sections IV and V make explicit the NAD's ultimate goal, namely, to make commissioned women fully equivalent to ordained men.

Today there are still a few activities that are not allowed to licensed and commissioned ministers. Unlike ordained ministers, licensed and commissioned ministers may not ordain local elders and deacons, they may not organize new churches, and they may not become presidents of conferences. Sections IV and V seek to remove all these limitations. If implemented, the results will include the election of women as local-conference and union-conference presidents and the establishment of commissioning as *fully equivalent* to ordination.

Because the Document avoids stating that commissioning is to be fully equivalent to ordination, some readers may not notice it. But on a moment's reflection, this goal becomes absolutely unmistakable. Forbidden to ordain women, the NAD proposes to commission them instead and then to make commissioning fully equivalent to ordination. The NAD is honoring the letter of the 1990 and 1995 decisions but can they be said to be honoring the spirit of them? Is it not *intentionally* making a distinction without a difference?

It should be noted that Section IV, which calls for changes in the *Church Manual*, can be implemented only if it wins approval at a five-year General Conference session. Section V, however, which asks only for a change in the *NAD Working Policy*, could win approval at any annual council of the General Conference executive committee, a much smaller gathering.

VI. Changes in the SDA Yearbook

The *Seventh-day Adventist Yearbook* gives the names and addresses of all denominational workers above a certain rank the world around and also lists all the ministers, commissioned ministers, and commissioned teachers in conferences around the world. As the church continues to grow, the number of names to be included grows larger and the *Yearbook* becomes ever more ponderous. For a long time, all licensed ministers were included by name, but a few years ago an editorial decision was made to leave out the licensed ministers, simply as a rational economy measure.

Section VI asks that the names of licensed ministers and licensed commissioned ministers be once again listed, at least in a NAD edition of the *Yearbook*. The motive appears to be to publicize the names of women who have been voted ministerial licenses.

VII. Encourage Conferences to Hire Women as Pastors

In order to make as clear as possible its intention to appoint women pastors in spite of the evident reservations of the world field expressed through two General Conference decisions, Section VII calls on conferences to set "realistic goals" to increase the number of women pastors in their territories. It offers to subsidize the salaries of some women interns for four years instead of the three years customary for young men. Additionally, it urges Adventist educational institutions to encourage young women to take ministerial studies if they "sense a call" to the ministry.

Many Seventh-day Adventists are concerned about the current emphasis on young women's "sensing a call" to the ministry. In view of what the Bible says about an elder's being "the husband of one wife," is it possible that a young woman who believes that she senses a call to the pastoral ministry should be encouraged to prepare instead for some other aspect of soul-winning ministry?

VIII. Data Base of Women Candidates for Openings
IX. Visibility of Women in Pastoral Ministry Roles
X. Articles in Church Journals
XI. Resource Center for Women in Ministry

Sections VIII-XI reiterate and expand subsections D, E, H, and L in Section II, asking that information about potential women pastors be made widely available, that women be invited to speak at major meetings of the church, and that our publications and videos deliberately give women ministers exposure "several times a year."

It is noteworthy that Section X asks that women ministers be shown working casually alongside of men, as if a mix of men and women in pastoral ministry were the normal thing to expect.

We may assume that the increased exposure of women pastors that we have been seeing recently in denominational periodicals is a response to this Section X.

XII. Goals for Gender Inclusiveness in Church Organization

Section XII may prove to be the section that will cause the greatest concern to Seventh-day Adventists who believe that the Bible teaches that men rather than women should serve as our church leaders.

Restrictions. Paragraph B (i) requires that "the Church Resources Consortium monitor and audit all NAD-produced and endorsed materials for compliance with a gender-inclusive model for ministry."

If this requirement is fully carried out, it will mean the complete elimination of all articles and even letters to the editor that oppose women's ordination or the employment of women in regular pastoral ministry. Already it is difficult to persuade the editors of our denominational periodicals to publish such articles and letters. Our publishing houses have also declined to publish books that take such positions. This proposed elimination becomes all the more worrisome when one realizes that the overwhelming majority of the representatives of Seventh-day Adventists around the world voted decisively in 1990 and 1995 in opposition to women's ordination. Why do our NAD editors choose not to allow articles in our church papers which favor the position voted by the representatives of the majority of our church members?

Hermeneutics. Even more worrisome than the restrictions is the statement in paragraph A that "there is urgent need to study and clarify the church's understanding and application of biblical hermeneutics" and that "this should take the form of: (i) multiple articles in denominational periodicals" and "(ii) a hermeneutics conference by the NAD and/or the GC."

What scholars call "hermeneutics" has to do, simply, with the *interpretation* of the Bible. Inasmuch as we are all concerned with interpreting the Bible, what is so worrisome about this recommendation? What is worrisome is that it doesn't call plainly for a clearer understanding of what the Bible teaches. The heading for this section, "Goals for Gender Inclusiveness in Church Organization," seems to imply that the Document is calling for Bible scholars to rally in support of women pastors.

Is it wrong to wish that this request for Bible study, instead of coming at the end of the document after all the decisions have been announced, had instead been placed at the beginning, before any decisions had even been made?

In February 1995, a few months before the Utrecht session, the NAD president said in the *Review,* "I have come to the conclusion that the church crossed the theological bridge when we voted to recognize the ordination of women as local elders" back in 1975. At the Utrecht session, however, the world church responded overwhelmingly to a presentation arguing *from the Bible* that women should not be made elders or pastors. Seeing this response to a theological presentation, the NAD leaders recognized that for many of our people the theological bridge was *not* crossed in 1975 and hasn't been crossed yet. Thus after all the NAD leaders sense a need to develop a theological argument from the Bible if they are ever going to win the world field—or even many of their own members—to the position which they have espoused in the Document.

In the meantime, it appears that what this Article XII is really calling for is a major effort to teach our people that in spite of 1 Timothy 2-3 and many other passages, the Bible really does teach that women may be appointed as senior pastors.

Is this *really* what Article XII means?

Yes! Indeed it has already been put into effect. Even before the Document was voted, when it was still in its early commission stage, a request came to the Seventh-day Adventist Theological Seminary of Andrews University to develop a whole book explaining that the Bible really does teach that women should be ordained as pastors.

For Seminary professors, who are trained in Bible study, this was a formidable challenge, for they all know that 1 Timothy 2-3 (along with numerous other passages) places a distinction between the roles of men and women in the church and, in this setting, specifies that an elder or pastor is to be "the husband of one wife."

Even more challenging has been the realization that the people who object to women's ordination are *conservative* Adventists, people who intend to take the Bible the way it reads.

The book, titled *Women in Ministry,* has appeared just as this issue is being readied for the press. As expected, it presents its arguments *in a manner calculated to persuade conservative Adventists.* This has been a real challenge! We are not surprised that the Seminary committee took longer to produce its book than was initially anticipated.

We expect to see copies of the book scattered widely at the expense of the North American Division. By God's grace, the staff of ADVENTISTS AFFIRM will send you a careful analysis of the book in 1999. [The book you are reading is the promised response, considerably enlarged.]

Meanwhile, we very much wish that Section XII in the NAD Document had asked more plainly for a clarification of what the Bible says.

So much for our *introduction* to the Document. Before presenting you with the Document itself, we would like to make a surprising new point, namely, that in view of this document, the issue is no longer ordination.

The Issue Is No Longer Ordination. All of us who have been opposing women's ordination over the past fifteen years have been doing so because in the Seventh-day Adventist church, as in most churches, up until very recent times ordination has been an essential preparation for pastoral ministry. We have not opposed ordination because we are opposed to the ordination of women as such. A century ago Ellen G. White allowed for a kind of ordination for a class of deaconesses. No, we have opposed ordination of women to the gospel ministry because the Bible says among many other things on the subject that an elder or pastor is to be "the husband of one wife," and no woman can meet this qualification whether ordained or commissioned.

We have not viewed the Bible's "husband" stipulation as something isolated, legalistic, or derogatory but rather as a vital aspect of the difference in roles that God since creation and the fall has lovingly assigned to men and women. From the very beginning, God has designed that men should provide the primary spiritual leadership at home and in the church.

Men who willingly surrender to women this God-given responsibility may be considered by some people to be generous, open-minded, and gracious, but God may not consider them so favorably. There is much reason to believe that God *expects* men to stand up and shoulder the leadership responsibilities that He has assigned to them.

So long as Seventh-day Adventists regarded ordination as an essential requirement for serving as an elder or pastor, it was enough to oppose women's ordination. But now that the NAD says that ordination need not be a requirement for serving as an elder or pastor and that commissioning is an alternate route to this goal, it is time to get to the heart of the issue. In order to be faithful to the Bible, we must point out that no woman can rightfully serve as an elder or pastor whether she be ordained or commissioned—or consecrated (as in some denominations) or elected or merely appointed. How she gets into the office is beside the point.

Now that the NAD leadership has shifted its strategy away from the 150-year-old Bible-based belief of Seventh-day Adventists that only men should serve as ordained pastors, it is time for us who desire a Bible-based ministry to refocus our approach. We recommend that in your local church as also in your conference you show people from the Bible that whether ordained or commissioned or consecrated or whatever, the elder or pastor of a church can only be "the husband of one wife."

Text of the Report presented to the Year-end Meeting of the North American Division (NAD) by the NAD President's Commission on Women in Ministry, accepted and approved in October 1997. COMMENTS IN ITALICS ARE BY ADVENTISTS AFFIRM. This document should be read in connection with the interpretive comments beginning on p. 5 [p. 393 in this book].

President's Commission on Women in Ministry—Report

At the 1995 Year-end Meeting in Battle Creek [*this was in October three months after the Utrecht vote against allowing North America to go its own way in respect to ordaining women ministers*], it was announced that a commission was being appointed to recommend ways to expand the role of women in ministry, recognize and deploy the gifts God has given to women, and affirm women in pastoral and other spiritual ministries [*in the wake of the 1990 and 1995 GC decisions*]. The membership and terms of reference were approved by NADCOA [*The North American Division Committee on Organization*] on February 28, 1996. The Commission met in June and July, 1996, and again in May, 1997.

The recommendations from the Commission are as follows:

I. Appointment of an Associate Ministerial Secretary

RECOMMENDED, That the NAD move with a sense of urgency to include a woman with ministerial background as ministerial secretary or an associate ministerial secretary. [*At the annual council of the General Conference held just recently in Brazil, a woman was elected to serve as an associate ministerial secretary of the General Conference Ministerial Association.*]

II. Needs to be Addressed by the Ministerial Association

RECOMMENDED, That the following needs be addressed by NAD administration for implementation through the Ministerial Association and/or any appropriate structure.

A. A professional association for women serving in pastoral ministry that would organize an annual retreat for the purpose of mutual support, affirmation and networking [*the sharing of ideas and experiences*]. Financial assistance which should be provided where local conferences are unwilling or unable to pay for travel, etc.

B. Development of an electronic linkage [*likely, via internet*] to connect more experienced women pastors with women who are ministerial students or intern pastors and desire a professional mentor.

C. Development of a newsletter for women in ministry that would publish affirmative success stories, list job vacancies of interest, announce relevant seminars and workshops, and provide other helpful information. This newsletter should also be sent to conference presidents and ministerial directors [*to encourage them to employ more and more women pastors*].

D. Development of a database [*a computerized listing*] of churches in the NAD which are likely to want women as pastors. (The newsletter and other information from the resource center should be provided to these churches on a regular basis.)

E. Development of a speaker's bureau for women in ministry which would solicit and market women speakers for camp meetings, seminars, weeks of prayer, retreats, etc. The NAD might provide travel subsidies for organizations seeking a woman speaker which could be managed by the resource center.

F. Appointment of an "ombudsman"—a person with insight in the system and denominational policies who can provide feedback and guidance when women in ministry encounter conflict with employing organizations, as well as provide mediation if necessary. [*If someone in authority objects conscientiously to having a woman pastor, the NAD should send a skillful person to quiet the opposition.*]

G. Development of training for women in ministry about conflict resolution skills and how to survive in a male-dominated milieu.

H. Development of a placement service that would provide a database where women in ministry could list their resumes and employing organizations could access this information. An adequate placement service should also include regular contacts with conference administrators and an identified list of local churches most likely to accept women as pastors; active promotion of qualified women, seeking to match these candidates with openings; and career counseling for women in ministry.

I. Development and regular distribution of information to conferences regarding the NAD's support for women in pastoral ministry and policies that encourage the hiring of women pastors.

J. Opportunities for the public affirmation to [*sic*] church administrators who have taken risks to support and employ women in ministry. [*If members so resist having women pastors that the conference president finds reelection at the next constituency meeting to be doubtful—that is, if he has "taken risks" to employ women—then the NAD should send a persuasive speaker to the constituency meeting to make sure he gets reelected anyway.*]

K. Development of a fund from which to provide financial assistance for travel expenses and registration fees for women in ministry to attend continuing education events when the employing organization cannot or will not provide these benefits.

L. Preparation and dissemination of educational materials in multiple media designed to raise awareness about women in pastoral ministry and the role of women in the church.

III. The Commissioning Service
RECOMMENDED, That the NAD, and its union and local conferences, be encouraged to promptly conduct commissioning services for those women who are eligible. [*The NAD opposed the "ordinations" conducted at Sligo and La Sierra, but here favors commissioning, which it wants to see treated as fully equivalent to ordination.*]

IV. Ministerial Function of Commissioned Ministers
RECOMMENDED, That the following changes be made in *The Church Manual:* [*Because the* Church Manual *can be changed only by the General Conference in session, this Section IV of the Report is only a recommendation.*]

A. Modify the language on page 46, in the section entitled "The Church Elder," as follows:

The ordination service is only performed by an ordained/<u>commissioned</u> minister with credentials from the local conference. [*The underlined word is to be added, thereby making commissioning equivalent to ordination and undermining the intent of the Utrecht decision.*]

B. Modify the language on page 52, in the section entitled "The Deacon," as follows:

A newly elected deacon cannot fill his office until he has been set apart by an ordained/<u>commissioned</u> minister who holds current credentials from the conference.

C. Modify the language on page 175, in the section entitled "Organization of a Church," as follows:

Churches are organized by an ordained/<u>commissioned</u> minister on the recommendation of a conference or field committee.

D. Modify the language on pages 176-177, in the section entitled "Uniting Churches," as follows:

In a duly called meeting, presided over by the conference president or the pastor or other ordained/commissioned minister, each church should vote on the question of union.

V. Working Policy Revisions

RECOMMENDED, That the following revisions be made in the NAD Working Policy. [*Because NAD Working Policy decisions have to be approved by the General Conference at an annual council or quinquennial session, these revisions haven't been made yet.*]

A. That gender-inclusive language be used throughout.

B. That the language of CA 10 05 Union Conference Constitution and By-laws be modified on page 100 as follows:

President: The president, who shall be an ordained/commissioned minister of experience. . . . [*The intention is to allow a woman to become a union president.*]

C. That the language of CA 20 05 Local Conference Constitution and By-laws be modified on page 110 as follows:

President: The president, who shall be an ordained/commissioned minister of experience . . . [*The intention is to allow a woman to become a conference president.*]

D. That NAD Working Policy L 21 Commissioned Minister be revised as follows:

L 21 ~~Associates in Pastoral Care~~ Commissioned Minister—Role and Status

L 21 05 Ministerial Employee— ~~An associate in pastoral care~~ A person is recognized as a ministerial employee when all of the following prerequisites have been satisfied: [*The document notes that* The rest of the paragraph is unchanged. *The intentions here are to eliminate the designation, "Associate in Pastoral Care," and to erase all procedural differences between men and women ministers.*]

VI. Changes in the SDA Yearbook

VOTED, To recommend that the NAD publish a NAD version of the NAD section of the *SDA Yearbook* with the licensed ministers and licensed commissioned ministers included in the listings. [*A few years ago the* SDA Yearbook *stopped listing any licensed ministers because the book was becoming too large.*]

VII. Encourage Conferences to Hire Women as Pastors

RECOMMENDED, In order to encourage conferences to hire more women in pastoral positions:

A. That the NAD extend a four-year internship budget (instead of the usual three-year internship budget) to each local conference which presently has no woman employed as a pastor and hires a women in the pastoral internship. [*Again, an attempt to overcome resistance to promotion of women as pastors, this time through a financial incentive.*]

B. That the NAD request local conferences to set realistic goals to increase the number of women in pastoral ministry in their field [*sic*] during the next three years. [*Further pressure on conferences to hire women pastors.*]

C. That Adventist colleges and universities in North America be encouraged to recruit young women who sense a call [*not the same as, "who are truly called"*] to pastoral ministry to pursue ministerial studies.

VII [*sic*]. Data Base of Women Candidates for Openings

RECOMMENDED, That the NAD departmental staff develop and disseminate a data base of women who might be candidates for vacancies on union and local conference staffs.

IX. Visibility of Women in Pastoral Ministry Roles

RECOMMENDED, That conferences be encouraged to invite women to speak during the Sabbath morning worship services and other general sessions at camp meetings. (Reference speaker's bureau.)

X. Articles in Church Journals

RECOMMENDED, That the NAD edition of the *Adventist Review* and other general church papers be asked to publish profiles of women serving in pastoral ministry several times a year [*We may expect to find women ministers being given exposure in the* Adventist Review *and in videos, with the apparent intention, again, of getting people used to seeing them up front*] and, that multiple exposures be given to models of gift-based ministry taking place in congregations throughout the NAD, including:

A. Concrete portrayal and affirmation of women in ministry

B. Indirect portrayals of women with men in creative approaches to pastoral ministry [*apparently in order to get people used to thinking of women in the same roles as men*]

C. Use of both print and video media

D. A cassette ministry of sermons and lectures supporting women in ministry

E. ACN "First Wednesday" segments highlighting women in ministry

XI. Resource Center for Women in Ministry

RECOMMENDED, That the NAD Church Resources Consortium create a resource center for women in pastoral ministry. It should provide the following services:

[*To save space, the remainder of Section XI is omitted. It is virtually identical to Section II, except that item L at the end of Section H is not repeated.*]

XII. Goals for Gender Inclusiveness in Church Organization

RECOMMENDED, A. That there is urgent need to study and clarify the church's understanding and application of biblical hermeneutics. This should take the form of:

   i. Multiple articles in denominational periodicals

  ii. A hermeneutics conference sponsored by the NAD and/or the GC. [*This recommendation seems ambiguous. Is it a clear call for Bible study? Coming, as it does, as the first item under the heading, "Goals for Gender Inclusiveness in Church Organization," is it not rather an "urgent" call for the development and dissemination of methods of Bible study that will support a gender-inclusive view of church leadership?*]

  B. That more of the advocacy for women in ministry be channeled through the union papers and other media of mass distribution, including:

   i. That the Church Resources Consortium monitor and audit all NAD produced and endorsed materials for compliance with a gender-inclusive model of ministry. [*Very few if any articles and letters opposing the use of women as pastors are to be allowed to appear in denominational publications.*]

  ii. That the NAD produce and endorse only gender-inclusive resource materials.

 iii. That the division president issue a clear call to the church for gender inclusiveness at all levels of the church—boards, committees, pastoral assignments, etc.

 iv. That materials be prepared for conference administrators and search committees that specifically address the need to consider qualified women as candidates.

Recommended Reading

Bible Passages Related to Women's Ordination

Genesis 1-3

Frame, John M. "Men and Women in the Image of God." In *Recovering Biblical Manhood and Womanhood,* ed. John Piper and Wayne Grudem, 225-232. Wheaton, Ill.: Crossway Books, 1991.

*Hasel, Gerhard F. "Man and Woman in Genesis 1-3." Mohaven Papers, 1976. Available in Adventist Heritage Center, Andrews University, Berrien Springs, Mich.

Ortland, Raymond C. "Male-Female Equality and Male Headship: Genesis 1-3." In *Recovering Biblical Manhood and Womanhood,* ed. John Piper and Wayne Grudem, 95-112. Wheaton, Ill.: Crossway Books, 1991.

Stitzinger, Michael F. "Genesis 1-3 and the Male/Female Role Relationship." *Grace Theological Journal* 2/2 (Fall 1981): 23-44.

1 Corinthians 11:2-16

Schreiner, Thomas R. "Head Coverings, Prophecies and the Trinity: 1 Corinthians 11:2-16." In *Recovering Biblical Manhood and Womanhood,* ed. John Piper and Wayne Grudem, 124-139. Wheaton, Ill.: Crossway Books, 1991.

1 Corinthians 14:33-36

Carson, D. A. "'Silent in the Churches': On the Role of Women in 1 Corinthians 14:33b-36." In *Recovering Biblical Manhood and Womanhood,* ed. John Piper and Wayne Grudem, 140-153. Wheaton, Ill.: Crossway Books, 1991.

Galatians 3:28

Davis, John Jefferson. "Some Reflections on Galatians 3:28, Sexual Roles, and Biblical Hermeneutics." *Journal of the Evangelical Theological Society* 19/3 (Summer 1976).

Johnson, S. Lewis. "Role Distinctions in the Church: Galatians 3:28." In *Recovering Biblical Manhood and Womanhood,* ed. John Piper and Wayne Grudem, 154-164. Wheaton, Ill.: Crossway Books, 1991.

*Kiesler, Herbert. "Exegesis of Galatians 3:26-28." Biblical Research Institute, February 7, 1987. Available from Biblical Research Institute, 12501 Old Columbia Pike, Silver Spring, MD 20904-6600.

Ephesians 5:21-33

Knight III, George. "Husbands and Wives as Analogues of Christ and the Church: Ephesians 5:21-33 and Colossians 3:18-19." In *Recovering Biblical Manhood and Womanhood,* ed. John Piper and Wayne Grudem, 165-178. Wheaton, Ill.: Crossway Books, 1991.

*Maxwell, C. Mervyn. "Mutual Submission: What is it?" *Adventists Affirm* 1/2 (Fall 1987): 23-26.

Colossians 3:18-19

Knight III, George. "Husbands and Wives as Analogues of Christ and the Church: Ephesians 5:21-33 and Colossians 3:18-19." In *Recovering Biblical Manhood and Womanhood,* ed. John Piper and Wayne Grudem, 165-178. Wheaton, Ill.: Crossway Books, 1991.

1 Peter 3:1-7

Grudem, Wayne. "Wives Like Sarah, and the Husbands Who Honor Them: 1 Peter 3:-17." In *Recovering Biblical Manhood and Womanhood,* ed. John Piper and Wayne Grudem, 194-208. Wheaton, Ill.: Crossway Books, 1991.

1 Timothy 2:9-15

Barnett, Paul W. "Wives and Women's Ministry (1 Timothy 2:11-15)." *Evangelical Quarterly* 61/3 (July 1989): 61-238.

Moo, Douglas J. "The Interpretation of 1 Timothy 2:11-15: A Rejoinder." *Trinity Journal* 2NS (1981): 198-222.

Moo, Douglas. "What Does it Mean Not to Teach or Have Authority Over Men?: 1 Timothy 2:11-15." In *Recovering Biblical Manhood and Womanhood,* ed. John Piper and Wayne Grudem, 179-193. Wheaton, Ill.: Crossway Books, 1991.

Knight III, George. *"Authenteo* In Reference to Women in 1 Timothy 2:12." *New Testament Studies* 30: 143-157.

Köstenberger, Andreas; Thomas R. Schreiner; H. Scott Baldwin. *Women in the Church: A Fresh Analysis of 1 Timothy 2:9-15.* Grand Rapids, Mich.: Baker Books, 1995.

"Saved Through Childbearing?" *Journal for Biblical Manhood and Womanhood* 2/4 (September 1997). Published by Council on Biblical Manhood and Womanhood, P.O. Box 7337, Libertyville, IL 60048.

*Veloso, Mario. "Exegesis and Theological Implications of 1 Timothy 2:8-15." Biblical Research Institute, n.d. Available from Biblical Research Institute, 12501 Old Columbia Pike, Silver Spring, MD 20904-6600.

Biblical Interpretation

*Damsteegt, P. Gerard. "New Light in the Last Days." *Adventists Affirm* 10/1 (Spring 1996): 5-13.

*_____. "Scripture Faces Current Issues." *Ministry* 72/4 (April 1999):23-27.

Foh, Susan T. *Women & the Word of God.* Presbyterian and Reformed Publishing Co., 1979.

*Hasel, Gerhard F. "Biblical Authority and Feminist Interpretation." *Adventists Affirm* 3/2 (Fall 1989): 12-23.

*_____. "Biblical Authority, Hermeneutics, and the Role of Women." Biblical Research Institute, 1988. Available from Biblical Research Institute, 12501 Old Columbia Pike, Silver Spring, MD 20904-6600.

*_____. "Hermeneutical Issues Relating to the Ordination of Women: Methodological Reflections on Key Passages." 1994. Available at Adventist Heritage Center, Andrews University, Berrien Springs, Mich.

*Holmes, C. Raymond. *The Tip of an Iceberg: Biblical Authority, Biblical Interpretation, and the Ordination of Women in Ministry.* Berrien Springs: Adventists Affirm & Pointer Publications, 1994.

*Henry III, Weiland. "Two or Three Witnesses." *Adventists Affirm* 10/1 (Spring 1996): 37-43.

*Koranteng-Pipim, Samuel. "Crisis Over the Word." *Adventists Affirm* 10/1 (Spring 1996): 14-25.

*_____. *Receiving the Word.* Berrien Springs: Berean Books, 1996.

*Maxwell, C. Mervyn. "Take the Bible as it Is." *Adventists Affirm* 10/1 (Spring 1996): 26-35.

*Nortey, J. J. "The Bible, Our Surest Guide." *Adventists Affirm* 9/1 (Spring 1995): 47-49, 67.

*Reid, George W. "Another Look at Adventist Methods of Bible Interpretation." *Adventists Affirm* 10/1 (Spring 1996): 50-56.

*Usilton, Kathy. "Depending on God's Word," *Adventists Affirm* 10/1 (Spring 1996): 57-59, 62.

*White, Ellen G. "How to Interpret the Scriptures: Principles Drawn from the Writings of Ellen G. White," *Adventists Affirm* 3/2 (Fall 1989): 18, 19.

*_____. "Guided Through the Written Testimony." *Adventists Affirm* 10/1 (Spring 1996): 60-62.

Feminism and Feminist Theology

Ayers, David J. "The Inevitability of Failure: The Assumptions and Implementations of Modern Feminism." In *Recovering Biblical Manhood and Womanhood,* ed. John Piper and Wayne Grudem, 312-331. Wheaton, Ill.: Crossway Books, 1991.

*Damsteegt, Laurel. "Feminism vs. Adventism: Why the Conflict?" *Adventists Affirm* 3/2 (Fall 1989): 33-40.

*_____. "Doctrines of Devils." *Adventists Affirm* 11/1 (Spring 1997): 41-52.

Kassian, Mary A. *The Feminist Gospel.* Wheaton, Ill.: Crossway Books, 1992.

O'Leary, Dale. *The Gender Agenda.* Lafayette, La.: Vital Issues Press, 1997.

Pride, Mary. *The Way Home: Beyond Feminism, Back to Reality.* Westchester, Ill.: Crossway Books, 1985.

Headship and Roles

*Bacchiocchi, Samuele. "Divine Order of Headship and Church Order: A Study of the Implications of the Principle of Male Headship for the Ordination of Women as Elders and/or Pastors." Biblical Research Institute, November 1987. Available from Biblical Research Institute, 12501 Old Columbia Pike, Silver Spring, MD 20904-6600.

*_____. "Recovering Harmonious Gender Distinctions." *Adventists Affirm* 9/1 (Spring 1995): 61-66.

Balasa, Donald A. "Is it Legal for Religious Organizations to Make Distinctions on the Basis of Sex?" In *Recovering Biblical Manhood and Womanhood,* ed. John Piper and Wayne Grudem, 332-341. Wheaton, Ill.: Crossway Books, 1991.

Clark, Stephen B. *Man and Woman in Christ.* Ann Arbor: Servant Books, 1980.

Elliot, Elisabeth. *Let Me Be a Woman.* Wheaton, Ill.: Tyndale House Publishers, 1976.

Hurley, James B. *Man and Woman in Biblical Perspective.* Grand Rapids, Mich.: Zondervan Publishing House, 1981.

*Jemison, Hedwig. "Our God-Appointed Roles: Should Women Be Ordained?" Mohaven Papers. Available at Adventist Heritage Center, Andrews University, Berrien Springs, Mich.

Johnson, Gregg. "The Biological Basis for Gender-Specific Behavior." In *Recovering Biblical Manhood and Womanhood,* ed. John Piper and Wayne Grudem, 280-293. Wheaton, Ill.: Crossway Books, 1991.

*Kiesler, Herbert. "Ephesians Four and the Role of Women." Biblical Research Institute, April 21, 1987. Available from Biblical Research Institute, 12501 Old Columbia Pike, Silver Spring, MD 20904-6600.

Knight III, George W. *The Role Relationship of Men and Women.* Chicago: Moody Press, 1985.

Patterson, Paige. "The Meaning of Authority in the Local Church." In *Recovering Biblical Manhood and Womanhood,* ed. John Piper and Wayne Grudem, 248-259. Wheaton, Ill.: Crossway Books, 1991.

Piper, John, and Wayne Grudem, eds. *Recovering Biblical Manhood and Womanhood.* Wheaton, Ill.: Crossway Books, 1991.

Rekers, George Alan. "Psychological Foundations for Rearing Masculine Boys and Feminine Girls." In *Recovering Biblical Manhood and Womanhood,* ed. John Piper and Wayne Grudem, 294-311. Wheaton, Ill.: Crossway Books, 1991.

*Wallace, Melissa. "Review: Let Me Be a Woman." *Adventists Affirm* 1/2 (Fall 1987): 32-34.

Church History and Women

*Damsteegt, Laurel. "S.M.I. Henry: Pioneer in Women's Ministry." *Adventists Affirm* 9/1 (Spring 1995): 17-19, 46.

*Fagal, William. "Ellen White and Women's Rights." *Adventists Affirm* 1/2 (Fall 1987): 40-42.

*Holmes, C. Raymond. "A Momentous Decision in the Christian Reformed Church." *Adventists Affirm* 9/1 (Spring 1995): 50-54.

*_____. "The Ordination of Women and the Anglican-Episcopal Experience: The Road to Schism." Biblical Research Institute: September 1987. Available from Biblical Research Institute, 12501 Old Columbia Pike, Silver Spring, MD 20904-6600.

*Maxwell, C. Mervyn. "Women in the Greco-Roman World." Biblical Research Institute: (Revised) February 1988. Available from Biblical Research Institute, 12501 Old Columbia Pike, Silver Spring, MD 20904-6600.

Ryrie, Charles C. *The Role of Women in the Church.* Chicago: Moody Press:, 1970.

Weinrich, William. "Women in the History of the Church: Learned and Holy, But Not Pastors." In *Recovering Biblical Manhood and Womanhood,* ed. John Piper and Wayne Grudem, 263-279. Wheaton, Ill.: Crossway Books, 1991.

History of Ordination, Adventist
Before 1995

*Damsteegt, Laurel. "Loyalty" [in the aftermath of Cohutta Springs]. *Adventists Affirm* 3/2 (Fall 1989): 44-48.

*_____. "Pushing the Brethren." *Adventists Affirm* 12/3 (Fall 1995): 13-17.

*Holmes, C. Raymond. "Review: *The Truth in Crisis.*" *Adventists Affirm* 1/2 (Fall 1987): 27-31.

*Hyde, Gordon M. "The Mohaven Council—Where it All Began." *Adventists Affirm* 3/2 (Fall 1989): 41-43.

*Maxwell, C. Mervyn. "Response to NAD President's Request to Annual Council." *Adventists Affirm* 9/1 (Spring 1995): 30-37, 67.

*Nelson, Ethel R. "'No Turning Back' on Ordination?" *Adventists Affirm* 9/1 (Spring 1995): 42-46.

Utrecht General Conference Session, 1995

*Damsteegt, P. Gerard. "A Response to the North American Division Ordination Request." Handout Presented at the 1995 General Conference at Utrecht, The Netherlands. July 5, 1995. Available from the Adventist Heritage Center, Andrews University, Berrien Springs, Mich. The presentation is available online at http://www.andrews.edu/~damsteeg/presentations.html.

*"Proceedings of the 13th Business Meeting, 56th General Conference, July 5, 1995." *Adventist Review,* July 7, 1995, 23-31. Audiotapes of this meeting are available from the Office of Archives and Statistics, General Conference of Seventh-day Adventists, 12501 Old Columbia Pike, Silver Spring, MD 20904-6600.

*Video of proceedings of the 13th Business Meeting, 56th General Conference Session, July 5, 1995. Available from Adventist Media Center, 101 W. Cochran St., Simi Valley, CA 93065

*Fagal, William. "Interesting Times." *Adventists Affirm* 10/1 (Spring 1996): 3-4, 13.

*Holmes, C. Raymond. "Post-Utrecht: Conscience and the Ecclesiastical Crisis." *Adventists Affirm* 10/1 (Spring 1996): 44-49, 56.

*Koranteng-Pipim, Samuel. "How the Spirit Leads the Church." *Adventists Affirm* 12/3 (Fall 1998): 28-35.

*[Maxwell, C. Mervyn.] "A Very Significant Development Regarding Women Pastors." *Adventists Affirm* 12/3 (Fall 1998): 5-13.

*"President's Commission on Women in Ministry—Report." *Adventists Affirm* 12/3 (Fall 1998): 13-17.

*Saelee, Terri. "Women of the Spirit." *Adventists Affirm* 9/2 (Fall 1995): 60-63.

Home as Prototype of Church

*Bacchiocchi, Samuele. "The Church and the Family: Structures and Roles." *Adventists Affirm* 1/2 (Fall 1987): 5-14.

*Fagal, William. "Family Church . . . Church Family." *Adventists Affirm* 1/2 (Fall 1987): 15-20.

*Hartlein, Betty Lou. "Follow God's Plan." *Adventists Affirm* 1/2 (Fall 1987): 21-22.

Knight III, George. "The Family and the Church: How Should Biblical Manhood and Womanhood Work Out in Practice?" In *Recovering Biblical Manhood and Womanhood,* ed. John Piper and Wayne Grudem, 345-357. Wheaton, Ill.: Crossway Books, 1991.

Polythress, Vern Sheridan. "The Church as Family: Why Male Leadership in the Family Requires Male Leadership in the Church." In *Recovering Biblical Manhood and Womanhood,* ed. John Piper and Wayne Grudem, 233-247. Wheaton, Ill.: Crossway Books, 1991.

Women in the Bible

Schreiner, Thomas R. "The Valuable Ministries of Women in the Context of Male Leadership: A Survey of Old and New Testament Examples and Teaching." In *Recovering Biblical Manhood and Womanhood,* ed. John Piper and Wayne Grudem, 209-224. Wheaton, Ill.: Crossway Books, 1991.

Women in Ministry

Brunner, Peter. *The Ministry and the Ministry of Women.* St. Louis, Mo.: Concordia Publishing House, 1971.

*Damsteegt, Laurel. "Shall Women Minister?" *Adventists Affirm* 9/1 (Spring 1995): 4-16.

*Dyer, Mercedes. "Thy Kingdom Come." *Adventists Affirm* 3/2 (Fall 1989): 49-54, 62.

House, H. Wayne. "Principles to Use in Establishing Women in Ministry." In *Recovering Biblical Manhood and Womanhood,* ed. John Piper and Wayne Grudem, 358-363. Wheaton, Ill.: Crossway Books, 1991.

*Slikkers, Dolores. "What Shall I Do For Thee?" *Adventists Affirm* 1/2 (Fall 1987): 43, 46.

*Wallace, Stephen Vincent. "A Question of Glory and Authority." An eight part presentation on audio cassettes available from American Cassette Ministries, P.O. Box 922, Harrisburg, PA 17108.

Zerbst, Fritz. *The Office of Woman in the Church.* St. Louis, Mo.: Concordia Publishing House, 1955.

Women's Ordination, General

*"Answers to Questions about Women's Ordination." *[Adventists] Affirm* 1/1 (Spring 1987): 1-8.

*Bacchiocchi, Samuele. *Women in the Church.* Berrien Springs, Mich.: Biblical Perspectives, 1987.

*Ball, Bryan. "The Ordination of Women—A Plea for Caution." Biblical Research Institute, n.d. Available from Biblical Research Institute, 12501 Old Columbia Pike, Silver Spring, MD 20904-6600.

*Holmes, C. Raymond. "Slavery, Sabbath, War, and Women." *Adventists Affirm* 3/2 (Fall 1989): 55-62.

*Koranteng-Pipim, Samuel. *Searching the Scriptures: Women's Ordination and the Call to Biblical Fidelity.* Berrien Springs, Mich.: Adventists Affirm, 1995.

*Lee, Rosalie Haffner. "Women's Ministry Without Ordination." Biblical Research Institute, n.d. Available from Biblical Research Institute, 12501 Old Columbia Pike, Silver Spring, MD 20904-6600.

*Maxwell, C. Mervyn. "Let's Be Serious." *Adventists Affirm* 3/2 (Fall 1989): 24-32, 40.

*Maxwell, S. Lawrence. "One Chilling Word." *Adventists Affirm* 9/1 (Spring 1995): 38-41.

*Reid, George W. "The Ordination of Women." Biblical Research Institute, January 1985. Available from Biblical Research Institute, 12501 Old Columbia Pike, Silver Spring, MD 20904-6600.

Scripture Index

Judges

2:30   114
4-5   89
4:1-2   92
4:4   92
4:4-5   90
4:4-6   96
4:5   91
4:6, 14   91
4:6-7   91
4:9   91
5:1   92
5:7   92, 104
4:17-22   91

1 Samuel

1:10   96, 378
2:22   93, 96, 357, 361, 378

2 Samuel

13:18-19   125
15:32   125

1 Kings

17:1-3   201
18:7-10   201
19:14   114
22   90

2 Kings

4:9-10, 20-37   378
17:15, 35, 36   114
22   201
22:13-14   96, 357
22:14-20   91-92, 378
22:15   92

1 Chronicles

25:5-6   96, 357
24   361

2 Chronicles

6:41   95
34:22-28   378

Ezra

2:65   96, 378
5:1-2   90

Nehemiah

8:2   96, 378
13:19   114
13:29   114

Job

1:5   94, 361
10:11   125
39:19   125

Psalms

10:14   77
22:11   77
22:28   85
54:4   77
59:17   332
68:24-25   358
116:15   333
119:168   77
132:16   95

Proverbs

1:8   96, 378
12:4   71
23:21   125

Song of Solomon

5:3   125
7:10   85

Isaiah

6:9   91
7:3   91
8:20   234, 300, 385
22:21   125
40:10   85
50:3   125
54:1   332
58:1   91
61:6   94
61:10   125

Jeremiah

1:10   91
2:2   91
7:2   91
20:1-2   201
37:11- 38:10   201
38   90

Ezekiel

2:3   91
6:2   91
20:20   372

Subject Index